Jerusalem Through the Ages

Jerusalem Through the Ages

From Its Beginnings to the Crusades

JODI MAGNESS

OXFORD

UNIVERSITY PRESS

Oxford University Press is a department of the University of Oxford. It furthers
the University's objective of excellence in research, scholarship, and education
by publishing worldwide. Oxford is a registered trade mark of Oxford University
Press in the UK and certain other countries.

Published in the United States of America by Oxford University Press
198 Madison Avenue, New York, NY 10016, United States of America.

Library of Congress Cataloging-in-Publication Data
Names: Magness, Jodi, author.
Title: Jerusalem through the ages : from its beginnings to the Crusades / Jodi Magness.
Description: New York, NY : Oxford University Press, [2024] |
Contents: The Explorers—Jebusite Jerusalem (1050 BCE)—Israelite Jerusalem (930 BCE)—
Judahite Jerusalem (587 BCE)—Post-Exilic (Persian) Jerusalem (333 BCE)—
Hasmonean Jerusalem (64 BCE)—Herodian Jerusalem (March 70 CE)—
Roman Jerusalem (Aelia Capitolina) (200 CE)—Byzantine
Jerusalem (633 CE)—Early Islamic Jerusalem (800 CE)—Crusader
Jerusalem (September 19, 1187)—British Mandatory Jerusalem (December 11, 1917).
Identifiers: LCCN 2023043049 | ISBN 9780190937805 (hardback) |
ISBN 9780197674994 (ebook) | ISBN 9780190937829 (epub)
Subjects: LCSH: Jerusalem—History. | Excavations (Archaeology)—Jerusalem.
Classification: LCC DS109.9 .M335 2024 | DDC 933/.442—dc23/eng/20231214
LC record available at https://lccn.loc.gov/2023043049

DOI: 10.1093/oso/9780190937805.001.0001

Printed by Sheridan Books, Inc., United States of America

Contents

Preface

Jerusalem attracts far more attention than it deserves.[1]

"WHY IS ANOTHER book on Jerusalem needed?" asked a friend of mine who is not an archaeologist. Plenty of books have been written about Jerusalem from a diversity of perspectives ranging from sweeping overviews to deep dives into its history, archaeology, religion, politics, and so on. Is it possible to say something new about Jerusalem or present it in a different light? My friend's question is one of the reasons I long dodged an invitation by Stefan Vranka, an editor at Oxford University Press, to write this book. But mainly I resisted because the more one knows about Jerusalem, the more one recognizes the limitations of that knowledge. Jerusalem is so rich in remains, so incredibly layered and complex, that it is impossible to know everything about it. Eventually, Stefan's persistence overcame my reluctance, and I agreed to write the book. Which brings us back to the question: Why is another book on Jerusalem needed? Although there are many excellent books about Jerusalem, most of those that cover the city's premodern history and archaeology fall into one of two categories: either they are broad surveys written by nonspecialists or edited volumes containing chapters by multiple specialists, or they are studies written by individual specialists focusing on a specific time frame or topic. This volume differs in presenting a broad survey authored by a single specialist.[2] An Israeli archaeologist was recently quoted as remarking that "People come to Jerusalem to hear a story. If you try to be very objective and show everything from every period, it is kind of boring."[3] But nothing about Jerusalem's story is boring, and I believe that, as specialists, we have a responsibility to share with the public—as objectively as possible—detailed and scientific information about Jerusalem's history and archaeology.

A book like this is not easy to write because it involves presenting granular archaeological data within a broad temporal framework. The presentation of such detailed information is precisely what differentiates this book from others and gives it value. Specifically, in response to another question my friend asked—"What will the reader learn that he or she doesn't already know?"—the answer is: hopefully, a lot. Of course, every reader will have his or her own prior knowledge about Jerusalem, and no two individuals will have the same background. But nearly every reader of this book will learn something new about Jerusalem, not only because of the broad but detailed coverage, but because it includes the most recent archaeological discoveries as well as my own original research.

My personal connection to Jerusalem goes back to 1974, when I arrived at the age of 18 to begin undergraduate studies in archaeology and history at the Hebrew University. I have been captivated by the city ever since and am indebted to the many teachers, colleagues, friends, and students from whom I have learned so much over the years. Although it is impossible to name them all, I must mention Yigal Shiloh and Nahman Avigad (as the material from their excavations was the subject of my PhD dissertation), and Alon de Groot, Hillel Geva, Shlomit Weksler-Bdolah, and Jane Cahill West—friends and colleagues whose seemingly boundless knowledge of Jerusalem is truly humbling. I am especially indebted to Alon, the anonymous outside reviewer, and Stefan for their helpful comments, although I alone am responsible for the contents. I am also grateful to the friends, colleagues, organizations, and institutions who generously granted reproduction permission and provided images for the illustrations in this book, including Jane Cahill West, David Hendin and the American Numismatic Society, Avital Mazar Tsa`iri, Ronny Reich, Felicity Cobbing (Palestine Exploration Fund), Megan Sauter (Biblical Archaeology Society), Joe Uziel (Israel Antiquities Authority), Gideon Avni (Israel Antiquities Authority), Shlomit Weksler-Bdolah (Israel Antiquities Authority), Hillel Geva (Israel Exploration Society), Yael Barschak (Israel Museum Jerusalem), Visual Archive (Israel Antiquities Authority), Daphna Tsoran (Institute of Archaeology at the Hebrew University), Nava Panitz-Cohen (Institute of Archaeology at the Hebrew University), Zvi Greenhut (Israel Antiquities Authority), Yosef Spiezer (Bar-Ilan University), the Studium Biblicum Franciscanum, Matanyah Hecht (Holyland Tourism, Ltd.), Leen Ritmeyer, Zev Radovan, Shay Hausman (Carta), and Oberlin College.

My original plan to write this book during a sabbatical in 2021–2022 was impacted in a positive way by the COVID-19 pandemic. After everything shut down in March 2020 and we were housebound, I took the opportunity to start writing. This turned out to be fortuitous, as I realized in retrospect that I could never have completed the book in just one year. Considering the hardships suffered by others during the pandemic, I was extremely fortunate. By the time my sabbatical began in August 2021, I was able to go to Wisconsin, where I spent an enjoyable and productive semester on a Kingdon Fellowship at the Institute for Research in the Humanities at the University of Wisconsin-Madison (UW). I am grateful to Steven Nadler (the Director) and Katie Apsey and Elizabeth (Lizzie) Neary (the staff) for their support and hospitality during my stay. I benefited from conversations and interactions with other fellows, particularly Katarzyna (Kat) Lecky (who kindly read and offered helpful comments on drafts of the first two chapters), as well as with colleagues at UW Madison including Nick Cahill, Lisa Cooper, Jeremy Hutton, William Aylward, and Jordan Rosenblum. While I was there, my in-laws in Middleton–Linda and Greg Dauck, their daughter Rose, and her husband Mike–made me feel at home.

In mid-January 2022, I traveled to Israel, where I spent a semester as a Fulbright Senior Research Fellow at Tel Aviv University while residing at the W. F. Albright Institute of Archaeological Research in Jerusalem as the Seymour Gitin Distinguished Professor. I am grateful to the Fulbright Scholar Program for their support and to Vered Noam for arranging the invitation at Tel Aviv University (TAU), as well as to Youval Rotman, Ronit Nevo, Anat Zion, and the other administrators and colleagues at TAU for their hospitality. I wish to express special appreciation of the Albright Institute, with which I have long been affiliated—beginning as a graduate student fellow in the mid-1980s, later as a member and officer of the Board of Trustees—and now, returning full circle, once again as both a fellow and member of the board. I am particularly grateful to Matt Adams, the Director at the time of my fellowship, for his hospitality and willingness to accommodate my needs during the difficult period of the pandemic, as well as the institute staff, including Aaron Greener, Nadia Bandak, Naual Herbawi, and Hisham M'farreh. For information about the institute, including how to support the current and future research of archaeologists and biblical scholars, visit www.aiar.org.

Finally, I wish to acknowledge the support of the University of North Carolina at Chapel Hill and the assistance of the Department of Religious Studies, especially the Chair, Barbara Ambros, and the Department Manager, Tracey Cave, who navigated the ever-changing paperwork requirements and travel restrictions during the pandemic. I am fortunate to have a loving family, including my father, Herbert Magness; my siblings, Alan and Lisa; and my step-nephew/adopted son Mike Miller. But, above all, I am grateful for the unconditional love and constant support of my husband, Jim Haberman, who patiently and uncomplainingly endured my extended absences during the sabbatical and prepared the illustrations for this book.

My mother, Marlene Z. Magness, passed away shortly before this book went to press, after a long period of declining health. She was so proud of my accomplishments, which would have been impossible without the support and encouragement that she and my father provided.

This book is dedicated to her memory.

Introduction

TOPOGRAPHY AND SOURCES

*Holy City of God, Jerusalem, how I long to stand even now at
your gates, and go in, rejoicing!*[1]

AROUND 600 CE, Sophronius, a monk from a monastery near Jerusalem who
had been posted to Egypt, Sinai, and North Africa, composed a poem expressing his
longing to return to the holy city—a wish that was fulfilled thirty years later when he
was appointed patriarch.[2] For Sophronius, not even Alexandria, the cosmopolitan
cultural capital of the Mediterranean, could compete with Jerusalem. Sophronius'
words echo Psalm 122:1–3, which was written hundreds of years earlier and attributed
to King David: "I was glad when they said to me, 'Let us go to the house of the Lord!'
Our feet are standing within your gates, O Jerusalem. Jerusalem—built as a city that
is bound firmly together."[3] Throughout the ages, pilgrims have shared Sophronius's
desire to stand in the gates of Jerusalem. Why has this poor and isolated mountain
town exerted such a powerful hold on billions of people worldwide over the course
of millennia? The simple answer is that for followers of the three Abrahamic faiths,
Jerusalem is the place where the presence of the God of Israel dwells and the Last
Judgment will take place. It is the meeting point of heaven and earth—the locus of
divine and human interaction.[4] This book explores how these beliefs came to be associated with Jerusalem by introducing readers to its complex and layered history.

A Holy City on a Mountain

*His holy mountain, beautiful in elevation, is the joy of all the
earth, Mount Zion.*

—Psalm 48:1–2

This psalm encapsulates Jerusalem's distinguishing characteristic as a city high in the Judean hills, dominated by a prominent rocky outcrop called Mount Zion, which is enshrined within a great esplanade (open platform) in the southeast corner of the modern Old City (Pl. 1A). This esplanade is known as the Temple Mount (Hebrew *har ha-bayit* [the mountain of the house]; in Arabic, *al-haram al-sharif* [the noble or sacred enclosure]), because it was the site of two successive temples to the God of Israel (Pl. 1B).[5] The rocky outcrop also came to be identified with Mount Moriah, where Abraham reportedly was prepared to sacrifice his son (Isaac in Jewish tradition; Ishmael in Islamic tradition).[6] Zion (pronounced in Hebrew tsee-YOHN) is another name for Jerusalem, as, for example, in Psalm 87:1–2: "On the holy mount stands the city he founded; the Lord loves the gates of Zion."[7] Today Mount Zion denotes an area outside the walls of the Old City. Jerusalem lies about 750 meters (2,460 feet) above sea level, straddling the watershed between the wooded Judean hills and fertile lowlands (Shefelah) to the west and the barren wilderness of Judea (Judean desert) to the east. The Dead Sea— the lowest point on earth at ca. 430 meters (1,410 feet) below sea level—is only 25 kilometers (15 miles) away.

Jerusalem's mountainous setting was shaped by geological processes in the distant past. Approximately 100 million years ago, Palestine (a term I use in the British Mandatory sense to denote modern Israel, Jordan, and the Palestinian territories) and neighboring regions were covered by an ancestor of the Mediterranean Sea called the Tethys Sea. After the Tethys Sea receded, the sediments that had accumulated on its floor hardened into layers of limestone, dolomite, and chalk interspersed with lenses of flint or chert. Tectonic movements lifted and folded these layers into a north-south anticline (ridge) called the Judean mountains or hills. On the west the ridge descends through foothills to the Mediterranean coast, while on the east it drops abruptly at the escarpment along the Dead Sea, which is the lowest point on earth. The sides of the anticline are scored by deep valleys which drain to the Mediterranean Sea or the Dead Sea.[8]

The prevailing winds carry moisture eastward from the Mediterranean, causing rain to fall as clouds rise and condense along the western side of the ridge but evaporating farther to the east, creating the Judean desert. As a result, the western side of the watershed (e.g., the modern West Jerusalem neighborhoods of Beit Hakerem and Katamon) receives more rain at ca. 550 millimeters (22 inches) per year than the Old City at ca. 500 millimeters (20 inches) per year, while 1 kilometer to the east the annual amount drops to 380 millimeters (14 inches).[9] Typical of a Mediterranean climate, the rainy season coincides with the cooler winter months (October–April/May), leaving a long hot season with little or no rainfall.[10] Until recently, Jerusalem's inhabitants relied heavily on rainwater collected in cisterns and pools, some of which can still be seen in the courtyards of houses in the Old City.[11] It was the Gihon spring—the most abundant perennial source of fresh water in the area—which attracted people to settle here over five thousand years ago. The spring produces approximately 1,500 cubic meters (40,000 gallons) of water daily and 550,000 cubic meters (146,000,000 gallons) annually.[12]

The different types of hard limestone and dolomite that make up Jerusalem's rocky landscape are easily distinguishable and are denoted by modern Arabic names: Mizzi Yahudi ("Jewish hard rock") is a dense gray dolomite; Mizzi Ahmar is a reddish dolomite; Meleke ("royal") is a white limestone; and Mizzi Hilu ("sweet") is a fine, yellowish-white limestone.[13] For example, Mizzi Ahmar is exposed in the cliffs of the Ben-Hinnom Valley; Meleke, which is more widespread, is also visible in the Ben-Hinnom Valley as well as in the Kidron Valley; and to the east of the Damascus Gate there are Mizzi Hilu outcrops.[14] As a medium-hard limestone, Meleke was preferred as a building material over the harder Mizzi Ahmar, which it overlies.[15] As rainfall seeps through cracks and fissures in the hard limestone and dolomite and collects between the layers it dissolves the rock, creating hollows and caves—a geological phenomenon called "karst." The Gihon spring is fed by water that has collected between layers of rock to form an underground aquifer. Gihon means "gushing" in Hebrew, referring to the spring's intermittent or fluctuating flow, which is a feature of some karstic formations.[16]

Despite Jerusalem's status as a holy city, it is an isolated mountain town that is poor in natural resources.[17] Throughout history, the major north–south routes through the country connecting Egypt and Syria have followed the flat land along the coast (the "Via Maris") or traversed the high mountain ridge to the east of the Dead Sea and Jordan River toward Damascus (the "King's Highway"), bypassing Jerusalem altogether.[18] Although Jerusalem lies at the intersection of two roads in the center of the country—one running north–south along the top of the Judean mountains and the other running west–east from the Mediterranean Sea across the Jordan Valley toward Amman—these have always been of secondary importance.[19]

The first arrivals to Jerusalem over five thousand years ago settled on a small hill that forms a spur to the south of the Temple Mount (Pl. 2A). The name "Jerusalem" does not mean "city of peace," as it was later understood, but rather "foundation of the god Shalem."[20] It was common practice in antiquity to name cities in honor of the patron deity, as for example Athens (named after Athena) or Jericho (named after the moon god). Shalem is thought to have been the god of twilight or the setting sun, who perhaps was worshiped on the rocky outcrop in the center of the Temple Mount that is now enshrined as the Foundation Stone in the Dome of the Rock.[21]

The small hill to the south of the Temple Mount that is the site of the earliest settlement in Jerusalem is referred to as the southeastern (or eastern) hill or the lower city. The southeastern hill is also called the City of David, based on an identification with the biblical city (2 Sam 5:11) that was first made by Raymond Weill, who conducted excavations in 1913–1914 (see Chapter 1). It is now part of the Palestinian neighborhood of Wadi Hilweh, which belongs to the poor and densely populated village of Silwan.[22]

Although the southeastern hill is small (somewhere between 11 and 28 acres in size) and lower in elevation than the surrounding hills (ca. 690–640 meters [2,265–2,100 feet] above sea level), Jerusalem's first inhabitants were attracted by its proximity to the spring, which gushes forth at the foot of the eastern slope.[23] The southeastern hill offered early inhabitants the additional advantage of natural protection, consisting of the Kidron Valley to the east and, to the west, the Tyropoeon (pronounced tie-rho-PEE-un) Valley (an ancient Greek name meaning the "Valley of the Cheesemakers"), which is sometimes called the Central Valley because it begins at the modern Damascus Gate and runs south through the center of the Old City (Figure 0.1). The eastern slope of the southeastern hill is particularly steep, rising at an angle of 25–30 degrees from the Kidron Valley and interspersed with vertical bedrock escarpments (Figure 0.2).[24] The Kidron and Tyropoeon Valleys meet at the southern tip of the southeastern hill, where they continue eastward (as the Kidron Valley) and empty into the Dead Sea. The bedrock of the southeastern hill is lowest at the southern tip (ca. 640 meters [2,100 feet] above sea level) and rises steadily to the north, culminating in the rocky outcrop that became the Temple Mount (745 meters [2,444 feet] above sea level). Most scholars identify the Ophel mentioned in the Hebrew Bible as the area between the northern end of the southeastern hill and the southern end of the Temple Mount (see Chapter 3).

By the latter part of the eighth century BCE—over two millennia after the first settlers arrived—Jerusalem's population could no longer be accommodated on the southeastern hill alone. As the city grew it spread westward, across the Tyropoeon Valley. This area, called the southwestern (or western) hill, is larger in size and higher in elevation than the southeastern hill (a maximum of ca. 775 meters [2,543 feet] above sea level) and therefore is also known as the upper city (in contrast to the southeastern hill, which is the lower city). The southwestern hill had the advantage of protection by natural valleys on three of four sides: on the east, the Tyropoeon Valley, which separates it from the Temple Mount and southeastern hill; on the west and south, the Ben-Hinnom Valley, which begins by the modern Jaffa Gate (the main gate in the middle of the west side of the Old City today) and joins the Kidron and Tyropoeon Valleys at the southern tip of the southeastern hill (Pl. 2B). The Ben-Hinnom Valley is notorious as the place

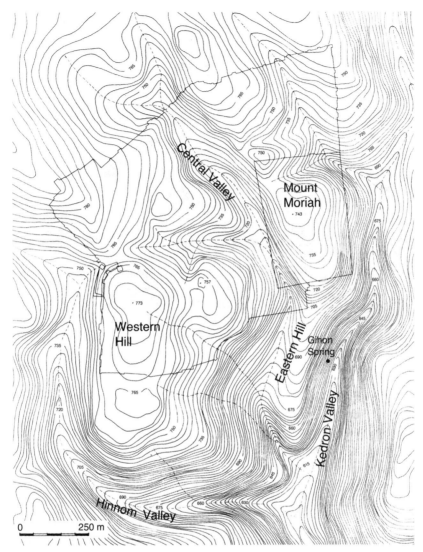

FIGURE 0.1 Topographic map of Jerusalem.
Credit: © by Leen Ritmeyer.

where some ancient Israelites reportedly offered child sacrifices, a Canaanite and
Phoenician practice that was condemned by the prophet Jeremiah (7:30–31): "For
the people of Judah have done evil in my sight, says the Lord; they have set their
abominations in the house that is called by my name, defiling it. And they go on
building the high place of Topheth, which is in the valley of the son of Hinnom
(Ben-Hinnom), to burn their sons and their daughters in the fire." As a result,
the Ben-Hinnom Valley—Hebrew *Gai Hinnom* (Valley of Hinnom)—became

FIGURE 0.2 Eastern slope of the southeastern hill looking south.
Credit: Photo by the author.

known as *Gehenna* in Greek, the place where the souls of the wicked will be tormented after death.[25]

The city never spread eastward to the Mount of Olives, which was used from the earliest periods as Jerusalem's necropolis (cemetery/burial ground) because of its location immediately outside the walls. The Mount of Olives is not a mountain but a ridge with several peaks. Today the northernmost peak is called Mount Scopus, which is the site of the campus of the Hebrew University and Hadassah Hospital. At ca. 830 meters (2,723 feet) above sea level, the Mount of Olives is the highest point in Jerusalem, rising to the east of the Kidron Valley before dropping steeply eastward down to the Dead Sea. In ancient times, Scopus (from the Greek word for "look-out") designated not the mountain to the northeast of the city but an area to the north, along the modern Nablus Road, approximately from the current Ammunition Hill to Sheikh Jarrah.[26] It was from this road that visitors caught their first glimpse of the city, as Titus did upon arriving to besiege Jerusalem in 70 CE: "Caesar [Titus], being joined during the night by the legion from Emmaus, next day broke up his camp and advanced to Scopus, as the place is called from which was obtained the first view of the city and the grand pile of the temple gleaming afar; whence the spot, a low prominence adjoining the northern quarter of the city, is appropriately named Scopus."[27]

Only Jerusalem's north side is not protected by deep natural valleys. Instead, a shallow ravine called the Transverse Valley marks the north end of the southwestern hill, running east from the modern Jaffa Gate to the Temple Mount, where it joins the Tyropoeon Valley. An even shallower valley branches off from the Transverse Valley to the south, creating two peaks on either side: a western peak at ca. 773 meters (2,536 feet) above sea level (corresponding to the modern Armenian Quarter) and an eastern peak at ca. 757 meters (2,483 feet) above sea level (corresponding to the west side of the modern Jewish Quarter).[28] In antiquity, Jerusalem usually was attacked from the north because of the lack of natural defenses. For example, in 70 CE, the Romans mounted an assault from the north even though this side was protected by three successive lines of walls.

The area we have just described—the southeastern hill, Temple Mount, and southwestern hill—constituted the city of Jerusalem until its destruction by the Romans in 70 CE (although by then settlement had expanded to the north). Nowadays, many visitors have the mistaken impression that the Old City is the ancient city of Jerusalem. In fact, the current walls of the Old City date to the Ottoman period (sixteenth century), and they enclose only part of the original ancient city but exclude the southeastern hill and the southern part of the southwestern hill (now known as Mount Zion). In other words, the walled city has shifted to the north since antiquity. This shift occurred when the Roman emperor Hadrian rebuilt Jerusalem in the second century CE as a pagan Roman city called Aelia Capitolina (see Chapter 8). The line of the current Ottoman walls reflects this later shift to the north.

The area enclosed within the walls of the Old City totals only 0.85 square kilometers (0.32 square miles).[29] Since the nineteenth century, this area has been divided into four quarters: the Jewish Quarter in the southern part of the Old City, around and opposite the Western Wall ("Wailing Wall") and the Temple Mount; the Christian Quarter in the northwest part, surrounding the Church of the Holy Sepulcher; the Armenian Quarter in the southwest corner; and the Muslim Quarter in the northeast part (Figure 0.3).[30] The esplanade of the Temple Mount occupies an area of ca. 150,000 square meters (37 acres) in the southeast corner of the Old City. The area in and around the walled Old City—sometimes called the "Holy Basin" due to the concentration of holy sites—has been a focus of Western interest since the nineteenth century (Pl. 3A).[31]

Throughout history, Jerusalem's buildings have been constructed of locally quarried stone, a readily available and abundant building material. Due to the scarcity of water and wood, buildings were not constructed of bricks or timber. In fact, the "knobby domes" described by Mark Twain and other nineteenth-century visitors as characteristic of the Old City were a result of the need to roof houses without wood (Figure 0.4).[32] Unlike other archaeological sites in the Near East/

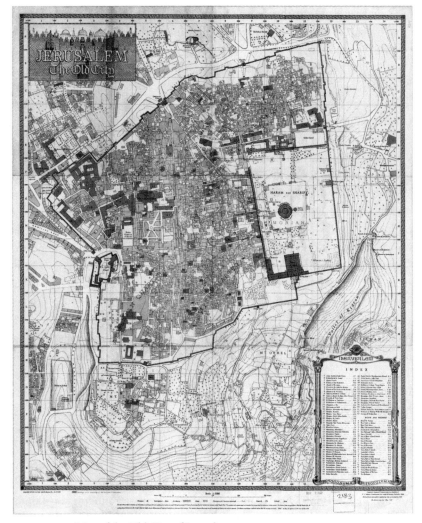

FIGURE 0.3 Map of the Old City of Jerusalem.
Credit: The Survey of Palestine.

Middle East, Jerusalem never became a classic tel/tell (artificial mound) because the stones in ruined buildings were pulled out for reuse, and often the remains were cleared to bedrock when new buildings were established. Due to this process, the earliest periods of settlement are poorly represented, and the remains are generally scattered and fragmentary.[33] Some structures—especially massive stone constructions such as the Middle Bronze Age fortifications or the stepped stone structure on the southeastern hill (see Chapter 2)—were maintained for centuries or even millennia after they were built or were repaired and reused after being damaged

FIGURE 0.4 Knobby domes in the Old City looking east towards the Temple Mount, with the Mount of Olives in the background.
Credit: Library of Congress, Matson (G. Eric and Edith) Photograph Collection, LC-M33- 8751-D.

or ruined. It is often difficult to determine the original construction date of these structures, especially as they often are founded on bedrock. Another difficulty presented by Jerusalem's conditions is that, as a living city, excavation areas tend to be small and scattered, making it difficult to reconstruct a coherent picture, especially for the earliest periods. For these reasons, the absence of evidence is not necessarily evidence of absence—a point that is central to the debates over Jerusalem's character and extent during the time of David and Solomon (see Chapter 3).[34]

Calculating Time

I, Daniel, perceived in the books the number of years that, according to the word of the Lord to the prophet Jeremiah, must be fulfilled for the devastation of Jerusalem, namely, seventy years.

—Daniel 9:2

The calculation of time has long been a human concern. In ancient Egypt, the calendar was tied to the annual flooding of the Nile River. In Jewish (and, later, Christian) circles, calendrical time became central to eschatological expectations about the end of days. For example, the biblical book of Daniel presents history as four kingdoms (represented by beasts) preceding the end times. The author reinterprets Jeremiah's prophecy of a seventy-year exile, extending it to his own time four hundred years later by making each of the seventy years a week of years. Calculating time is necessary to determine when peace will be restored in Jerusalem at the end of days.[35]

Different calendars and systems of periodization are still used around the world today. For scholars studying the Old World (the Mediterranean world and ancient Near East/modern Middle East), historical periods begin around 500 BCE because this is when Greek prose authors such as Hecataeus composed the first historical writings (historiographies).[36] Prehistoric periods (before ca. 500 BCE) are defined by the most advanced material used at the time to manufacture tools: Stone Age, Bronze Age, Iron Age. Each of these periods is further subdivided—for example, Old Stone Age (Paleolithic), Middle Stone Age (Mesolithic), New Stone Age (Neolithic), Early Bronze Age (EB), Middle Bronze Age (MB), Late Bronze Age (LB).

This system of periodization was developed in the nineteenth century, when scholars sought to impose order on the thousands of ancient artifacts from the Old World that had been amassed in museums and private collections. It is not a coincidence that in the nineteenth century—at the height of the Industrial Revolution—scholars devised a chronological framework defined by the materials used to make tools. This reflects the view current at that time that civilizations using stone tools were less advanced (or more "primitive") than those using metal tools, and especially iron. Of course, scholars now recognize the inherent bias of a system of periodization that ranks human progress according to materials used for tool making because there were highly developed civilizations in Mesoamerica and other parts of the world that never emerged from a "Stone Age." Nevertheless, because this terminology is entrenched, it is still used by scholars working in the Mediterranean world and the ancient Near East. In other parts of the world, such as the Americas, where interest in archaeological remains developed later, other systems of periodization are employed.

In the Old World, historical periods (after ca. 500 BCE) are dated according to events recorded in written sources. For example, in Palestine, the early Hellenistic period begins with Alexander the Great's conquest in 332 BCE and ends with the Maccabean revolt in 167 BCE. In contrast, although the Stone Age-Bronze Age-Iron Age system of periodization organizes artifacts in a relative sequence (meaning that, relatively speaking, the Stone Age is earliest and the Iron Age is the latest), it does not provide absolute dates for these periods. For the Iron Age (beginning ca. 1200 BCE), some dates can be gleaned from written sources such as the Hebrew Bible and Assyrian records. However, before the invention of radiocarbon dating in 1950, Egypt was the main chronological peg for prehistoric periods in the Mediterranean and Near East as it is the only country with a continuously dated calendar going back approximately 5,000 years (although scholars disagree about the precise dates of many events). Egyptian artifacts found at sites around the Mediterranean and Near East provided absolute dates for associated remains and levels. The reliance on Egyptian chronology underlies the tripartite division of the Bronze Age around the Mediterranean, with the Early Bronze Age corresponding roughly to the Old Kingdom in Egypt, the Middle Bronze Age to the Middle Kingdom, and the Late Bronze Age to the New Kingdom.[37]

Sources of Information
Archaeology

The information about Jerusalem presented in this book comes mainly from archaeological remains, written texts or documents, and ancient inscriptions. Both archaeologists and historians study the human past but draw on information from different sources. Archaeology is the study of the past based on human material culture—that is, anything that humans manufactured and left behind. These remains include *artifacts*, which are portable humanmade objects such as pottery vessels, tools, coins, and jewelry; and *features*, which are immovable humanmade structures such as buildings, installations, and tombs. Archaeologists conduct excavations to retrieve these remains, which comprise the data set they study. Other types of remains recovered in excavations, such as human or animal bones or botanical remains, are studied by specialists in related fields (such as biological archaeologists, zooarchaeologists, and paleobotanists, respectively) and provide information about ancient populations, diet, environment, and climate.

The main methods of dating used by archaeologists working in Palestine include radiocarbon dating (sometimes called Carbon 14 or C14 dating), coins, pottery, inscriptions, or other written materials found in excavations, and historical texts. Archaeology supplements our information about the past by bringing to light remains associated with groups that were often overlooked by ancient writers: the poorer classes, women, children, and slaves. Like other sciences, archaeology has limitations and can only provide certain types of information or answer certain types of questions. For example, although archaeology provides a great deal of information about the world of Jesus, including the appearance of Jerusalem and the temple in his time, there are no remains that can be associated with Jesus himself. Members of the lower classes, such as Jesus, rarely left behind identifiable remains in the archaeological record, such as monumental buildings with dedicatory inscriptions. And even when archaeologists can identify an excavated structure as a house, it generally is impossible to determine the number, familial relationships, ages, and gender of the occupants or the activities that took place in the various rooms. The material remains might indicate that people inhabited the building, but they do not usually inform us about their daily behavior, thoughts, and beliefs.

Archaeology is neither neutral nor objective. Excavated remains must be interpreted, and the act of excavation itself is an interpretive process. Even archaeologists who strive to be objective are influenced by personal views and biases. Nowhere is this more evident than in Jerusalem, where archaeology has been employed from the beginning of modern exploration for religious and nationalistic purposes, as Andrew Lawler notes: "Archaeologists in Jerusalem, more than anywhere else on the planet, have always confronted a past that remains stubbornly present."[38] Whereas Protestant explorers of the nineteenth century were motivated by millennial expectations, for many Israelis archaeology is a means of (re)establishing a physical connection to the land by bringing to light remains associated with the ancient Israelite and Jewish populations.[39] Religious and political interests influence many of the controversies surrounding archaeological finds discussed in this book, such as the claimed discovery of King David's palace or the road along which Jesus may have walked from the Pool of Siloam to the Temple Mount. In addition, religious and political motivations often dictate which excavated remains are preserved and how they are presented to the public. For example, the City of David Visitors' Center, which is in the midst of a Palestinian neighborhood, prioritizes remains of the Iron Age—the period of David and Solomon and their successors—in an attempt to establish Israeli claims to this part of the city.[40] Although addressing the (mis)use of archaeology for political or religious purposes in Jerusalem is not a primary concern of this book, its relevance to the ongoing debates will be apparent throughout the chapters.[41]

Texts

Texts—that is, literary or historical works—are a valuable source of information about the past because they can inform us not only about events (such as wars) and individuals, but also provide insight into the author's thoughts, beliefs, and world view. However, like archaeological remains, texts have limitations and must be used carefully and critically. For one thing, most texts were written by upper-class (elite) men and therefore reflect their interests, perspectives, and biases. This is the reason most ancient texts provide little information about the lives of lower-class individuals and women and children. In addition, although the earliest historical writings (historiographies) are generally dated to around 500 BCE, Greek and Roman authors sought to entertain their readers and used stories to teach a moral, rather than presenting "objective" history. Even ancient historical works that might be considered relatively objective by today's standards provide an incomplete and biased picture of the people and events they describe (as is true also of contemporary works). The notion that history writing should be objective—a modern ideal which many scholars believe is not fully attainable and perhaps not even desirable—did not exist in the ancient world.

Many ancient texts were composed not as histories but were written as literature or for religious purposes or for other reasons (and these categories sometimes overlap). For example, one of the most important sources for ancient Jerusalem is the Hebrew Bible (Old Testament). The Hebrew Bible is not a historical text but a collection of works relating the sacred (his)story of the covenant of the God of Israel with his people and containing the laws he is believed to have given them. Because the biblical writers had certain biases and agendas, their accounts must be evaluated critically.[42] Furthermore, many of the events described in the books of the Hebrew Bible occurred long before they were written, which calls into question the reliability of these accounts. This problem is most acute for the period prior to the arrival of the Israelites in Canaan (ca. 1200 BCE) since the process of writing the earliest books of the Hebrew Bible probably did not begin before the eighth and seventh centuries BCE, although scholars now debate the historicity of the biblical account even for the Iron Age (ca. 1200–586 BCE).[43] Nevertheless, most scholars agree that the Hebrew Bible contains historical information. The problem lies in identifying those pieces of information in the text and verifying their accuracy.

For the post-exilic and Second Temple period (586 BCE–70 CE), much of our literary information about Jerusalem comes from the writings of Flavius Josephus, the Jewish historian of the first century CE who was a native of the city. Other sources include the Dead Sea Scrolls (Jewish religious works and sectarian writings that were deposited by members of the Essene community at Qumran in the nearby caves); some of the books of the Hebrew Bible (e.g., Ezra and Nehemiah); apocrypha and pseudepigrapha (deutero-canonical and noncanonical books); and the New Testament.

For the period from Jerusalem's destruction in 70 CE to its surrender to the Muslims by 638 CE, our written information comes from rabbinic literature (the writings of the Jewish sages after 70 CE—primarily the Mishnah and Talmud[s]), the church fathers, and early Christian pilgrim accounts. Christian sources of the early Islamic period (after 638 CE) include Byzantine chroniclers, pilgrim accounts, and the writings of Christian clergy and monks who resided in the city and its environs, while Muslim sources include a world geography written ca. 985 by the Jerusalem native al-Muqaddasi, and a travelogue written by a Persian named Nasir-i-Khusraw, who visited Jerusalem in 1047. For the Crusader period, we possess a wealth of literary sources including ecclesiastical documents and pilgrims' accounts as well as a series of medieval European maps depicting Jerusalem.

Conclusion

In 2013, *National Geographic* released the giant-screen film *Jerusalem*, in which I am featured as an archaeologist. During the five years before the film's release, when I served as a consultant, the producers repeatedly asked me to address the questions: What makes Jerusalem special? How did it come to be so sacred and so contested? It is my hope that this book will provide readers with answers to these questions and will equip them with the information necessary to evaluate the claims made by various stakeholders. The book begins by introducing readers to the explorers and then tells Jerusalem's story from its beginnings to the Crusades—reflecting the periods in which I have expertise—with each chapter focusing on a key moment of transition in the city's long and turbulent history. A brief epilogue describes General Allenby's entry to Jerusalem in 1917, which consciously evoked millennia of biblical and historical precedents. The book concludes with guided tours of many of the sites described in the chapters.

I

The Explorers

"THE KNOBBIEST TOWN in the world"—so Samuel Clemens (aka Mark Twain) described Jerusalem in *The Innocents Abroad*, a travelogue of his visit to the Holy Land in 1867 (Figure 0.4).[1] He was struck by the Old City's small size; the small white domes protruding like knobs from the flat roofs of the tightly packed houses; the narrow, crooked, uneven stone-paved streets; the poverty and filth; and the throngs of beggars: "To see the numbers of maimed, malformed and diseased humanity that throng the holy places and obstruct the gates, one might suppose that the ancient days had come again, and that the angel of the Lord was expected to descend at any moment to stir the waters of Bethesda. Jerusalem is mournful, and dreary, and lifeless. I would not desire to live here."[2]

The nineteenth century witnessed the beginning of scientific exploration of the Holy Land as European colonial powers sought to gain a foothold in Ottoman Palestine amid growing scientific interest in using archaeology to verify the Bible. Thousands of Westerners—clerics, scholars, military men, pilgrims, adventure-seekers, and tourists—poured into the country.[3] Twain vividly describes the over-whelming experience of sightseeing in Jerusalem.

> We are surfeited with sights. Nothing has any fascination for us, now, but the Church of the Holy Sepulchre. We have been there every day, and have not grown tired of it; but we are weary of every thing else. The sights are too many. They swarm about you at every step; no single foot of ground in all Jerusalem or within its neighborhood seems to be without a stirring and important history of its own. It is a very relief to steal a walk of a hundred yards without a guide along to talk unceasingly about every stone you step upon and drag you back ages and ages to the day when it achieved celebrity. It seems hardly real when I find myself leaning for a moment on a ruined wall and looking listlessly down into the historic pool of

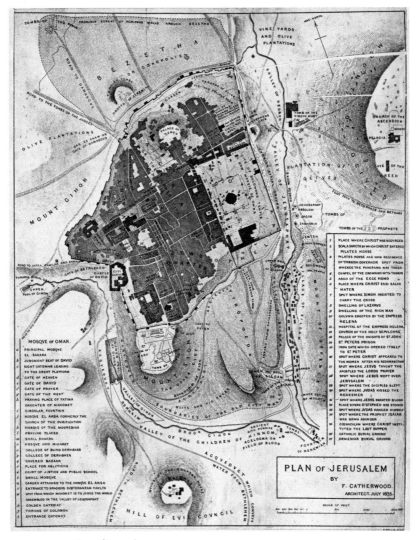

FIGURE 1.1 Map of Jerusalem.
Credit: by Frederick Catherwood, Library of Congress, Geography and Map Division, G7504.J4 1835.C3.

Bethesda. I did not think such things could be so crowded together as to diminish their interest. But in serious truth, we have been drifting about, for several days, using our eyes and our ears more from a sense of duty than any higher and worthier reason. And too often we have been glad when it was time to go home and be distressed no more about illustrious localities. Our pilgrims compress too much into one day. One can gorge sights to repletion as well as sweetmeats. Since we breakfasted, this morning, we have seen enough to have furnished us food for a year's reflection if we could have seen the various objects in comfort and looked upon them deliberately.[4]

Twain's remarks illustrate one of the great paradoxes of Jerusalem: it is small in size yet infinite in scope. Sites are jam-packed together, with multiple layers of occupation piled one atop another. These sites and the traditions associated with them have been described by countless visitors over the centuries. Between 1800 and 1878 alone, approximately two thousand authors produced at least one book, publication, or article each about their travels to the Holy Land.[5] As of 2010, Katharina Galor and Gideon Avni estimate that close to 1,850 excavations have been conducted in and around Jerusalem's Old City, with about one-quarter of the area of the ancient city investigated since 1995.[6] This chapter highlights some of the major excavation projects in Jerusalem, focusing especially on the work of European and American explorers and archaeologists before 1967 and Israeli archaeologists in the wake of the Six-Day War in 1967.

The Nineteenth Century

Napoleon's invasion ushered in the era of modern scientific exploration of Palestine because his army was accompanied by a corps of French geographers and engineers whose surveys were published in atlas form as *Jacotin's Map*. In 1799, Napoleon set out from Egypt with his troops, marching northward along the coast following same route the Crusaders had taken centuries earlier. He sought to bring down the Ottoman Empire and sever the British lines of communication with India.[7] But Napoleon's ambitions were thwarted when he failed to take Akko (Acre), a town north of Haifa that had been the last stronghold of the Crusader kingdom. After a long and costly siege, Napoleon returned to Egypt with his depleted forces. Ahmad al-Jazaar, the local Ottoman pasha (governor), and Sir Sidney Smith, the commander of the English fleet, successfully defended Akko and turned the tide against Napoleon.[8] Al-Jazaar's imprint on Akko is still visible today through a mosque he designed and built in 1781. The Mosque of al-Jazaar, with its prominent green dome, is the largest mosque in Israel outside of Jerusalem. It is sometimes called the White Mosque because it used to have a white dome. Al-Jazaar began his military career in Egypt and later allied with the Ottomans. Of Bosnian origin, he earned the nickname al-Jazaar ("the butcher") after brutally suppressing a Bedouin uprising. Bosnians have had a small but significant presence in Palestine. A century after al-Jazaar's time—in the 1870s and 1880s—the Ottomans settled Bosnians refugees on the ruins of Caesarea

(Kaisariyeh), to the south of Haifa. This settlement existed until the establishment of the state of Israel in 1948; some descendants of those Bosnian families
still live in the nearby Israeli town of Hadera.

After Napoleon's invasion, Palestine remained under the control of al-Jazaar
and succeeding Ottoman pashas until 1831, when the country was invaded by the
Egyptian Mohammed Ali and his adopted son Ibrahim Pasha.[9] Ali and Pasha
nearly succeeded in bringing down the Ottoman Empire, which survived only
because the European powers, mainly Russia and England, forced them to withdraw from Asia Minor. Ibrahim Pasha ruled Syria and Palestine for a decade,
until Ottoman rule in the country was reestablished after an uprising broke out,
thanks to European intervention.[10]

Despite an influx of Western scientists and scholars to Palestine in the wake
of Napoleon's invasion, for years the opposition of local Arabs to the desecration
of holy sites impeded the mapping and exploration of Jerusalem. As Yehoshua
Ben-Arieh remarks, "Indeed, surveyors were often threatened by stones and bullets while making measurements on the city walls."[11] Some of the earliest accurate maps and drawings of Jerusalem and its monuments were made in 1833, by
Frederick Catherwood, a British architect (Figure 1.1).[12] In the late 1830s, the
Scottish painter David Roberts and other Western artists also visited the Holy
Land, and their paintings and lithographs are invaluable sources of information
about sites and monuments that have since been damaged, lost, or destroyed.[13]

Edward Robinson and Eli Smith

Catherwood's maps of Jerusalem were a valuable source of information for Edward
Robinson, who Ben-Arieh describes as "the most important explorer of Palestine
in the 19th century."[14] Whereas most of the other nineteenth-century explorers
were European, Robinson was an American—the son of a Congregationalist
minister from Connecticut. He was a brilliant scholar who taught at Andover
Theological Seminary before becoming the first professor of biblical literature
at Union Theological Seminary. Robinson's interest in finding and identifying places mentioned in the Hebrew Bible (Old Testament) stemmed from the
Puritans' belief that they were the chosen people.[15] As part of his quest to better
understand the Bible and defend its accuracy, Robinson arrived in Palestine in
1837, with fellow Andover graduate Eli Smith. Smith had been sent to the Middle
East to master Arabic as part of Protestant missionary plans to translate the Bible.

Following in the footsteps of the Israelite tribes who fled Egypt by way
of the Sinai (or so they believed), Robinson and Smith made their way to
Jerusalem: "The country around Jerusalem is all of limestone formation; and not
particularly fertile. The rocks everywhere come out above the surface, which in

many parts is also thickly strewed with loose stones; and the aspect of the whole region is barren and dreary."[16] They spent the spring months in Jerusalem, documenting and measuring the sites and monuments precisely and in great detail, as for example the walls of the Old City: "One of the first measurements which I took in Jerusalem, was that of the circumference of the walls. This was done with a measuring tape of one hundred English feet, carried by our two servants, while I noted down the results. We measured as closely as possible to the walls, yet without regarding the short angles and smaller zigzags. We started first from the Yâfa Gate and proceeded first southwards and so around the city. This gives for the whole circumference a distance of 2 1/2 English miles less 74 yards; or very nearly 2 1/8 geographical miles."[17]

While exploring and documenting the city, Robinson and Smith made a number of important archaeological discoveries. Based on his knowledge of Josephus's writings and the observation of masonry styles in the temenos wall (the wall around the Temple Mount), Robinson confirmed that the Temple Mount was the site of the ancient temple, as tradition but not science had held until then.[18] He identified stones protruding from the upper southwest corner of the Temple Mount as part of an arch for a stairway, which ever since has been called "Robinson's Arch."[19] Robinson was also the first to identify remains of the Third Wall to the north of the Old City while walking from the Tombs of the Kings to Jaffa Gate.[20] Drawing upon his knowledge of Josephus, Robinson was able to confirm a proposal identifying the so-called Tombs of the Kings as the tomb of Queen Helena, a first-century CE convert to Judaism who moved to Jerusalem from Adiabene in Mesopotamia.[21] He also discovered the Siloam Tunnel (Hezekiah's Tunnel) and established that it carries water from the Gihon spring to the pool of Siloam.[22] Whereas nowadays it is an easy half-hour walk through the tunnel, in the nineteenth century the floor was covered with a thick layer of silt that reduced the height of the passage to a crawl space in some spots. It took Robinson's team two tries—one day penetrating the tunnel part-way from the pool of Siloam end and another day entering from the Gihon spring—to complete their examination. Robinson's observation that the tunnel must have been hewn by two teams of workmen who started at either end and met somewhere in the middle was confirmed in 1880, when an ancient Hebrew dedicatory inscription was found near the tunnel's outlet.[23]

Robinson and Smith published their findings in 1841, in a volume titled *Biblical Researches in Palestine, Sinai, Arabia Petraea and Adjacent Regions*, which earned Robinson the gold medal of the Royal Geographical Society, making him the first American to receive this prestigious award.[24] One hundred seventy pages in *Biblical Researches* are devoted to Jerusalem. Robinson and Smith returned to Palestine in 1852 to continue their research, focusing on parts of the country they had not visited previously.[25] The results were published in 1856, as *Later Biblical Researches in Palestine and the Adjacent Regions*. Traveling conditions were difficult in the nineteenth century, and Robinson's first and second visits—totaling only five months—were both cut short by illness. He died in the United States on 27 January 1863, at the age of sixty-nine, ten years after returning from his second trip to Palestine.[26]

In the period between Robinson and Smith's two visits to Palestine, Egyptian rule had ended and Ottoman control was reestablished. Under the terms of "Capitulations," the Ottomans granted European powers the right of official representation and legal and administrative jurisdiction over their own citizens. Beginning with the Tanzimat reforms in 1839, the sultan attempted to bring non-Muslims under Ottoman jurisdiction by providing for the equality of all subjects. It was during this period of transition that the European powers were granted permission for the first time to establish consulates in Jerusalem.[27] Whereas pilgrims to Jerusalem generally were housed in monasteries, the introduction of European-style hotels in the mid-nineteenth century attracted other types of visitors, greatly increasing foreign presence in the city.[28] As a result, "top-hatted European diplomats strolled through the streets of Jerusalem with their native bodyguards, or kawasses, anxious to promote the interests of their respective countries in the Holy Land."[29] The establishment in the 1860s and 1870s of organized tours by Thomas Cook and other agencies enabled large numbers of Western travelers to visit the Holy Land, including Twain, who arrived on the first organized tour from the United States.[30] The influx of Western visitors and increased scientific interest led James Finn, the British Consul in Jerusalem, to establish the Jerusalem Literary Society in 1849.[31]

Louis-Félicien Joseph Caignart de Saulcy

In the winter of 1850–1851, a Flemish explorer named Louis-Félicien Joseph Caignart de Saulcy arrived in Palestine. Despite being well-educated and proficient in Arabic, Greek, Latin, and some Hebrew, de Saulcy was an uncritical scholar who sought to make sensational discoveries confirming the Bible. Accompanied by a Catholic priest, he began his visit to the Holy Land with a twenty-one-day excursion to the Dead Sea, motivated primarily by a desire to find the biblical five cities of the plain: Sodom, Gomorrah, Admah, Zeboim, and Bela.[32] De Saulcy then turned his attention to Jerusalem, where he was drawn to a conspicuous ruin to the north of the Old City called the Tombs of the Kings. Over twenty years earlier, Robinson had confirmed the identification of this complex as the tomb of Queen Helena of Adiabene based on Josephus's testimony. De Saulcy sought to disprove Robinson, who was a Protestant, by showing that this was, in fact, the tombs of the last kings of Judah. Although the tomb was blocked with debris, de Saulcy managed to crawl inside and pulled out part of a limestone sarcophagus lid, which he promptly declared was the coffin of King David. As Neil Silberman remarks, de Saulcy was "a man who possessed the enviable talent of finding precisely what he was looking for."[33] He loaded the lid and other finds onto a ship bound for Paris, where they became part of a new Near Eastern antiquities collection at the Louvre.[34]

De Saulcy's first wife had passed away before his trip to Palestine, and, after his return to France, he married the daughter of the minister to Copenhagen, who was a close personal friend of the Empress Eugénie. Thanks to these connections, de Saulcy obtained high-ranking military and administrative appointments, and, in 1863, he returned to Palestine with the backing of the French government.[35] When local circumstances prevented further exploration of the Dead Sea, de Saulcy, now fifty-six years old, returned to the Tombs of the Kings, mounting the first full-scale archaeological excavation ever conducted in Jerusalem. His two assistants soon exposed the monumental rock-cut staircase leading to the courtyard in front of the tomb. Crawling into the burial chambers, de Saulcy removed a complete inscribed stone sarcophagus and other artifacts.[36] He describes finding a woman's skeleton dressed in a garment adorned with gold, which disintegrated when the sarcophagus was opened.[37] De Saulcy knew just enough Hebrew to make out the word "Queen" in the inscription (which is in Aramaic script, like the modern Hebrew alphabet) and promptly declared this the coffin of the wife of King Zedekiah, the last king of Judah.[38] Despite de Saulcy's brash pronouncement, Robinson was correct in identifying this as the tomb of Queen Helena of Adiabene (see Chapter 7). Ironically, de Saulcy was forced to depart the country hastily with the sarcophagus and other finds after his widely publicized claims about the discovery incited the ire of the local Jewish community who believed the burials of their royal ancestors had been desecrated.[39] Despite these shortcomings, de Saulcy contributed to the exploration of the Holy Land by producing high-quality maps and being the first in the country to use photography in archaeological research.[40]

Charles William Wilson

A year after de Saulcy's second visit, a water shortage in Jerusalem prompted the Jerusalem Water Relief Society in England to find ways to supply the city with water and improve its sanitation.[41] The Jerusalem Water Relief Society was an offshoot of a missionary organization called the London Society for Promoting Christianity among the Jews (abbreviated as the London Jews' Society), which was motivated by the Millennialist concern that Jews must return to Palestine and convert to Christianity as a prelude to the Second Coming of Christ.[42] Because many of the missionaries sent to Jerusalem became ill with cholera, the society decided to modernize the city's water system.[43] As this required having an accurate map of Jerusalem's topography, the Royal Engineers were enlisted in the effort, thanks to Lord Palmerston, a Millennialist serving as the British Foreign Secretary.[44] The Royal Engineers were led by Captain Charles Wilson, who had recently returned from surveying the border between the United States and British Columbia (Figure 1.2).[45] Over the course of eleven months in 1864–1865, Wilson and his team established a master grid over an area of more than twelve square miles in which every physical detail of Jerusalem was recorded and mapped.[46] The results were published a year later in three volumes as the *Ordnance Survey of Jerusalem.*[47]

Because the goal was to improve Jerusalem's water supply and sanitation, the survey paid special attention to underground features, including the series of pools and cisterns under the Temple Mount. Crawling through an underground sewer into an underground chamber just north of the Western Wall, Wilson

FIGURE 1.2 Charles Wilson in the Sinai, 1868–1869.
Credit: Photo by R.E. St. James MacDonald, Courtesy of the Palestine Exploration Fund, Surveyors in the Sinai, PEF-P-4991.

discovered the remains of a monumental bridge—now called Wilson's Arch—which, like Robinson's Arch nearby, was built by Herod the Great.[48]

Wilson's survey work led to the establishment in 1865 of the Palestine Exploration Fund (PEF), a society dedicated to the investigation of Palestine's archaeology, geography, geology, and natural history.[49] Although by the time the *Ordnance Survey of Jerusalem* was published the plans to improve the city's water supply had been scrapped, the PEF soon sent Wilson back to Palestine on a reconnaissance mission to prepare for a complete survey of the country.[50] When the PEF realized that a complete survey far exceeded their budget, they recalled Wilson to England and decided to focus on Jerusalem.[51] Wilson was serving as chairman of the PEF at the time of his death in 1905.[52]

Charles Warren

In 1867—the same year Mark Twain visited the Holy Land—Lieutenant Charles Warren was commissioned by the PEF to conduct a survey of Jerusalem. Like Wilson, the twenty-seven-year old Warren was an officer of the Royal Engineers, and he had previously scaled and surveyed the Rock of Gibraltar.[53] To circumvent the opposition of the local authorities and population to the exploration of Jerusalem's holy sites, Warren devised an ingenious method of excavation drawing on his experience in military mining. At various points surrounding the Temple Mount but at a distance from it, he sunk deep, rectangular shafts, up to 125 feet below ground level. The openings to the shafts were concealed by houses and piles of debris. From the base of the shafts Warren's team dug horizontal tunnels toward the Temple Mount. The tunnels revealed that the foundations of the southeast corner of the Temple Mount were 80 feet below ground level, and at the southwest corner 90 feet below ground level. Bedrock was reached at about 130 feet below ground level, indicating that the southwest side of the Temple Mount was founded on accumulated fill in the Tyropoean Valley.[54] From March–July 1867, Warren and his team dug twenty-seven shafts to the south and west of the Temple Mount, revealing that the foundations were constructed of huge ashlars with drafted margins like those visible in the lower courses of the Western Wall (these are well-cut blocks of stone with the four edges [margins] cut back—a typical feature of Herodian style masonry). Warren was the first to establish the relationship between the walls of the Temple Mount and the original bedrock.[55] Further exploration of the foundations of the Temple Mount's walls would have to wait another hundred years.

Warren also documented the cisterns and reservoirs on and around the Temple Mount, surveyed the area outside the walls of the Old City, and explored the southeastern hill, where he discovered an ancient water system now called

"Warren's Shaft."[56] During his stay in Jerusalem from February 1867 to April 1870, Warren conducted surveys in other parts of the country and was the first European to climb Masada by way of the Snake Path.[57] After Warren returned to England, he and Wilson published *The Recovery of Jerusalem* (1871), and, in 1876, he published *Underground Jerusalem*.[58]

The success of Wilson's and Warren's expeditions to Jerusalem prompted the PEF to sponsor a survey and mapping project of western Palestine, including archaeology, anthropology ("manners and customs"), topography, geology, botany, and zoology—in other words, the documentation of every natural and historical feature in the region. This project, called the Survey of Western Palestine (SWP), was carried out from 1871 to 1877 by a team of Royal Engineers led at various times by Wilson, Claude Reignier Conder, Charles Francis Tyrwhitt Drake (a civilian archaeologist), Horatio Herbert Kitchener (replacing Tyrwhitt Drake, who died of malarial fever in 1874 at the age of twenty-eight), and Warren. The result is a twelve-volume series of accurate topographic maps covering an area of some 6,000 square miles on a scale of 8 miles to 3 inches, marked with approximately 10,000 place names and accompanied by drawings of antiquities and plans of ruined sites (a thirteenth volume on the survey of eastern Palestine was published later).[59] The volume on Jerusalem, edited by Warren and Conder, was published in 1884.

The introduction to the first volume of the survey maps describes the motivation for the SWP as the investigation of the country's science and sacred history. There was also an underlying political motivation, specifically, British interest in the Suez Canal, which was being dug at that time under an agreement between the French authorities and the Ottoman governor of Egypt. The canal was opened in 1869. Six years later, Great Britain became the largest shareholder in the Suez Canal Company (which held the right to operate the canal). Seven years after that (in 1882), the British seized control of Egypt when a local uprising threatened access to the canal.[60] In advance of their invasion of Egypt, the British had dispatched Edward Henry Palmer to the Sinai. Palmer was a prominent Arabic scholar who had explored the Sinai twice and believed he could persuade the Bedouins there to support the British. After Palmer and two Royal Navy officers with him disappeared, Warren was sent to Sinai at the head of a search party. Warren discovered that Palmer and the officers had been murdered by the Bedouins for their money, and he arranged for their remains to be shipped back to England. Warren and Wilson, who was serving as the British consul general in Asia Minor, were put in charge of tracking down Palmer's murderers, who were tried and executed by the British in the presence of all the sheikhs of Sinai's Bedouin clans.[61]

In 1883, Warren was knighted. He continued to serve the British government with distinction in various capacities, including as chief commissioner of Scotland Yard (1886–1888) during the time of the "Jack the Ripper" murders, which he failed to solve.[62] Following another series of military postings, Warren was promoted to the rank of General in 1904. He died in 1927, after a long retirement.[63]

Charles Simon Clermont-Ganneau

Charles Simon Clermont-Ganneau arrived in Jerusalem in 1867, at the age of twenty-one, as dragoman-chancellor for the French consulate. He had already mastered a number of languages including Hebrew, Arabic, Turkish, and Persian. Two years after his arrival, Clermont-Ganneau became famous for his role in recovering and translating the Mesha Stone—an inscribed stele from Jordan dating to the ninth century BCE that records the victory of King Mesha of Moab over the Israelites—and facilitated its purchase and transfer to the Louvre.[64] In 1871, he discovered and published a complete Greek inscription from the *soreg* (stone balustrade) of the second temple—one of the only surviving relics belonging to the temple building. The inscription disappeared and eventually resurfaced in Istanbul, where it is still on display on the third floor of the Archaeological Museum.[65] Clermont-Ganneau conducted archaeological research and surveys in Jerusalem and in other parts of Palestine independently and on behalf of the PEF, which appointed him to their General Committee in 1875. He published his findings in the Palestine Exploration Fund's *Quarterly Studies* and in two large volumes titled *Archaeological Researches in Palestine* (1896, 1899).

In 1883, Clermont-Ganneau became embroiled in a public scandal called the "Shapira Affair." Moses Wilhelm Shapira, an antiquities dealer in Jerusalem who was a Jewish convert to Christianity, had obtained fifteen scroll fragments that reportedly were discovered by Bedouins in a cave near the Dead Sea. The fragments were blackened with a pitch-like substance and were inscribed in paleo-Hebrew (ancient Hebrew) script. Shapira claimed these were ancient copies of the book of Deuteronomy and offered to sell them to the British Museum for one million pounds sterling. Clermont-Ganneau had previously determined that supposedly Moabite artifacts (the so-called Moabite forgeries) sold by Shapira to the Prussian government were fakes. After briefly examining the scroll fragments, Clermont-Ganneau identified them as forgeries, too—a conclusion also reached by Christian David Ginsburg, who spent several weeks studying the manuscripts on behalf of the British Museum.[66] Disgraced, Shapira committed suicide by shooting himself in the head in a Rotterdam hotel.[67] In 1946–1947, the discovery of the first Dead Sea Scrolls in the same area where Shapira's fragments reportedly had been found raised the possibility that they were, in fact, authentic. But by then the fragments had disappeared.[68]

Most scholars accepted Clermont-Ganneau's and Ginsburg's identification of the Shapira fragments as forgeries. The controversy was reignited in 2021, when a young scholar named Idan Dershowitz published a book and article arguing in favor of their authenticity based on a reexamination of the documentary evidence, including Ginsburg's drawings of the fragments (there are no photographs). He claims that the fragments belong to a pre-exilic (pre-586 BCE) precursor to Deuteronomy, which, if true, would make it the oldest surviving copy of a biblical book.[69] Dershowitz's claim received extensive media coverage and has generated considerable scholarly debate.[70]

Clermont-Ganneau died in 1923, at the age of seventy-five. The PEF's obituary says that he "was remarkable for facility and brilliance and range of learning."[71] Based on my own familiarity with Clermont-Ganneau's work, I concur that he was a brilliant scholar, and therefore I would rely on his identification of the Shapira fragments as forgeries and reject the suggestion—made by some—that his determination was motivated by personal animus. As James Davila wrote in 2013 (before Dershowitz's publications): "no one would have been happier than Clermont-Ganneau to have Deuteronomy scrolls from the biblical period. I really can't imagine him rejecting a genuine epigraphic find of such importance, even if he was mad at Shapira about the Moabite forgeries."[72]

Conrad Schick

No site in Jerusalem outside of the Temple Mount has attracted more attention than the Church of the Holy Sepulcher. Originally built in fourth century CE by the Roman emperor Constantine, the church is revered by Roman Catholics and Eastern Orthodox Christians (but not by Protestants) as the site of Jesus's crucifixion and burial. Many nineteenth-century explorers sought to prove or disprove the authenticity of the church's location, usually along sectarian lines. For example, Robinson, who was a Protestant, argued against it.[73] The question of the church's authenticity is connected to the location of Jerusalem's city wall at the time of Jesus (the Second Wall) because, according to the Gospel accounts, he was crucified and buried outside the city.[74] Therefore, if the Church of the Holy Sepulcher lies inside the Second Wall, it cannot be the authentic spot (see Chapters 7 and 9).

After the Tanzimat reforms, the European powers began to lay claim to religious sites in the Holy Land and allied themselves with local Christian denominations.[75] Western intervention exacerbated tensions among the local communities and sometimes led to violence.[76] For example, the Crimean War erupted in

1853–1854 after a dispute between Roman Catholics and Greek Orthodox over control of the keys to the Church of the Nativity in Bethlehem, and repairs to the dome of the Church of the Holy Sepulcher pitted the French, British, and Ottomans against the Russians.[77]

In 1859, after the Crimean War ended, the Russian Orthodox Church acquired property adjoining the Church of the Holy Sepulcher, on which it later built the Alexander Nevsky Church (the Russian Alexander Hospice).[78] Prior to construction, the Russian Orthodox Palestine Society employed a German architect named Conrad Schick to conduct excavations on the site (Figure 1.3). Schick arrived in Jerusalem in 1846 as a missionary but became known for his knowledge of the city's architectural remains. He published occasional reports with the PEF and assisted Wilson in determining the level of the bedrock on which the city was founded. Schick was the first to report on the ancient Hebrew inscription in the Siloam Tunnel, which had been discovered by one of the students at his mission school.[79] In his excavations on the Russian property, Schick discovered part of the original Constantinian basilica as well as remains that were identified as belonging to the Second Wall, a finding that seemed to confirm the authenticity of the site of the Church of the Holy Sepulcher but eventually turned out to be erroneous.[80]

FIGURE 1.3 Conrad Schick on the right with his son-in-law L. Schoenecke at the Tombs of the Kings in Jerusalem, 1897.
Credit: Photo by Khalil Raad [?], Courtesy of the Palestine Exploration Fund, PEF-P-5037.

IN 1872, SCHICK was given unparalleled access to the Temple Mount (al-haram al-sharif) by the Ottoman authorities when he was commissioned to design a detailed model for display in the Great Exhibition in Vienna. He ended up making a series of models that include the cisterns and other subterranean features of the Temple Mount, some of which are still at Christ Church inside the Jaffa Gate and at the Schmidt's Girls' School opposite the Damascus Gate.[81] The Tabor House on the Street of the Prophets in West Jerusalem was designed and built by Schick and served as his residence until his death in 1901.[82] The building now houses the Swedish Theological Institute.

Charles George Gordon and the Garden Tomb

In 1883, General Charles Gordon visited Jerusalem. Two decades earlier, he had become famous for putting down the Taiping Rebellion in China, which earned him the nickname "Chinese Gordon." In 1873, Gordon entered the service of the Khedive (Ottoman viceroy) of Egypt with the consent of the British government (earning him the nickname "Gordon Pasha"), and later he became governor of Sudan (until 1880), where he worked to abolish the slave trade. Two years after visiting Jerusalem, Gordon lost his life in the siege of Khartoum, which the British had sent him to evacuate after the outbreak of a revolt in Sudan. Wilson participated in a failed attempt to end the siege and rescue Gordon, reaching Khartoum two days after the general fell into rebel hands and was killed.[83]

While in Jerusalem, Gordon visited the Church of the Holy Sepulcher, which he decided could not be the authentic site of Jesus's crucifixion and burial due to its location within the walls of the Old City. Like other Protestant Westerners, Gordon was put off by the dark, incense-filled interior of the Church of the Holy Sepulcher and the rites of the Latin and Eastern Orthodox denominations.[84] He therefore set out to find the authentic site. Imagining the city of Jerusalem as having the shape of a woman's body, Gordon identified a rocky outcrop to the north of Damascus Gate as Golgotha (Aramaic for "skull"), the hill on which Jesus was crucified, and one of the tombs cut into the outcrop as the site of his burial. The hill had been explored previously by others including Schick, with whom Gordon corresponded, and its resemblance to a skull had been noticed.[85] After Gordon's death, his sister published some of his letters. On 18 January 1883, he wrote: "I feel, for myself, convinced that the hill near the Damascus Gate is Golgotha. From it you can see the Temple, the Mount of Olives, and the bulk of Jerusalem. His [Jesus's] stretched-out arms would, as it were, embrace it all the day. . . . It is covered with tombs of Muslim [sic]; there are many rock-hewn caves; and gardens surround it . . . this hill is left bare ever since it was first used as a place of execution. . . . It is very nice to see it so plain and simple, instead of having a huge church built on it."[86] This spot appealed to Gordon's sensibilities because it was "plain and simple" and not enclosed within a "huge church."

Gordon's promotion of "Skull Hill" as the site of Golgotha and Jesus's tomb was widely publicized thanks to his fame and gained traction after his martyr-like death a couple of years later. In 1894, the property was purchased by the Garden Tomb Committee, a British group formed for this purpose, despite Wilson's protests that the Church of the Holy Sepulcher was probably the authentic site and the money would have been better spent funding legitimate archaeological excavations.[87] Since then, the Garden Tomb Committee has maintained the site, which is popular with Anglicans and other Protestants although archaeological investigations indicate that none of the tombs hewn into the rocky outcrop dates to the time of Jesus.[88]

Unlike the other explorers described in this chapter, Gordon's search for the authentic site of Jesus's crucifixion and burial was motivated entirely by his personal mystical faith without any concern for scientific evidence. Seth Frantzman and Ruth Kark characterize Gordon's approach as pseudo-scientific: "In his letters on topography and Bible, it is clear that although he was interested in biblical criticism his views were so intertwined with his own faith and beliefs that he merely created new biblical myths and illusions where old ones had been. . . . He did not question if the events portrayed in the Bible were true; he merely felt that they needed to be grounded and squared using modern tools."[89]

Frederick Jones Bliss

Frederick Jones Bliss was an American born in Lebanon, where his father was founder and president of the Syrian Protestant College, a missionary institution that later became the American University in Beirut.[90] He was sent to Palestine by the PEF in 1894, after being well-trained in stratigraphic excavation techniques by Sir Flinders Petrie in Egypt.[91] Bliss conducted excavations at Tell el-Hesi in 1891–1892, and he then was sent by the PEF to Jerusalem to excavate the southern end of the southwestern hill (Mount Zion) (in 1894–1897).[92] At the time, a debate raged among two prominent members of the PEF—George St. Clair and W. R. Birch—concerning whether the original City of David and tombs of the biblical kings were located on the southeastern hill (lower city) or southwestern hill (upper city).[93] St. Clair insisted that the wall encircling Mount Zion turned northeast to connect with the Temple Mount, whereas Birch believed it continued southeast to encircle the southeastern hill (which he argued was the City of David).[94]

Previous excavations had revealed a steep scarp along the southern edge of Mount Zion. Bliss followed the line of the scarp eastward, where he found the line of a wall with a gate and tower.[95] Lacking the funds necessary to purchase the properties along the wall, Bliss resorted to the same method of digging in shafts and tunnels that Warren had used.[96] He vividly describes the difficulties of digging underground: "Near the open drain, which pours its inky fluid into the Lower Pool of Siloam, the oozing galleries had to be sprinkled with carbolic acid, to the discomfiture of the long line of basket-boys."[97] Bliss discovered and documented the Byzantine church at the pool of Siloam, which has since been built over by a mosque, as well as an ancient dam across the southern end of the Tyropoeon Valley.[98] When Bliss collapsed from exhaustion and illness midway through the project, his Scottish architect, Archibald Dickie, took over until Bliss recovered.[99]

Bliss identified three distinct walls running along the southern edge of the southwestern hill and continuing toward the lower city (southeastern hill), which he concluded appear to "antedate the destruction of Jerusalem by Titus—parts of it to antedate Nehemiah; the second is apparently the wall of the Empress Eudocia, who, in the fifth century, included the Pool of Siloam within the city; and the third, undoubtedly mediaeval."[100] By digging a series of shafts from west to east, Bliss was able to determine the original depth and profile of the Tyropoeon Valley, and he discovered a stepped, paved street along its length, most of which was recently exposed.[101] In 1919, Bliss served as an adviser to General Edmund Allenby on the antiquities of Syria and Palestine.[102]

1900 to 1967
Robert Alexander Stewart Macalister

When Bliss's assistant Dickie resigned his commission with the PEF in 1898, Robert Alexander Stewart Macalister, a specialist in Irish archaeology from Dublin, was sent to Palestine to replace him (Figure 1.4).[103] After Bliss retired to Beirut two years later, Macalister continued excavating at sites around the country on behalf of the PEF—most prominently at the biblical tel of Gezer—until 1909, when he accepted a position at University College Dublin.[104] He returned briefly to Palestine in 1923, to conduct excavations on the Ophel with J. Garrow Duncan, who continued as director after Macalister returned to Dublin early in 1924.[105]

At Gezer, where Macalister excavated a huge trench, he has been criticized for digging hastily and carelessly.[106] In Jerusalem, he and Duncan opened an area at the northern end of the crest of the southeastern hill (City of David), where they found a wall with two towers which they dated to the "Jebusite period" (ca. 1200–1100 BCE) but later turned out to be a post-exilic fortification (dating after 586 BCE) at the top of an earlier massive stepped-stone structure (which they identified as the "Jebusite Ramp") (see Chapters 2 and 3).[107]

FIGURE 1.4 Robert Alexander Stewart Macalister (center) at Nablus, 1907.
Credit: Courtesy of the Palestine Exploration Fund, PEF-P-5849.

Louis-Hugues Vincent

Louis-Hugues Vincent was sent to Jerusalem from his native France in 1891, at the age of nineteen, one year after entering the Dominican novitiate (Figure 1.5). He remained in Jerusalem as a member of the convent of St. Stephen and a faculty member at the École biblique et archéologique française de Jérusalem—an institution for biblical studies on the grounds of the convent—until his death in 1960. Vincent soon established himself as a leading authority on Palestinian archaeology in general and the archaeology of Jerusalem in particular, publishing *Underground Jerusalem. Discoveries on the Hill of Ophel (1909–11)* (1911); with A.-M. Stève, *Jérusalem de l'Ancien Testament: recherches d'archéologie et d'histoire* (three volumes) (1954–1956); and with Félix-Marie Abel, *Jérusalem nouvelle* (two volumes) (1914–1922).[108]

In 1909, Montague Brownslow Parker, son of the Earl of Morley, arrived in the Holy Land. Spurred by claims made by a Finnish national named Valter H. Juvelius, Parker believed that the ark of the covenant and other ancient treasures were buried in tunnels explored by Warren and Bliss and Dickie to the south of the Temple Mount. Having raised a large sum of money and established the right connections, Parker obtained permission from the local authorities to begin excavations on the Ophel. Despite Parker's dubious motives, Vincent agreed to serve as his "archaeological advisor" in the hopes of extracting scientific information from the exploration of the tunnels. The Parker Expedition (as

FIGURE 1.5 Louis-Hugues Vincent during the Parker Expedition.
Credit: From *Vincent* 1911, unknown author.

it came to be called) ended in disgrace in 1911, after Parker and his men (not including Vincent) were caught digging under the rocky outcrop (Foundation Stone) enshrined in the Dome of the Rock and were forced to flee the country without having found any treasures.[109] However, Vincent was able to document Warren's Shaft, the Siloam Tunnel (which the Parker Expedition cleared of mud and silt), the Siloam Channel, and other components of the water system around the Gihon spring. He also discovered and correctly dated Early Bronze Age I pottery in burial caves on the southeastern hill, confirming that this is the original settlement in Jerusalem—the biblical City of David.[110]

Raymond Weill

All the explorers discussed to this point were Protestant or Catholic. The first Jewish archaeologist to conduct excavations in Jerusalem was Raymond Weill, a French Egyptologist who worked with Petrie in the Sinai Desert and co-founded the French Egyptological Society (Figure 1.6).[111] In 1913–1914 and 1923–1924, in the wake of the Parker Expedition, Weill was sent by Baron Éduard de Rothschild

FIGURE 1.6 Raymond Weill, from an obituary by Jacques Vandier in the *Revue d'Egyptologie* 8 [1951]: i–iv.
Credit: Courtesy of Ronny Reich.

to excavate land that he had acquired on the southeast slope of the southeastern hill. This property was encircled by the large southern bend of the Siloam Tunnel, which Clermont-Ganneau had suggested was intended to circumvent the location of the kings of Judah.[112]

Weill was the first archaeologist in Jerusalem to excavate above ground instead of being limited to tunnels.[113] His work exposed a large area with a Roman quarry that cut through earlier remains, including two long, vaulted, horizontal tunnels reached by vertical shafts which he identified as the tombs of the kings of Judah. Although Weill's identification has been widely rejected, in a cistern nearby he made his most significant discovery: the dedicatory inscription of a first century CE synagogue (the "Theodotos inscription").[114] After his first campaign on the southeastern hill, Weill returned to France and fought in World War I. He was severely wounded in battle and was awarded the Legion of Honor.[115] In 1923–1924, Weill again conducted excavations on Rothschild's property at the southern end of the southeastern hill.[116] Afterward he returned to France and, in 1931, was appointed professor of Oriental history at the Sorbonne. During the German occupation of France in World War II, Weill was stripped of his teaching post but was reinstated after the war ended.[117]

In the wake of World War I, the Ottoman Empire collapsed. In 1920, at the Conference of San Remo, representatives of the European powers granted the British a Mandate to control Palestine. Permanent Jewish involvement in the archaeological exploration of the country had begun in 1913, when a group of local Jewish intellectuals founded the Society for the Reclamation of Antiquities or the Jewish Society for the Exploration of Eretz-Israel, which was reorganized in 1920 as the Jewish Palestine Exploration Society (now the Israel Exploration Society [IES]).[118] The first excavation sponsored by the Jewish Palestine Exploration Society, with the approval of the British Mandatory authorities, was conducted by Nahum Slouschz (pronounced *Sloosh*) in 1920–1921 at Hammath Tiberias (south of Tiberias on the Sea of Galilee).[119] Since then, the society has sponsored dozens of excavation projects around the country, including in Jerusalem. The society's activities also include organizing conferences and publishing books and journals.[120]

John Winter Crowfoot

John W. Crowfoot was director of the British School of Archaeology in Jerusalem from 1926 to 1935, during which time he directed excavations at Jerash (Gerasa) in Jordan, Samaria-Sebaste, and Jerusalem.[121] In Jerusalem, Crowfoot conducted excavations with Gerald M. Fitzgerald on the eastern slope of the Tyropoeon Valley (the western slope of the southeastern hill) in 1927, exposing a 40-meter-long (131 feet) stretch of a well-preserved Byzantine street lined with houses that overlies significant earlier remains, including part of a massive structure that recently was identified as the Hellenistic period Akra fortress. After returning to England, Crowfoot served as chairman of the PEF (1945–1950).[122]

Robert William Hamilton

In an obituary, Roger Moorey described Robert William Hamilton as "the least well known of a remarkable trio of Oxford contemporaries who, in the 1920s, more by accident than by contrivance, entered upon careers in Near Eastern archaeology through which they were to define the British contribution to it for a generation."[123] The other members of the trio were Max Mallowan (who was married to Agatha Christie) and Kathleen Kenyon. Whereas Mallowan and Kenyon were above all field archaeologists, Hamilton was an imperial civil servant and museum administrator. His father served in the British administration in India, where Hamilton spent a year in 1911–1912. After graduation from Oxford in 1928, he joined the British School of Archaeology, which led to his participation in the excavations at Jerash, Megiddo, and Nineveh. In 1931, Hamilton was appointed Chief Inspector of Antiquities in Palestine under the British Mandatory administration, and, in 1938, at the age of thirty-three, he was made Director of Antiquities. Hamilton's term ended in 1947, with the end of the British Mandate. Afterward he spent time at the British School of Archaeology in Iraq, where he worked at Nimrud with Mallowan, taught for several years at Oxford, and was Keeper of the Ashmolean Museum from 1956 until his retirement in 1972.[124] Hamilton's publications include a study of *The Structural History of the Aqsa Mosque* (1949). His 1937–1938 excavations at the Damascus Gate provide important evidence for the construction history of the north wall of the Old City and are a model of stratigraphic techniques.[125]

Kathleen Mary Kenyon

In 1949, the renowned American biblical scholar and archaeologist William Foxwell Albright wrote in *The Archaeology of Palestine*,

> Women often make the best archaeologists, as is attested by a growing list of eminent women archaeologists. However, it is often wise to separate the sexes in excavating, since the presence of a mixed group in a camp far from a town greatly increases the expense of maintenance. In small expeditions it is difficult to mix the sexes unless the undertaking is very brief or is amply provided with funds. Some of the finest archaeological expeditions in the Near and Middle East have been all-women enterprises; excellent examples are provided by much of the work of Dorothy Garrod, Gertrude Caton Thompson, and Hetty Goldman. Where expeditions are mixed it is highly desirable to have the director's wife present, both to provide a feminine social arbiter and to avert scandal—which has brought not a few expeditions to grief.[126]

It was not until the mid-twentieth century that a woman broke the glass ceiling in the male-dominated field of archaeology in Jerusalem. Kathleen Mary Kenyon was the daughter of Fredric Kenyon, a biblical scholar who was director of the British Museum and president of the British Academy (Figure 1.7).[127] From 1930 to 1933 she worked with Robert E. Mortimer Wheeler and his wife Tessa Wheeler on the excavations at Verulamium (St. Albans), a Romano-British city. There Kenyon learned the new excavation technique developed by the Wheelers, which involved excavating in squares or trenches with detailed recording and careful attention to stratigraphy. During those same years, Kenyon worked on Crowfoot's

FIGURE 1.7   Kathleen Kenyon in Jerusalem, 1961–67, PEF-P-BART-9.
Credit: Photo by John R. Bartlett, courtesy of the Palestine Exploration Fund.

excavations at Samaria. She was instrumental in founding University College London's Institute of Archaeology in 1937 with Wheeler and served initially as its secretary and as acting director during World War II. Kenyon also was a member of the Executive Committee of the PEF and a fellow of the British Academy. In 1973, she was made a Dame Commander of the Order of the British Empire.

In 1951, Kenyon was appointed honorary director of the British School in Jerusalem, and from 1956–1967 she served as its director. In 1952–1958, Kenyon undertook excavations at Jericho, and, in 1961, she began excavations on Jerusalem's southeastern hill and in the Armenian Garden (with Roland de Vaux as co-director for the first three years and A. Douglas Tushingham as associate director for the duration). Her discoveries include identifying a section of the Bronze Age city wall halfway down the eastern slope of the southeastern hill and redating Macalister's "Jebusite wall" at the crest of the hill to the Second Temple period. Kenyon's method of digging in trenches with meticulous attention to stratigraphy rather than exposing large areas—the so-called Wheeler-Kenyon method—became a model for excavations in Palestine. However, Kenyon's rigid adherence to this method made it difficult to relate occupation layers to architectural remains, effectively divorcing the stratigraphy from its context. The limited size of the trenches also caused Kenyon to miss occupation periods that might have been represented in larger exposures. For example, due to the absence of Iron Age II, Hasmonean, and Herodian remains in a trench on the eastern slope of Mount Zion (the southwestern hill), Kenyon believed the Tyropoeon Valley was outside the city wall during these periods, thereby separating the southeastern and southwestern hills—a conclusion disproved by subsequent excavations.[128] Because of the limitations of Kenyon's method, nowadays archaeologists in Israel employ a modified version in larger excavation areas.

Kenyon's excavations ended after Israel took control of East Jerusalem in the Six-Day War.[129] Although Kenyon published a synthetic overview of the archaeology of Jerusalem (*Digging Up Jerusalem* [1974]), she died in 1978 without having produced a final report on her excavations. Andrew Lawler comments, "Kenyon's departure in the fall of 1967 marked the end of a century of archaeology dominated by Western Christians. . . . Now it was the Israelis' turn."[130]

The Years Following 1967

Since Israel's annexation of East Jerusalem in 1967, most of the excavations in and around the Old City have been carried out by Israeli archaeologists, either through the Israel Antiquities Authority (previously the Israel Department of Antiquities and Museums) or local universities, sometimes in collaboration with the Israel Exploration Society (IES).[131] After the Six-Day War, Israel mounted three large-scale excavation projects in East Jerusalem: the area around the southern and western sides of the Temple Mount, the Jewish Quarter in the Old City (the southwestern hill), and the southeastern hill.

Benjamin Mazar and Eilat Mazar

Benjamin Mazar is sometimes described as the doyen or dean of biblical archaeology (the archaeology of the Holy Land in the periods covered by the Hebrew Bible/Old Testament). Born in 1906, in Poland, as Binyamin Zeev Maisler, he studied Assyriology in Germany and emigrated to British Mandatory Palestine in 1928. From 1936 to 1939, Mazar conducted excavations at Beth Shearim under the auspices of the Jewish Palestine Exploration Society (now the IES, of which he later became the chairman). Mazar was professor of biblical history and archaeology at the Hebrew University of Jerusalem from 1951 to 1977 and served as rector for eight years during that time. From 1968 to 1978, Mazar conducted excavations outside the southern and western sides of the Temple Mount, which brought to light important remains of the late Second Temple period, the Roman period, the Byzantine period, and the early Islamic period. Following Mazar's death in 1995, his granddaughter Eilat Mazar, who was also an archaeologist, published final reports on the excavations and conducted her own excavations (Figure 1.8).[132] She died in May 2021, at the age of sixty-four.[133]

FIGURE 1.8 Eilat Mazar.
Credit: © Eilat Mazar, photo by Amihai Mazar, courtesy of Avital Mazar Tsa`iri.

Nahman Avigad

Nahman Avigad was born in Galicia (then Austria, now the Ukraine) and emigrated to British Mandatory Palestine in 1925 at the age of twenty. He worked at various sites around the country, including with B. Mazar at Beth She`arim. Much of Avigad's field work and research focused on Jerusalem, beginning with his Hebrew University PhD dissertation on rock-cut tombs in the Kidron Valley.[134] Avigad taught at the Hebrew University's Institute of Archaeology from 1949 until his retirement in 1974. He is best-known for directing excavations in Jerusalem's Jewish Quarter from 1969 to 1982, about which he published a semi-popular book.[135] Since Avigad's death in 1992, Hillel Geva (Avigad's assistant and director of the IES until 2022) has overseen the publication of the final reports on the Jewish Quarter excavations.[136]

Yigal Shiloh

Born in Haifa in 1937, Yigal Shiloh studied archaeology at the Hebrew University of Jerusalem and later joined its faculty (Figure 1.9).[137] From 1978 to 1987, he

FIGURE 1.9 Yigal Shiloh.
Credit: Courtesy of the City of David excavations, the Hebrew University of Jerusalem Institute of Archaeology.

directed excavations on the southeastern hill. At the time, Shiloh was relatively young, having received his PhD only three years earlier, and he had never directed an excavation. Nevertheless, Yigael Yadin (head of the Institute of Archaeology at the Hebrew University) and Joseph Aviram (director of the IES) selected Shiloh to lead the project because they felt he had the physical stamina, mental toughness, and organizational skills necessary to conduct a stratigraphic excavation on the southeastern hill's steep eastern slope. Shiloh, a strapping ex-paratrooper, proved them right, even taking on the difficult task of clearing Warren's Shaft. In Area G, Shiloh clarified the relationship and dates of the wall with towers and massive stepped stone structure at the crest of the hill that had been excavated previously by Macalister and Duncan and by Kenyon. In Areas B, D, and E— the land that had been purchased by Rothschild—Shiloh exposed additional stretches of the Bronze Age city wall discovered by Kenyon midway down the eastern slope.

I saw and heard B. Mazar speak on a few occasions, and I was in contact with Avigad before his death in 1992, because, for my PhD dissertation, I studied and published the pottery from his excavations in the Jewish Quarter. I also knew E. Mazar well. But Shiloh is the only archaeologist surveyed here with whom I studied. He was one of my professors when I was an undergraduate majoring in archaeology at the Hebrew University. Several of my classmates were staff members on Shiloh's excavations, and I worked on the Late Roman and Byzantine pottery for my dissertation. Personally, I did not care for Shiloh, who was a stereotypically brash *sabra* (native-born Israeli) with a lot of machismo. However, as I worked on the pottery from his excavations, I came to admire and appreciate the high scientific standards and stratigraphic techniques Shiloh employed and the first-rate staff he assembled. I benefited from the organizational skills that Yadin and Aviram noticed when I had to rely on excavation records and documentation for information after Shiloh's death.

Shiloh's excavations began shortly after Menahem Begin's Herut party came to power in Israel, ending the decades-long dominance of the Labor party. Israeli law requires the party that wins the most votes in an election to form a government with at least 61 out of 120 seats in the parliament (Knesset). If the majority party does not receive enough votes to control 61 seats, it must form a coalition with other parties. Begin's victory in 1977 ushered in a new era in which the religious parties, which previously had played a relatively small and marginal role in Israeli politics, now became part of the coalition government. Smaller parties extract concessions from the majority party in return for agreeing to join a coalition. Archaeology went from being the national pastime of Israel to an easy sacrificial lamb on the altar of political necessity. Since Begin's time, coalition governments have granted numerous concessions to religious parties, including limiting archaeological field work and especially any disturbance of supposedly Jewish burials.

Soon after Shiloh began excavations, ultra-orthodox Jews (*haredim*) launched massive demonstrations at the site, claiming that ancient Jewish graves were being desecrated despite the absence of any such remains. Even as thousands of *haredim* gathered in protest around Area G, Shiloh and his team—protected by police forces—continued to work. Shiloh brashly brushed off the protestors in a manner that Abraham Rabinovich described in a *Jerusalem Post* obituary as "provocatively combative." The ultra-orthodox retaliated by publicly cursing Shiloh. Soon thereafter, Shiloh was diagnosed with stomach cancer, which he battled bravely for the last two years of his life. He died in 1987, at the age of fifty. The ultra-orthodox viewed Shiloh's untimely death as divine retribution for his supposed transgressions, celebrating his passing in posters plastered on the walls of the Mea Shearim neighborhood: "In praise and thanksgiving to the Almighty, we inform the haredi public that the wicked heretic and defiler who destroyed Jewish graves on the slopes of the Temple Mount, Yigal Shiloh—may his name be blotted out—has died."[138] Just one week before he died, Shiloh was awarded the prestigious Jerusalem Prize in recognition of his contributions to the understanding of the city's archaeology and history. Since Shiloh's death, members of his team—many of them former students now at or approaching retirement—have continued to produce final reports on his excavations.

At the time of Shiloh's excavations and for a number of years afterward, the project's offices were housed in a building complex called Terra Sancta in the heart of West Jerusalem. The office space was leased from the Catholic Church, which owns the complex. The entrance is through a gate directly across from the Prime Minister's house. In the mid to late 1980s, I spent a lot of time in that office going through the excavation records and documentation in connection with my study of the Late Roman and Byzantine pottery. I still remember vividly the period following Shiloh's death, when those of us working in the office expected to see him walk through the door at any moment. Shiloh's oversized presence lingered with us long after he was gone.[139]

2

Jebusite Jerusalem (1050 BCE)

Historical Background

By the time of David's conquest (ca. 1000 BCE), Jerusalem had been inhabited for more than two millennia, from the beginning of the Bronze Age (ca. 3500 BCE).[1] The Hebrew Bible refers to the country's Bronze Age (pre-Israelite) population as "Canaanites," a term that denotes peoples who spoke a western Semitic precursor to the Iron Age languages of the region (e.g., Phoenician, Aramaic, Hebrew, etc.).[2] Jerusalem's first permanent inhabitants settled on the rocky slopes of the southeastern hill above the Gihon spring and cultivated the fertile soil in the Kidron Valley. The settlement seems to have been confined largely to this part of the southeastern hill throughout the Bronze Age and the beginning of the Iron Age. The remains of the earliest houses are built on bedrock. Typical of Early Bronze Age dwellings, they consist of a rectangular room surrounded by a stone bench, with an entrance in the long side (the "broad house" type).[3] Early Bronze Age I burial caves excavated by the Parker Expedition on the Ophel were published by Louis-Hugues Vincent.[4]

During the Middle Bronze Age II (ca. 2000–1550 BCE), some Canaanite towns and cities were fortified with walls and ramparts, forming great biblical tels/tells (artificial mounds) such as Megiddo, Hazor, and Lachish, each controlling the surrounding territory. Unlike Egypt, Canaan was never unified under a single ruler, although for much of the Bronze Age, parts of the country were under Egyptian hegemony. Most scholars agree that the earliest references to Jerusalem are found in the Execration Texts from Egypt, which are written in hieratic script. There are two groups, one earlier and one later, dating to the nineteenth and eighteenth centuries BCE. The Execration Texts are curses against rebellious cities and rulers, which were inscribed on clay bowls or figurines representing bound prisoners. The vessels and figurines were broken by Egyptian priests in a magical ritual to compel loyalty to the pharaoh. Among the Canaanite towns mentioned is *rwš3mm*, which is vocalized as *Rushalimum*—apparently a form of the name Jerusalem.[5]

The earlier group of Execration Texts mentions two rulers of *Rushalimum*, both of whom have Semitic names—*Šs 'n* (Shas`an) and *Yqr 'm* (Y'qar`am)— while the later group mentions one ruler (only the first syllable of his name is preserved).[6] Scholars understand the reduction from two rulers to one as per-haps reflecting Jerusalem's transition from a tribal society to a city-state.[7] By the Late Bronze Age (ca. 1550–1200 BCE), the eastern Mediterranean was ringed by powerful kingdoms including the New Kingdom in Egypt, the Hittite Empire in Anatolia (modern Turkey), and the Mycenean kingdoms in Greece. This period has been described as an international era due to the extensive contacts between these powers encompassing peaceful trade as well as violent conflicts. We know about these contacts thanks to ancient Egyptian texts and the discovery of imported objects at archaeological sites. In the Late Bronze Age, Jerusalem is mentioned again in texts from Egypt, specifically in the Amarna letters or tab-lets, so-called after the site where they were found. Ca. 1350 BCE, the Egyptian pharaoh Akhenaten (Amenhotep IV) established a new capital city at the site of Tell el-Amarna, which he named Akhetaten, reflecting his devotion to the sun god (Aten) above all other gods. After Akhenaten's death, Tell el-Amarna was abandoned as his successors reverted to the worship of the traditional Egyptian pantheon and moved the capital back to the area of Thebes. From an archaeo-logical point of view, Tell el-Amarna is important because, as a single-period site, everything found there must date to the short period in the mid-fourteenth cen-tury when it was occupied.[8]

The Amarna letters are clay tablets written in cuneiform script in the Akkadian language, the lingua franca of the period. Most of them are correspondence sent by rulers—many of whom were Egyptian vassals—to Akhenaten and his father, Amenophis III. They include six complete and one fragmentary letter sent to the pharaoh by Abdi-Hepa, the governor of *Urusalim* or *Urushalim* (Jerusalem).[9] In the letters, Abdi-Hepa repeatedly asks for military assistance against his oppo-nents and complains about neighboring rulers, as for example in EA (el-Amarna letter) 287:

> [Say to the kin]g, m[y] lord: [Message of [`Ab]di-Ḥeba, your servant. I fall at the feet [of the kin]g, my lord, 7 times and 7 times. . . . May the [kin]g know (that) all the lands are [at] peace (with one another), but I am at war. May the king provide for his land. . . . If this year there are archers, then the lands and the mayors will belong to the king, my lord. But if there are no archers, then the ki[ng] will have neither lands nor mayors. Consider Jerusalem! This neither my father nor m[y] mother gave to me.

The [str]ong hand: *zu-ru-uḫ* (arm) [of the king] gave it to me. Consider the deed! This is the deed of Milkilu and the deed of the sons of Lab`ayu, who have given the land of the king (to) the `Apiru. Consider, O king, my lord! *I am in the right*! . . . *A[nd] so i]f* he is going to send [troop]s into [Jerusalem], let them come with [*a garrison for*] (regular) *service*. May the king provide for them. . . . May the king, my lord, know (that) I am unable to send a caravan to the king, my lord. For your information! As the king has placed his name in Jerusalem forever, he cannot abandon it—the land of Jerusalem."[10]

In this letter, Abdi-Hepa mentions the `Apiru/Hapiru/Habiru, a term that occurs elsewhere in the Amarna tablets as well as in other ancient Near Eastern texts and appears to encompass various displaced groups or individuals who oper-ated on the margins of society. Scholars disagree about whether the similarity in names indicates that the `Apiru and the biblical Hebrews were related, in which case the Hebrews were perhaps a group of `Apiru, or is coincidental.[11]

The Hebrew Bible describes Jerusalem at the time of David's conquest as a Jebusite city called Jebus: "The king and his men marched to Jerusalem against the Jebusites, the inhabitants of the land" (2 Sam 5:6). The connection between the Jebusites and Canaanites is unclear. Many scholars propose that the Jebusites were related to the Hittites based on several biblical passages. Ezekiel 16:1–3 says, "The word of the Lord came to me: Mortal, make known to Jerusalem her abomi-nations, and say, Thus says the Lord God to Jerusalem: Your origin and your birth were in the land of the Canaanites; your father was an Amorite, and your mother a Hittite" (repeated in Ezek 16:45: "Your mother was a Hittite and your father an Amorite"). Uriah the Hittite was one of David's elite warriors (2 Sam 11:6; 23:39; 1 Chr 11:41). David erected an altar on a threshing floor that he purchased from a man named Araunah: "That day God came to David and said to him, 'Go up and erect an altar to the Lord on the threshing floor of Araunah the Jebusite'" (2 Sam 24:18;1 Chr 21:15, where he is called "Ornan"). Although Araunah is described as a Jebusite, his name might be Hittite or Hurrian.[12] The Amorites might cor-respond to western Semitic peoples from the region of Syria called *Amurru* in Mesopotamian texts.[13] Although composed centuries later, these biblical pas-sages suggest that, on the eve of David's conquest, Jerusalem's population was composed of different ethnic groups.

Archaeological Remains

There appears to be a disconnect between the picture of Middle and Late Bronze Age Jerusalem presented by texts and archaeology. The Execration Texts and

Amarna letters give the impression of an important city-state ruled by Egyptian vassals or petty kings. In contrast, archaeological remains indicate that, during this period, Jerusalem was a modest settlement of less than 11 acres in size, with an estimated population of around 1,000 inhabitants.[14] The architectural remains and other finds such as pottery are concentrated on the eastern slope of the hill and the crest above, perhaps indicating that the north end and west side of the southeastern hill were uninhabited.[15] However, the disconnect between text and archaeology is not as great as it seems, as Jerusalem is typical of the small fortified centers of the Middle Bronze Age. The population, including an urban elite, would have been supported by agricultural villages in the vicinity.[16]

The Water System

Most of the Bronze Age remains in Jerusalem date to the latter part of the Middle Bronze Age (Middle Bronze Age IIB = MB IIB; ca. 1750–1550 BCE) and are connected to the Gihon spring. Safe access to the spring was a major concern of Jerusalem's inhabitants, who sought to ensure that the water source was protected and safely accessible during times of war or siege. Beginning in 1995, excavations conducted around the spring by Ronny Reich and Eli Shukron brought to light a massive fortification and water system. The system includes tunnels and channels to convey water from the spring, pools for storing water, fortifications protecting the spring, and an underground system providing safe access to the water (Figure 2.1; Pl. 3B).

Reich and Shukron found that the spring was enclosed within an enormous, pi-shaped structure (the "Spring Tower") measuring ca. 16 × 16 meters (52 × 52 feet) (external dimensions), with walls up to 7 meters (23 feet) thick constructed of huge boulders weighing on average 3–4 tons.[17] The Siloam Channel (also called Channel II or the Canaanite Tunnel; not to be confused with the Siloam Tunnel = Hezekiah's Tunnel = Channel VIII) carried water from the spring southward along the foot of the eastern slope to a large storage pool. The northern half of the channel was cut into rock and was covered with massive stone slabs that form the foundations of the Spring Tower, while the southern half is a rock-cut tunnel (Figure 2.2). Reich and Shukron believe that the channel originally consisted only of the northern (rock-cut) portion. They theorize that it terminated at a storage pool in the Kidron Valley and was extended farther south (the tunnel portion) in the Iron Age II (eighth century BCE) to a large storage pool (the pool of Siloam or Birket el-Hamra) at the southern tip of the southeastern hill.[18] Contrary to Yigal Shiloh and his team, Reich and Shukron argue that openings along the sides of Channel II are not humanmade but are natural karstic voids that were blocked, and therefore the channel was not used to irrigate

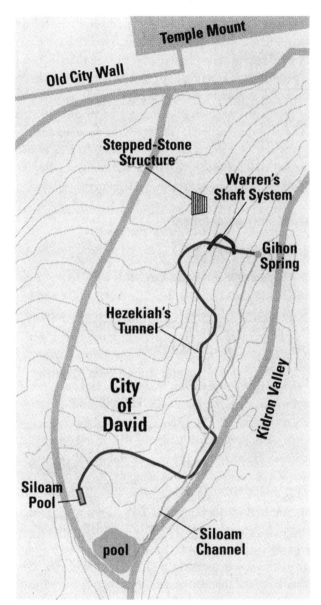

FIGURE 2.1 Plan of the ancient water systems in relation to the southeastern hill, from Reich and Shukron 1999: 25.
Credit: © Biblical Archaeology Society.

agricultural plots in the Kidron Valley.[19] In the Iron Age II, the excess water from the Gihon Spring was redirected through the Siloam Tunnel (= Hezekiah's Tunnel = Tunnel VIII), which is about 2.5 meters (8 feet) lower than Channel II and therefore replaced it (see Chapter 4).[20]

FIGURE 2.2 Inside Channel II.
Credit: Photo by the author.

Another channel (III) that branches off from Channel II fed a circular pool (the "Round Chamber") southwest of the Spring Tower. The Round Chamber is cut into the bottom of the eastern side of an enormous "Rock-Cut Pool" measuring ca. 15 × 10 × 10 meters (49 × 32 × 32 feet), which was accessed by a passage with steps hewn along its east side (Figure 2.3). On the western side of the Spring Tower and overlooking the northern side of the Rock-Cut Pool is another massive structure (the "Pool Tower"), with walls up to 3.5 meters (11 feet) thick constructed of huge boulders. The Pool Tower is not a tower but a gallery consisting of two parallel walls (the "Fortified Corridor") ascending the slope of the hill above the spring (Figure 2.4).[21] The gallery encloses a 2.3-meter-wide (7.5 feet) corridor or passage that provided protected access to the spring

FIGURE 2.3 The Rock-Cut Pool.
Credit: Photo by the author.

and/or the Round Chamber.[22] Despite its name, the Rock-Cut Pool could not have stored water from the spring because the Round Chamber in its north-east corner and Channel III, which feeds the Round Chamber, are 4–5 meters (13–16 feet) lower than the bottom of the pool. A geologist named Dan Gill determined that the Rock-Cut Pool was formed by quarrying the huge boulders used in the construction of the Spring Tower and Pool Tower. Nevertheless, it is not clear why the pool's walls were carefully smoothed if it was not intended to store water.[23]

The massive structures around the spring are connected to Warren's Shaft, which is named after Captain Charles Warren, who discovered the system in 1867.

FIGURE 2.4 The Pool Tower.
Credit: Photo by the author.

Warren's Shaft provided access to water from the Gihon spring through an underground tunnel, which was entered from within the fortification wall midway up the eastern slope. From the entrance a stepped diagonal passage led to a horizontal tunnel (Figure 2.5). For a long time, scholars thought the horizontal tunnel terminated at the top of a deep vertical shaft, at the base of which was a channel that conducted water from the spring (Figure 2.6). According to this understanding, water would have been drawn by dropping a bucket from a wooden platform at the top of the vertical shaft. However, Reich and Shukron's discoveries indicate that the horizontal tunnel originally bypassed the vertical shaft (which is a natural karstic formation) and instead terminated at the northwest corner

FIGURE 2.5 The stepped diagonal passage in Warren's Shaft.
Credit: Photo by the author.

of the Rock-Cut Pool (Figure 2.7).[24] In the Iron Age II, the floor level of the
horizontal tunnel was recut and lowered, exposing the top of the vertical shaft.[25]
Eyal Meiron and Zvi Abeles disagree with Reich and Shukron's conclusion that
the reason for the lowering of the floor in the Iron Age II is unknown and propose that the vertical shaft was used to draw water from a tunnel at its base that
brought water from the spring.[26]

Scholars also debate how other parts of the system functioned. Reich and
Shukron had assumed that Warren's Shaft provided access to water stored in
the Rock-Cut Pool but now acknowledge that the pool could not have been
filled with water.[27] In addition, the exit from Warren's Shaft terminates at the

FIGURE 2.6 The "shaft" in Warren's Shaft.
Credit: Photo by the author.

northwest corner of the pool in a sheer, 10-meter (32-foot) high rock face. The Round Chamber, located in the northeast corner of the pool, is 5 meters (16 feet) lower. The south wall of the Pool Tower would have blocked access from Warren's Shaft to the Round Chamber along the north side of the pool.

The function of the Pool Tower further complicates the picture. Reich and Shukron note that, on the one hand, the two parallel walls of the tower ascend the slope into a cave inside Warren's Shaft, suggesting they formed a passage (the Fortified Corridor) that provided an above-ground exit from the system.[28] Perhaps this is how water was accessed in Warren's Shaft, instead of at the northwest corner of the Rock-Cut Pool.[29] At the same time, however, Reich

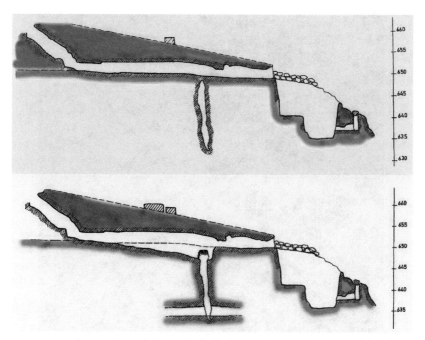

FIGURE 2.7 Section through Warren's Shaft, showing the original system (above), and the later cutting of the floor into the vertical shaft (below), from Reich 2011a: Fig. 107. Credit: Courtesy of Ronny Reich.

and Shukron found that the two parallel walls continue westward for a distance of ca. 24 meters (79 feet) up the slope above the spring, past Warren's Shaft.[30] They suggest that this reflects two phases: at first, the system consisted of two above-ground, parallel walls providing access to the Spring Tower, which later were replaced by an underground tunnel (Warren's Shaft). Reich and Shukron propose that the above-ground gallery continued to a fortress at the crest of the hill, although they were unable to trace the two parallel walls all the way to the top.[31]

The City Wall

The function and relationship of the components of the water system are connected to the question of whether Middle Bronze Age Jerusalem was fortified by a city wall. On the eastern crest of the hill above the Gihon spring, Macalister and Duncan uncovered a wall with two towers. They identified the wall as "Jebusite" and the towers as later additions. However, Kathleen Kenyon demonstrated that the wall and the towers date to the post-exilic period (after 586 BCE). Midway down the eastern slope above the spring, she discovered a 2-meter (7-foot) thick wall, which she identified as the Middle Bronze Age II city wall (Kenyon's Wall NB: renamed Wall 3 by Margreet Steiner in the final report).[32] At the north end of the exposed segment, the wall turns a corner toward the west, which led Kenyon to postulate that it was part of a gate providing access to the spring or marked the northern end of the city—a possibility suggested by the absence of the wall's continuation to the north.[33] On the slope immediately above and parallel to Wall 3, Kenyon found the remains of the Iron Age II (ca. 800 BCE) city wall, which she traced northward for a distance of 27.5 meters (90 feet) (Wall NA; renamed Wall 1 by Steiner).[34]

Kenyon's Wall 3 intersects the north wall of the Pool Tower/Fortified Corridor (Wall 108) at a 90-degree angle. Unfortunately, one of Parker's tunnels was dug at this spot in 1909–1911, destroying the connection between the two walls. Thus, it is impossible to determine their relationship, although Reich and Shukron believe that Kenyon's Wall 3 abuts and is later than Wall 108, and, therefore, the Pool Tower/Fortified Corridor.[35] In light of this evidence, Reich and Shukron argue that Kenyon's Wall 3 is not part of the Middle Bronze Age II city wall. Instead, they propose that the fortified settlement lay either to the north or south of the Pool Tower/Fortified Corridor.[36] However, Yuval Gadot and Joe Uziel argue that Walls 3 and 108 are bonded, which would indicate they are contemporary. Based on pottery found above and below a cobbled street abutting the western face of Wall 3, they date it and Wall 108 to the "early Iron Age IIB," that is, the early to mid-eighth century BCE.[37]

To the south of the Gihon spring, Shiloh discovered a massive wall founded on bedrock at the top of a cliff midway down the eastern slope (Shiloh's Area E), which he identified as the continuation of Kenyon's Walls 3 and 1 (Figure 2.8). The face of the northern part of the wall (designated Wall 285) is constructed of large boulders, while the upper courses are built of smaller stones (Wall 219). Shiloh identified Wall 285 as the MB IIB city wall and Wall 219 as a reconstruction dating to the Iron Age II.[38] This conclusion has been questioned by both Reich and David Ussishkin, who argue that the two walls appear to form a terrace wall rather than a fortification.[39] They identify a massive wall at the foot of the eastern slope (Reich and Shukron's Area J) as an extension of the Iron Age II fortifications (see Chapter 4).[40]

Shiloh, who cleared Warren's Shaft, dated it to the time of David and Solomon (ca. 1000 BCE) based on comparisons with Israelite water systems at sites such as Megiddo and Hazor.[41] However, archaeologists now date Warren's Shaft and the Siloam Channel (Channel II) to ca. 1800 BCE, as seems to be confirmed by Reich and Shukron's discovery of the Spring Tower, the Pool Tower, and the Rock-Cut Pool, which they date to the MB IIB. The date of Warren's Shaft is connected to the question of whether a city wall existed, as it clearly was intended to provide

FIGURE 2.8 The mid-slope wall.
Credit: Photo by the author.

safe underground access to the water in the spring from inside the wall. Indeed, the entrance to Warren's Shaft is located above (inside) Kenyon's Walls 1 and 3. Without a city wall, there would be no need for Warren's Shaft.[42]

The Water System and the City Wall

To summarize to this point: most archaeologists—including Reich and Shukron—date Warren's Shaft, the Siloam Channel, the Spring Tower, the Pool Tower, and the Rock-Cut Pool to the MB IIB (Reich and Shukron date the southern half of the Siloam Channel to the Iron Age II). Furthermore, many archaeologists identify Kenyon's Wall 3 and Shiloh's Wall 285 as the MB IIB city wall, which would mean the settlement was fortified.[43] However, Reich identifies Shiloh's Wall 285 as a terrace wall and Kenyon's Wall 3 as a "local" feature belonging to a fortification system around the spring rather than a city wall. The Pool Tower was an enclosed gallery that presumably provided protected access to a citadel at the crest of the hill above.[44] Kay Prag has concluded similarly that Kenyon's Wall 3 and the water system with its defensive system were the only Middle Bronze Age fortifications in Jerusalem, focusing on control of and access to the spring.[45]

In 2017, Uziel and Nahshon Szanton, who recently conducted excavations around the Gihon spring, published the radiocarbon dates of samples taken from layers of sediment under the northeast corner of the Spring Tower, with surprising results. The material from the lowest layer of sediment they sampled dates to the Middle Bronze Age, but the material taken from the uppermost layers, immediately below one of the huge boulders in the tower, dates to the late ninth century BCE (Iron Age IIA). This suggests that either the Spring Tower (and the associated components of the system) originally was built in the Middle Bronze Age and renovated in the Iron Age II, or the entire system was first established in the Iron Age II.[46] Reich rejects the possibility of an Iron Age II construction date on the grounds that the sediments from which the samples were taken could have washed in or been disturbed after the tower's initial construction. He points out that the huge boulders used to construct the Spring Tower and Pool Tower do not resemble the Iron Age fortification walls found by Kenyon and Shiloh (Walls 1 and 219), which are built of much smaller stones but are similar to Middle Bronze Age II fortifications at other sites around the country.[47] In contrast, Ussishkin proposes that the Spring Tower, the Pool Tower, the Rock-Cut Pool, and Warren's Shaft all date to the Iron Age II, which is when (he argues) the city wall was first built. He allows only for the Siloam Channel (Channel II) to be earlier in date (Early or Middle Bronze Age) as it carried water to a storage pool to the south and was not part of a defensive system around the spring.[48] This would mean that the entire system is nearly a millennium later in date than most archaeologists believe and would leave few identifiable remains of the Middle Bronze Age.[49]

The picture is further complicated by the sequencing of Warren's Shaft and the Pool Tower. According to Reich, the point at which the Pool Tower (the Fortified Corridor) emerges from Warren's Shaft was blocked by a wall dated to the Middle Bronze Age by potsherds found in the associated fills, indicating that this is when it went out of use.[50] As mentioned previously, Reich and Shukron distinguish two phases in the system: at first, two above-ground, parallel walls provided access to the spring from a fortress or citadel at the crest of the hill; these later were replaced by an underground tunnel (Warren's Shaft). Gill has concluded that the tunnels of Warren's Shaft are natural karstic formations adapted for use by humans. He therefore believes that Warren's Shaft antedates the Pool Tower.[51]

To conclude this part of our discussion: the only part of Jerusalem's early water system that all archaeologists seem to agree dates (or might date) to the Middle Bronze Age is the Siloam Channel (Channel II). Despite the results of radiocarbon dating of material under the Spring Tower and the uncertainty surrounding the relationship between the components of the system, most archaeologists date the Spring Tower, the Pool Tower, the Rock-Cut Pool, and Warren's

Shaft to the Middle Bronze Age IIB. There is less consensus about whether the Middle Bronze Age settlement was enclosed by a city wall (limited to the eastern crest and slope of the southeastern hill) or only the area around the spring and a possible citadel on the crest of the hill above were fortified.[52] The latter scenario calls into question the dating of Warren's Shaft to the Middle Bronze Age as its purpose was to provide underground access to the water in the spring from inside the city wall. Finally, according to a minority view, the Spring Tower, the Pool Tower, the Rock-Cut Pool, Warren's Shaft, and the city wall all were first built in the Iron Age II.

The modest size of the Jerusalem's Middle Bronze Age settlement—covering an area of less than 11 acres and with only about 1,000 inhabitants—raises the question: Who built the massive fortification and water systems? One possibility is that, in this period, Jerusalem became a regional center for surrounding villages thanks to the spring, which was venerated and utilized as a natural resource with a sacred mountain above.[53]

Jerusalem on the Eve of David's Conquest

The transition from the Late Bronze Age and Iron Age ca. 1200 BCE was marked by severe disruptions around the eastern Mediterranean, including the collapse of the Mycenean kingdoms in Greece, the New Kingdom in Egypt, and the Hittite Empire in Anatolia, which put an end to the era of internationalism. Scholars debate the causes of these disruptions—war, famine, plague, climate change, invasions—or some combination of these.[54] Raphael Greenberg believes the transition from the Late Bronze Age "palace prestige economy" (in which wealth and power were concentrated in the hands of a few) to the more "egalitarian" or collective societies of the early Iron Age was driven by an economic and demographic recovery.[55] Whatever the causes, the disruptions were accompanied by movements of peoples, some of whom contributed to the upheavals as invaders, while others were displaced refugees. Among these peoples were the Philistines, a group of "Sea Peoples" from the Aegean who settled along the Palestinian coast, while around the same time the Israelite tribes settled the country's hilly interior. If the Jebusites indeed were Hittite in origin, perhaps this is when they arrived in Jerusalem.[56] Most archaeologists now believe that most of the early Israelites did not arrive en masse in an exodus from Egypt but instead comprised peoples of different origins including Canaanites, who settled in the hill country in the early Iron Age and eventually unified as tribes around the worship of a national deity called `El or YHWH—the God of Israel.[57] The possibility that the early Iron Age Israelites included members of the native (Canaanite) population is suggested by elements of continuity in the country's material culture (e.g., pottery types).[58]

The earliest extrabiblical reference to Israel comes from Egypt and dates to this period. In the fifth year of his reign (1209 BCE), the pharaoh Merneptah recorded his military victories on a stele (inscribed stone slab), stating "Israel is laid waste and his seed is not." A special sign identifies Israel as a semi-nomadic or rural people rather than a territory or city-state, while the rest of the inscription suggests that they were located in Canaan.[59] By the time David conquered Jerusalem two centuries later, the Israelite tribes had united under the rule of a monarch.

According to the biblical account, the Israelite tribes settled the hilly interior of the country—from Galilee in the north to the northern Negev in the south—but were unable to take Jerusalem from the Jebusites, which remained a foreign enclave in the heart of the Israelite settlement until David's conquest. The Hebrew Bible implies that Jebusite Jerusalem was such a well-fortified stronghold that it could be defended even by the blind and the lame (2 Samuel 5:6). Again, however, there seems to be a disconnect between text and archaeology. As we have seen, there are questions about whether the Spring Tower, the Pool Tower, the Rock-Cut Pool, and Warren's Shaft date to the MB IIB, and there is even less consensus about the existence of a city wall. Furthermore, even if we agree with most archaeologists that the fortifications and water systems around the Gihon spring date to the MB IIB and continued in use through the Late Bronze Age,[60] almost no other Late Bronze Age remains have been discovered on the southeastern hill. Throughout the country, the transition from the Middle to Late Bronze Age (ca. 1550) is marked by the destruction or abandonment of sites accompanied by severe depopulation, reflecting a system-wide collapse.[61] Power and wealth were now concentrated in the hands of elite families living in palaces or manors who were vassals of Egypt's New Kingdom, while tenant farmers cultivated the land.[62]

Kay Prag, remarking on the demographic decline, describes Late Bronze Age Jerusalem as "little more than a garrisoned citadel," while Greenberg describes the evidence of settlement as "almost entirely circumstantial."[63] In contrast, while Jane Cahill acknowledges the lack of stratified remains dating to the beginning of the Late Bronze Age, she cites fragmentary architecture and pottery (including imports) of the fourteenth and thirteenth centuries from Macalister and Duncan's, Kenyon's, and Shiloh's excavations as evidence that Jerusalem was the capital of an Egyptian vassal city-state, consistent with the picture in the Amarna letters.[64] Cahill's view is supported by Eilat Mazar's discovery of "large quantities" of Middle Bronze, Late Bronze, and Iron Age I pottery under the large stone structure that she excavated at the top of the stepped stone structure (see below and Chapter 3).[65] In addition, in her 2009–2013 excavations on the Ophel, E. Mazar recovered nearly thirty seals and seal impressions dating to the Middle Bronze Age II, including some from Egypt, which were used for sealing documents and containers.[66] She also found a tiny fragment of a Late Bronze Age cuneiform tablet—the first ever discovered in Jerusalem. Cuneiform is a script (system of writing) that was used for international correspondence in the Near East during the Late Bronze Age. The Jerusalem tablet is roughly contemporary with the Amarna letters and is made of clay from the Jerusalem region. This indicates that the tablet was inscribed locally instead of having been delivered to Jerusalem from somewhere else. Presumably it is an archival copy of a letter that was sent to another recipient by the king of Jerusalem—perhaps Abdi-Hepa himself, although there is no definite indication of this.[67]

The Stepped Stone Structure

In their quest for an (assumed) Jebusite citadel, many archaeologists have focused their attention on the crest of the hill above the spring (Kenyon's Site A; Shiloh's Area G), where Robert Macalister and John Duncan found the "Jebusite" wall and two towers: the north tower, which they dated to the post-exilic period (after 586 BCE), and a larger south tower (or bastion), which they believed was added to the "Jebusite" wall by David and Solomon.[68] The wall and towers are perched atop a massive stone buttress (Macalister and Duncan's "Jebusite ramp"; now generally called the "stepped stone structure") constructed of roughly dressed limestone boulders rising in stepped courses from east to west at a 45-degree angle (Figure 2.9). The stepped stone structure forms a "mantle" connected to a rubble core underneath, which overlies a series of stone terraces or compartments formed by intersecting walls filled with earth and boulders.[69] Macalister and Duncan, Kenyon, Shiloh, and E. Mazar (who conducted excavations in 2007–2008) exposed parts of the stepped stone structure, the full extent of which is unknown.[70] In Shiloh's Area G alone, fifty-eight courses of masonry were exposed to a height of 17 meters (56 feet).[71] Cahill estimates the total preserved (exposed) height of the stepped stone structure at ca. 30 meters (98 feet), which originally could have reached 37.5 meters (123 feet) high if Kenyon was correct that it extended from the fortification wall (Wall 3) to the crest of the hill.[72]

Although archaeologists agree that Macalister and Duncan's "Jebusite" wall and towers are post-exilic, they disagree about the date, relationship, and function of the terraces and the stepped stone structure. Macalister and Duncan called the stepped stone structure the "Jebusite ramp" because they assumed it was a buttress to support the "Jebusite" wall above.[73] Kenyon dated the terraces to the thirteenth century BCE and thought they were intended to extend the built area on the ridge above. She believed that some of the terraces were rebuilt or repaired in the tenth century by Solomon and in the eighth century by Hezekiah and therefore corresponded to the biblical Millo (see Chapter 3).[74] According to Kenyon, the stepped stone structure was not connected to the terraces underneath but

FIGURE 2.9 The stepped stone structure.
Credit: Photo by the author.

instead was added in the Hasmonean period (second–first centuries BCE) as a buttress during repairs to the fortification wall and tower above (which she dated to the time of Nehemiah).[75] Like Kenyon, Shiloh assigned the terraces to the thirteenth century and thought they were unconnected to the stepped stone structure, which he dated to the time of David and Solomon (tenth century BCE).[76] Cahill and David Tarler, who supervised the excavations in Shiloh's Area G, identify the terraces and the stepped stone structure as a single unit dating to the Late Bronze-Early Iron Age transition (ca. 1200 BCE), while Reich agrees but dates the unit to the thirteenth century.[77] Steiner and Prag, who have each published material from Kenyon's excavations, have different views: Steiner dates the terraces to the twelfth century and the stepped stone structure to the tenth century, while Prag identifies them as a single unit dating to the tenth century.[78] Israel Finkelstein considers the terraces and stepped stone structure (or mantle) two separate units, with the former dating to the Bronze Age and the latter to the ninth or early eighth centuries BCE. He argues that the upper part of the stepped stone structure was renovated in the Hasmonean period to support the First Wall.[79] E. Mazar dates the stepped stone structure to the tenth century and claims to have found the remains of David's palace in the area above.[80] Thus, although it makes sense to assume that a fortified Bronze Age citadel occupied the crest of the hill above the spring, there is no consensus among archaeologists that any of the remains in this area antedate the tenth–ninth centuries.[81] We shall consider further the date of the stepped stone structure in the next chapter.

Warren's Shaft

Another element that some scholars have connected to the biblical account of David's conquest of Jerusalem is Warren's Shaft.

> The king and his men marched to Jerusalem against the Jebusites, the inhabitants of the land, who said to David, "You will not come in here, even the blind and the lame will turn you back"—thinking, "David cannot come in here." Nevertheless, David took the stronghold of Zion, which is now the City of David. David had said on that day, "Whoever would strike down the Jebusites, let him get up the *tsinnor* to attack the lame and the blind, those whom David hates." . . . David occupied the stronghold, and named it the city of David. (2 Sam 5:6–9; 1 Chronicles 11:4–7 adds that Joab, son of Zeruiah, was the first to go up the *tsinnor* and became David's commander.)

In modern Hebrew *tsinnor* means pipe or gutter (the kind used in plumbing), preserving the sense of its use in Psalm 42:7: "Deep calls to deep at the thunder of your cataracts (*tsinnorot* [plural])."[82] Some scholars therefore identify the *tsinnor* mentioned in the biblical account as a water system, specifically Warren's Shaft, which Joab managed to climb up to penetrate the city's defenses.[83] If this is correct, Warren's Shaft would have to predate David's conquest (as many archaeologists think it does). It might make sense to understand *tsinnor* as referring more broadly to the components of the water system around the Gihon spring, as Reich suggests.[84] However, because the term occurs nowhere else in the Hebrew Bible, its meaning is obscure and need not have anything to do with a water system.[85] For example, Prag proposes that the *tsinnor* might be a natural fault or break in the rock face, underlying the Stepped Stone Structure, which Joab managed to climb up.[86] Dan Bahat understands *tsinnor* as referring to an implement used magically to ward off the enemy—in accordance with the view of some scholars that the Jebusites placed the blind and lame on the walls to warn that attackers would suffer the same fate—or was a musical instrument used to conquer the city, similar to the trumpets blown outside the walls of Jericho.[87]

Temples and Shrines

Although presumably there were one or more temples or shrines in Jerusalem before David's conquest, there is no definite literary evidence or archaeological remains. It makes sense to suppose that the threshing floor of Araunah on the rocky outcrop rising to the north of the southeastern hill was a cultic spot even before David purchased it and erected an altar there (2 Sam 24:16–25; 1 Chr 21:15–28).[88] Gabriel Barkay has identified the site of a possible Late Bronze Age Egyptian temple to the north of Jerusalem's Old City. Excavations conducted on the grounds of the École Biblique in the late nineteenth century brought to light several objects including a stele inscribed with hieroglyphs and an offering table, which Barkay argues indicate the existence of a Late Bronze Age Egyptian temple on the road leading north from Jerusalem.[89] Because the evidence is inconclusive, reactions to this proposal have been mixed.[90]

Conclusion

It was the Gihon spring—a perennial source of water in a semi-arid environment—that attracted the first people to settle some five thousand years ago on the steep, rocky east slope of the southeastern hill. Water, of course, is necessary for survival, but its gushing forth from deep inside the earth must have been taken as a sign that the spring and the hill above were sacred. The importance of the spring is reflected in efforts to protect access to its water within the complex system of massive fortification walls and pools and tunnels constructed in the latter part of the Middle Bronze Age. Indeed, the remains associated with Middle and Late Bronze Age occupation are concentrated around the spring and on the slope above, leaving open the question of how far beyond that the settlement might have extended.

The concentration of remains in a small area around and above the spring, combined with their paucity elsewhere on the southeastern hill, contrasts with the impression of a fortified city-state conveyed in the Amarna letters and the biblical account, although the cuneiform tablet found on the Ophel indicates that Jerusalem had some international connections during this period.[91] In addition, pottery found in tombs around Jerusalem—including a surprisingly large number of imported vessels from Cyprus and Greece—is evidence of habitation in the vicinity. Nevertheless, the settlement on the southeastern hill appears to have been limited largely to the area around and above the Gihon spring, as Vincent concluded over a century ago: "in Jebusite times as in primitive times . . . the heart of the town was the summit of this hill directly linked with the spring."[92] This would have been the "stronghold of Zion" reportedly conquered by David (2 Sam 5:7).

3

Israelite Jerusalem (930 BCE)

Historical Background

The centuries following the upheavals that marked the transition from the Late Bronze Age to the Iron Age (ca. 1200 BCE) witnessed the emergence of a series of ethnic kingdoms and states in Canaan and its vicinity.[1] Some of these are mentioned in the Hebrew Bible as Israel's neighbors, including Ammon to the northeast (with its capital at Rabbath Ammon or Greater Ammon = modern Amman in Jordan), Moab to the east, and Edom to the southeast. The Philistines—one of the Sea Peoples—founded a kingdom on the southwestern coast with five major cities (a pentapolis) including Gaza and Ashkelon. Along the coast of modern Lebanon to the north, Phoenician cities such as Tyre, Sidon, and Berytus (modern Beirut) became major maritime powers.

Like the peoples around them, during the early Iron Age the Israelites underwent a process of ethnic formation (ethnogenesis), with the twelve tribes eventually uniting under Saul's rule. His successors, David and Solomon, expanded the territory they ruled by conquering neighboring peoples.[2] The period of David and Solomon—called the United Kingdom or United Monarchy—has been the subject of intense debate despite its brief, seventy-five-year duration (ca. 1005–928 BCE).[3] The kingdom would have been at its height in 930 BCE, shortly before Solomon's death resulted in its division (Pl. 4A). Controversies swirl around the nature and extent of the United Kingdom, ranging from scholars who follow the biblical description of David and Solomon as powerful kings with international contacts who ruled a territory extending from the Euphrates River to Egypt and Philistia (1 Kgs 4:21) (biblical "maximalists"), to those who argue that David was the tribal ruler of a small chiefdom, to those who claim that David and/or Solomon and the United Kingdom never existed but instead are inventions of later traditions and the biblical writers (biblical "minimalists").[4] Related to these controversies are disagreements over the dates when the various biblical books were first composed, with estimates ranging (depending on the book) from the latter part of the Iron Age (eighth–seventh centuries BCE) to the Hellenistic period (third–second centuries BCE).

Despite the lack of consensus, most scholars do not deny David's and Solomon's existence but instead debate the nature and extent of the United Kingdom in relation to the biblical account. Indeed, an inscription discovered at Tel Dan in 1993 and 1994 makes it difficult to maintain that David is a mythical invention rather than a historical figure (Figure 3.1). The inscription, incised on a stone slab (stele), records the victory of the Aramaean king of Damascus, apparently Hazael, over his enemies: "[I killed Jeho]ram son of [Ahab] king of Israel, and [I] killed [Ahaz]iahu son of [Jehoram kin]g of the House of David (*beit David*)."[5] After Solomon's death, the United Kingdom split into a northern kingdom (Israel) and southern kingdom (Judah). Jehoram was king of Israel and Ahaziah was king of Judah in the mid-ninth century, which must be the approximate date of the victory recorded in the inscription. Jehoram's description as "king of the House of David"—with "House" referring to a dynasty—means that a little over a century after David's assumed lifetime, the Israelite kings traced their ancestry

FIGURE 3.1 Tel Dan inscription in the Israel Museum Jerusalem.
Credit: Photo by the author.

to him, countering the argument that David is a mythical figure invented by later tradition or the biblical writers.[6]

As the capital of the United Kingdom, Jerusalem is central to these debates, with archaeological evidence cited to prove or disprove the historicity or accuracy of the biblical account. The main problem is that the Hebrew Bible, which is our only written source of information about the United Kingdom, is a complex collection of works composed, edited, and redacted by different authors over many centuries, long after the time of David and Solomon.[7] Although the authors' identities are unknown, their writings are colored by their theological agendas and biases as they sought to present God's covenant with his people within a narrative of Israel's sacred history. As Carol Redmount notes, "mythical and historical categories of thought were not mutually exclusive in antiquity."[8] While scholars agree that the Hebrew Bible must be read critically, they disagree about the extent to which it can be used as a source of information to reconstruct the history of Israel in general and the United Kingdom in particular.[9] Nevertheless, many of them do not doubt that the kingdom of David and Solomon existed, even while recognizing that the biblical writers may have exaggerated its size and influence.[10]

Using archaeology to prove or disprove the historicity and accuracy of the biblical account is problematic. For one thing, archaeology provides different types of information than do literary works such as the Hebrew Bible. For example, archaeologists might reasonably suppose that the massive, stepped stone structure near the crest of the southeastern hill above the Gihon spring was intended to buttress or support a citadel above. But archaeology does not indicate if this structure is the Millo mentioned in the Hebrew Bible in connection with David and Solomon (see below). If the stepped stone structure postdates the tenth century BCE—as some archaeologists claim—it could not be the Millo. Indeed, one of the biggest problems surrounding Davidic and Solomonic Jerusalem is the lack of chronological precision provided by archaeology. For the Bronze and Iron Ages, archaeologists generally date remains based on associated pottery types or radiocarbon dating of organic materials, both of which have long ranges. In addition, archaeologists disagree about the dating of Iron Age I and Iron Age II pottery types and, by way of extension, the associated remains. For example, some archaeologists claim that types that were assigned previously to the Iron Age I instead belong to the Iron Age II.[11] This is one reason the large building above the stepped stone structure can be dated either to the tenth century or the ninth century, and therefore may or may not be the palace of David.

The imprecise chronological resolution is exacerbated by indications that some monumental structures remained in use or were repaired and reused centuries or even millennia after they were constructed. For example, even archaeologists who accept that Middle Bronze Age Jerusalem was fortified with a city wall disagree about whether it continued in use through the Late Bronze Age and Iron Age—in which case, the wall would have been the fortification of the Jebusite city at the time of David's conquest.[12] Not least important, because of Jerusalem's continuous occupation, the reuse of building stones, construction down to bedrock, and the scattered and fragmentary nature of the remains, the absence of evidence is not necessarily evidence of absence. Therefore, a lack of identifiable monumental remains from the time of David and Solomon is not proof that none existed.[13]

Archaeology
Solomon's Temple and Palace

After David's conquest, Jerusalem became known as the City of David: "Nevertheless, David took the stronghold of Zion, which is now the city of David. . . . David occupied the stronghold, and named it the city of David" (2 Sam 5:7, 9). David made Jerusalem the political capital of his kingdom—a logical choice because it was a centrally located and neutral city that had not been occupied previously by any of the twelve tribes.[14] He also made Jerusalem the cultic center of the kingdom by transferring the ark of the covenant and the tabernacle there, and he erected an altar on a threshing floor that he purchased from Araunah on a spot identified by the author of Chronicles (the "Chronicler") as Mount Moriah—the future site of Solomon's temple (2 Sam 24:18; 1 Chr 21:15, 28–30; 22:1; 2 Chr 3:1, where Araunah is called "Ornan"; 2 Sam 6:17; 7:5–7). Perhaps the rocky outcrop was associated before David's conquest with the cult of Shalem, the original patron deity of Jerusalem, after whom the city was named. Indeed, Genesis 14:18 describes Melchizedek, the priest of God Most High who blessed Abraham (Abram), as king of Shalem (English: Salem).[15]

The Israelites and other ancient peoples believed that gods did not dwell in their midst but instead resided in the heavens (celestial deities) or on mountain peaks (like the Olympian gods) or underground (chthonic deities). The God of Israel was a celestial deity, which is why human interaction with him occurred on mountain tops, the loci of divine revelation (e.g., Mount Sinai, Jerusalem's Temple Mount, the Mount of Beatitudes).[16] Sacrifices were offered on altars to entice gods from their divine abodes to the earthly realm, where they could protect and ensure the well-being of humans. An ancient temple literally was the house of god, constructed as an earthly dwelling for a deity and located next to an altar.[17] The Hebrew term for the Temple Mount—*har ha-bayit*—means the mountain of the house (of the God of Israel), while the temple was simply "*the* house" (*ha-bayit*) (of the God of Israel). According to the Hebrew Bible, when the Israelites wandered in the desert, they carried a gold-plated wooden chest called the ark of the covenant which contained the stone tablets with the Ten Commandments that God gave Moses on Mount Sinai. On top of the ark was a gold "seat of mercy" that served as a throne for the divine presence (Ex 25:10–22). When they camped, the Israelites pitched a tent called the tabernacle to house the ark and offered sacrifices to keep God's presence dwelling in their midst (Ex 26–27).[18] After the Israelites settled in Canaan, the ark and tabernacle were placed in various locations including Shiloh, Baale-Judah (Kiryat Yearim), and perhaps Gibeon, until David brought them to Jerusalem. The ancient Israelites (and their post-exilic descendants, the Jews) offered sacrifices around the clock to the God of Israel to keep his presence dwelling in their midst as their protector.[19] The ancient Jewish historian Josephus expresses the belief that the second temple was destroyed in 70 CE after God abandoned the city and his people.[20]

Like other ancient peoples, the early Israelites worshipped many different gods with a national or patron deity at the top of the pantheon. Just as the goddess Athena was the patron deity of the city of Athens, which was named in her honor, YHWH was the national deity of the Israelites. YHWH (commonly vocalized as Yahweh) is a transliteration of the four Hebrew letters (Tetragrammaton) representing the sacred name of the God of Israel. Eventually many Israelites (and later, all Jews) came to believe that the God of Israel was a jealous god who would not tolerate the worship of other gods alongside him. The Hebrew Bible describes conflicts between Israelites who worshiped other gods alongside the God of Israel (inclusive Yahwists) and their opponents (exclusive Yahwists). In addition, some Israelites (and later, many Jews) came to believe that there should be only one house where the God of Israel dwells: on Jerusalem's Temple Mount—a principle reinforced in Deuteronomy, the Fifth Book of Moses. Nevertheless, literary and archaeological evidence indicates that there were ancient temples dedicated to the God of Israel outside of Jerusalem, including in Egypt, where the one at Leontopolis functioned until 73 CE, when it was shut down by the Roman emperor Vespasian.[21] Several Israelite shrines and temples dating to the Iron Age have been found outside Jerusalem, not all of which were necessarily dedicated to the worship of the God of Israel. One example is a "high place" (an elevated platform and an altar) at Tel Dan at the northern tip of Israel, in the territory of the ancient tribe of Dan.[22] It is thought to have been erected by Jeroboam, the king of northern kingdom of Israel after Solomon's death, who reportedly built a shrine at Dan. Because the biblical writers were exclusive Yahwists who supported the centralization of the cult in Jerusalem, they condemned the high place at Dan as a sin that doomed Jeroboam's dynasty (1 Kgs 12:28–29; 1 Kgs 13:28–29).

According to the biblical writers, David made preparations to build a permanent house (temple) for the God of Israel on Jerusalem's Temple Mount, but it was his son and successor Solomon who carried out the plans.[23] Solomon's name at birth was Jedidiah (pronounced yeh-dee-DEE-uh), which means "the delight (or beloved) of YHWH," while Solomon (Hebrew *Shlomo*) derives from the Hebrew word for peace (*shalom*) (2 Sam 12:25).[24] The author of 1 Chronicles 22:8–10 connects Solomon's name—which might have been given to him when he ascended the throne—with the reason he and not David, a man of war, was permitted by God to build the temple.[25] Perhaps, however, Solomon's name originally referred to his political and religious capital—Jerusalem—a possibility suggested by the fact that, by the Second Temple period, it was understood as meaning "city of peace."[26] In this case, just as Jerusalem was the city of David, it also came to be the city of Solomon.

Solomon expanded the city to the north to the Temple Mount, where he built a house for the God of Israel (the first temple) and a house (palace) for himself, establishing this natural high point as the acropolis. Although no archaeological remains survive of either building, the temple presumably was in the vicinity of the rocky outcrop (Foundation Stone), with the palace to its south. The temple's layout and appearance can be reconstructed based on biblical descriptions (see mainly 1 Kgs 6–7; 2 Chr 2–4) and comparisons to contemporary temples such as those at Tell Ta`yinat and at `Ain Dara` in Syria.[27] Important evidence is also provided by two Israelite temples discovered at Arad and Moza (or Motza) in Judah.

In the 1960s, Yohanan Aharoni discovered a shrine or small temple dated to the ninth–eighth centuries BCE in the Israelite citadel at Arad in southern Judah.[28] The structure consists of a broad house room surrounded by benches with an elevated cubicle at the back—apparently the holy of holies—which was accessed by three steps (Figure 3.2). Three stelae (stone slabs—Hebrew *massebot*) had been set up in the cubicle. Two stone incense altars stood on the top step. A stone altar in the courtyard had a plastered top with a channel to drain the blood of sacrifices.

In 2012–2013 and 2021, excavations by Shua Kisilevitz brought to light a Judahite temple that was constructed ca. 900 BCE at Moza, about 7 kilometers (4 miles) northwest of Jerusalem's Temple Mount.[29] The Moza temple is an elongated rectangular structure measuring 18 × 13 meters (26 × 43 feet) with stone benches lining the walls inside.[30] It was entered on the narrow east side through a porch with two pillars on stone bases. The west end of the building (where the holy of holies presumably was located) has not been excavated. The eastern part of the hall has a dirt and plaster floor, while the western part has a stone pavement at a higher level. A small elongated rectangular chamber abuts the north side of the building. A rectangular altar of unhewn field stones stood in the center of the courtyard in front of the temple. A refuse pit (*favissa*) adjacent to the altar contained the remains of sacrificial debris and offerings, including ash, animal bones,

FIGURE 3.2 Holy of holies in the Arad temple reconstructed in the Israel Museum Jerusalem.
Credit: Photo by the author.

and potsherds. A concentration of cultic vessels was found in the area between the refuse pit and a rectangular stone platform (or "podium") nearby. There were also four terracotta figurines of two bearded male heads and two horses. A stone block discovered in 2021 in secondary use (built into a later stone wall) might be carved with the legs of a deity.[31] The Moza temple is important because it might shed light on the layout of Solomon's temple—which is located only a few miles away and is roughly contemporary—and it provides direct evidence of Israelite cultic practices around Jerusalem unfiltered through the lenses of the biblical writers.

The biblical descriptions and archaeological parallels indicate that Solomon's temple was an elongated rectangular building with a flat roof measuring approximately 10 meters wide × 35 meters long × 15 meters high (32 × 115 × 50 feet), surrounded by two courtyards (inner and outer) (Figure 3.3).[32] The main entrance, which probably faced east, was flanked by two bronze columns (either freestanding or engaged) named Jachin and Boaz (meaning "He [God] will establish" and "in strength").[33] The temple building ("the house")—was divided into three successive rooms of unequal size: the *'ulam* (porch or vestibule), *heikhal* (sanctuary), and *debir* (the innermost room or holy of holies). The ark of the covenant

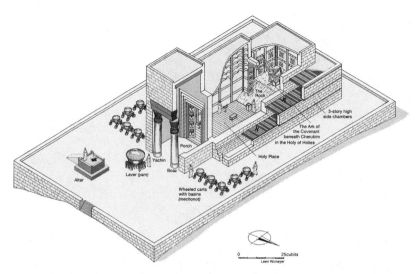

FIGURE 3.3 Reconstructed diagram of Solomon's Temple.
Credit: © by Leen Ritmeyer.

was housed in the *debir*, which apparently was separated from the *heikhal* by a curtain or wooden partition.[34]

According to the biblical account, Solomon gave wheat and oil to Hiram, king of Tyre in exchange for workmen and cedar and cypress wood to roof the temple and for paneling to cover the stone walls. The wood panels were carved with decoration and plated with gold. The sacred furniture (plated or inlaid with gold) in the *heikhal* included an incense altar, the showbread table (on which twelve loaves of unleavened bread were placed every sabbath), and ten lampstands. Inside the *debir*, two giant *cherubim* (cherubs = winged, sphinxlike creatures) carved of wood and plated with gold flanked the ark of the covenant, which was placed under their outstretched wings. The ark was a gold-plated wooden chest containing the two tablets of the law that Moses received on Mount Sinai.[35] The cherubs served as God's throne—the seat of mercy—while the ark was his footstool.[36]

The long sides and back of the building were surrounded by three stories of rooms used for storage and as treasuries.[37] The altar for burnt offerings and a huge bronze water basin or laver for priestly ablutions called the *yam* ("sea"; pronounced *yahm*) stood in the inner courtyard. The *yam* was supported by twelve bronze cattle, in groups of four facing each of the cardinal points, flanked by large, wheeled bronze stands (*mekhonot*) for bronze basins that were decorated with lions, cattle, and cherubs. Scholars disagree about whether the rocky outcrop (the Foundation Stone today enshrined in the Dome of the Rock) is the site of the altar of burnt offerings or was located inside the *debir* or was completely unassociated with the temple.[38]

The decoration and furnishings of Solomon's temple—God's earthly dwelling—indicate that it was conceived of as the Garden of Eden, that is, a divine pleasure garden. For example, the huge water basins in the inner court-yard (the *yam* and *mekhonot*) symbolized the river flowing from the Garden of Eden, which branched into four streams. The two bronze columns flanking the entrance to the building might have represented the Tree of Knowledge and the Tree of Life in the Garden of Eden.[39] The use of gold to decorate the dim interior and the fragrant scents of cedar wood and incense heightened the sensory experience. As Victor Hurowitz concludes, "All in all, Solomon's Temple is a luxurious divine residence in a mountaintop pleasure garden; and its general design focuses on the inner room, and is meant to glorify and magnify the Divine resident sitting on the cherub throne."[40]

Like the temple, the layout and appearance of Solomon's palace can be reconstructed based on biblical descriptions (1 Kgs 7:1–11) and archaeological parallels. The palace included units designated the "house of the Forest of Lebanon" (so-called because the wooden ceiling beams were supported by numerous pillars made of cedars of Lebanon), the "hall of Pillars" (which had a colonnaded porch), the "hall of the Throne" (where Solomon pronounced judgment), the house where he resided, and a separate house for Pharaoh's daughter, who was one of his wives. The biblical description gives the impression that Solomon's palace had the layout of a *bit-hilani*, a type of palace complex common in ancient Syria that was entered through a porch with columns.[41]

The Stepped Stone Structure

Robert Macalister and John Duncan were the first to expose part of the stepped stone structure, which they named the "Jebusite ramp" because they assumed it was a buttress to support a "Jebusite" fortification wall above.[42] Since then, excavations by Kathleen Kenyon, Yigal Shiloh, and Eilat Mazar have revealed additional portions of the stepped stone structure as well as remains above it. Although Macalister and Duncan's "Jebusite" wall dates to the post-exilic period (after 586 BCE), the evidence reviewed here supports their identification of the stepped stone structure as "Jebusite," as well as their assumption that it was built to buttress structures in the area above.

Nowadays many archaeologists view the stone terraces and overlying mantle (the stepped stone structure) as a single unit constructed either in the twelfth century or the tenth century BCE to support a major complex above. Before Solomon built the first temple and a new palace on the Temple Mount to the north, this natural high point would have been the acropolis of the city. For this reason, some scholars have identified the area above the stepped stone structure as the biblical fortress (or stronghold) of Zion—that is, the Jebusite and Davidic citadel: "Nevertheless, David took the stronghold of Zion, which is now the city of David" (2 Sam 5:7).[43] A twelfth-century date would mean the stepped stone structure was built by the Jebusites, presumably to support a citadel above, which was then taken by David. If the stepped stone structure dates to the tenth century, its construction could be attributed to David. The stakes are high because the construction of such a massive structure in the tenth century would accord with the biblical description of Jerusalem as the capital city of a large kingdom and support the view of scholars who believe that David was a king rather than a petty chief or an invented (mythical) figure.

Some archaeologists identify the stepped stone structure with the Millo mentioned in the Hebrew Bible in connection with David and Solomon—a possibility suggested by the term's apparent meaning of "filling":[44] "David occupied the stronghold, and named it the city of David. David built the city all around from the Millo inward" (2 Sam 5:9; also see 1 Chr 11:8).

Other passages crediting Solomon with the Millo's construction must mean its reconstruction, as is true of the city wall, which he also reportedly repaired.

> "This is the account of the forced labor that King Solomon conscripted to build the house of the Lord and his own house, the Millo and the wall of Jerusalem." (1 Kgs 9:15).
> "But Pharaoh's daughter went up from the city of David to her own house that Solomon had built for her; then he built the Millo." (1 Kgs 9:24)
> "Solomon built the Millo, and closed up the gap in the wall of the city of his father David." (1 Kgs 11:27)
> In the late eighth century BCE, Hezekiah "strengthened the Millo in the city of David." (2 Chr 32:5)[45]

Kenyon and Shiloh found Iron Age houses built on top of the stepped stone structure (Figure 3.4). The two most completely excavated houses were designated by Shiloh "the House of Ahiel" and "the Burnt Room House." They were destroyed at the time of the Babylonian conquest of Jerusalem in 586 BCE. Jane Cahill notes that not only are the houses built on top of the stepped stone structure and therefore postdate it, but, by the time they were constructed, parts of the stepped stone structure and underlying terraces had been removed, indicating that the stepped stone structure had ceased to serve a strategic function.[46] Therefore, the date when the houses were constructed provides a terminus ante quem (a "date before which") for the stepped stone

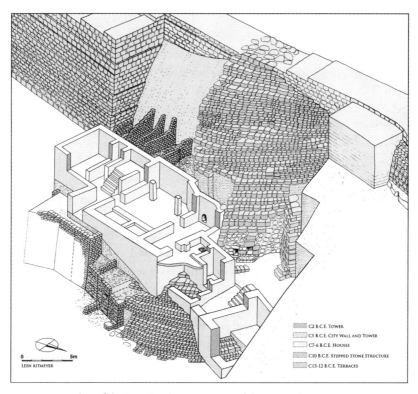

C2 B.C.E. TOWER
C5 B.C.E. CITY WALL AND TOWER
C7-6 B.C.E. HOUSES
C10 B.C.E. STEPPED STONE STRUCTURE
C13-12 B.C.E. TERRACES

0   5m
LEEN RITMEYER

FIGURE 3.4 Plan of the Iron Age houses on top of the stepped stone structure. Credit: © by Leen Ritmeyer.

structure. In other words, the stepped stone structure must have been constructed before the houses were built on top of it, by which time it had ceased serving its original function.

Following Kenyon and Shiloh, most archaeologists date these houses to the eighth and seventh centuries BCE.[47] However, Cahill assigns pottery found on and under the earliest floors in the House of Ahiel and the Burnt Room House to the tenth and ninth centuries.[48] Based on this evidence, she dates the construction of the houses to the tenth century BCE.[49] This would support Cahill's proposed date of ca. 1200 BCE for the stepped stone structure but makes a tenth century date unlikely as it would not allow enough time for its construction, use, and dismantling before the houses were built. However, the pottery discussed by Cahill appears to date to the Iron Age IIA–IIB transition as defined by Ze'ev Herzog and Lily Singer-Avitz—that is, the early ninth century.[50] If the houses were constructed in the early ninth century, the stepped stone structure could date as late as the tenth century. However, other evidence points to an earlier date.

A relatively small amount of pottery—mostly fragmentary—was recovered in probes in and under the stepped stone structure, and the types represented cannot be dated precisely but instead have broad ranges.[51] The latest datable sherds found in and under the stepped stone structure provide only a terminus post quem (Latin for "date after which") for its construction, meaning it could not have been built earlier than the latest types represented but could have been built at any time after that. Therefore, for example, if the latest pottery types have a range from the twelfth to tenth centuries, the stepped stone structure could have been constructed during that span of time or any time afterward. Margreet Steiner and Cahill advocate for a twelfth century date because the pottery types resemble Late Bronze Age forms (at the earlier end of the range), whereas E. Mazar cites the broad range in support of a tenth-century date.[52]

Perhaps the best evidence for the date of the stepped stone structure is provided by a nearly complete collared-rim pithos found on the floor of a room underneath it, which must have been crushed when the structure was built.[53] Collared-rim pithoi are large storage jars with a raised ridge encircling the base of the neck; the ridged "collar" is a hallmark of Iron Age I pithoi (Figure 3.5). E. Mazar argues for a broad range for the pithos and the other pottery found with it, but Steiner and Cahill each date these types to the Late Bronze Age II– Iron Age I transition. The presence of a few fragments of typical Iron Age I types (including collared-rim pithoi)—but nothing later—among the pottery found inside the stepped stone structure support the likelihood that it dates to the twelfth century.[54] Although in this case the stepped stone structure would have existed when David conquered the city, it is impossible to determine if it is the biblical Millo:[55] "David occupied the stronghold, and named it the city of David. David built the city all around from the Millo inward" (2 Sam 5:9).

The Large Building Above the Stepped Stone Structure (the Large Stone Structure)

As we have seen, most archaeologists agree that the stepped stone structure is a single unit built either in the twelfth or tenth century BCE to support a major complex above, which was the acropolis before Solomon expanded the city to the north to include the Temple Mount.[56] It makes sense to assume that the area above the stepped stone structure was the site of the Jebusite citadel, which David occupied after his conquest. And indeed, excavations conducted by E. Mazar from 2005 to 2007 brought to light remains of a monumental stone building (designated the "Large Stone Structure"), which she identifies as the palace of David mentioned in 2 Samuel 5:11: "King Hiram of Tyre sent messengers to David, along with cedar trees, and carpenters and masons who built David a

FIGURE 3.5 Collared-rim pithos from Shiloh in the Israel Museum Jerusalem. Credit: Photo by the author.

house."[57] E. Mazar's discovery has been highly publicized because, if this is the palace of David, it would seem to confirm the biblical account. However, some archaeologists have expressed reservations about E. Mazar's dating of the remains, suspecting that it might be influenced by her political views.[58]

There is no doubt that the building E. Mazar uncovered is monumental (Pl. 4B; Figure 3.6).[59] The structure's east wall (Wall 20), which was exposed for a length of more than 20 meters (65 feet), is nearly 5 meters (16 feet) thick. Several rooms (labeled A–E) and a possible courtyard were discovered inside the structure (west of Wall 20), although its full extent is unknown. E. Mazar's dating of this structure to ca. 1000 BCE is based mainly on pottery found in accumulations

FIGURE 3.6 The large stone structure (illuminated by rays of light from a walkway above). Credit: Photo by the author.

underneath the building and on top of or above floors inside the rooms. She also cites radiocarbon dated organic materials and optically stimulated luminescence (OSL) dating of the accumulations under the structure.[60]

Although the radiocarbon and OSL evidence cited by E. Mazar seems to support her claimed date, other evidence calls it into question. First, E. Mazar admits that nearly all the floors inside the structure were removed and many of the stones in the walls were robbed out in later periods.[61] This means that few undisturbed deposits have survived that can provide securely datable material associated with the structure's construction and occupation.[62] Second, it is reasonable to assume that parts of the structure were rebuilt or repaired over time, and walls or features such as benches were added. E. Mazar identifies some of the walls and features as additions based on the discovery of pottery that postdates ca. 1000 BCE but does not describe any stratigraphic or architectural indications (such as walls abutting instead of bonding with each other).[63] In other words, instead of identifying later additions based on visible signs such as abutting walls, E. Mazar seems to identify some walls and features as later additions only after pottery that postdates the tenth century was found in association with them. If this pottery is associated with the original construction instead of later additions or repairs, the entire structure could postdate ca. 1000 BCE, as some archaeologists argue.[64] As we shall see, however, other evidence indicates a twelfth century construction date, making it likely that these walls and features are indeed later additions.

According to E. Mazar, the large stone structure was constructed over accumulations of earth (including surfaces of beaten earth) with no remains of architecture. She therefore believes that the earth accumulated in an open area outside the main gate of the Middle Bronze Age–Late Bronze Age city, indicating that David built his palace in a previously vacant area to the north of the city.[65] Organic remains from the accumulations were dated by radiocarbon and OSL.[66] E. Mazar describes the earliest occupation level (stratum) inside the structure as the "Crucibles Layer" because it contained evidence of metal-working (such as smelting hearths, ceramic crucibles, blowpipes, and production waste). She associates the metal-working activity with the large stone structure's construction.[67]

Perhaps the best dating evidence for the large stone structure comes from Room E, where a cooking pot was found in situ in the earth accumulations, overlaid by a hearth belonging to the Crucibles Layer.[68] The cooking pot, which is typical of the Late Bronze II–Iron Age I transition, provides a terminus post quem of ca. 1200–1140 BCE for the structure's construction.[69] E. Mazar argues for the latest date in a supposedly long range for the type, from the thirteenth to eleventh (!) centuries, while acknowledging that the cooking pot is typical of the Late Bronze Age.[70] Nothing like it is illustrated by Amihai Mazar among Iron Age I cooking pots.[71] The cooking pot is important because the fact that it was found smashed but in situ indicates it was in use at or around the time the large stone structure was constructed, making unlikely a date much later than ca. 1140 BCE.

To the north of Room E, in Room D, E. Mazar found Late Bronze Age pottery in a thin layer of fill (L869) sealed by a paved installation or patchy surface abutting a wall.[72] Stone mallets apparently taken from the Crucibles Layer were incorporated as cobbles in the pavement, indicating that it postdates the construction of the large stone structure. The Late Bronze Age pottery found in the fill consists of large fragments, including a nearly complete Cypriot jug called a "bilbil" (Figure 3.7).[73] The large size of the Late Bronze Age pottery fragments and nearly complete condition of the bilbil make it unlikely that they were lying

FIGURE 3.7 Base Ring II Bilbil in the University of Pennsylvania Museum (not from Jerusalem) E15445, Distribution from the British School of Archaeology in Egypt, 1921. Credit: www.penn.museum/collections.

around for decades or centuries before the large stone structure was constructed. Therefore, like the cooking pot, these Late Bronze Age vessels provide a terminus post quem for the large stone structure's construction, with the nearly complete condition of the bilbil pointing to a date not much later than ca. 1300 BCE. However, unlike the cooking pot, as an import the bilbil might have been kept as an heirloom. In this case, the deposit sealed by the paved surface could date to the twelfth century but hardly later.

In several places, E. Mazar found pottery associated with floor levels or surfaces overlying the Crucibles Layer. An Iron Age I bowl (ca. 1200–1000) was found under the patchy paved surface or installation in Room E.[74] In another part of Room E, E. Mazar identified a disturbed earth layer overlying the Crucibles Layer as the earliest occupation level in the large stone building. Collared-rim pithoi, which are characteristic of the Iron Age I, were found in the earth layer.[75] Elsewhere in the large stone structure, E. Mazar found an assemblage of nearly complete pottery vessels which she believes were discarded when a wall (Wall 22) was added (L47). These vessels appear to better fit an early ninth-century date instead of the second half of the tenth century, as she claims.[76]

If the large stone structure was constructed in the twelfth century BCE, the dearth of finds antedating the ninth century could be the result of several factors. First, as already noted, severe damage to the structure in later periods, some of it caused by the robbing out of stones for reuse elsewhere, left few of the original floor deposits undisturbed. Second, while the structure was occupied, the rooms would have been kept clean and swept, preventing the build-up of deposits. When pottery vessels broke, they would have been removed. Thus, although the evidence is scanty, the large stone structure appears to have been constructed in the twelfth century and occupied at least until the early ninth century, making it contemporary with the stepped stone structure.

This review shows that the ceramic evidence supports a twelfth-century BCE construction date for both the stepped stone structure and the large stone structure. A seam visible between the walls that E. Mazar illustrates seems to indicate the two structures are not bonded.[77] If they were built together as one unit, the lack of bonding could be a technical feature or the result of later repairs or rebuilding. The pottery and other datable material associated with the latest floors inside the large stone structure indicate that it was occupied at least until the early ninth century—approximately the same time the stepped stone structure was partially dismantled and houses were built on top of it.

The Ophel

As noted in Chapter 1, most scholars identify the area between the north end of the southeastern hill and the south end of the Temple Mount as the Ophel (Greek *Ophlas*). This term occurs in several places in the Hebrew Bible with different meanings. Without the definite article, it means "hill" or "mound," as in Isaiah 32:14: "the hill (*ophel*) and watchtower will become dens forever."[78] When the definite article is used, the term denotes a specific hill or the citadel of a city, as in 2 Kings 5:24, referring to Samaria (the capital city of the northern kingdom of Israel): "When he came to the citadel (the Ophel)."[79] It is used with this same meaning in the Mesha Stele (Moabite Stone), an inscribed stone slab found in 1868 at Dhiban (ancient Dibon), the capital of Moab. The inscription, which dates to the ninth century BCE, commemorates a victory by Mesha, king of Moab, over King Omri of Israel, who boasts of having built in Karchah (Kerak) the "wall of the Ophel."[80]

The Ophel of Jerusalem is first mentioned in the Hebrew Bible in connection with Jotham, the son of Uzziah, who was king of Judah in the third quarter of the eighth century BCE: "He built the upper gate of the house of the Lord, and did extensive building on the wall of [the] Ophel" (2 Chr 27:3).[81] The next reference occurs in connection with Manasseh, the king of Judah in the first half of the seventh century: "Afterward he built an outer wall for the city of David west of Gihon, in the valley, reaching the entrance at the Fish Gate; he carried it around [the] Ophel" (2 Chr 33:14). After the return from Babylonian exile, temple servants living on the Ophel repaired the wall: "After him Pediah son of Parosh and the temple servants living on the Ophel made repairs up to a point opposite the Water Gate on the east and the projecting tower. After him the Tekoites repaired another section opposite the great projecting tower as far as the wall of [the] Ophel" (Neh 3:25–27; also see Neh 11:21: "But the temple servants lived on [the] Ophel"). It makes sense that the temple servants would have lived near the Temple Mount—that is, in the area immediately to the south. And indeed, Josephus refers to the area where the First Wall joined the southeast corner of the Temple Mount as the Ophel (Greek *Ophlas*): "and after passing a spot which they call Ophlas, finally joined the eastern portico of the temple."[82]

This evidence suggests that, by the eighth century BCE, the area between the Temple Mount and the north end of the southeastern hill had come to be known as the Ophel. Assuming Solomon built the first temple and a palace on the Temple Mount, we would expect the Ophel to have been built up at this time. Different archaeologists, including Charles Warren in the nineteenth century (who sank over fifty shafts, twenty of which reached bedrock) and Kenyon in the 1960s, explored this area. The most extensive excavations were conducted by Benjamin Mazar from 1968 to 1978 and were continued by E. Mazar in 1986–1987 (with B. Mazar) and in 2009–2013 (on her own).[83]

To the east of the southeast corner of the Temple Mount, these excavations revealed a group of monumental structures that were part of a fortification system. Among the remains identified by E. Mazar and B. Mazar are a gate comprised of a four-chambered inner gatehouse (Building C) and an outer gatehouse (Area E), at a ninety-degree angle to each other and flanking a large, fortified enclosure (the "Large Tower") (Pl. 5A; Figure 3.8). Another building, dubbed by E. Mazar the "Royal Structure" or "Royal Building" (Building D), adjoins the inner face of the Straight Wall, and an added tower (called by Warren the "Additional Tower" and by E. Mazar the "Extra Tower" or Area A) is located on the opposite side of the Straight Wall, abutting the Large Tower.[84]

Not all archaeologists agree with E. Mazar's identification of the remains as a gate complex,[85] and many date these structures to the ninth–eighth centuries BCE (or later) instead of the tenth century (the time of Solomon).[86] The reasons for the uncertainty are familiar: the remains were severely damaged by later construction, leaving few undisturbed contexts, and the pottery types—represented mostly by small sherds—have long ranges that make precise dating impossible. The best dating evidence appears to come from a room in the Royal Structure (Building D), where, in 1986, E. Mazar found a complete tiny black juglet in a

FIGURE 3.8 The Ophel Gate abutted on the lower right by a (later) *miqveh*; the Byzantine city wall is visible in the background under the road.
Credit: Photo by the author.

fill under the lower of two floors.[87] Black juglets of this type are typical of the Iron Age IIA (tenth–ninth centuries BCE).[88] Because the juglet was lying intact between the foundation stones of the room, it could have been deposited around the time the structure was built.[89] Nevertheless, E. Mazar acknowledges that she is unable to securely date the construction of the gate complex or the Royal Structure.[90]

In their final excavation report (published in 1989), E. Mazar and B. Mazar concluded that the lack of building remains on the northern Ophel which antedate the ninth century BCE suggests that Solomon's new acropolis on the Temple Mount was fortified independently of the rest of the city. The fortifications connecting the acropolis with the southern Ophel and southeastern hill were extended only in the ninth century at the earliest.[91] However, in her 2011 book, E. Mazar prefers a date in the second half of the tenth century, that is, the time of Solomon, saying that she was "overly cautious" in originally adopting the latest possible date in the tenth–ninth century range for the black juglet.[92] In support of a Solomonic date for the complex, E. Mazar also illustrates potsherds found in her 2009 excavations in the lowest fill layer of the inner gatehouse passage (Building C) and the earliest layers in a probe inside the Large Tower (Area E).[93]

Although she acknowledges that these pottery types are typical of the tenth and ninth centuries, E. Mazar argues, "It is therefore more reasonable to assume that the construction date of the two buildings [the inner gatehouse and the Large Tower] *would reflect the vessels' main period of use*, and neither their earliest appearance nor their last days. Given this, they point to a date of the late 10th century, corresponding to the biblical reference that announced the construction by King Solomon of a defensive wall around Jerusalem."[94] Although this argument sounds persuasive, it is methodologically unsound as various factors must be considered when using pottery as a means of dating. For example, the intact black juglet must have been deposited between the foundation stones of the room in the Royal Structure and buried shortly afterward, for, had it remained exposed, it would have soon been broken. Unfortunately, since this type of juglet has a tenth–ninth century range, it does not indicate the exact date of the Royal Structure's construction within that span of time. In contrast, small pottery fragments (sherds) provide only a very rough terminus post quem for associated remains because they were deposited only after the vessels were manufactured, used, broken, discarded, and deposited. Therefore, the potsherds found in the lowest layers of the inner gatehouse and Large Tower indicate only that these structures were constructed during or after the tenth–ninth centuries and not necessarily in the middle of that time frame, as E. Mazar claims.

The Solomonic City Wall

According to the biblical account, Solomon fortified Jerusalem with a wall: "he took Pharaoh's daughter and brought her into the city of David, until he had finished building his own house and the house of the Lord and the wall around Jerusalem" (1 Kgs 3:1). The Solomonic wall is as elusive as other remains of tenth-century Jerusalem. Many archaeologists who accept that the Middle Bronze Age city was fortified believe those fortifications continued in use through the Iron Age.[95] Others argue that the Iron Age city was fortified only in the ninth or eighth centuries BCE. 1 Kings seems to refer to a wall built by Solomon rather than the repair of an earlier wall. Therefore, finding a tenth-century fortification wall would support those who argue that the biblical description of the kingdom of David and Solomon and the capital city of Jerusalem is accurate, while the absence of a wall would support those who question it. So far, the question of whether the biblical reference to a wall built by Solomon is accurate remains unresolved.[96]

According to E. Mazar, the Straight Wall that runs north from her claimed gate complex is contemporary with the Royal Structure. She dates it to the third quarter of the tenth century and identifies it as part of the Solomonic

wall connecting the Ophel to the Temple Mount.[97] Other possible remains of
a Solomonic wall were discovered by Kenyon in her Site H, on the eastern crest
of the southeastern hill, just north of the large stone structure. Here, Kenyon
identified part of a casemate wall built on bedrock. A casemate wall is a double
wall with partitions dividing the interior space into a strip of rooms. Kenyon
dated this wall to the tenth century, noting that similar casemate walls attributed
to Solomon had been found at other sites such as Megiddo.[98] However, casemate
walls dating to the ninth century BCE and later—that is, after Solomon's time—
have been discovered elsewhere in Judah.[99]

Kenyon found no evidence that the casemate wall continued north from Site
H, contrary to what we would expect if it was the Solomonic fortification.[100]
And, as Cahill notes, it is not clear from the published photograph that the
remains uncovered by Kenyon are indeed a casemate wall. Instead, Cahill suggests they might be part of the Middle Bronze Age fortifications.[101] Farther
north, E. Mazar thought she found part of a Solomonic casemate wall on the
south side of the gatehouse complex. However, the remains were so damaged by
later construction that she questions the identification, calling it "The Casemate
(?) Fortification Line."[102]

The Straight Wall overlay an earlier structure consisting of a large rectangular
courtyard surrounded by casemate rooms (dubbed Building I or the "Fortified
Enclosure" or the "Far House"), which is represented by foundation trenches
cut into bedrock.[103] Because the walls were robbed out, little datable material
was found associated with this structure. Since it antedates the Straight Wall,
which she attributes to Solomon, E. Mazar assigns the structure to the time of
David, identifying it as the "Far House" mentioned in connection with Absalom's
rebellion against his father (2 Sam 15:17).[104] Specifically, E. Mazar proposes a date
in the second half of David's reign based on the pottery, which includes cooking
pots "characteristic of the Early Iron Age IIA (tenth century BCE)" from the
earliest phase of the structure.[105] Although E. Mazar is correct that these cooking
pots are characteristic of the Iron Age IIA, this does not mean they are from
the time of David.[106] In the past, archaeologists dated the Iron Age IIA to ca.
1000–900 BCE, but most now prefer a range of ca. 980/950 to 830/800 BCE.[107]
Therefore, it is unlikely that these cooking pots are from the time of David, and
they could easily date to the ninth century instead of the tenth century. No less
important, because these are small fragments instead of whole vessels, they would
have been deposited some time after being manufactured, used, and broken.
Furthermore, although E. Mazar associates the cooking pots with the earliest
phase (I) of the structure, she does not describe their context. As almost no
pottery is listed from the foundation trenches, the fragments likely come from
under or on top of the floors of Phase I rooms inside the structure.[108] This means

that the cooking pot fragments provide only a rough terminus post quem for the structure's construction.

There are other indications that the remains on the Ophel attributed by E. Mazar to the time of David and Solomon are, in fact, later in date. A structure dubbed Building II or the "Great Projecting Tower" cuts through one of the walls on the east side of the Far House (the Fortified Enclosure), and the Straight Wall was built against its west wall.[109] This means that the Far House is the earliest of the three structures, followed by Building II, and the Straight Wall is the latest. As we have seen, the pottery from the Far House indicates that it could date to the ninth century—a possibility supported by the finds from Building II. E. Mazar discovered fragments of pithoi (one bearing a Proto-Canaanite inscription) between the lowest floor of the building and the floor immediately overlying it. She therefore associates the pithoi with Building II's earliest occupation phase and dates them to mid-tenth century (Iron Age IIA), concluding that the building was a large tower that protected the Ophel before Solomon constructed the fortification wall.[110] However, this type of pithos, which is characterized by a globular body and flattened, flanged rim, does not date to the Iron Age IIA but instead is typical of the latter part of the Iron Age IIB—that is, the late ninth to mid-eighth century BCE.[111] Therefore, the Far House appears to date to the ninth century, while Building II (the Great Projecting Tower) dates to the first half of the eighth century (probably close to the middle of the century), and the Straight Wall was constructed no earlier than the second half of the eighth century. If these structures indeed postdate the tenth century, they cannot be connected to David and Solomon.[112]

On the northwest side of the southeastern hill, excavations conducted by Doron Ben-Ami and Yana Tchekhanovets from 2007 to 2017 in the Givati Parking Lot and by Kenyon in her Site M revealed no remains of Iron Age (or earlier) fortifications and almost no finds dating to the Bronze Age or the Iron Age I.[113] The Givati Parking Lot is 150 meters (492 feet) south of al-Aqsa Mosque, on the south and west sides of the junction of two modern roads: an east–west road that encircles the southern end of the Temple Mount and the Old City, and a road that branches off to the south along the Tyropoean Valley and western side of the southeastern hill. Originally a parking lot, since 2005, the Givati Parking Lot has become the site of the largest ongoing archaeological excavation in Jerusalem (Figure 3.9).[114] The earliest remains found consist of fragmentary, poorly constructed walls and floors overlying bedrock, which date to the Iron Age IB or IIA.[115] Based on this evidence, Ben-Ami concludes that the Iron Age city was unfortified prior to the eighth century, which is the date of the walls discovered by Kenyon and Shiloh on the east side of the southeastern hill. Ben-Ami believes that the steep slope of the Tyropoeon Valley makes it

FIGURE 3.9 View of the Givati Parking Lot looking east.
Credit: Photo by the author.

unlikely a fortification wall was located farther west, outside the excavation area.[116] However, more recent excavations conducted by a different expedition in the Givati Parking Lot indicate that the original channel (riverbed) of the Tyropoeon Valley passes some 100 meters (328 feet) west of the modern north–south road. By the early Iron Age, structures were built on the valley's east slope (i.e., the west side of the southeastern hill), where the bedrock descends in a series of natural and artificially hewn steps or terraces.[117] Therefore, the Iron Age (and perhaps Bronze Age) wall on the west side of the southeastern hill may lie to the west of the Givati Parking Lot, close to the original base of the Tyropoeon Valley.[118] Alternatively, a massive wall associated with the Hellenistic period Akra fortress discovered in this area might originally have been part of the Iron Age fortifications (see Chapter 6).

Other Remains

The remains of buildings dating to the tenth century BCE were discovered in Shiloh's Area E, the largest area in his excavations, located in the middle of the eastern slope of the southeastern hill.[119] Installations such as a *tabun* (oven) suggest the buildings were domestic dwellings. Two chalices (clay bowls on raised pedestals) found in one room, perhaps used for offerings, led Shiloh to identify this spot as a "cultic corner."[120] A large number of similar chalices from the Givati Parking Lot excavations—several with signs of burning inside—and a fragment from Kenyon's Site M led Kay Prag to suggest that a cultic building stood nearby.[121]

Jerusalem in the Time of David and Solomon

Many archaeologists agree that David conquered and occupied the Late Bronze Age (Jebusite) city and that the Middle Bronze Age fortifications enclosed at least the crest and east slope of the southeastern hill and continued in use through the Iron Age. As this review indicates, the stepped stone structure and the large stone structure appear to have been constructed in the twelfth century BCE, comprising the Jebusite and Davidic citadel of Jerusalem. Despite the difficulties surrounding the dating and identification of the remains uncovered by E. Mazar on the Ophel, they point to an expansion of the city to the north by the ninth century. On the other hand, the fortification wall reportedly built by Solomon has proved elusive. Hillel Geva estimates the population of Solomonic Jerusalem at ca. 2,000 inhabitants.[122]

A small but vocal group of archaeologists led by Israel Finkelstein argue that the absence of evidence is evidence of absence—that is, the relative paucity of remains indicates that the southeastern hill was unfortified and largely unsettled before the eighth century BCE. They date the stepped stone structure to the ninth–eighth centuries BCE and claim that the upper part was reconstructed in the late Hellenistic (Hasmonean) period (second–first centuries BCE).[123] In their view, the ancient city was centered not on the southeastern hill but on the Temple Mount, where it was later completely engulfed by Herod the Great's first-century BCE expansion—a theory they call "the mound on the Mount."[124] This proposal suffers from a greater lack of evidentiary support—that is, an even greater absence of evidence—than the majority view. For one thing, it is difficult to prove or disprove because archaeological excavations cannot be conducted on the Temple Mount. Nevertheless, the absence of remains in the surrounding area contradicts the possibility that the Temple Mount was the core of the ancient city. For example, the excavations conducted by E. Mazar and B. Mazar down to bedrock around the southern and western sides of the Temple Mount failed to bring to light Bronze Age and Iron Age I remains, leading Finkelstein and his colleagues to argue that these must have been cleared away by later activities.[125] In addition, the sifted fills removed from under al-Aqsa Mosque at the southern end of the Temple Mount have yielded few artifacts antedating the Iron Age II.[126] And even Finkelstein and his colleagues acknowledge the problem created by locating the settlement at such a distance from the water source (the Gihon spring).[127] For these reasons, this proposal has been widely rejected.[128]

The ongoing controversies surrounding Jerusalem in the time of David and Solomon concern whether the remains are consistent with what we would expect from the capital of a kingdom like the one described in the Hebrew Bible. Anthropological models suggest that tenth-century BCE Jerusalem should be characterized as a chiefdom because it lacks the features typical of a state such as an increased population, public works, the production of luxury items, and skilled artisanship.[129] Archaeologists who view tenth-century Jerusalem according to these criteria argue that the description of the kingdom of David and Solomon was created centuries later by the biblical writers as a foundation story for Israel.[130] In support of this view, Finkelstein, one of its main proponents, claims that virtually no remains antedating the eighth century have been discovered on and around the southeastern hill. However, this review indicates that remains dating to the twelfth–tenth centuries have been found in various spots, including the stepped stone structure and large stone structure. As Cahill notes, "the so-called 'meager' remains from the Late Bronze and early Iron Ages are comparable to and consistent with the remains of *every* other period evidenced in Jerusalem prior to the final phase of the Iron Age II."[131] Even so, tenth-century Jerusalem displays the characteristics of a chiefdom, not a state or kingdom.

In my opinion, this discrepancy is at least partly a result of modern scholarship—specifically, the imposition of anthropological categories on to the ancient world and the attempt to reconcile archaeological remains with the biblical text—two sources which provide different types of information. As Carol Meyers observes, "Yet the biblical record of monumental architecture in Jerusalem is not fictitious, and the discrepancy between textual records and material remains should not be used to discredit the former."[132] Jerusalem has always been a relatively impoverished and isolated mountain town, lacking in natural resources and removed from the major thoroughfares bisecting the country. Even today it is the poorest major city in Israel. Two thousand years from now, archaeologists could assume that Tel Aviv, not Jerusalem better fits the profile of the capital of the State of Israel. Similarly, future archaeologists would hardly guess that Harrisburg, as the thirteenth largest city in Pennsylvania, or Tallahassee, as the seventh largest city in Florida, are state capitals. Therefore, why must we assume that a relatively poor and impoverished mountain town like Jerusalem could not have been the capital of a minor state or kingdom? And, even so, is it not possible that the biblical writers embellished their description of Jerusalem when they wrote about the United Kingdom? Since the debates surrounding tenth-century Jerusalem and the United Kingdom stem from different scholarly approaches to the evidence, it is unlikely they will be resolved anytime soon.

4

Judahite Jerusalem (587 BCE)

AFTER EXPERIENCING A boom in growth and prosperity during the previous century, in 587 BCE Jerusalem was caught up in the power struggles between Egypt and Babylonia. Having been taken by the Babylonians after a siege just one decade earlier (597 BCE), the city was about to be besieged by the Babylonians again, this time with the direst consequences: the destruction of Solomon's temple and the forced exile of its inhabitants.

Historical Background

After Solomon's death (ca. 928 BCE), the United Kingdom split into a northern kingdom called Israel and a southern kingdom called Judah, each with its own king, administration, and capital city. Jerusalem was the capital of Judah, and Samaria eventually became the capital of Israel. The territories of the tribes of Judah and Benjamin belonged to Judah, whereas the territories of Ephraim, Manasseh, and the other northern tribes were part of Israel. As a result, the border between the two kingdoms passed just 10 miles (15 kilometers) north of Jerusalem, with Jerusalem and Samaria only about 36 miles apart.[1]

Although Solomon's temple served the inhabitants of both kingdoms, its location in Jerusalem privileged Judah, which controlled the cult—meaning access to the God of Israel—and the revenues derived from it, including sacrificial offerings, tithes, first fruit offerings, and so on. It is not surprising, therefore, that Jeroboam established other sanctuaries throughout his realm, including at Dan and Bethel on Israel's northern and southern borders, respectively:[2]

"So the king [Jeroboam] took counsel and made two calves of gold, and said to the people, 'You have gone up to Jerusalem long enough. Behold your gods, o Israel, who brought you up from the land of Egypt!' So he set

up the one in Bethel and the other he put in Dan; and this thing became a
sin to Israel." (1 Kgs 12:28–29; also see 1 Kgs 13:33–34)

The division of the United Kingdom was the result of long-standing differences between the northern and southern tribes.[3] The biblical writers present the
split as a turning point in the history of Israel. One of them—the author(s) of
the Deuteronomic or Deuteronomistic History (DH or DtrH)—relates the story in
the book of Kings (which was later divided into two books: 1–2 Kings). The DH is a
complex work that appears to have been composed and edited in stages over time, from
the pre-exilic (eighth century and/or late seventh century BCE) to post-exilic (post–586
BCE) periods.[4] Another version of the story is presented in the book of Chronicles
(later divided into 1–2 Chronicles), which was authored by the "Chronicler" in the
Persian period (fourth century BCE).[5] The versions of the story vary because the authors
drew upon different sources of information (including royal archives and annals) and
because the changing times and circumstances impacted their retrospective views of
the significance of the split. The author of the DH presents the fall of Israel to Assyria
in 722 BCE as God's punishment for straying from the covenant and as the rationale
for the reforms of kings Hezekiah and Josiah of Judah. The Chronicler, writing in the
post-exilic period, focuses on King David, the Jerusalem temple, and the lessons of the
split for Judah after the return from the Babylonian exile.[6]

The passages from 1 Kings condemning Jeroboam's sanctuaries at Dan and
Bethel are part of the DH and reflect the author's view that their establishment
brought about the end of the house (dynasty) of Jeroboam and contributed to
the fall of Israel. Ahab, who was king of Israel from 872–851 BCE, is presented
in similarly harsh terms as having provoked God's wrath by building a temple to
Baal (the chief deity of the Canaanite/Phoenician pantheon) in Samaria:

Ahab, the son of Omri, reigned over Israel in Samaria 22 years. But Ahab,
the son of Omri, did that which was evil in the sight of the Lord above all
who were before him. He took as wife Jezebel, the daughter of Ethbaal,
king of the Sidonians, and went and served the Baal and worshiped him.
Thus he erected an altar for Baal in the House of the Baal, which he built in
Samaria.... Ahab did more to provoke the jealousy of the Lord, the God of
Israel, than all of the kings of Israel who were before him. (1 Kgs 16:29–33)

The perspectives and biases of the biblical writers, which influenced how they
present the history of Israel and Judah, were shaped by their identities as elite
men associated with the Jerusalem priestly class. They were exclusive Yahwists
who believed that the God of Israel is a jealous deity who would not tolerate the
worship of other gods alongside him. Promoting the centralization of the cult

in Jerusalem put control of Solomon's temple and therefore access to the God of Israel—as well as the associated revenues—in their hands. Kings who conformed with this agenda are presented in a positive light while those like Jeroboam and Ahab who did not are condemned for invoking God's wrath.[7]

During the ninth and eighth centuries BCE, the Assyrian empire (based in the northern part of Mesopotamia [modern Iraq]) expanded its control throughout the Near East through coercion and conquest. The kingdom of Israel, which tried to resist, was dismantled, with Samaria falling to the Assyrians in 722 BCE. To uproot the local power base, the Samarian leaders and elites were deported, and other (non-Israelite) populations were settled in their place.[8] Eventually the dispersed Samarians became known as "the Ten Lost Tribes," referring to the ten northern tribes of Israel.

When Israel fell to the Assyrians, Hezekiah was king of Judah, which was spared by paying tribute as a vassal (727–698 BCE). After the Assyrian king Sargon II was killed in battle in 705 BCE, Hezekiah organized a revolt.[9] In 701 BCE, Sargon's successor Sennacherib arrived in Judah with his army. The Assyrian army ravaged the Judahite countryside, destroying many towns and cities including Lachish, the most important stronghold outside of Jerusalem. Hezekiah prepared Jerusalem for the onslaught by fortifying the extramural suburbs with walls and constructing a new water system.[10] The Assyrians besieged Jerusalem but ended up withdrawing without taking the city for reasons that are unclear.[11] Judah survived in a weakened state by reverting to being a vassal and was forced to pay a large indemnity and annual tribute and surrender some of its territories.[12] Despite the consequences of the revolt's failure, the biblical writers present Hezekiah in a positive light as a religious reformer who abolished non-Yahwistic cults and practices and centralized the worship of YHWH in the Jerusalem temple (it was perhaps at this time that the shrine at Arad went out of use).[13]

Hezekiah's son Manasseh ascended the throne at the age of twelve and ruled for fifty-five years—longer than any other Israelite king (698–642 BCE). Although Judah prospered under Assyrian domination, the biblical writers condemn Manasseh because he reversed his father's religious policies by restoring local sanctuaries and promoting non-Yahwistic cults and practices: "He did what was evil in the sight of the Lord, following the abominable practices of the nations that the Lord drove out before the people of Israel" (2 Kgs 21:3).[14]

For the author of the DH, writing in retrospect, Manasseh's deeds above all else caused God to punish his people in 586 BCE by allowing the Babylonians to destroy Jerusalem and Solomon's temple and exile the Judahites: "The Lord said by his servants the prophets, 'Because King Manasseh of Judah has committed these abominations. . . . I am bringing upon Jerusalem and Judah such evil that the ears of everyone who hears of it will tingle. . . . I will wipe Jerusalem as one wipes a dish, wiping it and turning it upside down. I will cast off the remnant of my heritage, and give them into the hand of their enemies'" (2 Kgs 21:10–15).

Manasseh was succeeded by his son Amon, who ruled only two years.[15] No king of Judah is presented in a more positive light than Amon's successor Josiah (639–609 BCE), who the biblical writers viewed as a second David because of his religious reforms.[16] The reforms are said to have been set in motion by the discovery of a new book of law (Torah) during repairs to the temple building (623/622 BCE): "At that time Hilkiah the high priest said to Shaphan the scribe, 'I have found a book of law in the House of the Lord'" (2 Kgs 22:8). Many scholars identify this "book of law" as Deuteronomy (the Fifth Book of Moses), or, more likely, an early form or portion of it, and they therefore refer to Josiah's reforms as "Deuteronomistic."[17] Deuteronomy (Greek for "second law") reiterates many of the laws in the other four books of Moses and promotes the centralization of the worship of the God of Israel and the elimination of non-Yahwistic cults and practices. The DH is so-called because the author(s)'s view is Deuteronomistic, with Israel being rewarded for observing the covenant and punished for breaking it. The DH's description of Josiah's reforms indicates that non-Yahwistic cults and practices were still widespread in Judah in the late seventh century BCE, penetrating even into the Jerusalem temple:[18]

> Then the king [Josiah] commanded Hilkiah, the high priest . . . to bring out of the Temple of the Lord all the vessels that were made for the Baal and the Asherah and for all the host of the heavens; and he burned them outside Jerusalem in the limekilns by the Kidron, and carried away their ashes to Bethel. He also did away with the idolatrous priests, whom the kings of Judah had ordained to offer sacrifices in the high places in the cities of Judah and in the sanctuaries around Jerusalem; and to those who offered sacrifices to the Baal, to the sun, the moon, and the constellations, and all the host of the heavens. Moreover he brought the Asherah from the House of the Lord outside Jerusalem to the Kidron Valley and burned it at the Kidron Valley, and ground it to powder, and cast the powder of it upon the graves of the common people.
>
> Furthermore, he tore down the houses of the devotees of the fertility cult which were in the House of the Lord, where the women wove tunics for the Asherah. Then he brought all the priests from the cities of Judah and defiled the high places, where the priests offered sacrifices, from Geva to Beersheba. (2 Kgs 23:4–8)

During Josiah's reign, the Assyrian empire weakened while Babylonia (in southern Mesopotamia = modern Iraq) grew more powerful. In 609 BCE, the

Egyptian pharaoh Necho (or Neco/Necco) II sent an army to bolster Assyria against Babylonian expansion. As the Egyptian army exited a pass through the Carmel mountains by the major biblical tel of Megiddo, Josiah arrived and was slain by Necho: "In his days Pharaoh Necho, king of Egypt, went up to the king of Assyria to the Euphrates River; and King Josiah went to meet him; and Pharoah Necho slew him at Megiddo, as soon as he saw him" (2 Kgs 23:29).

Although it is unclear why Necho killed Josiah—Did he oppose the Egyptian army and ally with Babylonia as the Chronicler (2 Chr 35:20–24) writes?—for the biblical writers, this was a tragedy that ended their hopes for a revived Davidic kingdom under Josiah.[19] Because of Megiddo's strategic location, throughout history many important battles were fought in its vicinity.[20] As a result, and because Josiah—a second David—lost his life at Megiddo, the author of the Book of Revelation identified it as the site where the final apocalyptic battle will take place at the end of days: "They are demon spirits that perform wonders, and they go out to the kings all over the world to muster them for battle on the great day of God Almighty. . . . So they mustered the kings at the place called in Hebrew Armageddon" (Rev 16:14–16). "Armageddon" is the Greek version of the Hebrew name of the site: Har (Mount) Megiddo.

Necho's attempt to bolster Assyria failed and the Assyrian empire collapsed in 612 BCE, replaced by the Neo-Babylonian empire as the dominant power in the Near East. Over the next several decades, Judah was caught up in a power struggle between Egypt and Babylonia, resulting in the division of Jerusalem's leaders into factions with shifting allegiances. The prophet Jeremiah predicted dire consequences if Judah did not side with Babylonia: "For thus says the Lord: . . . And I will give all Judah into the hand of the king of Babylon; he shall carry them captive to Babylon, and shall kill them with the sword" (Jer 20:4). In 597 BCE, the Babylonians took Jerusalem after a siege. Josiah's grandson Jehoiachin (or Jechoniah), who had been king of Judah for only three months, surrendered and was exiled to Babylon with other members of the royal household and the Jerusalem elite, including the prophet Ezekiel. The Babylonians appointed a new king, Zedekiah, who was Jehoiachin's uncle and the last son of Josiah to rule Judah. A decade later Judah joined other Babylonian vassal states in a rebellion supported by Egypt.[21] The revolt was brutally suppressed by the Babylonians, who took Jerusalem in 586 BCE after an eighteen-month-long siege: "In the fifth month, on the seventh day of the month—this was in the nineteenth year of King Nebuchadnezzar, king of Babylon—Nebuzaradan, the commander of the guard, a servant of the king of Babylon, came to Jerusalem and burned the House of the Lord and the King's House; and all the houses of Jerusalem" (2 Kgs 25:8).

Solomon's temple was ransacked by the Babylonians. Later Jewish tradition commemorates its destruction on the ninth day of the month of Av (August).

Zedekiah was captured near Jericho as he tried to escape: "Then they took the king and brought him up to the king of Babylon at Riblah; and they pronounced judgment against him. They also slew the sons of Zedekiah before his eyes and put out his eyes and bound him fetters and carried him to Babylon" (2 Kgs 25:5–7). The last thing Zedekiah saw before being blinded was the death of his sons. The rest of Jerusalem's leaders and the elite were sent into exile with Zedekiah:[22] "Nebuzaradan the captain of the guard carried into exile the rest of the people who were left in the city and the deserters who had defected to the king of Babylon—all the rest of the population. But the captain of the guard left some of the poorest people of the land to be vinedressers and tillers of the soil. . . . So Judah went into exile out of its land" (2 Kgs 25:11–12, 21).

Jeremiah stayed behind at Mizpah (Tell en-Nasbeh, 12 kilometers [7.5 miles] north of Jerusalem) with the remaining Judahites under the administration of a prominent Jerusalemite named Gedaliah, who was appointed governor by the Babylonians. A few months later Gedaliah was assassinated, and Jeremiah fled to Egypt.[23] Unlike what the Assyrians had done to Israel, the Babylonians did not settle a different population to replace the Judahite exiles. Instead, Jerusalem remained desolate, and its environs were depopulated.[24]

Archaeology
The City Wall

Most archaeologists believe that the Middle Bronze Age wall discovered by Kathleen Kenyon and Yigal Shiloh midway down the east slope of the southeastern hill was in continuous use through the Iron Age, with repairs or reconstructions dating between the Middle Bronze Age (MB) II and the ninth–eighth centuries (Iron Age II) having been identified.[25] By this time, the settlement in Jerusalem had expanded into previously uninhabited areas, indicating an increase in population. The city's growth is reflected by the establishment of fortifications to protect neighborhoods that sprang up outside the walls. Archaeologists disagree about to what extent the expansion—much of it dating to the ninth–eighth centuries—was due to an influx of refugees from the northern kingdom of Israel and the countryside of Judah.[26] Ronny Reich and Eli Shukron's excavations (their Areas J and A) brought to light a 2-meter (6.5-foot) thick wall at the foot of the east slope of the southeastern hill, which encloses a residential quarter that developed outside the line of the Middle Bronze Age wall. They identify this as a new line of fortification to protect the residential quarter, although some archaeologists object that the wall is too narrow to have served as an effective line of defense and suggest it was part of a network of terraces on which the houses were built.[27] Reich and Shukron date both the wall and the residential quarter to the eighth century, whereas Shiloh's team claim the area was settled no later than the ninth century BCE as an extramural neighborhood, before being enclosed by a wall in the eighth century.[28]

By the eighth century, settlement had spread onto the southwestern hill, which was also enclosed within a wall (Figure 4.1). Sections of this wall were discovered by Nahman Avigad, including a 7-meter (23-feet) thick stretch on the

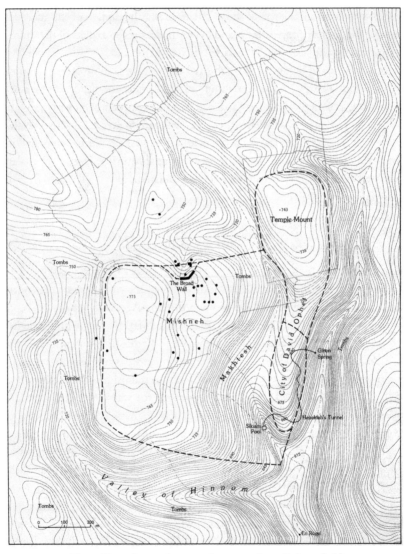

FIGURE 4.1 Plan of Jerusalem in the seventh century, from E. Stern [ed.] 1993: 707. Credit: With permission of Hillel Geva and the Israel Exploration Society.

north side of the hill (following the crest along the south side of the Transverse Valley) (Avigad's Area A) (Figure 4.2). Avigad dubbed this the "Broad Wall," from biblical references to a wall repaired by Nehemiah (Neh 3:8; 12:38; see Chapter 5).[29] The Broad Wall was built over preexisting houses, putting them out of use. The finds from the houses indicate that the wall was constructed in the late eighth century, apparently as part of Hezekiah's preparations for the Assyrian siege, and show that by then the southwestern hill was settled. This date is confirmed by the absence of *lmlk* seal impressions (see below) from the occupation level (stratum) associated with these houses versus the large numbers found in the stratum associated with the wall, as these seals first appeared in Judah during

FIGURE 4.2 The Broad Wall.
Credit: Photo by the author.

Hezekiah's reign.[30] Thus, the settlement on the southwestern hill began as an unfortified suburb before being enclosed by a wall in the late eighth century.

Avigad found that the Broad Wall does not run in a straight east–west line along the north side of the southwestern hill but has a deep southerly bend in the middle. The bend is placed at the point where a shallow valley branches off from the Transverse Valley to the south.[31] Although Avigad originally thought there was an opening for a gate in the middle of the bend, he and Hillel Geva later concluded that this part of the wall had been robbed out.[32] Earth fills and structures covering the Broad Wall indicate that it went out of use by the mid-seventh century BCE, perhaps having been damaged during the Assyrian siege.[33]

Some time in the seventh century, the Broad Wall was replaced by an east–west line of wall without a bend, which included a well-preserved tower that was incorporated into the Hasmonean period (second–first century BCE) fortifications (Avigad's Areas W and X–2).[34] Avigad proposed that the tower was the northeast corner of a four-chambered gate, a type of fortification typical of the Iron Age. However, this would mean the wall was connected to the middle of the gate on either side (leaving half of the gate outside the line of wall and half inside), whereas these gates typically lie completely inside the line of wall. Therefore, Geva suggests that the tower was a bastion projecting on the outside of the gate, while the gate itself lay inside the line of wall.[35] An ash layer with arrowheads at the foot of the tower is evidence of the Babylonian destruction in 586 BCE. Round stones made of flint found by the tower and wall, each weighing about half a pound, probably were projectiles fired by the Assyrians or Babylonians.[36]

In addition to the remains discovered by Avigad along the north side of the southwestern hill, segments of the late eighth-century wall have been found by other archaeologists along the western side of the hill, including in the Citadel (by Jaffa Gate) and the Armenian Garden.[37] These discoveries indicate that the extension of the fortifications to the southwestern hill brought the Pool of Siloam (Birket el-Hamra) into the walls of the city.[38] Geva concludes: "It appears that the two major building projects carried out by Hezekiah in Jerusalem—cutting the tunnel and fortification of the Southwestern Hill—were related. . . . Hezekiah created a massive and effective system of defenses in Jerusalem that proved itself when the Assyrian army besieged the city in 701 BCE, but failed in its attempt to conquer it."[39]

Avigad identified the southwestern hill with the Mishneh (Hebrew for "second"), a suburb mentioned in the Hebrew Bible that was the residence of Huldah the prophetess (2 Kgs 22:14; also see Neh 11:9). The seventh-century prophet Zephaniah refers to the Mishneh and to the Makhtesh (Hebrew for "mortar"), which Avigad proposed refers to the slopes of the Tyropoeon Valley: "On that day says the Lord, a cry will be heard from the Fish Gate, a wail from the Second

Quarter (Mishneh); a loud crash from the hills, the inhabitants of the Mortar (Makhtesh) wail" (Zeph 1:10–11).[40]

By the late eighth century BCE, the area enclosed within the walls totaled ca. 650 dunams (160.5 acres)—fourteen times the size of the Bronze Age and Early Iron Age city, although the southwestern hill was only sparsely settled.[41] With scattered dwellings and substantial areas under cultivation, the southwestern hill would have appeared more like a rural village than an urban settlement. A small number of residents lived outside the wall, to the north of the Temple Mount and north of the southwestern hill, an area that was quarried extensively for building stone in the ninth and eighth centuries.[42] Geva estimates Jerusalem's total population in the late eighth century at no more than 7,000–8,000—a fourfold increase from the time of David and Solomon.[43] Many archaeologists attribute the city's expansion in the eighth century, at least in part, to an influx of refugees from the northern kingdom, although other factors such as the security and prosperity under Assyrian hegemony could have spurred internal growth while attracting migrants from other parts of the country.[44] However, the establishment of the extramural quarter at the foot of the eastern slope of the southeastern hill by the ninth century shows that the city's population might have been growing even before the eighth century.[45]

After 701 BCE, the residential quarter at the southeast end of the southeastern hill, the neighborhood at the foot of the east slope of the southeastern hill, and the area outside the north wall of the southwestern hill appear to have been abandoned, although there is evidence of continued occupation near the Gihon spring.[46] Around this time—in the mid-seventh century, possibly during the reign of Manasseh—the earlier (Middle Bronze Age) wall discovered by Kenyon and Shiloh midway down the east slope of the southeastern hill was rebuilt.[47] Perhaps this is when the wall and tower replacing the Broad Wall were built. Jerusalem's fortifications on the eve of the Babylonian destruction in 586 BCE encompassed the southeastern hill, the Ophel and Temple Mount, and the southwestern hill. Although archaeologists disagree about whether there are signs of contraction and decline in the seventh century (perhaps followed by a modest recovery at the end of the century), many consider the eighth century, particularly the latter part, as the period when Iron Age Jerusalem reached the peak of its size and prosperity. The city seems never to have recovered fully from Sennacherib's siege in 701, and, by 586, BCE the population had decreased to around 6,000.[48]

Official Buildings: The Ophel

The buildings on the Ophel discovered by E. Mazar and B. Mazar continued in use until 586 BCE. Mazar and Mazar believe that, at the time of its destruction, the

"Royal Structure" (Building D) was used as a bakery (the "Building of the Royal Bakers"), based on their reconstruction of a paleo-Hebrew inscription incised on a pithos (large storage jar) found in one of the rooms. Paleo-Hebrew is a slightly modified version of the Canaanite-Phoenician alphabet that was adopted by the Israelites (whereas modern Hebrew is written in Aramaic script). The inscription reads, "to the minister of the O," which they restore as "to the minister of the bakers (*ophim*)."[49] Presumably the pithoi found in this building were used to store food products such as flour, oil, and honey. A palm tree incised on a pithos from another room in the building suggests that some of the jars contained date honey.[50] The pithoi were found lying on the floors of the building, where they were crushed when it was destroyed in 586 BCE. An intact black juglet dating to the tenth–ninth centuries was associated with an earlier floor below.[51] A large number of complete but smashed pottery vessels, including storage jars, was also discovered in the Babylonian destruction level in Building C (the "inner gatehouse") on the Ophel.[52]

In 2009, excavations by E. Mazar uncovered piles of refuse that had been discarded against Building D's outer wall. The debris included fragments of pottery vessels, ivory inlays, terracotta figurines, and bullae (small lumps of clay used to seal documents and containers). One bulla is stamped in paleo-Hebrew script with the personal seal of King Hezekiah: "Belonging to Hezekiah [son of] Ahaz King of Judah."[53] These finds support E. Mazar's and B. Mazar's identification of this area as a royal or official quarter.

Official Buildings: The North End of the Southeastern Hill

Part of a massive, two-story high, pillared late Iron Age building (Building 100) constructed of ashlars (large, well-cut blocks of stone), apparently a public structure, was uncovered recently in the Givati Parking Lot excavations. The rooms were filled with debris, in some places to a height of 2.3 meters (7.5 feet), including collapsed stones, ash, and burnt wood (some apparently belonging to furniture) from the Babylonian destruction in 586 BCE.[54] Several seals and bullae were found in this building, including a bulla stamped in paleo-Hebrew: "(Belonging to) Natanmelek Servant of the King." The title "Servant of the King" indicates that Natanmelek was a member of the Judahite king's court. The name Natanmelek (Hebrew for "the [divine] King has given") occurs only once in the Hebrew Bible, in connection with Josiah's reforms: "He [Josiah] removed the horses that the kings of Judah had dedicated to the sun, at the entrance to the house of the Lord, by the chamber of the eunuch [Hebrew *saris*] Nathan-melech [Natanmelek], which was in the precincts; then he burned the chariots of the sun with fire" (2 Kgs 23:11).[55] Since Building 100 was destroyed only a couple of decades after

Josiah's death, it is possible, although not provable, that the Natanmelek Servant of the King named on the bulla is the same individual described as a eunuch in 2 Kings (the term "eunuch" originally denoted an officer rather than an emasculated male). Either way, the size and high quality of construction and the finds from Building 100 suggest it was used for administrative purposes.

A rare find from Building 100 is a semi-precious stone seal inscribed in paleo-Hebrew with the name of a woman: "[belonging] to Elihana bat [daughter of] Gael."[56] Elihana is an otherwise unknown feminine variant of the name Eli. Seals and bullae with female names are rare because ancient families were patriarchal, with the male head of the household responsible for supporting and protecting the women and children. Unmarried women were dependent upon their fathers until they married, when they became part of their husband's household. Widows and orphans are frequently singled out in the Hebrew Bible as vulnerable because they had no male head of household to support and protect them. Few women had the financial means and independence to conduct business in their own name, as Elihana did. She undoubtedly was a member of the Jerusalem elite. The fact that the seal names Elihana's father but not her husband indicates that either her family was more prominent than her husband's or she was an unmarried woman or widow who lived with her father's household.

Three stone capitals of a type called "proto-Aeolic," "proto-Ionic," or "volute" were discovered at the north end of the southeastern hill: a large capital (broken into two pieces) from Kenyon's Area A (=Shiloh's Area G); a fragment of a similar (but not identical) capital from E. Mazar's 2012 excavations on the Ophel; and a fragment belonging to a smaller capital from the Givati Parking Lot excavations. The capital from Kenyon's excavations was found among debris from the 586 BCE destruction, while the Ophel fragment was built into a Herodian period pool and the Givati Parking Lot fragment was mixed with post-Iron Age fills.[57] The capitals are so-called because the distinctive central triangle design flanked by two volutes (curlicues that resemble the ends of a rolled-up scroll) recalls Greek Aeolic and Ionic capitals (the element at the top of a column) (Figure 4.3). Proto-Aeolic capitals have been found at Iron Age sites around Palestine, including Ramat Rahel, Megiddo, Samaria, Dan, and Hazor, as well as in Moab and Ammon (in modern Jordan).[58] Although in the past archaeologists dated some of these capitals to the time of David and Solomon, they apparently appeared in Palestine no earlier than the ninth century BCE and are most common in the eighth and seventh centuries.[59]

Proto-Aeolic capitals are associated with monumental buildings constructed of ashlar masonry such as palaces, administrative centers, fortresses, and gates. They were placed atop pillars or piers (square pillars constructed of ashlars), usually on either side of an entrance or doorway, with the decorated side facing the

FIGURE 4.3 Proto-Aeolic capitals in the Israel Museum Jerusalem.
Credit: Photo by the author.

passage, or were used as balustrades in windows. The different sizes of the proto-Aeolic capitals from Jerusalem suggest that they derive from three different monumental buildings at the north end of the southeastern hill, by the Ophel.[60] The capital from the Givati Parking Lot excavations might originally have been part of Building 100, although it was found in a later context nearby.[61]

Private Residences/Houses

Kenyon and Shiloh found that Iron Age houses were built on top of the stepped stone structure after it went out of use, apparently in the early ninth century BCE or later (Shiloh's Area G; see Chapter 3) (Figure 4.4).[62] The houses were

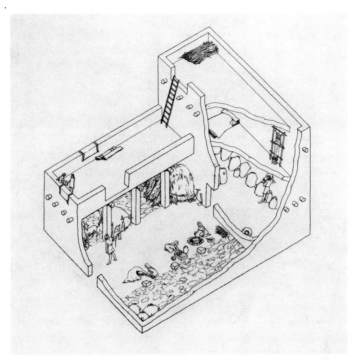

FIGURE 4.4 Four-room house, Israel Museum.
Credit: Chamberi, CC BY-SA 3.0, via Wikimedia Commons.

occupied through the eighth and seventh centuries and were destroyed in 586 BCE. They all represent a common Israelite type called by archaeologists a "four-room house" because the ground floor plan typically is divided into three long (parallel) spaces, with a short space running along the width at the back. The three long spaces consisted of a central open courtyard with pillared porches on either side. Animals could be stabled in the porches, while the courtyard was used for cooking, spinning and weaving, and other work. The room at the rear of the house was used for storage. The sleeping quarters were upstairs, away from the noise, dirt, and animals on the ground floor, accessed by a staircase abutting the outside of the house.

Shiloh dubbed the most complete house (ca. 8 × 12 meters [26 × 40 feet]) in Area G the "House of Ahiel" because this name appears on two ostraca (inscribed potsherds) found in the vicinity (Figure 4.5).[63] Nevertheless, we do not know whether anyone named Ahiel owned or lived in this house. Stones steps along the outer wall led to the second story, and three service rooms were attached to the back. One of the service rooms contained thirty-seven storage jars, while another room had a thick plastered floor and a toilet seat set over a cesspit. The seat is a square limestone block measuring about half a meter on each side, with a concave

FIGURE 4.5 The House of Ahiel.
Credit: Photo by the author.

top pierced by a keystone-shaped hole (Figure 4.6). John Duncan found an identical toilet seat in this area in 1925, and another was found in situ in Shiloh's excavations in Area E. Altogether, seven stone seats dating to the late Iron Age have been found on Jerusalem's southeastern hill, some still set over cesspits.[64] Another stone toilet seat was discovered in 2019–2020, in the garden of a late Iron Age villa in the modern neighborhood of Armon Hanatziv to the south of the Old City (see below). It was at the bottom of a hewn cesspit that contained a large quantity of pottery and animal bones—apparently waste that was disposed of in the cesspit.[65] Similar stone toilet seats have been discovered at Lachish in southern Judea and at other sites in the region.[66]

An analysis of the soil from the cesspit of the toilet in the House of Ahiel revealed that the inhabitants suffered from intestinal parasites (tapeworm and whipworm) and indicated that their diet included salad plants, potherbs, and spices.[67] Similar results were obtained from analyses of the sediment associated with the toilet in Armon Hanatziv, which contained the remains of four different families (taxa) of intestinal parasites: whipworm, beef/pork tapeworm, roundworm, and pinworm.[68] These parasites are common in unsanitary conditions and are caused by fecal contamination and the consumption of poorly cooked beef and pork. Parasites were spread widely through the use of human excrement as

FIGURE 4.6 Toilet in the House of Ahiel, from Cahill et al. 1991: 64. Credit: Reproduced with permission of Jane Cahill West.

agricultural fertilizer ("night soil"). A passage in Ezekiel indicates that human excrement was even used as fuel:

> You shall eat it as a barley-cake, baking it in their sight on human dung (*be-gellalei tse'at ha-adam* [literally, "dung that comes out of/is excreted by a human"]). The Lord said, "Thus shall the people of Israel eat their bread, unclean, among the nations to which I will drive them." Then I said, "Ah Lord God! I have never defiled myself; from my youth up until now I have never eaten what died of itself or was torn by animals, nor has carrion flesh come into my mouth." Then he said to me, "See, I will let you have cow's dung instead of human dung on which you may prepare your bread." (Ezek 4:12–15)

In this passage, Ezekiel objects to using human excrement as fuel not on account of hygiene but due to ritual purity concerns.[69] As private toilets were a luxury that only the elite could afford, the presence of parasites indicates that even ancient Jerusalem's wealthiest inhabitants suffered from painful and potentially deadly intestinal diseases.[70]

Shiloh excavated a room in another house across an alley from the House of Ahiel. He called it the "Burnt Room House" because it was filled with ash and carbonized wooden ceiling beams from the Babylonian destruction in 586 BCE.

The debris included fragments of charred wood with carved decoration belonging to furniture. Analyses indicate that some of the wood is *Pistacia atlantica*—a local species—while the more finely carved fragments are imported boxwood.[71]

A small part of another four-room house excavated by Shiloh in Area G is dubbed the "House of the Bullae" because it yielded a cache of 51 bullae (singular: bulla). Because there were no envelopes in antiquity, documents were rolled up and tied with string (or similar material). Documents and containers were sealed by placing a small lump of raw clay over the string and impressing it with a small stone or gemstone incised with the owner's name or personal symbol, which typically was worn as a ring or pendant. To open the document, the seal had to be broken by removing the lump of clay. Bullae are rare finds because unfired clay turns back into mud. In this case, the bullae were preserved as a result of the Babylonian destruction of 586 BCE, which burned the scrolls originally stored in this house but fired the clay sealings. These bullae are important because they have a documented and securely dated archaeological context, whereas many ancient bullae in museums and private collections were purchased on the antiquities market and were illegally looted from archaeological sites or are modern forgeries.

The bullae from the House of the Bullae are stamped in paleo-Hebrew script with the names of the owners of the seals. As is common in many parts of the Middle East today, ancient Jerusalemites did not have a first and last name but instead were identified as someone's son or daughter. This is reflected in the typical formula that appears on seals and bullae: "belonging to X son of Y." One example from the House of the Bullae reads "belonging to ʿAzaryahu son of Hilkiyahu," which, like many of the names on the bullae, contains the theophoric suffix –*yahu* (deriving from YHWH). Although many of the names are known from the Hebrew Bible, in most cases, it is impossible to determine if they are the same individuals who made the impressions on the bullae, as these were common names in seventh-century Judah. However, at least one bulla bears such an unusual name that it almost certainly is the same person mentioned in the Hebrew Bible: "belonging to Gemaryahu son of Shaphan." Gemaryah[u] son of Shaphan is mentioned in Jeremiah 36:10 as a scribe in the court of Jehoiakim the king of Judah (the son of Josiah), who reigned from ca. 609 to 598 BCE (Figure 4.7). A scribe is the sort of person we would expect to seal documents, and the timing corresponds well with the archaeological evidence since the House of the Bullae was destroyed in 586 BCE.[72] The finds from the houses in Area G indicate that the residents were members of the Jerusalem elite, including royal officials. The houses are located just below the summit of the north end of the southeastern hill and the Ophel, an area that apparently served as the administrative center of Jerusalem until its destruction in 586 BCE.

FIGURE 4.7 Gemaryahu son of Shaphan bulla.
Credit: Courtesy of Zev Radovan/BibleLandPictures.com.

Recent excavations on the slope just above the Gihon spring brought to light private dwellings that were inhabited from the eighth century to 586 BCE. The earliest occupation phase in one house (Building 17081) ended with the collapse of the upper parts of the walls. Pottery vessels typical of the eighth century BCE were found lying on the floor, smashed into pieces under the collapse.[73] Animal bones in the debris consist mainly of sheep and goats, with smaller quantities of cattle, gazelles, waterfowl and chickens, and fish—species typical of the ancient diet in this region. In addition, the complete skeleton of a small pig (less than seven months old) was found wedged between the smashed pottery vessels, where it was caught when the building collapsed. Pig remains are unattested at many Iron Age sites in Judah, and, even when they are represented, they comprise less than two percent of the animal bone (faunal) assemblage.[74] The discovery of this pig suggests that the biblical ban on pork consumption did not exist yet, or, if it existed, was not observed by all Judahites.[75] The excavators propose that the walls were toppled by an earthquake in the middle of the eighth century.[76] This may be the same earthquake mentioned in the biblical book of Amos, which chronicles the activities of that prophet around the years 765–755 BCE: "The words of Amos, who was among the shepherds of Tekoa, which he saw concerning Israel in the days of King Uzziah of Judah and in the days of King Jeroboam son of Joash of Israel, two years before the earthquake" (Amos 1:1).[77] The area around the Great Rift Valley (the Afro-Syrian Rift) is prone to tectonic activity, resulting in frequent earthquakes. Indeed, earthquake damage dating to the eighth century BCE has been identified at other archaeological sites around the country. The mid-eighth-century earthquake (or, possibly, a pair of earthquakes) was so devastating that it was mentioned more than two centuries later by the prophet Zechariah: "and you shall flee as you fled from the earthquake in the days of King Uzziah of Judah" (Zech 14:5).[78]

An increase in Jerusalem's population in the eighth century BCE is evident not only from the expansion of the settlement onto the southwestern hill but also the crowding of houses along the east slope of the southeastern hill, which was densely occupied.[79] Due to the steep topography, the houses were built on bedrock terraces, and sometimes even rooms within a single building were located on different terraces (e.g., the "Terrace House").[80] One large structure dubbed the "Pavement Building" extends westward from the city wall and might have been a public building.[81] In another building nearby, a stone toilet seat was found, possibly still set over a cesspit.[82] The settlement spilled outside the city wall down to the base of the east slope (Shiloh's Areas B, D1, and E2). This extramural quarter, which was fortified by its own wall during the eighth century, was abandoned after the Assyrian siege in 701 BCE. In contrast to the houses excavated elsewhere on the east slope of the southeastern hill, the thin, flimsy walls and relatively poor finds indicate that these were lower-class dwellings.[83]

The abandonment of the extramural quarter after the Assyrian siege suggests that the settlement in Jerusalem contracted and declined during the seventh century BCE. A similar picture is evident in the densely built-up neighborhoods inside the city wall on the east slope of the southeastern hill, where some of the houses were abandoned. At the end of the seventh century, spacious, well-constructed dwellings were built inside the city wall over the earlier houses, some of which were lying in ruins.[84] One of these is the "Ashlar House," a large (13 × 13 meters [43 × 43 feet]) structure spread over two terraces (Shiloh's Area E1). It is so-called because the outer walls are built of roughly hewn ashlar stones. Although the structure has the plan of a four-room house, Shiloh's team believe it was a public building.[85] The Ashlar House was (re)occupied in the early Persian period (late sixth century BCE), perhaps only on a small scale, despite lying in ruins at the time. A stone toilet seat found lying on the floor of a room from this phase probably originated in the pre-586 BCE occupation level.[86] A small stone column belonging to a decorative window balustrade is associated with another building nearby (Building 2011).[87] The construction of the Ashlar House and other structures hints at a revival late in the seventh century—at least on the southeastern hill—although the city did not recover in size and population to the same level as prior to the Assyrian siege in 701 BCE.[88]

The architectural remains and finds on the southwestern hill are much sparser and poorer, leading Geva to conclude that the southeastern hill remained the administrative center of the city until 586 BCE. One structure on the southwestern hill (Building 363) resembles a farmstead with a central courtyard surrounded by rooms. Built before the southwestern hill was enclosed by the Broad Wall, the structure was protected by its own fortifications.[89] Unlike the southeastern hill, the southwestern hill seems to have declined continuously without recovering before the destruction in 586 BCE.[90]

In 2019–2020, an extramural villa or mansion was discovered in the modern neighborhood of Arnona or Armon Hanatziv about 2 kilometers (1.2 miles) south of the Old City.[91] Armon Hanatziv (the Governor's Palace) is so-called because, under the British Mandate, it was the seat of the High Commissioner (it is now the United Nations headquarters). The villa, which dates to the end of the Iron Age (second half of the seventh century BCE), is perched on the high point of a ridge overlooking the Temple Mount and southeastern hill to the north. The structure was richly appointed, as indicated by the discovery of three intact, medium-sized, finely carved proto-Aeolic capitals, and a series of tiny proto-Aeolic capitals, which, together with small stone columns, formed part of a window balustrade. All three medium-sized capitals are carved on both long sides, indicating that they stood atop free-standing pillars or piers inside a passageway. A stone toilet seat (above) was found in the villa's garden, which was planted with shade trees and fruit trees. These finds indicate that this was an estate belonging to a member of the Jerusalem elite, likely a member of the royal family.

The Water System: The Rock-Cut Pool

In the late eighth century BCE, changes were made to the water system around the Gihon spring, which had continued to function since the Middle Bronze Age. These include the lowering of the floor level of the horizontal tunnel in Warren's Shaft, the extension of the Siloam Channel southward to the pool of Siloam (according to Reich and Shukron), and the reconstruction or construction of the Spring Tower (see Chapter 2). A simple private dwelling was constructed on top of a 3-meter-thick (10-foot) layer of fill covering the floor of the Rock-Cut Pool. The fill consisted of debris that had been dumped into the pool around 800 BCE judging from the pottery it contained.[92] By sifting the fill, Reich and Shukron recovered ten seals and scarabs and fragments of hundreds of clay bullae, over

170 of which are stamped with impressions. The bullae are fragmentary because the recipients broke them when opening the sealed documents and packages. Analyses of impressions visible on the reverse of bullae from E. Mazar's excavations on the Ophel indicate that they sealed papyrus and linen, the latter perhaps from sacks, pouches, or jar covers.[93] In contrast, the bullae found by Shiloh in the House of the Bullae are intact because the documents were still sealed when they were burned in the Babylonian destruction in 586 BCE.[94] For this reason, whereas the bullae from the House of the Bullae bear the names of local officials who sealed the documents that were stored there, none from the Rock-Cut Pool has writing in any Semitic language (e.g., Hebrew, Phoenician, Aramaic). Several have Egyptian hieroglyphic or pseudo-hieroglyphic signs, but most are impressed with figured images and other decorative motifs, including humans, real and mythical animals (such as sphinxes and griffins), ships, and proto-Aeolic capitals.

The lack of writing on the bullae from the Rock-Cut Pool versus those from the House of the Bullae and the Ophel (E. Mazar's excavations and the Givati Parking Lot) reflects their different dates: in the ninth century, individuals used decorative motifs on their seals for personal identification, whereas by the late eighth century, it had become common to inscribe one's name.[95] The motifs depicted on some of the bullae from the Rock-Cut Pool indicate that they sealed documents or packages sent to Jerusalem from Phoenicia and other areas outside Palestine.[96] The excavators posit that the bullae were disposed of together with other refuse from an otherwise unknown administrative or commercial center near the pool.[97] Additional bullae inscribed with names dating from the late eighth to early sixth centuries were found in more recent excavations by the Gihon spring.[98] The concentration of bullae in the vicinity of the spring suggests there was an administrative center nearby that controlled the access to and distribution of the water.[99]

The sifting of the fill from the Rock-Cut Pool also produced 10,600 fish bones belonging to fourteen different families of fish.[100] About ninety percent are bream and mullet from the Mediterranean. Other species represented include Nile perch from the Nile Delta, which is found at sites around the eastern Mediterranean and apparently was marketed widely. Isotope studies indicate that the Egyptian species include Gilthead seabream from the Bardawil Lagoon in the northern Sinai.[101] About one-third of the bones recovered from the pool belong to the fish head, while two-thirds are from the trunk. The fish were dried, salted, or smoked prior to transport. The bones must have been discarded with other refuse from a market nearby.[102] The Hebrew Bible refers to a Persian period gate in Jerusalem called the Fish Gate, the location of which is unknown (Zeph 1:10; Neh 3:3, 12:16; 2 Chron 33:14; see Chapter 5). Perhaps a gate with the same name existed in the Iron Age near the market that is assumed to be the source of the fish bones.[103]

The quantity of fish bones from the Rock-Cut Pool is greater than that found at any other Iron Age site in Israel. This is partly a result of the sifting of the fill, which retrieved tiny bones that otherwise would have been missed. Another 215 fish bones were discovered in Shiloh's excavations, 183 of which are from eighth–seventh century BCE contexts.[104] Eighty-eight bones come from a stone-lined pit in the House of Ahiel, and six were found in the cesspit of the toilet in that house, apparently having been tossed in with garbage rather than being part of the fecal matter. As in the Rock-Cut Pool, most of the fish from Shiloh's excavations are bream and mullet.[105] The bullae and fish bones are evidence of Jerusalem's commercial contacts with other parts of the eastern Mediterranean.[106] The remains from the Rock-Cut Pool and other excavations on the southeastern hill and the Ophel include hundreds of bones belonging to scaleless fish, represented mostly by catfish together with smaller quantities of shark's teeth and eel. This is surprising because biblical law prohibits the consumption of scaleless fish (Lev 11:9–12; Deut 14:9–10). In contrast to pig bones, which are rare even at non-Israelite and Judahite sites in the region, scaleless fish appear to have been a common part of the local diet through the Persian period. This suggests that the biblical ban on scaleless fish was new, whereas the prohibition on pork consumption was in line with preexisting dietary habits.[107]

Although sharks presumably were imported to Jerusalem for human consumption like the other marine species, isotope studies indicate that some of the shark's teeth are fossils of the Late Cretaceous period some 80 million years ago! Furthermore, the fossil teeth might have been brought to Jerusalem from the southern Negev desert—a distance of up to 90 kilometers (56 miles) away—where they are commonly found in chalky outcrops.[108] What the teeth were used for is a mystery. Thomas Tütken, the head of the team that conducted the isotope studies, said, "Our working hypothesis is that the teeth were brought together by collectors, but we don't have anything to confirm that. There are no wear marks which might show that they were used as tools, and no drill holes to indicate that they may have been jewelry. We know that there is a market for shark's teeth even today, so it may be that there was an Iron Age trend for collecting such items. This was a period of riches in the Judean Court. However, its too easy to put 2 and 2 together to make 5. We'll probably never really be sure."[109]

The Water System: The Siloam Tunnel (Hezekiah's Tunnel)

In preparation for the Assyrian siege, Hezekiah equipped Jerusalem with a new water system: the Siloam Tunnel (= Hezekiah's Tunnel = Channel VIII). Unlike

Warren's Shaft and the Siloam Channel (Channel II), water still flows through the Siloam Tunnel today (Figure 4.8). The tunnel begins at the Gihon spring and ends at a storage pool (the current Pool of Siloam) on the southwest side of the southeastern hill. The Siloam Tunnel is a marvel of ancient engineering. It is entirely underground and was hewn through bedrock by two teams of men who started at either end (i.e., one team at the Gihon spring and the other team at the outlet end with the pool), as indicated by the cutting marks left by iron tools. The difference in the level of the floor from beginning to end is 30 centimeters (12 inches)—a gradient of just 0.05 percent![110] Although the tunnel winds back and forth for a distance of more than 500 meters—about twice the distance from

FIGURE 4.8 The Siloam Tunnel (Hezekiah's Tunnel) (3782613123). Credit: Ian Scott, CC BY-SA 2.0, via Wikimedia Commons.

the spring to the pool as the crow flies—the two teams met roughly in the middle. How they managed to do this is a mystery. According to one theory, the teams followed existing karstic cracks in the bedrock through which water was already flowing.[111] But if this is true, why is the ceiling of the tunnel so much higher at the outlet end than at the spring end (dropping from about 5 meters [16 feet] to about 2 meters [7 feet] in height)?[112] Why would the workers have expended so much unnecessary effort? Furthermore, false starts are clearly visible in the tunnel—that is, places where the teams began to cut through the bedrock in one direction, but then stopped and continued in another direction—which makes no sense if they were following an existing stream of water.

Reich and Shukron propose the following solution to the mystery of the Siloam Tunnel. Although the channel was hewn by two teams beginning at either end, the work was not simultaneous, nor was it completed according to a preconceived plan. Instead, work commenced at the pool of Siloam (outlet) end, with the goal of connecting to the Siloam Channel (Channel II). The ceiling of the Siloam Tunnel at the outlet end is very high (ca. 5 meters [16 feet]) because the tunnel's floor would have been at the same level as the Siloam Channel, which is about 2.5 meters (8 feet) higher than the Siloam Tunnel's floor as completed. At some point, this plan was abandoned in favor of hewing a deeper tunnel under the Siloam Channel to connect with the Gihon Spring. The floor level at the southern end of the Siloam Tunnel was deepened and the tunnel was continued eastward and southward, passing underneath the Siloam Channel, from which it is separated by only 50–100 centimeters (20–40 inches) of rock.[113] In the meantime, workers had begun to hew the northern end of the tunnel in the vicinity of the Gihon Spring. They cut an opening through the north wall of the Rock-Cut Pool (Tunnel IV) and continued westward before winding around to the south. The tunnelers were able to work without being flooded because water from the spring was still flowing through Channel II. Reich and Shukron propose that a small channel dug to the east of Channel II—Channel I—provided a point of reference to the water level, and that a small amount of water was allowed to flow through the Rock-Cut Pool into the tunnel.[114] Existing karstic cracks in the bedrock might have been utilized to guide the course of the northern part of the tunnel.[115] Once the two teams met, the opening to the Siloam Channel was blocked and the water was directed into the Siloam Tunnel.[116]

A group of geologists (Amihai Sneh, Ram Weinberger, and Eyal Shalev) reject Reich and Shukron's proposal, noting that we would expect a sudden drop in the height of the ceiling after the initial plan was abandoned instead of a gradual decrease in height. Instead, they propose that the two teams followed existing but not necessarily interconnected karstic cavities in the bedrock.[117] In short, how the Siloam Tunnel was hewn remains an unsolved mystery.[118]

Why did Hezekiah find it necessary to provide Jerusalem with a new water system when the other two systems were still functioning? According to 2 Chr 32:2–4,

> When Hezekiah saw that [the Assyrian king] Sennacherib had come and intended to fight against Jerusalem, he planned with his officers and his warriors to stop the flow of the springs that were outside the city; and they helped him. A great many people were gathered, and they stopped all the springs and the wadi (or stream) that flowed through the land, saying, "Why should the Assyrian kings come and find water in abundance?"

This passage indicates that Hezekiah commissioned a new water system to prevent the Assyrians from having access to the water in the Siloam Channel ("the wadi or stream that flowed through the land"). Once the extramural quarter at the foot of the east slope of the southeastern hill was fortified, the Siloam Channel was enclosed within a wall. Nonetheless, had the Assyrians succeeded in penetrating the wall, they would have gained access to the water because the channel is above ground.[119] Therefore, Hezekiah blocked the Siloam Channel and redirected the water into a new underground tunnel (the Siloam Tunnel = Hezekiah's Tunnel), which carried the runoff from the Gihon spring to the southwest side of the southeastern hill. The water was stored in a pool called the Pool of Siloam (Birket el-Hamra), which had been fed by the Siloam Channel and was enclosed within Hezekiah's new city wall:[120] "This same Hezekiah closed the upper outlet of the waters of Gihon and directed them down to the west side of the city of David" (2 Chr 32:30).

Reich and Shukron's excavations reveal that the Pool of Siloam was an enormous reservoir (ca. 60 × 50 meters [197 × 165 feet) at the southern end of the Tyropoeon Valley and the southeastern hill. The remains date to the late Second Temple period (first century BCE to first century CE) but probably occupy roughly the same spot as the Iron Age pool.[121]

In 1880, children from the nearby village discovered an inscription high up on the wall of the Siloam Tunnel, close to the pool at the outlet end. The inscription is in biblical Hebrew and is written in paleo-Hebrew script (Figure 4.9). This remarkable document commemorates the completion of the tunnel—the moment when the two teams of men were so close that they could hear the others' voices through the bedrock and finally met.

> [T]he tunnelling (was finished). And this was the matter of the tunnel: While [the hewers wielded] the axe, each man toward his fellow, and while there were still three cubits to be he[wn, there was hear]d a

FIGURE 4.9 The Siloam Tunnel inscription.
Credit: Courtesy of Zev Radovan/BibleLandPictures.com.

man's voice call/ing to his fellow; for there was a crack (?) in the rock on the right and [on the lef]t. And at the end of the tunnelling the hewers hacked each man toward his fellow, axe upon axe. And there / flowed the waters from the spring toward the reservoir for two hundre[d and] a / thousand and cubits. And a hu[nd]red cubits was the height of the rock above the head(s) of the hewers.[122]

The Siloam Tunnel is often called Hezekiah's Tunnel although the inscription does not name that king or any other individual and contains no date. Most scholars understand 2 Chronicles as referring to a new water system commissioned by Hezekiah in advance of the Assyrian siege and identify this system as the Siloam Tunnel. In this case, the inscription would be associated with Hezekiah and therefore would date to the late eighth century BCE.[123] However, some scholars date the tunnel—and with it the inscription—to the early eighth century or to the seventh century or later.[124] For example, Reich and Shukron argue that the scale of the project indicates that the Siloam Tunnel took years rather than months to complete and therefore was hewn by one of Hezekiah's predecessors in the early eighth century.[125] On the other hand, based on their estimates that the Siloam Tunnel took at least four years to complete, Sneh, Weinberger, and Shalev believe the system could not have been hewn by Hezekiah in advance of the Assyrian siege. Instead, they attribute the Siloam Channel to Hezekiah and date the Siloam Tunnel to the seventh century, perhaps the reign of Manasseh.[126] However, the association of the Siloam Tunnel with Hezekiah is still accepted by most scholars and is supported by scientific analyses including radiometric dating of the original plaster covering the tunnel's floor, which show that it was hewn around 700 BCE.[127]

Ten years after its discovery, the Siloam inscription was hacked out of the tunnel's wall by local villagers and broken into pieces. Since Palestine was under Ottoman rule at the time, the Ottoman authorities confiscated the fragments.[128] Since then, the inscription has been displayed in the Istanbul Archaeological Museum. According to an announcement made in March 2022, in the wake of the visit of Israel's president to Ankara and improving Turkish–Israeli relations, the Siloam inscription will be returned to Israel.[129]

Stamped Jars

The handles or bodies of ancient storage jars were sometimes stamped with seal impressions bearing names and symbols. A type called *lmlk* stamps (vocalized as *lamelekh*) is common in Jerusalem in the late eighth and seventh centuries (Figures 4.10 and 4.11). *Lamelekh* means "of [or belonging to] the king" or "royal." The stamps are so-called because they have an inscription that begins with the word *lmlk*, followed by the name of one of four cities: Hebron, Ziph, Socoh, or *mmšt* (an unidentified city).[130] The inscriptions are accompanied by a depiction of a four-winged scarab or a two-winged solar disk. The stamps are impressed on a distinctive type of storage jar with four handles. In many cases, all four handles were stamped, whereas in other cases only one or two handles were stamped.[131] Although there is no doubt that the stamps indicate royal oversight or authority, their purpose is unknown: Do they indicate that the jars contained goods paid as taxes, or were these emergency food provisions stored in the four cities, or did the jars store produce from royal estates?[132]

Some jar handles are stamped with personal names, apparently belonging to officials. In a few cases, the same names or motifs are stamped on both jar handles and bullae.[133] For example, the bulla stamped with Hezekiah's name from E. Mazar's excavations on the Ophel displays a two-winged solar disk flanked by *ankh* symbols (the Egyptian symbol of life). The two-winged solar disk seems to have replaced the four-winged scarab on Judahite royal seals in the late eighth century. Both symbols originated in Egypt, where they were associated with the sun god Ra, but became popular throughout the Near East as representations of divine power and protection.[134]

In the late seventh century BCE, *lmlk* stamps were replaced by stamps with a rosette motif (a series of dots surrounding a central dot that resemble a schematic flower). Like the winged scarab and solar disk, the rosette was a common Near Eastern symbol of divine kingship.[135] Although *lmlk* impressions are found in much greater numbers than rosette impressions, both were

FIGURE 4.10 Iron Age storage jar with stamped handles from Lachish in the Israel Museum Jerusalem.
Credit: Photo by the author.

stamped on handles of the same types of jars and seem to have served the same purpose. Jane Cahill's 2003 publication of rosette impressions from the Jewish Quarter documents 283 *lmlk* stamped handles from sites in Jerusalem (out of a total of more than 1,700 known stamps) and 84 rosette stamped handles from sites in Jerusalem (versus 145 from outside Jerusalem).[136] She notes that the larger ratio of rosette stamped handles to *lmlk* handles in Jerusalem (1:2 versus 1:4) suggests that royal administrative and economic activity became more concentrated in the capital city in the late seventh century than it was previously.[137]

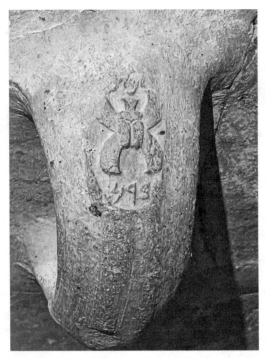

FIGURE 4.11 Iron Age storage jar from Lachish, with a handle stamped with a four-winged scarab and the inscription "of the king, Hebron" in the Israel Museum Jerusalem. Credit: Photo by the author.

The large numbers of stamped jar handles and bullae found around and above the Gihon spring are consistent with other evidence that the summit of the north end of the southeastern hill and the Ophel served as the administrative center of Jerusalem until its destruction in 586 BCE.[138] Large concentrations of stamped jars and jar handles have also been discovered on the southwest outskirts of modern Jerusalem—at Ramat Rahel and in the Arnona neighborhood (near the U.S. Embassy)—an agricultural area where the goods collected and stored in the jars were produced.[139]

Terracotta Figurines

Although terracotta figurines (small clay statuettes) are found at sites around Judah in the eighth and seventh centuries BCE, they are represented in much larger numbers in Jerusalem than elsewhere.[140] Diana Gilbert-Peretz's 1996 publication of figurines from Shiloh's excavations documented nearly 2,000 figurines from Jerusalem to that point, leading her to observe that, "No site has yielded even a quarter of the finds recovered from Jerusalem."[141] Within Jerusalem, the largest concentration of figurines comes from the southeastern hill, with 1,309 from Shiloh's excavations alone.[142]

The figurines are anthropomorphic (human-shaped) or zoomorphic (animal-shaped). Zoomorphic figurines—almost twenty percent of which are horses (some with riders)—are the most common type, comprising about three-quarters of the corpus from sites in Judah. Anthropomorphic figurines, which comprise approximately twenty percent of the corpus, all belong to the same type: Judean pillar figurines (JPFs) depicting women (Figure 4.12). They are so-called because the body is a hollow or solid cylinder that widens at the base, representing an ankle-length garment.[143] The upper part of the cylinder is formed into the shape of a woman who cradles her breasts in her hands or holds an object to her breasts.[144] The head was formed either in a mold or by pinching the clay. Although zoomorphic figurines outnumber the JPFs, both types were manufactured from the same clays, come from the same contexts, and are sometimes found together.[145] In most cases, the original painted decoration, which indicated details such as clothing and hair, has not survived.[146]

FIGURE 4.12 Judean Pillar Figurines (JPFs).
Credit: Photo by David Hendin, courtesy of David Hendin.

The function and significance of these figurines are unknown. Were anthropomorphic figurines votive offerings representing human devotees or perhaps images of deities or supernatural (semi-divine) beings that were divine intermediaries?[147] Were the zoomorphic figurines offered as substitutes for animal sacrifices, or were they an attribute or symbol of a deity? Or could they have been something as mundane as toys?[148]

Although found in large numbers in Jerusalem at a time when the earliest books of the Hebrew Bible were composed or written down, there are no explicit biblical references to these figurines.[149] Nevertheless, some scholars connect the horses to a solar cult and the worship of YHWH, as in the DH's description of Josiah's reforms: "He [Josiah] removed the horses that the kings of Judah had dedicated to the sun, at the entrance to the house of the Lord, by the chamber of the eunuch Nathan-melech, which was in the precincts; then he burned the chariots of the sun with fire" (2 Kgs 23:11).[150] However, the non-Yahwistic cultic images mentioned in the Hebrew Bible were housed in shrines and temples and therefore would have been larger and made of metal rather than clay, whereas most of the figurines come from domestic (household) contexts.[151]

The prominent breasts of the JPFs suggest an association with fertility, and many scholars identify them with Asherah or Astarte—a female consort of the chief male deity.[152] However, in a recent study, Erin Darby rejects both assumptions, concluding that the JPFs were used mostly in household contexts among all sectors of Judahite society for protection and healing.[153] She notes that these figurines appeared while Judah was under Assyrian domination and remained common through the reforms of Hezekiah and Josiah, which suggests they were not connected to an "official" or state-sponsored cult.[154]

The discovery of zoomorphic figurines and JPFs in different contexts—mostly domestic (houses) but also funerary (tombs)—suggests they were used for different purposes.[155] "Cultic corners" have been discovered in some houses on the southeastern hill, consisting of standing stones or stelae (*mazzeboth*), decorated clay chalices and cultic stands, and/or concentrations of figurines (one house contained sixty-six figurines!). Alon de Groot believes these provide evidence of domestic or household cult while cautioning, "Such figurines appear in every structure in Jerusalem in the eighth-seventh centuries, however, and one should not automatically assume that their presence attests to a cultic site."[156] Indeed, Darby notes that the JPFs are not usually found with other cultic objects.[157] The possibility that the figurines were used for apotropaic purposes or in magical rituals is supported by signs that many were broken deliberately and discarded. In this case, the figurines might have been destroyed by their users after serving their purpose.[158]

Two characteristics of these figurines are especially noteworthy: (1) they are concentrated in Jerusalem and especially on the southeastern hill, and (2) they date to the eighth and seventh centuries BCE. Although the figurines and espe-cially the JPFs are distinctive to Judah, other types of anthropomorphic and zoomorphic clay figurines were common around the eastern Mediterranean in this period. Their popularity shows that the inhabitants of Jerusalem were not divorced from their broader Near Eastern context but employed some of the same practices and rituals as the peoples around them.[159] The appearance of zoo-morphic figurines and JPFs in the eighth and seventh centuries and their large numbers in Jerusalem and especially on the southeastern hill are one aspect of Jerusalem's growth and prosperity under Assyrian influence (domination?). This explains their disappearance from Jerusalem after 586 BCE. Similar factors account for foreign influence on tombs and burial customs in this period.

Tombs

Although most Israelite burials in Jerusalem were extramural, according to the Hebrew Bible David and his successors were laid to rest inside the city: "Then David slept with his ancestors, and was buried in the city of David" (1 Kgs 2:10). The description of the rebuilding of Jerusalem's walls under Nehemiah indicates that the graves of David and his successors were located at the south end of the southeastern hill: "After him Nehemiah son of Azbuk, ruler of half the district of Beth-Zur, repaired from a point opposite the graves of David as far as the arti-ficial pool and the house of the warriors" (Neh 3:16). Some scholars identify the "Garden of Uzzah" mentioned in 2 Kings 21:18 with the royal cemetery where Manasseh and his successors were buried:[160] "Manasseh slept with his ancestors, and was buried in the garden of his house [palace], in the garden of Uzza." The association of the garden with the royal palace suggests it was within the city walls, close to the Temple Mount. Perhaps these are the royal tombs condemned by Ezekiel due to their proximity to the temple:[161] "The house of Israel shall no more defile my holy name, neither they nor their kings, by their whoring, and by the corpses of their kings at their death. . . . Now let them put away their idolatry and the corpses of their kings far from me" (Ezek 43:7, 9). In this case, whereas the tombs of David and his successors were located at the south end of the south-eastern hill, those of the later Judahite kings (Manasseh and his successors) might have been in the northern part of the city.[162]

The royal tombs of Judah have never been found. In 1863, Louis-Félicien de Saulcy erroneously identified the tomb of Queen Helena of Adiabene—a monumental first century CE tomb complex to the north of the Old City—as the tombs of the House of David, since which time it has been called the "Tombs of the Kings" (see Chapters 1 and 7). At the end of the nineteenth century, after Charles Clermont-Ganneau suggested that the large bend in the southern part of the Siloam Tunnel was cut to circumvent the tombs of David and his successors, Frederick Bliss and Archibald Dickie conducted excavations immediately to the south of the bend but failed to find the tombs. A couple of decades later, Raymond Weill excavated the area north of the bend and identified large rock-cut spaces including a large, vaulted tunnel as the tombs of David and his successors, although this claim is now widely rejected. Reich identifies the rock-cut spaces as belonging to late Second Temple period dwellings.[163]

Nowadays visitors to Jerusalem are shown David's tomb on Mount Zion (the southern tip of the southwestern hill). How is this possible when the Hebrew Bible says David was buried in the City of David? As a synonym for Jerusalem, the term "Zion" originally denoted the City of David (and, from Solomon's time, the Ophel and Temple Mount as well). However, by the late Second Temple period, the southwestern hill—which is where Herod the Great and the Jerusalem elite lived—had become known as Mount Zion. The site of David's tomb moved with the name Mount Zion to the southwestern hill. Since the Byzantine period or later, tradition has located David's tomb at the southern tip of the southwestern hill, which today is called Mount Zion (see Chapter 9).[164]

The Israelites (and later, the Jews) did not cremate or expose their dead but disposed of the whole corpse (inhumation), mostly in ways that have left few traces in the archaeological landscape. Biblical law mandates burial within twenty-four hours of death even for the worst criminals (Deut 21:23). Often, the bodies of the deceased were laid to rest in trench graves dug into the ground (similar to the way we bury our dead today). This kind of grave is called a "cist" if it is lined with stone slabs or is hewn into the top of a rocky outcrop. Typically, the corpse was wrapped in a shroud and sometimes placed in a coffin (usually of wood) and then laid in the grave. Trench graves are rarely discovered because they are easily covered or plowed over or destroyed, and, when found, they are difficult to date because of the lack of burial goods accompanying the deceased.

In the eighth and seventh centuries BCE, Jerusalem's wealthy residents interred family members in burial caves cut into the rocky outcrops surrounding the city.[165] These rock-cut tombs are associated with the elite, who could afford to pay someone to hew them out of bedrock as a lasting memorial in the city's landscape. Each rock-cut tomb belonged to a family and was used over the course of generations. Except for the royal burials mentioned above, graves in Jerusalem were located outside the city walls. Therefore, their distribution may reflect the extent of the city in different periods.[166] For example, Geva postulates that tombs discovered north of the Damascus Gate indicate that, in the eighth–seventh centuries, people lived outside the southwestern hill's north wall.[167] B. Mazar found rock-cut square shafts leading to spacious plastered underground chambers on the east slope of the southwestern hill (along the Tyropoeon Valley). He and

E. Mazar identify these as a common Phoenician type of tomb that was adopted by the Jerusalem elite and suggest they were emptied and abandoned when the city wall was extended to the southwestern hill in the late eighth century.[168] However, because the underground chambers were emptied of their original contents and modified later for other uses, it is uncertain that they were tombs.[169]

Dozens of rock-cut tombs of the eighth and seventh centuries have been discovered to the west, north, and east of the Old City. They include tombs at Ketef Hinnom (on the northwest side of the Ben-Hinnom Valley), St. Étienne (St. Stephen's Monastery or the École Biblique, to the north of the Old City), and in the Silwan (Siloam) village (across the Kidron Valley from the southeastern hill). Most of the tombs consist of a single burial chamber entered through an unadorned opening cut into a rocky outcrop, but some are larger and more elaborate.

In 1968–1970, David Ussishkin documented approximately fifty tombs cut into the cliffs and rocky outcrops of Silwan, the Arab village on the lower southeast slope of the Kidron Valley, directly across from the southeastern hill.[170] One group of tombs is characterized by an elongated chamber with a gabled bedrock ceiling and hewn, bathtub-shaped burial troughs with a rock-cut "pillow" for the head of the deceased. The tombs in another group have two or three large burial chambers with flat ceilings lined up in a row one behind the other, with few or no burial troughs. A small group of tombs is exceptional in consisting of an above-ground (free-standing) rock-cut cube.[171] The best example of this type is the "Tomb of Pharaoh's Daughter," so-called because the cube terminates in an Egyptian cornice (a concave molding) and originally was surmounted by a pyramidal roof (Figure 4.13). The tomb contains a single burial chamber. An inscription in paleo-Hebrew script was carved above the entrance, but only the last two letters are preserved.[172]

Another free-standing rock-cut cube, named the "Tomb of the Royal Steward," contains two side-by-side burial chambers. It is so-called because two paleo-Hebrew inscriptions on the façade indicate that it belonged to a "Steward of the House" (Hebrew *asher al-habbayit*, literally "[he] who is over the house"), a biblical term denoting a royal administrative official.[173] The inscriptions were discovered in 1870, by Clermont-Ganneau, who removed them and sent them to the British Museum "to ensure their preservation," where they are still housed.[174] One inscription is three lines long and the other is only one line, and both are badly damaged. Although Clermont-Ganneau was able to read only one word ("house") in the longer inscription, it appeared to him to be part of the phrase "who is over the house."[175] Clermont-Ganneau's hunch was confirmed when Avigad deciphered the full inscription over eighty years after its initial discovery: "This is [the sepulchre of . . .]yahu who is over the house. There is no silver

FIGURE 4.13 Tomb of Pharoah's Daughter in Silwan (on left).
Credit: Photo by the author.

and no gold here but [his bones] and the bones of his slave-wife [Hebrew *amah*] with him. Cursed be the man who will open this!"[176] *Amah* refers to an Israelite free-born young woman who was sold by her father as a slave-wife and was inferior in status to a legally married wife.[177] Presumably, tomb-robbers would have been literate enough to read the inscription or there would have been no point in inscribing the curse on the façade. The inscription indicates that gold, silver, and other valuables were deposited in tombs with the deceased.[178]

Many scholars identify the official named in the inscription with Shebna, a steward who lived in Hezekiah's time and was rebuked by the prophet Isaiah for hewing a rock-cut tomb on a prominent high spot: "Thus says the Lord God of hosts: Come, go to this steward, to Shebna, who is master of the household ["who is over the house"], and say to him: what right do you have here? Who are your relatives here, that you have cut out a tomb here for yourself, cutting a tomb on the height, and carving a habitation for yourself in the rock?" (Isa 22:15–16). Shebna is an abbreviated version of the biblical name Shebanyahu, in which case the inscription would have read, "This is [the sepulchre of Sheban]yahu who is over the house." Not only does the Tomb of the Royal Steward's location on a cliff in Silwan accord with Isaiah's reference to a rock-cut tomb "on the height," but the dates fit because Shebna lived during the time of Hezekiah and the inscription is dated to ca. 700 BCE based on paleography (letter forms).[179]

Soon after deciphering the first inscription from the Tomb of the Royal Steward, Avigad succeeded in reading the second inscription, which is incomplete and badly damaged: "(Tomb-) chamber in the side (or slope) of the rock (or mountain) . . ."[180] Ussishkin explains this inscription as referring to the side chamber (second chamber) inside the tomb, in which case it should be understood as "a burial-chamber in the side of the rock-cut burial-chamber" or "a burial-chamber in the side of the rock-cut tomb (with reference to the monolithic tomb above ground)."[181]

A number of rock-cut tombs have been found to the north of the Old City, including around the Garden Tomb (see Chapter 7). Two exceptionally large and elaborate tombs are located nearby on the grounds of the École Biblique.[182] In both, a forecourt leads into a main hall surrounded by several burial chambers. The rooms are carefully hewn with architectural details that reflect Assyrian influence, including protruding door sockets, carved rectangular panels on the walls, and a double cornice at the junction between the walls and ceiling. A pit cut into the floor of the main hall in one of the tombs contained a decorated metal box with fowl bones, perhaps representing a foundation deposit.[183] Each burial chamber is surrounded on three sides by rock-cut benches on which the bodies of the deceased were laid. The benches have raised edges and horseshoe-shaped headrests with curled ends, recalling the headdress of the Egyptian goddess Hathor. Pits used as repositories were cut under one of the benches in each burial chamber. When the benches were filled and space was needed for new burials, the earlier remains (bones and burial gifts) were deposited in the repository.

Similar tombs are hewn into the slopes of the Ben-Hinnom Valley west of the Old City.[184] Between 1979 and 1988, Gabriel Barkay excavated seven late Iron Age rock-cut tombs cut into a rocky outcrop under the Church of St. Andrew, at a site called Ketef Hinnom.[185] Quarrying activity in later periods exposed the interiors of the tombs, each of which had a chamber surrounded on three sides by rock-cut benches (Figure 4.14). Nearly all of Jerusalem's rock-cut tombs were plundered of their contents long ago.[186] However, in one of the Ketef Hinnom tombs, Barkay found a repository that was undisturbed because the rock ceiling had collapsed, burying and concealing the contents.[187] The repository contained large numbers of skeletons belonging to at least ninety-five individuals, as well as burial gifts including ceramic vases and oil lamps, jewelry, seals, a rare early coin, and two silver amulets.[188] The amulets are thin silver plaques that were rolled up like tiny scrolls, each about the size of a cigarette butt, and would have been worn on a string like a charm.[189] Both amulets are lightly incised with versions of the priestly blessing (Num 6:24–26; Deut 7:9).

FIGURE 4.14 Interior of a rock-cut tomb at Ketef Hinnom.
Credit: Photo by the author.

Amulet I:

". . .]YHW. . . the grea[t . . . who keeps] the covenant and [G]raciousness toward those who love [him] and (alt: those who love [hi]m;) those who keep [his commandments . . . . . .]. the Eternal? [. . .]. [the?] blessing more than any [sna]re and more than Evil. For redemption is in him. For YHWH is our restorer [and] rock. May YHWH bles[s] you and [may he] keep you. [May] YHWH make [his face] shine . . . ."[190]

Amulet II:

"[For PN, (the son/daughter of) xxxx]h/hu. May h[e]/sh[e] be blessed by Yahweh, the warrior [or: helper] and the rebuker of [E]vil: May Yahweh bless you, keep you. May Yahweh make his face shine upon you and grant you p[ea]ce."[191]

These amulets preserve the earliest known citations of biblical texts. Their discovery in a late Iron Age tomb shows that this blessing—which was incorporated into the Five Books of Moses—originated before 586 BCE.[192]

Many of the elements in Jerusalem's larger and more elaborate rock-cut tombs reflect Egyptian, Assyrian, and especially Phoenician influence (including Egyptian styles transmitted through Phoenician intermediaries).[193] The diversity of the tombs shows that the Jerusalem elite were well-integrated into their larger

Near Eastern context and borrowed freely from other cultures to display their status and wealth.

Jerusalem at the End of the Iron Age

Jerusalem prospered as an Assyrian vassal despite suffering some decline after the siege in 701 BCE. Thanks largely to an influx of refugees from the northern kingdom, the city exploded in size and population in the eighth century. By the eve of the Babylonian destruction in 586 BCE, the walled settlement encompassed the southeastern hill, the Ophel and Temple Mount, and the southwestern hill, comprising a much larger city than in the time of David and Solomon. Not only was the eighth–seventh century city large but it was prosperous, as indicated by the remains of spacious residences built of ashlar masonry, some with passageways or window balustrades decorated with proto-Aeolic capitals, and/or equipped with private toilets, and by the tombs of elite families hewn into the rocky slopes outside the city. The surprisingly large number of fish bones recovered in excavations is evidence of Jerusalem's commercial contacts with other parts of the eastern Mediterranean, while the concentration of stamped jar handles and bullae around and above the Gihon spring attests to the city's importance as an administrative and economic center in eighth and seventh century Judah.

Although Jerusalem's inhabitants worshiped the God of Israel as their chief deity in his house on the Temple Mount, the biblical accounts and archaeological evidence indicate that they also adopted non-Yahwistic cultic practices. In fact, the influence of foreign practices and styles reflects the city's integration into a wider Near Eastern context. Although this influence is especially visible among the elite (e.g., rock-cut tombs, proto-Aeolic capitals, the designs on bullae and stamped jar handles), it impacted all sectors of Jerusalem society to some degree (e.g., terracotta figurines).

586 BCE is a watershed in the history of Jerusalem and its inhabitants, marking the end of the Iron Age and the First Temple period and the fall of the kingdom of Judah, on the one hand, and the beginning of the Babylonian exile, on the other hand. This traumatic epoch ended some sixty years later when the Persian king allowed the exiled Judahites to return to Jerusalem and rebuild the temple to the God of Israel on the Temple Mount.

5

Post-Exilic (Persian) Jerusalem (333 BCE)

IN 333 BCE, Jerusalem was on the brink of a momentous event that would transform the Near East for centuries to come: the conquest of Alexander the Great. Alexander had just defeated the Persian king Darius III a second time—at Issus in Cilicia—and he and his army were making their way south along the Mediterranean coast. But living in an era before mass communication and the internet, Jerusalem's residents were unaware of Alexander's approach, and, indeed, the significance of his conquest was recognized in Jewish tradition only in retrospect. Instead, in 333 BCE, life in Jerusalem continued as it had for the previous two centuries under Persian rule.

Historical Background

The trauma of the Babylonian destruction in 586 BCE left lasting scars on Jerusalem and its inhabitants. The city's leaders and elite were deported in 597 BCE (with Jehoiachin) and, in 586 BCE (with Zedekiah), while the poor were left behind: "no one remained except the poorest people of the land" (2 Kgs 24:14).[1] Jerusalem was abandoned and lay in ruins throughout most of the sixth century.[2] Unlike the Assyrians, the Babylonians did not disperse exiled peoples but resettled them together as communities in border regions, a policy that enabled the Judahites to preserve their identity.[3] Other members of the Jerusalem elite, including the prophet Jeremiah, settled in Egypt. In 539 BCE, less than fifty years after Jerusalem's destruction, the Neo-Babylonian empire fell to the Achaemenid Persian king Cyrus II ("the Great"), who united Persia and Media under his rule and conquered territories extending through Asia Minor.

Whereas the Assyrians and Babylonians uprooted the ruling classes of conquered peoples to destroy the local power bases, the Persians repatriated those who were dispersed and tolerated or restored their native cults.[4] This policy was aimed at ensuring the loyalty of subject peoples while bolstering the king's claims to piety. Piety was not merely a concern about image but had real consequences, for by venerating gods the king hoped to gain their protection and support. In addition, satisfied subjects and rebuilt temples generated increased revenues for the imperial coffers.[5] Accordingly, Cyrus allowed the exiled Judahites to return to their homeland and rebuild the Jerusalem temple. The author of the book of Ezra presents Cyrus as moved by God's will to issue a decree:

> In the first year of King Cyrus of Persia, in order that the word of the Lord by the mouth of Jeremiah might be accomplished, the Lord stirred up the spirit of King Cyrus of Persia so that he sent a herald throughout his kingdom, and also in a written edict declared: "Thus says King Cyrus of Persia: The Lord, the God of heaven, has given me all the kingdoms of the earth, and he has charged me to build him a house at Jerusalem in Judah. Any of those among you who are of his people—may their God be with them!—are now permitted to go up to Jerusalem in Judah, and rebuild the house of the Lord, the God of Israel—he is the God who is in Jerusalem." (Ezra 1:1–3)

The decree attributed to Cyrus in Ezra 1:2–4 has similarities to the Cyrus Cylinder, an inscribed cylindrical clay tablet that commemorates his conquest of Babylon in 539 BCE and refers to his restoration of other temples, showing that the rebuilding of the Jerusalem temple was part of a wider policy.[6]

> I am Cyrus, king of the world, great king. . . . I returned to (these) sacred cities on the other side of the Tigris, the sanctuaries of which have been ruins for a long time, the images which (used) to live therein and established for them permanent sanctuaries. I (also) gathered all their (former) inhabitants and returned (to them) their habitations. . . . May all the gods whom I have resettled in their sacred cities ask daily Bel and Nebo for a long life for me and may they recommend me (to him).[7]

The enthusiastic response to Cyrus's decree is reflected in the writings of "Second Isaiah" (Deutero-Isaiah), who apparently was a Judahite exile living in Cyrus's time. Whereas Isaiah 1–39 is associated with an eighth-century BCE prophet by that name, chapters 40–55 are attributed to a different figure who describes the Persian king not only as God's instrument but as the "messiah"—the only non-Israelite/Jew so designated in the Hebrew Bible:[8] "who says of Cyrus, 'He is my shepherd, and he shall carry out all my purpose'; who says of Jerusalem,

'It shall be rebuilt,' and of the temple, 'Your foundation shall be laid.' Thus says the Lord to his anointed [messiah], to Cyrus" (Isa 44:27–45:1).

Small numbers of exiles trickled back to Judah—now a Persian district (*medinah*) called Yehud—while many chose to stay in Babylonia, forming the core of a Diaspora community that flourished for centuries. The first returnees were led by Sheshbazzar, a "prince of Judah" (perhaps the Shenazzar mentioned as a son of Jehoiachin in 1 Chr 3:18), who was appointed governor (*peha*) of Yehud, as well as by Zerubbabel and Joshua (or Jeshua).[9] Under Sheshbazzar, the rebuilding of the temple commenced but did not progress beyond the laying of the foundations, although the altar was rebuilt and sacrifices resumed (Ezra 3:1–7, 5:16; contradicted by Ezra 3:6).[10]

In 525 BCE, Cyrus's son Cambyses added Egypt to the Persian Empire. He was succeeded by Darius I (522–486 BCE), who is remembered in Western tradition for invading Greece in 490 BCE. Two years after Darius's accession to the throne, a second wave of Judahite exiles returned to Jerusalem under Zerubbabel, who was now the governor, and the high priest Joshua. Zerubbabel and Joshua shared power as a diarchy.[11] Like Sheshbazzar, Zerubbabel's name is Babylonian ("seed of Babylon"), indicating some degree of assimilation during the dispersion.[12] Zerubbabel was the grandson of the Davidic king Jehoiachin (who died in exile in Babylon), while Joshua was the son of Jehozadak (or Jozadak), the last pre-exilic chief priest in Jerusalem.[13] Joshua is the first priest in the Hebrew Bible designated "high priest" (*ha-kohen ha-rosh*), whereas his pre-exilic predecessors had the title "chief priest" (*ha-kohen ha-gaddol*), a change that reflects the increased importance of the office.[14] Spurred on by the prophets Haggai and Zechariah, Zerubbabel and Joshua renewed construction work on the temple, which was consecrated in 516–515 BCE.[15] The prophets' description of the renewal of the temple cult under a Davidic king and a Zadokite high priest is cloaked in messianic and eschatological language:[16]

> The word of the Lord came a second time to Haggai on the twenty-fourth day of the month: Speak to Zerubbabel, governor of Judah, saying, I am about to shake the heavens and the earth, and to overthrow the throne of kingdoms; I am about to destroy the strength of the kingdoms of the nations, and overthrow the chariots and their riders; and the horses and their riders shall fall, every one by the sword of a comrade. On that day, says the Lord of hosts, I will take you, O Zerubbabel my servant, son of Shealtiel, says the Lord, and make you like a signet ring, for I have chosen you, says the Lord of hosts. (Haggai 2:20–23)
>
> Take the silver and gold and make a crown, and set it on the head of the high priest Joshua son of Jehozadak; say to him: Thus says the Lord of

hosts: Here is a man whose name is Branch: for he shall branch out in his place, and he shall build the temple of the Lord. (Zech 6:11–12)

Branch (Hebrew *tsemach*) occurs in Isaiah 11:1 as a reference to the coming Davidic messiah, while in Zechariah the term apparently denotes Zerubbabel.[17] Christian tradition preserves Zerubbabel's association with messianic expectations by listing him among Jesus's ancestors (Matt 1:12–13; Luke 3:27).

Darius I was succeeded by Xerxes I (486–465 BCE), who, like his father, is known in Western tradition for invading Greece (480–479 BCE). During the reign of his successor, Artaxerxes I (465–424 BCE), Ezra and Nehemiah arrived in Jerusalem. Nehemiah was a Judahite exile who attained the office of cupbearer to the Persian king and was appointed governor of Yehud.[18] Ezra was a priest and scribe sent to ensure that the people observed divine law (apparently some form of Pentateuchal legislation) and royal (Persian) law.[19] Nehemiah served two terms as governor, beginning in 445 BCE, while scholars disagree about whether Ezra arrived before or after that.[20] The biblical books of Ezra and Nehemiah (which originally were one book) and Chronicles, which are dated roughly to the fourth century BCE, are important sources for Jerusalem in this period.[21] Much of the book of Nehemiah, which is written in the first person, is thought to be based on Nehemiah's own account (called the "Nehemiah Memoir" [NM] by scholars).[22]

Nehemiah oversaw the repair of Jerusalem's walls, which had lain in ruins since 586 BCE. The work, carried out by the city's inhabitants, was completed in just fifty-two days (Neh 6:15).[23] The book of Nehemiah describes the opposition of neighboring governors including Sanballat of Samaria and Tobiah the Ammonite (the area around modern Amman in Jordan), who probably viewed a fortified city of Jerusalem as a potential threat.[24] Under Nehemiah, a new citadel (the *birah*) was constructed adjacent to the temple.

The rebuilding of Jerusalem's walls is symbolic of a central concern of Ezra and Nehemiah: the establishment of boundaries between Israel (now the Judeans/ Jews) and other peoples.[25] They condemned mixed marriages as defiling the land and demanded that Jewish men divorce their foreign wives.[26] One particularly evocative passage describes Ezra gathering the people outside the temple on a cold and rainy December day.

Then all the people of Jerusalem of Judah and Benjamin assembled at Jerusalem within the three days; it was the ninth month, on the twentieth day of the month. All the people sat in the open square before the house of God, trembling because of this matter and because of the heavy rain. Then Ezra the priest stood up and said to them, "You have trespassed and married foreign women, and so increased the guilt of Israel.

Now make your confession to the Lord the God of your ancestors, and
do his will; separate yourselves from the peoples of the land and from the
foreign wives." (Ezra 10:9–11)

The rebuilding of Jerusalem's wall also enabled Nehemiah to enforce the
observance of the Sabbath by closing the gates to prevent commercial activity.

When it began to be dark at the gates of Jerusalem before the sabbath,
I commanded that the doors should be shut and gave orders that they
should not be opened until after the sabbath. And I set some of my servants over the gates, to prevent any burden from being brought in on the
sabbath day. (Neh 13:19)

Ezra and Nehemiah's concern with ethnic purity reflects an elitist world view
that privileged the exiled Judahites over the lower classes who had remained in
Judah after 586 BCE—the "people of the land." The census and genealogy lists
they present were also intended to establish the right of the returning exiles to
reclaim their families' ancestral property holdings (Ezra 2; Neh 7:5–66).[27] For
Ezra and Nehemiah, the exiles were the "true Israel," in contrast to the native
Judahite population, many of whom had intermarried in the intervening years.[28]
They considered Israel's ethnic purity necessary to ensuring that they retained
possession of the land given to them by God.[29] According to Joseph Blenkinsopp,
because foreigners were excluded from the Jerusalem temple, participation in
the city's political and cultic life required the population to be Jewish, resulting in a policy of "ritual ethnicity."[30] Ezra's prohibition of intermarriage is an
expansion of Deuteronomy 7:1–5, in which Moses instructs the Israelites not
to intermarry with native peoples but without mandating separation from non-
Israelite spouses.[31]

Ancient elites used intermarriage as a means of uniting the most powerful
families and to create alliances with the ruling classes of neighboring peoples.
Therefore, it is not surprising that even high priests are named in Ezra 10:18
among the returning exiles who had intermarried.[32] Although the prohibition
eventually became normative in rabbinic Judaism, intermarriage had a long
history among Israelites, Judahites, and Jews, from Solomon's marriages to the
daughter of the Egyptian pharaoh and to Moabite, Ammonite, Edomite, and
Phoenician ("Sidonian") women (1 Kgs 11:1–3), to the marriages of Herod the
Great and his family members to non-Jews.

Not only did Ezra and Nehemiah reject the remaining Judahites as part of
Israel but they erased their very existence by describing an empty land resettled
by tens of thousands of returning exiles.[33] However, there is no archeological

evidence of significant spikes in population during the Persian period, suggesting that no more than a few thousand Judahites returned from exile, most of whom apparently assimilated with the local population.[34]

Although the land was not empty at the time of the return, it was severely depopulated and impoverished. The district (*medinah*) of Yehud covered a much smaller area than the pre-exilic kingdom of Judah (from which its name derives), measuring roughly 40 × 50 kilometers (25 × 30 miles), or about 2,000 square kilometers (800 square miles).[35] The northern boundary remained roughly the same as before, passing just north of Mitzpah and Bethel, while the Jordan River and Dead Sea including Jericho and Ein Gedi still marked the eastern border. But the southern boundary of Yehud excluded Hebron and southern Judah, which in the meantime had been settled by Edomites (now called Idumaeans), while to the west the boundary extended up to the Shephelah (the lowlands between the Judean Mountains and the Mediterranean coast).[36] After Alexander the Great's conquest, this district became known as Judea—the Greek version of the Aramaic name Yehud and Hebrew Judah. Later, the Romans established a province called Judea that included Judea, Samaria, Idumaea, Peraea, Galilee, and the Golan (i.e., much of the area within the borders of modern Israel and the Palestinian Territories, as well as some territories east of the Jordan River).

It is estimated that, at the beginning of the Persian period, Yehud had less than one-third of its pre-exilic population and less than half as many settlements.[37] Even Jerusalem with its newly rebuilt temple and reconstructed walls had contracted to the southeastern hill and Temple Mount. According to modest estimates, the city's population numbered only around 400–500 at the beginning of the Persian period, increasing to ca. 1,000–1,500 by the time of Alexander's conquest.[38]

After the Assyrian and Babylonian conquests, the division of Israelite society into twelve tribes largely disappeared as the Judahite exiles returned instead in family groups (clans).[39] Together with Judahites who remained behind and assimilated with the returning exiles, this population came to be known as Judeans/Jews.[40] The term derives from the Hebrew/Aramaic *Yehudi* and Greek *Ioudaios* (plural *Ioudaioi*), referring to the inhabitants of Judea. *Ioudaioi* were people of Judahite/Judean ancestry who worshiped the God of Israel as their national deity and (at least nominally) lived according to his laws. In English usage, the term "Judean" highlights identity based on geographical or ethnic origins whereas "Jew" emphasizes the religious dimension.[41] By the Persian period, sizable Diaspora communities of Judahite/Judean origin were scattered around the Mediterranean world and Near East, including in Egypt and Mesopotamia. In addition, Yahwistic populations such as the inhabitants of Samaria (Samarians/Samaritans) claimed descent from the northern tribes of Israel and worshiped the same national deity as the Judeans/Jews.[42]

Lester Grabbe concludes, "The Persian period is important for the Jews because at that time the Jews were not important. Yehud was a small, backward province with a rural subsistence economy. Jerusalem, the only urban area, held still no more than a few thousand people at best."[43] Nevertheless, it was during this period that the final writing and editing of the Pentateuch (Five Books of Moses), the Former Prophets, Psalms, Chronicles, and some of the other biblical books were carried out—writings which not only became canonical in the three Abrahamic faiths but enabled Judaism to survive the permanent loss of the temple after 70 CE.[44] The Persian period also witnessed the rise of Jewish boundary-making and separatism, creating divisions that spawned the formation of the sects of the late Second Temple period (second century BCE–first century CE).[45]

After the battle of Issus in 333 BCE, Alexander marched south, taking the powerful Phoenician city of Tyre after a seven-month-long siege. Continuing along the coastal road to Egypt, he and his army bypassed the tiny, impoverished, inland district of Yehud. Only in later centuries would the impact of Alexander's conquest be registered in Jewish tradition, which came to connect this event with eschatological expectations through prophecies in the book of Daniel.

Archaeological Remains

Stories of the construction (or reconstruction) of temples and city walls, including those connected with Nehemiah and (later) the Maccabees in Jerusalem are literary tropes that served to legitimize rulers and therefore do not necessarily reflect historical reality.[46] Nevertheless, most scholars do not question that a second temple was dedicated on the Temple Mount and Jerusalem's walls were rebuilt in the late sixth and fifth centuries BCE. There is, however, substantial disagreement about the temple's appearance, the wall's circuit, and the size of the settlement.[47]

The Temple

The reconstruction of the temple initiated by Sheshbazzar did not progress beyond laying the foundations, although sacrifices were already being offered on an altar set up by Zerubbabel and Joshua even before rebuilding resumed (Ezra 3:3). Information about the building's appearance comes from literary sources, primarily the book of Ezra and later writings such as *The Letter of Aristeas* and Josephus's *Antiquities*. Ezra 6 contains another version of Cyrus's decree (in Ezra 1) concerning the temple:[48]

In the first year of his reign, King Cyrus issued a decree: Concerning the house of God at Jerusalem, let the house be rebuilt, the place where sacrifices are offered and burnt offerings are brought; its height shall be sixty cubits and its width sixty cubits, with three courses of hewn stones and one course of timber; let the cost be paid from the royal treasury. Moreover, let the gold and silver vessels of the house of God, which Nebuchadnezzar took out of the temple in Jerusalem and brought to Babylon, be restored and brought back to the temple in Jerusalem, each to its place; you shall put them in the house of God. (Ezra 6:2–5)

This passage describes the temple as built of stone interspersed with timber beams and measuring 60 cubits (ca. 30 meters) in height and width (Ezra 5: 8, 6: 3–4).[49]

Archaeologists disagree about whether identifiable remains survive of the temple building consecrated in 516–515 BCE (Zerubbabel's temple) or the courtyard(s) around it, which expanded over time. According to Joseph Patrich, Zerubbabel's temple building stood in the middle of a fortified inner court (Hebrew `ezra`), which he identifies as Nehemiah's *birah* (see below), surrounded by an unpaved and unfortified courtyard.[50] Thirty-two meters (105 feet) north of the southeast corner of the Temple Mount, a prominent vertical straight joint ("seam") is visible in the temenos wall (Figure 5.1). The masonry on the south side of the seam is Herodian in style, indicating that it belongs to Herod the Great's extension of the Temple Mount. The Herodian masonry clearly is built up against and therefore postdates the section of the wall north of the seam, which appears to represent a Hellenistic or Hasmonean period reconstruction or extension based on the masonry style (see Chapter 6). Forty meters (131 feet) north of the seam (73 meters [240 feet] from the southeast corner of the Temple Mount), the lowest courses adjacent to the Golden Gate consist of very large stone blocks with drafted margins and irregular bosses (meaning the edges of the surface are cut back, leaving an uneven raised panel in the center) (Figure 5.2). Since these courses apparently belong to a construction phase that antedates Alexander's conquest, they likely date to the Persian period (Zerubbabel's temple) or the First Temple period.[51]

Cyrus allowed Sheshbazzar to return some of the sacred vessels from Solomon's temple that had been looted by the Babylonians, although the ark of the covenant, the two tablets of the Law, and the Urim and Thummim (oracular devices used by the chief priest) had disappeared (Ezra 1:6–7, 6:5–6).[52] The new building was not nearly as impressive as its predecessor because the returning exiles lacked Solomon's wealth and resources. Those old enough to have seen the first temple reportedly wept with disappointment as construction proceeded.[53]

But many of the priests and Levites and heads of families, old people who had seen the first house on its foundations, wept with a loud voice when

FIGURE 5.1 The straight joint ("seam") in the southeast wall of the Temple Mount.
Credit: Photo by the author.

they saw this house, though many shouted aloud for joy, so that the people
could not distinguish the sound of the joyful shout from the sound of
the people's weeping, for the people shouted so loudly that the sound was
heard far away. (Ezra 3:12–13)

The prophet Haggai expressed similar disappointment.

Speak now to Zerubbabel son of Shealtiel, governor of Judah, and to Joshua
son of Jehozadak, the high priest, and to the remnant of the people, and say,
Who is left among you that saw this house in its former glory? How does it
look to you now? Is it not in your sight as nothing? (Hag 2:2–3)

Ezra 10:9, which describes the prophet assembling the people in front of the temple
in the rain, indicates that the building stood in an open square (*rehov*)—perhaps

FIGURE 5.2 The Golden Gate, produced by David Castor [userdcastor].
Credit: Creative Commons CC0 1.0 Universal Public Domain Dedication.

the outer court.[54] Storerooms for first fruits and tithes surrounded the court (Neh 12:44).[55] *The Letter of Aristeas*, a pseudonymous work relating in a fictional manner the story of the translation of the Five Books of Moses into Greek (the Septuagint), contains a description of the Jerusalem temple. Although the work was composed in the latter part of the second century BCE, it might include details about the temple that go back to the Persian period.[56]

> The Temple faces the east and its back is toward the west. The whole of the floor is paved with stones and slopes down to the appointed places, that water may be conveyed to wash away the blood from the sacrifices, for many thousand beasts are sacrificed there on feast days. And there is an inexhaustible supply of water, because an abundant natural spring gushes up from within the temple area. There are moreover wonderful and indescribable cisterns underground, as they pointed out to me, at a distance of five furlongs all round the site of the temple, and each of them has countless pipes so that the different streams converge together. And all these were fastened with lead at the bottom and at the sidewalls, and over them a great quantity of plaster has been spread, and every part

of the work has been most carefully carried out. (*The Letter of Aristeas* 88–90)[57]

How much of this description is accurate is unclear because the author blended real features with realistic (but fictitious) elements to present an image of Jerusalem as the ideal city.[58] For example, since there are no perennial sources of water on the Temple Mount, the "abundant natural spring" may refer to water brought by aqueduct from sources outside it.[59] Or, perhaps the author was influenced by the ancient tradition that the huge water basins in the courtyard of Solomon's temple symbolized the river flowing from the Garden of Eden, which branched into four streams. Nevertheless, *The Letter of Aristeas* seems to be accurate in mentioning subterranean cisterns under the Temple Mount, some of which are very large and many of which date to the late Second Temple period.[60] Much of our information comes from the documentation of nineteenth-century explorers such as Charles Wilson and Conrad Schick, who mapped the cisterns.[61] Because large quantities of water were required for the sacrificial cult, it is reasonable to assume that by the fifth and fourth centuries, there were cisterns in the area of the temple.[62]

The Birah

In addition to rebuilding Jerusalem's walls, Nehemiah commissioned new wooden gates for the *birah*, a fortified citadel associated with the temple that apparently was garrisoned by Persian troops (Neh 2:8; 7:2).[63] Although no remains survive, many archaeologists believe the *birah* was located on the natural high point at the northwest corner of the Temple Mount, where the Hasmoneans built a fortress called the *baris* and Herod the Great built the Antonia fortress (see Chapters 6 and 7).[64] Others have suggested that the entire city was a *birah*, that is, a fortified settlement with a Persian garrison and civilian population, or that the *birah* was a fortification wall with gates surrounding the temple, or that it corresponded to the entire Temple Mount with no relationship to the *baris*.[65]

The Walls and Gates

Nehemiah's main accomplishment was rebuilding the walls of Jerusalem (Figure 5.3). This project is described in detail in Nehemiah 2–6, beginning with a secret inspection of the ruined walls under cover of night, during which he found the eastern slope of the southeastern hill impassable.

I went out by night by the Valley Gate past the Dragon's Spring and to the Dung Gate, and I inspected the walls of Jerusalem that had been broken

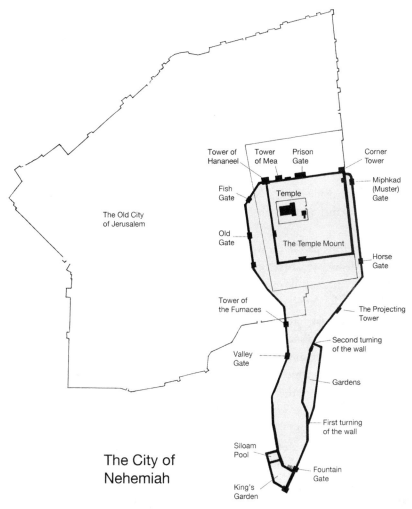

The City of
Nehemiah

FIGURE 5.3 Plan of Persian period Jerusalem.
Credit: © by Leen Ritmeyer.

down and its gates that had been destroyed by fire. Then I went on to the
Fountain Gate and to the King's Pool; but there was no place for the animal I was riding to continue. (Neh 2:13–14)

Although 2 Kings 25:10 says that the Babylonians "broke down the walls around
Jerusalem," this does not mean they tore down the entire circuit. Instead, they
would have breached the wall in spots and set fire to the wooden doors of the
gates, rendering the city defenseless. When Nehemiah arrived 140 years later, he
found the wall lying in ruins where it had been breached. In addition, in some

places the upper part of the wall had crumbled or collapsed, and the gates had no doors. Therefore, the reconstruction focused on patching the breaches, repairing damage to the towers and the upper parts of the wall, and installing wooden doors to close the gates.

Nehemiah divided the work among the inhabitants of Jerusalem and nearby towns such as Gibeon and Mizpah. Each family was assigned a different section of wall or a gate or a tower, for example:

> The sons of Hassenaah built the Fish Gate; they laid its beams and set up its doors, its bolts, and its bars. Next to them Meremoth son of Uriah son of Hakkoz made repairs. Next to them Meshullam son of Berechiah son of Meshezabel made repairs. (Neh 3:3–4)

Women also took part in the work: "Next to him Shallum son of Hallohesh, ruler of half the district of Jerusalem, made repairs, he and his daughters" (Neh 3:12).

The description follows the course of the wall in a counterclockwise direction. Despite the details provided—including the names of numerous gates and towers—there is no consensus among scholars regarding the wall's circuit as few of the features mentioned can be located with certainty.[66] Because gates typically were named for the direction or landmark they faced, most scholars locate the Valley Gate—from which Nehemiah set out on his night-time inspection—on the west side of the southeastern hill, adjacent to the Tyropoeon Valley.[67] Biblical references indicate that some of the features mentioned in Nehemiah's account existed before 586 BCE. For example, the Fish Gate mentioned by the seventh-century BCE prophet Zechariah (1:10) presumably is the same gate named in Nehemiah 3:3 and 12:16 and 2 Chronicles 33:14.[68]

2 Chronicles 26:9 attributes to Uzziah, king of Judah from ca. 791–739 BCE, the construction of towers by the Corner Gate and the Valley Gate, indicating that these gates also existed before 586 BCE.[69] Other gates are more difficult to identify. For example, Nehemiah (2:6) refers to a gate called *Yeshanah* (or *Jeshanah*), a word that means "old" but was also the name of a town in the territory of Benjamin, north of Jerusalem. Therefore, some scholars believe the name indicates that the gate was located on the north side of the Temple Mount, in the direction of the town of Jeshanah.[70] Other scholars propose emending the Hebrew name to the Mishneh Gate, referring to the Mishneh or second quarter of Jerusalem on the southwestern hill—an area that was outside the Persian-period city walls. Michael Avi-Yonah pointed out that the names of the gates reflect locations outside the city to which they led, not locations inside the walls. Therefore, if the Mishneh Gate is the correct name, it would indicate that it led to an area on the southwestern hill that was outside the walls.[71]

The paucity of Persian-period remains on the southwestern hill confirms that settlement was limited to the southeastern hill and Temple Mount.[72] Oded Lipschits characterizes Persian-period Jerusalem as "a temple with a settlement alongside it."[73] Even this small area was sparsely inhabited, as Nehemiah reports: "The city was wide and large, but the people within it were few and no houses had been built" (Neh 7:3).[74] The size of the population, numbering no more than a few hundred, explains why the inhabitants of towns outside of Jerusalem were pressed into service on the wall. To increase the number of residents, Nehemiah required priests, Levites, officials, and one-tenth of the rest of the population of Yehud to settle in the city: "Now the leaders of the people lived in Jerusalem; and the rest of the people cast lots to bring one out of ten to live in the holy city Jerusalem, while nine-tenths remained in the other towns" (Neh 11:1). Hanan Eshel suggests that Nehemiah was influenced by contemporary Greek rulers (tyrants) who forced local peoples to build fortification walls and then required one-tenth of them to settle in the city.[75]

As only the southeastern hill and Temple Mount were inhabited in the Persian period, it makes sense to assume—as many scholars do—that only the wall surrounding this small area was repaired by Nehemiah. This would explain how the project could have been completed in just fifty-two days (Neh 6:15). However, Nehemiah's account mentions ten gates, which seems to far exceed the number needed. In comparison, the Ottoman period wall of Jerusalem (which still encircles the Old City today) has only six gates, two of which are posterns.[76] Some scholars reduce the number of gates by locating one or more of them on the Temple Mount, while others argue that some gates had more than one name.[77] For example, Eshel places eight gates in the city wall and the remaining gates on the Temple Mount.[78] Nevertheless, fitting even eight gates into a wall that encircled only the southeastern hill and Temple Mount crowds them together.[79] It also makes little sense because gates are the most vulnerable point in a defensive system and therefore generally are kept to a minimum.[80] Eshel locates four gates (Sheep Gate, Fish Gate, Old Gate, Ephraim Gate) in the short, 200-meter (656-foot) section of wall on the north side of the Temple Mount, which is the only side of the city not protected by natural valleys. He suggests that Nehemiah deliberately installed these gates along Jerusalem's weakest flank to reassure the Persian king that the refortified city would not pose a threat of rebellion.[81] Hillel Geva locates three of the gates along the sides of the southeastern hill (the Valley Gate on the west; the Dung Gate on the south [and the adjacent Fountain Gate connected to the Pool of Siloam]; and the Water Gate on the northeast side), while the other gates were in the wall surrounding the Temple Mount or inside the temple complex.[82]

Although archaeologists assume there was a Bronze Age and early Iron Age wall along the west side of the southeastern hill (following the Tyropoeon

Valley), no definite remains have been found. And any such wall would have been superseded by the new line of fortification built around the southwestern hill by the eighth century.[83] Therefore, if Nehemiah's reconstruction was limited to the southeastern hill and Temple Mount, it would have entailed repairing an (assumed) wall along the Tyropoeon Valley that had been abandoned centuries earlier. Eshel argues that this wall would have been in better condition than the rest of the circuit because it had been an interior wall since the eighth century and therefore would not have been damaged by the Babylonians. He identifies this with the 1,000-cubit (ca. 500-meter/1,640-foot) section of wall between the Valley Gate and the Dung Gate (at the southern end of the southeastern hill), which was repaired by one group alone:[84] "Hanun and the inhabitants of Zanoah repaired the Valley Gate; they rebuilt it and set up its doors, its bolts, and its bars, and repaired a thousand cubits of the wall, as far as the Dung Gate" (Neh 3:13).

Some archaeologists claim that Nehemiah repaired the entire circuit of the late Iron Age (eighth century BCE) wall, even while acknowledging that the southwestern hill was uninhabited.[85] Although this would accommodate the large number of gates, it is difficult to understand why Nehemiah would have invested his limited manpower and resources in fortifying the southwestern hill when even the southeastern hill was only sparsely settled.[86] It also seems unlikely that such an extensive project could have been completed in just fifty-two days. The problem can be summarized as follows: either Nehemiah's wall encircled only the southeastern hill and Temple Mount and had as many as ten gates crowded into its circuit, or it included the uninhabited southwestern hill.[87] Most scholars agree that Nehemiah's wall encircled only the southeastern hill and Temple Mount, although their opinions differ regarding the identification and placement of the gates and other features.

Nehemiah's description of the wall includes references to elements of Jerusalem's water system. During his night-time inspection, Nehemiah exited through the Valley Gate (on the west side of the southeastern hill), "past the Dragon's Spring (`ayn ha-tanin) and to the Dung Gate, on to the Fountain Gate and to the King's Pool" (Neh 2:13–14). From here he found the path impassable and returned the way he had come. Although Nehemiah's description proceeds toward the southern tip of the southeastern hill, the identity of the "Dragon's Spring" is unknown. Perhaps it should be identified with Ein Rogel, a spring located to the south of the junction of the Kidron, Tyropoeon, and Ben-Hinnom Valleys.[88]

Two more pools—the Pool of Shelah and the artificial pool—are mentioned in connection with Nehemiah's account of the rebuilding of the wall.

> And Shallum son of Col-hozeh, ruler of the district of Mizpah, repaired the Fountain Gate; he rebuilt it and covered it and set up its doors, its

bolts, and its bars; and he built the wall of the Pool of Shelah of the king's garden, as far as the stairs that go down from the City of David. After him Nehemiah son of Azbuk, ruler of half the district of Beth-zur, repaired from a point opposite the graves of David, as far as the artificial pool and the house of the warriors. (Neh 3:15–16)

The "artificial pool" is otherwise unknown. Its position in the sequence suggests it might have been an extramural irrigation pool in the Kidron Valley.[89] The Pool of Shelah refers to the Pool of Siloam, the large storage pool at the southern tip of the southeastern hill that was fed by the Siloam Tunnel. "Siloam" is the Greek form of the Hebrew term *shelah*, which means "sent." This pool is sometimes referred to by its modern Arabic name, Birket el-Hamra. A reference in Nehemiah 3:15 to the "wall of the pool of Shelah" probably denotes a tower or fortification that protected the pool, which in the Persian period apparently lay outside the city wall.[90] Some scholars speculate that the King's Pool is another name for the Pool of Shelah/Siloam because the "King's Garden" was adjacent to it.[91] The Pool of Shelah might be the "Lower Pool" and the "reservoir between the two walls" mentioned by Isaiah:[92]

> On that day you looked to the weapons of the House of the Forest, and you saw that there were many breaches in the city of David, and you collected the waters of the lower pool. You counted the houses of Jerusalem, and you broke down the houses to fortify the wall. You made a reservoir between the two walls for the water of the old pool. (Isa 22:8–11)

Nehemiah's account places the Fountain Gate in the vicinity of the Pool of Shelah and the King's Garden (Neh 2:14, 3:15, 12:37). Perhaps its name indicates that it gave access to Ein Rogel (which might be the Dragon's Spring).[93] This is the route Zedekiah took when he fled Jerusalem under cover of night in 586 BCE: "the king with all the soldiers fled by night by way of the gate between the two walls, by the king's garden" (2 Kgs 25:4; also see Jer 39:4). Many archaeologists identify the Fountain Gate with a gate ("P") discovered by Raymond Weill to the north of the dam that crosses the southern end of the Tyropoeon Valley (see Chapter 6).[94] Nehemiah also mentions a Water Gate on the northeast side of the southeastern hill in the vicinity of the Ophel (Neh 3:26 and 12:37), which presumably was so-called because it gave access to the Gihon spring.[95] Ezra gathered the people in a square (*rehov*) in front of the Water Gate for a public reading of the Law (Neh 8:1, 3), an act that some scholars view as a precursor to the institution of the synagogue—that is, a Jewish assembly mainly for the purpose of reading the Law.

Nehemiah's account refers twice to the "Broad Wall," the position of which in the sequence suggests it was on the northwest side of the city:

"they restored Jerusalem as far as the Broad Wall." (Neh 3:8)

"and I followed them with half of the people on the wall, above the Tower of the Ovens, to the Broad Wall." (Neh 12:38)

Nahman Avigad identified a 7-meter (23-foot) thick wall attributed to Hezekiah (late eighth century BCE) on the north side of the southwestern hill as the Broad Wall mentioned by Nehemiah (Figure 4.2). Since Avigad's excavations indicate that the southwestern hill was not reoccupied in the Persian period, he believed that the Broad Wall is referred to in Nehemiah's account as a landmark or point of reference, not because it was rebuilt. Specifically, Avigad suggested that the Broad Wall is mentioned as the spot where the pre–586 BCE wall on the north side of the southwestern hill joined the western wall of the southeastern hill.[96] The biblical name referred not to the wall's thickness but to the large area it enclosed—that is, the southwestern hill.[97]

During his night-time inspection, Nehemiah was unable to proceed northward from the Pool of Siloam due to the massive collapse covering the east slope of the southeastern hill: "Then I went on to the Fountain Gate and to the King's Pool; but there was no place for the animal I was riding to continue" (Neh 2:14). Possible remains of Nehemiah's wall were found on this side of the city, on the eastern crest of the hill above the Gihon spring. Here Robert Macalister and John Duncan uncovered a 30-meter (98-foot) long section of wall with two square towers ("bastions") at the top of the stepped stone structure (their "Jebusite ramp") (Figure 2.9; Pl. 6B). They identified the wall as "Jebusite," the large south tower as Davidic or Solomonic, and the smaller north tower as post-exilic in date.[98]

Macalister and Duncan's wall and towers were re-excavated by Kathleen Kenyon (her Area A). Unfortunately, Macalister and Duncan had completely trenched (cleared) both sides of the wall (which Kenyon designated "Wall 1"), leaving no associated material that could be used for dating purposes. However, Kenyon found that the south tower was built over debris of the Babylonian destruction of 586 BCE, indicating that it is post-exilic.[99] To the north of the north tower, she excavated an additional stretch of the wall (a continuation of Wall 1) founded on the bedrock scarp. At least two different construction phases are visible in this section of wall. The north tower (designated "Wall 2" by Kenyon) abuts (is built up against) the outer face of the wall, indicating it was added after the second construction phase. Since the north tower was built over

Persian-period (fifth–fourth century) debris, Kenyon dated it to the Hasmonean period and attributed the wall (Wall 1) to Nehemiah.[100]

Because Kenyon found that the Iron Age wall midway down the east slope (Kenyon's Wall NA=Steiner's Wall 1) was not rebuilt after 586 BCE, she reasoned that Nehemiah constructed a new wall along the crest of the hill to avoid clearing the debris below.[101] The establishment of a new wall may explain why Nehemiah's account says a larger number of teams was assigned to the eastern side.[102] Building the wall at the top of the hill increased its distance from the Gihon spring, which apparently was blocked by debris.[103] However, the Siloam Tunnel still functioned, and water was drawn from the original Pool of Siloam (Birket el-Hamra), which was fortified.[104]

Yigal Shiloh's excavations in Area G revealed that the stepped stone structure was overlaid by a massive Hellenistic or Hasmonean period earthen glacis (rampart), parts of which had been discovered previously by Macalister and Duncan and by Kenyon. Under the glacis and on top of the stepped stone structure were remains associated with the Babylonian destruction of 586 BCE—architectural elements, pottery, and other debris that had collapsed from the structures above or been dumped onto the slope. Walls associated with Persian-period pottery, bullae, and other artifacts were found above the destruction debris on top of the stepped stone structure and underneath the glacis (Shiloh's Stratum 9).[105] These finds provide evidence of Persian-period occupation in the area but do not confirm that the wall above was built by Nehemiah.

Shiloh dated Macalister and Duncan's "Jebusite" wall—that is, the section of Wall 1 between the north and south towers (which he designated Wall 309)— as well as the towers to the Hasmonean period (ca. 100 BCE) because he associated them with the glacis: "We thus assume that there is a direct connection between the support of the slope at this spot and the general construction of the 'First Wall' under the Hasmoneans. We may assume that it served here as an architectural-defensive element down to the destruction of Jerusalem at the end of Stratum 6 [70 CE]."[106] Nonetheless, Shiloh acknowledged that parts of this wall might have been built by Nehemiah.[107]

The question of whether Macalister and Duncan's "Jebusite Wall" (= Kenyon's Wall 1 = Shiloh's Wall 309 = E. Mazar's Wall 27) dates to the time of Nehemiah or is later depends on the relationship between the wall, on the one hand, and the glacis and the layers underlying it, on the other. Kenyon describes finding "midden tips" (dumped material) "lapping up against" the base of the wall, indicating that the material was deposited after the wall was built. Because the midden tips contained artifacts of the fifth to early third centuries BCE, Kenyon concluded that this material was deposited incrementally beginning in the fifth century, indicating that the wall dates to the time of Nehemiah.[108] However, Margreet Steiner identifies Kenyon's "midden" as part of the Hellenistic or Hasmonean period glacis. The

Persian-period layers ("deposits") found by Kenyon underneath the "midden" abut the rock scarp below the wall but not the wall itself, and therefore antedate it.[109] Steiner concludes that the Persian-period material comes from a building that stood on the summit above and was cleared in the fifth century BCE and dumped onto the slope when the wall was built. In the Hellenistic or Hasmonean period, the wall was rebuilt, and the glacis was added.[110]

In 2007–2008, Eilat Mazar dismantled the north tower and excavated underneath it.[111] She found that the section of Wall 1 to the north of the north tower that had been discovered by Kenyon is part of the east wall of the large stone structure of the Iron Age (Mazar designates this Wall 20). The continuation of this wall to the south, that is, the section between the north and south towers (Macalister and Duncan's "Jebusite" wall = Shiloh's Wall 309, designated by E. Mazar "Wall 27"), is built on top of the east wall of the large stone structure (E. Mazar's Wall 20).[112] Therefore, this line of wall (Keyon's Wall 1, including the sections to the north and south of the north tower) reused or incorporated the east wall of the large stone structure. Although Shiloh correctly identified this wall as the Hasmonean-period First Wall, the question remains whether it originally was built in the time of Nehemiah. E. Mazar answers in the affirmative, as the latest material she found under the north tower dates to the first half of the fifth century, suggesting it was built around the mid-fifth century and not in the Hasmonean period, as Kenyon thought.[113] The wall (Wall 1) must be earlier than the tower, which abuts it, and later than the east wall of the large stone structure, which it reuses (Figure 5.4). Therefore, E. Mazar concludes that Wall 1 must postdate 586 BCE, when the large stone structure was destroyed, and antedate the mid-fifth century BCE, when she believes the tower was added.[114] E. Mazar suggests that the tower guarded a postern gate, which she reconstructs about 2.5 meters (8 feet) to the north.[115]

E. Mazar describes finding two layers under the north tower, which sloped down to the east: a lower (earlier) layer of light brown soil containing pottery and other artifacts dating to the sixth and early fifth centuries BCE, and an upper (later) brown soil layer with pottery and other artifacts dating to the late sixth century and first half of the fifth century BCE.[116] She dates the upper layer no later than the mid-fifth century based on the absence of *yhwd* stamps (see below), imported Greek (Attic) pottery, and coins, all of which are characteristic of the latter part of the Persian period.[117] The upper layer was covered by a 0.3–0.6 meter-thick (11–23-inch) layer of clay that E. Mazar says is distinct from the overlying glacis and which she believes was laid to stabilize the north tower.[118] The lowest two courses of the tower were sunk into the clay layer.

Sandwiched between the clay layer and the lowest course on the tower's east side, E. Mazar found a burial of two dogs covered with a layer of loose yellow

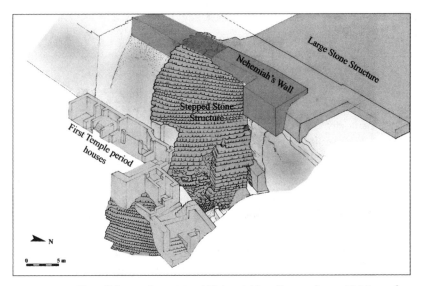

FIGURE 5.4 Plan of the north tower and Nehemiah's wall according to E. Mazar, from E. Mazar 2019a: 52 bottom.
Credit: Eilat Mazar; drawing based on plan by Alexander [Sasha] Pachuro, color by Yiftah Shalev, with permission of Avital Mazar Tsa`iri.

earth. The dogs had been laid (inhumed) on their sides next to each other, with no burial gifts.[119] An analysis of the bones indicated that the dogs—one large and one small—had died of old age and were buried together.[120]

Dog burials have been discovered at other Persian-period sites in Israel. By far the largest number has been found in Persian-period contexts at Ashkelon, where the excavators recorded 1,238 "dog finds" representing a minimum of 436 dogs, although the original number was probably at least 600–700 animals.[121] Of these, sixty-two percent were puppies, thirty-three percent were adults, and five percent were subadults. Paula Wapnish and Brian Hesse, who analyzed and published the skeletons, note that these percentages are consistent with a population of unmanaged urban dogs, as puppies and older dogs have higher rates of mortality than young adults.[122] There are no indications that these were household pets. The Ashkelon burials resemble those in Jerusalem in consisting of the interment (inhumation) of single dogs in shallow, unlined, unmarked pits with no grave goods. The absence of signs of trauma to the skeletons suggests the Ashkelon dogs died of natural causes and were buried over the course of several decades.

Dogs were venerated in some ancient Near Eastern religions, especially in Egypt, where they were held in high esteem and mummified, and in Persia, where they played a key role in funeral rites as protectors of the deceased on the journey to the next world. However, in Persia, dogs were not buried.[123] Elsewhere around the eastern Mediterranean and Near East, dogs had a mixed image. For example, dogs were thought to have therapeutic powers and therefore were venerated in healing cults in Mesopotamia and Greece, but in other contexts were avoided because of their association with ritual impurity and ill omens.[124] Lawrence Stager connects the Ashkelon dog burials to an otherwise unknown sacred precinct or temple at the site. He associates them with the Phoenician population that was the dominant element in Persian-period Ashkelon.[125]

The Jerusalem dog burials appear to resemble those in Ashkelon as well as a small number of examples known from other Persian-period sites in Israel.[126] However, the Jerusalem dog burials are the only ones found in a Jewish context. In biblical tradition, dogs have a negative image as filthy scavengers associated with ritual impurity.[127] In Exodus 22:31, God instructs the Israelites to give dogs "road kill": "you shall not eat any meat that is mangled by beasts in the field; you shall throw it to the dogs." Calling someone a dog was an insult: "The Philistine [Goliath] said to David, 'Am I a dog, that you come to me with sticks?'" (1 Sam 17:43). Dogs roamed the streets scavenging garbage: "Each evening they come back, howling like dogs and prowling about the city. They roam about for food, and growl if they do not get their fill" (Ps 59:14–15). When Jezebel, the wife of the Israelite king Ahab was thrown from the window of her palace during a coup, her corpse was devoured by dogs before she could be buried: "But when they went to bury her, they found no more of her than the skull and the feet and the palms of her hands. . . . In the territory of Jezreel the dogs shall eat the flesh of Jezebel" (2 Kgs 9:35, 37).[128] Even in Rome, dogs gnawed on corpses left lying in the streets and dug up human remains buried in shallow pits, depositing body parts around the city, as reflected in Suetonius's *Life of Vespasian* (5:4): "Once when he [the emperor Vespasian] was taking breakfast, a stray dog brought in a human hand from the cross-roads and dropped it under the table." Apparently, dogs also scavenged sacrificial remains in Jerusalem, a situation that might be alluded to in Jesus's Sermon on the Mount: "Do not give what is holy to dogs" (Mt 7:6).[129]

Although the Jerusalem dog burials are paralleled at Ashkelon and other Persian-period sites in Israel, their discovery in a Jewish context is puzzling considering the negative image of dogs in biblical tradition. While the placement of the burials immediately under the north tower resembles a foundation deposit, there is no other evidence of such a practice among ancient Jews. And it was the large number of dog burials at Ashkelon that suggested to Stager an association with cult. Even if Stager is correct, it cannot be assumed that the small number of Persian-period dog burials at other sites, including Jerusalem, is cultic. Nevertheless, a reference in Nehemiah leaves open the possibility that the Jerusalem dog burials were associated with Phoenicians: "Tyrians also, who lived in the city, brought in fish and all kinds of merchandise and sold them on the sabbath to the people of Judah, and in Jerusalem" (Neh 13:16). As noted above, Nehemiah 3:3 mentions a Fish Gate, presumably so-called after a market nearby. The reference to Tyrian merchants appears to be historically reliable, although it is not clear if they were resident aliens (and therefore subject to local—that is, Torah—law) or members of a resident trading enclave (in which case they might have been subject to Persian or Tyrian law).[130] Perhaps the dog burials in Jerusalem were associated with these resident Tyrians. Alternately, they might reflect the adoption of a Phoenician practice by members of Jerusalem's Jewish population. Interestingly, the reference to Tyrian merchants is embedded in a passage describing Nehemiah's attempt to enforce sabbath observance.[131] Ronny Reich translates the Greek word *tyros* in the Tyropoeon Valley's name not as cheese ("the valley of the Cheesemakers") but as Tyrians ("the valley where the Tyrians were"), citing in support Nehemiah's reference to Tyrian merchants in the city.[132]

Some archaeologists have dismissed E. Mazar's dating of the wall (Wall 1) and the north tower to the Persian period, noting that the material found under the tower provides only a terminus post quem, which means it could have been constructed at any time from the mid-fifth century BCE on.[133] Alon de Groot concludes that the tower postdates the Persian period, and argues that the wall is much earlier (Iron Age) because the Persian-period fill below the tower abuts the lower courses of the wall.[134] Steiner dates the wall to the Hasmonean period because she associates it with the glacis.[135] Hillel Geva claims that since the north tower sat on top of the layers excavated by E. Mazar, the surviving courses of stones must belong to the tower's foundations, which might explain the poor construction.[136] This means the ground level at the time of the tower's construction would have been above the layers that E. Mazar excavated, and the tower's foundations were sunk down to the level of the Persian layer. Geva posits that the upper layers were removed by Macalister and Duncan, leaving the tower's foundations exposed on top of the Persian layer, and therefore the tower must postdate the Persian period. He says that the wall between the towers (Wall 1) appears to be contemporary with the south tower, which he dates to the Hasmonean period based on its construction style. Since the north tower abuts this wall, it must be later in date. Geva therefore identifies Wall 1 and the towers as part of the Hasmonean period First Wall and proposes that Nehemiah rebuilt the old Bronze Age–Iron Age wall midway down the east slope of the southeastern hill, while admitting there is no evidence that this wall was reused in the Persian period.[137] Geva argues that identifying the wall on the crest of the southeastern hill as Nehemiah's wall would leave insufficient space for an intermural settlement. He therefore proposes that the wall midway down the slope was abandoned and a new wall was established on the crest above in the Hasmonean period, when Jerusalem's settlement expanded onto the southwestern hill and all these areas were fortified with a new wall—the First Wall.[138]

Although Geva's analysis is persuasive, it assumes that the south tower (which he dates to the Hasmonean period) is contemporary with Wall 1. However, it is possible that the south tower abuts Wall 1 instead of being bonded with it, in which case the tower would be later than the wall.[139] Recent discoveries suggest that the south tower and glacis might be part of the Seleucid Akra fortress and that the Hasmonean period First Wall reused parts of the Akra's fortifications (see Chapter 6).[140] Geva's argument also relies on an absence of evidence, both with regard to the layers around the tower which may have been removed by Macalister and Duncan and with regard to a supposed Persian-period reconstruction of the Bronze Age–Iron Age wall midway down the east slope.[141] And although Geva probably is correct in identifying at least some of the tower's surviving courses as foundations, E. Mazar describes a foundation trench cut into the clay layer, into which she says the tower's south wall (W293) was laid.[142] In addition, recent discoveries in the Givati Parking Lot demonstrate that the Persian-period settlement on the southeastern hill extended farther west than previously thought, countering Geva's argument that the wall on the eastern crest would leave insufficient space for intermural settlement.

Thus, while it is true that the latest artifacts found under the north tower provide only a terminus post quem, the absence of later finds suggests a construction date in the mid-to-late fifth century.[143] The dog burials immediately under the lowest course of the tower are perhaps the strongest piece of evidence supporting a Persian-period date as they appear to have been placed intentionally at the time of construction.[144] However, the north tower clearly was added to the wall (Wall 1). Therefore, it is only possible to conclude that the north tower dates to the Persian period (apparently the mid- to late fifth century), while the wall is earlier. Because the wall reused or incorporated the east wall of the large stone structure, it likely postdates the Iron Age. In this case, the wall could date to the mid-fifth century while the tower was added later in the fifth century. Even many archaeologists who date the wall to the Hellenistic or Hasmonean period acknowledge the possibility that it originally was built in the Persian period, as evidenced by the different styles of masonry visible in its construction.[145]

The Settlement Inside the Walls

Based on the paucity of remains, Israel Finkelstein argues that the Persian-period settlement was restricted to the center of the southeastern hill, an area of only about 20–25 dunams (5–6 acres). He claims that Nehemiah's account is not based on a Persian-period reality but was written in the Hasmonean period and describes the city walls at that time (second half of the second century to first half of the first century BCE).[146] However, the three hundred years between Nehemiah's time and the Hasmonean period seem insufficient for the creation of a myth without any historical basis—a scenario which assumes that Jerusalem residents living at the time the wall supposedly was built in the second century BCE accepted its attribution to the fifth century BCE.[147] It is also likely that Persian-period remains were obliterated by large-scale building activities in later periods, a well-known phenomenon in Jerusalem.[148]

Finkelstein's claim that settlement was limited to the center of the southeastern hill is contradicted by discoveries in the Givati Parking Lot excavations and along the east slope, which was covered by Persian-period debris dumped outside the city wall.[149] If Nehemiah's wall was located on the eastern crest of the hill, it would have enclosed a narrow strip along the summit no more than 80–100 meters (262–328 feet) wide and about 350 meters (1,148 feet) long, yielding an area of ca. 28–30 dunams (7–7.5 acres).[150] Including the Ophel but not the Temple Mount, the total area of the city was ca. 50 dunams (12 acres).[151] Kenneth Ristau proposes that, before the mid-fifth century, when Nehemiah rebuilt the walls, the settlement did not exceed 20–25 dunams, and consisted mainly of the limited reoccupation of late Iron Age buildings along the eastern slope but did not include the Ophel.[152] From the mid-fifth century on, the settlement spread to other parts of the southeastern hill and the Ophel, eventually reaching a size of approximately 40 dunams.[153] Even then, not all the area within the walls was settled or built up.

Many of the Persian-period finds on the southeastern hill come from Shiloh's Area E, which is located at the center of the east side. Before 586 BCE, this was a neighborhood inside the city wall midway down the slope. A large structure in Area E called the "Ashlar House," which might have been a public building before 586 BCE, was reoccupied in the early Persian period, perhaps only on a small scale, despite lying in ruins at the time. De Groot proposes that the "Ashlar House" was reoccupied in the late sixth century BCE by the first waves of returnees prior to Nehemiah.[154] By the fifth century, the "Ashlar House" was abandoned and covered by a layer of gravel or stone chips.[155] Similar layers of stone chips dating to the Persian period were found in Shiloh's Area D to the south and east of Area E, in Weill's excavations adjacent to Area D, and elsewhere along the east slope. The stone chips are a product of extensive quarrying activities along the rock scarp above, presumably connected to the construction of Nehemiah's wall and other structures.[156]

Recent discoveries in the Givati Parking Lot indicate that the Persian-period settlement extended farther down the west slope of the southeastern hill than previously thought. The massive late Iron Age public building (Building 100), which was destroyed in 586 BCE, was partially cleared and reoccupied early in the Persian period.[157] Although the remains are limited to poorly built walls and a large pit, the finds are surprisingly rich, including 133 fish bones—the largest quantity found so far in a Persian-period context in Jerusalem. Walls, floors, and *tabuns* (ovens) associated with domestic structures of the Persian period were found to the south of Building 100.[158]

In the early Hellenistic period (third-second century BCE), a large public building (Building 110) was built over Building 100.[159] Building 110's size and the finds, which include bullae stamped with images from Greek mythology, suggest it was used for administrative purposes. The excavators of the Givati Parking Lot propose that settlement along the Tyropoeon Valley intensified in the Persian and Hellenistic periods due to its proximity to the Pool of Siloam (at the outlet of the Siloam Tunnel), which replaced the Gihon spring as the main point of access to Jerusalem's water supply.[160] As direct access to the spring was no longer needed, much of the east slope of the southeastern hill was left in ruins and instead was used for burials, agriculture, and as a garbage dump.[161]

Stamped Jars

Much of the evidence of Persian-period occupation on the southeastern hill is provided by seal impressions stamped on the handles and bodies of storage jars, which appeared in Jerusalem in the late eighth and seventh centuries and remained common through the second century BCE, although the inscriptions and images in the impressions changed over time. Many of the Persian-period impressions are stamped with a variant of the word *yhwd* (Yehud) in Aramaic script. Others are stamped with the Aramaic words *phw* (province) or *hph'* (*ha-peha*, "the governor") (sometimes including the name of the governor), or with motifs such as lions, wheels, or crosses.[162] As the lingua franca of the Persian Empire, Aramaic—a language related to Hebrew—now became the common language of the inhabitants of Judea. Nearly all the hundreds of seal impressions on jars have been found on Jerusalem's southwestern outskirts at Ramat Rahel and Arnona and on Jerusalem's southeastern hill, with a majority coming from Ramat Rahel. This pattern of distribution suggests that Ramat Rahel was the main administrative center for the collection and distribution of the goods contained in the jars.[163] Analyses of the clay indicate that the stamped jars were manufactured in the Jerusalem area of local (Motza) clay.[164]

Lipschits and David Vanderhooft conclude that jars with Yehud seal impressions were produced in a single workshop in Jerusalem's vicinity and were sent to nearby production centers, where they were filled with wine, oil, or other liquids. Once filled, the jars were transported to the administrative centers for warehousing. The concentration of stamped jars and handles at Ramat Rahel and Arnona and in Jerusalem suggests that the jars' contents were emptied into other containers (such as skins) for redistribution to other sites.[165] The fact that the largest numbers of stamped jars and handles in Jerusalem have been found in the vicinity of the large stone structure indicates that the north end of the southeastern hill remained the city's administrative center through the Persian period.[166]

Coins

Evidence of Persian-period settlement in Jerusalem is also provided by coins, which first appeared at sites in Palestine in the sixth–fifth centuries BCE.[167] Coins are lumps of metal stamped with seal impressions, including some of the same motifs and inscriptions found on jars. Coinage was invented in western Asia Minor, either by the East Greeks or by indigenous peoples such as the Lydians. Scholars disagree about exactly when coinage was invented, but there is no doubt it existed by ca. 600 BCE. Whoever was responsible for inventing coinage drew on two existing traditions: (1) small lumps of precious metals called "dumps" had long circulated in trade and commerce, and (2) seals carved with inscriptions or designs had been used for millennia to make impressions on the raw lumps of clay used to seal documents and containers. Coins differ from dumps in being stamped with the seal of a minting authority, which guaranteed the purity and weight of the lump of precious metal. Many of the earliest coins are made of electrum, a natural alloy of gold and silver common in western Asia Minor. They are stamped on the obverse with the symbol of the minting authority and have cuttings on the reverse to show that the metal was pure all the way through, not just coated. Soon after the invention of coinage, it became common practice to stamp the reverse with a design rather than cuttings. Eventually ridges were added around the edges of some coins to track wear and the loss of metal content (weight).

Originally the value of a coin was equal to the value of its weight in precious metal. This is reflected in the names given to some coin denominations, such as the ancient Jewish sheqel, the Greek drachma, and the British pound. The right to mint coins has always been a prerogative of the central governing authority, although in antiquity rulers sometimes allowed individuals, cities, or provinces to mint their own coins—usually small, inexpensive denominations made of bronze or copper rather than precious metals.[168] Even today only the federal government, not individual states can issue currency in the United States. Using coins in trade and commerce eliminated the need to weigh metals for the purposes of payment as they were minted in standard weights that were guaranteed by the governing authority. Nevertheless, coin circulation remained limited for a long time, and even the most advanced ancient civilizations were never fully monetized.

By the fifth century BCE, various kingdoms and city-states around the eastern Mediterranean minted their own coinage. The coins of Athens circulated widely because they were made of high-quality silver from the mines at Laurion in Attica. Athenian coins are stamped on the obverse with the head of Athena in profile and on the reverse with an owl and olive branch (both attributes of Athena) and the inscription "Athe[nae]." The coins of Athens were so popular that other cities minted imitations, including the coastal Phoenician cities and the former Philistine cities of Gaza, Ashkelon, and Ashdod.

In the fourth century BCE, numerous cities and districts around Palestine issued their own low denomination silver coins, most of which are minute in size and bear a wide variety of motifs including heads of deities, figures of animals and mythological creatures, ships, and buildings. The motifs reflect the authority of different local officials responsible for minting. Yehud coins display the same diversity of motifs (even the bust of the goddess Athena), but typically include an eagle and a lily flower, which probably represented the Jerusalem temple (a symbol that the State of Israel adopted for its one-sheqel coins) (Figure 5.5).[169] These were issued by the governing authority in Jerusalem, as indicated by specimens minted immediately before Alexander the Great's conquest with the legend "Yehezkiah the governor (*ha-peha*)"—perhaps the high priest Ezechias mentioned by Josephus, who lived at the end of the fourth century.[170] A Yehud coin minted shortly after Alexander's conquest inscribed "Yohanan the priest" shows that high priests were among the minting authorities in Jerusalem. The coin

FIGURE 5.5 Yehud coin showing the eagle/falcon and lily.
Credit: American Numismatic Society Cultural Change 2.5; ANS collection gift of Abraham and Marian Sofaer, courtesy of David Hendin.

depicts an owl on the reverse and a human face—perhaps Yohanan himself?—on the reverse, indicating that even high priests did not object to figured images, in contrast to later centuries when Jewish art was largely aniconic.[171]

Tombs

After Jerusalem's elite were dispersed in 586 BCE, most of the rock-cut tombs that belonged to these families went out of use. However, an undisturbed repository in a late Iron Age burial cave at Ketef Hinnom that was excavated by Gabriel Barkay contained pottery and other finds indicating that the tomb continued in use after 586 BCE (see Chapter 4).[172] The repository also yielded the earliest coin discovered until now in Palestine—a rare silver issue from the Greek island of Kos, dated to 570 BCE. The worn condition of the tiny coin indicates that it was in circulation for a while before being deposited.[173] The finds from the repository are important evidence of continued but limited Jewish presence in or around Jerusalem through the sixth century BCE.

Conclusion

Thanks to the reconstruction of the temple, the Persian period laid the foundation for the increasing importance of Jerusalem in Jewish religious life in the following centuries—a message reinforced in the biblical books composed during this era, such as Chronicles, which contains twenty-two percent of all references to the city in the Hebrew Bible.[174] These Persian-period works consciously emphasize themes of continuity with the past and of restoration, such as repeated references to the return of the temple vessels. Lee Levine notes, for example, that although the menorah in the second temple was modeled after the first-temple period precedents, the second temple had only a single menorah whereas Solomon's temple reportedly had at least ten.[175] Indeed, the restored temple was founded, literally and conceptually, on its destroyed predecessor. Thus, the Persian period can be viewed as a bridge between the past (pre-exilic period), present (post-exilic period), and future (messianic era). Nevertheless, under Persian rule and for nearly two centuries after Alexander's conquest, Jerusalem remained the tiny and impoverished center of a provincial backwater. It was only in the latter part of the second century BCE, when Jerusalem became the capital of an independent Jewish kingdom, that it grew significantly in size and importance.

6

Hasmonean Jerusalem (64 BCE)

Historical Background

In 64 BCE, Jerusalem was in turmoil. For nearly eighty years, the city had increased in size and importance as the capital of an independent Jewish kingdom. But now that was about to end as a civil war erupted between two brothers, both of whom laid claim to the throne. Their struggle opened the door to annexation by Rome.[1]

In the centuries since Alexander the Great conquered the Persian Empire, the ancient Near East had been transformed. In 332 BCE, Judea (Persian Yehud), including Jerusalem, had come under Alexander's rule. After Alexander's death in 323 BCE, Judea became part of the kingdoms of his Greek successors: first the Ptolemies (based in Egypt) and then the Seleucids (based in Syria). Administratively, Judea was a semi-autonomous unit within these kingdoms, with the population governed by a council of elders (*Gerousia*) and following— at least to some degree—biblical Jewish law (the laws in the Torah/Pentateuch/ Five Books of Moses).[2] Although many Greeks and Romans considered Jewish customs such as circumcision, abstention from pork, and Sabbath observance peculiar, they respected Judaism as an ancient religion and referred to the laws in the Torah as "the ancestral laws of the Jews."

Despite the freedom to observe biblical law, Jews were influenced to varying degrees by Greek culture—a process called *Hellenization*.[3] Under Alexander and his successors, Greek customs spread throughout the Near East, affecting all aspects of life including language, religion, architecture and art, entertainment, education, governance, dress, and diet and dining habits. Local elites eagerly embraced the Greek lifestyle in emulation of the ruling class. The Jerusalem elite—primarily wealthy priestly families—were not immune to these influences, although the Greek way of life sometimes contradicted biblical law or Jewish customs.

In 175 BCE, the Seleucid king Antiochus IV Epiphanes allowed Jason (Hebrew name Jeshua), the brother of the high priest Onias III, to purchase the office of high priest for himself and granted him permission to refound Jerusalem as a Greek city (*polis*) named Antiochia. Having the status of a *polis* entitled the city's citizens to certain benefits and status, including tax breaks and the right to send athletes to international competitions. Nevertheless, the practice of Judaism was still permitted, and the Jerusalem temple remained dedicated to the God of Israel. In 172 BCE, a temple official named Menelaus outbid Jason for the office of high priest. Jason fled to Ammon, the area around modern Amman in Jordan. Onias III was assassinated and his son, Onias IV, fled to Egypt, where he established a Jewish temple at Leontopolis (Heliopolis), over which he and his descendants (the Oniads) presided. The Oniads were Zadokite high priests, so-called because they traced their ancestry back to Zadok, the high priest appointed by Solomon to officiate in the first Jerusalem temple, whereas Menelaus was from a non-Zadokite priestly family.[4]

In 168 BCE, Antiochus IV invaded Egypt, taking advantage of the weakness of the Ptolemies. Afraid that Antiochus's annexation of Egypt would make the Seleucid kingdom too powerful, the Romans intervened and forced him to withdraw. In the meantime, a civil war had broken out in Judea. Antiochus quelled the unrest and established a fortified citadel in Jerusalem called the Akra garrisoned with soldiers to keep order.

The following year (167 BCE) Antiochus IV issued a decree, as reported by the author of 1 Maccabees.

> Then the king wrote to his whole kingdom that all should be one people, and that all should give up their particular customs. All the Gentiles accepted the command of the king. Many even from Israel gladly adopted his religion; they sacrificed to idols and profaned the sabbath. And the king sent letters by messengers to Jerusalem and the towns of Judah; he directed them to follow customs strange to the land, to forbid burnt offerings and sacrifices and drink offerings in the sanctuary, to profane Sabbaths and festivals, to defile the sanctuary and the priests, to build altars and sacred precincts and shrines for idols, to sacrifice swine and other unclean animals, and to leave their sons uncircumcised. They were to make themselves abominable by everything unclean and profane, so that they would forget the law and change all the ordinances. He added, "And whoever does not obey the command of the king shall die." (1 Macc 1:41–50)

The Jerusalem temple was rededicated to Olympian Zeus (the chief deity of the Greek pantheon), and the Samarian (or Samaritan) temple on Mount Gerizim (where the God of Israel was also worshiped) was rededicated to Zeus Hellenios. Shines and altars to Greek gods were established elsewhere around Jerusalem and the countryside. The reason Antiochus issued this decree is unclear; perhaps it was an attempt to use Hellenization as a means of subduing the ongoing unrest in Judea and uniting the Jews with other peoples in his kingdom.[5]

Antiochus IV's decree sparked the outbreak of a Jewish rebellion led by the Hasmonean family—the elderly patriarch and priest Mattathias and his five sons—from the town of Modiin (about midway between Tel Aviv and Jerusalem). Mattathias's third son, Judah Maccabee (a nickname meaning Judah "the hammer"; in Greek, Judas Maccabeus), led the rebels in a bloody civil war aimed at eliminating internal opponents and an external war against the Seleucids, successfully employing guerilla tactics. After Antiochus IV Epiphanes died in 164 BCE, his son, Antiochus V, canceled his father's decree and issued an edict granting the Jews full religious freedom and amnesty. Judah and his brothers seized the Jerusalem temple, which they rededicated to the God of Israel in mid-December. According to later tradition, they found only a one-day supply of ritually pure oil to light the temple's seven-branched lampstand or candelabrum (menorah). Miraculously, the lamp burned for eight days, until they were able to obtain more oil. The rededication of the temple in 164 BCE is celebrated by the holiday of Hanukkah, when a "Hanukkah menorah" with eight branches is lit—one for each day the oil burned (plus an additional branch to light the others).[6]

Fighting continued even after the temple's rededication, and, by 140 BCE, the Jews had captured and demolished the Akra fortress and gained independence from the Seleucids. A Jewish kingdom was established, ruled by Judah's brothers and their descendants—the Hasmonean dynasty.[7] Under the Hasmoneans, the kingdom expanded beyond Judea, beginning with John Hyrcanus I (134–104 BCE), who added territories to the east (Transjordan = ancient Peraea), south (Idumaea), and north (Samaria). Josephus reports that John Hyrcanus I forced the Idumaeans and other non-Jewish inhabitants of these conquered territories to convert to Judaism or go into exile: "Hyrcanus also captured the Idumaean cities of Adora and Marisa, and after subduing all the Idumaeans, permitted them to remain in their country so long as they had themselves circumcised and were willing to observe the laws of the Jews. And so, out of attachment to the land of their fathers, they submitted to circumcision and to making their manner of life conform in all other respects to that of the Jews. And from that time on they have continued to be Jews."[8]

Judah Aristobulus I (104–103 BCE) conquered Galilee and the Golan, perhaps converting to Judaism the Ituraeans, a native Semitic people.[9] Alexander Jannaeus (103–76 BCE) added the Palestinian coast and parts of Transjordan (including the city of Pella, which he destroyed when the inhabitants refused to covert to Judaism). As a result, under Jannaeus's rule the Hasmonean kingdom reached its greatest extent.[10] After Jannaeus died, his widow Salome Alexandra succeeded him to the throne—the only woman to rule the Hasmonean kingdom as queen (76–67 BCE). Salome is the Greek version of her Hebrew name, Shelamzion.[11] Because only men could serve in the Jerusalem temple, Salome Alexandra appointed her older son John Hyrcanus II as high priest.

Salome Alexandra's reign was relatively peaceful, but after her death a civil war erupted over the succession between her older son, John Hyrcanus II, and her younger son, Aristobulus II. Hyrcanus II was supported by Antipater, a wealthy and influential Idumaean Jew who, like his father (Herod the Great's grandfather Antipas), had served as governor of Idumaea under the Hasmoneans. Antipater exploited the conflict between the brothers to advance himself, supporting the weak Hyrcanus II over the ambitious Aristobulus II. When the two sides reached a stalemate, the brothers turned to the Romans for help. This was the period of the Late Republic in Rome. During the first century BCE, a series of powerful generals seized the reins of power illegally, establishing themselves as dictators. At the time Hyrcanus II and Aristobulus II made their plea for help, the Roman general Pompey was campaigning in Asia Minor (the area of modern Turkey). As a result, Pompey invaded Judea and besieged Jerusalem, which he took with the aid of Hyrcanus II. He desecrated the temple by entering the Holy of Holies, which was off-limits to everyone except the high priest, who went in only on the Day of Atonement (Yom Kippur). The Roman historian Tacitus describes Pompey's astonishment at finding the Holy of Holies empty: "The first Roman to subdue the Jews and set foot in their temple by right of conquest was Gnaeus Pompey: thereafter it was a matter of common knowledge that there were no representations of the gods within, but that the place was empty and the secret shrine contained nothing."[12]

Pompey rewarded Hyrcanus II for his support with the high priesthood but punished the Jews for refusing to submit peacefully by dismembering the Hasmonean kingdom. Only territories with high concentrations of Jews (including the Yahwistic population of Samaria) were left under the administration of the high priest: Judea, Galilee, eastern Idumaea, Samaria, and Peraea. To strengthen the pro-Roman elements within the country, the Romans formed a league of the most Hellenized cities called the Decapolis (the ten cities of the New Testament), which included Beth Shean/Scythopolis, Pella, Gadara, and Abila. These were part of the newly established Roman province of Syria with its capital at Antioch. The province was under the administration of a governor titled a proconsul or consul—a title later modified to legate, reflecting his dual role as a civil administrator and military (legionary) commander.

Ancient Jewish Sectarianism: Sadducees, Pharisees, and Essenes

Although the Hasmoneans established an independent Jewish kingdom roughly the size of the kingdom of David and Solomon, not all Jews supported their rise to power. Early on, the Maccabees' opponents included pro-Seleucid members of the Jerusalem elite, among them priestly families. By around 100 BCE, a number of groups, sects, and movements had emerged among the Jewish population, including the Sadducees, Pharisees, and Essenes (see, e.g., Josephus, *War* 2.119), and, later, Jesus's movement.[13]

The Sadducees

When Jason and Menelaus (and later the Hasmoneans) usurped the high priesthood, the Zadokites lost control of this office and never regained it. The Zadokite line splintered into several branches.

1. *The Oniads*: After the high priest Onias III was assassinated in Antioch, his son Onias IV fled to Egypt, where he established a temple at Leontopolis (Heliopolis), over which he and his descendants officiated until it was shut down by Vespasian in 73 CE.
2. *The Essenes/Qumran sect*: Another branch of the Zadokite family was involved with the sect that eventually became known as the Essenes, some members of which settled at Qumran.
3. *The Sadducees*: A third branch of the Zadokite family remained in Jerusalem, forming an alliance with the ruling powers and becoming an integral part of Jewish society for the next two centuries. They were called Sadducees, a term apparently derived from the name Zadok/Zadokite.

The Sadducees were the wealthiest members of Jewish society—particularly the Jerusalem elite—including the higher-ranking priestly families and aristocracy. Because the Sadducees sought to maintain their standing by preserving the status quo, they were political conservatives who accommodated with the ruling powers. They were also religious conservatives who opposed religious innovations. They recognized only the authority of written law as divinely ordained and adhered to it literally, rejecting Pharisaic oral tradition which opened the door to human innovation and interpretation. For example, the Sadducees rejected the Pharisaic doctrine of individual, physical resurrection of the dead because it is not explicitly mentioned in the Torah.

The Pharisees

Although the Pharisees are familiar to many Westerners today from the Gospel accounts, our information about them is patchy and incomplete.[14] We do not even know why they were called Pharisees. The name appears to derive from the Hebrew word *parash*, which means "to separate." But separate from what? Some scholars speculate that the Pharisees were so-called because they kept themselves apart from other Jews, who they considered lax in their observance of ritual purity laws and held themselves to a higher standard. It is not clear whether the Pharisees referred to themselves by this term, or if it was a name used by others to describe them. In writings associated with the Pharisees, they usually refer to themselves by other names including friend (*haver*), scribe, or sage (*rabbi*). Interestingly, the only two ancient Jews who self-identify in our sources as Pharisees were Diaspora Jews: Saul/Paul of Tarsus, and the Jewish historian Flavius Josephus, who spent the last three decades of his life in Rome.

Although Pharisees sometimes addressed each other as "rabbi," the term was not exclusive to them. Rabbi simply means "my master" or "one who is greater than me." Jews used it as an informal title of respect to address men who were considered experts in the Torah. Unlike today, ancient rabbis did not undergo a formal process of ordination and were not necessarily synagogue leaders. The occasional references to Jesus as a rabbi in the Gospel accounts do not indicate he was a Pharisee but rather that his followers respected him as an expert in Jewish law.

The Pharisees came from diverse backgrounds in urban and rural areas. They are known for an innovative approach to the Torah called "oral law" because it allows for human interpretation and expansion on the written law, in contrast to the Sadducees, who accepted only the authority of written law as divinely ordained. Ultimately, Pharisaic beliefs, including the innovation of oral law prevailed as they were shared by the rabbis—a group of sages who became the leaders of Judaism in the centuries following the destruction of the second temple in 70 CE and who are responsible for the "rabbinic Judaism" that is normative today. In fact, it was the flexibility of the Pharisaic approach to the interpretation of the Torah that enabled Judaism to survive the temple's destruction, an event which made it impossible to continue to offer sacrifices as mandated by biblical law.

The Essenes

The Essene sect apparently was established by dispossessed Zadokite priests, as reflected by the founder's nickname or sobriquet: the Teacher of Righteousness

(Hebrew *tzedek* [righteousness]), which is a pun on *tzadok* (Zadok/Zadokite). This branch of the Zadokite family regarded the non-Zadokite priests in control of the Jerusalem temple as usurpers who polluted the temple and the sacrifices offered there. They withdrew, apparently refusing to participate in the sacrificial cult, and awaited the day when they would regain control of the temple. In the interim, the sect constituted itself as a substitute temple (or, more precisely, the wilderness tabernacle), with each full member living his everyday life as if he were a priest (although most members were not necessarily from priestly families).

The Dead Sea Scrolls were deposited in caves surrounding Qumran by members of the Essene sect who lived at the site, which apparently served as a community center, from ca. 80 BCE to 68 CE. The remains of approximately 1,000 different scrolls were found in eleven caves, all of which represent Jewish religious writings. They include the earliest copies of the books of the Hebrew Bible that have ever been discovered; Aramaic translations of biblical books (*targumim*; singular: *targum*); commentaries on biblical—and especially prophetic—books (*pesharim*; singular: *pesher*); apocryphal works, such as Tobit and Ecclesiasticus/ the Wisdom of Ben Sira (books that are included in the Catholic canon of sacred scripture but not in the Hebrew Bible or Protestant Bible); and pseudepigrapha (books such as Enoch and Jubilees, which were not included in the Jewish, Protestant, or Catholic canons of sacred scripture but are sometimes preserved in the canons of other churches). The scrolls from the Qumran caves also include sectarian works, which were composed by members of the sect and describe or reflect their distinctive outlook, beliefs, and practices. Sectarian works include the Damascus Document, the Community Rule (Manual of Discipline), the War Scroll, the Pesher Habakkuk, and the Pesher Nahum.

Members of the Essene sect lived in towns and villages around Palestine, including in Jerusalem, but some practiced desert separatism—that is, some lived apart in the wilderness, as at Qumran (the only such community identified so far). Although many members were married and had families, only physically and mentally unblemished adult Jewish men were eligible to apply for full membership (the same qualifications required for priests serving in the Jerusalem temple). Applicants underwent a process of initiation that lasted two to three years. After a candidate passed the initial stages of initiation, he surrendered all personal property, as the sect pooled their possessions.

The sect attracted members because it promised salvation to them alone, for this was an apocalyptic group that anticipated the imminent arrival of the end of days, which would be ushered in by a forty-year-long war between the Sons of Light (= good = themselves) and the Sons of Darkness (= evil = everyone else). In contrast to the Pharisees and Sadducees, the Essenes believed in predeterminism, meaning that everything is preordained by God and there is no human free will at all. Therefore, the forty-year-long war and its outcome—victory for the Sons of Light—were preordained by God. Another peculiarity of this sect was their expectation of not one but two messiahs: in addition to the usual royal messiah of Israel descended from David, they anticipated a second, priestly messiah descended from Aaron (and, possibly, a third, prophetic messiah).

While all three sects differed in their approaches to biblical law, particularly relating to the temple cult, the Sadducees and Pharisees were also involved in politics. The Sadducees were active mainly in Jerusalem, where some lived in mansions on the southwestern hill that were excavated by Nahman Avigad. The Pharisees appear to have been active in Jerusalem as well as in other parts of the country, such as Galilee, where they exerted some influence among the local population. Although none of the sects was large, and most Jews did not belong to any of them, the Essenes were especially small and marginal.[15]

A reference by Josephus to "the gate of Essenes" in Jerusalem suggests there might have been an Essene quarter at the southern end of the southwestern hill (today's Mount Zion). This reference is embedded in Josephus's description of the circuit of the Hasmonean wall along the western and southern sides of the southwestern hill: "Beginning at the same point in the other direction, westward, it descended past the place called Bethso to the gate of the Essenes, then turned southward above the fountain of Siloam."[16] Yigael Yadin understood Josephus's passage in light of legislation in the Temple Scroll, the longest intact scroll from Qumran. Although most scholars do not consider the Temple Scroll a sectarian composition, it appears to have had some authority among the Essenes.[17] Much of the scroll, which is written in the first person as if God himself is speaking, provides a blueprint for a future ideal (but real, not heavenly or eschatological) city of Jerusalem dominated by a temple of gargantuan size. One passage mandates the placement of the toilets (called in Hebrew "the place of the hand") 3,000 cubits to the northwest of the city.[18] Yadin proposed that the gate of the Essenes mentioned by Josephus was used by Essenes (presumably) living nearby to access toilets outside the city, as Bethso may derive from the Hebrew *beth tsoah* ("house of excrement"), referring to a toilet or latrine.[19] Josephus's description indicates that Bethso and the gate of the Essenes were located on the west side of the southwestern hill, and the gate's name might indicate that there was an Essene quarter in the vicinity.[20] Bargil Pixner, a Benedictine monk and scholar who lived in a monastery on Mount Zion, identified the remains of a gate on the southwest side of the southwestern hill as the gate of the Essenes and the area inside it as an Essene quarter. According to Pixner, after using the toilet the Essenes purified themselves in *miqva'ot* (ritual baths) located outside the gate, in accordance with their view that defecation caused ritual impurity (a view not shared by most other Jews).[21] However, *miqva'ot* were used by all Jews for ritual purification and are found in large numbers in and around Jerusalem, including outside the walls.[22] Other scholars place the gate and a possible Essene quarter at locations elsewhere along the First Wall.[23] Because there is no unequivocal archaeological evidence of Essene presence in Jerusalem, the existence of such a quarter remains speculative.

Archaeological Remains

Most of our historical information about Hasmonean Jerusalem comes from 1 and 2 Maccabees and Josephus's *Jewish Antiquities* (*Ant.*) and *The Jewish War* (*War*) (for Josephus, see Chapter 7).[24] 1 and 2 Maccabees are apocryphal works included in the Catholic Bible but not in the Hebrew Bible or Protestant Bible. 1 Maccabees was written shortly after 129 BCE in Hebrew but is preserved only in Greek translation. It begins with Antiochus IV Epiphanes (169 BCE) and ends with the death of Simon—the youngest of the Maccabean brothers—in 134 BCE. 1 Maccabees is a dynastic narrative written by a Hasmonean supporter, probably a member of the court and perhaps even John Hyrcanus I himself.[25] 2 Maccabees was written in Greek and was completed not before 124 BCE. It begins with Seleucus IV and the high priest Onias III and ends with Judah Maccabee's victory against the Seleucids in 161 BCE. The author, who might have been a Diaspora Jew, tells us that 2 Maccabees is an abridged version (epitome) of an otherwise unknown five-volume work by a certain Jason of Cyrene.[26] Both 1 and 2 Maccabees were written to defend the legitimacy of the Hasmonean dynasty by telling its founding myth: the rededication of the Jerusalem temple.[27] Despite the authors' agendas, 1 and 2 Maccabees and Josephus's works are important sources of information about Jerusalem in the Hasmonean period.

The Temple

The Mishnah, a compilation of rabbinic law edited ca. 200 CE, describes the Temple Mount as a square: "The Temple Mount measured five hundred cubits by five hundred cubits" (m. Middoth 2:1).[28] The length of a cubit—originally the distance from a person's elbow to fingertips—varied in antiquity. In the case of the 500 × 500-meter square Temple Mount mentioned in the Mishnah, 1 cubit appears to measure 20.6 inches (or 52.5 cm), which equals a total of 262.50 meters or 861 feet.[29] Because Herod the Great's expansion of the Temple Mount to the north, west, and south created a rectangular esplanade, the Mishnah seems to refer to a pre-Herodian Temple Mount. Scholars have speculated about the date of the square Temple Mount and its location relative to the Herodian esplanade.[30] For example, Leen Ritmeyer attributes the square Temple Mount to Hezekiah (eighth century BCE), while Joseph Patrich and Marcos Edelcopp associate it with John Hyrcanus I.[31] Based on Josephus's account of the Roman general Pompey's siege of Jerusalem in 63 BCE, Patrich and Edelcopp reconstruct the Hasmonean Temple Mount as a square fortified precinct measuring 500 × 500 cubits. Inside the walled precinct of the outer court, a second wall surrounded an inner court (Hebrew ʿ*azarah*), within which the temple building stood. A fence (Hebrew *soreg*) between the walls of the outer and inner courts created a barrier into which gentiles (non-Jews) were prohibited from entering (see Chapter 7).[32]

The prophet Ezekiel, a Judahite priest exiled to Babylonia in the early sixth century BCE, describes a vision in which he was shown a future temple with a 500 × 500-cubit inner court, surrounded by a huge outer court measuring 3,000 cubits square (Ezek 40–43).[33] The Temple Scroll, which was probably composed in the last quarter of the second century BCE, describes a future temple surrounded by three square courts instead of two: inner, middle, and outer.[34] The middle court's dimensions of 480 × 480 cubits are strikingly close to the Mishnah's outer court of 500 × 500 cubits, although the Temple Scroll adds a gigantic outer court that would have covered the entire city of Jerusalem.[35] These elements and others in Ezekiel and the Temple Scroll were inspired by biblical descriptions of the tabernacle (wilderness sanctuary).[36] However, the Mishnah's reference suggests that a pre-Herodian square Temple Mount measuring 500 × 500 cubits—whatever its date—did exist, and this might have influenced the descriptions in Ezekiel and the Temple Scroll.[37]

Although the second temple presumably stood on the site of the first temple (Solomon's temple), there is no agreement about its exact location and orientation within the Temple Mount.[38] Most scholars assume that the rocky outcrop (the Foundation Stone) enshrined in the Dome of the Rock was inside the temple's innermost room (the Holy of Holies), or, less likely, was underneath the altar in the courtyard in front of the temple.[39] According to Ritmeyer, when Herod rebuilt the temple, the building's foundations were so high that only the top of the rock was left exposed inside the Holy of Holies, and, centuries later, the Crusaders cut back the rocky outcrop to its present dimensions.[40] In contrast, Patrich concludes that the floor level inside Herod's temple was 6 cubits higher than the top of the rocky outcrop. This allows him to divorce the temple's location from the rocky outcrop, placing the building to the southeast of the Dome of the Rock.[41]

Whereas most scholars (including Ritmeyer) believe the temple faced east (or, less likely, west), Patrich argues that the building faced southeast. This is based on his belief that the laver—a giant basin between the temple porch and the altar used by the priests for washing their hands and feet—was fed by Cistern 5.[42] Cistern 5 is a huge reservoir under the Temple Mount that has a distinctive shape, consisting of an elongated gallery running northwest–southeast and two perpendicular arms branching off to the south (Figure 6.1). Both Ritmeyer and Patrich identify Cistern 5 with the Golah cistern mentioned in the Mishnah: " 'The Golah Chamber'—the Golah cistern was there, and a wheel was set over it, and from thence they drew water enough for the whole Temple Court"

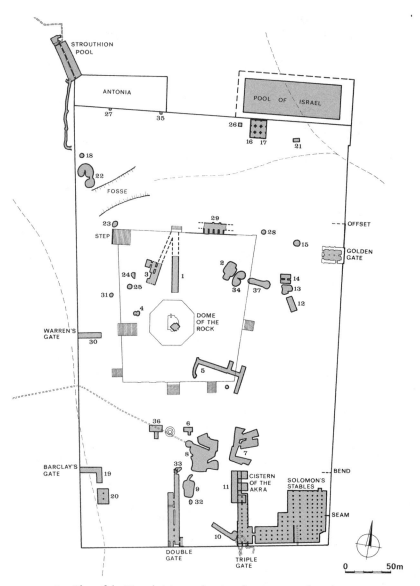

FIGURE 6.1 Plan of the Temple Mount showing the cisterns and pools.
Credit: © by Leen Ritmeyer.

(m. Middoth 5:4).[43] Based on Cistern 5's layout and the Mishnah's description, Patrich proposes that the water was drawn by means of a water wheel, a second-century BCE invention.[44] He therefore reconstructs the temple along the north side of Cistern 5 and with the same orientation to the southeast.[45]

Thirty-two meters (105 feet) north of the southeast corner of the Temple Mount, a prominent vertical seam or straight joint is visible in the wall (Figure 5.1). The masonry on the south side of the seam is Herodian in style, indicating that it is part of Herod's expansion of the Temple Mount. The Herodian masonry clearly is built up against and therefore postdates the section of the wall north of the seam. Most scholars identify the masonry north of the seam as a Hellenistic or Hasmonean period reconstruction or extension to the east wall of the Temple Mount, although recent discoveries in the Givati Parking Lot indicate that it is not part of the Akra fortress, as Yoram Tsafrir suggested.[46] Others propose that it represents an expansion of the Temple Mount to the south early in Herod's reign, to which the section south of the seam was added later in his reign.[47]

The Baris

On the natural high point at the northwest corner of the Temple Mount, John Hyrcanus I (re)constructed a fortress called the *baris*.[48] The relationship between the Persian period *birah* and the Hasmonean *baris* is unclear. Whereas the *baris* was a fortress, scholars disagree about whether the *birah* mentioned in Nehemiah 2:8 was an earlier fortress on the same spot or whether the term refers to the fortified Temple Mount or even the entire Persian-period settlement in Jerusalem (see Chapter 5).[49] Josephus says that John Hyrcanus I built the *baris* next to the temple, where he lived most of the time and stored the garments of the high priest (*Ant.* 18.91). The *baris* therefore served as a palace before the Hasmoneans built a separate residence on the southwestern hill, and Herod used it as a palace early in his reign.[50] Remains of the *baris* are elusive as it was largely obliterated when Herod constructed the Antonia fortress on this spot.[51] Dan Bahat associates cuttings in the bedrock at the northwest corner of the Temple Mount and two cisterns with the *baris*, which he believes was larger than the Antonia. According to Bahat, the cuttings are part of a channel (aqueduct) that brought rainwater from the Tyropoeon Valley to the *baris*. The channel is cut by the Struthion pools and the western temenos wall of Herod's expanded Temple Mount.[52] Ritmeyer places the *baris* to the south of the Antonia, at the northwest corner of the Hasmonean Temple Mount (which was smaller in size than Herod's Temple Mount), where he believes the Ptolemaic (not Seleucid) Akra stood.[53] Dominique-Marie Cabaret locates the *baris* farther to the north, on a rocky hill on the north side of a fosse (dry moat) that separated it from the Hasmonean Temple Mount.[54] According to

Cabaret, the Second Wall (which he dates to the Hasmonean period) terminated at the northwest corner of the *baris*, and the Struthion pools (which he also dates to the Hasmonean period) were alongside the wall.

The First Wall

With the establishment of Hasmonean rule, Jerusalem increased greatly in importance as the capital of an independent kingdom. The fortification wall along the crest of the southeastern hill (at the top of the stepped stone structure) was repaired and one or more towers were added. The city quadrupled in size as settlement spread onto the southwestern hill for the first time since 586 BCE (Pl. 5B). At first the settlement on the southwestern hill was sparse, consisting of industrial installations, workshops, and houses separated by agricultural plots, but, by the first century BCE, it became more densely built-up.[55] With the construction of the First Wall, the fortified area—the southeastern hill, the Temple Mount, and the southwestern hill—reached the same extent as on the eve of the Babylonian destruction in 586 BCE: ca. 650 dunams (160.5 acres).[56] Jerusalem's maximum population in the Hasmonean period is estimated at ca. 8,000–10,000 to 30,000.[57]

With the expansion of settlement, the late eighth-century BCE fortification wall surrounding the southwestern hill was rebuilt. The wall had been lying in ruins since it was breached by the Babylonians in 586 BCE, although parts were still standing. Under the Hasmoneans, the breaches were patched, the surviving portions of wall were repaired, and towers were reconstructed or added. Josephus calls this the "First Wall" because it is the earliest of three successive lines of wall built to protect the city before 70 CE: "Of the three walls, the most ancient, owing to the surrounding ravines, and the hill above them on which it was reared, was well-nigh impregnable. But, besides the advantage of its position, it was also strongly built, David and Solomon and their successors on the throne having taken pride in the work."[58] It was, of course, not David and Solomon but their successors (as Josephus says)—specifically Hezekiah—who originally built this wall.

Remains of the First Wall dating to the late Iron Age and Hasmonean period have been discovered at various points around the southwestern hill.[59] Different construction styles visible in the wall indicate that the initial reconstruction at the beginning of the Hasmonean period was carried out in stages. Occasional repairs were made afterward including substantial work by Herod, who added three towers at the northwest corner of the First Wall and built his palace to the south, partially overlying the wall.[60] Hillel Geva notes that although all the towers are square, the Hasmonean towers in the Citadel (at the northwest corner of the First Wall/southwestern hill) are solid while those on the north and south sides of the southwestern hill are hollow.[61] Solid towers may have been needed as emplacements for heavy artillery (catapults and ballistas) to protect the northwest corner of the southwestern hill, which lacks natural defenses.[62]

On the northeast side of the city, the First Wall presumably crossed the Tyropoeon Valley on a bridge that also carried the low-level aqueduct to the Temple Mount, at roughly the same spot as Wilson's Arch of the Herodian period. The bridge was built on a dam wall with openings in its base that allowed flood waters to pass through.[63] Radiocarbon dating of charred organic remains from this wall yielded a probable age of ca. 90–45 BCE—that is, the Hasmonean period.[64] However, since the dam wall postdates the "Masonic Hall," which was built early in Herod's reign, it might be contemporary with Herod's later expansion of the Temple Mount (see Chapter 7).[65] The First Wall crossed the southern end of the Tyropoeon Valley on a massive dam about 140 meters (460 feet) in length, at the point where it flows into the Kidron Valley. Spillways allowed flood waters to pass through the dam, the outer (east) face of which was reinforced with buttresses.[66] The wall and dam enclosed and protected the Pool of Siloam (Birket el-Hamra), renewing fortifications which, like the tunnel and pool, originally were established in the eighth century BCE. Gates flanked by towers on the north and south sides of the dam provided entry into the city.[67]

Although archaeological evidence indicates that the First Wall was reconstructed at the beginning of the Hasmonean period, scholars disagree about which ruler was responsible. Geva argues that the project could not have been undertaken until after Simon captured the Akra in 141 BCE but must have been completed before Antiochus VII Sidetes, a claimant to the Seleucid throne, invaded Judea and besieged Jerusalem.[68] Scholars disagree about the date and length of Antiochus VII's siege; Donald Ariel recently proposed that it took place in 133 or 132 BCE and lasted only a few months.[69] The siege ended when John Hyrcanus I negotiated terms of surrender, which included demolishing the city walls and becoming a vassal of Antiochus VII.[70] Since the First Wall was standing at the time of the siege, Geva concludes that it must have been built by Simon after he took the Akra, or at the very beginning of John Hyrcanus I's reign, between 141–133 BCE.[71] The demolition of the city walls in the capitulation to Antiochus VII likely entailed creating breaches, which John Hyrcanus I repaired after the Seleucid king died in 129 BCE while on military campaign in Parthia.[72] Even if Geva is correct, construction must have continued for decades afterward, as indicated by the radiocarbon dates of ca. 90–45 BCE yielded by samples taken from the bridge carrying the First Wall across the Tyropoeon Valley to the Temple Mount.[73]

FIGURE 6.2 Section of the First Wall in the Citadel.
Credit: Photo by the author.

Apparent evidence of Antiochus VII's siege has been discovered in the Citadel, a fortified enclosure at the northwest corner of the southwestern hill, adjacent to the modern Jaffa Gate. Although much of the enclosure and its buildings are medieval or later in date, earlier remains including a segment of the First Wall and towers are preserved in the courtyard (Figure 6.2).[74] Excavations outside the wall and towers brought to light hundreds of ballista stones (stone projectiles or cannon shot), dozens of Hellenistic arrowheads, iron spear butts, and lead sling projectiles (sling shot) which are typical of the second century BCE. Many of these were concentrated outside one of the Hasmonean towers (the Middle Tower) (Figure 6.3). Scattered ballista stones were also found under the foundations of a Herodian tower (the so-called Tower of David) and under and inside a wall (Wall 110), which apparently was constructed after the siege but before the Herodian tower was built.[75] The arrowheads, some of which are stamped with a Greek monogram composed of the letters B and E (*beta* and *epsilon*), appear to be associated with mercenary archers in the service of Antiochus VII Sidetes. Arrowheads stamped with the same monogram have been discovered in the Givati Parking Lot and on the east side of the southeastern hill, suggesting that fighting also occurred at these spots during Antiochus VII's siege.[76]

FIGURE 6.3 Ballista stones by a Hasmonean tower in the First Wall in the Citadel. Credit: Photo by the author.

The Second Wall

By the time Jerusalem was destroyed by the Romans in 70 CE, the north side of the city was fortified by three successive lines of wall, which Josephus calls the First Wall, the Second Wall, and the Third Wall: "The city was fortified by three walls, except where it was enclosed by impassable ravines, a single rampart there sufficing."[77] Although there is no consensus about its circuit, archaeologists agree that the Third Wall—the outermost and latest of the three walls—was begun in the mid-first century CE by Herod Agrippa I, the grandson of Herod the Great, and completed on the eve of the outbreak of the First Revolt. However, the circuit and the date of the Second Wall are unclear. Josephus says, "The second wall started from the gate in the first wall which they called Gennath, and, enclosing only the northern district of the town, went up as far as Antonia."[78] Nahman Avigad proposed identifying a gate that he found in the middle of the north side of the First Wall as the Gennath Gate, although some archaeologists place it farther to the west.[79] And whereas some archaeologists reconstruct the Second Wall as enclosing a relatively small area to the northeast of the First Wall as far as the Antonia (at the northwest corner of the Temple Mount), according to others it enclosed a larger area extending along the northern part of the Tyropoeon Valley as far as the Damascus Gate in the north wall of the Old City.[80]

The Second Wall must have been built after the First Wall (in the second half of the second century BCE) and before the Third Wall (in the mid-first century CE). But although Josephus tells us who built the First and Third Walls, he does not mention who was responsible for the Second Wall. Many scholars consider Herod the Great the best candidate in light of his extensive building activities in Jerusalem, when the population increased.[81] Others argue that had the Second Wall been built by Herod the Great, Josephus would have mentioned it.[82] They also cite Josephus's description of Herod's siege of Jerusalem in 37 BCE, which refers to the Temple Mount being taken after the north wall of the city was breached, as indicating that the Second Wall already existed.[83]

Possible evidence that the Second Wall was constructed in the Hasmonean period (first century BCE) was found in the Jewish Quarter excavations. Massive earth fills were dumped against the outer face of the First Wall in Areas W and X–2, in the middle of the north side of the southwestern hill. The pottery and other finds indicate that the fills were dumped in the second half of the second century and the beginning of the first century BCE. Since the fills appear to have been deposited after this section of the First Wall went out of use, Geva connects them to the construction of a new fortification—the Second Wall—farther to the north.[84] Geva proposes that the Second Wall was constructed to protect the markets along the Tyropoeon Valley as well as a Hasmonean aqueduct that channeled surface runoff water to the *baris* from the vicinity of the modern Damascus Gate to the north.[85] However, Geva's explanation does not account for similar earth fills that were deposited around the same time in other places outside the First Wall, including in the Citadel and on the west side of the southwestern hill.[86] It also does not explain why these fills were deposited for only a brief period. If this is garbage, why did the dumping stop?

The Akra

In 168 BCE, Antiochus IV Epiphanes established a fortified citadel in Jerusalem called the Akra, which he garrisoned with gentile troops and pro-Seleucid Jews.

The citadel was a thorn in the side of the Jewish population until 141 BCE, when Simon captured it: "In those days things prospered in his hands, so that the Gentiles were put out of the country, as were also those in the city of David in Jerusalem, who had built themselves a citadel [Akra] from which they used to sally forth and defile the environs of the sanctuary, doing great damage to its purity" (1 Macc 14:36).[87] It is unclear if Antiochus IV's Akra is related to a Ptolemaic period Akra in Jerusalem mentioned in the Letter of Aristeas and by Josephus.[88]

The location of the Seleucid Akra, which apparently was a sizeable fortress, has been the subject of much speculation, with scholars placing it at various points around the city.[89] The fortress's name—which means "high point" in Greek—suggests that it occupied an elevated spot, while the passage from 1 Maccabees cited above indicates proximity to the Temple Mount. In a brilliant analysis of the literary sources and topography of Jerusalem published in 1989, Bezalel Bar-Kochva located the Akra at the north end of the southeastern hill, which was the site of the city's citadels since the Bronze Age and Iron Age.[90] Bar-Kochva was proved right in 2015, when excavations in the Givati Parking Lot brought to light a Hellenistic-period fortification system which Doron Ben-Ami and Yana Tchekhanovets have identified persuasively as the Akra.[91] Part of the fortification wall was first exposed by Kathleen Kenyon in her Site M, which is in the Givati Parking Lot. Kenyon identified the wall as "Maccabean" but rejected an association with the Akra, which she placed on the southwestern hill.[92] Rather than occupying a high point overlooking the Temple Mount (as many scholars assumed), the Akra controlled the main access to it from the southeastern hill through the Ophel.[93]

The remains uncovered in the Givati Parking Lot include a massive wall up to 3.5 meters (11 feet) thick running northeast-southwest and a large tower (salient), both abutted on the west (outer) side by a glacis (sloping layers of fill). The wall was built on a deep bedrock shelf that is part of a series of artificial terraces or steps hewn along the northeastern slope of the Tyropoeon Valley. The fortification system originally consisted only of the wall and tower, to which the glacis was added later.[94] The glacis is composed of two distinct layers that were deposited outside the wall and tower at different times: a lower (earlier) fill consisting of layers of gravel sloping down toward the northwest and an upper (later) fill with enormous quantities of broken pottery sloping down toward the southwest.[95] The pottery, coins, and other finds indicate that the wall and tower were constructed in the first half of the second century BCE, while the lower (gravel) glacis was added early in the second half of the second century BCE and the upper (pottery) glacis dates to the later 130s–120s BCE.[96] In the late second or early first century BCE, the fortifications were dismantled, the area was leveled, and a large Hasmonean-period ashlar building (4001) was erected above.[97]

Based on this evidence, the excavators identify the wall and tower in the Givati Parking Lot as part of the Akra built by Antiochus IV Epiphanes.[98] The lower (gravel) glacis appears to have been added by Simon, in accordance with 1 Macc 13:52: "He [Simon] strengthened the fortifications of the temple hill alongside the citadel." The upper (pottery) glacis dates to the reign of John Hyrcanus I and presumably was added after Antiochus VII Sidetes's death in 129 BCE.[99]

The finds in the Givati Parking Lot resolve the discrepancy between 1 Maccabees' statement that Simon strengthened the Akra and settled his own garrison there after capturing it (1 Macc 14:37) and Josephus's account that Simon destroyed the Akra and leveled the hill on which it was built (*Ant.* 13:215–217; *War* 5.139).[100] Whereas 1 Maccabees was composed during the reign of John Hyrcanus I, Josephus's works date to the 70s and 80s of the Common Era. When 1 Maccabees was written, the Akra was still standing and had been strengthened and garrisoned by Simon and John Hyrcanus I. Afterward—in the late second century or early first century BCE—the fortress was destroyed and the area was leveled, as Josephus reports, although he erroneously attributed the demolition to Simon.[101] Instead, it appears that Akra was demolished and ashlar Building 4001 were constructed during the reign of Alexander Jannaeus.

The remains of the Akra were first discovered and identified by John Crowfoot and George Fitzgerald to the south of the (present) Givati Parking Lot.[102] In 1927, in a 20-meter (66- foot)-wide trench across the Tyropoeon Valley, Crowfoot and Fitzgerald reached bedrock at a depth of 11 meters (36 feet) below ground level on the east and 17 meters (56 feet) below ground level on the west.[103] Their excavations revealed massive stone walls running northeast–southwest, still standing in places to a height of over 6 meters (19 feet), with a gate (opening measuring 3.5 meters [11 feet]) flanked by two towers over 8 meters (26 feet) thick (Pl. 6; Figure 6.4). The wall and towers were built on a broad bedrock shelf below the western crest of the hill.[104] Crowfoot and Fitzgerald observed that "though the towers contained Maccabaean work, the plan of the gate was very much more ancient. The masonry of different parts of the walls varies, as the illustrations show, and it is plain that they have been patched and repaired in the course of time, like most other city walls; but the mere dimensions prove to our mind without possibility of doubt that our walls belong in origin to a much earlier age."[105] They concluded that the fortifications were constructed in the Bronze Age, or, at the latest, in the early Iron Age, and were used during the late Iron Age, the Persian period, and the Second Temple period until 70 CE. Crowfoot and Fitzgerald proposed an association with the Akra and noted at least one Hasmonean-period repair including the reconstruction of the north tower.[106]

THE OLD GATE, FROM THE NORTH-WEST. *(Photo; Père Savignac, 17 July.)*

FIGURE 6.4 The gate uncovered by Crowfoot and Fitzgerald, from Crowfoot and Fitzgerald 1929: Frontispiece.
Credit: Courtesy of the Palestine Exploration Fund.

Although Crowfoot and Fitzgerald did not identify a glacis, they describe a thick layer of debris overlying the bedrock outside the wall and towers, which contained a large quantity of Hellenistic pottery.[107] One hundred thirty-three coins tentatively dated to the fourth century BCE were found along the outside of the south gate tower (Area 17).[108] In addition, a hoard of 319 "Maccabaean" coins was discovered immediately west (outside) of the gate, at a depth of 10.8 meters (35 feet) below the surface and 1.5–2 meters (6–8 feet) above bedrock, indicating that this was the ground level at the time they were deposited.[109] Eight of the coins are issues of John Hyrcanus I and 303 are of Alexander Jannaeus, suggesting a connection to the demolition of the Akra and the construction of Building 4001 in the Givati Parking Lot.[110]

In 1928, Crowfoot excavated a 28-meter-long (31-yard) stretch of wall to the south of the south gate tower, running along the western crest of the Ophel, which he designated the "long wall."[111] Only one or two of the lowest courses were preserved—apparently the foundations—embedded in a layer of stone chips that belong to construction debris. A hoard of twenty-four coins of Antiochus III (ruled 223–187 BCE) embedded in the chips must have been deposited at the time of construction. The coins and hundreds of stamped Rhodian amphora handles found in the vicinity suggested to Crowfoot that the wall dates to within twenty to thirty years of Antiochus III's death.[112] On this basis, he concluded that "the long wall we have described is most probably to be identified as part of this Akra."[113] Because the gate and towers appear to be earlier (perhaps Bronze Age or early Iron Age), Crowfoot surmised that they were attached to a fortification wall that predates the "long wall" and was located farther to the west.[114] His conclusion that the Akra did not overlook the temple but instead controlled access to it has since been proven correct.[115]

Apparent remains of the Akra were also found on the northeast side of the southeastern hill. Below the fortification wall on the eastern crest, a "thick earth glacis" overlay debris from the Babylonian destruction and the Persian period fills that covered the stepped stone structure. Yigal Shiloh described the glacis as "made up of layers of earth, chalky earth, and gravel and cobbles, tipped one over the other alternately . . . [which] contained much Iron Age II and Hellenistic pottery."[116] The latest pottery dates to ca. 100 BCE. Shiloh assumed that the glacis is contemporary with the fortification wall above, which he identified as the First Wall.[117] Ben-Ami and Tchekhanovets note that the south tower in the wall above the stepped stone structure (the First Wall) lies due east of the gateway uncovered by Crowfoot and Fitzgerald.[118] In fact, nearly ninety years earlier, Crowfoot suggested that Macalister and Duncan's "post-exilic" wall corresponded to the "long wall" that he found on the western side of the Ophel and identified as part of the Akra.[119] As in the Givati Parking Lot, photographs from Macalister and Duncan's excavations suggest that the glacis was added later to the outside of the south tower in the wall above the stepped stone structure, in which case the tower may be part of the Akra, as Ben-Ami and Tchekhanovets propose.[120] Thus, the Hasmonean-period First Wall reused the Akra's fortifications.[121] Whether or not this previously was Nehemiah's wall, it incorporated the east wall of the Iron Age large stone structure. Crowfoot and Fitzgerald remarked that "the wall to which our gate and towers belong was maintained long after it had ceased to be the external wall of the city [on the west side of the southeastern hill], as a second line of defence to give additional protection to the oldest quarter of the city."[122]

The Hasmonean Palace

Josephus reports that the Hasmoneans built a palace on a high point overlooking the city and the Temple Mount, apparently on the southwestern hill.[123] Geva proposes identifying the fragmentary remains of an impressive Hasmonean-period structure in the Citadel as the Hasmonean palace. Like the podium of Herod's palace which overlies it, this structure was built on a natural high point on the southwestern hill, inside the northwest corner of the First Wall.[124] However, Josephus's description makes clear that the Hasmonean palace was separate from Herod's palace and was used by members of the Hasmonean family until the First Jewish Revolt. Herod built his own palace in Jerusalem because he was not a Hasmonean and therefore could not use their palace. Similarly, at Jericho, Herod established a new winter palace complex adjacent to the Hasmonean palaces rather than on the same spot.[125] Therefore, presumably the Hasmonean palace in Jerusalem was located elsewhere on the southwestern hill, perhaps near but not on the site of Herod's (later) palace.

Water Supply

Before the Hasmonean period, Jerusalem's main water source was the Gihon spring (including the Pool of Siloam). In addition, each house was equipped with one or more cisterns that stored enough rainwater for the needs of the residents over the course of a year.[126] The expansion of settlement onto the southwestern hill and the accompanying population growth resulted in an increased demand for water, including for the sacrificial cult in the temple, for which the cisterns on the Temple Mount no longer sufficed. In response to this need, the low-level aqueduct was constructed in the Hasmonean period to bring more water into the city, and a second channel, called the high-level aqueduct, was added in the Herodian period (Figure 6.5).[127] Both aqueducts were first explored and documented in the nineteenth century by Charles Wilson and especially by Conrad Schick.[128] The aqueducts carried water to Jerusalem from three enormous reservoirs called Solomon's Pools, which lie in a valley called Wadi Artas (or Urtas) southwest of Bethlehem (Figure 6.6). The name was given by modern Western travelers who associated the pools with Solomon based on Ecclesiastes 2:6: "I made myself pools from which to water the forest of growing trees."[129] The pools and aqueducts are located on the Judean hills watershed and were fed by four different springs as well as by surface runoff.[130] Because the ridge on which the watershed lies rises in elevation to the south of Jerusalem, the water flowed by gravity through the aqueducts to the city. At Solomon's Pools, the low-level aqueduct's elevation is 765 meters (2,510 feet) above sea level, with the terminus at the Temple Mount

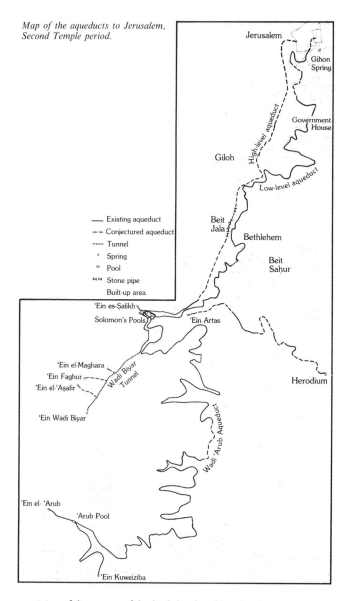

Map of the aqueducts to Jerusalem,
Second Temple period.

FIGURE 6.5 Map of the routes of the high-level and low-level aqueducts, from E. Stern [ed.] 1993: 747. Credit: with permission of Carta.

at ca. 735 meters (2,411 feet) above sea level.[131] Amihai Mazar estimates that the pools could hold up to 288,000 cubic meters (76,081,551 gallons) of water, while the springs produce up to 500,000 cubic meters (132,086,026 gallons) of water annually.[132]

FIGURE 6.6 Solomon's Pools: the third or lower pool, looking northeast.
Credit: LOC Matson Collection 22407: hdl.loc.gov/loc.pnp/matpc.22407.

The low-level aqueduct is so-called because it consists of a plastered channel built on top of the ground or hewn through rocky outcrops. The channel winds for 21.5 kms (ca. 13 miles) from Solomon's Pools to Jerusalem, which is twice the straight-line distance between the two points.[133] The low-level aqueduct remained in use through the Ottoman period, when a clay pipe was inserted into the channel, and water still flowed through sections of the pipe in British Mandatory times.[134] The aqueduct entered Jerusalem from the southwest and ran along the western side of the Ben-Hinnom Valley, below the modern neighborhood of Mishkenot Sha'ananim (next to the King David Hotel) and along the Sultan's Pool before crossing the valley on a bridge to Mount Zion. From there the aqueduct continued eastward, wrapping around the south side of the southwestern hill. It then crossed the Tyropoeon Valley to the Temple Mount, apparently on the same bridge that carried the First Wall.[135] The water was stored in large cisterns on the Temple Mount.[136]

Miqva'ot (Jewish Ritual Baths)

Like other ancient peoples, the Israelites/Jews had laws regulating interaction between the divine and human realms, including the requirement to be ritually pure in the presence of a deity.[137] According to the laws in the Five Books of

Moses, the main causes of impurity are certain skin diseases (including on clothing and walls), certain types of bodily secretions, and contact with certain categories of living things and corpses. The sources of impurity appear random to us, ranging, for example, from touching mildew on the walls of a house to touching a lizard to having a menstrual period (for a woman) or a nocturnal (seminal) emission (for a man). Ritual impurity in Judaism is a mechanical category, meaning it does not make a person bad or sinful (in the Christian sense of the word) or physically dirty or unhygienic. Ritual impurity is unavoidable as it affects every human being repeatedly and at various times. The methods of purification vary depending on the status of the affected person (layperson versus priest) and the nature of the impurity (corpse impurity is the most severe and requires a complicated purification procedure). But, in most cases, purification is effected by washing or immersing in water and waiting for the passage of a certain amount of time (usually until sundown).

The need to observe biblical purity laws was limited to certain times or situations—mostly when entering the presence of the God of Israel in the Jerusalem temple or when producing goods destined for the temple and priests. Therefore, everyone—including Jesus and Paul—took for granted that ritual purification was required first. For example, Acts 21:26 says that Paul entered the temple after "having purified himself." But most of the time, most ancient Jews were ritually impure. Priests observed the ritual purity laws on a more regular basis due to their service in God's presence in the Jerusalem temple. Judaism was distinguished from other ancient religions in that some groups or sects in the late Second Temple period (such as the Essenes and Pharisees) extended the observance of ritual purity beyond the boundaries of the temple cult, reflecting their belief that God's presence was not limited to the Jerusalem temple.

Because there are few natural bodies of water such as lakes, rivers, streams, springs, and pools of rainwater, by ca. 100 BCE Jews in Judea began to create immersion pools for ritual purification, which are called *miqva'ot* (singular *miqveh*).[138] Ancient *miqva'ot* typically are plastered pools dug into the ground or hewn into bedrock, with a broad set of steps running along the width of the pool, from top to bottom, which facilitated immersion in the water. Many ritual baths have other features, such as low partitions running down the steps (to separate pure from impure), staggered broad and narrow steps (with the broad steps used as bathing platforms depending on the level of the water), and a deep basin at the bottom to enable immersion when the water reached its lowest level. Most *miqva'ot* were filled by rainwater or spring water, which flowed by gravity through a channel.

The earliest *miqva'ot* date to the late second–early first century BCE, indicating that, by the Hasmonean period, Jews understood biblical law as requiring

FIGURE 6.7 *Miqveh* south of the Temple Mount.
Credit: Photo by the author.

full-body immersion in undrawn water for purification. It is unclear whether the absence of ritual baths before ca. 100 BCE indicates that earlier Israelites/Jews used other methods of purification such as washing only parts of the body or limited purity requirements to individuals with certain afflictions such as leprosy, who immersed in natural bodies of water.[139] Either way, the proliferation of *miqva'ot* in the first century BCE and first century CE attests to the increased observance of biblical purity laws among broad sectors of the Jewish population.[140] Not surprisingly, ritual baths are concentrated especially in and around Jerusalem, reflecting the need for purity in connection with the temple cult. Although a majority of *miqva'ot* date to the Herodian period (40 BCE–70 CE), Hasmonean-period examples are found in houses on Jerusalem's southwestern hill and in public areas around the Temple Mount (Figures 3.8 and 6.7).[141]

Amphoras

Amphoras are large jars designed for transporting goods on ships. They have a long, narrow neck with two handles extending from the rim or neck to the shoulder, and a teardrop shaped body narrowing to a pointed base. This design allowed for easy loading onto ships by grasping the handle with one hand and lifting the base with the other. Wine, olive oil, fish sauce, and grain were shipped around the Mediterranean in amphoras. Variations in the shape of amphoras signaled to consumers the contents and/or the place of origin, in much the same way that Coca-Cola or fine wines today have distinctively shaped bottles. Local (Judean) storage jars of the Hellenistic, Roman, and Byzantine periods look nothing like amphoras. They are characterized by a short, narrow neck and a large, "bag-shaped" body with rounded base and two small ring handles on the shoulders (Figure 6.8). With their bulky body and awkward shape,

FIGURE 6.8 Bag-shaped storage jar.
Credit: Photo by the author.

FIGURE 6.9 Rhodian amphora.
Credit: Metropolitan Museum of Art, www.metmuseum.org/art/collection/search/239942.

bag-shaped jars were designed for storage rather than transport. The rounded base was set onto a dirt floor or on a stand. These differences make amphoras easily distinguishable from Judean bag-shaped jars. Most of the Hellenistic period amphoras found in Jerusalem come from the Aegean—predominantly Rhodes—and contained wine (Figure 6.9).[142] The handles are often stamped with the name or symbol of the city or island that produced the wine, the overseeing official(s), and (sometimes) the date of production. These features make it possible to reconstruct trading patterns around the Mediterranean.

Approximately two thousand stamped amphora handles have been found in excavations in Jerusalem, most of which date from the mid-third to mid-second century BCE, and ninety-five percent of which come from the southeastern hill.[143] The concentration of stamped amphora handles on the southeastern hill, especially at the north end, many of which date to 170–160 BCE, suggests an association with the Akra, whose gentile (and perhaps Hellenized Jewish) occupants were the primary consumers of imported wine in Jerusalem.[144] The latest stamped amphora handles found on the southeastern hill date to ca. 150–149 BCE, roughly coinciding with the beginning of the siege of the Akra by Judah Maccabee's brother Jonathan.[145]

Recently, a large number of amphoras from Rhodes and Kos, including more than forty stamped handles was discovered in rescue excavations about 2 kilometers (1 mile) north of the Old City, near the modern neighborhood of Mea Shearim. The stamps date between 143 and 132 BCE, clustering mostly at the end of the range. Since this coincides with the date of Antiochus VII Sidetes' siege (probably in 133 or 132 BCE), Ariel associates the deposit with Seleucid siege camps to the north of the First Wall, suggesting that imported Greek wine was among the troops' provisions.[146] Ariel proposes that stamped amphora handles found elsewhere to the north and west of the First Wall may reflect the location of other siege camps of Antiochus VII.[147]

Only fifty-six Rhodian stamped amphora handles have been found on the southwestern hill, together with a smaller number of other Greek stamped handles and Latin stamped handles.[148] In addition, most of the stamped handles from the southwestern hill date to the late second and first centuries BCE through the reign of Herod the Great.[149] As noted above, the concentration of stamped amphora handles at the north end of the southeastern hill indicates a preference for imported Greek wine by the soldiers stationed in the Akra. The paucity of stamped amphora handles on the southwestern hill is due in part to the fact that this area was uninhabited before the mid-second century BCE.[150]

Could the steep decline in numbers of stamped amphora handles after the mid-second century BCE indicate that Jerusalem's Jewish inhabitants refrained from consuming imported wine due to the observance of dietary and purity laws? In the late Second Temple period (first century BCE and first century CE) and the following centuries, some Jews came to associate gentiles or gentile products with ritual impurity. Biblical purity laws do not apply to gentiles because they were prohibited from entering the presence of the God of Israel (the Jerusalem temple). However, gentile lands (territories outside the land of Israel) were considered polluted by idolatry (the worship of other gods). Therefore, in the late Second Temple period, some Jews began to consider products imported from gentile lands impure, including amphoras (which are made of clay—a substance that is susceptible to ritual impurity according to biblical law), and, perhaps, their contents. Scholars disagree about when prohibitions on gentile products began to develop and to what extent they were observed.[151] The low number of stamped amphora handles in Hasmonean- and Herodian-period contexts in Jerusalem probably indicates that some Jews refrained from consuming imported goods because they considered these containers and their contents impure. As we have seen, the appearance of ritual baths in the late second century and first century BCE reflects the increased observance of biblical purity laws among broad sectors of the Jewish population. On the other hand, the discovery of small numbers of imported amphoras including stamped handles through the Herodian period indicates that not all Jerusalem's residents considered gentiles impure or were concerned with the impurity of gentile products, as Avigad noted: "It would seem that there have always been more and less observant Jews."[152]

Stamped Jars

Seal impressions stamped on the handles and bodies of local (bag-shaped) storage jars first appeared in Jerusalem in the late eighth and seventh centuries and continued through the second century BCE. Although, like their predecessors, Hasmonean-period jars were stamped with a variant of the name of the province (*yhwd* [Yehud]), in the second half of the second century BCE, the inscriptions were written in paleo-Hebrew (ancient Hebrew) script instead of Aramaic. In addition, a new motif was introduced, which consists of the letters *yršlm* (Yerushalem = Jerusalem) in paleo-Hebrew script between the rays of a five-pointed star. The Hasmoneans used the paleo-Hebrew script on stamped jar handles and on coins to connect themselves to the biblical kingdom of Judah and to highlight Jerusalem's status as their capital.[153]

Whereas a majority of Persian and early Hellenistic seal impressions have been found at Ramat Rahel, in the second half of the second century BCE most come from Jerusalem, reflecting the increased importance of the city as the capital of the Hasmonean kingdom. The concentration of seal impressions on the southeastern hill indicates that it remained the administrative center of the city. The discovery of only a few seal impressions dating to the second half of the second century BCE on the southwestern hill—and none from the Persian and early Hellenistic periods—confirms that this area was resettled only in the Hasmonean period.[154] Geva suggests that *yršlm* seals were introduced after Simon conquered the Akra in 141 BCE. By the end of the second century BCE, seal impressions on jars disappeared altogether, perhaps replaced for administrative purposes by coins, which are stamped with seal impressions including some of the same motifs and inscriptions found on jars.[155]

Coins

The Hasmoneans minted their own coins in Jerusalem beginning with the first autonomous issues of John Hyrcanus I ca. 125 BCE.[156] All the Hasmonean coins are small, low-value, bronze denominations called a *prutah*. Perhaps the Hasmoneans refrained from minting higher value silver coins because it was more cost effective to use other silver currencies that were in circulation, especially Tyrian tetradrachmas[157] (672 *prutot* are estimated to equal one Tyrian tetradrachma).[158] Alexander Jannaeus minted huge quantities of bronze coins, apparently numbering in the millions.[159] His coins are so common that large numbers remained in circulation for decades afterward, through the reign of Herod and into the first century CE.[160]

In addition to bronze coins, Alexander Jannaeus minted small lead coins or tokens for a brief period around 79/78 BCE. Lead was rarely used for coinage in antiquity because it is soft and friable and had only a fraction of the value of its weight in bronze. Therefore, the minting of lead coins suggests an urgent need for cash combined with a shortage of bronze.[161] It is unclear why Alexander Jannaeus would have been cash-strapped in 79/78 BCE. A year earlier, he had returned to Jerusalem in triumph after three years of successful military campaigns which added territories to the Hasmonean kingdom. Despite being in declining health due to heavy drinking, Alexander Jannaeus then embarked on a new series of campaigns, succumbing to illness in 76 BCE while conducting a siege in the territory of Gerasa (Jerash in Jordan).[162] Perhaps he issued lead coins to supplement a shortfall of bronze coinage needed to pay for his campaigns. Or perhaps these were not coins but tokens given as gifts by Alexander Jannaeus to his subjects, which could be redeemed for food or other commodities.[163]

Many of the motifs depicted on Hasmonean coins—including helmets, anchors, cornucopias (horns of plenty), wreaths, diadems, stars, and palm branches—are borrowed from Hellenistic types symbolizing victory and military achievement, kingship, and prosperity (Figures 6.10 and 6.11).[164] Other designs include a pomegranate and a flower usually described as a lily—a motif characteristic of the earlier Yehud coins—which are thought to be symbols of Jerusalem.[165] However, unlike other Hellenistic rulers, the Hasmoneans refrained from putting their own portraits or other figured images on their coins. This reflects a growing trend toward aniconism (avoiding the depiction of figured images) among the Jewish population of the Hasmonean period, apparently reflecting a stricter interpretation and observance of the second commandment. Lee Levine suggests that perhaps the Hasmoneans promoted aniconism because they associated figured images with idolatry.[166]

FIGURE 6.10 Coin of Alexander Jannaeus with the Greek inscription "of King Alexander" around an inverted anchor, 2017.38.19; ANS collection gift of Abraham D and Marian Scheuer Sofaer.
Credit: Courtesy of David Hendin.

   In addition to Greek and Aramaic, the Hasmoneans used paleo-Hebrew script on their coins, as they did as on stamped jar handles. Many of the inscriptions give only the ruler's Hebrew name, not his Greek name: Yehohanan for John Hyrcanus I, Yehudah for (Judah) Aristobulus I, Yehonatan or Yonatan for Alexander Jannaeus.[167] The inscriptions reflect the increasing integration of the Hasmoneans into the Hellenistic world; whereas the coins of John Hyrcanus I are inscribed in paleo-Hebrew and use only his Hebrew name and Jewish titles (high priest and [head of] the council [*hever*] of the Jews), those of Alexander Jannaeus give both his Hebrew and Greek names, add the Greek title king (*basileios*) to the Jewish titles, and are inscribed in paleo-Hebrew, Greek, and Aramaic.[168]

FIGURE 6.11 Coin of Alexander Jannaeus with the paleo-Hebrew inscription "Yehonatan the King" between the rays of star with eight rays within a diadem, 2017.38.19; ANS collection gift of Abraham D and Marian Scheuer Sofaer.
Credit: Courtesy of David Hendin.

After the Roman annexation in 63 BCE, the Hasmonean kingdom was revived briefly in 40 BCE when the Parthians (an ancient Iranian people) overran Syria-Palestine. Antigonus II Mattathias (Mattathias Antigonus), the son of Aristobulus II, seized the opportunity to claim the Hasmonean throne. He ruled until 37 BCE, when Jerusalem fell to Herod and the Roman governor Sosius after a siege. Although Mattathias Antigonus minted bronze coins like those of his Hasmonean predecessors, one of his types is unique in depicting two objects that are emblematic of the Jerusalem temple (Figures 6.12 and 6.13). One side of the coin shows a menorah—the seven-branched candelabrum or lampstand—accompanied by the Greek inscription "of King Antigonus." The other side depicts the showbread table, with or without stacks of bread, surrounded by the

FIGURE 6.12 Coin of Mattathias Antigonus showing the menorah with the Greek inscription "of King Antigonus," 2013.63.446; ANS collection gift of Abraham D and Marian Scheuer Sofaer.
Credit: Courtesy of David Hendin.

FIGURE 6.13 Coin of Mattathias Antigonus showing the showbread table with the paleo-Hebrew inscription "Mattatayah the High Priest," 2013.63.446; ANS collection gift of Abraham D and Marian Scheuer Sofaer.
Credit: Courtesy of David Hendin.

paleo-Hebrew inscription "Mattatayah the high priest." Mattathias Antigonus might have issued these coins in his final days to rally support among the Jewish population.[169]

Tombs

After 586 BCE, most of Jerusalem's rock-cut tombs went out of use because the wealthy families who owned them were dead or dispersed. Rock-cut tombs reappeared in the Hasmonean period when Jerusalem became the capital of the Hasmonean kingdom and elite presence in the city increased.[170] In the meantime, in 353 BCE, a local dynast named Mausolus of Caria died and was buried in a monumental tomb in his capital city of Halicarnassus (modern Bodrum on the southwest coast of Turkey). Due to the ravages of humans and nature, little survives of the tomb of Mausolus, which became known as the Mausoleum at Halicarnassus. However, ancient literary accounts and depictions on coins indicate that it consisted of a Greek-temple style building surrounded by columns with a pyramidal roof on a tall, raised podium (in which the burial chamber was located). The tomb was decorated with hundreds of statues and reliefs carved by the most famous Greek sculptors of the day (most of the surviving sculpture is now in the British Museum in London). It was because of the high quality and lavishness of the decoration that the tomb of Mausolus became one of the seven wonders of the ancient world. Since then, it has become conventional to refer to all monumental tombs as mausolea (singular: mausoleum).

The Mausoleum at Halicarnassus inspired rulers and elites around the Mediterranean to construct their own tombs in imitation. When an autonomous Jewish elite emerged in Judea after the Maccabean revolt, they, too, adopted this type of monumental tomb. Ironically, although the Maccabees were renowned for their opposition to the imposition of Greek customs on the Jews, the Hasmonean rulers show signs of Hellenization soon after the establishment of their kingdom. Nowhere is this better illustrated than by the monumental family tomb and victory memorial built by Simon in their hometown of Modiin, in which he interred the remains of his parents and brothers. Although no remains of this tomb survive, the descriptions provided in 1 Maccabees and by Josephus leave little doubt that it was inspired by the Mausoleum at Halicarnassus.

> And Simon built a monument over the tomb of his father and his brothers, he made it high so that it might be seen, with polished stone at the front and back. He also erected seven pyramids, opposite one another, for his father and mother and four brothers. For the pyramids he devised an elaborate setting, erecting about them great columns, and

on the columns he put suits of armor for a permanent memorial, and beside the suits of armor he carved ships, so that they could be seen by all who sail the sea. This is the tomb that he built in Modein; it remains to this day. (1 Macc. 13:27–30)

But Simon sent to the city of Basca and brought back the bones of his brother, which he buried in Modeei, his birthplace, while all the people made great lamentation over him. And Simon also built for his father and brothers a very great monument of polished white marble, and raising it to a great and conspicuous height, made porticoes round it, and erected monolithic pillars, a wonderful thing to see. In addition to these he built for his parents and his brothers seven pyramids, one for each, so made as to excite wonder by their size and beauty; and these have been preserved to this day.[171]

These descriptions indicate that, like the Mausoleum at Halicarnassus, the tomb of the Maccabees consisted of a tall podium with a temple-like building surrounded by columns and capped by a pyramidal roof (or, in the case of the tomb of the Maccabees, seven pyramids, one for each family member including Simon).

The wealthy Jews of Jerusalem soon began to imitate the new tomb style introduced by Simon. They revived the ancient custom of interring family members in rock-cut tombs used over the course of several generations, making space for new burials by depositing the earlier remains elsewhere in the tomb. However, new features introduced into these tombs reflect foreign influences and fashions. These features include niches (Latin: loculi [sgl. loculus]; Hebrew: *kokhim* [sgl. *kokh*]) hewn in the walls of the burial chamber instead of benches to accommodate the bodies and decorating the tomb's exterior, sometimes with a Greek-style porch and a pyramid or other monumental marker (Figure 9.3). These features remained characteristic of Jewish rock-cut tombs in Jerusalem until the end of the Second Temple period. The differences between individual rock-cut tombs mostly concern their size and degree of elaboration; that is, the number of burial chambers, the presence or absence of a porch (with or without columns), the addition of decoration (typically around the entrance to the burial chambers and/or on the porch façade), and the presence or absence of one or more monumental markers. Many burial chambers are encircled by narrow rock-cut benches below the loculi, on which the bodies of the deceased could be placed as they were prepared for interment.

The most prominent Hasmonean period rock-cut tomb in Jerusalem is Jason's Tomb (Figure 6.14).[172] Discovered in 1956 during construction in Rehavia, a neighborhood on the west side of the city, Jason's Tomb was excavated by the

FIGURE 6.14 Jason's Tomb.
Credit: Photo by the author.

Israeli archaeologist Levy Yitzhak Rahmani. The tomb was entered through a long, narrow, open passage (*dromos*) cut into the slope of a hill, subdivided into a series of three successive courts which provided access to a porch in front of the burial chambers. A single column with a Greek Doric-style capital was set between the jambs of the porch (an arrangement called in Greek *in-antis*, meaning between the antae [thickened jambs]). The tomb itself consists of two chambers cut into bedrock: a burial chamber with loculi (A) to one side of the porch and a charnel room (B) at the rear of the porch. Like the repositories in late Iron Age tombs, the remains cleared out of the loculi to make space for new burials were deposited in the charnel room. A monumental stone pyramid was erected above the tomb. Jews of the late Second Temple period referred to monumental grave markers as a *nefesh* (Hebrew for "soul").[173] The finds from Jason's Tomb indicate that it was constructed in the second half of the second century BCE, apparently during the reign of John Hyrcanus I, and was used until it collapsed in the earthquake of 31 BCE.[174]

Graffiti drawn in charcoal and incised in the plaster on the porch walls include several inscriptions in Aramaic and Hebrew and one in Greek. One Aramaic inscription enjoins visitors to lament the death of Jason—hence the name given to the tomb by archaeologists: "A powerful lament make for Jason son of P . . . (my brother). Peace. . . . Who hast built thyself a tomb and *nefesh*. Rest in peace."[175] The inscription apparently was written by Honio (Onias), Jason's brother.[176] The Greek inscription is a common type of Hellenistic funerary exhortation intended to console mourners: "[You] the living, rejoice! For the rest . . . drink and eat."[177]

The graffiti from Jason's Tomb include depictions of figured images such as a resting stag with raised head (which Rahmani identified as a red deer), showing that the trend toward aniconism was not universally observed. There are also five seven-branched menorahs accompanied by an object which might be the showbread table.[178] The menorahs and showbread table depicted in Jason's Tomb and on the coins of Mattathias Antigonus are the earliest representations of these objects.[179] There is also a graffito of three ships with unfurled sails: two war galleys flanking a merchant ship or fishing vessel (Figure 6.15). The right-hand galley, which is equipped with a battering ram on the prow, appears to be in pursuit of the merchant ship. Inside the galley's prow is a forecastle with two helmeted warriors, one holding a bow and arrow and the other a spear. Rows of oars descend into the water from the sides of the galley. Above them, a row of shields along the bulwark protects the rowers. A helmsman in a tent on the

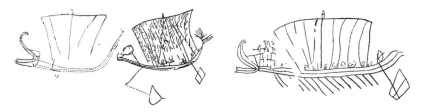

FIGURE 6.15　Graffito of ships in Jason's Tomb, from Rahmani 1967: 70–71. Credit: With permission of Hillel Geva and the Israel Exploration Society.

stern steers the ship with a heavy rudder. A pointed oval standard at the top of the mast contains a symbol resembling the Greek letter *lambda* or *alpha*. The sail of the merchant ship appears to be wind-blown. The mast head is topped with a palm-shaped standard, and below the stern is a rudder in the water. A triangular object attached by a line to the fore of the ship might be a dragnet, identifying it as a fishing vessel. The merchant ship's crew hold round shields. The left-hand galley is poorly preserved but has a battering ram on the prow like the other war galley.[180]

The significance of these graffiti—including who made them and why—is unknown. Based on ancient references to Jewish pirates, Rahmani speculated that the family who owned the tomb made their fortune through piracy at sea.[181] In contrast, Dan Barag connects the owners to the merchant ship, identifying this as a scene of the liberation of a family member(s) from a maritime attack.[182] Whatever the meaning of these graffiti, there is little doubt that Jason's Tomb belonged to a priestly family. This is indicated by the names Honio/Onias and Jason (which were common in priestly families in the second century BCE), the depiction of menorahs and possible showbread table (alluding to the temple), and the tomb's size and ostentation.[183] The loculi in Jason's Tomb, which are the earliest examples found so far in a Jewish tomb, the use of the Doric order, and the Greek inscription reflect Hellenistic influence on this priestly family.[184]

The finds from the tomb include a fragment of a hair net from the charnel room (B).[185] Hair nets typically were worn with Greek-style (Eastern) attire but not with Roman (Western) dress and seem to have been standard for Jewish women. Because they are made of organic material, hair nets are rarely preserved. Four hair nets were found at Masada in contexts dating to the time of the First Jewish Revolt against the Romans (66–73 CE). Two still had human hairs stuck in them which indicate that the nets matched the wearer's hair color: light-colored nets for fair-haired women and darker nets for dark-haired women. The nets were edged with a braided or woven ribbon sewn along one side of the opening and had a draw string on the other side that was knotted to the ends of the ribbon. The net was worn by placing the ribbon across the brow, pulling the ends of the draw string at the base of the nape, and then tying the draw string around the top of the head.[186] Whereas the Masada hair nets are made of wool—the common material used for clothing in Judea in the late Second Temple period—the hair net from Jason's Tomb is cotton, which would have been imported from India or the Bahrain region.[187]

The wealthy priestly owners of Jason's Tomb built it on the southern edge of a sprawling estate covering some 8,750 dunams (= 2,162 acres).[188] Situated on a ridge overlooking the road from Jerusalem to Gaza (the same route that originates today at the Jaffa Gate in the Old City), the tomb with its large pyramidal monument would have been visible to all passersby.[189] The estate may have included a settlement called "Jason's village" (Latin *Iasonis pagus*), which is mentioned in a medieval text as located west of Jerusalem.[190] Pottery vessels inscribed in Hebrew before firing with the name "Jason" or "son of Jason" have been found in a huge industrial site on the city's western edge.[191] The site, which was a pottery manufacturing center in the Hasmonean, Herodian, and Roman periods has different names after the modern properties on which excavations have been conducted: Givʿat Ram, the Crowne Plaza Hotel, and Binyanei Ha'uma (Jerusalem's convention center). The pottery manufacturing center seems to be part of the estate that belonged to the owners of Jason's Tomb, and the inhabitants of "Jason's village" might have worked as potters at the site. Not far away, also on the western side of the city, a rock-cut tomb of the first century CE contained an ossuary inscribed with the name Jason (Iasion) in Greek and Hebrew, and another inscribed in Greek, "Aristobulus son of Jason (Iasion)."[192] Excavations along Jaffa Road near the convention center brought to light a stone column of the first century CE, which is inscribed in Hebrew "Hananiah bar [son of] Daedalus from Yerushalayim [Jerusalem]" (Figure 6.16). Hananiah's father might have been named Daedalus (in which case he might have been a convert to Judaism), or perhaps Hananiah was a potter who adopted the name of the Greek mythological figure famed as a master architect and craftsman.[193]

Conclusion

Jerusalem's elevation from the tiny and impoverished center of a provincial backwater to capital of the Hasmonean kingdom had a significant impact, and, by 64 BCE, the city had reached its pre–586 BCE size and population. The fortification wall surrounding the southwestern hill (the First Wall) had been rebuilt, and another line of wall to the north (the Second Wall) may have been added by this time to the north. Under the Hasmoneans, the city was increasingly integrated into the Hellenistic world but also became visibly more "Jewish," with the appearance of *miqva'ot*, the use of paleo-Hebrew script on coins and seals, and the depiction of temple symbols combined with a dearth of imported amphoras and a trend toward aniconism. Although the Roman annexation in 63 BCE marked a sharp historical break by ending Jewish independence, from an archaeological perspective, Jerusalem's development by the Hasmoneans laid the groundwork for its continued growth under Herod the Great and his successors. By the time of the Roman destruction in 70 CE, the city was larger and more prosperous than ever before. Living in 64 BCE, the Jews of Jerusalem could

FIGURE 6.16 Column inscribed "Hananiah son of Daedalus from Jerusalem" in the Israel Museum Jerusalem.
Credit: Photo by the author.

not foresee that, twenty-four years later, Herod would be appointed client king of Judea on behalf of the Romans and that his building projects would transform the city. Nor could they imagine the lasting global impact of the birth of a Jewish child in Bethlehem—just 5 miles (8 kilometers) south of Jerusalem—some fifty-seven years later.

7

Herodian Jerusalem (March 70 CE)

Historical Background

Of all the catastrophes that affected Jerusalem throughout the ages, arguably none had a greater or more lasting impact than the fall of the city to the Romans at the end of the First Jewish Revolt in 70 CE, which resulted in the destruction of the second temple—a disaster reportedly foretold by Jesus: "As Jesus came out of the temple and was going away, his disciples came to point out to him the buildings of the temple. Then he asked them, 'You see all these, do you not? Truly I tell you, not one stone will be left here upon another; all will be thrown down'" (Mt 24:1–2). What no one could foresee was that this event eventually would lead to the "parting of the ways," as in the following centuries Jews continued to await the rebuilding of the Jerusalem temple while Christians accepted Jesus's sacrifice as the path to salvation instead.[1]

Jerusalem was at an apogee when the First Jewish Revolt against the Romans erupted in 66 CE. Never had the city been so large and populous, and never had it been filled with so many monuments, chief among them the second temple, which had been rebuilt by King Herod the Great. Estimates of Jerusalem's population at its height range from ca. 20,000 or fewer to 80,000–100,000, numbers that swelled when tens of thousands more Jews poured into the city for the three pilgrimage holidays to the temple: Sukkot (the Feast of Tabernacles), Passover, and Shavuot (the Feast of Weeks or Pentecost).[2] This is the city in which Jesus spent his final days on earth and where he was laid to rest after being crucified. But within four decades of Jesus's death, Jerusalem had been transformed. In March 70 CE, the city was crowded with refugees who had fled other parts of the country in advance of the Roman army. In-fighting among bands of rebel extremists worsened the already dire conditions. The following month, the Roman siege began, which ended a half a year later when the Romans destroyed the temple and took the southwestern hill—the last part of the city to fall.

Flavius Josephus

Much of our information about late Second Temple period Judea in general, and Jerusalem in particular, comes from the writings of Flavius Josephus.[3] Josephus was born Joseph son of Mattathias in Jerusalem in 37 CE, the same year Gaius Caligula became emperor. He was from a priestly family and claimed to be related to the Hasmoneans on his mother's side. When the First Revolt erupted in 66 CE and the Jews organized a provisional government, Josephus was put in charge of the district of Galilee. In 67 CE, he surrendered to the Romans at Jotapata (Yodefat), a fortified town in Galilee, and was taken captive by Vespasian. During Titus's siege of Jerusalem, Josephus walked around the walls on behalf of the Romans and tried unsuccessfully to convince the besieged to submit. After the fall of Jerusalem, Josephus settled in Rome. He was awarded Roman citizenship and became a client of the Flavians, whose family name he assumed: Titus Flavius Josephus. Josephus spent his time in Rome writing histories of the Jewish people and the First Revolt, until his death around 100 CE.

Josephus's first work is his seven-volume account of *The Jewish War*, which was completed in the late 70s–early 80s—that is, about a decade after the First Revolt ended. *War* was written as a cautionary tale for subject peoples living under Roman rule not to consider the possibility of revolt, as well as an apologetic intended to exonerate most of the Jews who participated in the revolt, especially the upper classes including Josephus himself. Around 93–94 CE, Josephus completed a 20-volume work called *Jewish Antiquities* (or *Antiquities of the Jews*; Greek *Archaeologia* [Archaeology]), in which he presented to a Greek and Roman audience the entire scope of Jewish history beginning with creation and ending on the eve of the First Revolt. The first ten volumes are based on the books of the Hebrew Bible, while the second ten volumes cover the rest of Jewish history up to the revolt. There is much overlap in the material covered by *War* and *Antiquities*, but with significant differences and even some contradictory information. Instead of warning subject peoples against rebellion, *Antiquities* seeks to elevate the Jews and Judaism in the eyes of the Greco-Roman world—a goal reflecting Josephus's own changed circumstances and perspective as a Diaspora Jew living in Rome. By recounting the history of Jews based on sacred scripture, Josephus sought to demonstrate the antiquity of the Jewish people and, by way of extension, the continued power of the God of Israel and the need to observe biblical law.

Josephus was an eyewitness to some of the events he describes—such as the siege of Jerusalem—and in other cases he drew on literary sources that have since been lost. His works are complex for various reasons, including (1) much of the information is drawn from lost or unknown sources, (2) the works were aimed at different audiences and therefore were intended to convey different messages, and (3) Josephus wrote with biases and apologetic tendencies aimed at exonerating his Roman patrons from responsibility for the outcome of the revolt and to justify and glorify his own behavior. As a result, scholars have become increasingly skeptical of Josephus's credibility and therefore less confident of our ability to reconstruct history based on his accounts.

Christians preserved Josephus's works because he was an important witness to events during and after Jesus's lifetime. Christian authors such as Eusebius, who was bishop of Caesarea in the early fourth century, used Josephus's writings to blame the Jews for Jesus's death, a crime for which (in their view) God had punished the Jews by allowing the destruction of the Jerusalem temple. One passage in *Antiquities* (18.63–64) even refers to Jesus, although scholars disagree about whether it was written by Josephus (and reworked later by Christians) or inserted by Christian copyists. Other passages that are believed to have been written by Josephus but later reworked refer to John the Baptist (*Ant.* 18.116–119) and James the brother of Jesus (*Ant.* 20.200). Josephus is the last ancient Jewish author to write about the history of the Jews whose works have survived. A vast corpus of Jewish literature was produced after 70 by the rabbis (sages), which contains their rulings on biblical law and other matters related to religious life. However, they were not interested in the writings of Jewish authors such as Josephus, as these have no relevance to the rabbinic approach to Torah interpretation through oral law. Moreover, the rabbis viewed the Jewish rebels as crazed fanatics who brought disaster on Israel. Jews would later reject Josephus in reaction to Christians who appropriated his works to express anti-Jewish sentiments.[4]

Herod the Great

The disastrous events of 70 CE were largely a result of decades of Roman maladministration, which exacerbated existing tensions among different sectors of the local population.[5] In 40 BCE, the Roman Senate appointed Herod client king of Judea—encompassing the Jewish and Judaized territories of Judea, Galilee, Idumaea, and Peraea. He spent the next three years fighting Mattathias Antigonus, a Hasmonean claimant to the throne. In 37 BCE, Herod and Sosius, the Roman governor of Syria took Jerusalem after a prolonged siege and executed Mattathias Antigonus. During the early years of his reign, Herod faced threats from members of the Hasmonean family who sought to reestablish their rule, and from Cleopatra VII, a descendant of the Ptolemies who was romantically involved with Herod's patron Mark Antony. Herod also faced widespread opposition among the Jewish population, who refused to accept him as a legitimate king because he was not a Hasmonean despite his marriage to a Hasmonean princess named Mariamme (or Mariamne), nor even Judean (he was an Idumaean Jew on his father's side of the family, while his mother was Nabataean [Arab]).

Mark Antony's involvement with Cleopatra led to growing tensions with his co-ruler Octavian, which culminated in 31 BCE in a naval battle at Actium off the coast of Greece. Mark Antony and Cleopatra were defeated and fled to Egypt, where they committed suicide. Mark Antony's death paved the way for Octavian to assume sole rule of Rome. In 27 BCE, the Roman Senate bestowed upon Octavian the title Augustus, an event that marks the transition from the Roman Republic to the Empire. Mark Antony and Cleopatra's defeat and subsequent deaths removed Cleopatra's threat to Herod's kingdom. However, because Mark Antony had been his patron, after the battle of Actium Herod met with Octavian to pledge his loyalty, asking him to consider not "whose friend, but how loyal a friend" he had been (*War* 1.390). Herod was so persuasive that not only did Octavian reconfirm him as king, but soon thereafter he increased the size of Herod's kingdom. Over time, Herod's kingdom was expanded to include much of the coast, Samaria, the Golan, and territories northeast of the Golan, until it was almost as large as the Hasmonean kingdom had been at its greatest extent.

Herod was a ruthless and paranoid ruler who executed anyone he perceived as a potential threat, including members of his immediate household: Hyrcanus II, Mariamme, her mother, her younger brother, two of her sons (by Herod), and another son by a different wife. Herod's reputation apparently led Augustus to quip in Greek, "It is better to be Herod's pig (*hus*) than his son (*huios*)."[6] If Augustus indeed said this, the pun on the words *hus* and *huios*, which sound similar, would reflect his fluency in Greek. It also suggests that Augustus either knew or assumed that Herod, like other Jews, abstained from eating pork, and, therefore, pigs were safe from slaughter whereas his own sons were not. Herod's reputation for executing his sons might have given rise to the story of the massacre (or slaughter) of the innocents as reported in Matthew 2:16: "When Herod saw that he had been tricked by the wise men, he was infuriated, and he sent and killed all the [male] children in and around Bethlehem who were two years old or under, according to the time that he had learned from the wise men."

Ironically, although this story is the reason for Herod's lasting infamy, it is an atrocity he probably did not commit. The episode is not mentioned in any sources aside from the Gospel of Matthew, where it is presented as part of Jesus's birth narrative. This means there is no independent confirmation that this event ever occurred. Furthermore, Herod's command echoes Pharaoh's order to have all first-born Hebrew males put to death (Exodus 1:22), thereby presenting Jesus as a new Moses. In fact, Matthew's account is filled with allusions to the Exodus, as Herod's edict is immediately preceded by the story of Joseph and Mary's flight to Egypt (Mt 2:13–15). For these reasons, many scholars believe that the massacre of the innocents never occurred, but instead was inspired by Herod's reputation for executing his own sons.[7]

Herod suffered from an agonizing disease in the final days of his life and died in his palace at Jericho in 4 BCE. His body was carried in a procession to Herodium, where he was laid to rest in a monumental tomb marked by a tholos (circular structure), which was discovered in 2007 by the Israeli archaeologist Ehud Netzer.[8]

The Division of Herod's Kingdom Among His Sons

Augustus confirmed Herod's will that the kingdom be divided among three of his sons, but gave them lesser titles than king:

1. *Herod Archelaus*, the elder son of Malthace the Samaritan, was made ethnarch of Judea, Samaria, and Idumaea (4 BCE–6 CE). He inherited the parts of his father's kingdom that were thoroughly Jewish/Judaized and Yahwistic/Samaritan. He had the shortest reign of Herod's three sons due to his inability to rule effectively. The Jews and Samaritans complained so bitterly about his cruelty that, in 6 CE, Augustus removed Archelaus and banished him to Gaul (France).

2. *Herod Philip*, the son of Cleopatra of Jerusalem, was made tetrarch of the northern territories of Trachonitis, Batanaea (biblical Bashan), Auranitis (biblical Hauran), Gaulanitis (Golan), Paneas (Banyas), and Ituraea (4 BCE–33/34 CE). Philip is the only one of Herod's three sons who ruled until his death. His territory—consisting of the Golan and areas farther to the north and east—was populated mostly by gentiles. Philip established a new capital for his territory by the springs of Paneas (Banyas), one of the sources of the Jordan River, naming the city Caesarea Philippi in honor of the emperor and himself. Philip died childless after a reign of thirty-seven years, although he was married to Herodias, the daughter of Herod's sister Salome (his first cousin). After Philip's death, his territory was placed under the direct administration of the legate in Syria.

3. *Herod Antipas*, Herod's youngest son and offspring of Malthace, was made tetrarch of Galilee and Peraea (4 BCE–39 CE). He had the longest reign of the three brothers, having inherited the Judaized territories of Galilee and Peraea. Antipas initially chose Sepphoris, a Jewish town in the heart of Lower Galilee, as his capital. He renamed the town *Autokratoris* (Latin *Imperatoria*) in honor of Augustus, and reportedly rebuilt it as a Greco-Roman city. Sepphoris figures prominently in debates about the historical Jesus, as the small hamlet of Nazareth was only 4 miles (6.5 kilometers) away. Around 20 CE, Antipas

moved his capital to a newly established city on the western shore of the Sea of Galilee, which he named Tiberias in honor of the emperor Tiberius (Augustus's successor).

Antipas's marriage to the daughter of the Nabataean king ended when he fell in love with Herodias, the wife of his brother Philip. Antipas and Herodias divorced their spouses and married each other, violating a biblical law that prohibits marriage to a brother's wife. Antipas is probably best-known for his execution of John the Baptist, which the Gospels attribute to his condemnation of his unlawful marriage to Herodias: "For Herod [Antipas] had arrested John, bound him, and put him in prison on account of Herodias, his brother Philip's wife, because John had been telling him, 'it is not lawful for you to have her' " (Mt 14:3; also see Mk 6:14–29; Lk 3:1–2). However, Josephus reports that Antipas executed John the Baptist because he feared that John's movement might lead to unrest: "Herod [Antipas] decided therefore that it would be much better to strike first and be rid of him before his work led to an uprising, than to wait for an upheaval, get involved in a difficult situation, and see his mistake."[9]

The Herod mentioned in these passages in the Gospels and Josephus is Antipas, not Herod the Great. According to these accounts, Antipas executed John the Baptist at Machaerus in Peraea, one of Herod the Great's fortified desert palaces (now in Jordan, east of the Dead Sea).

The Roman Governors and Later Successors of Herod

Eventually, the territories ruled by Herod's sons were placed under the administration of Roman governors, titled prefects or procurators, who administered Judea independently on behalf of the emperor but ultimately were subordinate to the legate in Syria. Because they did not have the authority to command a legion, the main military force in the region remained stationed in Antioch, where the legate was based. Only one cohort (approximately 500 soldiers) was stationed permanently in Jerusalem, in the Antonia fortress. Whereas Jerusalem had been the capital city and administrative base of Herod the Great and Archelaus, the Roman governors chose to reside at Caesarea Maritima, which had a harbor that facilitated communication with Rome and offered the amenities of a Greco-Roman city. Pontius Pilate (26–36 CE), who served as the fifth prefect, is notorious for having Jesus sentenced to death.[10]

Herod's kingdom was revived briefly under Herod Agrippa I (Marcus Julius Agrippa) (37–44 CE), the grandson of Herod and Mariamme (and the brother of Herodias, who divorced her husband Philip to marry Herod Antipas).[11] Agrippa I was fantastically popular with the Jewish population and is described by the rabbis in glowing terms, although he had been raised in Rome and was not an observant Jew. For example, most of his coins depict human images, including the Roman emperor, himself, and even pagan temples and deities. He had statues of his daughters set up at Caesarea and Samaria-Sebaste. In contrast, Christian tradition describes Agrippa I as a persecutor of the developing Church. He had James the son of Zebedee beheaded and Peter arrested, although the latter escaped from prison (Acts 12:1–3).[12]

After Agrippa I died suddenly in Caesarea at the age of fifty-four, the emperor Claudius decided not to appoint his oldest son, Herod Agrippa II—who was only sixteen or seventeen years old—to succeed him. Instead, Agrippa I's kingdom was made part of the Roman province of Syria and placed under the administration of procurators. Their inability to deal with the diverse populations and unstable conditions exacerbated the deteriorating situation, and they often overreacted to perceived threats by employing military force. One of the procurators, Tiberius Julius Alexander (46–48 CE), was the nephew of the Jewish philosopher Philo of Alexandria and apparently had renounced Judaism. Tiberius Julius Alexander advised Titus as second-in-command during the siege of Jerusalem in 70 CE. His younger brother, Marcus Julius Alexander, was married to Berenice III (aka Julia Berenice), the daughter of Agrippa I and sister of Agrippa II. After Marcus Julius Alexander's premature death in 44 CE, Berenice married twice more. Her second marriage was to her uncle, Herod of Chalcis, who died in 48 CE, and she abandoned her third husband. Later, Berenice became the mistress of Titus, who was eleven years her junior. Eventually, Titus had to send Berenice away due to the Roman public's disapproval of his involvement with an eastern Jewish princess.[13]

During the administration of the next procurator, Ventidius Cumanus (48–52 CE), local unrest increased, as reflected by an incident that occurred during Passover involving a Roman soldier posted on one of the porches overlooking the temple: "The usual crowd had assembled at Jerusalem for the feast of unleavened bread, and the Roman cohort had taken up its position on the roof of the portico of the temple. . . . Thereupon one of the soldiers, raising his robe, stooped in an indecent attitude, so as to turn his backside to the Jews, and made a noise in keeping with his posture."[14] The insult was even worse than it seems because Roman soldiers wore no undergarments under their tunics. Offended, the crowd of worshipers called on Cumanus to punish the soldier. When they began to throw stones, he called in reinforcements. Josephus reports that in the ensuing stampede, 20,000–30,000 Jews were killed. Although ancient crowd estimates are notoriously unreliable and often exaggerated, Josephus's account indicates that a large number of pilgrims lost their lives that day.

The next procurator, Marcus Antonius Felix (or Claudius Felix) (52–60 CE), was known in Roman circles for his three marriages, all to members of royal families. His first wife was the granddaughter of Mark Antony and Cleopatra. Felix's second wife was Drusilla, the daughter of Herod Agrippa I and sister of Herod Agrippa II and Berenice III. As a young teenager, Drusilla was married to the king of Emesa (in Syria). When Felix became procurator of Judea, she was about fourteen years old. Felix was so taken by Drusilla's great beauty that he persuaded the sixteen-year-old to divorce her husband and marry him (54 CE). Conditions grew increasingly anarchic during Felix's administration. Josephus reports that Jewish urban terrorists called *sicarii* assassinated their compatriots by concealing daggers (Latin *sica*) under their cloaks and mingling in crowds, then sneaking up on their targets and stabbing them: "But while the country was thus cleared of these pests, a new species of banditti was springing up in Jerusalem, the so-called *sicarii*, who committed murders in broad daylight in the heart of the city. The festivals were their special seasons, when they would mingle with the crowd, carrying short daggers concealed under their clothing, with which they stabbed their enemies. Then, when they fell, the murderers joined in the cries of indignation and, through this plausible behavior, were never discovered."[15]

Messianic and prophetic figures contributed to the unrest. One Egyptian Jew attracted thousands of followers, promising them that he would destroy the walls of Jerusalem with a command while standing on the Mount of Olives. Felix sent his troops against the crowds, killing or capturing hundreds, but the Egyptian Jew escaped. According to Acts 21:38, a Roman tribune confused Paul with this Egyptian: "Then you are not the Egyptian who recently stirred up a revolt and led the four thousand assassins out into the wilderness?" This episode occurred after Paul was arrested while on pilgrimage to the Jerusalem temple. Because he was a Roman citizen, Paul was escorted by five hundred soldiers to Caesarea Maritima, where it was up to the procurator to determine his fate. Felix held Paul in custody at Caesarea for nearly two years, during which time they reportedly spoke frequently: "Some days later when Felix came with his wife Drusilla, who was Jewish, he sent for Paul and heard him speak concerning faith in Christ Jesus" (Acts 24:24).

Herod Agrippa II (Marcus Julius Agrippa) was the son of Agrippa I and the brother of Drusilla and Berenice III. Considered by the Romans too young to inherit his father's throne, he was made king of Chalcis in Lebanon as well as some of the northern territories that had been part of his father's and great-grandfather's kingdoms. Agrippa II was also given oversight of the Jerusalem temple and the right to appoint the high priests. After her second husband died, Berenice moved into the palace at Caesarea Philippi with her bachelor brother, leading to rumors that the two had an incestuous relationship.

When they were in Jerusalem, Agrippa II and Berenice stayed in the old Hasmonean palace on the southwestern hill, which overlooked the Temple

Mount. Agrippa II added another floor to the palace with a dining room that provided a view of the activities in the temple, including the sacrifices. This aroused the ire of the priests and Sanhedrin, who responded by erecting a high wall around the temple precincts. Because the wall also blocked the view of the Roman soldiers standing guard on the temple porticoes, the Roman procurator Porcius Festus (60–62 CE) became involved in the dispute. Both sides appealed to the emperor Nero, who allowed the Jews to leave the wall up, a decision attributed to the influence of his mistress (and later wife) Poppaea, who Josephus describes as "God fearing" (i.e., a Jewish sympathizer).

When the First Revolt broke out in 66 CE, Agrippa II's attempts to keep the peace were rebuffed and he was forced to leave Jerusalem. He sided with the Romans, providing military assistance and accompanying Titus during the siege of Jerusalem in 70. Agrippa II died around 92 CE, unmarried and childless.

When Porcius Festus replaced Felix as procurator in 60 CE, he found Paul still in custody at Caesarea. Shortly after Festus's arrival, Agrippa II and his sister Berenice visited Caesarea to greet the newly installed procurator. Festus took the opportunity to consult with them about Paul's case: "So on the next day Agrippa and Bernice came with great pomp, and they entered the audience hall with the military tribunes and the prominent men of the city. Then Festus gave the order and Paul was brought in" (Acts 25:23). Although the Jews demanded to try Paul in Jerusalem, Paul invoked his right as a Roman citizen to be judged by the emperor. Therefore, Festus sent Paul to Rome, where he was probably executed a couple of years later.

Festus died in office in 62 CE, leaving an interval when there was no procurator in Judea. In the interim, the high priest Ananus (or Annas) took advantage of the opportunity to have James "the Just," the brother of Jesus and leader of Jesus's followers in Jerusalem brought before the Sanhedrin on a charge of violating biblical Jewish law. This was almost certainly a trumped-up charge, as James had a reputation as a Torah-observant Jew who had consecrated himself to God by taking Nazirite vows (see Numbers 6:1–21). James's arrest likely was due to his outspoken opposition to and condemnation of the ostentatious lifestyle of the Jerusalem elite, who included Ananus and other priests. The exact charge is unknown, but the fact that Ananus was found guilty and sentenced to death by stoning suggests he was accused of blasphemy. The possibility that James's arrest and execution were motivated by political factors rather than by a violation of Jewish law is indicated by the opposition of moderate Jews and the Pharisees. These groups complained to Agrippa II and the newly installed procurator (Albinus), who deposed and replaced Ananus.

Gessius Florus (64–66 CE) was the last procurator before the outbreak of the First Jewish Revolt. His most egregious act was taking money from the Jerusalem temple under the pretense that Nero wanted it. As these events unfolded, all-out war was sparked by a conflict between Jews and gentiles at Caesarea Maritima over access to a synagogue.

The First Jewish Revolt Against Rome (66–70 CE)

Outbreaks of violence quickly spread from Caesarea across the country. Agrippa II and Berenice tried unsuccessfully to restore peace. In Jerusalem, the traditional sacrifices offered in the temple on behalf of the Roman state and emperor were halted by Eleazar son of Ananias, a young high priest who was captain of the temple. Jewish insurgents took the Upper City (southwestern hill) and burned down the house of the high priest, Agrippa II's palace (the Hasmonean palace), and the public archives office, which was targeted because it housed tax and loan records. When the rebels captured the Antonia fortress and slaughtered its garrison, Agrippa's troops and supporters took refuge in Herod's palace. They left after capitulating, but the Roman cohort, which was holed up in the three towers adjacent to Herod's palace, was massacred by the insurgents, who reneged on a promise of safe conduct after offering terms of surrender. The rebels also murdered the high priest, who had been hiding in the palace.

To put down the unrest, Cestius Gallus, the Syrian legate, marched south from Antioch at the head of approximately 30,000 soldiers. Upon arrival in Jerusalem, he set up camp on Scopus (the area north of the city) and began his assault by burning the northern suburb of Bezetha, but his troops were repelled when they attacked the Temple Mount. For reasons that are unclear, Cestius then ordered his army to retreat to the coast. Pursued by the Jews and unable to regroup, the Roman soldiers were ambushed in the mountain pass at Beth-Horon. Cestius made it back to Antioch with his life and only a fraction of his army, having lost 6,000 soldiers (more than a legion) and much of his equipment and animals. The Jewish rebels plundered the corpses, collected the abandoned military equipment, and returned victorious to Jerusalem.

With Cestius's humiliating defeat, all-out war became inevitable. Strongly pro-Roman Jews fled Jerusalem, and moderate pro-Romans now had to cast their lot with the anti-Roman rebels. Because the country was no longer under Roman rule, the Jews set up a government with moderates and high priests in control, though by the end of the revolt, extremists had taken over. The country was divided into seven districts under the administration of military governors: Jerusalem, Idumaea, Peraea, Jericho, Western Judea, Northeast Judea, and Galilee (including Gamla [or Gamala] in the Golan). Josephus was put in charge of Galilee. He was opposed by John son of Levi of Gischala (Gush Halav) in Upper Galilee, who was the leader of a powerful rebel band. Another band of extremists led by Simon bar Giora of Gerasa was active in other parts of the country. Both John and Simon played prominent roles in the siege and fall of Jerusalem in 70.

When the emperor Nero heard of Cestius's defeat, he dispatched his general Vespasian to Syria to restore order. After assembling his forces in Antioch in the spring of 67, Vespasian moved into Galilee, taking Josephus into captivity at Jotapata. By November 67, when the rainy season had set in, the entire northern part of the country had been subdued by the Romans. Vespasian settled his troops in winter quarters at Caesarea Maritima and Scythopolis (Beth Shean in the Jordan Valley), planning to resume his campaign in the spring. By now, Jerusalem was swollen with refugees who had poured into the city in the wake of the Roman subjugation of Galilee. Among them were extremists such as John of Gischala and his followers, creating additional factions that began fighting with each other. The extremists soon took over, eliminating rival leaders, moderates, and anyone suspected of pro-Roman sympathies. According to the fourth-century writer Eusebius, by this time the early Christian community of Jerusalem had abandoned the city for Pella in Peraea.

As the rainy season ended (spring 68), Vespasian renewed his campaign, intending to isolate Jerusalem by subduing the rest of the country first. However, Nero's suicide in Rome delayed his plans, as Vespasian awaited orders from the next emperor to proceed. The delay was extended when the situation in Rome deteriorated, after a civil war erupted with a rapid succession of claimants to the throne ("the year of the four emperors"). While awaiting word from Rome, Vespasian subdued the rest of Judea and Idumaea aside from Jerusalem. By the late spring of 69 CE, the only remaining holdouts were Herod's fortified palaces at Herodium, Machaerus, and Masada, which were in the hands of Jewish rebels. By this time Simon bar Giora and his followers were camped outside the walls of Jerusalem, killing anyone they caught leaving the city. The situation inside the city was equally dire, with various rebel factions including John of Gischala's followers terrorizing the population.

Eventually the people of Jerusalem admitted Simon into the city, hoping he could rid them of John—a solution that only worsened the situation by escalating the sectarian violence. As a result, the city was divided among three extremist factions: John of Gischala's band held the outer court of the temple and part of the southeastern hill; a faction led by Eleazar ben Simon occupied the inner court of the temple; and Simon bar Giora's band, which was the largest and most powerful (and included about 5,000 Idumaeans [*War* 5.249]), controlled the southwestern hill and part of the southeastern hill. The Roman historian Tacitus describes as follows the conditions in Jerusalem: "There were three generals, three armies: the outermost and largest circuit of the wall was held by Simon, the middle of the city by John, and the temple was guarded by Eleazar. John and Simon were strong in numbers and equipment, Eleazar had the advantage of position: between these three there was constant fighting, treachery, and arson, and a great store of grain was consumed."[16]

The situation in Rome eventually stabilized when Vespasian was proclaimed emperor and assumed the throne. In the summer of 70 CE, he departed for Rome, leaving his older son Titus to oversee the siege of Jerusalem. As Tacitus indicates, during the ongoing violence in Jerusalem much of the grain stores—a critical food supply for the upcoming siege—was consumed by fire as buildings around the city went up in flames. Similarly, Josephus relates: "At all events the result was that all the environs of the temple were reduced to ashes, the city was converted into a desolate no man's land for their domestic warfare, and almost all the corn, which might have sufficed them for many years of siege, was burnt up."[17] Centuries later, the Babylonian Talmud recalled the famine caused by the senseless destruction of Jerusalem's grain supply: "The *biryoni* [Zealots] were then in the city. The Rabbis said to them: Let us go out and make peace with them [the Romans]. They would not let them, but on the contrary said, Let us go out and fight them. The Rabbis said: You will not succeed. They then rose up and burnt the stores of wheat and barley so that a famine ensued" (b. Gittin 56a).[18]

After assembling his forces at Caesarea, Titus reached Jerusalem and set up camp on Mount Scopus just before Passover (April–May) 70 CE—that is, at the time of the spring harvest season. He commanded four legions and a large number of auxiliary units. Tiberias Julius Alexander, who was intimately familiar with Jerusalem, accompanied Titus as his chief advisor. Even now, the in-fighting within the city continued. When Eleazar opened the gates to the inner court of the temple for the Passover celebration, John's band launched a surprise attack and took over, reducing to two the number of factions in the city: his and Simon's. However, once the Roman assault began, the factions united. Titus launched his offensive against the north side of the city, which, although enclosed by three successive walls, lacks the natural protection of a deep valley like the other sides. The outermost (Third) wall, which enclosed a large but relatively unbuilt-up area (the suburb of Bezetha) was breached after fifteen days of being assaulted with battering rams. The Romans breached the Second Wall after five days but were repelled by the defenders and took it only after another four days of fighting. Each of the four legions now began raising earth ramps for battering rams against the First Wall, which was defended by Simon bar Giora, and the Antonia fortress, which was defended by John of Gischala.

While the Roman troops were busy erecting the siege works, Titus dispatched Josephus in an unsuccessful attempt to persuade the defenders to surrender—as Josephus describes here, referring to himself in the third person: "Josephus, accordingly, went round the wall, and, endeavoring to keep out of range of missiles and yet within ear-shot, repeatedly implored them to spare themselves and the people, to spare their country and their temple. . . . Josephus, during this exhortation, was derided by many from the ramparts, by many execrated, and by some assailed with missiles."[19]

With food supplies dwindling inside the city, famine spread, and the inhabitants fought each other for every scrap. Those unfortunates caught trying to flee the city were tortured and put to death by John and Simon, or by the Romans. Josephus vividly describes how the Romans tried to intimidate the Jews into submission by returning prisoners to the city with their hands cut off and by crucifixion near the walls: "They were accordingly scourged and subjected to torture of every description, before being killed, and then crucified opposite the walls. . . . The soldiers, out of rage and hatred amused themselves by nailing their prisoners in different postures; and so great was their number, that space could not be found for the crosses nor crosses for the bodies."[20] When Syrian auxiliaries found a refugee picking gold coins he had swallowed for safekeeping out of his feces, the soldiers began cutting open other deserters in the hopes of finding more hidden treasure.

After seventeen days, the legions finished piling massive earthen ramps against the First Wall. The defenders destroyed these by tunneling underneath, buttressing the tunnels with timbers smeared with pitch and bitumen which they set on fire, causing the mounds of earth to collapse. Titus commanded his men to construct a siege wall encircling the city to ensure that none of the besieged could escape and that no supplies or assistance could reach them. The wall—completed in only three days—worsened the famine within the city, as Josephus describes: "For the Jews, along with all egress, every hope of escape was now cut off; and the famine, enlarging its maw, devoured the people by households and families. The roofs were thronged with women and babes completely exhausted, the alleys with the corpses of the aged; children and youths, with swollen figures, roamed like phantoms through the market-places and collapsed wherever their doom took them."[21] As the famine became more severe, Josephus reports that a starving mother slaughtered and cannibalized her infant son.[22]

After another three weeks, the Romans re-erected the ramps against the Antonia, which they took and razed to the ground after fierce fighting. Incredibly, despite the famine, fighting, and atrocities, the daily sacrifices in the temple had continued until now. But Josephus reports that on the day the Antonia was razed, the sacrifices ceased, probably because there were no more lambs. Later, the rabbis lamented this disastrous day, saying, "Five things befell our fathers on the 17th of Tammuz . . . the Daily Whole-offering (Hebrew *tamid*) ceased" (m. Taanith 4.6).[23]

Josephus, who had been continuing his rounds outside the walls, again attempted to persuade the defenders to surrender but was rebuffed. Once the

Antonia was razed, Titus instructed his troops to construct a ramp by the temenos wall of the Temple Mount. After the wall was breached, fighting spread onto the roofs of the porches on the Temple Mount, which were set ablaze. The Romans raised another ramp against the fortification wall surrounding the temple (inside the Temple Mount), which they breached by setting fire to its gates. Although, according to Josephus, the temple burned down when a rogue Roman soldier flung a burning timber into it, he blames the temple's destruction on the Jewish defenders for having taken refuge inside the building. In fact, Josephus repeatedly attempts to exonerate Titus, claiming that he would never have ordered the temple's destruction, which was done against his wishes.

It is true, as Josephus says, that "the Romans would never venture, except under the direst necessity, to set fire to the holy places."[24] However, Josephus's account of Titus's reluctance to destroy the Jerusalem temple is contradicted by Sulpicius Severus's reference to the same event: "On the other hand, others, and Titus himself, expressed their opinion that the Temple should be destroyed without delay, in order that the religion of the Jews and Christians should be more completely exterminated."[25] Sulpicius Severus was a late fourth–early fifth century CE Christian writer from Gaul (France), which means he was far removed in time and space from the destruction of the Jerusalem temple. His account is relevant to our discussion because a mid-nineteenth-century scholar named Jacob Bernays suggested that Sulpicius's description of the temple's destruction derives not from Josephus but from a lost section of Tacitus's *Histories*. Since then, most scholars have preferred Sulpicius's version that Titus ordered the temple destroyed on the assumption that Tacitus would be a less biased source than Josephus, whose apologetic tendencies are well-known. On the other hand, it is possible that Sulpicius's version is based on Josephus's account, not a lost passage from Tacitus, and was rewritten to show that God destroyed the temple to punish the Jews.[26] Whether or not Titus ordered the temple's destruction, this disagreement is a reminder that Josephus and other ancient sources are not always accurate or reliable and therefore must be read critically.

As the temple burned, Titus and his commanders rushed into the building and looted its treasures, including the menorah (seven-branched candelabrum) and the showbread table, which were taken to Rome. Other sacred objects from the temple were turned over to Titus by priests who had held them in safekeeping and were captured or surrendered. With the temple still in flames, the Roman troops set up their standards in the temple court and sacrificed to them, hailing Titus as *imperator* (commander)—a title usually reserved for the emperor.

The desecration of the Jerusalem temple by pagan sacrifices might be the desolating sacrilege mentioned in the Gospel accounts as a fulfillment of Jesus's prophecy that the temple would be destroyed, echoing earlier predictions of the end of days in the book of Daniel. The book of Daniel is believed to have been written ca. 167–164 BCE, that is, at the time of the Maccabean revolt. It refers to the tumultuous events that occurred in Judea when Antiochus IV Epiphanes outlawed Judaism and rededicated the Jerusalem temple to the Greek god Olympian Zeus. Daniel 9:24–27 contains the prophecy of seventy weeks, in which Daniel ponders the meaning of Jeremiah's prediction (25:11–12 and 29:10) that Jerusalem would remain desolate for seventy years. Daniel is told by the angel Gabriel about various things that would take place within a period of seventy weeks of years (each week = one year), including the setting up of an abomination of desolation or desolating sacrilege (Hebrew *shikutz meshomem*) in the temple. "Abomination" is the Hebrew term for an idol.

> After the sixty-two weeks, an anointed one [the Jewish high priest Onias III] shall be cut off and shall have nothing, and the troops of the prince [Antiochus IV] who is to come shall destroy the city and the sanctuary. Desolations are decreed. He [Antiochus IV] shall make a strong covenant with many [Hellenizing Jews] for one week, and for half of the week he shall make sacrifice and offering cease; and in their place shall be an *abomination that desolates*, until the decreed end is poured out upon the desolator. (Daniel 9:26–27; also see 11:31–32)

> From the time that the regular burnt offering is taken away and the *abomination that desolates* is set up, there shall be one thousand two hundred ninety days. (Daniel 12:11)

The desolating sacrilege is also mentioned in 1 Maccabees:

> Now on the fifteenth day of Kislev, in the one hundred forty-fifth year; they erected a *desolating sacrilege* on the altar of burnt offering. . . . On the twenty-fifth day of the month they offered sacrifice on the altar that was on top of the altar of burnt offering. (1 Macc. 1:54, 59; also see 6:7)

The desolating sacrilege of Daniel and 1 Maccabees seems to refer to an altar to Zeus erected by Antiochus IV in the Jerusalem temple.

According to the Gospel accounts, Jesus foretold the destruction of the Temple and described signs of the end of days.

> So when you see the *desolating sacrilege* standing in the holy place, as was spoken of by the prophet Daniel (let the reader understand), then those in Judea must flee to the mountains. (Mt 24:15–16)

But when you see the *desolating sacrilege* set up where it ought not to be (let the reader understand), then those in Judea must flee to the mountains. (Mk 13:14: NRSV; also see Lk 21:20–21)

Jesus's statement implies that the prophecy of the desolating sacrilege in Daniel 9:27 is about to be fulfilled.

What is the desolating sacrilege of the Gospel accounts? The answer depends partly on whether they were composed before or after 70 CE. Notice the difference between Mark and Matthew.

But when you see the desolating sacrilege set up where it ought not to be. (Mark)

So when you see the desolating sacrilege standing in the holy place. (Matthew)

Mark is generally thought to be the earliest Gospel, written around the time of the First Revolt or soon thereafter, while Matthew is usually dated ca. 80–90 CE. Therefore, the authors of these Gospels did not necessarily understand the desolating sacrilege to be the same thing. Depending on the date of composition, the author of the Gospel of Mark might have thought the desolating sacrilege was a statue that the Romans would set up in the temple (in the future), as the emperor Caligula had intended to do in 39–40 CE. The author of the Gospel of Matthew might have understood the desolating sacrilege as the Roman standards set up in the temple in 70 CE, to which Titus's troops offered sacrifices.

Josephus says that the second temple was destroyed on the tenth day of the month of Av (29 August)—the same day that the first temple was destroyed according to Jeremiah 52:12–13 (2 Kgs 25:8–10 places the destruction of the first temple on the seventh day of Av). Apparently, however, the second temple was destroyed a day earlier, on the ninth of Av. Like Josephus, the rabbis harmonized the chronology of these two disasters by assigning both destructions to the same day. But whereas Josephus adopted the day when the first temple was destroyed (the tenth of Av), rabbinic tradition follows the day of the destruction of the second temple (the ninth of Av).[27]

The destruction of the temple did not mark the end of the siege of Jerusalem, which continued for another month. While the temple was ablaze, the Romans set fire to the Ophel and the southeastern hill (Lower City) because the Jewish defenders had fled to the southwestern hill (Upper City). Titus instructed his troops to erect ramps against the First Wall at the northwest and northeast corners of the Upper City—a difficult task due to the shortage of wood around

Jerusalem, which had been stripped bare of trees during the siege. After eighteen days the Romans completed the siege works and breached the wall but met with little resistance from the starved and exhausted defenders, many of whom were caught fleeing through underground sewers. One such sewer was excavated recently beneath a paved street along the Tyropoeon Valley, which connected the Pool of Siloam at the southern tip of the southeastern hill with the Temple Mount. John of Gischala was among those who took refuge in the sewers but surrendered after emerging due to starvation. Simon bar Giora was captured later, after surfacing from a tunnel beneath the temple.

Josephus reports that, as the Romans overran the Upper City, they massacred the inhabitants, and ransacked and burned down the houses: "Pouring into the alleys, sword in hand, they massacred indiscriminately all whom they met, and burnt the houses with all who had taken refuge within."[28] On Titus's orders, the Roman soldiers rounded up all the survivors, executing the very young, the elderly, the infirm, and anyone who resisted or was a known insurgent. Seven hundred of the tallest and handsomest youths were selected to be paraded in the triumph at Rome, while able-bodied men were shipped off to Egypt for hard labor in mines or were saved for use in gladiator and animal fights. Women and children under the age of seventeen were sold into slavery. One young woman was sold in Puteoli, Italy, to a freedman of the emperor, who freed and married her and buried her when she died, as her tombstone records: "Claudia Aster [Esther], a captive from Jerusalem. Tiberius Claudius Masculus, a freedman of the emperor, took care of the grave... she lived twenty-five years."[29] As Benjamin Isaac notes, most of the survivors of the siege of Jerusalem were less fortunate than Claudia Aster, and their fates are unknown.[30] According to Josephus, "The total number of prisoners taken throughout the entire war amounted to ninety-seven thousand, and of those who perished during the siege, from first to last, one million one hundred thousand."[31] Although these numbers are unreliable and surely inflated, they give an impression of the scale of the loss of life. It is at this point—the end of the siege of Jerusalem—that Josephus concluded Book 6, the penultimate book of *The Jewish War*.

Archaeological Evidence

Archaeologists conventionally designate the time beginning with the reign of Herod the Great and ending with the fall of Jerusalem in 70 CE as the Herodian period. Although ancient authors never called Herod "the Great," and on his own coins Herod titled himself "king" but not "the Great," modern scholars use this term to distinguish him from other family members named Herod.[32] Herod's building program transformed Jerusalem's appearance and left a lasting imprint

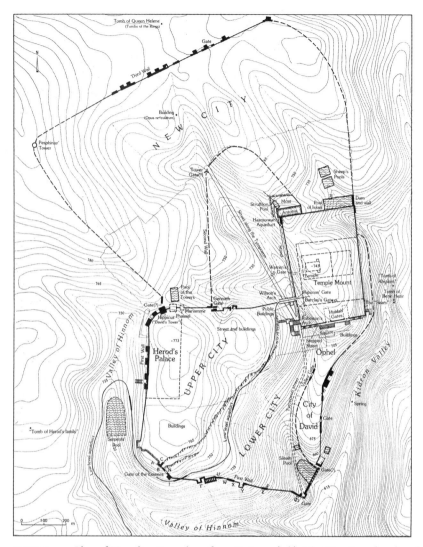

FIGURE 7.1 Plan of Herodian Jerusalem, from E. Stern (ed.), *The New Encyclopedia of Archaeological Excavations in the Holy Land*, New York: Simon and Schuster, 1993, vol. 2, p. 718.
Credit: With permission of Carta.

that is still visible today. During the Herodian period, the area enclosed within the walls reached the greatest extent in the city's history (Figure 7.1). Many of the monuments were built or begun during Herod's reign, although construction work continued for decades afterward.[33] Chief among these projects was Herod's reconstruction and expansion of the second temple, which further elevated Jerusalem's status as a temple city.[34]

The Temple

Herod's greatest monument in Jerusalem, and arguably anywhere, was the second temple. He also dedicated temples to Augustus and Rome at Caesarea Maritima and Samaria-Sebaste—demonstrating his loyalty to the emperor—and rebuilt the Pythian temple on Rhodes.[35] Herod's motives for rebuilding the Jerusalem temple included a desire to win the support of the Jewish population. Josephus says that Herod claimed to rule by the will of God, a statement which suggests that Herod, who ruled a revived kingdom of David and Solomon, rebuilt the Jerusalem temple to connect himself to Solomon and demonstrate that he enjoyed God's favor. Through these actions Herod may have intended to present himself as fulfilling biblical prophecy as the Davidic messiah, according to God's will.[36] Herod's reconstruction of the Jerusalem temple and his dedication of pagan temples in non-Jewish territories suggest he shared the Roman worldview that all gods demanded respect and piety.[37] Indeed, Hellenistic and Roman rulers were expected to demonstrate their piety through benefactions to temples. Herod's reconstruction of the Jerusalem temple also stimulated the local economy by employing laborers and generated revenue by increasing the number of pilgrims and visitors.[38]

Josephus's works and the Mishnah (especially the tractates Middoth and Tamid) contain detailed descriptions of the second temple and the Temple Mount after Herod's reconstruction.[39] However, there are numerous contradictions between these sources as well as internally within each one, including differences in the construction dates and dimensions of the Temple Mount and the number of gates in and around it.[40] These discrepancies apparently are the result of the information deriving from sources that date to different periods. For example, although *Antiquities* was written a couple of decades after *War*, it contains a description of the temple in an earlier period—shortly after Herod's construction of the building—whereas *War* depicts the temple as it appeared at the time of Titus's siege of Jerusalem in 70 CE. The Mishnah (edited ca. 200 CE) incorporates information about the temple extending as far back as the Hasmonean period, although much of it seems to derive from the period shortly before 70 CE.[41]

Translations of Josephus's works and the New Testament do not always distinguish between the temple and the Temple Mount—that is, the temple building and the esplanade on which it stood. For example, many New Testament editions describe Jesus's overturning of the tables of the money changers as having occurred "in the temple": "And he entered the temple (*hieron*) and began to drive out those who were selling and those who were buying in the temple, and he overturned the tables of the moneychangers and the seats of those who sold doves; and he would not allow anyone to carry anything through the temple" (Mk 11:15–16). This episode is described as taking place in the *hieron*, which derives from the Greek word for sacred, holy, or divine. In the New Testament and Josephus, *hieron* denotes one of the courts surrounding the temple on the Temple Mount or even the entire Temple Mount, whereas the Greek word *naos* refers to the temple building.[42] This means that the tables of the moneychangers were not located inside the temple building but in the area outside it, a matter to which we shall return.

We begin, however, with the temple building (henceforth "the temple," in distinction from the Temple Mount). As there are no archaeological remains of the temple, all our information about its appearance comes from literary sources such as Josephus and the Mishnah.[43] In addition, coins minted at the time of the Bar-Kokhba Revolt (the Second Jewish Revolt against the Romans; 132–135 CE) and a wall painting in the mid-third-century CE synagogue at Dura Europos in Syria depict the façade of the temple and show that it had a flat roof. Built of Jerusalem limestone resembling white marble, parts of the building's exterior including the entire east façade were plated with gold that gleamed in the sun (Figure 7.2).[44]

FIGURE 7.2 The second temple in the Holyland Model.
Credit: With permission of Matanyah Hecht; all winnings are from Holyland Tourism [1992] Ltd.

Like Solomon's temple and the pre-Herodian second temple, Herod's rebuilt temple was a rectangular building probably oriented to the east and was divided into three successive rooms: the *'ulam* (porch or vestibule), *heikhal* (sanctuary), and *debir* (the innermost room or holy of holies). The *'ulam* was wider than the rest of the building, measuring 100 cubits (about 61 meters [200 feet]) in height and width, while the rear (west) end of the building was 30 cubits narrower, creating a T-shaped plan.[45] A huge open portal 70 cubits high approached by twelve steps provided access into the *'ulam*, which was only eleven cubits deep.[46] Two columns flanked the doorway from the *'ulam* to the *heikhal*, which had a gold-plated double door covered by a veil, and a vine with large clusters of grapes made of gold hanging over it.[47] The sacred furniture (plated or inlaid with gold) in the *heikhal* included an incense altar flanked by the showbread table and a menorah (seven-branched lampstand). The *debir* was separated from the *heikhal* by two curtains and had an elevated floor approached by twelve steps. Inside, the *debir* was empty as the ark with the stone tablets of the law from Solomon's temple disappeared after 586 BCE.[48] A second-story level above the *heikhal* and *debir* contained the Upper Chamber (*'aliyah*), which was accessed by a staircase on the north side. There were three stories of small storage rooms around the north, west, and south sides, occupying the space between the walls of the *heikhal* and *debir* and the outer walls of the building. Altogether the temple was 100 cubits or about 61 meters [200 feet] high.[49]

Although literary sources provide much information about the temple, many elements remain unclear. For example, most—but not all—scholars agree that the temple was oriented to the east (as assumed here), and there is no consensus about its location on the Temple Mount. According to the Mishnah, a rock called the Foundation Stone protruded above the floor in the *debir*: "After the Ark [of the Covenant] was taken away [in 586 BCE], a stone remained there from the time of the early Prophets, and it was called 'Shetiyah' [Foundation]. It was higher than the ground by three fingerbreadths" (m. Yoma 5:2).[50] Many scholars assume that the Foundation Stone is the same rocky outcrop enshrined within the Dome of the Rock today, in which case this would be the location of the Holy of Holies in the second temple.[51] Others identify the rocky outcrop in the Dome of the Rock as the site of the altar in front of the temple.[52] Some scholars divorce the temple from the rocky outcrop altogether and place it elsewhere on the Temple Mount. For example, Joseph Patrich argues that the top of the rocky outcrop in the Dome of the Rock was lower than the floor level inside the *debir* and therefore was not part of the temple. He locates the temple to the east of the Dome of the Rock, orienting it southeast–northwest alongside Cistern 5 (see Chapter 6).[53]

The temple stood on a raised platform surrounded by a series of open courts (Pl. 7). The innermost (or inner) court, inside which the temple stood, was subdivided into smaller courts or spaces. Immediately in front of the temple was the Court of the Priests, with the sacrificial altar, laver (for priestly ablutions), and the area for slaughtering animals. Along the east side of the Court of the Priests was the Court of the Israelites, a narrow space where Jewish men and women could watch in silence as the sacrifices were offered.[54] The inner court was surrounded by a high wall with several gates.[55] Porches along the north and south sides of the court gave access to the gates and to chambers used for the preparation of the sacrifices and the meetings of the high court or Sanhedrin (the Chamber of Hewn Stone).[56]

In front (to the east) of the inner court was the Women's Court, a square, open courtyard with four corner chambers used by Nazarites, lepers, and for the storage of wood and oil. Despite its name, Jewish men, women, and children congregated in the Women's Court for nonsacrificial ceremonies and rituals. Fifteen semicircular steps ascended from the Women's Court to Nicanor's Gate, which provided access to the Court of the Israelites. The Levites sang and played musical instruments while standing on these steps.[57] Nicanor's Gate is so-called because the Corinthian brass doors were donated to the temple by a wealthy Alexandrian Jew named Nicanor, whose family tomb was discovered on Mount Scopus (see below).[58] Unlike the other temple gates, Nicanor's was left ungilded to commemorate a miracle that reportedly occurred while the gate was being transported by sea from Alexandria. According to the story, to lighten the load during a storm, the sailors threw one of the gates overboard but were unable to jettison the second gate because Nicanor held onto it. The storm ceased immediately, and when the ship reached the port at Akko (Acre), the first gate surfaced from beneath it.[59]

The temple and its courts stood on an elevated platform surrounded by a wall with towers (the `azarah).[60] The main entrance through the wall was by way of a gate on the east side—perhaps the "Beautiful Gate" mentioned in Acts 3:2: "One day Peter and John were going up to the temple (hieron) at the hour of prayer, at three o'clock in the afternoon. And a man lame from birth was being carried in. People would lay him daily at the gate of the temple (hieron) called the Beautiful Gate so that he could ask for alms from those entering the temple (hieron)" (also see Acts 3:10).[61] This gate—on the east side of the Women's Court—was larger than the others and was capped by a tower connected to an underground passage to the Antonia fortress, providing Herod with a secret escape route from the Temple Mount.[62] The elevated platform projected ten cubits from the `azarah, creating a terrace called the hel (pronounced kheyl), which was surrounded by steps descending to the level of the Temple Mount esplanade.[63]

FIGURE 7.3 The author seated next to the *soreg* inscription in the Istanbul Archaeological Museum.
Credit: Photo by Jim Haberman.

Encircling the base of the elevated platform was a stone barrier or balustrade called the *soreg* in m. Middoth 2:3, which marked the sacred area into which only ritually pure Jewish women and men could enter.[64] This space might correspond with the pre-Herodian, 500 ×500-cubit-square Temple Mount.[65] Greek and Latin inscriptions set into the balustrade warned gentiles from entering within on pain of death. Two of the Greek inscriptions were discovered to the north of the Temple Mount. The more complete inscription was found in 1871 and was published by Charles Clermont-Ganneau.[66] It subsequently disappeared and later resurfaced in Istanbul, where it is now displayed in the Archaeological Museum (Figure 7.3). The second, fragmentary inscription was discovered in 1935 and was published by the British archaeologist John Iliffe. It is on display in the Israel Museum in Jerusalem.

The complete inscription reads: "No foreigner is to enter within the balustrade and forecourt around the sacred precinct (*hieron*). Whoever is caught will himself be responsible for his consequent death."[67] Notice that the agent of death is not mentioned—only that trespassers will die. Josephus provides a remarkably similar description of the *soreg* inscriptions: "Within it [the first court] and no far distant was a second one, accessible by a few steps and surrounded by a stone balustrade with an inscription prohibiting the entrance of a foreigner under threat of the penalty of death" (*Ant.* 15:417; also see m. Kelim 1:8).[68] Many ancient temples had similar restrictions on entry to the most sacred areas—a custom that is still observed in some parts of the world today.[69]

Paul was arrested and taken into protective custody after the Jews charged him with taking a gentile into the temple—apparently the area marked off by the *soreg*.

> Then Paul took the men, and the next day, having purified himself, he entered the temple (*hieron*) with them, making public the completion of the days of purification when the sacrifice would be made for each of them. When the seven days were almost completed, the Jews from Asia, who had seen him in the temple (*hieron*), stirred up the whole crowd. They seized him, shouting, "Fellow Israelites, help! This is the man who is teaching everyone everywhere against our people, our law, and this place; more than that, he has actually brought Greeks into the temple and has defiled this holy place." For they had previously seen Trophimus the Ephesian with him in the city, and they supposed that Paul had brought him into the temple (*hieron*). Then all the city was aroused, and people rushed together. They seized Paul and dragged him out of the temple, and immediately the doors were shut. While they were trying to kill him, word came to the tribune of the cohort that all of Jerusalem was in an uproar. (Acts 21:26–31)

This passage indicates that Paul observed the biblical requirement to purify himself before entering the temple. Paul was not recognized by the Judeans (who did not know him), but by Jews from the Roman province of Asia (= Asia Minor) because he was from Tarsus. They also recognized the gentile with the Greek name Trophimus, who was from Ephesus (also in Asia Minor). The Romans took Paul into protective custody, fearing that the Jewish mob was about to lynch him. Paul was imprisoned at Caesarea Maritima for a couple of years before being shipped off to Rome for trial.

The Temple Mount

The temple and the area enclosed within the *soreg* stood in the midst of an enormous, open-air, paved esplanade—the Temple Mount (Figure 7.4). In contrast to the temple, which does not survive, the current Temple Mount is a product of Herod's reconstruction. In addition, whereas for the temple we are dependent on literary sources, archaeological explorations have provided a great deal of information about the rest of the Temple Mount. According to Josephus (*Ant.* 1.401), Herod doubled the size of the Temple Mount by extending it to the north, west, and south, while the steep slope of the Kidron Valley prevented expansion to the east. The extension

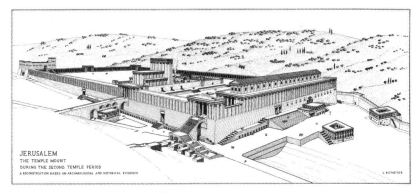

FIGURE 7.4 Reconstruction of the Herodian Temple Mount.
Credit: © Leen Ritmeyer.

to the south is clearly visible 32 meters (104 feet) north of the southeast corner of the Temple Mount, where Herodian style masonry abuts an earlier section of wall on the south side of a vertical seam or straight joint (see Chapter 6). The expanded trapezoidal esplanade measures 485 meters (1,620 feet) on the west, 315 meters (1,050 feet) on the north, 470 meters (1,550 feet) on the east, and 280 meters (930 feet) on the south, for a total area of ca. 144,000 square meters (1,550,000 square feet).[70] Herod surrounded the Temple Mount with retaining walls that supported the esplanade to create a temenos, a Greek word referring to a sacred space that is cut off or separated from the profane. The temenos walls are founded on bedrock and are constructed of huge Herodian ashlars—rectangular stones with drafted margins and paneled bosses (meaning the four edges [margins] are trimmed and the central part [the boss] is raised but flat).[71] Portions of the temenos walls survive on all four sides of the Temple Mount. The upper parts have been repaired and rebuilt over time, although not to their original height. At the south end of the Temple Mount, where the bedrock is lowest, the temenos wall reached a total height of ca. 50–55 meters (165–180 feet). Originally, the walls towered some 30 meters (98 feet) above the surrounding ground level.[72]

The upper part of the temenos walls was decorated with engaged pilasters (square pillars built into the wall), which broke up the monotony of the masonry by creating a play of light and shadow in the bright sunlight.[73] Pieces of broken pilasters can be seen lying among the heaps of stones—some showing signs of burning—that fell from above onto a paved Herodian street on the southwest side of the Temple Mount, evidence of the violence wrought by the Roman destruction in 70 CE (Figure 7.5).[74] The bases of a few pilasters are preserved in situ in an underground tunnel on the northwest side of the Temple Mount, under later buildings abutting the temenos wall.[75] The Western ("Wailing") Wall

FIGURE 7.5 Street along the western side of the Temple Mount with collapsed stones. Credit: Photo by the author.

is part of Herod's temenos wall around the Temple Mount, not part of the temple building itself (which was located on the esplanade above, inside the temenos).[76] The Jewish tradition ascribing special sanctity to the site of the Western Wall (as opposed to other sections of the Herodian temenos wall) developed after 1546, when an earthquake destroyed the buildings on this spot, making the wall accessible. Until the Crusader period, Jews prayed at all four walls surrounding the Temple Mount.[77] Today only seven courses of Herodian ashlars are visible above the floor level of the Western Wall plaza (Pl. 8A). Shafts dug by Charles Warren in the nineteenth century indicate that there are another nineteen courses of Herodian ashlars at depth of 21 meters (68 feet below), down to bedrock.[78]

FIGURE 7.6 The southwest corner of the Temple Mount.
Credit: Photo by the author.

The Temple Mount is built over uneven bedrock that slopes down from north to south and from west to east (Figure 7.6). To support a level pavement for the esplanade, the spaces inside the temenos walls that extended into the Tyropoeon Valley to the west and the Bezetha Valley to the north were filled with dirt.[79] On the south and southeast sides, where the bedrock descends toward the southeastern hill and the Kidron Valley, the expanded platform was supported on a series of underground arches or vaults called a *cryptoporticus* (Figure 7.7). The cryptoporticus supported the pavement of the esplanade and the buildings above, but without creating the outward pressure and danger of collapse that would have resulted from filling the space with dirt. The arches of the cryptoporticus still survive (although the area is closed to the public). They are now called "Solomon's Stables," a name that originated when Jerusalem was part of the Crusader kingdom in the Middle Ages. At that time, different orders of knights occupied or were given different parts of the city. One order of knights occupied the Temple Mount, and therefore became known as the Knights Templar. They attributed the cryptoporticus to Solomon (as the Temple Mount had been the site of Solomon's temple) and used the area for stabling their horses. Although Solomon's Stables as they appear today are post-Herodian—perhaps dating to the early Islamic period—scholars disagree about whether the cryptoporticus originally was built

384 Solomon's Stables. Salomonische Ställe. Ecuries de Salomon.

FIGURE 7.7 Solomon's Stables.
Credit: LoC Matson matpc 06646.

by Herod or was constructed in the seventh and eighth centuries in connection with the construction of the Dome of the Rock and al-Aqsa mosque.[80]

Although Israel has controlled the Old City and East Jerusalem since 1967, the Muslim religious authority (the Waqf) remains in charge of the Temple Mount (Arabic al-haram al-sharif). In 1999, the Waqf began clearing the accumulated fill inside Solomon's Stables to convert the space for use as a mosque (the Marwan or Marwani Mosque). Controversy ensued due to the sensitive religious nature of the site and because the work was conducted without any archaeological supervision. In response, a group of Israeli archaeologists formed a project to sift the fill, which was dumped in the Kidron Valley. Many ancient artifacts have been retrieved through the sifting, although their scientific value is reduced by the lack of an excavated context.[81]

The esplanade was surrounded on the east, north, and west sides by porticoes (porches with columns that supported the wooden beams of a roof), which provided shelter from the sun and rain for the masses of pilgrims. Josephus associates the east portico with Solomon, perhaps reflecting the notion (at his time) that the older stretch of temenos wall below—to the north of the seam or straight joint—was part of Solomon's temple.[82] That visitors to the Temple

Mount congregated in these porches is illustrated by references to Solomon's Portico in Acts.

> While he clung to Peter and John, all the people ran together to them in the portico called Solomon's Portico. (Acts 3:11)[83]

> Now many signs and wonders were done among the people through the apostles. And they were all together in Solomon's Portico. (Acts 5:12)

According to the Gospel of John, it was in Solomon's Portico that the Jews demanded to know if Jesus was the messiah.

> At that time the festival of the Dedication [Hanukkah] took place in Jerusalem. It was winter, and Jesus was walking in the temple, in the portico of Solomon. (Jn 10:22–23)

A monumental, two-story high building called the Royal Stoa or Royal Basilica (Greek *stoa basileios*) occupied the south end of the esplanade (encompassing the area occupied today by al-Aqsa mosque, but much larger) (Figure 7.8).[84] Like

FIGURE 7.8 The Royal Stoa in the Holyland Model.
Credit: With permission of Matanyah Hecht; all winnings are from Holyland Tourism [1992] Ltd.

other Greek and Roman stoas and basilicas, Herod's Royal Stoa was a rectangular structure with columns built alongside a public space and was used for various non-cultic purposes including judicial assemblies and commercial activities.[85] Although today we tend to think of the Temple Mount exclusively in religious terms, it was a commercial center as well. The thousands of visitors to Jerusalem's Temple Mount included not only Jewish pilgrims but gentiles, who could enter the Temple Mount except for the sacred precinct inside the *soreg*. The enormous esplanade with the Royal Stoa and porticoes bustled with merchants and vendors, many of them selling sacrificial animals and birds. In fact, Herod's Temple Mount is analogous to ancient agoras and forums, which typically consisted of a large open paved space surrounded by public buildings such as stoas, basilicas, theaters, and temples, although the temple typically was placed on one side instead of in the center.[86]

The commercial activity on the Temple Mount is the background to the Gospel story of Jesus's cleansing of the temple: "Then they came to Jerusalem. And he entered the temple (*hieron*) and began to drive out those who were selling and those who were buying in the temple, and he overturned the tables of the money changers and the seats of those who sold doves; and he would not allow anyone to carry anything through the temple (*hieron*). He was teaching and saying, 'Is it not written, "My house shall be called a house of prayer for all the nations?" But you have made it a den of robbers'" (Mk 11:15–17; also see Mt 21:12–15; Lk 19:45–46; Jn 2:13–16).

Although nowadays this episode is often understood as stemming from Jesus's objection to commercial activity in the temple, the term *hieron* indicates that it occurred not inside the temple but somewhere on the Temple Mount. Furthermore, it is anachronistic to suppose that Jesus would have opposed buying and selling on the Temple Mount since commercial activity associated with temples was taken for granted in the ancient world. Instead, Jesus likely was motivated by a concern for the poor, as suggested by his singling out of money changers and dove sellers. Pigeons and doves were the cheapest form of sacrifice, offered by impoverished people who could not afford more expensive animals such as sheep and goats. The money changers served pilgrims who needed to pay the temple tax, which helped pay for cultic and sacrificial expenses. Biblical law requires a one-time payment or tax of Israelites who reached adulthood. Shortly before Jesus's time, this requirement was changed to an annual payment for the maintenance of the Temple cult.[87] Furthermore, the tax had to be paid in only one kind of currency—Tyrian tetradrachmas (silver sheqels)—which apparently was preferred by the temple authorities due to the high quality of the silver (ninety-two percent silver or better).[88] Money changers exchanged currency for Jewish pilgrims so they could pay the tax in Tyrian tetradrachmas. Scraping together the cash needed to exchange and purchase the Tyrian silver coins annually must have been a great hardship on the poor. Other Jewish groups of the late Second Temple period including the Qumran sect also opposed the institution of an annual temple tax.[89] Some scholars identify the Royal Stoa as the setting for Jesus's cleansing of the temple because it was used for commercial purposes, in which case the term *hieron* in the Gospel accounts of this episode would denote the entire Temple Mount instead of one of its courts.[90]

Gates in the west, south, and east walls of the temenos provided access to Herod's expanded Temple Mount. Their remains are still visible today, specifically (proceeding from west to south to east): Warren's Gate, Wilson's Arch, Barclay's Gate, Robinson's Arch (west); the Huldah Gates (south); and the Eastern Arch and Golden Gate (east). The Eastern Arch is close to the southeast corner of the Temple Mount. Only the lower part of the gate is preserved, consisting of stones forming two side-by-side doorways with a single large threshold stone. Since the threshold is much lower than the pavement of the Herodian esplanade, the gate presumably provided access to the area below the Royal Stoa.[91] The Golden Gate, a double arched gate in the middle of the east wall of the temenos is later—probably Byzantine or early Islamic (Figure 5.2). Some scholars speculate that a Herodian gate called the Shushan (Susa) Gate, which is mentioned in the Mishnah (Middoth 1:3) might have been located on this spot.[92]

Warren's Gate, which is named after Charles Warren although it was discovered by Charles Wilson, is an arched opening that provided access through an underground passage on the west side of the Temple Mount. The arched opening is the product of a later reconstruction of the original Herodian period gate.[93] Nowadays the gate is located inside the tunnel running northward from the Western Wall plaza.[94] In the stretch of wall between Warren's Gate and Wilson's Arch is a singular course of stones called the Western Master Course.[95] This is a row of four enormous stones equaling the height of three courses in the rest of the wall. The largest complete stone is 12 meters (39 feet) long, 3 meters high (10 feet), and ca. 4 meters (13 feet) thick, and is estimated to weigh around 400 tons. Another stone is 13.5 meters (44 feet) long, but its original height is unknown as the upper part is missing.[96] Scholars speculate that these four stones were placed here to support a (lost) vaulted structure under the pavement of the esplanade that abutted the temenos wall.[97]

Wilson's Arch, named after Charles Wilson, was part of a bridge carried by arches that provided access to the Temple Mount from the Tyropoeon Valley.[98] Today the underside of the bridge's first (easternmost) arch abuts the north side of the Western Wall in an underground area reserved for men's prayers (but open to the public for visits at certain times) (Figure 7.9). Below and slightly to the west of Wilson's Arch is a monumental building from the early years of Herod's

WILSON'S ARCH.

FIGURE 7.9 Wilson's Arch.
Credit: LoC Matson cph 3b21110.

reign. The building was first discovered in the nineteenth century by Warren, who called it the "Masonic Hall." Recent excavations indicate that the building was divided into a central area with a water reservoir and fountain flanked by two rooms that apparently were used as triclinia (formal dining rooms). The building is constructed of ashlar masonry, and the walls of the rooms are decorated with finely carved square pilasters with Corinthian capitals. The excavators propose identifying this building as a *prytaneion* (a dining facility for public officials), perhaps associated with the council house (*bouleterion*), which is thought to have been located nearby. It was constructed early in Herod's reign and went out of use in the first third of the first century CE.[99]

The "Masonic Hall" was located on the south side of a road that led eastward from the southwestern hill (on the line of the First Wall) to the Kiponos (or Coponius) Gate in the western wall of the pre-Herodian Temple Mount. Later in Herod's reign, the road level was raised when a massive concrete-like wall was constructed, concealing the north façade of the monumental building. The excavators call this the "dam wall" or "foundation wall" because it crossed the Tyropoeon Valley as a dam that carried the road. It is not clear if the newly elevated road led to an earlier gate—possibly the Kiponos Gate mentioned in m. Middoth 1:3—or to Wilson's Arch, which replaced an earlier gate when Herod expanded the Temple Mount.[100] Wilson's Arch was part of a bridge supporting a staircase that led to the gate (today in the vicinity of the Gate of the Chain). The staircase apparently turned ninety degrees into the Tyropoeon Valley below—now the Western Wall plaza.[101] It is also possible that a west–east staircase on top of the foundation wall led up to Wilson's Arch.[102] Radiocarbon dating indicates that the construction of Wilson's Arch began during Herod's reign and continued for two decades after his death, and that the bridge carried on the arch was doubled in width between 30 and 60 CE.[103] After Hadrian refounded Jerusalem as Aelia Capitolina in the second century CE, an arched bridge called the "great causeway" was constructed on top of the dam wall.

According to Josephus, Herod constructed three entertainment arenas in Jerusalem: a theater, a hippodrome (for horse and chariot races), and an amphitheater (for gladiator and animal fights).[104] The location of all three arenas is unknown and has generated much debate.[105] Because of the lack of identifiable archaeological remains, some scholars speculate that one or more of the arenas were temporary wooden structures that left no traces.[106] In 1994–1996, Ronny Reich and Yaacov Billig found six stone theater seats built into the walls of an early Islamic palace at the southwest corner of the Temple Mount. Presumably, the seats originated in a theater nearby that was dismantled for building material after it went out of use. This discovery raised the possibility that Herod's theater was located between Wilson's Arch and Robinson's Arch to the north or between the early Islamic buildings and the Dung Gate to the south.[107] However, excavations in 2015–2018 by Joe Uziel, Tehillah Lieberman, and Avi Solomon brought to light a tiny theater-like structure—perhaps an odeion (a roofed theater)—tucked under Wilson's Arch and abutting the Temple Mount's western temenos wall. Since the structure dates to the second century CE (the Roman period), it has nothing to do with Herod's theater (see Chapter 8). Furthermore, the seats found by Reich and Shukron match the seats in the theater-like structure, indicating that it was the likely source.[108] Therefore, the whereabouts of Herod's theater and the other arenas remain unknown.

To the south of Wilson's Arch, the remains of Barclay's Gate—named for a mid-nineteenth-century American missionary and medical doctor, James Thomas Barclay—are preserved on the south side of the Western Wall (in the women's section) (Figure 7.10). The visible part consists of the upper courses of the northern doorpost and a massive lintel, and the original passage blocked by smaller stones.[109] The gate's threshold (which is below the current ground level) lay thirteen feet above the Herodian street that runs along the outside of the temenos wall. The gate was accessed by an arched bridge that supported steps leading up from the street.[110] The southern half of the upper part of Barclay's Gate is obscured by a bridge leading to the Mughrabi Gate above, which is the only gate through which non-Muslims are permitted to enter the Temple Mount today (Pl. 8B). The Mughrabi Gate is so-called because, until 1967, the

FIGURE 7.10 Barclay's Gate.
Credit: Photo by the author.

neighborhood around it was inhabited by North Africans who had immigrated from the Maghreb in the time of Saladin (twelfth century CE). After taking possession of the Old City in the Six-Day War, the Israeli government demolished the houses and forcibly relocated the residents to create an open plaza in front of the Western Wall.[111] The current bridge was supposed to be a temporary replacement for an earthen ramp that collapsed in 2004.

Robinson's Arch, named after the nineteenth-century explorer Edward Robinson, is located at the southwest corner of the Temple Mount, visible as the beginning of a large arch projecting from the temenos wall (Figure 7.11).[112] The arch carried a staircase that provided access to the Royal Stoa. It was long thought

FIGURE 7.11 Robinson's Arch.
Credit: Photo by the author.

that Robinson's Arch was a bridge carried on arches across the Tyropoeon Valley, from the southwestern hill to the Temple Mount. However, excavations conducted by Benjamin Mazar after 1967 around the southern and western sides of the Temple Mount brought to light a staircase which indicated that Robinson's Arch turned a ninety-degree angle into the Tyropoeon Valley below.[113] A broad street paved with thick stone slabs that was lined by shops ran along the western side of the Temple Mount (the same street crushed in 70 CE by falling stones from the temenos wall above). The road along the Tyropoeon Valley (the line of modern el-Wad Street) seems to have become a main commercial artery already in the Hasmonean period.

FIGURE 7.12 View of the southern end of the Temple Mount with the Hulda Gates in the Holyland Model.
Credit: With permission of Matanyah Hecht; all winnings are from Holyland Tourism [1992] Ltd.

The Huldah Gates are two gates in the south wall of the Temple Mount (both are now blocked) (Figure 7.12). They provided the main access for pilgrims to the Temple Mount, who could purify themselves first in the large *miqva'ot* outside the gates or in the Pool of Siloam to the south. Unlike the other gates just described, which are named after nineteenth-century explorers, Huldah is an ancient name (m. Middoth 1:3), perhaps referring to the nearby (lost) tomb of the prophetess Huldah or deriving from the Hebrew word for mole (the animal), as the gates led to underground passages.[114] The western gate has two doorways with flat lintels and is sometimes called the Double Gate (Figure 7.13). The eastern or Triple Gate has three arched doorways (Figure 7.14). Scholars agree that the double portal of the western gate is original although the projecting decorative elements above the doorways are Umayyad (early Islamic) additions. Because the triple arches of the eastern gate are a later modification of the Umayyad period, it is unclear if the Herodian gate had two or three portals.[115]

The Mishnah seems to indicate that the Huldah Gates worked as a pair, with the eastern (Triple) gate used for entrance to the Temple Mount and the western (Double) gate used as the exit: "There were five gates to the Temple Mount: the two Huldah Gates on the south, that served for coming in and for going out"

FIGURE 7.13 The western Hulda Gate (Double Gate).
Credit: Photo by the author.

FIGURE 7.14 The eastern Hulda Gate (Triple Gate).
Credit: Photo by the author.

FIGURE 7.15 Carved decoration from the ceiling of the Hulda Gate (double gate) (displayed in the Citadel).
Credit: Photo by the author.

(m. Middoth 1:3).[116] Both gates led to underground passages below the Royal Stoa that brought visitors into the Temple Mount. Part of one of the doorways of the western gate is still visible today, including the doorpost and lintel (with a flat arch above the lintel). The portal is blocked by smaller stones, while the rest of the gate is covered by a Crusader tower built up against the southern temenos wall. The ceiling of the passageway inside the Double Gate has four shallow domes covered with delicate carved and stuccoed geometric designs, including early Islamic additions to the original Herodian decoration (Figure 7.15).[117] The staircase that led to the western (Double) gate is 65 meters (213 feet) wide while than the staircase in front of the eastern (Triple) gate is only 15 meters (49 feet) wide. The broader staircase was designed to accommodate the crowds of pilgrims exiting the Temple Mount and to provide a place to sit. The steps are alternately narrow and wide and are broken up at intervals by broad landings.[118] A paved street running along the south wall of the Temple Mount terminated at the east end in a sloping ramp carried on arches.[119]

Although the temple itself was built in 23/22 or 20/19 BCE, construction on the massive complex surrounding it continued until 64 CE, a situation alluded to by the author the Fourth Gospel: "Jesus answered them, 'Destroy this temple, and in three days I will raise it up.' The Jews then said, 'This temple has been under construction for forty-six years, and will you raise it up in three days'?"

(John 2:18–19).[120] Excavations around the southwest side of the Temple Mount confirm this picture. For example, under Robinson's Arch, Reich and Eli Shukron excavated a *miqveh* (ritual bath) under the lowest course of the temenos wall. When Herod expanded the Temple Mount, the *miqveh* was put out of use. It was filled with dirt and debris and covered with stone slabs and the temenos wall was built on top of it. Coins dating to 17/18–24/25 CE and Herodian (wheel made) oil lamps (a common first-century CE type) were found in the *miqveh*'s fill.[121] The latest coin found under the pavement of the street that runs along the western side of the Temple Mount and below Robinson's Arch dates to the time of Pontius Pilate (26–37 CE).[122] These discoveries indicate that construction work on the southwest side of the Temple Mount continued for several decades after Herod's death. They also mean that the Royal Stoa must have been constructed in the first century CE, and not by Herod.[123] In fact, the northwest corner of the Temple Mount was never completed. The bedrock, which rises steeply at this spot, was left unhewn, blocking the street running alongside the western temenos wall.[124]

In 4 BCE, as Herod lay dying, two men (described by Josephus as *sophistai* and identified by many scholars as Pharisees) incited a mob of youths to tear down a golden eagle the king had erected over one of the temple's gates, probably in a pediment. The perpetrators subsequently were executed by Herod.

> Hearing now that the king was gradually sinking under despondency and disease, these *sophistai* threw out hints to their friends that this was the fitting moment to avenge God's honor and to pull down those structures which had been erected in defiance of their fathers' laws. It was, in fact, unlawful to place in the temple either images or busts or any representation whatsoever of a living creature; notwithstanding this, the king had erected over the great gate a golden eagle. This it was which these *sophistai* now exhorted their disciples to cut down. . . . At mid-day, accordingly, when numbers of people were perambulating the temple (*hieron*), they let themselves down from the roof by stout cords and began chopping off the golden eagle with hatchets.[125]

It is unclear if the gate with the golden eagle was part of the temple building or one of the gates in the court surrounding the temple or one of the gates in the temenos wall of the Temple Mount.[126] Josephus's reference to the great gate suggests it was the gate on the east side of the Women's Court (perhaps the Beautiful Gate mentioned in Acts 3).[127] Many scholars follow Josephus in attributing the eagle incident to Jewish opposition to the depiction of figured images in accordance with the second commandment, especially in Pharisaic circles. Some speculate that the Jews found the eagle offensive because it was a symbol of the Roman Empire. But even if the *sophistai* were Pharisees and the incident reflects opposition to the depiction of images, it is evident that not all Jews objected to the golden eagle, which had been erected over a decade earlier. Furthermore, there is no evidence of opposition to the eagles depicted on some of Herod's coins and on the Tyrian tetradrachmas that were required for payment of the temple tax.[128] Josephus describes Herod's anger at the golden eagle's removal: "at great length he denounced the men as sacrilegious persons who, under the pretext of zeal for the law, had some more ambitious aim in view, and demanded that they should be punished for impiety."[129] In Herod's view—a view presumably shared by other Jews—the golden eagle's erection was an act of piety and therefore its removal was a sacrilege.

Eagles were associated with celestial deities in the ancient world including the God of Israel and Zeus/Jupiter, the chief god of the Greco-Roman pantheon, who was often represented by an eagle carrying a thunderbolt.[130] Just as Augustus was considered Jupiter's agent on earth, so Herod may have conceived of himself as the agent of the God of Israel, through whose will he claimed to rule. Therefore, eagles in the ancient Mediterranean and Near East functioned as a royal symbol and as a divine attribute connecting the king to the chief deity. It seems unlikely that Herod's golden eagle was intended to be a symbol of Roman imperial power, as some scholars have suggested, even if it might have been understood as such by some Jews. Instead, the golden eagle probably represented a divine instrument or intermediary connecting Herod as king and builder/dedicator of the temple to the God of Israel.[131] This would explain why Herod considered the eagle's erection over the temple gate to be an act of piety and its removal a sacrilege. If the *sophistai* who incited the youthful mob to tear it down were indeed Pharisees, this incident might reflect sectarian divisions among the population. These divisions were based not only on different interpretations of or approaches to biblical law but also stemmed from class distinctions as well as opposition to Herod's claim of divine agency.

The Antonia Fortress

At the northwest corner of the Temple Mount, Herod erected a massive fortress with four corner towers named the Antonia in honor of Mark Antony, indicating that it was built before the battle of Actium in 31 BCE (Figure 7.16). The fortress was situated on a tall, rocky outcrop overlooking the Temple Mount, largely obliterating the Hasmonean *baris*, which was located on roughly the same spot. Herod garrisoned the Antonia with a cohort of Roman soldiers to monitor the masses of pilgrims and quell any unrest.[132] The fortress, which was probably the first building constructed by Herod in Jerusalem, also served as the king's residence for the first ten years of his reign, until his palace was completed.[133]

FIGURE 7.16 The Antonia Fortress in the Holyland Model.
Credit: With permission of Matanyah Hecht; all winnings are from Holyland Tourism [1992] Ltd.

Although Josephus provides a detailed description of the Antonia, its dimensions have been the subject of much debate. Today the area where the Antonia was located is bisected by a road called the Via Dolorosa, which runs parallel to the north side of the Temple Mount. The Via Dolorosa (Latin for "Way of Sorrow") is so-called because, according to Christian tradition, this is the route along which Jesus carried his cross, beginning with his sentencing by Pontius Pilate and ending with his crucifixion and burial (now enshrined within the Church of the Holy Sepulcher). A convent called the Church of the Sisters of Zion now lies along the north side of the Via Dolorosa. The convent was founded in 1858, by Marie-Alphonse Ratisbonne, a French Jew who converted to Catholicism and became a priest. During the construction of the convent, a series of ancient remains came to light. The remains consist of large pools or cisterns called the Struthion (Greek for "sparrow") Pools, which are overlaid by a stone pavement (today identified as the Lithostratos) and a monumental, triple-arched gateway sitting on top of the pavement (today called the arch of Ecce Homo) (although the gate's piers are founded on bedrock). Modern Christian tradition identifies the pavement and arched gateway as the places where, according to the Gospel of John, Jesus was sentenced by Pontius Pilate and clothed with a purple robe and a crown of thorns.

When Pilate heard these words, he brought Jesus outside and sat on the
judge's bench at a place called The Stone Pavement (*lithostratos*). (Jn 19:13)

So Jesus came out, wearing the crown of thorns and the purple robe. Pilate
said to them, "Behold the man" (*ecce homo*)!" (Jn 19:5)

These remains were long thought to be part of the Antonia, with the pools used
for water storage inside the fortress, the pavement belonging to an inner courtyard, and the arched gateway providing access to the fortress. If they were part
of the Antonia, there would be no contradiction with Christian tradition, as
the Antonia was built over half a century before Jesus's death. However, most
scholars now agree that the Antonia was much smaller than previously thought
and did not extend to the area north of the Via Dolorosa, thereby excluding the
remains in the Church of the Sisters of Zion.[134] Furthermore, only the Struthion
Pools seem to antedate 70 CE, and they were located in an open moat outside
the Antonia fortress. The arch and pavement, which clearly are contemporary,
were part of a forum that the emperor Hadrian established on this spot in the
second century CE (see Chapter 8).[135] The Lithostratos pavement and the arch of
Ecce Homo cannot be identified with the places mentioned in the Gospel of John
because they did not exist in the time of Jesus.

Today the Via Dolorosa begins on the north side of the Temple Mount
because, according to modern Christian tradition, this is where Jesus took up
the cross after being sentenced to death by Pontius Pilate. In other words, modern Christian tradition identifies the Antonia as the place where Jesus was sentenced to death. However, the Gospel accounts mention the praetorium, not the
Antonia: "Then the soldiers of the governor took Jesus into the praetorium" (Mt
27:27). The praetorium—the palace of the Roman governor in Jerusalem—was
Herod's palace, not the Antonia fortress.[136] Therefore, Jesus would have been sentenced to death and taken up the cross not in the area to the north of the Temple
Mount but on the western side of the city. This means that the route walked by
Jesus is different from the one walked by modern pilgrims (the Via Dolorosa),
which is based on a relatively late Christian tradition.

Herod's Palace and the Three Towers

When Jerusalem fell to Herod in 37 BCE, the walled settlement consisted of
the Temple Mount (with the pre-Herodian second temple), the southeastern hill, and the southwestern hill. The Temple Mount and southeastern hill
had been resettled after the return from Babylonian exile and fortified under
Nehemiah, while the wall surrounding the southwestern hill (the First Wall)
was constructed in the Hasmonean period (following the line of the late Iron

Age wall). On the northwest side of the southwestern hill, Herod built a palace for himself as he could not use the palace of the Hasmonean family. Josephus describes Herod's palace as consisting of two wings separated by pools and gardens. Herod named the wings the Caesareum, in honor of Augustus, and the Agrippaeum, in honor of Marcus Agrippa, Augustus's son-in-law and designated heir (who died in 12 BCE, predeceasing Augustus). Herod formed a close friendship with Marcus Agrippa, who visited Judea and toured Herod's kingdom in 15 BCE. Although excavations have been conducted in the area where Herod's palace was located (the modern Armenian Garden), the superstructure has not survived. Instead, most of the remains belong to a massive subterranean podium on which the palace was built.[137] Underground channels carried water to the palace from Hezekiah's pool (the Amygdalon Pool; see Josephus, *War* 5.468), which was located outside the First Wall to the north of the three towers (Pl. 5A). From the palace, water and sewage drained through channels into the Ben-Hinnom Valley.[138]

At the northwest corner of the First Wall and on the north side of his palace, Herod erected three large towers (Figure 7.17). These towers served two purposes: (1) to reinforce the city's vulnerable northern flank, which was not bounded by a deep natural valley like the other sides; and (2) to protect Herod's

FIGURE 7.17 The three towers in the Holyland Model.
Credit: With permission of Matanyah Hecht; all winnings are from Holyland Tourism [1992] Ltd.

palace, which was surrounded by its own fortifications. Josephus tells us that Herod named the largest tower Phasael (in honor of his older brother, who committed suicide in 40 BCE), the middle-sized tower Hippicus (after a friend), and the smallest tower Mariamme (in honor of his beloved Hasmonean wife, who he executed). Josephus reports that when Jerusalem fell in 70 CE, Titus left the towers standing as a testament to the strength of the city he conquered: "And when, at a later period, he demolished the rest of the city and razed the walls, he left these towers as a memorial of his attendant fortune, to whose co-operation he owed his conquest of defences which defied assault."[139]

Today the lone surviving Herodian tower lies inside a fortified enclosure called the Citadel, next to Jaffa Gate, in the middle of the west wall of the modern Old City (Figure 7.18). Most of the remains in the Citadel are much later than the Roman period, dating to medieval and Ottoman times. However, some earlier remains are enclosed within the Citadel, including the northwest corner of the First Wall, into which the Herodian tower is set. Only the lower part of the tower has survived, which is constructed of characteristic Herodian-style masonry: large ashlar stones with smooth, drafted margins and a flat, paneled boss. The upper part of the tower was reconstructed later using much smaller stones. The current moniker, "David's Tower," reflects a popular (and incorrect) association with King David that stems from a later tradition (see Chapter 9).[140] The tower is visible immediately to the right (south) after entering Jaffa Gate, within the walls of the Citadel, as well as inside the courtyard of the Citadel. Sometimes modern visitors confuse "David's Tower" with the minaret of an Ottoman mosque that is also located inside the courtyard of the Citadel. Because of its large size, which seems to be close to the dimensions provided by Josephus, many scholars identify the tower as Phasael. However, Hillel Geva proposes that it is Hippicus, which Josephus says was the westernmost of the three towers.[141] The towers were probably arranged in a row at the northwest corner of the First Wall instead of in a triangular formation as reconstructed in the Holyland Model (a scale model of Jerusalem before its destruction in 70, so-called because originally it was on the grounds of the Holyland Hotel in Jerusalem but is now in the Israel Museum). Geva proposes that the other two towers disappeared because they lost their strategic importance when the Third Wall and later city walls moved the fortification line farther to the west.[142]

The Southwestern Hill

In the late Second Temple period, the southwestern hill was Jerusalem's upper-class residential quarter. This is where the Hasmonean and Herodian palaces were

FIGURE 7.18 The Herodian tower in the Citadel ("David's Tower").
Credit: Photo by the author.

located and where Jerusalem's wealthiest Jews lived. In addition to offering a stunning view across the Tyropoeon Valley to the Temple Mount, the southwestern hill remains cooler in summer thanks to its relatively high elevation. Although remains of the Hasmonean palace have not been found, literary sources suggest it was located on the north side of the southwestern hill, to the east of Herod's palace. The bouleterion (council hall) and a mysterious building called the Xystus (perhaps a gymnasium complex or forum or promenade) probably were located between the Hasmonean palace to the west and the "Masonic Hall" to the east.[143] In other words, there appears to have been a row of important royal and public buildings along the north side of the southwestern hill, following the line of the First Wall: Herod's palace, the Hasmonean palace, the bouleterion, the Xystus, and the "Masonic Hall." It makes sense that Herod would have built his own palace in proximity to the Hasmonean palace.

While under Jordanian rule from 1948 to 1967, Jerusalem's Jewish Quarter, which occupies the northeast part of the southwestern hill was leveled. After capturing the Old City in the 1967 Six-Day War, the State of Israel rebuilt the quarter. In advance of the renewal project, Nahman Avigad conducted excavations in the Jewish Quarter. Because the Old City is a densely built-up, living city, archaeologists rarely have an opportunity to conduct excavations on such a large scale. Avigad's excavations brought to light remains of various periods, including urban villas of the Herodian period belonging to the Jerusalem elite (Figure 7.19).[144] The largest villa, which Avigad dubbed "the palatial mansion," covers an area of some 600 square meters (6,400 square feet).[145] Each villa consisted of two or three stories of rooms (including a basement for storage) surrounding a central courtyard. Unlike contemporary houses in North America, which have large windows opening on to lawns and gardens surrounding the house, in the ancient Mediterranean and Near East, houses focused on a central courtyard surrounded by rooms. This arrangement provided privacy for the house's residents, with windows and doorways in the walls facing the courtyard providing light and air to the surrounding rooms.

FIGURE 7.19 Herodian houses in the Jewish Quarter.
Credit: Bukvoed, CC BY 4.0, via Wikimedia Commons.

The villas discovered by Avigad were decorated in Roman fashion with mosaic floors, wall paintings (frescoes) in the Second and Third Pompeian Styles (wall paintings imitating colored stone panels and other architectural elements), and stucco decoration including the First Pompeian Style (plaster molded in imitation of marble panels and other architectural shapes) (Pl. 9). Some rooms had been repainted or remodeled more than once, to keep up with changing styles of interior decoration.[146] The villas also were furnished with expensive Roman-style stone tables (carved of local Jerusalem chalk) and provided with sets of Eastern Terra Sigillata pottery—fine dining dishes with a glossy, dark orange-red slip that were imported from Phoenicia. The occupants of the palatial mansion owned a beautiful, mold-made glass vase signed by Ennion, a famous Phoenician master craftsman (Figure 7.20).[147] A complete glass vase manufactured in the same mold is in the collection of New York's Metropolitan Museum of Art (it was acquired on the antiquities market, so its provenience is unknown). The discovery of the vase in the Jewish Quarter excavations provides a context for dating Ennion's products to the first century CE.

The size and lavish decoration of these urban villas indicates that the residents were members of the Jerusalem elite. Clearly these wealthy Jews were "Romanized"—that is, they had adopted many aspects of a Roman lifestyle.[148] At the same time, it is evident that they observed Jewish law and customs. For example, although the interior decoration is Hellenistic or Roman in style, it lacks the figured images that characterize Roman art. Furthermore, each villa was equipped with one or more *miqva'ot* and yielded large numbers of chalk dining dishes and other stone vessels, attesting to the observance of purity laws (Figure 7.21).[149] Many Jews of the late Second Temple period came to believe that stone cannot contract ritual impurity, whereas a pottery vessel that becomes impure cannot be purified and must be destroyed. Although stone vessels were more difficult to produce than pottery and therefore more costly, the investment paid off for Jews who were concerned about the observance of purity laws and could afford the expense. The stone vessels found in the Jewish Quarter villas include knife-pared stone "mugs"—which are found at many sites around Palestine and might have been used for ritual hand-washing before meals—as well as sets of more expensive lathe-turned dining dishes and large jars. The stone dining dishes might have held offerings of produce (Hebrew *terumah*) given to priests, which had to be consumed in a state of ritual purity. John describes Jesus turning water stored in stone jars into wine at a wedding at Cana in Galilee: "Now standing there were six stone water jars for the Jewish rites of purification, each holding twenty or thirty gallons" (Jn 2:6).

FIGURE 7.20 Ennion's glass vase from the Jewish Quarter, mold blown, signature inscription in Greek, Jerusalem, first century C.E. Collection of the Israel Antiquities Authority. Credit: Photo © The Israel Museum, Jerusalem.

The large numbers of *miqva'ot* and stone vessels, which reflect a high level of purity observance, indicate that some of the wealthy residents of the Jewish Quarter villas were priests. This is not surprising as priestly families (and especially high priestly families) were members of the Jerusalem elite. Priestly presence is suggested by a graffito depicting a menorah with the showbread table and altar, which was incised on the wall plaster of one of the villas (Figure 7.22).[150] Avigad discovered evidence of priestly presence in another villa that he dubbed "the Burnt House." This villa is so-called because the basement rooms (the only part of the house that survived) were covered with layers of ashy soot from the

FIGURE 7.21 Stone vessels in the Israel Museum Jerusalem.
Credit: Photo by the author.

destruction of the house in 70 CE. The finds from the rooms—stoves, grinding stones, cooking pots, weights, and measuring devices—suggest this was the villa's service wing, including a kitchen.[151] Other finds including pottery, stone vessels, and coins fell into the basement when the upper stories burned and collapsed. A stone weight found in one of the rooms is inscribed with the name of a known priestly family—Bar Kathros (or Qatros)—presumably, the villa's owners.[152] On a step leading down to the basement, Avigad found the skeletal arm of a young woman about twenty years of age, who might have starved to death during the siege of Jerusalem or was crushed when the burning house collapsed on top of her (Figure 7.23).[153] Although Avigad assumed that the villa burned down and was ransacked by the Romans when the city fell in 70 CE, it appears to have been destroyed during the siege—apparently as a result of the in-fighting among the Jewish rebel factions or the Roman artillery assault.[154] After Avigad completed his excavations, a yeshiva (Kollel) was built over the site. The urban villas were preserved and restored in the complex's basement together with artifacts from the excavations, and the site was opened to the public as the Wohl Archaeological Museum.

The "Herodian Quarter" excavated by Avigad constituted a densely built-up, residential quarter that spread from the top of the southwestern hill down the eastern slope toward the Tyropoeon Valley below. The villas were separated by narrow streets and alleys, reflecting the high cost of this prime real estate and its intensive development since the Hasmonean period. Similar urban villas were discovered on Mount Zion, at the south end of the southwestern hill. As in the Jewish Quarter, these residences were equipped with miqva'ot and were

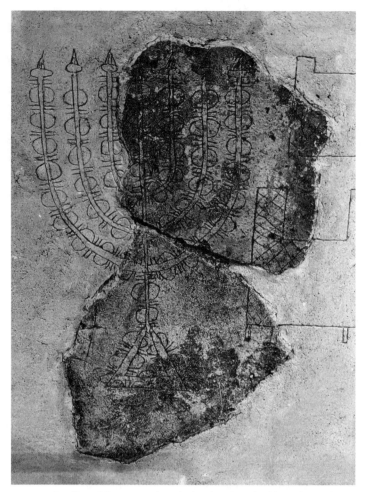

FIGURE 7.22 Graffito of the menorah with the showbread table and altar from a house
in the Jewish Quarter, Israel Museum Jerusalem.
Credit: Photo by the author.

decorated with high quality wall paintings and stucco. But whereas no figured
images (representations of living creatures) were discovered in the Jewish Quarter
villas, the motifs in the wall paintings from Mount Zion include birds. As the
excavator, Magen Broshi, concluded, "The location of our site on the summit of
the Upper City and the elegant, sophisticated murals leave no doubt that this
quarter was occupied by the more affluent residents of Jerusalem."[155] Interestingly,
Christian tradition identifies this area as the location of the house of the high
priest Caiaphas. The only other figured images found to date in a domestic
Jewish context of the late Second Temple period in Jerusalem were discovered

FIGURE 7.23 Skeletal arm in the Burnt House.
Credit: Courtesy of Zev Radovan/BibleLandsPictures.com.

in a residential quarter to the south and west of the Temple Mount. Benjamin Mazar's excavations in this area brought to light fragments of a stuccoed animal frieze including a lion, lioness, antelope, rabbit, and pig (!).[156]

Archaeologists have assumed that Jerusalem's lower classes lived in crowded conditions along the slopes of the Tyropoeon Valley, as depicted in the Holyland Model. However, recent excavations on the lower western slope of the valley across from the Pool of Siloam brought to light remains of spacious, well-built, terraced dwellings equipped with *miqva'ot*.[157] This indicates that Jerusalem's elite quarter covered a larger area than previously thought, and points to a high level of prosperity among much of the city's population.

The Third Wall and the Bezetha Quarter

By the time Jerusalem was destroyed by the Romans in 70 CE, the north side of the city was fortified by three successive lines of wall, which Josephus calls the First Wall, the Second Wall, and the Third Wall. The First Wall was built by the Hasmoneans to enclose the southwestern hill within the city's fortifications. However, there is no consensus among scholars about the circuit of the Second and Third Walls, nor does Josephus indicate whether the Second Wall was built by the Hasmoneans or Herod. Josephus does inform us that the Third Wall—the outermost and latest of the three walls—was begun in the mid-first century CE by Herod Agrippa I, the grandson of Herod the Great. Construction work was halted either by order of the emperor Claudius due to fears of a Jewish revolt or by Herod Agrippa I's untimely death.[158] Two decades later, the wall was completed by the inhabitants of Jerusalem on the eve of the outbreak of the First Revolt.

There are two schools of thought among scholars regarding the circuit of the Third Wall: the minimalists and the maximalists. According to the minimalists, the current north wall of the Old City is built over the line of the Third Wall (Figure 7.24). The minimalists point to possible remains of the late Second Temple period at the site of the Damascus Gate, although the ancient gate visible under the modern passage dates to the time of Aelia Capitolina (second century CE).[159] However, some archaeologists associate the possible late Second Temple period remains with the Second Wall, not the Third Wall. Excavations in other spots along the north wall of the Old City have not yielded definite evidence of a wall antedating the third–fourth centuries CE. The maximalists identify a fortification wall located ca. 450 meters (1,476 feet) to the north of the Old City as the Third Wall (I refer to this wall as "the northern line") (Figure 7.25). The northern line was first discovered in 1838, by Edward Robinson.[160] It is sometimes called the Sukenik-Mayer wall because large sections were excavated by Eleazar Lipa Sukenik and Leo Aryeh Mayer in 1925–1928 and 1940.[161] Additional sections were excavated by Sara Ben-Arieh and Ehud Netzer in 1972–1974, and by a team of IAA archaeologists led by Vassilios Tzaferis from 1990 to 1992. The route of the wall was recently mapped using Geographic Information System (GIS) (Pl. 10A).[162]

Altogether the northern line can be traced for some 1000 meters (3,280 feet), extending on the east from the W. F. Albright Institute of Archaeological Research (formerly the American School of Oriental Research), westward along Amr Ibn Al A`as Street, and past the former U.S. Consulate building in East Jerusalem to the Russian Compound on the west. For the most part only the wall's foundations are preserved, consisting of small stones set in a hard, concrete-like mortar. In a few spots the first course of the wall is preserved on top of the foundations, which

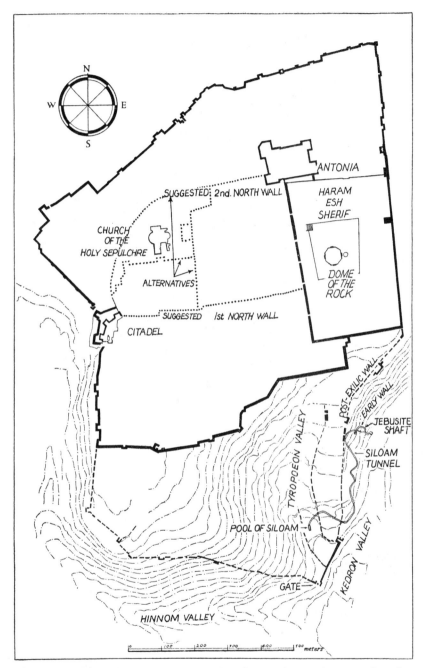

FIGURE 7.24 Plan of the Second and Third Walls according to the minimalists, from Kenyon 1974: 233 figure 38.
Credit: By permission of A&C Black Publishers.

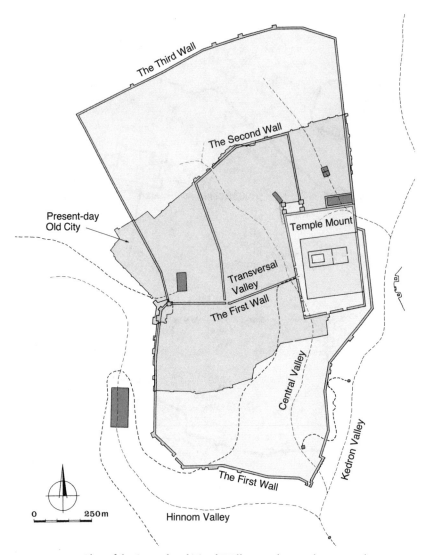

FIGURE 7.25 Plan of the Second and Third Walls according to the maximalists. Credit: © by Leen Ritmeyer

is built of Herodian-style ashlar stones, some in apparent reuse (Figure 7.26).[163] The maximalists identify the northern line as the Third Wall due to its careless appearance, which accords with Josephus's account that the wall was completed on the eve of the outbreak of the First Revolt, and on first-century CE pottery and coins found in the foundation trenches and adjacent levels.

Although the minimalists reject the identification of the wall to the north of the Old City as the Third Wall, the alternative proposals they have put forward

FIGURE 7.26 Remains of the Third Wall.
Credit: Photo by the author.

are unconvincing. For example, the fact that the towers in the wall are on the outer side facing north contradicts its identification as Titus's siege wall, and there is no evidence that any such wall was built at the time of the Bar Kokhba Revolt in 132–135 CE, nor is there any evidence that the Jews built a fourth wall on the north side of the city at the time of the First Jewish Revolt.[164] The debate over the Third Wall reflects political as well as archaeological considerations, with the maximalists represented by Israeli archaeologists and some Americans, and the minimalists represented by British, French, and Australian archaeologists. Thus, according to the Israeli (maximalist) view, the area enclosed within the walls reached its greatest extent at the end of the Second Temple period, when Jerusalem was a Jewish city.

Sukenik and Mayer's 1940 excavations on the east side of the Albright Institute's courtyard brought to light a section of the northern line and a square tower, which was partially destroyed when the back fence was built. Another 150 meters (492 feet) to the east, outside the grounds of the Albright Institute, they discovered additional remains of the wall and a tower measuring at least 7.50 meters (24 feet) wide by 20 meters (66 feet) long—the largest tower associated so far with the northern line. The tower's size and its position on a high rocky outcrop suggest that it marked the northeast corner of the northern line, from which point the wall presumably turned southward to join the northeast corner of the Temple Mount.[165]

According to Josephus, the western section of the Third Wall ran from Herod's Hippicus tower northward to a tower called Psephinus, and then turned to the east.[166] The Psephinus tower was especially large and octagonal in shape, and stood on a high point from which it was possible to see the Mediterranean Sea to the west and the mountains of Moab across the Dead Sea to the east: "But as wonderful as was the third wall throughout, still more so was the tower Psephinus, which rose at its north-west angle and opposite to which Titus encamped. For, being seventy cubits high, it afforded from sunrise a prospect embracing both Arabia and the utmost limits of Hebrew territory as far as the sea; it was of octagonal form."[167] The minimalists locate the Psephinus tower at the northwest corner of the wall of the Old City. However, excavations conducted in 1971–1972 indicate that the tower on this spot is medieval in date ("Goliath's Tower").[168] According to the maximalists, the Psephinus tower stood on a natural high point to the northwest of the Old City now occupied by the Russian Compound (Figure 7.27). The site is so-called because in the nineteenth century the land was sold by the Ottomans to the Russian Empire, which built a cathedral, hospital, hospice, and other facilities for pilgrims. Many of the buildings are now used by the Israeli government and Jerusalem municipality. The Russian Compound is located at the northwest end of a large hill to the north of the Old City that is bordered on the east by the Tyropoeon Valley and on the west by the Ben-Hinnom Valley. The hill forms

FIGURE 7.27 The church in the Russian Compound.
Credit: Photo by the author.

a ridge along the east side of the Ben-Hinnom Valley, rising to its highest point (798 meters/2,618 feet above sea level) at the Russian Compound.[169] According to the maximalists, the Third Wall would have continued south from the Russian Compound, roughly following the line of Jaffa Road today and along the west side of the Old City to the Jaffa Gate, where the Hippicus tower was located.[170]

Finds from excavations conducted in 2016 by Rina Avner and Kfir Arbib in the Russian Compound support the maximalists' identification of the northern line as the Third Wall. The excavations revealed the base of a fortification wall oriented north–south and a projecting square or rectangular tower, constructed of small stones in a hard, concrete-like mortar similar to other parts of the northern line. Eighty-two ballista and slingshot stones lay on the ground outside (west) of the wall and tower, covered by a burnt layer. The pottery from inside the foundations and the associated ground level dates to the first century CE. This appears to be part of the western stretch of the Third Wall, which Josephus reports had ninety towers along it.[171] The Psephinus tower must be located a short distance to the north inside the Russian Compound.[172] The ballista and slingshot stones apparently were fired by light artillery during the Roman siege in 70 CE. According to Josephus, Titus attacked the city on the north at three points: the Hippicus tower, the Psephinus tower, and north of the Antonia, where the Third Wall was breached. Avner and Arbib associate the concentration of ballista and slingshot stones with the Roman assault by the Psephinus tower.[173]

The northern line/Third Wall doubled the area of the walled city to ca. 450 acres or 1,800 dunams.[174] The area it enclosed included a suburb called Bezetha, as Josephus describes: "This wall was built by [Herod] Agrippa [I] to enclose the later additions to the city, which were quite unprotected; for the town, overflowing with inhabitants, had gradually crept beyond the ramparts. Indeed, the population, uniting to the hill the district north of the temple, had encroached so far that even a fourth hill was surrounded with houses. This hill, which is called Bezetha, lay opposite Antonia, but was cut off from it by a deep fosse. . . . The recently built quarter was called in the vernacular Bezetha, which, might be translated into Greek as New Town (Caenopolis)."[175]

The Bezetha quarter occupied the eastern part of the area enclosed within the Third Wall, to the north of the Temple Mount and Antonia fortress. The Bezetha Valley ran southward through the middle of the quarter, turning east by the northeast corner of the Temple Mount to join the Kidron Valley at the site of the modern Lions' Gate in the Old City. Today the Via Dolorosa follows the southern end of this valley, running along the north side of the Temple Mount and bordered by the Kidron Valley (outside the Lions' Gate) at the east end and the Tyropoeon Valley (el-Wad Street) at the west end. Two large reservoirs stored rain and flood water that collected behind a dam at the southern end of the

Bezetha Valley: the Bezetha (or Bethesda or Sheep's) Pool on the north side of the Via Dolorosa, and the Pool of Israel (Birket Isra`il) a short distance to the south, along the north side of the Temple Mount.[176] The Antonia fortress and northwest corner of the Temple Mount occupied the southern end of the hill bordered on the east by the Bezetha Valley and on the west by the Tyropoeon Valley.[177]

Bezetha (or Bethzatha) is an Aramaic word meaning "olive grove," indicating that much of the area north of the First and Second Walls was cultivated. The area north of the Temple Mount appears to have become known as Bezetha before the Third Wall was built, whereas after the wall was built the entire area within it including the Bezetha quarter became known as New Town (Caenopolis).[178] Because the Third Wall was completed only at the time of the First Revolt, the area within it was much less densely built up than the rest of the city, as indicated by the sparse archaeological remains. These remains show that the Bezetha quarter was settled during the first century CE, as the population increased and conditions inside the First and Second Walls grew increasingly crowded.[179]

"Holy Garbage"

On the northeast side of the southeastern hill, a glacis associated with the Akra fortress that was made of layers of earth, gravel, and cobbles was found overlying the stepped stone structure (see Chapter 6).[180] The glacis was buried in layers of debris that had been dumped over the crest of the hill and had accumulated to a depth of more than 10 meters (32 feet). Based on the pottery and coins he found in the debris, Yigal Shiloh assumed it was cleared and dumped from the top of the hill after 70 CE.[181] Since then, other archaeologists have noticed that nearly the entire east slope of the southeastern hill is covered in similar debris, extending as far as the southeast corner of the Temple Mount.[182] Pottery and coins from recent excavations indicate that the debris was deposited from the mid-first century BCE to 70 CE, and not following Jerusalem's destruction. As debris was dumped it was set on fire, and the layers were covered with soil, forming a giant landfill (midden). It is now clear that in the late Second Temple period, when the east slope of the southeastern hill lay outside the city wall and was uninhabited, it was used as a municipal garbage dump.[183]

Excavations in the landfill have recovered large numbers of animal bones dominated by sheep, goat, and, to a lesser degree, cattle, as well as fowl (e.g., chickens and pigeons), but no pig bones or other non-kosher species—evidence that Jerusalem's population observed biblical dietary laws.[184] Most of the bones belong to young animals, indicating that they were slaughtered and butchered for their meat rather than being raised to adulthood for secondary products (such as milk or wool) or to serve as beasts of burden (in the case of cattle). Differences in the composition of the remains, such as the presence or absence of pigeons (which were common offerings of the poor) and chickens (which were raised in domestic contexts), and juvenile versus adult animals suggest that the garbage dumped at the north end of the southeastern hill derived from the temple, whereas at the south end it appears to represent household waste.[185] In addition to the animal bones, 591 fish bones were recovered in excavations at the south end of the land-fill, with more than half that could be identified belonging to freshwater species (mostly carp). This is a much higher proportion of freshwater species than in ear-lier fish bone assemblages from Jerusalem (e.g., Iron Age II and Persian-period contexts), which are dominated by marine and Nilotic species. Omri Lernau, who analyzed the fish bones, proposes that the freshwater fish were imported from Tarichaea (Migdal/Magdala) on the western shore of the Sea of Galilee, which was known in this period for its fish pickling and salting industry.[186]

The enormous size of the landfill is attributable to an increase in Jerusalem's population in the late Second Temple period as well as the larger numbers of pilgrims visiting the temple. The predominance of juvenile animals, especially in the dump at the north end of the southeastern hill, suggests that many of the bones are sacrificial remains. The animals were slaughtered and butchered in the temple, and the parts not burned on the altar were divided among the priests and pilgrims. The sacrificial meat was boiled in cooking pots and consumed on the Temple Mount and around the city.[187] Because biblical law requires pottery vessels to be destroyed if they become ritually impure, the cooking pots were disposed of together with the bones. It seems likely that cooking pots are repre-sented in higher proportions at the north end of the landfill because they are part of the refuse associated with the temple sacrifices rather than everyday household waste.[188] Large numbers of whole cooking pots discovered in several spots in the Kidron Valley at the base of the southeastern hill might also have been discarded by pilgrims to the temple.[189]

A long stretch of the paved street along the west side of the Temple Mount (below Robinson's Arch) was excavated by Reich and Shukron (Figure 7.5). They observed that the street was covered by a thin layer of earth mixed with broken pottery, coins, and other artifacts. Most of the coins date to the time of the First Revolt. The earth was overlaid by large stones belonging to the upper part of the temenos wall, which collapsed onto the street as a result of the Roman destruc-tion in 70 CE. Reich and Shukron conclude that, during the first century CE, the street was maintained by municipal authorities who were responsible for keeping public spaces clean. When the revolt broke out, the municipal services ceased to function, and debris accumulated on the street.[190] During the siege, the cisterns in the palatial mansion (and presumably in other residences) were filled with gar-bage, which could no longer be dumped outside the city walls.[191]

Water Supply

The growth of Jerusalem's population including pilgrims and the increased volume of sacrifices offered in the temple resulted in a need for more water.[192] Under Herod, a new channel—the high-level aqueduct—was constructed to bring water to the city. Like the Hasmonean-period low-level aqueduct, the high-level aqueduct originated at Solomon's Pools near Bethlehem. But whereas the low-level aqueduct meanders for twice the straight-line distance between the beginning and end points, the high-level aqueduct follows a relatively direct route along a distance of 13 kilometers (8 miles). For long stretches, the high-level aqueduct is a rock-cut channel, hewn completely underground or running along the surface of the ground and covered with stone slabs.[193] One section near Bethlehem is visible as a massive pipe constructed of individual stone links carefully fitted together. For a long time, archaeologists dated the high-level aqueduct to the second century CE because some of the stone links have Latin inscriptions associated with the Tenth Roman Legion. It therefore was assumed that the aqueduct brought water to the legionary camp established after 70 CE on Jerusalem's southwestern hill.[194] However, in the early 1990s, an examination by David Amit revealed that this section of the high-level aqueduct spans a valley. When Herod established the high-level aqueduct, he built a bridge supported on arches to carry the channel across the valley. After 70 CE, when the Tenth Legion rebuilt the channel, they filled in the arches with stones and constructed the stone-link pipe on top of it.[195]

Eventually, another aqueduct was constructed to provide additional water to Solomon's Pools from a spring in Wadi el-Biyar, about 4 kilometers (2.5 miles) to the south.[196] A recent study was unable to determine whether the Wadi el-Biyar aqueduct was established in the mid-first century CE (perhaps during the administration of Pontius Pilate) and renovated in the second century (during the time of Aelia Capitolina), or dates entirely to the second century.[197] Whereas the low-level aqueduct supplied the Temple Mount, the high-level aqueduct served the needs of the residents of the Upper City and particularly Herod's palace, probably terminating at Hezekiah's Pool, just north of the modern Jaffa Gate on the western side of the Old City.[198] The amount of water stored in Solomon's Pools was increased even more by another aqueduct that brought water from springs in the `Arrub valley (Wadi `Arrub), south of Bethlehem. Although the straight-line distance from the beginning to the end of the `Arrub aqueduct is only about 10 kilometers (6 miles), the channel meanders for 39 kilometers (24 miles) due to the steep and uneven topography.[199] The `Arrub aqueduct might be the aqueduct that Josephus says was constructed by Pontius Pilate: "On a later occasion he [Pontius Pilate] provoked a fresh uproar [among the Jews] by expending upon the construction of an aqueduct the sacred treasure known as *Corbonas*; the water was brought from a distance of 400 furlongs."[200]

Corban (Hebrew *korban*)—a sacrifice or gift to God—is mentioned in Mark 7:11–13, where Jesus responds to the Pharisees and scribes for criticizing his disciples for not washing their hands before eating: "But you say that if anyone tells father or mother, 'Whatever support you might have had from me is Corban' (that is, an offering to God)—then you no longer permit doing anything for a father or mother, thus making void the word of God through your tradition that you have handed on." Jesus calls his critics hypocrites because they prohibit using a gift vowed to God to support one's parents, thereby violating the commandment to honor your father and mother.

By the first century CE, Jerusalem was ringed by large, open-air reservoirs that created a moat-like barrier protecting the city. The pools lay inside valley beds and were fed by surface runoff (rainwater), water channeled from sources to the north and south of the city (including the Gihon spring), and the aqueduct system.[201] Moving counterclockwise from the northeast corner of the Temple Mount, they include Birket Isra`il (the Pool of Israel) and the Bezetha (or Bethesda or Sheep's) Pool to the north, both of which provided water for the needs of the temple; the Struthion (Sparrow) Pools, north of the Antonia fortress; Hezekiah's Pool (the Amygdalon Pool or Pool of the Towers), north of Herod's three towers and palace; the Serpent's Pool (perhaps the current Sultan's Pool [Birket Sultan] in the Ben-Hinnom Valley, on the southwest side of the southwestern hill); and the Pool of Siloam (Birket el-Hamra) at the southwest tip of the southeastern hill.[202]

The Sheep's Pool and the Pool of Siloam are mentioned in the Gospel of John in connection with Jesus's miraculous healings. Despite John's Christological agenda, his Gospel contains a number of references to topographical features in Jerusalem and at other sites around the country which are not mentioned in the other three Gospels. Scholars disagree about whether these references preserve accurate historical information from the time of Jesus.[203] In John 5:2–9, Jesus heals an invalid at the Bezetha Pool while in Jerusalem for a festival.

Now in Jerusalem by the Probatica [the Sheep's Gate or Sheep's Market] there is a pool, called in Hebrew Beth-zatha, which has five porticoes. In these lay many invalids—blind, lame, and paralyzed. One man was there who had been ill for thirty-eight years. When Jesus saw him lying there and knew that he had been there a long time, he said to him, "Do you want to be made well?" The sick man answered him, "Sir, I have no one to put me into the pool when the water is stirred up; and while I am making my way, someone else steps down ahead of me." Jesus said to him, "Stand up, take your mat and walk." At once the man was made well; and he took up his mat and began to walk. (my adaptation from the NRSV)

John's reference to the Bezetha Pool suggests it should be identified with the reservoir in the Bezetha quarter to the north of Birket Isra`il (Figure 7.28).[204] The Bezetha Pool (commonly rendered as Bethesda) is often called the Sheep's Pool because John says it was located by the Sheep's Gate or Sheep's Market (Greek Probatica), presumably because that is where sacrificial animals were sold to pilgrims. Excavations have revealed that the Bezetha Pool was divided into two large basins separated by a barrier wall. Based on John's reference, archaeologists

FIGURE 7.28 The Bezetha (Bethesda) Pool.
Credit: Photo by the author.

reconstruct four rows of columns (porticoes) around the sides of the pool and a fifth row on the barrier wall.[205] No remains of columns have been found at the site, probably having been carried away for reuse over the centuries.[206]

Shimon Gibson identifies the southern basin of the Bezetha Pool as an enormous miqveh based on the massive hewn steps descending along its western side, which are lacking in the northern basin.[207] The southern basin appears to have been designed to accommodate the throngs of pilgrims who needed to purify themselves before entering the temple. Gibson suggests that a channel through the barrier wall separating the northern and southern basin, which could be opened by a sluice gate to allow water through, may have caused the stirring of the water mentioned in John's account.[208] He concludes that "those precluded from admission to the Temple, owing to disabilities and bodily defects, would have sought miraculous healing at these pools and this is the background for the healing accounts in the Gospel of John."[209]

Gibson's conclusion is possible but speculative. Biblical law requires immersion in water for purification from certain types of impurity. A state of purity was required to enter God's presence, which Jews of the late Second Temple period believed dwelled in the Jerusalem temple. According to biblical law, the main causes of impurity are certain skin diseases (including on clothing and walls), certain types of bodily secretions (such as nocturnal emissions for men and menstruation for women), and contact with certain categories of living things and corpses. However, there is no indication in any sources—literary or archaeological—that Jews immersed in *miqva'ot* for purposes other than purification, such as seeking miraculous healings. Neither of the men healed by Jesus suffered from a condition or affliction that required ritual purification. This does not prove that Jews never immersed in a *miqveh* for the purposes of miraculous healing, only that this practice is unattested outside of John's account.[210]

Although John's testimony might provide evidence of this practice, there is another possibility. After 70 CE, the Bezetha Pool was the site of a healing sanctuary dedicated to Serapis (it usually described in scholarly literature as a sanctuary to Asclepius or an Asclepeion). Ancient sources describe Asclepius and Serapis as gods that healed patients through a combination of bathing in water and dreaming while sleeping on the grounds of the sanctuary (a process called "incubation"). John's description of the Sheep's Pool—surrounded by invalids lying on mats—sounds more like the incubator of an Asclepeion than pools used for ritual purification as prescribed by biblical law. John refers to the invalid's bed as a *krabbatos*, which in New Testament Greek denotes the pallet or mattress used as bedding by the poor. John's story better fits a post-70 than pre-70 CE reality in Jerusalem, and a scene of invalids sleeping on mats by a pool hoping for a miraculous healing would have made more sense to a gentile than Jewish audience. In other words, although it is possible that some Jews sought healing at the Sheep's Pool (in which case the tradition associating Jesus with healing at this site would antedate 70), it is just as likely that this tradition postdates 70 CE.[211]

Several early church fathers who were natives of Palestine describe the Sheep's Pool as divided into two parts surrounded by porticoes—a detail not mentioned in the Fourth Gospel.[212] They include Origen (writing in the first half of the third century CE), and Eusebius (writing in the latter part of the third century to first half of the fourth century), who says: "Bezetha, a pool in Jerusalem, which is the Probatica, once having had five porticoes. It is shown now to have twin pools, one of which is fed normally by rainwater and the other has wondrously red water, the remains—it is said, of victims who had formerly been washed here. The name Probatic comes from the animals which were sacrificed here."[213] Cyril, the bishop of Jerusalem in the third quarter of the fourth century, explicitly describes the Sheep's Pool as two basins surrounded by porticoes on four sides and a fifth row of columns on the partition wall: "By the Sheep Market in Jerusalem there used to be a pool with five colonnades, four of which enclosed the pool, while the fifth spanned it midway."[214] These descriptions might indicate the pool's appearance after 70 CE.

John's account of Jesus's healing of a blind man at the Pool of Siloam differs from the account of the Bezetha Pool: "As he [Jesus] walked along, he saw a man blind from birth. . . .When he had said this, he spat on the ground and made mud with the saliva and spread the mud on the man's eyes, saying to him, 'Go, wash in the pool of Siloam' (which means Sent). Then he went and washed and came back able to see" (Jn 9:1, 6–7). Unlike the episode at the Bezetha Pool, there is no indication of a setting recalling a healing sanctuary, only a single, random blind man. Indeed, although John refers to the Pool of Siloam, the healing is not described as taking place at the pool. Instead, Jesus tells the blind man to wash in the pool after being healed. It is impossible to determine whether Jesus and other Jews utilized the water (and mud) of the Pool of Siloam for healing purposes and not just for ritual purification. Interestingly, unlike Jerusalem's other large reservoirs, the Pool of Siloam and the Bezetha Pool apparently were used as *miqva'ot*—that is, Jesus's miraculous healings reportedly occurred at pools in which Jews immersed.

Ya`akov Meshorer suggests that, after 70 CE, a sanctuary of Hygieia (the goddess of health and hygiene) was associated with the Pool of Siloam, based on a series of city coins depicting the goddess sitting on a rock (which he believes must be the source of a spring) and feeding a snake.[215] Nicole Belayche rejects this proposal on the grounds that there is no supporting archaeological or literary evidence.[216] Either way, John's account does not imply that the Pool of Siloam was used as a healing sanctuary. John may have presented it as the setting for Jesus's

FIGURE 7.29 The Pool of Siloam.
Credit: Photo by the author.

performance of a miracle because of Isaiah 8:6, in which the waters of Shiloah (Siloam) symbolize the Davidic dynasty.[217]

Most of the Pool of Siloam (Birket el-Hamra) is now occupied by a large, privately owned garden or orchard. Excavations by Reich and Shukron on the east side indicate that the pool was an enormous trapezoid measuring approximately 60 × 50 meters (196 × 164 feet).[218] The pool was surrounded by stone steps arranged in groups of five separated by broad landings, indicating that it was used for ritual purification by the masses of pilgrims who ascended from this point to the Temple Mount (Figure 7.29). The steps facilitated access to the pool, with bathers standing on landings to immerse if the water level was high enough.[219]

Since immersion without clothing is required for Jewish ritual purification, Reich and Shukron speculate that temporary structures might have been erected in the pool to separate male and female bathers.[220]

Below the stone steps surrounding the pool is an earlier set of steps made of rubble (uncut stones) and cement covered with plaster. Coins indicate that the earlier steps date to the mid-to-late first century BCE, while the stone steps appear to date to the first century CE.[221] Presumably, the late Iron Age–Persian-period Pool of Shelah mentioned in Nehemiah 3:15 is located under this pool.[222] The Pool of Siloam was fed by a channel that brought water from the outlet of the Siloam Tunnel some 70 meters (229 feet) to the north. After Jerusalem was destroyed in 70 CE, the pool went of use and silted up, and its location was forgotten. In the Byzantine period (fifth century CE), a new but smaller pool—the current pool of Siloam—was built next to a church farther to the north, at the outlet of the Siloam Tunnel.[223]

The First Wall crossed the southern end of the Tyropoeon Valley on a massive dam that enclosed and protected the Pool of Siloam. In the Hasmonean period, gates flanked by towers on the north and south sides of the dam provided entry into the city.[224] In the first century CE the southern gate was replaced by another gate some 60 meters (196 feet) farther south, at the point where the First Wall turns to climb the southwestern hill. This gate provided access to a paved street that followed the Tyropoeon Valley northward by the Pool of Siloam and continued along the western side of the Temple Mount.[225] This is the same paved street that runs underneath Robinson's Arch and was covered by the stone collapse of the upper temenos wall of the Temple Mount.

On the north side of the Pool of Siloam, Reich and Shukron found a stone-paved plaza or esplanade that was separated from the pool by a portico.[226] The paved street continues northward from the esplanade, where it ascends in alternating wide and narrow steps along the Tyropoeon Valley (Figure 7.30).[227] The esplanade and paved street were covered with stone collapse from the destruction of the city in 70 CE.[228] A drainage channel underneath the street is large enough for a person to move through it in a crouched position. It was filled with debris including coins from the time of the First Revolt and intact cooking pots.[229] In several spots the paving stones of the street had been removed, apparently to allow entry into the drain. Reich and Shukron connect this to Josephus's description of inhabitants desperately attempting to escape the Romans through "underground passages"—apparently the sewers—after the city fell in 70 CE:[230] "A last and cherished hope of the tyrants and their brigand comrades lay in the underground passages, as a place of refuge where they expected that no search would be made for them, intending after the complete capture of the city and the departure of the Romans to come forth and make their escape."[231]

FIGURE 7.30 The stepped street from Siloam along the Tyropoeon Valley. Credit: Photo by the author.

As mentioned above, coins found under the continuation of this paved street to the north in the vicinity of Robinson's Arch date to the time of Pontius Pilate (26–37 CE), indicating that construction around the Temple Mount continued for decades after Herod's death.[232] Excavations have been conducted by various archaeologists at other points along this street, including a large-scale project about 220 meters (721 feet) north of the Pool of Siloam and 360 meters (1,181 feet) south of the Temple Mount, directed from 2013–2016 by Nahshon Szanton and Joe Uziel. Altogether 101 coins were discovered under the street in different excavations, including one specimen dated to 16–29 CE found under the street at the top of the staircase that led to Wilson's Arch.[233] Because the latest coins from all these contexts date to 30/31 CE, Szanton and his team conclude that Pontius Pilate was responsible for paving the street.[234] Previously, Reich and Shukron had associated the paved street with Herod Agrippa II since the latest coins found under it indicate only that the pavement was laid no earlier than 30/31 CE. They connect the project with Josephus's reference to the completion of work on the Temple Mount under Agrippa II, which resulted in mass layoffs.[235] Agrippa II refused the people's request to employ the laborers by raising the height of Solomon's Portico on the east side of the Temple Mount but agreed to pave the streets: "Just now, too, the temple (*hieron*) had been completed. The people therefore saw that the workmen, numbering over eighteen thousand, were out of work and would be deprived of pay, for they earned their living by working on the temple (*hieron*) ... but he did not veto the paving of the city with white stone."[236]

When Herod Agrippa I was given rule over Judea in 41 CE, he began to mint large numbers of coins in Jerusalem. Szanton's team point to the absence of coins of Agrippa I as evidence that the street must have been paved by his predecessor, Pontius Pilate, who they note was responsible for constructing a new aqueduct.[237] Although this is a persuasive argument, it is not the only plausible interpretation. The coins come from fills that presumably were imported from other locations and were deposited to level the street before the pavement was laid. These fills likely were taken from garbage dumps (middens). The coins only provide a terminus post quem for the deposition of the material in the middens, not the date when those fills were brought from the middens to level the street. Therefore, the absence of coins of Herod Agrippa I does not negate the possibility that Herod Agrippa II was responsible for paving the street after being given oversight of the Jerusalem temple in 48–49 CE.[238] The street's dating has far-reaching historical and religious implications because if it was paved shortly after 30/31 CE, Jesus could have walked the route from the Pool of Siloam to the Temple Mount during his final days in Jerusalem. Following the excavations, the street was opened to the public on 30 June 2019, in a highly publicized ceremony.[239]

Since Yigal Shiloh's 1978–1987 excavations, Israeli archaeological work on the southeastern hill has become increasingly politicized due to the involvement of El-Ad (or Elad = the Ir David Foundation), a right-wing settler organization that seeks to legitimize Israeli claims to the land by finding evidence of earlier Jewish (or even Israelite) presence. El-Ad has underwritten excavations on Palestinian properties it acquired around the southeastern hill, including the ongoing excavations in the Givati Parking Lot and the development of the "City of David" as a tourist attraction. The work has been widely criticized because the focus on Jewish or Israelite remains effectively erases the history of other peoples who have lived on the southeastern hill, including (and especially) the current Palestinian residents.[240]

The excavations funded by El-Ad on the southeastern hill have also generated controversy because in some areas the work was carried out underground. Archaeological methodology involves digging in a systematic manner from top to bottom. In areas where El-Ad was unable to acquire Palestinian properties, excavations have been conducted entirely below ground level. For example, the paved street was dug by tunnelling under the modern street along the Tyropoeon Valley. The underground excavations are problematic on legal, ethical, and scientific grounds. Legally, they raise the question of ownership of the land on which a house sits. Ethically, the process of tunnelling under some of the Palestinian houses has destabilized the foundations and caused structural damage. Scientifically, digging tunnels runs counter to the archaeological endeavor by divorcing the remains from their context, even if the excavations are conducted by qualified professional archaeologists.[241] Consequently, much of Israel's archaeological community is divided among those supporting the excavation work and those who condemn it.

Synagogues

Acts 6:9 refers to synagogues in Jerusalem with congregations of Diaspora Jews: "Then some of those who belonged to the synagogue of the Freedmen (as it was called), Cyrenians, Alexandrians, and others of those from Cilicia and Asia, stood up and argued with Stephen." A split in the Jerusalem church between Hellenists and Hebrews mentioned in Acts 6:1 might reflect differences between Greek-speaking Diaspora Jews and locals.[242] The Tosefta (a rabbinic work) refers to an Alexandrian congregation: "R. Eleazar b. R. Sadoq purchased the synagogue of the Alexandrians which was located in Jerusalem."[243]

Although scholars debate exactly when and where synagogues originated, there is no doubt that they existed by the first century BCE–first century CE, as indicated by references in Josephus, Philo, and the New Testament. The term "synagogue" can denote a Jewish assembly as well as a building to house such an assembly.[244] The earliest synagogue buildings have benches lining the walls to accommodate the congregation but lack features such as permanent liturgical furniture and Jewish decorative symbols and motifs, which were introduced in later centuries.[245]

Archaeological remains associated with a first century CE synagogue were discovered in excavations at the south end of the southeastern hill in 1913–1914, when Raymond Weill found an inscribed stone block that had been dumped in a cistern with other architectural fragments.[246] The inscribed block is now on display in the Israel Museum in Jerusalem (Figure 7.31). The inscription, which is in Greek, commemorates a synagogue built by Theodotos son of Vettenos.

FIGURE 7.31 The Theodotos synagogue inscription in the Israel Museum Jerusalem. Credit: Photo by the author.

> Theodotos son of Vettenos, priest and archisynagogos, son of an archisynagogos, grandson of an archisynagogos, built the synagogue for the reading of the Law and teaching of the commandments, and the guesthouse and the (other) rooms and water installations(?) for the lodging of those who are in need of it from abroad, which (=the synagogue) his forefathers, the elders and Simonides founded.[247]

Presumably, the building associated with the inscription was located nearby and was destroyed in 70 CE.[248] Although Theodotos is a common Greek name (equivalent to the Hebrew Yehonatan [John] or Netanel [Nathaniel]), Vettenos appears to be Latin, suggesting this was an immigrant family.[249] *Archisynagogos*—Greek for "head of a synagogue"—is the most common leadership title associated with ancient synagogues. It is unclear whether this title indicates that the bearer had any liturgical and/or administrative responsibilities or was purely honorific. The fact that Theodotos was a priest and a third-generation *archisynagogos* and had the means to dedicate a synagogue indicates this was an elite family. The inscription states that the synagogue was built "for the reading of the Law [Torah] and the teaching of the commandments," which are still central to synagogue liturgy. However, there is no mention of prayer, as institutionalized communal prayer in synagogues developed only in the centuries after 70 CE.[250]

It is unclear if Theodotos's synagogue served an immigrant or Diaspora congregation like those mentioned in Acts, or if it replaced an earlier building on the same spot, or if the guest house (hostel) was intended for pilgrims visiting Jerusalem.[251] Some scholars have speculated that the Theodotos synagogue is the "synagogue of the Freedmen" of Acts 6:9 because Tacitus and Philo mention that Jews brought to Rome as captives were soon freed. According to this view, the Vettenos family would have been descended from Jews taken into captivity when Pompey annexed the Hasmonean kingdom in 63 BCE.[252] However, John Kloppenborg refutes this suggestion, noting that if Theodotos was a freedman or the son of a freedman, he should be named Theodotos Vettenos (or, technically, Caius Vettennius Theodotos), not Theodotos *son of* Vettenos.[253] And the widespread assumption that Vettenos is a Latin name, although reasonable, is unproved. To the contrary, the lack of a reference to the family's origin in the inscription (e.g., Theodotos son of Vettenos of Rome), which might be expected if they were immigrants, leaves open the possibility that they were natives of Judea.[254]

Glass

Although glass had been invented centuries earlier, it was an expensive and rare product before the Herodian period. During the Hellenistic period, mold-made glass bowls became common. Late in the first century BCE, the invention of glass blowing revolutionized glass production. Blown glass is made by blowing hot glass through a tube into the desired shape. This invention made glass vessels much less costly and therefore more common. Phoenicia (where Ennion worked) and Palestine were centers of glass-making in the Hellenistic and Roman periods. In the Jewish Quarter excavations, Avigad discovered glass refuse in the fill of a *miqveh* that was sealed by a stone pavement during the reign of Herod the Great. The refuse, which represents waste from a glass factory, consists of glass fragments, wasters (misfired glass), pieces of raw glass, and slag. The objects represented among the fragments include cast bowls, small blown glass perfume bottles, applicators or stirring rods ("kohl sticks"), spindle whorls, gaming pieces, and inlays. This is the earliest archaeological evidence of blown glass found anywhere. Although Avigad was surprised to find evidence of glass manufacturing in a major urban center and not closer to a source of silica sand, raw glass is usually transferred to workshops from areas close to sources of sand and fuel.[255]

Although glass is not listed among the materials from which vessels that acquire impurity are made (Num 31:22–23)—presumably because it was not yet in use when this legislation was written—after 70 CE, the rabbis ruled that glass vessels are susceptible to impurity. It is not clear whether any groups before 70 CE (including the Pharisees) considered glass susceptible to impurity. It is possible that some groups such as the Sadducees took the omission of glass from the list

in Numbers to mean that it is insusceptible to impurity, as perhaps suggested by
the finds from the Jewish Quarter mansions, which include locally produced and
imported luxury glass vessels such as an exquisite vase signed by the Sidonian
craftsman Ennion (Figure 7.20).[256]

Coins

Herod the Great issued his own bronze coins, most of which were minted in
Jerusalem and are undated. Many of the coins bear motifs similar to those used
by the Hasmoneans (anchors, cornucopias, and wreaths), accompanied by the
Greek inscription "of King Herod."[257] He might have been concerned not to
offend the Jewish population by putting figured images on his coins.[258] However,
one series minted by Herod bears non-figured symbols that appear to be pagan
or at least are ambiguous, such as an altar or table on top of which is a helmet or
cap with a star—perhaps the cap of the Dioscuri, the sons of Zeus (Figures 7.32
and 7.33). This series was minted for a short time, possibly at the non-Jewish site
of Samaria-Sebaste, and had limited circulation.[259] Herod Agrippa I and Herod
Agrippa II minted coins bearing figured images (including busts of the emperor
and portraits of themselves and other family members) and depictions of pagan
temples for circulation in non-Jewish territories.[260]

During the First Revolt, the Jews issued their own coins as a proclamation
of independence.[261] These coins, which were minted in silver and bronze, carry
symbols and slogans alluding to Jerusalem and the temple (Figures 7.34 and 7.35).
The symbols include a chalice (a vessel used in the temple) and a branch with
three pomegranates (perhaps a staff used by the priests). The coins are inscribed
in paleo-Hebrew script with Hebrew slogans alluding to Jerusalem and the
temple (and the revival of an independent Jewish kingdom), such as "Jerusalem
the holy" and "for the freedom of Zion." The designation of these coins as
sheqels—an ancient system of weights—also alludes to the revival of the biblical
kingdom. The coins carry dates from Year One to Year Five (of the revolt), with
the establishment of a new calendar being another proclamation of independence
from Roman rule. Minting continued even while Jerusalem was under siege.[262]

After the fall of Jerusalem, Vespasian and his sons celebrated their victory
over the Jews by minting Judea Capta coins—a special series which David
Hendin describes as "the broadest and most diverse series of coins commemorating a Roman victory issued to that time."[263] The head of the emperor is
depicted on the obverse, while the reverse shows various motifs such as a young
woman (symbolizing the Jewish people) mourning under a date palm (symbolizing the province of Judea), and a Jewish male captive with hands bound
behind his back standing on the other side of the tree (Figures 7.36 and 7.37).

FIGURE 7.32 Coin of Herod showing pagan images: a helmet with a star (perhaps the cap of the Dioscuri on an altar) (1944.100.62798; ANS collection bequest of E. T. Newell). Credit: Courtesy of David Hendin.

FIGURE 7.33 Coin of Herod showing pagan images: a tripod with *lebes* (ceremonial bowl) surrounded by the Greek inscription "of King Herod," flanked by date "year 3" and a monogram (1944.100.62798; ANS collection bequest of E. T. Newell). Credit: Courtesy of David Hendin.

The coins are so-called because some bear the Latin inscription *Iudaea Capta*— Judea has been conquered.[264]

Stone Weights

Weights used to weigh commodities were common in the ancient world. However, whereas in the Hellenistic and Roman periods most weights were made of lead, in Herodian Jerusalem they are all made of the local limestone. A majority are cylindrical while the others are shaped like cubes. The stone

FIGURE 7.34 Silver sheqel of the First Jewish Revolt showing a chalice with pearled rim with the letter "One" [Year One] above surrounded by the paleo-Hebrew inscription "Sheqel of Israel" (2010.69.3. ANS collection gift of Abraham D and Marian Scheuer Sofaer).
Credit: Courtesy of David Hendin.

FIGURE 7.35 Silver sheqel of the First Jewish Revolt showing a staff with three pomegranate buds and the paleo-Hebrew inscription "Jerusalem the holy" (2010.69.3. ANS collection gift of Abraham D and Marian Scheuer Sofaer).
Credit: Courtesy of David Hendin.

weights appear to be distinctive to Jerusalem, where ninety-five percent of all known examples have been found. Approximately one-third of the stone weights come from the villas in the Jewish Quarter, including the one inscribed with the name of the priestly family Bar Kathros.[265] A large number was also found in the municipal landfill along the east slope of the southeastern hill, where they appear to have been dumped with other refuse. The stone weights

FIGURE 7.36 Judea Capta coin of Vespasian (ANS 1947.2.430).
Credit: Courtesy of David Hendin.

FIGURE 7.37 Judea Capta coin of Vespasian (ANS 1947.2.430).
Credit: Courtesy of David Hendin.

date from Herod's reign until Jerusalem's destruction in 70 CE, although the weighing systems changed over time.[266] Signs of recalibration on some of the weights are evidence that the system was strictly controlled by central authorities. The original weight was restored to stone weights that lost mass over time by filling a small, drilled hole with cast lead.[267]

The large number of weights found in the Jewish Quarter villas, including one inscribed with the name of a priestly family, might indicate that some were used to weigh priestly offerings (tithes).[268] This would account for the exclusive preference for stone, a material that many Jews considered insusceptible to ritual impurity.[269]

Tombs and Ossuaries

The features that appeared in the Hasmonean period in Jason's Tomb remained characteristic of Jewish rock-cut tombs in Jerusalem until 70 CE.[270] The differences between individual rock-cut tombs of the Herodian period mostly concern their size and degree of elaboration; that is, the number of burial chambers, the presence or absence of a porch (with or without columns), the addition of decoration (typically around the entrance to the burial chambers and/or on the porch façade), and the presence or absence of one or more monumental tomb markers. Many burial chambers are encircled by rock-cut benches just below the loculi, on which the bodies of the deceased could be placed as they were prepared for interment.

In the middle of Herod's reign, around 20–15 BCE, ossuaries first appeared in Jerusalem's rock-cut tombs. Ossuaries were used as containers for bones removed from loculi (after the flesh had decayed), in contrast to sarcophagi (coffins), which accommodated a corpse still with the flesh (an inhumation). Ossuaries are much smaller than sarcophagi—only big enough to accommodate individual bones—whereas sarcophagi were designed to contain a whole corpse. Most ossuaries from Jerusalem are made of locally quarried stone, usually soft chalk or, rarely, harder limestone. They have flat, rounded, or gabled lids. The ossuaries can be plain or decorated (most decoration consists of incised or chip-carved designs, rarely in relief, and sometimes with painting). Sometimes the name(s) of the deceased (and infrequently other information such as their title or occupation) were incised on the front, back, side, or lid of the ossuary. Most of the inscriptions are in Aramaic, Hebrew, or Greek, and usually they are crudely executed, having been added inside the tomb by family members involved in collecting the remains.[271]

There is not necessarily a correlation between the relative wealth and status of the deceased and the ornamentation of the ossuary, since undecorated ossuaries have been found in tombs belonging to some of ancient Jerusalem's most prominent families. The same is true of the tombs themselves, as indicated by the modest size and appearance of a tomb belonging to the Caiaphas family. This tomb was discovered in 1990, to the southwest of the Old City and was excavated by Israeli archaeologists. Two of the ossuaries from the tomb are inscribed with the name Caiaphas (Aramaic *Capha*), including one inscribed "Joseph son of Caiaphas" (Figure 7.38). Because Caiaphas is an unusual name and Joseph son of Caiaphas is known to have served as high priest from 18–36 CE, this tomb likely belonged to the family of the same high priest who presided over the trial of Jesus according to the Gospel accounts.

Whereas there is no doubt that ossuaries were used as containers for bones removed from loculi, scholars question why they were introduced into Jerusalem's

FIGURE 7.38 The Caiaphas ossuary in the Israel Museum Jerusalem.
Credit: Photo by the author.

rock-cut tombs around 20–15 BCE and why they disappeared from Jerusalem after 70 CE (with evidence of their use on a smaller and more modest scale in southern Judea and Galilee until the third century). An Israeli archaeologist named Levy Yitzhak Rahmani connected the appearance of ossuaries with the Pharisaic belief in the individual, physical resurrection of the dead. The anticipation of a future, physical resurrection of the dead is accepted today as part of normative, rabbinic Judaism. This doctrine became popular among the Pharisees in the late Second Temple period. However, the Sadducees rejected the belief in individual, physical resurrection of the dead on the grounds that such a doctrine is nowhere explicitly stated in the Pentateuch (Torah). Rahmani connected the introduction of ossuaries to the spread of a belief in the future, physical resurrection of the dead. Prior to the introduction of ossuaries, the remains of burials in rock-cut tombs such as Jason's Tomb were collected in pits, repositories, or charnel rooms. The skeletons therefore were mingled and susceptible to separation, breakage, and even loss. This means that, in the event of a physical resurrection, an individual would be restored to life missing vital body parts. According to Rahmani, ossuaries were introduced into Jerusalem's rock-cut tombs to preserve the remains of each individual intact. Rahmani also argued that the collection of bones in an ossuary corresponds to the Pharisaic notion connecting the decay of the flesh to the expiation of sin. In other words, each individual's remains were preserved intact in an ossuary, in a sinless state, awaiting future resurrection.[272]

Many scholars have pointed to difficulties with Rahmani's explanation. For example, ossuaries frequently contain the bones of more than one individual, and sometimes parts of the skeleton are missing. In fact, according to rabbinic law it was not necessary to collect all the bones. Furthermore, even in tombs with ossuaries, some skeletons continued to be deposited in pits or repositories. Another difficulty with Rahmani's explanation is that the monumental rock-cut tombs with ossuaries belonged to Jerusalem's elite, many of whom were Sadducees—the same group who reportedly rejected the doctrine of individual, physical resurrection of the dead. In fact, some of these tombs and ossuaries belonged to high priestly families, such as the tomb of Bene Hezir and the tomb and ossuaries of the Caiaphas family. In other words, ossuaries were used by some of the same members of Jerusalem society who reportedly rejected the concept of individual, physical resurrection of the dead. It is not a coincidence that, outside of Jerusalem, the largest cemetery with rock-cut loculus tombs containing ossuaries is at Jericho, which was the site of the Hasmonean and Herodian winter palaces and the center of a priestly community.

Instead of associating ossuaries with expectations of an afterlife or other religious beliefs, their appearance should be understood within the context of foreign (specifically, Roman) influence on the Jerusalem elite, just like other features of rock-cut tombs. In the late first century BCE and first century CE, cremation was the prevailing burial rite among the Romans. The ashes of the deceased were placed in small stone containers called *cineraria* (cinerary urns), which are usually casket-shaped and have gabled lids. Sometimes they have carved decoration and/or inscriptions. Cinerary urns were in widespread use around the Roman world, including Rhodes, Asia Minor, and North Africa. Small stone containers or chests used for the secondary collection of bones (called *ostothecai*) are also found in Asia Minor. Like their Judean counterparts, these stone boxes can have carved decoration and sometimes contain the remains of more than one individual. This evidence suggests that the appearance of ossuaries in Judea is related to funerary customs and fashions that were prevalent in the Roman world instead of to Jewish expectations of resurrection.

Rahmani has objected to the possibility that ossuaries were inspired by Roman cinerary urns on the grounds that Jerusalem's elite could not have imitated a practice with which they were unacquainted. However, other Hellenized features in tombs and burial customs were adopted by Jerusalem's elite without personal contact or familiarity (as were other aspects of Hellenistic and Roman culture). Monumental tombs marked by a pyramid became a raging fashion after Simon constructed the family tomb at Modiin. The ultimate source of inspiration for these tombs was the Mausoleum at Halicarnassos, which presumably none of Jerusalem's elite in the Hasmonean period—not even Simon—ever saw. Loculi, which also originated in the Hellenistic world, quickly became universal in Jerusalem's rock-cut tombs. The spread of these features has little or nothing to do with religious beliefs in the afterlife and everything to do with social status. Jerusalem's elite were prohibited by Jewish law from cremating their dead. Instead, they could and did adopt the external trappings of cremation by depositing the bones of the deceased in ossuaries (urns). Like loculi, once ossuaries appeared, they quickly became universal in rock-cut tombs.

By 70 CE, Jerusalem was surrounded by rock-cut tombs, mostly to the north, east, and south, nearly a thousand of which have been documented to date.[273] Well-known examples include the tomb of Bene Hezir, the tomb of Queen Helena of Adiabene (the so-called Tombs of the Kings), and the tomb of Nicanor. Most of Jerusalem's rock-cut tombs are more modest than these examples, having an undecorated or simply decorated entrance and a single burial chamber with loculi.

The Kidron Valley Tombs

A series of monumental tombs of the late Second Temple period is in the Kidron Valley, at the foot of the western slope of the Mount of Olives. They are positioned to be visible from the Temple Mount above. Their size, location, and decoration indicate that they belonged to some of the wealthiest and most prominent families among Jerusalem's elite. There are three monuments in a row, from north to south: the monument (or tomb) of Absalom (and the associated cave of Jehoshaphat), the tomb of Bene Hezir (pronounced "bin-EH kheh-ZEER"), and the tomb of Zachariah (Pl. 10B).[274]

The tomb of Bene Hezir is cut into the bedrock cliff at the foot of the Mount of Olives (Figure 7.39). It has a porch with two Doric columns and a Doric entablature with a triglyph and metope frieze, and three burial chambers containing loculi and arcosolia (arched burial niches). A recess with a false doorway is hewn into the bedrock surface on the north side of the porch. Originally there was a false window with a tower-like structure at the top of the recess, which served as a monumental grave marker (*nefesh*).[275]

The tomb is so-called because an inscription on the porch's architrave states that this is the tomb and *nefesh* of the family of Bene (Hebrew for "the sons of") Hezir: "This [is the] tomb and the monument (nefesh) of El`azar Ḥonyoh Jo`ezer Jehudah Shim`on Joḥanan sons of Joseph son of `Obed Joseph and El`azar sons of Ḥonyoh priests of [the] sons of Ḥezir."[276] In other words, according to the inscription, six brothers who were the sons of Joseph son of

FIGURE 7.39 The tombs of Bene Hezir (left) and Zachariah (right).
Credit: Photo by the author.

`Obed, and two brothers who apparently were the sons of one of the six broth-
ers (Ḥonyoh = Onias), were interred in the tomb—all of them priests of the
sons of Ḥezir. The priestly family of Ḥezir is mentioned in 1 Chronicles 24:15
and Nehemiah 10:20.[277] It is not surprising that the elite families who owned
rock-cut tombs included priests, many of whom were among the wealthiest
Jews.[278]

A passage cut through the rock cliff on one side of the porch connects the
tomb of Bene Hezir with the tomb of Zachariah, just to the south. The tomb
of Zachariah is a misnomer because it contains no burial chambers and was not
associated with that prophet. Instead, the tomb of Zachariah is a solid rock cube
hewn from the bedrock cliff at the foot of the Mount of Olives. The stepped base
of the cube, the Ionic semi-columns carved around its sides, and the pyramidal
roof recall the Mausoleum at Halicarnassos. The tops of the columns (just under
the Ionic capitals) are encircled by carved notches that indicate the beginning
of fluting, instead of being fluted along their entire length. This feature long ago
suggested to scholars that the tomb of Zachariah was modeled after a lost building in late Second Temple-period Jerusalem. And indeed, in the 1970s, Avigad's
excavations in the Jewish Quarter brought to light the remains of an enormous
Ionic capital (and matching column base) with this same peculiar treatment.[279]

Although we do not have the remains of the building to which the column found by Avigad belonged, this discovery confirmed that the columns on the tomb of Zachariah were inspired by a contemporary monument.

Avigad dated the tomb of Bene Hezir to the mid-second century BCE based on its architectural style.[280] The tomb of Zachariah, which was hewn after the tomb of Bene Hezir, is thought to date to the early part of the Herodian period, that is, the second half of the first century BCE.[281] The inscription on the porch of the tomb of Bene Hezir was probably added around this time, and it is likely that the *nefesh* it mentions refers to the tomb of Zachariah rather than the original, tower-like monument to the north, which perhaps had been damaged.[282] This means that the tomb of Zachariah was added as a giant *nefesh* marking the tomb of Bene Hezir.

The northernmost of the monuments in the Kidron Valley is the monument (Hebrew *yad*) of Absalom (Figure 7.40). The bottom part is a free-standing cube cut from the cliff of the Mount of Olives, while the upper portion is built of stone blocks. The sides of the cube are encircled by Ionic columns with a Doric triglyph and metope frieze, capped by a cone topped with a lotus flower instead of a pyramid. Unlike the tomb of Zachariah, the monument of Absalom contains burial chambers (holes in the sides of the stone cube were made by grave robbers who plundered its contents long ago). A large rock-cut tomb with loculi (the cave of Jehoshaphat) cut into the cliff immediately behind the monument of Absalom provided additional space for burials and presumably belonged to the same family. In other words, the monument of Absalom served as both a tomb and a *nefesh* for the burial cave behind it.[283] Avigad dated the monument and the cave behind it to the early first century CE.[284]

The association of the tomb of Zachariah with the prophet of that name originated in the Byzantine period, when a chapel was built at the foot of the cliff under the tomb of Bene Hezir. Scholars thought that the chapel was erected to enshrine the (supposed) burials of James the brother of Jesus (James "the Just"), Zachariah, and Simeon. This assumption was disproved in 2000, when Joe Zias noticed faint Greek inscriptions dating to the fourth–fifth centuries CE above the original entrance to the monument of Absalom. One inscription reads, "This is the funerary monument of Zachariah, martyr, a very pious priest, father of John," while another mentions Simeon.[285] These inscriptions indicate that early Christians believed Zachariah and Simeon were interred in the monument of Absalom. Since the inscriptions do not refer to James, presumably his remains were believed to be interred elsewhere, perhaps in or near the chapel at the foot of the tomb of Bene Hezir.[286] The chamber in the base of the tomb of Zachariah was hewn at this time, apparently in connection with the settlement of monks and hermits around the chapel.[287]

FIGURE 7.40 The monument of Absalom and the cave of Jehoshaphat.
Credit: Photo by the author.

Zachariah and Simeon were priests in the second temple at the time of the
First Revolt. According to Josephus (*War* 4.334–343), Zachariah was falsely
accused of treason and was executed by the Zealots, who threw his body into the
valley below the Temple Mount. The Zachariah whose remains were believed to
be interred in the monument of Absalom is a conflation of two different figures.
In early Christian tradition, Zachariah the priest and martyr was confused with
Zachariah, the father of John the Baptist, as reflected in the inscription's reference to "Zachariah, martyr, a very pious priest, father of John."[288] By the later
Middle Ages, the chapel at the foot of the tomb of Bene Hezir had disappeared

and Zachariah's name had come to be associated with the stone cube now known as the tomb of Zachariah.[289]

Like the tomb of Zachariah, the monument of Absalom has no connection to the biblical figure of that name. It is so-called because by the Middle Ages it had come to be associated with a monument mentioned in 2 Samuel 18:18:[290] "Now Absalom in his lifetime had taken and set up for himself a pillar that is in the King's Valley, for he said, 'I have no son to keep my name in remembrance'; he called the pillar by his own name. It is called Absalom's Monument (*yad*) to this day." Because of this association, it became traditional for visitors to stone the monument while cursing Absalom for rebelling against his father King David. Etchings from the seventeenth century on and late nineteenth century photographs show it engulfed in stones.[291]

In 2007, Netzer discovered Herod's tomb at Herodium: a Hellenistic-style mausoleum halfway up the side of the mountain. The mausoleum consisted of a square podium surmounted by two stories and a conical roof, measuring approximately 25 meters (82 feet) in height, with vaulted burial chambers inside. The monument of Absalom is clearly an imitation of Herod's mausoleum, except that its tholos is not surrounded by columns. This indicates that members of the Jerusalem elite, who emulated other aspects of Herod's lifestyle, modeled their own family tombs after his.[292]

The Tombs of the Kings (the Tomb of Queen Helena of Adiabene)

To the north of the Old City, between the Albright Institute and the American Colony Hotel, is a monumental tomb of the first century CE, which has been in the custody of the French government since the late nineteenth century.[293] Popularly known as the Tombs of the Kings because of a mistaken association with the burials of the last kings of Judah, this is, in fact, the family tomb of Queen Helena of Adiabene. The royal house of Adiabene, an ancient kingdom on the upper Tigris River in northern Mesopotamia (ancient Parthia/modern Iraqi Kurdistan), was perhaps the most illustrious Diaspora Jewish family in first-century CE Jerusalem.[294] Helena was the daughter of Izates I, the king of Adiabene. She was married to her brother Monobazus (I), who succeeded their father as king, and bore two sons, Monobazus (II) and Izates (II). She and Izates II converted to Judaism, and, after her husband's death (ca. 30 CE), Helena moved to Jerusalem, escorted part of the way by Izates II. According to the Mishnah (Nazir 3:6), Helena arrived in Jerusalem after fulfilling Nazarite vows.[295] Izates II also sent five of his sons (Helena's grandsons) to Jerusalem to study. Helena stayed in Jerusalem for twenty-four years. She was a generous benefactress who provided the people of Jerusalem with food during a famine and is commemorated in the Mishnah for her donations to the Temple: "King Monobaz[us] made of gold all the handles for the vessels used on the Day of Atonement. His mother Helena set a golden candlestick over the door of the Sanctuary. She made a golden tablet on which was written the paragraph of the Suspected Adulteress" (m. Yoma 3:10).[296]

Josephus mentions that Helena's palace in Jerusalem was located inside the Akra (*War* 5.253; 6.355), while other family members had palaces elsewhere in the Lower City (southeastern hill), including Helena's son Monobazus II (*War* 5.252) and a relative named Grapte (*War* 4.567). Another Monobazus, who was related to the king, fought on the side of the Jews at the battle of Beth-Horon early in the First Revolt (*War* 2.520), and the sons and brothers of Izates were taken into captivity by the Romans at the end of the siege of Jerusalem in 70 CE (*War* 6.356).

Excavations by Doron Ben-Ami and Yana Tchekhanovets in the Givati Parking Lot brought to light the northeast corner of a monumental building dating to the late Second Temple period, which they suggest might be Helena's palace.[297] The remains consist of elongated basement halls that were roofed with vaults. The massive walls are built of huge field stones, some weighing hundreds of kilograms. Fragments of colorful paneled frescoes found in the collapse indicate that the upper stories were richly decorated, while column bases, capitals, drums, and shafts belonging to the building were incorporated into the walls of a Late Roman structure above. A series of plastered water installations including cisterns and *miqva'ot* (described by the excavators as a "purification annex") are located to the north of the structure. The discovery of the remains of the Akra fortress in the Givati Parking Lot excavations accords with Josephus's description of Helena's palace as lying inside the Akra.

Helena returned to Adiabene after Izates's death. When Helena died soon thereafter (ca. 60 CE), Josephus reports that her son Monobazus "sent her bones and those of his brother to Jerusalem with instructions that they should be buried in the three pyramids that his mother had erected at a distance of three furlongs from the city of Jerusalem."[298] He mentions that the tomb was located to the north of the city, outside the Third Wall: "The third [wall] began at the tower Hippicus, whence it stretched northwards to the tower Psephinus, and then descending opposite the monuments of Helena (queen of Adiabene and daughter of king Izates)."[299]

The tomb of Queen Helena is the only Judean tomb mentioned by the second-century CE Greek traveler Pausanias, who singled it out together with the Mausoleum at Halicarnassus.

I know many wonderful graves, and will mention two of them, the one at Halicarnassus and one in the land of the Hebrews. The one at Halicarnassus was made for Mausolus, king of the city, and it is of such vast size, and so notable for all its ornament, that the Romans in their great admiration of it call remarkable tombs in their country "Mausolea." The Hebrews have a grave, that of Helen, a native woman, in the city of Jerusalem, which the Roman Emperor razed to the ground. There is a contrivance in the grave whereby the door, which like all the graves is of stone, does not open until the year brings back the same day and the same hour. Then the mechanism, unaided, opens the door, which, after a short interval, shuts itself. This happens at that time, but should you at any other try to open the door you cannot do so; force will not open it, but only break it down.[300]

The tomb of Queen Helena was still a landmark in the fourth century, as indicated by reports of the Church Fathers Eusebius and Jerome.[301] In 1863, Félicien de Saulcy began excavations at the site, erroneously believing it to be the tombs of the kings of Judah. The tomb is a huge underground complex that was surmounted by three pyramidal markers (Figure 7.41). In front of it is an enormous open courtyard hewn out of bedrock accessed via a monumental rock-cut staircase.[302]

FIGURE 7.41 The Tombs of the Kings.
Credit: Photo by the author.

A large *miqveh* at the base of the staircase was used by visitors and mourners.[303] The burial chambers, located on the courtyard's west side, were entered through a porch that originally had two columns. The porch's entablature is carved with a triglyph and metope frieze decorated with vegetal designs including bunches of grapes. The entrance to the burial chambers was sealed by a round rolling stone on the outside and a hinged stone door on the inside. A mechanism operated by water pressure might have moved the rolling stone—perhaps the device described by Pausanias.[304] The burial chambers, loculi, and benches are cut more finely and evenly than most other Judean tombs. Five rooms (I–V) inside the tomb contained fifty loculi and arcosolia. The innermost room (C), which is aligned with the center of the porch façade, might have contained the burial of Queen Helena.[305]

Five sarcophagi found by de Saulcy were taken to the Louvre. The names "Ṣadan the Queen" and "Ṣada the Queen" are inscribed in Aramaic on one of the sarcophagi.[306] De Saulcy reported that a woman's skeleton dressed in a garment adorned with gold disintegrated when the sarcophagus was opened.[307] De Saulcy also found fragments of ossuaries, pottery vessels, oil lamps, glass and alabaster vessels, gold jewelry, and coins. According to Amos Kloner and Boaz Zissu, "the archaeological finds support the identification of the tomb with that of the family of Helene of Adiabene."[308]

The Tomb of Nicanor

A large tomb complex discovered in 1902, on Mount Scopus, belonged to the family of Nicanor of Alexandria, who donated a set of bronze gates to the temple.[309] The complex contains five burial halls with numerous loculi and was entered through a porch with two square pillars. Kloner and Zissu describe the tomb as "one of the most elaborate in Jerusalem: the quality of the quarrying is excellent, and the very exact design of the tomb into separate burial units exploited the possibility for burials at different levels in the depth of the rock."[310] Seven ossuaries were discovered in the tomb, as well as fragments of a stone sarcophagus, pottery, and oil lamps.[311] One ossuary is inscribed in Greek, "The ossuary of Nicanor of Alexandria, who made the gates," followed in formal Jewish script (a development or variant of Aramaic script) by the inscription "Nicanor the Alexandrian."[312] The tomb is now located in the Botanical Gardens of the Hebrew University of Jerusalem's Mount Scopus campus.

The Akeldama Tombs

In 1989, the so-called Akeldama tombs, consisting of three adjacent burial caves on the western slope of the Kidron Valley near the confluence with the Ben-Hinnom Valley were excavated by Gideon Avni and Zvi Greenhut.[313] All three caves were sealed and showed no signs of modern disturbance. Only Cave 1 was completely excavated. It has four burial chambers containing loculi and arcosolia. Cave 2 (the "Eros Family Tomb") has three burial chambers with loculi and arcosolia, and Cave 3 (the "Ariston Family Tomb") has four burial chambers, also with loculi and arcosolia.[314] The opening to one of the chambers (C) in Cave 2 was sealed by a hinged stone door with an iron locking device.[315] The entrance to Chamber C in Cave 3 was adorned by a recessed frame topped by an arch and closed by a pivoting, paneled stone door. The door was locked by an elongated stone that was inserted into it through a narrow rock-cut crevice. The walls of this chamber (C) were decorated with incised geometric panels painted in red, and architectural elements carved in low relief (Pl. 11).[316] Avni and Greenhut observe that the quality and ornamentation of the burial caves indicate they belonged to affluent Jewish families.[317]

Forty ossuaries and one sarcophagus were found in the three burial caves, some decorated and some inscribed (mostly in Greek).[318] The names in the inscriptions suggest that the families buried in the three caves were related and came from Apamaea and Seleucia in Syria.[319] These include an ossuary from Cave 3 inscribed "Ariston of Apamea," and an ossuary from Cave 2 inscribed "Eiras (daughter/wife) of Seleukos(?)."[320] The excavators speculate that Ariston might be the same individual mentioned in the Mishnah as bringing first-fruits to the temple: "Ariston brought his First-fruits from Apamia and they accepted them from him, for they said: He that owns [land] in Syria is as one that owns [land] in the outskirts of Jerusalem" (m. Hallah 4:11).[321] Another ossuary from the Akeldama tombs is inscribed in Greek "Of Megiste the priestess." Scholars generally understand the title "priestess" as meaning that Megiste was the wife or daughter of a priest rather than indicating that she served in a cultic role.[322] Ariston's ossuary was also inscribed "Yehuda the proselyte," indicating that at least one convert was buried in the tomb.[323]

One unusual large and fine ossuary made of hard limestone is carved in high relief on the front with two rosettes and schematic bucrania (ox skulls) on the short sides. This is the only example of a bucranium motif in the art of late Second Temple-period Jerusalem.[324] A Greek inscription above one of the bucrania records the name of the artist who made this ossuary: "Erotas. Beroutos made (this ossuary)? ZA."[325] This ossuary and the Megiste ossuary come from the same chamber (B) in Cave 2. Beroutos apparently was interred in Cave 3 (Chamber

D), as indicated by an ossuary inscribed in Greek "(Son) of Dimos. Berouthos (son) of Dimos."[326] Jonathan Price notes that it is "highly unusual" for an artist's signature to be recorded on an ossuary, but without considering why this artist was interred in the tomb.[327] Since rock-cut tombs belonged to families, Beroutos must either have been a family member (which is possible but seems unlikely as this clearly was an elite family) or was included as a client of the family. In Rome, household members including freedmen and slaves were placed in family tombs, but to my knowledge this was not common practice in Jerusalem.[328]

The pottery from the Akeldama tombs includes an imported Parthian glazed amphoriskos (a small jar) from Cave 1—a type rarely found in Jerusalem.[329] Tal Ilan concludes that the occupants of the Akeldama tombs "were most likely Syrian Jews, some of them converts, who came to Jerusalem either to settle or be buried."[330] Price and Haggai Misgav are more reserved, saying that it is impossible to determine if the families resided in Jerusalem or lived elsewhere and had their bones brought to the city for burial after their deaths.[331] Price and Misgav's observation is based on the inscriptions without taking into account that loculi, arcosolia, and sarcophagi were used for primary burials. There is no doubt that the arcosolia in the Akeldama tombs were used for primary burials because they contain hewn troughs that were sealed by stone slabs, as Avni and Greenhut note: "like the loculi, they clearly served for primary burials, prior to the collection of the bones and their deposition in ossuaries."[332] Therefore, in my opinion there can be no doubt that at least some of the occupants of the Akeldama tombs were members of elite Syrian immigrant families in Jerusalem. It is noteworthy that some of the largest and most lavishly decorated tombs belonged to émigré families living in Jerusalem, including the tomb of Queen Helena of Adiabene, the Akeldama tombs, and Nicanor's tomb. Perhaps these families constructed especially large and lavish tombs to establish their standing among the local elite.

Tombs and Burial Customs of the Lower Classes

In the late Second Temple period, Jerusalem's wealthier Jews buried their dead in rock-cut family tombs that were used over the course of several generations.[333] However, only the more affluent members of Jewish society, who comprised a small percentage of the population, could afford rock-cut tombs. A majority of the population was disposed of in a manner that left few traces in the archaeological landscape. Many individuals were buried in graves dug into the ground, analogous to the way we bury our dead today. The body of the deceased, wrapped in a shroud and sometimes placed in a wooden coffin, was laid in a pit or a trench dug into the ground. Sometimes the burial at the base of the trench was sealed off with stone slabs or mud bricks before the trench was filled in with dirt. Often a headstone was erected to mark the site of the grave. The bodies of the poorest members of society, including executed criminals, were thrown into pits in potter's fields or were disposed of randomly. Similarly, according to tradition Judas's blood money was used to pay for a potter's field in Jerusalem (Matt 27:5–8).

Because pit graves and trench graves are poor in finds and are much less conspicuous and more susceptible to destruction than rock-cut tombs, relatively few examples are recorded, and the lack of grave goods makes those that are found difficult to date. Qumran (the site where the Dead Sea Scrolls were discovered) provides the best evidence for the use of trench graves in late Second Temple-period Judea, where the cemetery is preserved and visible because it is in the desert and was never built over, covered up, or plowed. When graves of this type are found at other sites, scholars often identify them as Essene burials. Although it is possible that some or all of those buried in these cemeteries were Essenes, there is no archaeological evidence to support this assumption.

The Death and Burial of Jesus

In the ancient world, the method of execution used for capital crimes varied depending on the nature of the crime and the socioeconomic status of the criminal. [334] Those found guilty by the Sanhedrin (Jewish law court) of violating Jewish law were executed by stoning, burning, decapitation, or strangulation, depending on the crime. Because he was a Roman citizen, Paul was entitled to a trial in Rome (where he apparently was sentenced to death and executed). In contrast, as a lower-class Jew from Galilee, Jesus was sentenced to death by Pontius Pilate and executed by crucifixion. The Romans used crucifixion to punish non-Roman citizens for incitement to rebellion and acts of treason. Roman crucifixion involved using ropes or nails to affix the victim to a wooden stake and crossbeam, a type of hanging that caused slow asphyxiation. This method of execution was generally reserved for lower-class criminals because it was a painful process that could last for days.

According to the Gospel accounts, Jesus was nailed to the cross and expired on the eve of the Sabbath (Friday afternoon; John seems to place the crucifixion on Thursday). A wealthy, prominent Jewish follower of Jesus named Joseph of Arimathea received permission from the Roman governor, Pontius Pilate, to inter Jesus's body in his own family's tomb. The synoptic Gospels (Mark, Matthew, and Luke) are in broad agreement in their description of this event. Mark 15:42–46 says: "Although it was now evening, yet since it was the Preparation Day, that is, the day before the Sabbath, Joseph of Arimathea, a highly respected member of the council, who was himself living in expectation of the reign of God, made bold to go to Pilate and ask for Jesus's body. . . . And he [Joseph] bought a linen sheet and took him down from the cross and wrapped him in the sheet, and laid him in a tomb that had been hewn out of the rock, and rolled a stone against the doorway of the tomb." Matthew 27:57–60 differs in describing Joseph as a rich man, adding that the linen shroud was clean and the tomb was new, while Luke 23:50–54 describes Joseph as a good and righteous man who was a member of the council and states that no one had ever been laid in the tomb.

Joseph of Arimathea seems to have been motivated by a concern for the observance of Jewish law. On the one hand, biblical law requires burial within twenty-four hours of death even for those guilty of the worst crimes. On the other hand, Jewish law prohibits burial on the Sabbath and festivals. Because Jesus expired on the cross on the eve of the Sabbath, he had to be buried before sundown on Friday because waiting until after sundown on Saturday would have exceeded the twenty-four-hour time limit. Since there was no time to prepare a grave, Joseph of Arimathea placed Jesus's body in his family's rock-cut tomb.

In 1968, a rock-cut tomb was discovered in a northern neighborhood of Jerusalem. One of the ossuaries (inscribed with the name Yohanan [John]), contained the remains of a man who had been crucified, as indicated by a nail that was stuck in his heel bone.[335] This is an extraordinary discovery because the methods by which victims were affixed to crosses usually leave no discernable traces in the physical remains or archaeological record. Some victims were bound with ropes, which were untied when the body was removed from the cross. When nails were used, they were pulled out when the body was removed from the cross. The nail in Yohanan's heel bone was preserved only because it bent after hitting a knot in the wood and therefore could not be removed from the body.

The Gospel accounts of Jesus's burial appear to be largely consistent with the archaeological evidence. In other words, although archaeology does not prove there was a follower of Jesus named Joseph of Arimathea or that Pontius Pilate granted his request for Jesus's body, the Gospel accounts describing Jesus's removal from the cross and burial accord well with archaeological evidence and with Jewish law. The source(s) of these accounts were familiar with the manner in which wealthy Jews living in Jerusalem during the time of Jesus disposed of their dead. The circumstances surrounding Jesus's death and burial can be reconstructed as follows.

Jesus expired on the cross shortly before sundown on Friday. Because Jesus came from a lower-class family that did not own a rock-cut tomb, under ordinary circumstances he would have been buried in a pit grave or trench grave. However, there was no time to prepare (dig) a grave before the beginning of the Sabbath. Joseph of Arimathea, a wealthy and prominent follower of Jesus, was concerned to ensure that Jesus was buried before sundown in accordance with biblical law. Therefore, Joseph hastened to Pilate and requested permission to take Jesus's body. Joseph laid Jesus's body in a loculus in his own rock-cut tomb, an exceptional measure due to the circumstances as rock-cut tombs were family tombs. When the women entered the tomb of Joseph of Arimathea on Sunday morning, the loculus where Jesus's body had been laid was empty. The theological explanation for this phenomenon is that Jesus was resurrected from the dead. However, once Jesus had been buried in accordance with Jewish law, there was no prohibition against removing the body from the tomb after the end of the Sabbath and reburying it elsewhere. It is therefore possible that followers or family members removed Jesus's body from Joseph's tomb after the Sabbath ended and buried it in a pit grave or trench grave, as it would have been unusual to leave a non-relative in a family tomb. No matter which explanation one prefers, the fact that Jesus's body did not remain in Joseph's tomb means that his bones could not have been collected in an ossuary, at least not if we follow the Gospel accounts.

The Death and Burial of James

After Jesus's death his brother James became the leader of Jerusalem's early Christian community (technically these were not early Christians, but rather a Jewish sect of Jesus's followers). [336] James apparently was an observant Jew whose pious and ascetic lifestyle earned him the nickname "the Just." We have little direct information about James since he was marginalized in later western Christian tradition. The New Testament contains the Epistle or Letter of James, although scholars debate whether James was the author of this work or whether someone else wrote it and attributed to James (in which case it is a pseudepigraphic or falsely attributed work). Either way, the attribution of this work to James suggests that he was known for his opposition to the accumulation of wealth and the lifestyle of the wealthy, as illustrated by the following passages:

> Let the believer who is lowly boast in being raised up, and the rich in being brought low, because the rich will disappear like a flower in the field. For the sun rises with its scorching heat and withers the field; its flower falls, and its beauty perishes. It is the same way with the rich; in the midst of a busy life, they will wither away. (1:9–11)

> Has not God chosen the poor in the world to be rich in faith and to be heirs of the kingdom that he has promised to those who love him? But you have dishonored the poor. Is it not the rich who oppress you? Is it not they who drag you into court? (2:5–6)

> Come now, you rich people, weep and wail for the miseries that are coming to you. Your riches have rotted, and your clothes are moth-eaten. Your gold and silver have rusted, and their rust will be evidence against you,

and it will eat your flesh like fire. You have laid up treasure for the last days. Listen! The wages of the laborers who mowed your fields, which you kept back by fraud, cry out, and the cries of the harvesters have reached the ears of the Lord of hosts. You have lived on the earth in luxury and in pleasure. (5:1–5)

The negative views on wealth expressed in the Letter of James are consistent with the nature of the early Christian community in Jerusalem, which Acts describes as having a communal and impoverished lifestyle, although some members came from wealthy families. In this regard, the early Christian community in Jerusalem resembled the Qumran community.

In 62–63 CE, the Roman governor of Judea died suddenly while in office, and several months passed before his successor arrived from Rome. In the interim, the Jewish high priest Ananus took advantage of the opportunity to condemn James on charges of violating Jewish law and had him executed by stoning. James's opposition to the wealthy, who of course included the high priests, might explain why Ananus had him put to death, since James was otherwise known as a pious and law-abiding Jew. The possibility that the charges were trumped-up is also suggested by the fact that the Pharisees protested James's execution when the new Roman governor arrived, and Ananus was removed from office. Josephus provides a contemporary account of this event: "And so he [Ananus the high priest] convened the judges of the Sanhedrin and brought before them a man named James, the brother of Jesus who was called the Christ, and certain others. He accused them of having transgressed the law and delivered them to be stoned."[337]

According to a slightly later source—the second-century CE church historian Hegesippus—James was buried just below the Temple Mount (presumably in the area of the Kidron Valley or Mount of Olives). Hegesippus mentions that in his time the headstone marking the grave could still be seen.

So they went up and threw down the Just, and they said to one another, "Let us stone James the Just," and they began to stone him since the fall had not killed him, but he turned and knelt saying, "I beseech thee, O Lord, God and Father, forgive them, for they know not what they do." And while they were thus stoning him one of the priests of the sons of Rechab, the son of Rechabim,[2] to whom Jeremiah the prophet bore witness, cried out saying, "Stop! what are you doing? The Just is praying for you." And a certain man among them, one of the laundrymen, took the club with which he used to beat out the clothes, and hit the Just on the head, and so he suffered martyrdom. And they buried him on the spot by the temple, and his gravestone still remains by the temple.[338]

Although we do not know if the grave that Hegesippus mentions contained James's remains, his testimony indicates that within a century of James's death, Christian tradition recalled that he had been buried in a pit grave or trench grave marked by a headstone. This tradition is supported by other evidence. James came from a family of modest means that presumably could not afford a rock-cut tomb. He was the leader of a community whose members lived in communal poverty, and he was known for his ascetic lifestyle and his opposition to the accumulation of wealth and the lifestyle of the wealthy. And, unlike Jesus, James did not expire on the cross on the eve of the Sabbath but was executed by the Sanhedrin by stoning. Because according to biblical law even the worst criminals are entitled to burial within twenty-four hours, the Jewish law court only employed methods of execution such as stoning—but not crucifixion—that resulted in immediate death. Therefore, unlike the case of Jesus, James would not have been executed in a manner that precluded burial within twenty-four hours.

The Talpiyot Tomb

The so-called Talpiyot tomb is a modest, single chamber loculus tomb that was discovered in 1980, during construction work in Jerusalem's East Talpiyot neighborhood (southwest of the Old City). [339] The tomb was excavated by Joseph Gat on behalf of the Israel Department of Antiquities, and a final (scientific) report was published in 1996, by Kloner. Ten ossuaries were found in the tomb, four of which are plain and the other six inscribed (five in Hebrew and one in Greek). The tomb has attracted attention because some of the names on the inscribed ossuaries correspond to figures mentioned in the New Testament in association with Jesus, specifically Yeshua (Jesus), Mariamene (Mary), and Yosé (Joseph). It is mainly on this basis that the claim has been made that this is the [lost] tomb of Jesus and his family—a claim that was the subject of a Discovery Channel program first broadcast in March 2007. If the Talpiyot tomb is the tomb of Jesus and his family, it would mean that the Church of the Holy Sepulcher does not enshrine the site of Jesus's crucifixion and burial, a tradition that goes back at least to the time of Constantine (early fourth century CE). Furthermore, if true, this claim would mean that Jesus was married and had an otherwise unknown son named Judah (as one ossuary is inscribed "Yehudah son of Yeshua") and that Jesus was not resurrected (because his remains were gathered in an ossuary).

The identification of the Talpiyot tomb as belonging to Jesus's family flies in the face of all available evidence and contradicts the Gospel accounts, which are our earliest sources of information about Jesus's death and burial. This claim is also inconsistent with evidence from these sources indicating that Jesus was a lower-class Jew. Even if we accept the unlikely possibility that Jesus's family had the means to purchase a rock-cut tomb, it would have been located in their hometown of Nazareth, not in Jerusalem. For example, when Simon, the last of the Maccabean brothers and one of the Hasmonean rulers built a large tomb or mausoleum for his family, he constructed it in their hometown of Modiin, not in Jerusalem. In fact, the Gospel accounts indicate that Jesus's family did not own a rock-cut tomb in Jerusalem, for, if they had, there would have been no need for Joseph of Arimathea to take Jesus's body and place it in his own family's rock-cut tomb. If Jesus's family did not own a rock-cut tomb, it means they also had no ossuaries.

A number of scholars, including Kloner, have pointed out that the names on the ossuaries in the Talpiyot tomb are very common among the Jewish population of Jerusalem in the first century. Furthermore, the ossuary inscriptions provide no indication that those interred in this tomb were Galilean (not Judean) in origin. On ossuaries in rock-cut tombs belonging to Judean families it was customary to indicate the ancestry or lineage of the deceased by naming the father, as, for example, Judah son of John (Yohanan); Shimon son of Alexa; and Martha daughter of Hananya. But in rock-cut tombs owned by non-Judean families (or which contained the remains of family members from outside Judea), it was customary to indicate the deceased's place of origin, as, for example, Simon of Ptolemais (Akko/Acre), Papias the Bethshanite (of Beth Shean), and Gaios son of Artemon from Berenike. If the Talpiyot tomb indeed belonged to Jesus's family, we would expect at least some of the ossuary inscriptions to reflect their Galilean origin, by reading, for example, Jesus [son of Joseph] of Nazareth (or Jesus the Nazarene), Mary of Magdala, and so on. However, the inscriptions provide no indication that this is the tomb of a Galilean family and instead point to a Judean family.

The claim that the Talpiyot tomb belongs to Jesus's family is based on a string of problematic and unsubstantiated claims, including adding an otherwise unattested Matthew (Matya) to the family of Jesus (as one ossuary is inscribed with this name), identifying an otherwise unknown son of Jesus named Judah (and assuming that Jesus was married), and identifying the Mariamene named on one of the ossuaries in the tomb as Mary Magdalene by interpreting the word *Mara* (which follows the name Mariamene) as the Aramaic term for "master" (arguing that Mariamene was a teacher and leader). Individually each of these points weakens the case for the identification of the Talpiyot tomb as the tomb of Jesus's family, but collectively they are devastating.

To conclude, the identification of the Talpiyot tomb as the tomb of Jesus and his family contradicts the canonical Gospel accounts of the death and burial of Jesus and the earliest Christian traditions about Jesus. This claim is also inconsistent with all available information—historical and archaeological—about how Jews in the time of Jesus buried their dead and specifically the evidence we have about lower class, non-Judean families like that of Jesus. Finally, the fact that not a single ancient source preserves any reference to or tradition about any tomb associated with Jesus aside from Joseph of Arimathea's is a loud silence indeed, especially since Paul's writings and some sources of the synoptic Gospel accounts antedate 70 CE. Had Jesus's family owned a rock-cut tomb in Jerusalem, presumably some of his followers would have preserved the memory of its existence (if not its location) and venerated the site. In fact, our earliest sources contradict the identification of the Talpiyot tomb as the tomb of Jesus and his family. For example, Hegesippus refers to James's grave in the second century CE but seems to describe a pit grave or trench grave marked by a headstone and makes no reference to James having been interred with his brother Jesus in a rock-cut family tomb.

The "James Ossuary"

The so-called James ossuary is an ossuary with an Aramaic inscription that reads, "James son of Joseph brother of Jesus." [340] While there is little doubt that the ossuary is authentic and ancient, the inscription is the subject of an ongoing controversy. The problem is that the ossuary was not discovered by archaeologists but surfaced in 2002, in the hands of an antiquities collector in Israel. Put into "CSI" terms, this means that there is no chain of custody. The ossuary presumably was looted (illegally excavated) and was purchased by the collector on the antiquities market. Without scientific documentation describing the ossuary's original appearance and context, it is impossible to determine whether the inscription is authentic and ancient, or whether all or part of the inscription is a modern forgery added to enhance the value of the ossuary after its discovery or purchase.

The evidence that James was buried in a pit grave or trench grave renders moot the controversy surrounding the "James ossuary." Even if the inscription is authentic, it could not refer to James the Just, the brother of Jesus. Ossuaries were introduced into rock-cut tombs to collect the remains removed from loculi. They are not associated with pit graves or trench graves, as there was no reason to exhume the remains and place them in an ossuary to make space for new burials. Instead, new graves were dug as the need arose. In other words, if the inscription on the "James ossuary" is authentic and ancient, it must refer to another individual, not James the Just, the brother of Jesus. This is possible as the names James (Hebrew Yaakov/Jacob), Jesus (Hebrew Yeshua/Joshua), and Joseph (Hebrew Yosef or Yose) were common among the Jewish population of the late Second Temple period. In fact, it has been estimated that at least twenty different individuals in first-century CE Jerusalem could have had this combination of names.

Archaeology and Jesus

The claims about the Talpiyot tomb and the "James ossuary" reflect a broader interest in identifying remains associated with Jesus in the archaeological record. This accounts for the continued public fascination with the Shroud of Turin and the quest for the Holy Grail. The search for a physical connection with Jesus has existed since the earliest centuries of Christianity, when pilgrims began to visit holy sites and acquire relics. Of course, Jerusalem has always been a focal point of Christian interest. And, indeed, archaeology allows us to reconstruct the world of Jesus with a high degree of accuracy, from Galilean villages to Jerusalem and the temple. We have a wealth of information about the houses of rich and poor, their lifestyles, their diets, and their burials. What archaeology generally does not provide, however, is information about individuals, especially non-elites. Usually, only very wealthy and prominent members of society, such as King Herod or Queen Helena, left identifiable traces in the archaeological record, either because they built monuments that are described by ancient writers and have survived or been discovered, or because they are mentioned in inscriptions (hence the controversy about the "James ossuary"). Lower-class individuals such as Jesus did not leave such remains. For example, how could we know that a cup found in an excavation is the Holy Grail unless it has an authentic, ancient inscription indicating its date and identifying it as the vessel out of which Jesus drank at the Last Supper? Nevertheless, by providing information about Jesus's setting, archaeology indirectly sheds light on him as an individual and provides a context for better understanding Jesus's teachings as related in the Gospel accounts.

Conclusion

Jerusalem as Jesus knew it was filled with monuments built by Herod the Great (some of which were still under construction): the Antonia fortress, Herod's palace protected by the three towers, a sophisticated water system with a new aqueduct and large pools ringing the city, and paved streets—all dominated by the rebuilt second temple, made of white stone covered in gold plating that gleamed in the bright sun atop the hugely expanded esplanade (the Temple Mount), with the Royal Stoa towering along its southern side. In the densely built-up area inside the First Wall, the sprawling and richly appointed villas of the elite—standing two or three stories high—afforded spectacular views of the Temple Mount. Although construction of the Third Wall would not begin until after Jesus's death, settlement had already spread northward, outside the Second Wall. The city was a hub of commercial activity, especially along the Tyropoeon Valley and around the Temple Mount, where shops and vendors catered to the multitudes of pilgrims. In the crowded streets, Jews and gentiles from around the Mediterranean and Near East jostled side by side with pack animals, wagons, and carts laden with produce and other goods, and with animals and birds being brought for sacrifice. The air was filled with a cacophony of languages, including Aramaic, Greek, Latin, and Palmyrene, and with the sounds of animals—donkeys braying, chickens clucking, sheep and goats bleating, and cows mooing. The huge amounts of waste generated by people and animals alike were disposed of in an enormous landfill along the east side of the southeastern hill. The burning of the garbage added to the smoke rising from the sacrifices offered in the temple around the clock.

In March 70 CE, some three decades after Jesus's death, Jerusalem had been transformed, and not for the better. Although many of the same monuments still stood and sacrifices continued to be offered in the temple, most of the members of the elite had abandoned the city, their elegant villas burned down during sectarian in-fighting or occupied by squatters. The refugees who poured into Jerusalem from other parts of the country crowded into every quarter, desperately looking for food as fighting among rebel factions destroyed the grain supplies. Garbage accumulated in the streets or was dumped into cisterns as municipal services ceased to operate. The hardship and suffering inside the city increased after Titus mounted his siege a month or two later. In July, sacrifices ceased after no more lambs could be found. A month later, the temple was destroyed, marking a watershed moment in the history of Judaism and Christianity.

8

Roman Jerusalem (Aelia Capitolina)
(200 CE)

IN THE 130 years since its destruction, Jerusalem had been transformed. It was no longer a Jewish city dedicated to the God of Israel who was worshiped in his house on the Temple Mount. Instead, Jerusalem was a pagan Roman city in appearance and population, named Aelia Capitolina in honor of its new chief deity, Capitoline Jupiter, who (in the minds of the Romans), had vanquished and replaced the Jewish God. Whereas until 70 CE the core of the city was centered on the southeastern hill, the Temple Mount, and (later) the southwestern hill, now the settlement had shifted to the north, excluding the southeastern hill and the southern part of the southwestern hill (modern-day Mount Zion). Although the current walls of the Old City date to the sixteenth century (Ottoman period), the area they encompass and the layout of the streets within reflect the changes that occurred after 70.

Historical Background
The Roman Empire

The Flavian dynasty, which was founded by Vespasian, ended when his younger son Domitian, an unpopular ruler, was assassinated in 96 CE. The Roman Senate nominated the next emperor, an elderly but highly regarded statesman named Nerva. Nerva established the long-lived Antonine dynasty but ruled for only two years before dying of natural causes. He was succeeded by his adopted heir, Trajan, the first Roman emperor from the provinces (Spain), although born to an Italian family. Trajan was a popular emperor who enjoyed a long and successful reign (98–117 CE). An accomplished general, Trajan spent much of his time on military campaigns. He added the province of Dacia (modern Romania) to the Roman Empire, using the spoils to fund a building program in Rome that included a sprawling marketplace complex. Trajan also added to the Roman Empire the province of Arabia, which included the Nabataean kingdom (106 CE).

Trajan adopted as his successor a relative named Hadrian, who was also born to an Italian family in Spain (ruled 117–138 CE). Hadrian was a Philhellene—a lover of Greek culture and philosophy—so much so that he was mockingly nicknamed the *Graeculus* ("Little Greek"). He lavished monuments and other benefactions on Athens, which had lost its claim to cultural supremacy and was a relatively impoverished, provincial backwater. The people of Athens reciprocated by proclaiming Hadrian a "second Theseus," that is, a second founder or refounder of the city. Hadrian was an amateur architect who enjoyed designing his own buildings. His most famous monument, the Pantheon or temple of all gods, still stands in Rome today. The Pantheon literally turned the concept of an ancient temple inside-out. Using the latest innovations in Roman concrete technology, Hadrian created a huge domed space, shifting the focus of temples from the exterior to the interior. The dome has a large opening (*oculus*) in the center, through which the sun and heavens are visible above. Hadrian also designed a sprawling country villa at Tivoli outside Rome, periodically adding new buildings that were inspired by his travels. Although Hadrian is known for constructing a fortification wall in Britain that bears his name (Hadrian's Wall), aside from the Bar Kokhba Revolt his reign was relatively peaceful.

The Antonine dynasty ended with the death of Commodus in 192 CE. The next dynasty was established by Septimius Severus, the first emperor of non-Italian descent (he was North African, and his wife was Syrian), who ruled until 211 CE. After the last member of the Severan dynasty died in 235, a prolonged period of civil war broke out, precipitating a crisis that affected the Roman Empire through much of the third century.

Judea

After 70 CE, Judea was made an independent province with a governor who was no longer subordinate to the Syrian legate, and the Tenth Legion was camped permanently in Jerusalem. This reflects a major administrative adjustment made by the Romans in the wake of the First Revolt. Until now, the closest legions to Judea had been stationed at Antioch in Syria, a distance of approximately 800 kilometers (500 miles), under the command of the legate there. The changes ensured that forces were always present to keep order, although the legate resided at Caesarea.[1]

Following the siege of Jerusalem, Titus ordered the entire city razed except for the three towers adjacent to Herod's palace (Phasael, Hippicus, Mariamme), which were left standing as a testament to the strength of Jerusalem's defenses.

Titus also left intact the wall encircling the western side of the southwestern hill (that is, the western circuit of the First Wall), where the Tenth Legion was now camped. Since Josephus's accounts end with the First Revolt, we have much less information about events in Judea after 70 CE. For information we must rely on rabbinic literature and incidental references by classical (Greek and Roman) authors and the Church Fathers.

After Jerusalem's destruction, Jewish scholars established an academy in the southern coastal town of Jamnia (Hebrew Yavneh), under the leadership of Rabbi Yohanan Ben Zakkai (ca. 1–80 CE) and his successor, Gamaliel II (ca. 80–120). Yohanan Ben Zakkai is said to have faked his own death during the siege of Jerusalem and was smuggled out of the city in a coffin. He became the first *Nasi* (Prince or Patriarch) of the academy, which replaced the Sanhedrin as the body responsible for administering Jewish law.

After 70, the Jews awaited permission from the Romans to rebuild the Jerusalem temple. They expected this to happen soon, and never imagined Judaism without a temple two thousand years later. After all, only sixty years had passed between the destruction of the first temple and its replacement by the second temple. But as the decades passed and Roman permission was not forthcoming, the Jews of Palestine and the Diaspora grew increasingly anxious.

The Diaspora Revolt (115–117 CE)

Toward the end of Trajan's reign, a Jewish revolt erupted among Jewish communities in the Diaspora. In contrast to the First Jewish Revolt against the Romans, we have little information about the Diaspora Revolt. The unrest started in Egypt and spread to Cyrene (North Africa), Cyprus, and Mesopotamia. The revolt seems to have been fueled by messianic expectations, perhaps under the leadership of a messianic figure named Loukouas (Lucas). Pent-up hostilities between Jews and gentiles were also a factor. The uprising lasted for three years and seems to have been brutally suppressed. The Jews of Egypt, including the large and well-established community at Alexandria, were especially hard hit by violent reprisals from Roman soldiers joined by the local Greeks and Egyptians. As a result, many of Egypt's Jewish communities were wiped out, and those that survived never fully recovered.[2]

The Bar Kokhba Revolt (the Second Jewish Revolt Against the Romans) (132–135/136 CE)

Hadrian spent much of his reign traveling around the Roman provinces.[3] In 129–130 CE he toured Syria-Palestine and visited Jerusalem, which was still in ruins. Hadrian decided to refound Jerusalem as a Roman colony called Aelia Capitolina with a temple to Capitoline Jupiter on the Temple Mount (see below), dealing a crushing blow to Jewish expectations. Soon afterward, in 132 CE, the Second Jewish Revolt against the Romans (Bar Kokhba Revolt) erupted in Judea. It was led by a messianic figure named Simeon bar Kosiba (Bar Kokhba), who reportedly was supported by the highly respected Rabbi Akiba.

Most of our limited historical information about the Bar Kokhba Revolt comes from a third-century CE Roman author named Cassius Dio. In fact, before ancient documents were discovered in caves in the Judean Desert in the 1960s, even Bar Kokhba's real name was unknown. His followers called him Bar Kokhba—the son of a star—alluding to his messianic status. But rabbinic literature refers to him as Bar Koziba—the son of a liar or deceiver—because he was a false messiah who led a failed revolt.

The Jewish rebels learned the lessons of the First Revolt and enjoyed early success against the Romans. Instead of engaging the enemy in open battle or attempting to hold out under siege, they conducted a campaign of guerilla warfare. The Jewish population dug warrens of underground tunnels and took advantage of natural caves around the countryside. Whole villages disappeared into these hiding places, which also served as bases from which Jewish insurgents could ambush Roman troops under cover of night. The Roman army was not trained in this kind of warfare and as a result suffered many casualties, including the loss of an entire legion (the XXII Deiotariana). Hadrian ended up sending over a third of the Roman army to Judea to suppress the revolt.[4]

Inevitably, the tide turned against the rebels. Cassius Dio reports that 580,000 Jews were killed, and 50 fortified towns and 985 villages were destroyed. Although it is impossible to assess the accuracy of these numbers, they give an impression of the revolt's impact. Most of the fighting took place in Judea, with Jews in other parts of the country participating to a lesser degree or not at all.[5] One of the long-term consequences of the Bar Kokhba Revolt was the obliteration of many of the settlements in Judea, which resulted in the concentration of the Jewish population in the north (Galilee and the Golan) in the following centuries. The Bar Kokhba Revolt ended when the last stronghold, Bethar (near Bethlehem) fell to the Romans and Bar Kokhba was killed. Although according to Jewish tradition this occurred on the ninth of Av (August) in 135 CE, recent studies suggest the revolt ended early in the following year.[6]

The Bar Kokhba Revolt was as disastrous for the Jews as the First Revolt. First, it exacted a terrible toll in human lives, with Judea hit especially hard. Second, the revolt sealed the fate of the Jerusalem temple, ensuring that it would not be rebuilt in the foreseeable future. Hadrian proceeded to rebuild Jerusalem as a Roman colony dedicated to Capitoline Jupiter and prohibited Jews from living in the city and its environs. To further punish the Jews, Hadrian instituted bans restricting or prohibiting some Jewish practices such as circumcision and Sabbath observance. For the first time, Jews living under Roman rule were subject to persecution under the law for practicing their religion. Finally, to obliterate the memory of this troublesome people, Hadrian changed the name of the province from Judea to Syria-Palaestina (or simply Palaestina/Palestine), reviving the name Philistia—the ancient kingdom of the Philistines.[7]

Aelia Capitolina was named after Hadrian (whose full name was Publius Aelius Hadrianus), following the precedent established by Alexander the Great centuries earlier, and in honor of Capitoline Jupiter, who replaced the God of Israel as the city's patron deity. The name Aelia stuck for centuries; even under Islamic rule (after 640 CE) the city was sometimes referred to as "Ilya." But Aelia Capitolina was Roman in more than name alone. Because of Hadrian's prohibition, few if any Jews lived in Jerusalem until after the Muslim conquest of ca. 638 CE—a period of some five hundred years.[8] During these centuries, Jews were allowed to enter the city once a year, apparently on the ninth of Av, to mourn the destruction of the temple.[9]

Aelia Capitolina was a military colony that included the soldiers stationed in the legionary camp, which apparently was located on the southwestern hill, and veterans and family members who lived outside it.[10] Hannah Cotton Paltiel and Avner Ecker point out that Hadrian's foundation of Aelia Capitolina as a colony rather than another type of municipality was an act of generosity, not a punishment, which benefited its population.[11] The benefits included the awarding of Roman citizenship to all free residents, including the non-Roman wives and children of veterans who had completed their service and settled in the camp's environs.[12] The Tenth Legion remained in Jerusalem until the emperor Diocletian transferred it to Aila (modern ʿAqaba) on the Red Sea around 300 CE.[13]

Archaeological Evidence

Archaeological remains associated with Aelia Capitolina have proved to be among the most elusive in Jerusalem's long history, resulting in a lack of scholarly consensus relating to the city's extent and the location of key features such as the Capitolium and the camp of the Tenth Legion. There are a number of reasons for these difficulties, including the paucity and problematic nature of our historical sources, the obliteration of Roman remains by Byzantine and later overbuilding, and the fact that until recently the local pottery types of the second and third centuries were virtually unknown. Roman Jerusalem has also attracted less attention than periods when the city was Canaanite, Israelite/Judahite, Jewish, or Christian.

Shu'afat

Due to a lack of archaeological remains, it is unclear if anyone other than Roman soldiers resided in Jerusalem between the two revolts (70–132 CE), although new discoveries indicate that Jews lived just outside the city.[14] In 2003–2007, excavations in the Arab neighborhood of Shu'afat on Jerusalem's northeast outskirts brought to light a large settlement dating to ca. 70–130 CE. Because this discovery was made during the construction of Jerusalem's light rail, only a narrow north–south strip cutting through the ancient settlement was excavated (ca. 500 meters (1,640 feet) long but only 8 meters (26 feet) wide), exposing small parts of buildings.[15] Nevertheless, the remains of at least ten spacious dwellings were identified, arranged in *insulae* (blocks) along a grid plan. Miqva'ot and stone vessels found in the houses indicate that the residents were Jews who observed purity laws. There are also two public bath houses with Roman hypocaust heating systems.[16] The finds include pottery from the Roman legionary kiln works at Binyanei Ha'uma (see below). This appears to have been a settlement of upper-class Jews including priestly families who adopted aspects of a Roman lifestyle while continuing to follow biblical laws.

The settlement is located at the foot of Tell el-Ful (Arabic for "the mound of horse beans"), which is identified with biblical Gibeah (Hebrew Giv`at Shaul), the hometown of Saul (Judges 20). In the 1960s, King Hussein of Jordan began construction of a royal palace atop the tell, but the project was abandoned after Israel captured East Jerusalem and the West Bank in the 1967 Six-Day War. The unfinished structure still stands, visible from the highway from Jerusalem north to Nablus (ancient Shechem/Flavia Neapolis). Josephus reports that in 70 CE, Titus and the Roman army camped at this spot as they approached Jerusalem: "Leading his army forward in this orderly array, according to Roman usage, Titus advanced through Samaria to Gophna, previously captured by his father and now garrisoned. After resting here one night he set forward at dawn, and at the end of a full day's march encamped in the valley which is called by the Jews in their native tongue, 'Valley of thorns,' close to a village named Gabath Saul, which means 'Saul's hill,' at a distance of about thirty furlongs from Jerusalem."[17] The excavated settlement is in the vicinity of Gibeah, although since the remains postdate 70 CE they cannot be identified with certainty as the same village mentioned by Josephus.[18]

After 70, the Romans created a new administrative unit to replace Jerusalem. This new unit was a toparchy—that is, a territory with a collection of villages—called Orine (pronounced OH-ree-nay; Greek for "hilly country"). Orine is one of ten toparchies in Judea mentioned by Pliny the Elder in a list that postdates 70.[19] Each toparchy had a main village that served as the administrative center.

Orine existed only until Hadrian's foundation of Aelia Capitolina, which became the capital of a newly established municipal territory. The excavated settlement, which dates to the period between the two revolts, therefore belonged to the toparchy of Orine, although it is impossible to say if it was the main village.[20] As the settlement was located on the main approach to Jerusalem from the north, it could have existed only with Roman permission. The excavators speculate that the inhabitants supplied the Tenth Legion, which was permanently camped in Jerusalem after 70, with food and provided roadside services.[21] The inhabitants, among them priestly families, lived in proximity to Jerusalem while awaiting the rebuilding of the temple. That, of course, never came to pass, and the settlement was abandoned shortly before the outbreak of the Bar-Kokhba Revolt. It appears that the inhabitants packed their valuables and departed in a hasty but orderly manner, although some of the buildings show signs of destruction by fire.[22]

The Camp of the Tenth Legion

Josephus reports that after the siege ended in 70, Titus left the Tenth Legion camped permanently in Jerusalem: "As the local garrison [Titus] Caesar decided to leave the tenth legion, along with some squadrons of cavalry and companies of infantry."[23] And indeed, inscriptions, stamped bricks, roof tiles, ceramic pipes, and other finds discovered around the city that bear the name or symbols of the Tenth Legion confirm its presence. Most scholars agree that the legionary camp would have had a typical Roman military layout: roughly square with the four sides oriented to the cardinal points and a gate in the middle of each side leading to two main roads bisecting it.[24] But although the camp would have included barracks, headquarters (*principia*), stables, and bakeries enclosed within a fortification wall, it left almost no traces in the archeological record.[25] The dearth of identifiable remains is even more surprising in view of the legion's lengthy stay in Jerusalem.[26]

Remains of the legionary camp have proven elusive for a couple of reasons. First, there is little identifiable architecture, perhaps because the barracks were obliterated by later construction or were made of perishable materials such as wood or because they were dismantled when the legion was transferred to Aila by Diocletian, as Shlomit Weksler-Bdolah proposes. A second problem concerns the dating of stamped roof tiles, bricks, and pottery produced in the legionary kiln works, which are among the clearest indicators of legionary presence. However, stamped roof tiles and bricks do not appear to have been produced in Jerusalem's legionary kiln works before the early second century and perhaps not until after 130 CE, while some of the legionary pottery types cannot be dated precisely to before or after Hadrian's reign. Furthermore, stamped roof tiles and bricks are found in civilian structures and remained available for use (or reuse) at least through the fourth century.[27] This means that these artifacts do not necessarily provide evidence of legionary presence before 130 CE and, at least in some cases, could be associated with civilian settlement outside the camp after the foundation of Aelia Capitolina.

The paucity of archaeological remains has given rise to a multiplicity of theories about the camp's size and location, ranging from suggestions placing it on or around the Temple Mount or in the vicinity of the Church of the Holy Sepulcher (in the northwest part of the Old City).[28] According to another proposal, the city itself was the legionary camp, with the soldiers billeted in the buildings they were constructing.[29] Most scholars accept Josephus's testimony that the legion was camped on the southwestern hill, in the area formerly occupied by Herod's palace, sheltered by the three towers and the western stretch of the First Wall: "[Titus] Caesar ordered the whole city and the temple to be razed to the ground, leaving only the loftiest of the towers, Phasael, Hippicus, and Mariamme, and the portion of the wall enclosing the city on the west: the latter as an encampment for the garrison that was to remain."[30] Locating the camp on the southwestern hill is not only supported by Josephus's testimony but makes sense as it was a high, flat, and easily defensible position supplied with water by the high-level aqueduct, which was repaired by the Tenth Legion.[31] However, even among scholars who agree that the camp was on the southwestern hill, there is no consensus about its precise location and extent.[32]

Weksler-Bdolah argues that the camp occupied the entire southwestern hill (the Citadel, the Armenian and Jewish Quarters, and Mount Zion), citing fragmentary architectural remains and artifacts scattered throughout the area.[33] However, the meagerness of the remains requires accepting her claim that the barracks were completely dismantled, and the southwestern hill was left vacant after the legion's transfer to Aila. In addition, there is no conclusive evidence that even the few structures Weksler-Bdolah documents are legionary rather than civilian, nor in most cases can they be dated precisely within a second–fourth century range. This does not negate the possibility that she is correct, only that the evidentiary support is weak and not unequivocal.[34]

More substantial remains associated with the Tenth Legion have been discovered in excavations southwest of the Temple Mount. These include a group of public buildings—a latrine, a Roman-style bath house (with a hypocaust heating system and another latrine), and a bakery—and hundreds of stamped legionary roof and floor tiles.[35] Weksler-Bdolah describes this as "the largest group of Roman-period public buildings known to date in Jerusalem."[36] The finds from these buildings include a rectangular terracotta die from the bakery with the Latin inscription PRIM that might be a bread stamp, and a bronze statuette of a

Moorish rider (cavalry soldier) with dreadlocks and a beard.[37] Guy Stiebel notes that a Latin tombstone found in North Africa commemorates a soldier who served in the Tenth Legion and returned to Mauretania (the Maghreb) after his discharge.[38] An imperial document of the late fourth century CE called the *Notitia Dignitatum* ("List of Offices") lists three military units stationed in Palaestina Prima (Judea, Idumaea, Samaria, and the coast), one of which was a Moorish cavalry unit (the *Equites Mauri Illyriciani*) stationed in Aelia Capitolina.[39]

Based on the concentration of military finds, Stiebel and Eilat Mazar have each proposed that the Tenth Legion's camp was located around the southwest side of the Temple Mount.[40] Both suggest that, after 70, the legion was camped on the southwestern hill in the area of the Citadel and Armenian Garden but moved to the vicinity of the Temple Mount either before or at the time of the establishment of Aelia Capitolina.[41] Weksler-Bdolah acknowledges the possibility that the camp relocated to the area around Temple Mount but notes that as these buildings are not necessarily military facilities, this could have been a civilian quarter.[42] Similarly, Werner Eck questions Stiebel's assertion that the PRIM die belonged to a soldier-baker named Primus or is an abbreviation for *panis primus* ("bread of the first quality"), concluding that it is impossible to determine if it is associated with the Tenth Legion.[43]

To summarize: Josephus's testimony and the concentration of legionary pottery and stamped tiles, bricks, and ceramic pipes in the Citadel and Armenian Garden support the view that, after 70, the legionary camp occupied the area of Herod's former palace and the three towers and reused the western stretch of the First Wall and perhaps portions of its northern stretch. Whether or how much the camp extended beyond this, or whether it moved to the southwest side of the Temple Mount in the decades after 70 remain matters of speculation.

The Damascus Gate

With Hadrian's foundation of Aelia Capitolina, the city was rebuilt with a typical Roman city plan: a roughly square layout, with the four sides oriented toward the cardinal points and one main gate in the center of each side (Figure 8.1). These gates gave access to two main roads that bisected the city from north to south and east to west and intersected in the center. Other roads were laid out parallel to the two main roads, creating a grid of streets running north–south and east–west. The Romans called a north–south road a *cardo* and an east–west road a *decumanus*. The main north–south road was the cardo maximus, and the main east–west road was the decumanus maximus. This type of plan is related to the layout of Roman military camps and represents an adaptation of the Hippodamian town plan common in the Hellenistic world, which had a grid of streets running north–south and east–west but did not have a regular (square) layout or two main roads bisecting the city.

Valuable evidence for the layout and appearance of Aelia Capitolina comes from the Madaba Map—a map of the Holy Land that decorates the mosaic floor of a Byzantine church in the town of Madaba in Jordan (Pl. 12A).[44] Jerusalem is depicted prominently in some detail but without the southeastern hill, which is not preserved, and without the Temple Mount. The map represents the Holy Land around 600 CE, when the mosaic was laid, and therefore includes monuments and features added after Hadrian's time. Nevertheless, it is an important

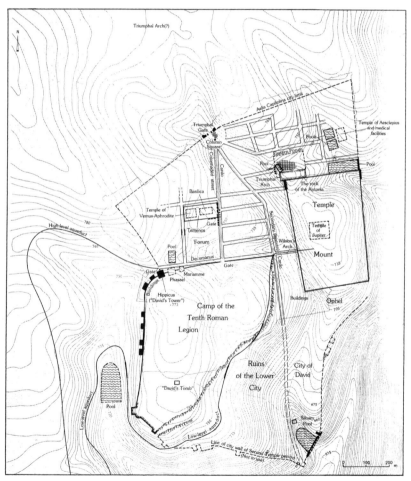

FIGURE 8.1 Plan of Aelia Capitolina without the northern line (from E. Stern [ed.] 1993: 758).
Credit: With permission of Hillel Geva and the Israel Exploration Society.

source of information about Aelia Capitolina because the city did not experience any major destructions or reconstructions in the intervening 400–500 years. In fact, the modern Old City of Jerusalem still preserves the main features of Aelia Capitolina as never again has the city been razed and rebuilt from scratch. These features, which can be seen in the Madaba Map, include a gate at the north end of the city, the cardo maximus (the western cardo) and a second main cardo (the eastern cardo), and the decumanus maximus. Over the centuries the location of these features has remained the same, although the ground level has risen as debris accumulated, streets were repaved, and new buildings were constructed.

Unlike modern maps, the Madaba Map is oriented with east at the top. It shows the entrance to the city on the north (left) dominated by a gate with an arched passageway flanked by two towers. This is the site of the modern (Ottoman) Damascus Gate, which is built over the remains of the Roman gate. Steps leading down to the modern gate from the street outside the north wall of the Old City show how much the ground level has risen since the sixteenth century (Figure 8.2). In Hadrian's time the gate consisted of three arched passageways—a large central passage flanked by two smaller ones, with towers on either side—but by the time the Madaba Map was made, the side passages were blocked and only the central one was still in use.

Of the three original (Hadrianic) arched passageways, only the small eastern one has survived, with its flanking tower (Figure 8.3). The gate and tower are constructed of Herodian-style stones (large ashlars with drafted margins and flat paneled bosses) in secondary use. Aelia Capitolina's monuments typically incorporate reused Herodian stones, which were readily available because they belonged to buildings that had been lying in ruins since 70 CE. One stone immediately above the keystone of the passageway's arch has a Latin inscription on its lower margin that reads "the colonia Aelia Capitolina (built this) by decree of the city councillors."[45] The stone's battered condition and its off-center position relative to the arch's keystone indicate that it is in secondary use, apparently having originated in a building erected by decree of Aelia Capitolina's city council.[46] The Hadrianic triple-arched gate originally was a free-standing monument and only later was incorporated into a city wall. The Romans often erected free-standing gates to mark entrances to public spaces or as commemorative monuments. For example, the arch of Titus is a free-standing victory monument that straddles the Sacred Way at the entrance to the Roman Forum. Gregory Wightman describes the Hadrianic triple-arched gate at the Damascus Gate as "essentially a fortified city gate into which was set a triple-portal decorative arch."[47]

The Madaba Map shows a large oval plaza just inside the Hadrianic gate on the north side of the city. Although the ground level has risen since then, there is still an open area inside the Damascus Gate today. Originally the oval plaza

PLATE 1A Aerial view of the Old City looking north.
Credit: Photo by Avraham Graicer © Creative Commons Share Alike 4.0 International.

PLATE 1B Aerial view of the Temple Mount looking northwest.
Credit: Photo by אסף.צ, © Creative Commons Share Alike 3.0 Unported.

PLATE 2A Aerial view of the southeastern hill and Temple Mount looking north.
Credit: Photo by Avraham Graicer © Creative Commons Share Alike 3.0 Unported.

PLATE 2B Aerial view of the Old City looking northeast.
Credit: Photo by Avraham Graicer © Creative Commons Share Alike 4.0 International.

PLATE 3A View from the Citadel looking northeast, with the Church of the Holy Sepulcher on the left and the Dome of the Rock on the right, and Hezekiah's Pool in the foreground.

Credit: Photo by the author.

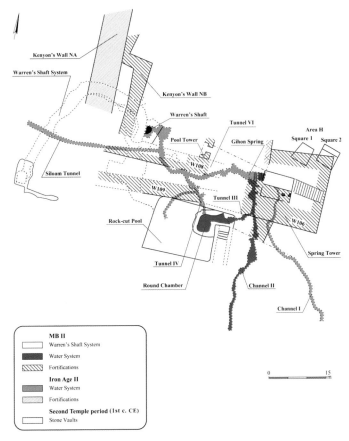

PLATE 3B Plan of the ancient water systems around the Gihon spring, from Reich and Shukron (2021b, figure 13.1).

Credit: © Biblical Archaeology Society.

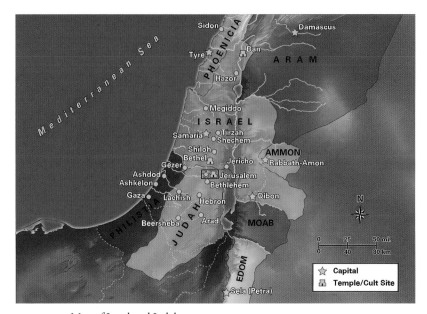

PLATE 4A Map of Israel and Judah.
Credit: From Bible Odyssey; www.bibleodyssey.org.

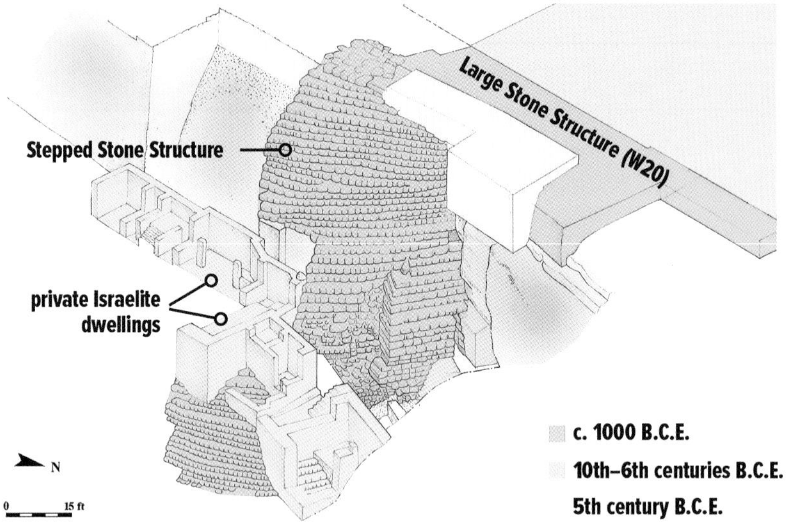

PLATE 4B Plan of the stepped stone structure, drawing by Alexander Pachorou, color by Yiftah Shalev.
Credit: © Eilat Mazar, Courtesy of the Biblical Archaeology Society and Avital Mazar Tsa`iri.

PLATE 5A Plan of the Ophel gate (drawing by Gary Lipton).

Credit: © Eilat Mazar, from E. Mazar 1989: 43 and E. Mazar 2015a: 462, courtesy of the Biblical Archaeology Society and Avital Mazar Tsa`iri.

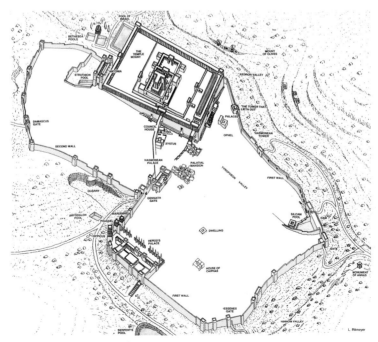

PLATE 5B Plan of Jerusalem with the First Wall and conjectured line of the Second Wall.

Credit: © Leen Ritmeyer.

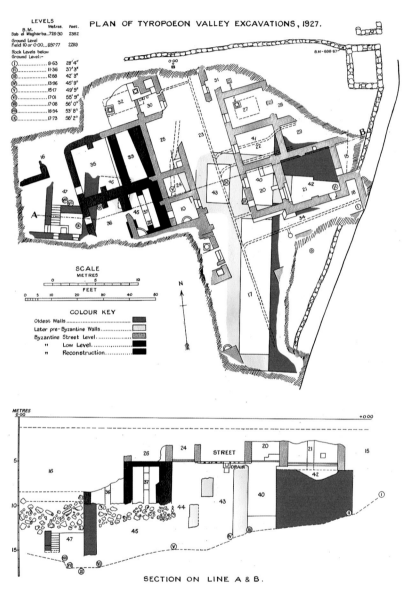

PLATE 6 Plan of Crowfoot and Fitzgerald's excavations in the Tyropoeon Valley, from Crowfoot and Fitzgerald (1929: plate XXII).

Credit: Courtesy of the Palestine Exploration Fund.

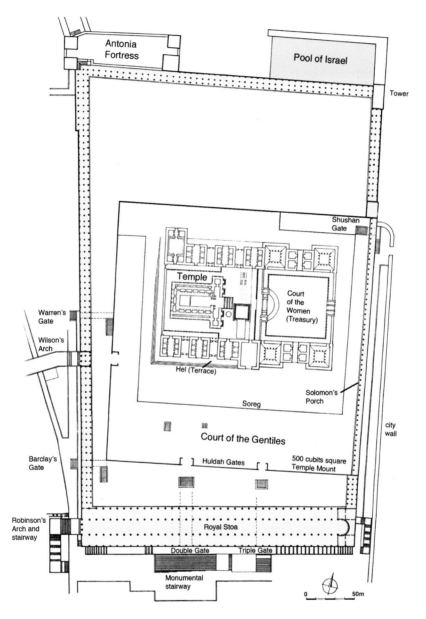

Antonia
Fortress

Pool of Israel

Tower

Shushan
Gate

Temple

Court
of the
Women
(Treasury)

Warren's
Gate

Wilson's
Arch

Hel (Terrace)

Solomon's
Porch

Soreg

city
wall

Court of the Gentiles

Barclay's
Gate

Huldah Gates

500 cubits square
Temple Mount

Robinson's
Arch and
stairway

Royal Stoa

Double Gate

Triple Gate

Monumental
stairway

0   50m

PLATE 7 Plan of the Herodian Temple Mount.
Credit: © Leen Ritmeyer.

PLATE 8A The Western Wall.

Credit: Photo by author.

PLATE 8B The western wall of the Temple Mount with the Mughrabi Gate bridge on the right and the Dome of the Rock above.

Credit: Photo by author.

PLATE 9 Herodian house in the Jewish Quarter.
Credit: Bukvoed, CC BY 4.0, via Wikimedia Commons.

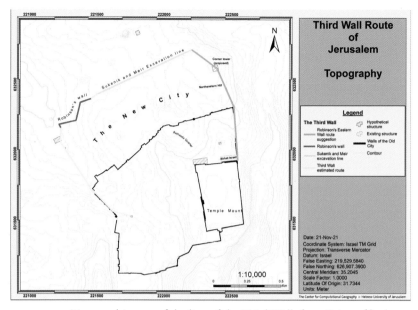

PLATE 10A Topographic map of the line of the Third Wall, from Spiezer (forthcoming: figure 9).

Credit: Prepared by and reproduced with the permission of Yosef Spiezer.

PLATE 10B The Kidron Valley tombs (the monument of Absalom on the far left is partly obscured by a tree).

Credit: Photo by author.

PLATE 11 Akeldama tombs, Cave 3, Chamber C. From Avni and Greenhut (1996: color plate; photograph by Doron Adar).

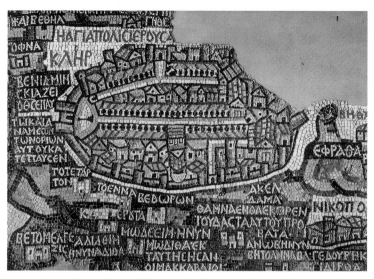

PLATE 12A Jerusalem in the Madaba Map (unknown author, public domain).
Credit: Wikimedia Commons, https://commons.wikimedia.org/wiki/File:Madaba_map.jpg.

PLATE 12B Rotunda of the Church of the Holy Sepulcher.
Credit: Photo by author.

PLATE 13A The Bird Mosaic.

Credit: Photo by Dickran Kouymjian, via Wikimedia Commons.

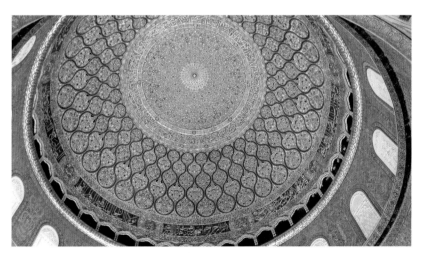

PLATE 13B The dome of the Dome of the Rock.

Credit: Aseel zm, CC BY-SA 4.0, via Wikimedia Commons.

PLATE 14A The Dome of the Rock and the Dome of the Chain (right front).
Credit: Ralf Roletschek, GFDL 1.2, via Wikimedia Commons.

PLATE 14B Interior of the Dome of the Rock.
Credit: Eassa, CC BY-SA 3.0, via Wikimedia Commons.

PLATE 15A Interior of the Dome of the Rock.
Credit: Virtutepetens, CC BY-SA 4.0, via Wikimedia Commons.

PLATE 15B Monumental Umayyad buildings southwest of the Temple Mount.
Credit: Photo by author.

PLATE 16   The Church of St. Anne.
Credit: Photo by author.

FIGURE 8.2 The Damascus Gate.
Credit: Photo by the author.

(which was paved with large flagstones) was dominated by a monumental column topped by a statue of Hadrian. By the time the map was made, the statue had been removed but the column was still standing and is depicted in the center of the oval area. In fact, the modern Arabic name of Damascus Gate—Bab al-ʿAmud (the Gate of the Column)—takes its name from the monumental column, although it disappeared long ago.[48] A similar oval plaza is preserved at Gerasa (modern Jerash in Jordan), a Decapolis city visited by Hadrian during his tour of the region in 129–130 CE.

The Eastern Cardo

The Madaba Map shows two main streets radiating from the oval plaza, bisecting the city from north to south. The more prominent of the two streets, which runs due south, is the main cardo (the cardo maximus or western cardo), while the other follows a more easterly course (the eastern cardo). Roman cities typically did not have two main cardos (Latin plural: *cardines*). Hadrian gave Jerusalem a second main cardo—the eastern cardo—because of a prominent topographic feature that could not be ignored: the Tyropoeon Valley. In fact, the modern street that lies above and follows the line of the eastern cardo is called "the street

FIGURE 8.3 The Hadrianic gate under the Damascus Gate.
Credit: Photo by the author.

of the valley" (Arabic: Tariq al-Wad[i]; Hebrew: Rehov ha-Gai). The Madaba
Map depicts both cardos as broad, stone-paved boulevards with columns lining
the curbs of the sidewalks on one or both sides. The columns supported pitched,
red-tiled roofs that covered the sidewalks and provided shelter for pedestrians
browsing in shops alongside them. The paved thoroughfares accommodated the
passage of animals, carts, chariots, and other vehicular traffic. The main east–west
street (decumanus maximus) of Aelia Capitolina is not depicted as prominently
on the Madaba Map due to a lack of space in the mosaic. Part of it can be seen
originating at an arched gate in the middle of the western side of the city (the
site of the modern Jaffa Gate) and continuing eastward to the intersection with

the western cardo. This main decumanus (modern David Street/the Street of the Chain) follows the line of the Transverse Valley along the north side of the south-western hill.

From 2005 to 2010, Weksler-Bdolah and Alexander Onn excavated a 50-meter (164-foot) long stretch of the eastern cardo alongside the Western Wall plaza.[49] Although other sections of the eastern cardo have been exposed by other archaeologists, Weksler-Bdolah and Onn's discoveries are noteworthy because they claim to have found evidence of Hadrianic construction that predates the Bar-Kokhba Revolt. The section they excavated consists of an eight-meter wide paved street running parallel to the western wall of the Temple Mount, bounded by raised sidewalks (1.5 meters [5 feet] wide) with columns on either side (Figure 8.4).[50] A large drainage channel runs north–south under the center of the street. The bedrock of the lower slope of the southwestern hill was cut back to create a vertical cliff to accommodate the street and the portico and shops along its west-ern side. Earlier buildings were leveled, and the area was filled before the street was paved. Two parallel streets led from the eastern side of the cardo toward the Temple Mount.[51]

Weksler-Bdolah and Onn distinguish two phases of construction in the eastern cardo, both associated with Hadrian: first, the preparation of the infra-structure and then the paving of the street and construction of the structures alongside it. As part of the preparatory activity, a deep, abandoned quarry pit on the east side of the street was filled with military debris, which they describe as "the Roman refuse dump." The pit yielded three military bread stamps, a rich assemblage of broken pottery and glass vessels, a large quantity of pig bones, and organic material that appears to have been burned on site.[52] The latest coin is an issue of Domitian dating to 86/87 CE. The names on the bread stamps indicate a date no later than ca. 100 CE, while the pottery and glass types are characteristic of the period between the two revolts.[53] An undated coin of Hadrian was found in an unsealed but undisturbed fill under the cardo, a few centimeters below the street level.[54]

The finds from the Roman refuse dump provide evidence of Roman military presence in the area before 130 CE, while the absence of clearly later artifacts led Weksler-Bdolah to conclude that preparatory work on the eastern cardo com-menced early in Hadrian's reign rather than around the time of his visit to the East in 129/130 CE. She therefore dates the preparation of the infrastructure to the first third of the second century (ca. 100–130 CE), arguing that work began ca. 120 CE.[55] Weksler-Bdolah suggests that either Hadrian's visit in 130 CE or the outbreak of the Bar-Kokhba Revolt brought an end to the work, which is the reason the western portico of the eastern cardo was never completed.[56] If correct, this would mean that nearly all the eastern cardo was completed by 130–132 CE.

FIGURE 8.4 The eastern cardo (from Weksler-Bdolah et al. 2009: figure 2).
Credit: Courtesy of the Israel Antiquities Authority and Shlomit Weksler-Bdolah; photo
by Shlomit Weksler-Bdolah.

Whereas according to Weksler-Bdolah the evidence from the eastern cardo
indicates that Hadrian planned to refound Jerusalem as Aelia Capitolina long
before his visit in 129/130, Cassius Dio presents the visit as the cause of the
revolt: "At Jerusalem he [Hadrian] founded a city in place of the one which
had been razed to the ground, naming it Aelia Capitolina, and on the site
of the temple of the god he raised a new temple to Jupiter. This brought
on a war of no slight importance nor of brief duration, for the Jews deemed
it intolerable that foreign races should be settled in their city and foreign
religious rites planted there. So long, indeed, as Hadrian was close by in

Egypt and again in Syria, they remained quiet . . . but when he went farther away, they openly revolted."[57]

In contrast, Eusebius, a Church Father writing in the early fourth century, says that Hadrian founded Aelia Capitolina after the revolt to punish the Jews, in which case the foundation would date to ca. 135/136: "The war raged most fiercely in the eighteenth year of Hadrian . . . and thus, when the city [Jerusalem] had been emptied of the Jewish nation and had suffered the total destruction of its ancient inhabitants, it was colonized by a different race, and the Roman city which subsequently arose changed its name and was called Aelia, in honor of the emperor Aelius Hadrianus."[58]

Cassius Dio's testimony is supported by the discovery of coins of Aelia Capitolina in archaeological contexts that antedate the revolt. Among them are coins from caves in the Judean Desert where Jews took refuge during the Bar Kokhba Revolt and a coin found on the floor of a building in the Shu`afat settlement, which was abandoned before the outbreak of the revolt.[59] Based on Cassius Dio's testimony and these finds, most scholars agree that Hadrian founded Aelia Capitolina around the time of his visit in 129/130 and believe that this was the cause of the revolt.[60] Eusebius's presentation of the foundation of Aelia Capitolina as Hadrian's punishment of the Jews in the wake of the revolt reflects his Christian supersessionist views.[61]

A few scholars including Weksler-Bdolah cite two later sources—Epiphanius of Salamis (second half of the fourth century) and the *Chronicon Paschale* (seventh century)—as evidence that Hadrian founded Aelia Capitolina in 117/118 or 119/120, during an otherwise unknown visit to Judea around the time of the Diaspora Revolt. They argue that the testimony of these sources is more reliable than that of Cassius Dio and Eusebius.[62] According to Weksler-Bdolah, the finds from the eastern cardo are consistent with this early date and indicate that Hadrian's plans for Aelia Capitolina were well advanced and preparatory work was underway long before his visit to the region in 129–130 CE.[63] However, most scholars reject an early date for the foundation of Aelia Capitolina on the grounds that Epiphanius's chronology is erroneous and refers to Hadrian's visit in 129/130 CE, not an earlier visit.[64]

Weksler-Bdolah supports her claim that the eastern cardo was constructed ca. 120–130/132 CE instead of ca. 130–138 CE by pointing to legionary pottery types in the Roman refuse dump that date from ca. 70/75 to 120/125 CE.[65] However, some of these types have longer ranges, while in the final report the burnt seeds are given later dates than in the preliminary publications.[66] And since the refuse appears to have been brought to this spot from one or more other sites, the latest artifacts indicate only when the material was disposed of at the point of origin and not necessarily when it was transported to the cardo.[67] Therefore, the finds from the Roman refuse dump are not proof that work on the eastern cardo commenced early in Hadrian's reign. A date around 130 CE is equally possible, in which case work might have been brought to a halt by Hadrian's death in 138 instead of at the time of Hadrian's visit in 129/130 or with the outbreak of the Bar-Kokhba Revolt in 132.[68]

The ten-year difference between the two dating ranges is significant for a couple of reasons. First, although numismatic evidence had already indicated that Hadrian refounded Jerusalem as Aelia Capitolina before the outbreak of the Bar-Kokhba Revolt (instead of in its wake, as some scholars once thought), an earlier date would mean that these plans were not a consequence of his visit to the region in 129/130 CE but had been in the works long before then. As Weksler-Bdolah states: "The Hadrianic date for both phases of construction of the Eastern Cardo—the preparation of the infrastructure (probably around the 120s, as stated above) and the actual paving of the street (some time later)— implies, in my opinion, that the decision to rebuild Jerusalem as a Roman city was made by Hadrian shortly after his accession to the throne in 117/118 CE. . . . The construction of the new Roman city of Aelia Capitolina is generally thought to be associated with Hadrian's well-known visit to Judaea around 129/130. On the basis of the finds from the Eastern Cardo, we now suggest that the Roman city was planned and its main thoroughfares paved in the early years of Hadrian's reign, about a decade before his visit to the East."[69] Second, the pottery from the Roman refuse dump is now being cited as a fixed reference point for dating some of the types produced in Jerusalem's legionary kiln works to the period between the two revolts, particularly to the Flavian period (for the kiln works, see below).

The establishment of a local ceramic typology dating to ca. 70–130 CE is crucial for identifying remains of this period at other sites around Jerusalem. However, as mentioned above, some of the fine wares have ranges that extend beyond the Flavian period, while many of the other types have long ranges and cannot be closely dated. In other words, although the evidence from the Roman refuse dump and the eastern cardo confirms that some of these pottery types were produced in Jerusalem's legionary kiln works before ca. 130 CE, this is not neces- sarily their terminal date. Accepting a 130 CE cut-off date for production has the potential to create a circular argument in which these pottery types are used to date other sites to the period between the two revolts.[70] Similarly, the glass vessels from the Roman dump are dated to ca. 75–125 CE because this is the assumed date of the dump—but then are cited by Weksler-Bdolah as proof that this is the date of the dump.[71]

A circular argument is also evident in Weksler-Bdolah's claim that the establishment of the eastern cardo early in Hadrian's reign is proof that he founded Aelia Capitolina long before his visit in 129/130 CE: "Another important contribution to the chronology of the foundation of Aelia Capitolina comes from archaeological excavations along the Eastern Cardo in the Western Wall Plaza. There, it was found that the Cardo was paved in the early Hadrianic reign. As this street constituted a main traffic construction, it helps date the foundation of the Roman city to about a decade earlier than the well-known visit of Hadrian to Judaea in 129/130 CE and well before the Bar-Kokhba war."[72] Of course, this claim is based on her early dating of the eastern cardo.

The Western Cardo and North Wall of Aelia Capitolina

Because Jerusalem has not experienced another catastrophic destruction and renewal since Hadrian's time, scholars long assumed that the area of the modern Old City corresponds to Aelia Capitolina as depicted in the Madaba Map. It was not until the 1970s that archaeologists were able to excavate along the western cardo, which runs through the middle of the densely inhabited Old City. This opportunity arose when Nahman Avigad was invited to conduct excavations on the southwestern hill as part of Israel's reconstruction of the Jewish Quarter. Avigad discovered important remains from various periods, including the Herodian-period villas and the late Iron Age "Broad Wall."

Below the modern street that follows the line of the western cardo (Khan ez-Zeit/Beit ha-Bad Street), Avigad discovered a broad, stone-paved boulevard with columns lining the curbs of the sidewalks, corresponding to the depiction in the Madaba Map (Figure 8.5). He was surprised to find coins and pottery dating to the sixth century CE in fills sealed by the stone pavement of the ancient street, with no signs of an earlier street dating to Hadrian's time below. Avigad concluded that this part of the street is a sixth-century extension of the Hadrianic cardo to the south of the intersection with the main decumanus.[73] The main decumanus followed the Transverse Valley from modern Jaffa Gate and the Citadel eastward to the Temple Mount. Nowadays the street to the west of this intersection is called (in Hebrew) David Street, while to the east it is called (in Arabic) al-Silsilah Street (the Street of the Chain). According to Avigad, Aelia Capitolina occupied only the northern half of the modern Old City—the area north of the western decumanus—while the area to the south was unsettled. Avigad noted that the concentration of legionary inscriptions in the northern half of the Old City supports this picture. This would mean that Hadrian's city was laid out not as a square but as a narrow, elongated strip, with a truncated main (western) cardo terminating at the intersection with the main decumanus (instead of intersecting in the middle of the city).

Weksler-Bdolah proposes that the area south of the main decumanus was unsettled from ca. 300 CE until the fifth–sixth centuries because this is where

FIGURE 8.5 The western cardo.
Credit: Photo by the author.

the legionary camp had been located.[74] She believes this accounts for the slightly different alignment of the northern and southern halves of the western cardo (i.e., north and south of the intersection with the main decumanus); whereas the southern half originally was the main north–south road through the legionary camp (the *via principalis*), the northern half was established by Hadrian as the western cardo of Aelia Capitolina. Weksler-Bdolah reconstructs the legionary camp's north gate in the middle of the north side of the First Wall—the same spot that later became the intersection of the western cardo and main decumanus of Aelia Capitolina. Four columns arranged in a square that are still preserved in a building called Café Bashourah might belong to a Roman tetrapylon (a four-sided gate) at this intersection and would have marked the *caput viae*—the starting point of imperial roads to and from Jerusalem.[75]

Avigad's discovery that the southern half of the western cardo dates to the Byzantine period led to a reassessment of assumptions about Aelia Capitolina's layout. Most scholars believe that Hadrian's city of Aelia Capitolina was unwalled, with free-standing gates marking the main entrances on the north, west, east, and south sides: on the north at the site of the modern Damascus Gate; on the east near the modern Lion's Gate; on the south at the end of the eastern cardo; and on the west near the modern Jaffa Gate.[76] The legionary camp (which was likely walled) occupied all or part of the southwestern hill, while the civilian settlement was located to its north and east (corresponding to the northern half of the Old City). This view of the extent of the Hadrianic city is based on Avigad's findings that "the built-up area of Aelia Capitolina was restricted to the northern part of the town, while the Tenth Legion camped in the south."[77]

The only surviving gate of the four that marked the entrances to the city is on the north side, under the modern Damascus Gate. Excavations conducted at the Damascus Gate by different archaeologists, beginning with Robert Hamilton in 1937–1938, brought to light the remains of the triple-arched gateway discussed above, which scholars generally agree is Hadrianic.[78] Evidence that this gate was incorporated into a wall around 300 CE comes from Hamilton's Sounding A, which was dug against the western face of the west tower of the Damascus Gate and exposed a small portion of the adjacent section of fortification (curtain) wall.[79]

Hamilton's findings support the view that the Hadrianic triple-arched gateway under the Damascus Gate was free-standing until ca. 300 CE, when it was incorporated into a wall that corresponds with current line of the north wall of the Old City. In my opinion, however, Hadrian did not intend Aelia Capitolina to be unfortified. Instead, I have proposed that the wall to the north of the Old City, which Israeli archaeologists identify as the Third Wall, is also the north wall of Hadrianic Jerusalem (Pl. 10A; Figure 8.6).[80] This wall—which I call the "northern line"—lies about 450 meters (1,476 feet) to the north of and parallel to the north wall of the Old City. Recent excavations by Rina Avner and Kfir Arbib seem to confirm that this wall was constructed in the first century CE, in which case it could have been reused by Hadrian.[81] If the northern line was the north wall of Aelia Capitolina, the triple-arched gateway under the Damascus Gate would have been a free-standing gate marking the entrance to the oval plaza inside the city rather than its northern end (Figure 8.7).[82]

In 1903, Charles Clermont-Ganneau reported the discovery of two incomplete monumental Latin inscriptions to the north of the Old City.[83] The inscriptions came to light during construction work by Nablus Road, about 100 meters (328 feet) northwest of the Church of St. Stephen (the École Biblique) and ca. 400 meters (1,312 feet) north of the Damascus Gate—that is, in the vicinity of the northern line.[84] There were also pieces of columns and large stone blocks, all in secondary use in later structures. Although the site was not excavated, the remains were photographed by James E. Hanauer of the nearby Christ Church and reported in a letter to the Palestine Exploration Fund (PEF), and by Raphaël Savignac of the École Biblique, who published a description of the remains including a plan.[85] The inscriptions were also published by Clermont-Ganneau, who associated them with an unknown monument of Aelia Capitolina.[86]

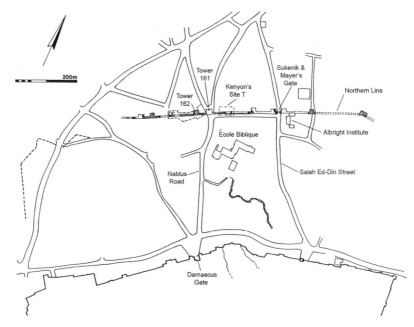

FIGURE 8.6 Plan of the north wall of Aelia Capitolina.
Credit: Prepared by Jim Haberman

In 2014, another fragment of one of the inscriptions was discovered in excavations in this area, allowing it to be restored in full.[87] The complete (restored) inscription, which I designate Inscription 1 for the purposes of this discussion, reads,

> To the Imperator Caesar Traianus Hadrianus Augustus, son of the deified Traianus Parthicus, grandson of the deified Nerva, high priest, invested with tribunician power for the 14th time, consul for the third time, father of the country (dedicated by) the 10th legion Fretensis Antoniniana.[88]

The second (incomplete) inscription was built into a later structure but originally belonged to a monument that was dedicated to Hadrian, or, less likely, to Antoninus Pius, by a freedman and built by detachments of at least five legions. This inscription, which I designate Inscription 2, reads,

> For Imperator Caesar Traianus Hadrianus Augustus, son of the deified Traianus Parthicus, grandson of the deified Nerva [— name —]us, his freedman (had erected/built this) with the help of the vexillations of the legions . . . and X Fretensis and II (Traiana?) and . . . and . . . and XII Fulminata.[89]

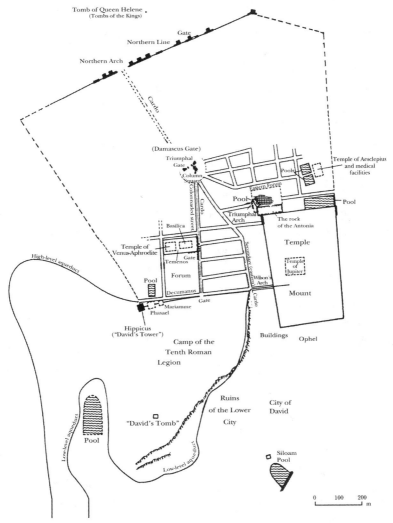

FIGURE 8.7 Plan of Aelia Capitolina with the northern line.
Credit: Prepared by the author.

Most scholars associate Inscription 1 and perhaps also Inscription 2 with a lost monumental arched gateway at this spot.[90] I have proposed that this gateway, which I call the "northern arch," was the main point of entry through the northern line, which marked the northern limit of Aelia Capitolina, while the triple-arched gateway at the Damascus Gate was inside the city.[91] Other scholars suggest that the northern arch marked the *pomerium* (boundary) of Aelia Capitolina but was not part of a city wall.[92] Ecker identifies the area between the Damascus Gate and the northern line as Aelia Capitolina's *campus* (military training ground).

He associates the inscriptions with monuments erected at the entrance to the *campus*, while the *pomerium* was marked by the Damascus Gate.[93] According to Ecker, Inscription 1 did not decorate an arched gateway but was on the base of a monumental column (*cippus*). In support, he cites similar letter sizes on an inscribed commemorative column base from Lambaesis, a Roman legionary base in Algeria.[94] However, the letter sizes of Inscription 1 and Inscription 2 are comparable to those in inscriptions associated with other monumental (but lost) arches erected in Aelia Capitolina, including two found in the vicinity of the Temple Mount: one dedicated to Septimius Severus ca. 202–205 CE, with letters 12.5–10 centimeters (4–5 inches) high, and the second of unknown date, with letters 11.5 centimeters (4.5 inches) high.[95]

Ecker claims that the monuments associated with the inscriptions stood in a space that belonged to the legion that dedicated them (such as a *campus*), not to the colony or other civic body.[96] However, as Weksler-Bdolah notes, Inscription 1's reference to the Tenth Legion alone indicates that either the associated monument was dedicated before the foundation of the colony, or the colony did not participate in its dedication.[97] The inscription's date—between December 129 and July–August 130—indicates that the associated monument was dedicated in honor of Hadrian's visit and before his foundation of the colony of Aelia Capitolina.[98] Ecker's claim that the monument(s) associated with the inscriptions must have stood in a space that belonged to the legion and not the colony or other civic body therefore is irrelevant as the colony did not yet exist. At the time of Hadrian's visit, Jerusalem was a military settlement with the Tenth Legion camped somewhere on the southwestern hill amid the ruins of the city, probably surrounded by scattered residences of veterans and their families. The monument associated with Inscription 1 and perhaps Inscription 2—apparently an arched gateway—was erected by the legion to honor Hadrian on the occasion of his visit, as indicated by the inscriptions' contents and the use of Latin.[99] Monumental arched gateways at Timgad (Thamugadi) in Algeria carried inscriptions announcing its foundation by Trajan as a military colony for veterans, through the work of his legate and the III Legion Augusta. For example, one inscription reads,

> The Emperor Caesar, son of the divine Nerva, Nerva Trajan Augustus, Conqueror of the Germans, Pontifex Maximus, with tribunician powers for the fourth time, elected consul three times, Father of the Fatherland, established the Colony Marciana Traiana Thamugadi through the Third Augustan Legion and the propraetorian legate Lucius Munatius Gallus.[100]

Like Jerusalem Inscription 1, the Timgad inscription is in Latin and commemorates the dedication of a monument—apparently an arched gateway—by the legion in honor of the emperor. Unlike the Jerusalem inscription, the Timgad inscription honors the emperor for having founded the colony. This is because Timgad was a de novo foundation, that is, a colony established on previously unoccupied land about 24 kilometers (15 miles) from the legionary camp in Lambaesis. In contrast, in Jerusalem the legionary camp was located amid the ruins of the city. No one lived at Timgad before the emperor founded the colony there, whereas in Jerusalem the legionary camp existed before the colony's foundation. This explains why the earliest inscriptions dedicated by the legion at Timgad, which adorned monumental arched gateways, acknowledge the imperial foundation of a colony there, while Inscription 1 from Jerusalem contains no reference to a colony—because it was dedicated before the colony was founded.

During his tour of the region in 129–130 CE, Hadrian visited Gerasa (modern Jerash), a Decapolis city now in Jordan. In advance of his visit, the inhabitants erected a free-standing arched gateway (which I designate here "the free-standing arch") straddling the main approach to the city. About 460 meters (1,509 feet) to its north, another arched gateway—the South Gate—which was also rebuilt under Hadrian, marked the entrance into Gerasa's famous oval plaza (Figure 8.8).[101] This mirrors the arrangement in Jerusalem, where the northern arch is located about 400 m to the north of the Hadrianic arched gateway at the Damascus Gate and the plaza inside it.

The dedicatory inscription on the free-standing arch at Gerasa reads,

> For the safety of Emperor Caesar, son of divine Trajan Parthicus, grandson of divine Nerva, Trajan Hadrian Augustus, Pontifex Maximus, holding tribunician authority for the 14th (time), consul the 3rd (time), father of his country; and for the good fortune and perpetuity of his entire house— the city of the Antiochenes, on the Chrysoroas, the former Gerasenes, in accordance with the will of Flavius Agrippa, (has dedicated) the gateway, with a triumph, in the year 192.[102]

Because at the time of Hadrian's visit Gerasa was neither a legionary base nor a colony (a status the city attained much later), the dedication was made by the citizens of the city alone. The letters are comparable in height (12–13 cm/4.5– 5 inches) to those in the Jerusalem inscriptions. Although the free-standing arch could have been incorporated subsequently into the line of an extended walled circuit had the situation arisen (much as the Damascus Gate was appropriated for the purposes of the new defenses provided for Jerusalem in the early fourth century CE), its construction was not predicated upon considerations of defense. Rather, the free-standing arch, just like the northern arch in its original form, was intended as a display of loyalty to the emperor upon his visit.

FIGURE 8.8 The oval plaza at Gerasa (Jerash).
Credit: Photo by the author.

Shimon Gibson and Alla Nagorsky agree that Hadrian intended the northern line to serve as the north wall of Aelia Capitolina and that the inscriptions and architectural pieces derive from a monumental gateway in it.[103] However, because no remains of a gateway have been discovered in the vicinity of the inscriptions, they conclude that there was no such structure at this spot. Instead, they associate Inscriptions 1 and 2 and the column pieces and large stone blocks with a gate in the northern line about 300 meters (984 feet) to the northeast, by Salah ed-Din Street. This gate was discovered in Eleazar Lipa Sukenik and Leo Aryeh Mayer's 1925–1928 excavations along the northern line (which they identified as the Third Wall), outside the northwest corner of the fence surrounding the W. F. Albright Institute of Archaeological Research (formerly the American School of Oriental Research) (Figure 8.9).[104] The first buildings on the grounds of the Albright Institute were completed in 1924–1925, shortly before Sukenik and Mayer's excavations.[105] Gibson and Nagorsky's proposal is attractive because, even today, Salah ed-Din Street is a major north–south thoroughfare north of the Old City. However, as Ecker points out, the sizes and weights of the inscribed stone blocks (Inscription 1 weighs a total of ca. 1.5 tons and Inscription 2 weighs ca. 430–500 kg) and the other architectural pieces make it unlikely they were moved such a distance.[106]

The remains uncovered by Sukenik and Mayer include a tower projecting 7.5 m (24 feet) from the north face of the wall immediately west of Salah ed-Din

FIGURE 8.9 Sukenik and Mayer's excavation of the Third Wall in front of the Albright Institute.
Credit: From the Herbert May collection at Oberlin College, Courtesy of Oberlin College Libraries, Special Collections.

Street. On the east side of the tower, they found a square room that appears to be ancient but was not bonded with the tower (and therefore presumably is a later addition). The continuation of the wall was discovered 6 meters (19 feet) to the east of the room, up to the front fence of the Albright Institute (which is on the east side of Salah ed-Din Street). At this point the wall is 5.7 meters (18 feet) wide, which is about 1 meter (3 feet) wider than other sections of the northern line. According to Sukenik and Mayer, this section was an opening in the wall (a gate) that was later blocked by row of large stones. On the other (east) side of the Albright Institute's fence (inside the fence), they found the continuation of the wall but no traces of a tower, while farther to the east, inside the courtyard of the institute, there were no traces of the wall at all.[107]

Sukenik and Mayer identified the remains by Salah ed-Din Street as a gate because of the tower, the thickness of the wall immediately east of the tower, and the later blockage of large stones. A recent survey conducted by Matt Adams using Ground Penetrating Radar (GPR) indicates that the east tower lies inside the Albright Institute's fence, confirming that there indeed was a gate at this spot.[108] Nevertheless, Gibson and Nagorsky's claim that no monumental gateway existed farther to the west, near the findspot of the inscriptions is an unconvincing argument from silence in light of the extremely limited exploration of this area, which consists of the observation by passersby of a construction site in 1903, and the 2014 excavation of two squares measuring 5 × 3–4.5 meters (16 × 10–15 feet) each.[109] Furthermore, in his letter to the PEF, Hanauer describes the "remains of a massive building and gateway," although the nature of these remains cannot be verified.[110] Other considerations support the existence of a monumental gateway near the findspot of the inscriptions. First, this spot lies on a route (modern Nablus Road) that presumably was always the major north–south thoroughfare from the site of the Damascus Gate. In fact, there is now a rotary at this spot, where Nablus Road intersects with Amr Ibn Al A`as Street and bifurcates into two branches to the north. The former US Consulate in East Jerusalem, which closed in March 2019, is on the north side of the rotary, between the two branches.[111] In front of the former consulate building is a large block of stone with drafted margins that belongs to the north face of a tower in the northern line, which was uncovered by Sukenik and Mayer (Figure 8.10). During Sara Ben-Arieh and Ehud Netzer's 1972–1974 excavations in this area, the digging of a sewer trench revealed a stone belonging to the west face of this tower, which they designated Tower 161. Ben-Arieh and Netzer discovered two more towers in the wall to the west of this, about 30–32 meters (90–104 feet) apart from each other, which they designated towers 162 and 163.[112] After a break, the continuation of the northern line to the east of Tower 161 is visible on the north side of Amr Ibn Al A`as Street, where a row of large ashlar blocks has been exposed since Charles Wilson's survey in the mid-nineteenth century (Figure 7.26). In the 1960s, as part of Kathleen Kenyon's excavations in Area T, Emmett Hamrick dug two narrow trenches against the north face of these ashlars.[113]

The 30–32 meters (90–104 feet) separating Towers 161, 162, and 163 from each other and the fact that only the bedding of the wall was found by Ben-Arieh and Netzer leaves open the possibility that a monumental gateway was set between two of these towers. In my opinion, the large size of Tower 161, which projects over 11 meters (36 feet) from the wall, suggests it was part of the gateway. In contrast, the other towers along the northern line project no more than 9 meters (29 feet), with the tower by Salah ed-Din Street and the Albrght Institute projecting only 7.5 meters (24 feet) from the wall.[114] Therefore, it seems likely, as most scholars have assumed, that Inscription 1 and perhaps Inscription 2 originated in a monumental arched gateway in the northern line that was located close to their findspot. This gate (the northern arch) probably replaced an earlier gate in the Third Wall, substantial sections of which must still have been standing even if parts were breached, in ruins, or robbed out.[115] Inscription 1 commemorates the gate's dedication by the Tenth Legion in 129/130 CE, while Inscription 2 might

FIGURE 8.10 A section of the Third Wall in front of the former US Consulate in East Jerusalem.
Credit: Photo by the author.

be associated with a later repair of the structure—perhaps after the Bar-Kokhba Revolt—or with the erection of another monument nearby.[116]

The evidence reviewed here supports the view held by many scholars that Hadrian announced the foundation of the colony of Aelia Capitolina on the occasion of his visit in 129/130.[117] In advance of his arrival, the Tenth Legion honored the emperor by erecting a monumental arched gateway (the northern arch) to the north of the legionary camp and the ruins of the city, probably on the site of an earlier gate in the Third Wall. Hadrian's plans for Aelia Capitolina included reconstructing the Third Wall as a strategic line of defense to protect the vulnerable north side of the colony in the wake of the two recent Jewish revolts (the First Revolt and the Diaspora Revolt). In fact, city walls were considered a "functional necessity" for Roman colonial foundations.[118]

The possibility that the northern line was the north wall of Aelia Capitolina is supported by the distribution of Roman burials of the second–fourth centuries only to the north of it, not inside the wall to the south.[119] Tombs cut into the northern line indicate that it was abandoned by ca. 300 CE, when the current line of the north wall of the Old City appears to have been established. The need to fortify the north side of the city with a new line of wall probably resulted from Diocletian's transfer of the Tenth Legion to Aila, or perhaps occurred with the rapid growth of the city's population after Constantine's legalization of Christianity in 313 CE.[120] The testimony of the pilgrim of Bordeaux indicates that Jerusalem was walled by the time of his visit in 333 CE.[121] The fact that the northern line began to be dismantled by the late third or early fourth century suggests that its construction may never have been completed. This would account for the absence of Roman architectural remains inside it, which, as at Gerasa, appears to enclose a Hadrianic quarter that never developed.[122] The possibility that the northern line was never completed recalls the unfinished state of the eastern cardo. Although Weksler-Bdolah attributes the eastern cardo's unfinished state to the outbreak of the Bar Kokhba Revolt, perhaps it was Hadrian's death that ended work on both projects.

The Great Causeway (or "Giant Viaduct") and the Western Wall of the Temple Mount

Before 70 CE, a 14-meter (46-foot) wide, concrete-like wall (the "foundation wall" or "dam wall") was constructed at the eastern end of the First Wall, which functioned as a dam across the Tyropoeon Valley.[123] Archaeologists long assumed that the dam carried a road that provided access to the Temple Mount through a gate approached by an arched bridge. Various parts of the bridge, which has two abutting rows of arches (a north row and a south row), have been explored and dated differently over time. The easternmost arch is called Wilson's Arch, which today projects from the north side of the Western Wall in an underground area reserved for men's prayers but is open to the public for visits at certain times. The westernmost arch (Arch 100) spanned the eastern cardo. Based on excavations that they conducted beginning in 2007, Weksler-Bdolah and Alexander Onn conclude that the arched bridge—dubbed the "Great Causeway" or "Giant Viaduct"—is a Roman (post–70 CE) structure that incorporates Second Temple-period remains including the dam and Wilson's Arch (Figure 8.11).[124] A corridor between the Great Causeway and buildings constructed to the south later in the Roman period is known as the "secret passage."[125] An undated Latin building inscription of the Tenth Legion was discovered in the wall of one of these buildings (Building G) and is associated with its original construction.[126]

The piers (square supports) of both rows of arches were founded on top of the dam wall. Since the southern row of arches appears to abut the northern row, the northern row must have been constructed first. Because Arch 100 fits the combined width of both rows of arches and was adjusted to the orientation and level of the eastern cardo, Weksler-Bdolah and Onn conclude that the Great Causeway and the eastern cardo are contemporary. In their opinion, the northern row of

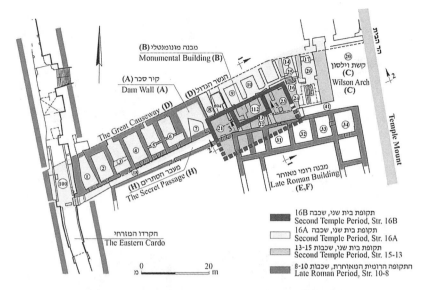

FIGURE 8.11 Plan of the Great Causeway (from Onn and Weksler-Bdolah 2016: figure 2). Credit: Courtesy of the Israel Antiquities Authority and Shlomit Weksler-Bdolah.

arches was a narrow bridge dating to the period between the two revolts (70–130 CE), antedating the foundation of Aelia Capitolina. Later, under Hadrian, the bridge was widened by the addition of the southern row of arches, and the pavement of the decumanus maximus was laid on top of it. Weksler-Bdolah and Onn propose that the narrow bridge provided access from the legionary camp on the southwestern hill to the Temple Mount while the soldiers cleared the surrounding area. The widening of the bridge and paving of the decumanus maximus support the view that Hadrian established a Capitolium on the Temple Mount (see below).

During excavations in 2015–2018, Joe Uziel, Tehillah Lieberman, and Avi Solomon discovered a tiny theater-like structure (their terminology)—perhaps an odeion (roofed theater)—sandwiched between the western wall of the Temple Mount and the pier of Wilson's Arch (Figure 8.12). The structure has a semi-circular cavea (for the banks of seats) and a stage area ca. 2 meters (7 feet) wide × 10 meters (32 feet) long. The orchestra (the semi-circular floor between the stage and the cavea) is only 6 meters (19 feet) in diameter, making this the smallest known theater-like structure in the eastern Roman Empire.[127] Although construction was never completed, the excavators estimate that there would have been 6–8 rows of seats with a capacity of 150–200 spectators.[128] Six stone theater seats built into the walls of an early Islamic palace at the southwest corner of the Temple Mount probably originated in this structure. Pottery found in the cavea's

FIGURE 8.12 The odeion under Wilson's Arch.
Credit: Photo by Assaf Peretz. Courtesy of Joe Uziel, Tehillah Lieberman, and the Israel Antiquities Authority.

foundations and radiocarbon dating of charred organic remains indicate a date in the first half of the second century and suggest that construction commenced before the Bar Kokhba Revolt. In this case, it may have been the outbreak of the revolt or Hadrian's death that put an end to the project before its completion.[129]

The Temple Mount and the Capitolium

Hadrian renamed Jerusalem Aelia Capitolina in honor of Capitoline Jupiter, the city's new patron god and the chief deity of the Roman pantheon. Capitoline Jupiter was worshiped together with Juno (Greek Hera) and Minerva (Greek Athena) around the Roman Empire. Temples dedicated to the Capitoline triad are known as Capitoliums, a name that derives from the temple of Jupiter Optimus Maximus (the best and greatest Jupiter) on the Capitoline Hill in Rome. The establishment of a Capitolium, often on a hill, as in Rome, was a characteristic feature of Roman colonies.[130] Although there is little doubt that Hadrian built a Capitolium in Aelia Capitolina, there is no consensus about its size or location due to the confused testimony of our literary sources and a lack of archaeological evidence. The information provided by literary sources reflects the Christian biases of the writers or later editors who emphasized the Temple Mount's ruinous state, which they viewed as a fulfilment of Jesus's prophecy about the second temple's destruction and the "desolating sacrilege" foretold by Daniel. Scholars are divided on whether the Capitolium was on the Temple Mount or the site of the (later) Church of the Holy Sepulcher.[131] The following is a review of some of the sources supporting a location on the Temple Mount. The site of the Church of the Holy Sepulcher is discussed below in the section on Hadrian's western forum.

The earliest literary testimony about the Capitolium's location is provided by Cassius Dio who, as noted above, attributes the outbreak of the Bar Kokhba Revolt to Hadrian's foundation of Aelia Capitolina: "At Jerusalem he [Hadrian] founded a city in place of the one which had been razed to the ground, naming it Aelia Capitolina, and *on the site* (Greek *eis ton topon*) of the temple (*naon*) of the god he raised a new temple (*naon*) to Jupiter."[132] This passage is often taken at face value as meaning that Hadrian built the Capitolium on the site of the second temple on the Temple Mount. However, some scholars translate the Greek as "*instead of* the temple of the god he raised a new temple to Jupiter," in which case Cassius Dio's testimony would only indicate that Hadrian built a Capitolium somewhere in Aelia Capitolina but not necessarily on the Temple Mount.[133] These scholars also note that Cassius Dio's testimony might not be accurate as it is preserved only in an abridged version by an eleventh-century monk named Xiphilinius of Constantinople.[134] In my opinion, the use of the term *topos*, which means "place," and the term *naos*, which denotes a temple building rather than a sacred precinct, support the view that the Capitolium was built on the site of the second temple, which it replaced.[135]

In 333 CE, a Christian pilgrim from Burdigala (modern Bordeaux in France)—the so-called "pilgrim of (or traveler from) Bordeaux"—visited the Holy Land. He wrote a travelogue describing his travels, including an eyewitness account of the Temple Mount: "And in the sanctuary itself (Latin *in aede ipsa*), where the Temple stood which Solomon built, there is marble in front of the altar which has on it the blood of Zacharias—you would think it had only been shed today. All around you can see the marks of the hobnails of the soldiers who killed him, as plainly as if they had been pressed into wax. Two statues of Hadrian stand there, and, not far from them, a pierced stone which the Jews come and anoint each year" (591).[136] The pilgrim does not mention a Capitolium or Jupiter, only the two statues of Hadrian. It is not clear if the sanctuary (*aedes*) he saw was the ruined second temple or a Hadrianic shrine or temple to Jupiter in its place.[137] Some scholars believe the pilgrim of Bordeaux mistakenly identified the second statue he saw as Hadrian and that it was more likely a statue of his successor, Antoninus Pius (138–161 CE). In this case, perhaps the statue originally stood on an inscribed base dedicated to Antoninus Pius that is built into the south wall of the Temple Mount above the western (Double) Hulda Gate.[138] The inscription, which is in Latin, reads,

> For Titus Aelius Hadrianus Antoninus Pius Augustus, father of his country, pontifex, augur (a statue was erected) by the decision of the city councilors at public expense.[139]

In his commentaries on Matthew and Isaiah, written in the late fourth–early fifth century, the early Church Father Jerome, who is known for his translation of the Bible into Latin (the Vulgate), mentions a statue of Jupiter and an equestrian statue of Hadrian (a statue of Hadrian on horseback) on the site of the ruined second temple.[140]

> Now this [the abomination of desolation mentioned in Mt 24:15] can be interpreted either literally of the Antichrist, or of the image of Caesar that Pilate placed in the Temple, or of the equestrian statue of Hadrian, which stands to the present day in the very location of the Holy of Holies.[141]

> In the place where once there was the temple and religion of God, there was set up a statue of Hadrian and an *idol* of Jupiter.[142]

The *Chronicon Paschale* (*Easter Chronicle*), an early seventh-century chronicle of world history by an anonymous author, presents dated events arranged in chronological order beginning with creation. Despite the author's Christian perspective and his interweaving of biblical and secular material, the work contains valuable historical information.[143] This includes a list of buildings in Aelia Capitolina attributed by the author to Hadrian: two *demosia* (public bath houses?), a theater, a *trikameron*, a *tetranymphon* (a nymphaeum or fountain house with four porticoes—perhaps the pool of Siloam?), and a *dodekapylon*— a structure with four gates—that formerly was called *anabathmoi* (a staircase), and the *kodra*.[144] The identification of these buildings is unclear and the author's source(s) are unknown. Although the information is generally considered reliable, most scholars believe the description relates to the third–fourth centuries rather than the time of Hadrian (second century).[145] Perhaps the *trikameron*—a Greek word meaning a building with three rooms—refers to the Capitolium, which was dedicated to the Capitoline triad and therefore would have had three cellas (cult rooms). The *kodra* (Latin *quadra* or *quadrum*—a square) is usually understood as denoting all or part of the Temple Mount.[146] But even if the *trikameron* is the Capitolium and the *kodra* is the Temple Mount, the list does not link them together and therefore does not indicate where the Capitolium was located.

Two other seventh-century sources refer to the Temple Mount as the "Capitol" (*Kapitolion* or *Kapitolin*). Both sources relate legendary stories set in Jerusalem shortly after the Muslim conquest. Although the references to the "Capitol" are incidental to the stories, the name seems to preserve the memory of the location of Hadrian's temple to Jupiter on the Temple Mount.[147] However, some scholars propose that the identification of the Temple Mount with the Capitolium developed only in the sixth–seventh centuries and therefore does not prove this was the site of Hadrian's temple to Jupiter.[148]

Despite the difficulties understanding these sources, many scholars believe that Hadrian erected the Capitolium on the Temple Mount, on or near the ruins of the second temple. This is supported by the site's physical prominence and the construction of the Great Causeway, which was a narrow bridge between 70 and 130 CE. The bridge was widened after the foundation of Aelia Capitolina to accommodate the eastern end of the main decumanus, which terminated at the Temple Mount.[149] There would be no reason to provide access to the Temple Mount unless something significant was located on it.[150] The establishment of a Roman temple on the site of the former Jewish temple makes sense in light of the Roman view that the God of Israel had been vanquished and his cult replaced by that of Capitoline Jupiter.[151] It also accords with a phenomenon known to archaeologists as the "continuity of cult," in which a site remains sacred over time even if the religions or the god(s) worshiped changed. It is impossible to determine if the Capitolium was a full-scale temple building or a modest shrine. However, the literary references to statues of Hadrian suggest that the emperor was worshiped alongside Jupiter.[152] Indeed, the city's name—Aelia Capitolina—indicates that Hadrian identified himself with Jupiter.

The Forums of Aelia Capitolina

The northern arch and the Hadrianic arch at the Damascus Gate originally were free-standing monuments, although both were later incorporated into different lines of city walls. There were at least five other monumental arches in Aelia Capitolina, all of which seem to have been free-standing: the so-called arch of Ecce Homo at the northern forum, an arch in the western forum, and three other inscriptions apparently associated with arches—a dedication to Hadrian found east of the Church of the Holy Sepulcher; a dedication to Septimius Severus (ca. 202–205 CE) found reused in the pavement of an early Islamic palace to the south of the Temple Mount, which perhaps originally was in an arch at the southern entrance to the city; and an inscription of unknown date and provenance in the Islamic Museum on the Temple Mount.[153] Here we consider the forums of Aelia Capitolina.

The Northern Forum

Hadrian established two forums (markets or commercial centers) in Aelia Capitolina, one to the north of the Temple Mount and the other on the western side of the city. Both were open paved spaces surrounded by temples and public monuments, with the entrances marked by free-standing, triple-arched gateways similar to the one at the Damascus Gate. The northern forum was in the area occupied by Herod's Antonia fortress before 70 CE. Today this area is bisected by the Via Dolorosa, on the north side of which is a convent called the Church of the Sisters of Zion. The ancient stone pavement ("Lithostratos") and triple-arched gate ("arch of Ecce Homo") preserved inside the convent, which once were thought to belong to the Antonia fortress and are associated in modern Christian tradition with Jesus's passion, instead are part of Hadrian's northern forum (Figures 8.13–8.15). Specifically, the triple-arched gateway was a free-standing monument marking the entrance to the forum, and the Lithostratos was the flagstone pavement of the forum. The pavement was laid above the Struthion pools, which originally were open-air pools in the moat outside the Antonia fortress (Figure 8.16). Excavations indicate that the triple-arched gateway is contemporary with the pavement.[154]

The meager archaeological evidence suggests that the Via Dolorosa was a center of cultic activity in Aelia Capitolina. In the Herodian period this side of the city was protected by the Bezetha (or Bethesda or Sheep's) Pool (Figure 7.28). Today this pool lies on the grounds of the Crusader period Church of St. Anne. It is so-called because this is where sacrificial animals presumably were sold to pilgrims visiting the second temple. After 70 CE, the pool was the site of a healing sanctuary dedicated to Serapis (usually described in scholarly literature as a sanctuary to Asclepius or an Asclepeion).[155] Asclepius and Serapis were believed to heal patients through a combination of bathing in water and dreaming while sleeping on the grounds of the sanctuary (a process called incubation). Interestingly, John (5:1–9) describes Jesus's miraculous cure of an invalid at the Sheep's Pool, suggesting that either the pool was associated with healing even before 70, or this story (which is reported only in the Fourth Gospel) originated after 70 (see Chapter 7).

In the nineteenth century, Clermont-Ganneau conducted excavations in caverns below the basements of houses on the north side of the Via Dolorosa, to the west of the Sheep's Pool. Among his discoveries were two unusual vases decorated with figured images in relief, which he correctly dated to the time of Aelia Capitolina (Figure 8.17). The images on these vases (now in the Palestine Exploration Fund in London) appear to be Mithraic.[156] They include snakes and depictions of Mercury (who was associated with the cult of Mithras as

FIGURE 8.13 The Arch of Ecce Homo above the Via Dolorosa.
Credit: Photo by the author.

the planetary god of Wednesday and the protective deity of the lowest grade of initiates). Mithraism was a cult that originated in the Near East but became popular among Romans, especially soldiers, in the first to third centuries CE. The cult centered on a mythical figure named Mithras and promised salvation and an afterlife to its adherents (all of whom were men; women were prohibited from joining). Mithraism was a mystery cult, meaning that only initiates could participate in the rituals, which were conducted in cave-like shrines. The discovery of vases decorated with Mithraic imagery in underground caverns by the Via Dolorosa suggests this was the site of a Mithraeum (a shrine of Mithras), a possibility supported by the cult's popularity among Roman soldiers.

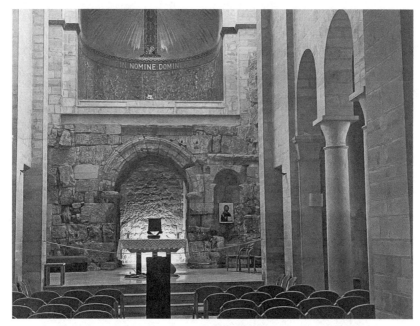

FIGURE 8.14 The Arch of Ecce Homo in the Church of the Sisters of Zion.
Credit: Photo by the author.

FIGURE 8.15 The Lithostratos.
Credit: Photo by the author.

FIGURE 8.16 The Struthion Pools.
Credit: Photo by the author.

The Western Forum

Hadrian established another forum on the western side of the city, in the area today occupied by the Church of the Holy Sepulcher. It was entered from the western cardo through a free-standing, triple-arched gateway. Two buildings were erected on the north side of the forum: a basilica (on the east) and a temple (on the west).[157] As was typical in the Roman world, the basilica—a multifunctional civic hall—was arranged with the long axis of the building running east–west, so that the long side faced the forum. A staircase led from the western cardo on the east to a courtyard (atrium) in front of the basilica. Nowadays the remains

FIGURE 8.17 Mithraic vases.
Credit: Photo by Rupert Chapman. Courtesy of the Palestine Exploration Fund.

on the northeast side of the forum, including columns lining the west side of the western cardo, the triple-arched gateway (only a small part of which has survived), the staircase and façade of the atrium and basilica, and the forum's stone pavement are preserved in the Alexander Nevsky Church (the Russian Alexander Hospice) (Figures 8.18 and 8.19). This property, which adjoins the Church of the Holy Sepulcher, was acquired in 1859 by the Russian Orthodox Church.[158]

When these remains were discovered during the hospice's construction in the nineteenth century, they were believed to be associated with the Hasmonean- or Herodian-period Second Wall. Specifically, the south wall and part of the east wall of the atrium/basilica or the temple's temenos wall were identified as the Second Wall because they are built of Herodian-style stones (which are in secondary use, typical of Hadrianic construction in Jerusalem).[159] If these remains belong to the Second Wall, it would prove that the Church of the Holy Sepulcher (which is located to the west) was outside the city walls at the time of Jesus. This is important because, according to the Gospel accounts, Jesus was crucified and buried outside the city walls, but the Church of the Holy Sepulcher was not built

FIGURE 8.18 The basilica in the Alexander Nevsky Church.
Credit: Photo by the author.

until three hundred years after his death. In addition, a stone threshold adjoining the southeast corner of the atrium was at first identified as the gate through which Jesus was taken to be crucified. A huge image of Jesus bearing the cross is still displayed on the threshold. Nevertheless, most scholars agree that these remains did not exist in the late Second Temple period but instead are part of Hadrian's western forum.[160] The Hadrianic basilica was converted into a church (a Christian hall of worship) by the emperor Constantine in the fourth century.

The temple to the west of the basilica was built over Golgotha (Calvary)—the rocky outcrop venerated as the site of Jesus's crucifixion—and the rock-cut tomb in which many Christians believe his body was laid. The temple was demolished around 326 CE when Constantine ordered the construction of the Church of the Holy Sepulcher. Scholars disagree about whether the temple was dedicated to Aphrodite/Venus (the Greco-Roman goddess of love) or Jupiter. Eusebius, a Church Father who was the bishop of Caesarea (on the coast of Palestine) in the early fourth century, reports that Hadrian built a temple to Aphrodite/Venus on a raised podium over the site of Jesus's tomb.

Indeed with a great expenditure of effort they brought earth from somewhere outside [the city] and covered up the whole place. Then once

FIGURE 8.19 The arched gateway in the Alexander Nevsky Church.
Credit: Photo by the author.

the embankment had been levelled at a certain height, they paved it, and so
hid the divine cave [the tomb] somewhere down beneath a great quantity
of soil. Then as though they had everything finished, above the ground
they constructed a terrible and truly genuine tomb, one for souls, for dead
idols, and built a gloomy sanctuary to the impure demon of Aphrodite;
then they offered foul sacrifices there upon defiled and polluted altars.[161]

In the fifth century, Sozomen (or Sozomenos), a native of a village near Gaza
wrote an Ecclesiastical History in which he, too, reported that the Church of the
Holy Sepulcher was established on the site of a temple to Aphrodite/Venus.

[T]he Greeks [pagan Romans] had heaped up mounds of earth upon the holy places, and, the more effectually to conceal them, had enclosed the place of the resurrection and Mount Cavalry within a wall, and had moreover ornamented the whole locality, and paved it with stone. A temple and statue dedicated to Venus had also been erected on the same spot by these people.[162]

Based on the testimony of Eusebius and Sozomen, many scholars believe the temple at Hadrian's western forum was dedicated to Aphrodite/Venus. Perhaps, they suggest, this is reflected in the layout of the Rotunda of the Church of the Holy Sepulcher (the domed structure that enshrines the tomb of Jesus), as some Roman temples to Aphrodite/Venus were circular.[163] Others identify the temple at Hadrian's western forum as the Capitolium, citing a late fourth-century letter sent by Jerome to Paulinus of Nola: "From the days of Hadrian until the reign of Constantine, roughly 180 years, the pagans worshiped a likeness of Jupiter set up in the place of the resurrection and a marble statue of Venus on the rock of the cross."[164] It has been suggested, however, that Jerome might have inserted the reference to Jupiter as a literary parallel to Venus and to emphasize the extent of the desecration of the Christian holy site.[165]

Scholars who locate the Capitolium by Hadrian's western forum maintain that Aphrodite/Venus was worshiped there alongside Jupiter. They identify fragmentary walls under the Church of the Holy Sepulcher as the remains of a tripartite (three-room) temple that must be the Capitolium.[166] Others, however, associate these remains with the temple of Aphrodite/Venus or with the original Constantinian church.[167] Those who identify the temple by Hadrian's western forum as the Capitolium argue that the ruined and desolate Temple Mount "was not a suitable environment for the great Capitoline god."[168] In their opinion, one or more statues of Hadrian (and perhaps his successor Antoninus Pius) were set up on the Temple Mount independently of the Capitolium, which was on the other side of the city by the western forum.[169] If true, it would mean that Hadrian established a temple to Capitoline Jupiter not on the site of the former Jewish temple but on the spot where Jesus—who Christians believe is divine— was crucified and buried, and which, in turn, was replaced by the Church of the Holy Sepulcher. This is a Christian supersessionist view that equates/substitutes the chief deity of the Roman pantheon not with the God of Israel but with Jesus and moves the locus of divine presence from the Temple Mount to the Church of the Holy Sepulcher.[170] It also makes no sense, as in Hadrian's time the Romans equated Capitoline Jupiter not with Jesus but with the God of Israel (who, they believed, had been vanquished by Jupiter).[171] And, in my opinion, it was Hadrian's plan to establish a shrine or temple to Capitoline Jupiter on the Temple

Mount as part of his refoundation of Jerusalem as Aelia Capitolina that provoked the Jews to revolt.

The Kiln Works of the Tenth Legion

A sprawling site on the western outskirts of Jerusalem was a pottery manufacturing center in the Hasmonean, Herodian, and Roman periods. It has different names after the modern properties on which excavations have been conducted: Giv`at Ram, the Crowne Plaza Hotel, and Binyanei Ha'uma (Jerusalem's convention center). In the Hasmonean and Herodian periods, Jewish potters who might have lived in "Jason's village" produced cooking pots, cooking pot stands, and storage jars at the site (see Chapter 6). Although after 70 the site contracted in size to the area around the Crowne Plaza Hotel, pottery production continued. New types were introduced to serve the needs of the Roman army: unstamped bricks, roof tiles, ceramic pipes, and large, coarse vessels. The continued use of kilns and *miqva'ot* that antedate 70, the production of Herodian-period types of cooking pots, and the absence of pig bones suggest that the potters were Jews who manufactured products for the Tenth Legion.[172]

Some time between 117 and 130 CE, the pottery manufacturing site moved about 100 meters (328 feet) north from the Crowne Plaza Hotel to the area of Jerusalem's convention center (Binyanei Ha'uma).[173] There is no evidence of Jewish presence or potters at the new site: the miqva'ot went out of use, the production of native pottery types ceased, and stone vessels disappeared. Instead, new kilns were established which produced a different repertoire of terracotta and ceramic vessels: roof and floor tiles and pipes stamped with the name and symbols of the Tenth Legion and pottery types that are distinctively Roman and alien to the native Palestinian tradition (analyses demonstrate that the clay is local, indicating that the vessels are not imports). Roman legions typically manufactured their own stamped terracotta tiles and pipes, but they rarely produced their own pottery. Instead, legions usually imported some vessels and purchased the rest from local potters. However, Jerusalem's remote location relative to the major Roman pottery production centers in the western Mediterranean made it too costly to import pottery, and Jewish potters apparently were no longer employed at the kiln works after the Diaspora Revolt and the Bar Kokhba Revolt. Therefore, the Tenth Legion in Jerusalem commissioned military potters to produce many of the vessels they needed.[174] The ceramic repertoire includes a number of distinctive types with close parallels in the potters' quarter at Brigetio—the site of a legionary camp on the Danube in the Roman province of Pannonia (modern Hungary)—suggesting that some of the military potters in Jerusalem came from this region. The possibility of such a connection is supported by the discovery of a Bar Kokhba coin at Brigetio, which apparently was taken home as a souvenir by a returning solder.[175] Roman presence at the Jerusalem kiln works after 130 CE is further indicated by the appearance of pig bones among the faunal remains, as pork was a staple of the Roman diet but was generally avoided by Jews due to the biblical prohibition.

Why did the Roman legion replace the Jewish potters with their own military potters around 117–130 CE? Perhaps this is connected to administrative changes made by Trajan in the wake of the Diaspora Revolt or to unrest in Judea during the governorship of Lusius Quietus in 117 CE.[176] Or, perhaps the new legionary kiln works were established in connection with Hadrian's visit and foundation of Aelia Capitolina in 130 CE, which would have required the production of large quantities of construction materials and pottery.

The pottery produced in Jerusalem's legionary kiln works consists of fine table wares and cooking vessels, which were used to prepare and serve Roman types of cuisine. They differ in shape and decoration from the pottery types characteristic of Jerusalem before 70 CE, reflecting a sea-change in culinary and dining habits. For millennia, bread has been the dietary staple in the eastern Mediterranean, dipped in olive oil, bean spreads (analogous to hummus), and/or vegetable or lentil-based soups, stews, and gruels. From the late Iron Age on, Judean cooking pots were characterized by having a large globular body, short neck, and relatively narrow mouth—an ideal design for boiling the soups, stews, and gruels that were a basic component of the local diet. The small opening (mouth) minimized evaporation and spillage and required any meat added to be cut into small chunks. Boiling softened the ingredients—an advantage in an era when tooth loss was common—and the liquid base was an economical way to stretch the meal.

The pottery types produced in Jerusalem's legionary kiln works reflect Roman dietary preferences. They include mortaria, which are large, shallow bowls or basins with thick, coarse walls and everted rims that were an essential part of the Roman kitchen. The Romans, who liked flavorful food, used mortaria for grinding herbs and nuts such as garlic, mints, celery seed, rosemary, lovage, thyme, oregano, sage, parsley, coriander, cumin, aniseed, and juniper. The spices flavored elaborate sauces that were served with roasted or boiled meats, fowl, fish, vegetables, or eggs. The Romans also used fish sauces such as *garum* as seasonings and condiments. The fish sauces were made by fermenting fish such as anchovies or mackerel together with additional ingredients including fish intestines, gills, fish blood, and salt. The taste is said to recall modern Asian fish sauces.[177]

Patinae and *patellae*, which are similar to a quiche or frittata, were also popular among the Romans. They were made by pouring a beaten egg mixture over chopped vegetables, meat, fish, and/or fruit, and then baking or cooking it in a broad, shallow, flat-based pan. Some pans of this type that were manufactured in

FIGURE 8.20 Fine table wares from Binyanei Ha'uma.
Credit: From Magness 2005b: 76 photos 7–9.

Italy are called Pompeian Red Slip Ware because they are coated with a thick, non-stick red slip. The discovery of a small number of imported pans in the Herodian-period villas on Jerusalem's southwestern hill indicates that, before 70 CE, the city's Jewish elite adopted Roman culinary habits even while observing biblical dietary laws. The pans from Binyanei Ha'uma differ from the earlier examples in being locally manufactured and are found in greater numbers, reflecting the popularity of these egg dishes in Aelia Capitolina.

Decorated sets of table ware (dining dishes) were also manufactured in the legionary kiln works. They include red-slipped dishes in the tradition of Western Terra Sigillata (a type of fine ware manufactured in Italy and Gaul [modern France]), and unslipped, eggshell-thin cups and beakers with delicate relief designs (Figure 8.20). Many of the table wares are decorated with depictions of Roman deities such as Dionysos (Bacchus), the god of wine—the first examples of figured images like this on pottery made in Jerusalem. Dionysos and symbols associated with his cult (such as grapes and grape vines) were appropriate motifs for decorating vessels used for serving and drinking wine. After the legionary kiln works ceased producing pottery around 200 CE, local potters began manufacturing types that imitated the Roman wares, but usually without the figured decoration.[178] The legionary kiln works had a lasting impact on local ceramic traditions, as imitation Roman wares continued to be produced in Jerusalem for centuries afterward.

Coins

As in the First Revolt, during the Bar Kokhba Revolt the Jews minted their own coins dated from the first year of the revolt as a proclamation of independence. The Bar Kokhba rebels increased the insult to Rome by over-striking (reminting) Roman coins. Frequently, the original Roman designs and inscriptions are visible beneath those added by the Jewish rebels.[179] These coins, decorated with sacred

FIGURE 8.21 Silver Bar Kokhba coin with a lulav and ethrog and the paleo-Hebrew inscription "Year 2 of the Freedom of Israel" (ANS 1944.100.63042; ANS collection bequest of E. T. Newell).
Credit: Courtesy of David Hendin.

vessels such as chalices and kraters, instruments such as trumpets and lyres, and ritual objects such as the *lulav* and *ethrog* (the bundle of branches and citron fruit used in the celebration of the Feast of Tabernacles), clearly proclaimed the revolt's goal—the overthrow of Roman rule, the reestablishment of Jewish independence under the leadership of a messianic figure, and the rebuilding of the Jerusalem temple (Figure 8.21). One series of coins is decorated with the earliest surviving depiction of the Jerusalem temple. It shows a flat-roofed building with four columns in front, framing an arched element that might be a doorway or the showbread table inside (Figure 8.22). Some Jews living at the time of the Bar Kokhba Revolt would have remembered the appearance of the temple, which had been destroyed a little over sixty years earlier. Therefore, scholars generally assume that this coin displays an accurate depiction of the main features of the second temple.[180]

Like the coins of the First Revolt, the Bar Kokhba coins are inscribed in the paleo-Hebrew script with Hebrew slogans alluding to Jerusalem and the temple, such as "year one of the redemption of Israel," "for the freedom of Jerusalem," and "Jerusalem" (the last surrounds the depiction of the temple façade). Some coins are inscribed with the name of the revolt's leader, "Simeon" (Hebrew Shimon), sometimes accompanied by the title "prince (*nasi*) of Israel." Others are inscribed "Eleazar the priest," implying that Bar Kokhba had appointed a high priest to officiate in the rebuilt temple.[181] However, there is no evidence that construction of a temple building commenced before the revolt ended. In fact, archaeological evidence suggests that the Jewish rebels never managed to gain control of Jerusalem, which was occupied by the Tenth Legion when the revolt began.[182]

FIGURE 8.22 Silver Bar Kokhba coin with the temple façade surrounded by the paleo-Hebrew inscription "Jerusalem" (ANS 1944.100.63042; ANS collection bequest of E. T. Newell).
Credit: Courtesy of David Hendin.

To strengthen the non-Jewish elements among the local population, after 70 CE, the Romans began to urbanize the country by dividing it into municipal territories, each centered on a major Hellenized-Romanized city.[183] Hadrian's foundation of the colony of Aelia Capitolina was part of this process. Like the other cities, Aelia Capitolina was granted the right to mint its own bronze coins. The first coins, minted under Hadrian, show the emperor ploughing a furrow with an ox and cow—an ancient Roman ceremony representing the establishment of a city by marking its boundary (*pomerium*).[184] Other coins are decorated with symbols of the Tenth Legion such as the eagle and the boar.[185] One coin type depicts the Capitolium as a temple with Jupiter seated in the center flanked by Minerva and Juno.[186] After Hadrian's time, coins were minted depicting other deities worshiped in the city, such as Serapis, Dionysus, Asclepius, and Tyche (the city-goddess).[187]

Conclusion

Even after Hadrian's foundation of Aelia Capitolina, the Romans considered Jerusalem an insignificant city on the eastern periphery of the empire. Whatever the exact extent of the settlement, there is no doubt the city had shrunk in size and population compared with the apex reached under Herod and his successors before 70. Although some estimates place Aelia Capitolina's population as high as 80,000, the true number is certainly much lower—perhaps only 4,000 inhabitants or less.[188]

In the 130 years since the destruction in 70, Jerusalem had been transformed from a Jewish city dominated by a single temple dedicated to the God of Israel to a Roman colony with a legionary camp under the protection of its new patron deity, Capitoline Jupiter. The features that distinguished Jerusalem as a Jewish temple city, including *miqva'ot*, stone vessels, a lack of pig bones, an almost complete absence of figured decoration, and, most importantly, Jews were gone. Aelia Capitolina's inhabitants—legionaries, military veterans and their families, and other non-Jews—worshiped a multiplicity of deities at shrines around the city, many of them depicted on the city's coins. Aelia bore little resemblance to its predecessor, with its new Roman layout characterized by broad colonnaded streets and free-standing, arched gateways. Forums on the north and west sides of the city served as commercial centers, while games incised on the Lithostratos pavement show that residents congregated here for social and leisure activities as well. Latin, which is hardly attested in Jerusalem before 70 CE, is common in Aelia's inscriptions. The dishes used by the inhabitants, which were designed to prepare and serve typically Roman types of cuisine, many containing pork, were decorated with figured images. The tiny "theater-like" structure under Wilson's Arch suggests that Aelia Capitolina offered its residents other amenities typical of a Roman colony. Peace was secured through the establishment of a fortification wall and the Tenth Legion's presence and by ethnic cleansing through the expulsion of the Jewish population—a process that was repeated centuries later when the Crusaders slaughtered or banished Jews and Muslims from the city (see Chapter 11).

In retrospect, 200 CE stands as a midpoint between the destruction in 70 and Constantine's legalization of Christianity and construction of the Church of the Holy Sepulcher, which catapulted Jerusalem again to a position of prominence. But it was not until after the Muslim conquest in the seventh century that permanent Jewish presence was reestablished in the city.

9

Byzantine Jerusalem (633 CE)

CONSTANTINE'S LEGALIZATION OF Christianity in 313 CE had a profound effect on the Holy Land in general and Jerusalem in particular, which was transformed from a small and insignificant colony on the periphery of the Roman world to one of its most important cities. By the time the Madaba Map was made (ca. 600 CE), Jerusalem had attained a size and level of prosperity that were not reached again until the latter part of the twentieth century.[1] The map shows a city packed with churches, which are represented as basilicas with pitched, tiled roofs, and, most prominently, the Church of the Holy Sepulcher in the center. Even the area outside the walls was filled with churches and monasteries, many of which have come to light in archaeological excavations. Christian officials, clergy, monks, and pilgrims poured into the city, seeking blessings by visiting the holy sites. Prayers recited during solemn processions and ceremonies in incense-filled churches replaced the animal sacrifices offered in the temple on the Temple Mount, which now lay in ruins. And yet, at its apex in 633 CE, Byzantine Jerusalem was on the precipice of another transition—this time to Muslim rule.

Historical Background

After Severus Alexander, the last member of the Severan dynasty died in 235 CE, a prolonged period of civil war broke out. Over the next fifty years there was a rapid succession of claimants to the Roman throne, only one of whom died a natural death (the others were assassinated or killed in battle). The instability on the throne affected all aspects of Roman life, resulting in inflation and devaluation of the currency, and hostile invasions as foreign tribes overran the borders of the empire. For the first time in centuries, a new fortification wall was built around the city of Rome.

The crisis of the third century ended when a general named Diocletian became emperor in 284. He is known for having implemented the "Diocletianic persecution"—the last great persecution of Christians in the Roman Empire. Diocletian instituted wide-ranging reforms that affected nearly every aspect of Roman life, including changing the monetary system to deal with rampant inflation and the devaluation of the currency and establishing a series of border forts to protect the empire. Diocletian even reformed the system of government. He realized that the empire had grown too large for one man to manage alone and that the principle of dynastic succession was a source of instability. Therefore, Diocletian split the empire into two halves, east and west, and appointed an emperor (called an Augustus) to rule over each half. He also appointed two co-rulers with the title Caesar to assist the emperors, one each for the east and west. The Caesars were intended to ensure a peaceful and orderly transition to the throne by replacing the Augusti when they died or retired. Diocletian's system of rule by four men (two Augusti and two Caesars) is called the *Tetrarchy*, and each of the four rulers is called a *tetrarch*.

In 305, Diocletian retired to a palace in the town of Split (Spalato), in his native Illyria (modern Croatia). He forced the other Augustus to retire as well, intending that the two Caesars would take over. Instead, a civil war erupted between the other co-rulers and their sons. In 312, Constantine (the son of the Caesar of the west) defeated Maxentius (the son of the Augustus of the west) at the battle at the Milvian Bridge. Before this battle, Constantine reportedly had a dream or vision in which he saw two winged Victories (angels) holding a banner bearing the Chi-Rho symbol (the Greek monogram of Christ). Constantine vowed to become a Christian if he won the battle, although he was not baptized until he was on his deathbed. After his victory in the battle, Constantine assumed rule of the western half of the Roman Empire. In 313 Constantine and Licinius (the ruler of the eastern half of the empire) issued the Edict of Milan legalizing Christianity, which until now had been outlawed.

In 324, Constantine defeated Licinius in battle and became the sole ruler of the Roman Empire. Two years later, he established a new imperial capital at Byzantium, a city strategically located on the land bridge between the continents of Europe and Asia. Following the precedent set by Alexander the Great centuries earlier, Constantine refounded the city and named it after himself: Constantinople (Constantinopolis—"the city of Constantine" = modern Istanbul in Turkey). Constantine's new capital city was modeled after Rome, including being built on seven hills and having a palace complex overlooking a hippodrome (like the Palatine Hill overlooking the Circus Maximus in Rome). But, unlike Rome, the new capital was filled with Christian churches, not pagan temples. Constantine dedicated the churches to personified concepts or ideals that had been worshiped as pagan gods, such as Holy Wisdom (Hagia Sophia) and Holy Peace (Hagia Eirene).

Constantine was succeeded to the throne by his son, Constantius II (337–361), who was also a Christian. After Constantius II died, the new emperor Julian ("the Apostate") tried to turn the clock back by restoring the ancient (pagan) cults of the Roman Empire, including reinstituting animal sacrifices in temples. As part of this program of restoration, Julian announced the rebuilding of the Jerusalem temple and the renewal of the sacrificial cult to the God of Israel, to the joy of Jews and dismay of Christians. However, soon after work commenced on clearing the ruins of the second temple and/or the Capitolium, it was halted by a natural disaster—apparently an earthquake that caused a fire to break out. Christian sources describe the event in miraculous terms, embellishing the story with details such as crosses appearing in the sky or on the clothing of Jerusalem's inhabitants. Before the project could resume, Julian lost his life in battle in Persia (16 June 363). As all the succeeding emperors were Christians, Julian's death put an end to Jewish hopes that the temple would be rebuilt anytime soon.[2]

In the winter of 1880–1881, some of the stones in the upper (post-Herodian) courses at the southeast corner of the Temple Mount collapsed. During the repair work, Conrad Schick discovered a statue made of green marble measuring slightly less than 1 meter (2 feet 4 inches) high, which was broken into two joining pieces.[3] The statue depicts a standing eagle (the beak and feet are broken off) with a medallion hanging from a band around its neck. The medallion is inscribed with a Greek monogram of the name "Julian." Eagles were an attribute of Jupiter and the sun god, with whom the Roman emperors were identified. The medallion explicitly associates Julian with these two deities, in the guise of an eagle.[4] The statue's reuse in the Temple Mount wall suggests a connection to the reconstruction work under Julian. A second possible piece of evidence for activity around the Temple Mount during Julian's reign is a Hebrew inscription discovered by Benjamin Mazar on the temenos wall below Robinson's Arch. The inscription is a modified quote from Isaiah 66:14: "You shall see and your heart shall rejoice and their bones like grass (shall flourish)." B. Mazar proposed that it was inscribed in the fourth century in reaction to Julian's announcement about the rebuilding of the temple.[5] However, Ronny Reich and Ya`akov Billig associate the inscription with a small medieval cemetery that they excavated along the wall.[6]

In 380 CE, Theodosius I decreed that the official Christianity of the Roman Empire would be "Catholic" in an attempt to eliminate non-orthodox beliefs and practices.[7] As Christianity spread, hundreds of monasteries populated by thousands of monks were established in the deserts of Egypt, Palestine, and Syria. Many monastic communities formed when a holy man seeking solitude and an ascetic lifestyle attracted a following, while others were established in proximity to holy sites. The Jordan Valley and Judean Desert, and especially the area around Jericho, attracted large numbers of monks due to the region's proximity to Jerusalem and the concentration of sites with biblical associations.

The later Roman emperors issued legislation targeting Christian heresies, Judaism, and pagan religions. Theodosius II had these laws systematized and compiled into the Theodosian Code, which was presented to the Senates in Rome and Constantinople in 438.[8] The final book of the Code (Book 16) contains laws relating to religion. These laws reflect a concern to prevent the spread of Judaism by limiting the rights of Jews.[9] The Jewish Patriarchate—an institution that had provided leadership for Jewish communities in Palestine and the Diaspora since ca. 200 CE—ended around 425, perhaps having been abolished by the later Roman authorities.[10] At the same time, literary sources and archaeological evidence attest to growing hostility and outbreaks of violence between Christians and Jews around the empire, including the occasional destruction of synagogues.[11] Although many of the anti-Jewish laws were not enforced, and although Christian writers present an exaggerated narrative aimed at demonstrating the victory of Christianity over Judaism, conditions for the Jewish population did indeed worsen from the late fourth century on.[12] Nevertheless, archaeology indicates that synagogues continued to be built around the Roman world, and, even as Christianity spread in Palestine, the population of Eastern Galilee and the southern Golan remained overwhelmingly Jewish.[13]

After Theodosius I died in 395, the empire split into two halves—east and west—ruled by his sons. With a brief exception, never again was the Roman Empire united under a single emperor. Soon after the split, foreign tribes began to overrun and occupy parts of the western half of the empire, including the Ostrogoths in Italy, Vandals in North Africa, Franks in France, and Visigoths in Spain. The territories they settled eventually were transformed into the states of medieval Europe. The unstable situation in the western half of the empire culminated in 410 with the sack of Rome by Alaric and the Goths.

The eastern half of the Roman Empire eventually became known as the Byzantine Empire, after the capital city (formerly named Byzantium), although the Byzantines considered themselves Romans. In fact, many scholars refer to the fourth to sixth centuries as the Late Roman period, not the Byzantine period (although most archaeologists working in Palestine call it Byzantine). This period is also sometimes referred to as "late antiquity." In contrast to the west, the eastern half of the empire remained unified and secure through the sixth century. Justinian, the Byzantine emperor from 527–565, attempted to reunify the empire by conducting a "reconquest" of the western half of the Mediterranean. Justinian was a great builder who reconstructed Constantine's Hagia Sophia (which still stands today in Istanbul) and sponsored the construction of many other churches and monasteries around the empire, including the monastery of St. Catherine at the foot of Mount Sinai. He also established a series of forts to protect the empire's borders from invasions. Justinian is known for having persecuted pagans and Jews, and he closed the last schools of Greek philosophy that were still operating in Athens.

Justinian's reconquest bankrupted the imperial treasury. After his death, the Byzantines lost control of the western half of the Mediterranean and began to suffer invasions of their own borders. In 614 CE, Syria and Palestine were conquered by the Sasanid (or Sassanian) Persians, who massacred much of Jerusalem's Christian population and exiled many others to Persia, headed by the patriarch Zacharias together with the True Cross (the relic of the cross on which Jesus was believed to have been crucified).[14] The Sasanids were aided by the local Jewish population, who had suffered under Byzantine Christian rule and hoped for permission to rebuild the Jerusalem temple. Jewish hopes were dashed when the Sasanids accommodated with the Christian majority before being ousted by the Byzantines in 628, who promptly expelled the Jews again from Jerusalem.[15] However, the Byzantine reconquest of Syria and Palestine was short-lived. Beginning in 634, Palestine fell to Muslim tribes from Arabia, never to be retaken by the Byzantines. In Jerusalem the transition to Muslim rule was peaceful, as the city surrendered without resistance to the caliph Umar some time between 634 and 638 CE.[16] Caesarea, the last major city in Palestine to fall to the Muslims, was taken in 641 or 642 CE after a seven-month-long siege, when the embattled Byzantine administrators and elite boarded ships to Constantinople. By the seventh and eighth centuries the territories under Byzantine rule were limited to Asia Minor and Greece, although the Byzantine Empire survived until 1453, when the Ottoman Turks conquered Constantinople.

Archaeological Evidence

Jerusalem benefited greatly from the legalization of Christianity, becoming one of only five Patriarchate cities (the seat of a Patriarch) in the entire Roman Empire. Pilgrims poured into the city, bringing with them money that boosted the economy and fueled a building boom. Since Christianity was outlawed and Christians could not worship openly until Constantine issued the Edict of Milan, the earliest churches were built during his reign. Not surprisingly, Constantine focused much of his attention on the Holy Land and especially Jerusalem, where he built the Church of the Holy Sepulcher, and the Eleona Church on the Mount of Olives (Eleona derives from the Greek word for olives)—a large complex including a monastery and a circular chapel marking the spot where Jesus is believed to have ascended to heaven (see Luke 24:50–52). Constantine also constructed the Church of the Nativity in Bethlehem over the grotto in which Jesus is believed to have been born. Other churches and monasteries were the beneficiaries of imperial patronage. For example, in 438, Eudocia, the wife of the emperor Theodosius II, visited Jerusalem at the invitation of Melania the Younger (see below). In 441, after becoming estranged from her husband, Eudocia settled in Jerusalem, where she sponsored a number of building projects including churches, monasteries, and a new city wall.[17]

Accounts written by early Christian pilgrims and archaeological remains provide a wealth of evidence about Jerusalem in the Byzantine period. Other literary sources include a biography of Justinian written by the historian Procopius with a detailed description of the emperor's construction of the Nea Church in Jerusalem. In addition, the Madaba Map shows Jerusalem at the height of its expansion (ca. 600 CE), when the city extended from the line of the current north wall of the Old City to Mount Zion and the southeastern hill on the south (Pl. 12A). The southwestern hill, which was vacated by the Tenth Legion ca. 300 CE, became a residential area. Numerous churches erected along the streets originally laid out by Hadrian are visible on the map as basilical structures with red-tiled roofs. Dozens of churches, monasteries, and cemeteries surrounded the walled city. Estimates of Jerusalem's population on the eve of the Muslim conquest range from a maximum of ca. 150,000 to a minimum of 15,000.[18] The true number likely lies in-between, at ca. 50,000–70,000 (i.e., about the same as it was at the height of the Herodian period).[19] In both periods, the city attracted throngs of immigrants and pilgrims from distant locales. Under Byzantine rule the city's official name was Aelia (the reference to Capitoline Jupiter having been removed), but, in pilgrims' accounts, it generally called *Ierousalem/Hierusalem* or *Hierosolyma* (Greek/Latin for "temple of peace").[20] In the Madaba Map, Jerusalem is labeled in Greek "the holy city of Jerusalem" (*he hagia polis Ierousalem*).

The Temple Mount

Jerusalem's most conspicuous feature—the Temple Mount—is not shown on the Madaba Map. The reason is simple: during the Byzantine period, the Temple Mount was abandoned, without any buildings standing on it. The second temple had been destroyed centuries earlier, and many of its architectural fragments had been robbed out for reuse. Hadrian's shrine or temple to Capitoline Jupiter—whether it was on the Temple Mount or by the western forum—was razed after Christianity was legalized. Ancient sources suggest that, during the Byzantine period, the Temple Mount was used as a garbage dump.[21] Eusebius, a Church Father writing in the early fourth century, describes the despoliation of the Temple Mount in light of the biblical prophet Micah's statement (3:12) about the destruction of Jerusalem.

So Aquila says, "Therefore for your sake the land of Zion shall be ploughed, and Jerusalem shall be a quarry of stone," for being inhabited by men of foreign race it is even now like a quarry, ✦ the inhabitants of the city choosing stores from its ruins as they will for private as well as public buildings. And it is sad for the eyes to see stones from the Temple itself, and from its ancient sanctuary and holy place, used for the building of idol temples, and of theaters for the populace.[22]

The Christian population deliberately left the Temple Mount lying in ruins because they considered this proof of Jesus's prediction that the second temple would be destroyed (e.g., Mark 13:1–4). The despoiled esplanade served as a witness to the truth of Jesus's prophecy and a visual symbol of the triumph of Christianity over Judaism. For Christians, the center of Jerusalem, and indeed the world, had shifted from the Temple Mount to the Church of the Holy Sepulcher, which is revered as the site of Jesus's crucifixion and resurrection and is displayed prominently in the Madaba Map.[23]

The City Walls and Gates and the Western Cardo

Since ca. 300 CE, Jerusalem has been fortified with a wall that corresponds to the line of the north wall of the Old City. By ca. 600 CE, the area within the walls extended from the site of the Damascus Gate on the north to the southwestern and southeastern hills to the south (Figure 9.1). Early Christian pilgrims to Jerusalem mention its fortifications and gates.[24] Eucherius, the Bishop of Lyons from ca. 434–449, wrote a letter to a monk named Faustinus describing the walls of Jerusalem as including the southwestern hill: "The site of the city *is almost forced into a circular shape*, and is enclosed by a lengthy wall, which now embraces Mount Sion, though this was once just outside" (v 125.3).[25] This area corresponds to the depiction of Jerusalem in the Madaba Map, which clearly shows the expansion of the walled city since Hadrian's time. The main elements of Aelia Capitolina are visible on the north (left) side of the map: the arched gateway and semicircular plaza at the Damascus Gate; the colonnaded western cardo and eastern cardo and decumanus maximus; and arched gateways on the east and west sides of the city. In the Roman and Byzantine periods, the gate at the site of the Damascus Gate was called the Neapolis Gate as it gave access to the road running north to that city (modern Nablus).[26] By the fifth century, many Christians called it St. Stephen's Gate, after the saint who was believed to have been stoned nearby (see the Church of St. Stephen below). The west gate (modern Jaffa Gate) was known as David's Gate, after the Tower of David (in the Citadel) next to it. The east gate (by the modern Lion's Gate) was called the Gate of Benjamin or the

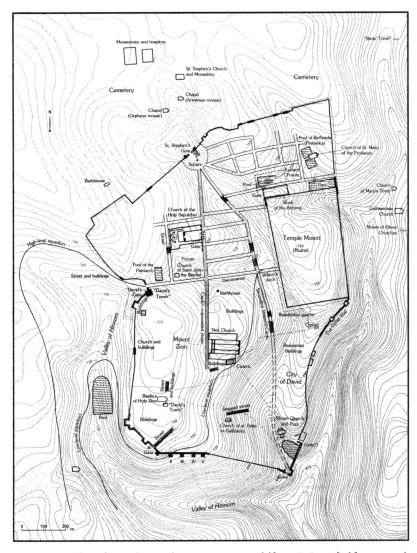

FIGURE 9.1 Plan of Jerusalem in the Byzantine period (from E. Stern [ed.] 1993: 769). Credit: With permission of Hillel Geva and the Israel Exploration Society.

Gate of the Sheep's Pool.[27] Gates are also shown at the southern ends of the two cardos. Eucherius's description of Jerusalem as almost circular and its depiction as an oval in the Madaba Map were intended to convey that it had the shape of an ideal city.[28]

The Madaba Map also shows the monumental column in the semicircular plaza by the Damascus Gate, although the statue of Hadrian that originally stood on top of it had been removed long before, possibly replaced by a cross.[29]

Most scholars believe that the terminal points of the western cardo and eastern cardo depicted on the Madaba Map mark the southern extent of the wall of Aelia Capitolina, corresponding roughly with the south wall of the Old City. The areas to the south—modern Mount Zion (the southern end of the southwestern hill) and the southeastern hill—today lie outside the walls of the Old City but are shown on the Madaba Map as part of the walled city. This means that some time between ca. 300 and 600 CE, a new fortification wall must have been added around the southern end of the southwestern hill and the southeastern hill.[30]

And, indeed, remains of a Byzantine-period wall have been discovered around the southwestern and southeastern hills, roughly following (and sometimes reusing) the ruins of the First Wall from centuries earlier. Substantial portions of the Byzantine wall including towers and gateways and a massive dam across the southern end of the Tyropoeon Valley were excavated by Frederick Jones Bliss and Archibald Dickie in 1894–1897.[31] A similar portion of wall first discovered by Charles Warren extends to the south and southwest from the southeast corner of the Temple Mount. Kathleen Kenyon and Benjamin Mazar and Eilat Mazar uncovered additional stretches of this wall with square towers, which runs southwest along the inside of the current Ophel Road before disappearing underneath it (Figure 3.8).[32] Many scholars believe it was Eudocia who extended the wall to the south, based on the accounts of sixth-century pilgrims who attributed the rebuilding of Jerusalem's walls to the empress in fulfillment of Psalm 51:18 (Septuagint version): "Graciously bestow your goodwill (Greek *eudokia*) upon Sion and build the walls of Jerusalem."[33] If Eudocia built this wall, it would date to 438, when she first visited Jerusalem, or to ca. 444–460, when she resided in the city until her death. Eucherius's letter to Faustinus was written around the time Eudocia was in Jerusalem but does not attribute the wall to her.[34] The archaeological finds (mainly pottery) associated with the wall's construction indicate a date range from ca. 300–450 CE. This leaves open the possibility that the southern extension was indeed built by Eudocia—as many scholars believe—or was constructed earlier and attributed to her.[35] After a strong earthquake struck Jerusalem in 1033 and damaged the walls, the southern extension was abandoned and a new wall was built to the north, along the current line of the south wall of the Old City. Since then, the southern part of the southwestern hill (Mount Zion) and the southeastern hill have been outside the city walls.

In the 1970s, Nahman Avigad conducted excavations along the line of the western cardo. Below the modern street (Khan ez-Zeit/Beit ha-Bad Street), south of the intersection with the main decumanus (modern David/al-Silsilah Street), he discovered a broad, stone-paved boulevard with columns lining the curbs of the sidewalks, corresponding to the depiction in the Madaba Map (Pl. 12A). Because the pottery and coins found under the paving stones indicate that the street dates to the sixth century, Avigad suggested that Justinian extended the Hadrianic western cardo south of the intersection with the main decumanus, to facilitate religious processions and pilgrimage between the Church of the Holy Sepulcher and his newly built Nea Church.[36] Indeed, Avigad's excavations elsewhere in the Jewish Quarter as well as excavations by other archaeologists indicate that settlement on the southwestern hill was not renewed until the fifth and sixth centuries. Shlomit Weksler-Bdolah proposes that the southwestern hill was unsettled after ca. 300 CE because this is where the legionary camp had been located, whereas Oren Gutfeld attributes the absence of settlement to an avoidance of areas still covered with heaps of ruins from the destruction of the city in 70. Gutfeld notes that instead of reusing the Herodian street along the western side of the Temple Mount, Hadrian's eastern cardo was established some 90 meters (295 feet) to the west, perhaps to bypass the piles of debris covering the earlier street.[37] By the time Justinian built the Nea Church and extended the western cardo to the south, the southwestern hill had been resettled.

In 614 CE, the Sasanid Persians overran Syria and Palestine. Although Jerusalem initially surrendered peacefully, the Christian population soon rebelled. The Sasanids responded by besieging the city, which fell in May 614 after a twenty-day long siege. Contemporary Christian accounts describe the destruction of churches and monasteries (including the Church of the Holy Sepulcher) and the massacre of Christian clerics and civilian inhabitants.[38] The Persians carried off the most precious Christian relic—the True Cross—and took Zacharias, the Patriarch of Jerusalem, to captivity in Persia. The *Chronicon Paschale*, a contemporary source, describes the fall of Jerusalem.

> In this year in about the month of June, we suffered a calamity which deserves unceasing lamentations. For, together with many cities of the east, Jerusalem too was captured by the Persians, and in it were slain many thousands of clerics, monks, and virgin nuns. The Lord's tomb was burnt and the far-famed temples of God and, in short, all the precious things were destroyed. The venerated wood of the Cross, together with the holy vessels that were beyond enumeration, was taken by the Persians, and the Patriarch Zacharias also became a prisoner.[39]

Other accounts of the siege and sack of Jerusalem are provided by the seventh-century Armenian chronicler Sebeos, and by Antiochus Strategius, a monk at the Mar Saba monastery in the Judean Desert who was taken captive by the Sasanids but managed to escape.[40] Strategius concludes his account with a list of the dead, who were buried at thirty-five locations around Jerusalem by a group of Christians led by a certain Thomas and his wife.[41]

Only limited archaeological evidence has been found of damage to or destruction of Jerusalem's churches and monasteries in the early seventh century.[42] One example is a Byzantine monastic complex at Sheikh Bader (Giv'at Ram) to the west of the city, which Michael Avi-Yonah excavated in 1949 and identified as the church of St. George "before" the Holy City (or Extramuros) mentioned in literary sources.[43] He associated the thick layer of ash covering the complex with the Persian invasion, as illustrated by Strategius's testimony.

> And I [Thomas] found in the church of the holy martyr George, which is outside the town, and I began from this spot to search for corpses and to bury them in the grottos. We found at the altar of the holy church seven persons lying. The Lord and Saint George gave us strength and we buried them.[44]

More recently, Gabriel Barkay identified a large Byzantine church that he excavated at Ketef Hinnom (the ridge of the Ben-Hinnom Valley) as the church of St. George.[45]

Despite the limited archaeological evidence, the remains of early seventh century mass burials in various locations to the north and west of the city suggest that the Sasanid sack took a devastating toll on the inhabitants.[46] There are also signs that the Sasanids breached the city wall in at least one spot. In his 1937–1938 excavations by the Damascus Gate, Robert W. Hamilton found a layer of rubble that represents the collapse from a breach in the wall and can be dated to the early seventh century based on the associated pottery and coins. After the siege, the breached wall lay in ruins and the area became a garbage dump. Eventually debris accumulated to a depth of 4.5 meters (15 feet), completely burying the stump of the wall.[47] In 1964–1966, Crystal-Margaret Bennett and John Basil Hennessy investigated more fully the area around the Damascus Gate that had been excavated previously by Hamilton. Gregory Wightman, who published Bennett's and Hennessy's excavations, notes that the accumulations dating to the sixth century were covered by a thick layer of ash, earth, and stones, which he associates with the Sasanid Persian invasion.[48]

These remains suggest that there was fierce fighting at the site of the Damascus Gate. The Sasanids apparently managed to break through the north wall of the city next to the west tower by the Damascus Gate. They burned and stormed the gate, as indicated by the thick layer of ash, earth, and stones just outside it (on the western side of the east tower). The archaeological evidence accords with the descriptions provided by ancient literary sources. According to Strategius, the Persians "shot from their balistas with such violence that on the twenty-first day (of the siege) they broke down the city wall."[49] An ode by Sophronius, the patriarch of Jerusalem at the time of the siege, refers to burning under the foundations of the walls. As Charles Clermont-Ganneau demonstrated, this means the Persians sapped and breached the city walls by digging underground tunnels, which were supported by a wooden framework and then set on fire, causing the collapse of the wall above.[50] Sebeos provides a similar account: "Then Khoream, that is Erazmiozan, gathered his troops, went and camped around Jerusalem, and besieged it. He attacked it for nineteen days. Having mined the foundations of the city wall from below, they brought down the wall."[51] The Arabic version of Strategius's account refers to "the place where the breach had been made in the enclosing wall."[52] Sophronius and Strategius also refer to the use of siege engines (*mangana* or *mangonels*) by the Persians.[53] This part of the city wall appears to have remained in ruins until the first half of the eighth century, when the accumulated garbage was cleared away to expose the stump, and a patch was inserted to seal the breach.[54]

In 622, the Byzantine emperor Heraclius launched a counter-offensive against the Sasanid Persians. By 629, the Sasanids ceded to him the territories and captives they had taken. On 21 March 630, Heraclius entered Jerusalem as a "new David" at the head of a procession and restored the True Cross to its place in the Church of the Holy Sepulcher.[55] Despite Jerusalem's significance to Christians, Heraclius is the only Christian Roman emperor who ever visited the city.[56]

According to Christian tradition, Heraclius made his triumphal entrance through the Golden Gate (Figure 5.2). This is the only gate in the east wall of the Temple Mount, and today its two arched passageways are blocked up. The Golden Gate's architectural style and decoration point to a Byzantine or Umayyad date of construction, although it might be built over the ruins of an earlier gate. Early Christians thought this was the Beautiful Gate mentioned in Acts 3:2 and identified it as a remnant of the temple. For example, the Piacenza Pilgrim, a native of that city in Italy who visited Jerusalem ca. 570, writes, "This gate of the city is next to the Gate Beautiful which was part of the Temple, and its threshold and entablature are still in position there."[57] By the seventh century, it had come to be called the Golden Gate, perhaps because the Greek word for beautiful (*oraia*) sounds the same as golden in Latin (*aurea*).[58] After the Byzantine reconquest of Jerusalem, Christians began to identify the Golden Gate as the gate through which Jesus entered the Temple Mount on Palm Sunday (John 12:13), describing Heraclius's return of the True Cross in similar terms.[59] In fact, Dan Bahat proposes that the current gate was constructed on the occasion of Heraclius's entry, following Cyril Mango's observation that it is aligned with the Church of the Holy Sepulcher, not the Dome of the Rock.[60] Other archaeologists associate its construction with the early Islamic (Umayyad) building program on and around the Temple Mount.[61]

The Church of the Holy Sepulcher

Constantine built the Church of the Holy Sepulcher after his mother Helena reportedly found the remnants of the True Cross at this spot during a visit to Jerusalem in 326/327 CE, although the story of the discovery appears to be a later tradition.[62] In 326 CE, Constantine ordered the temple on the north side of Hadrian's western forum (dedicated to Aphrodite/Venus or Capitoline Jupiter; see Chapter 8) razed to expose the rocky outcrop of Golgotha/Calvary on which Jesus is believed to have been crucified and the nearby tomb in which his body is believed to have been laid. He enshrined these spots in an enormous complex measuring ca. 130 × 60 meters (426 × 196 feet), which was consecrated in September 335 CE, although work on the structure surrounding the tomb (the Rotunda) continued for a number of years afterward (Figure 9.2).[63] After the temple was razed, the rocky outcrop was found to contain rock-cut tombs with loculi, which are typical of the late Second Temple period. A few loculi belonging to this cemetery are still preserved outside the walls of the Rotunda, which modern Christian tradition identifies as the tombs of Joseph of Arimathea and Nicodemus (Figure 9.3). The presence of these loculi indicates that this area was a Jewish cemetery in the time of Jesus and therefore lay outside the walls of the city.[64] And indeed, according to Eusebius, the "divine grotto" where Jesus was resurrected came to light when the temple was razed. Nevertheless, archaeology cannot prove that Jesus's body was laid to rest in one of these tombs.[65] Constantine cut back the outcrop to isolate the burial chamber which reportedly had contained Jesus's body and enclosed it within a small structure (edicule).[66]

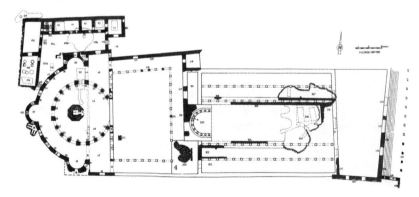

FIGURE 9.2 Plan of Constantine's Church of the Holy Sepulcher (from Corbo 1981: Tavola 3).
Credit: With permission of the Studium Biblicum Franciscanum Photographic Archive.

FIGURE 9.3 Loculi outside the Rotunda of the Church of the Holy Sepulcher.
Credit: Photo by the author.

Over the centuries, the Church of the Holy Sepulcher has suffered much
damage from human agents and natural catastrophes such as earthquakes,
although the damage caused by the Sasanid Persians in 614 CE apparently was
not severe and was repaired by the patriarch Modestus.[67] Because little survives
of the Constantinian church, our information about its layout and appearance
comes from a variety of sources including early Christian pilgrim accounts and
archaeological evidence. One of the most important sources is Eusebius's *Life of
Constantine*, which provides a description of the church around the time of its
construction.[68] In addition, the Madaba Map prominently depicts the church on
the west side of the western cardo, from which it was approached by a set of steps.
The basilica is shown as a large, rectangular building with a pitched, red-tiled
roof. Immediately below (to the west of) the basilica a gilded dome is visible,
representing the Rotunda.[69]

The large size of the Church of the Holy Sepulcher and its representation
in the middle of the city convey the Christian supersessionist message that the
site of Jesus's death and resurrection replaced the ruined and desolate Temple
Mount as the center of the world. This message is expressed by early Christian
writers who transferred to the church concepts relating to the temple and Temple
Mount, such as the belief that it contained the altar where Abraham offered his

son for sacrifice—an episode that for Christians prefigured Jesus's crucifixion—
and the identification of Mount Moriah with Golgotha. Similarly, the small
structure (edicule) enclosing the tomb seems to have been modeled after contemporary Jewish depictions of the Holy of Holies in the Jerusalem temple, while the
entry of the bishop into the tomb on Sunday mornings may have been conceived
of as paralleling the entry of the high priest into the Holy of Holies.[70] Eusebius
explicitly identifies the Church of the Holy Sepulcher as the "New (Christian)
Jerusalem" that superseded the Old (Jewish) Jerusalem (the Temple Mount/tem-
ple), which now lay desolate due (in the eyes of Christians) to God's punishment.

> New Jerusalem was built at the very Testimony to the Savior, facing the
> famous Jerusalem of old, which after the bloody murder of the Lord had
> been overthrown in utter devastation, and paid the penalty of its wicked
> inhabitants. Opposite this then the Emperor erected the victory of the
> Savior over death with rich and abundant munificence, this being perhaps
> that fresh new Jerusalem proclaimed in prophetic oracles[71]

The construction of the Church of the Holy Sepulcher as a replacement for
the temple situated Constantine as a successor to David and Solomon.[72]

The architect of the Constantinian church was a Syrian named Zenobius.[73]
Although scholars disagree about some details, the main elements can be reconstructed as follows, proceeding from east to west. The complex was entered from
the western cardo to the east by way of steps leading to an atrium (courtyard)
surrounded by columns. Small holes in the walls of the atrium and basilica preserved in the Alexander Nevsky Church indicate that marble veneer (revetment)
originally was affixed to the stones.[74] The church itself consisted of the Hadrianic
basilica or temple temenos, which Constantine converted to a Christian basilica
(hall of worship).[75] From the late fourth century on, early Christian sources refer
to the basilica as the Martyrion (Greek) or Martyrium (Latin)—that is, a holy
place associated with a martyr (a witness to the truth of Christianity).[76] The hall
was divided by four rows of columns into a central nave flanked by four aisles (two
on each side), with a large apse (semicircular niche) at the west end of the hall
containing the altar. Twelve columns lining the apse symbolized the apostles.[77]
Whereas in most early Christian churches the apse (which indicates the direction
of prayer) was oriented to the east, in Constantine's basilica it faced west, toward
the tomb of Christ. Part of the original Constantinian apse is preserved beneath
the existing apse, which is at the east end of the Crusader basilica. The apse of the
Crusader basilica faces east instead of west—that is, away from the tomb.[78]

There was a series of rock-cut grottos under the Constantinian basilica. The
first grotto—the Chapel of St. Helena—today is accessed by steps that descend

FIGURE 9.4 Graffito in the Chapel of St. Vartan in the Church of the Holy Sepulcher. Credit: Photo by the author.

eastward from the ambulatory of the Crusader basilica. From there, a stairway descends eastward to another grotto now called the Chapel of the Invention (or Discovery) of the Cross. The grottos were created by quarrying activity in the Iron Age and Second Temple period.[79] The Chapel of the Invention of the Cross apparently was a cistern under the Constantinian basilica before being converted to a chapel in the eleventh century.[80] Another quarry on the north side of the Chapel of St. Helena and the Chapel of the Invention of the Cross is now an Armenian chapel dedicated to St. Vartan. Inside the chapel is a stylobate wall (foundation for columns) belonging to the Constantinian basilica. One of the stones in the wall has an ink drawing of a boat accompanied by the Latin inscription *DOMINE IVIMUS* ("Lord, we have gone") (Figure 9.4). The bow of the boat faces left, and the stern is to the right. The mast is lying on its side, suggesting this was a large vessel with a retractable mast, and there are two rudders by the stern. The inscription might be an allusion to the Latin version of Psalm 121:1 (MT 122:1): *In domum Domini ibimus* ("Let us go to the house of the Lord").[81] The excavator, Magen Broshi, believes the graffito was made by a pilgrim, apparently before the construction of Constantine's church was completed as it is on a foundation stone. The use of Latin indicates that the pilgrim(s) came from the western part of the Roman Empire—Italy, Gaul, Spain, or North Africa.[82]

To the west of the Constantinian basilica, an open courtyard surrounded by columns called the "Holy Garden" (Triforum or Triportico) opened to the Rotunda.[83] The Holy Garden was so-called on account of John 19:41: "Now there was a garden in the place where he was crucified, and in the garden there was a new tomb in which no one had ever been laid."[84] A chapel in the southeast corner of the courtyard enshrined a 9–14 meter (30–46-foot) high rocky outcrop venerated as Golgotha (Greek) or Calvary (Latin), based on its identification as the place where Jesus was crucified according to the Gospel accounts.[85] Steps on the north side of the outcrop provided access to the top, which was surmounted by a large cross covered by a canopied structure (*ciborium*).[86] By the latter part of the fourth century, Christian tradition located Adam's tomb at Golgotha instead of on the Temple Mount (Mount Moriah) as Jewish tradition had it.[87] Nowadays a vertical fissure in the rocky outcrop is visible through a glass pane in the Crusader chapel of Adam, which is located under the chapel of Golgotha. When Jesus was crucified, his blood is said to have flowed through the crack and revived Adam.[88]

In Constantine's time the tomb—consisting of the isolated rock-cut burial chamber—was enclosed within a small structure (edicule) consisting of a porch with columns on the front (east) side and surrounded by columns supporting a conical roof.[89] The edicule with the tomb inside it were enshrined, either during Constantine's lifetime or after his death, within a circular domed structure originally called the "Anastasis" (Greek for "resurrection") but is now known as the Rotunda.[90] It draws on a tradition of circular mausolea, sometimes roofed with domes, that developed in the Roman and late Roman world. The Rotunda's outer wall is 36.58 meters (120 feet) in diameter and contains three apses facing north, west, and south.[91] The west apse—today a chapel belonging to the Syrian Orthodox church—is partly hewn into the rocky outcrop that contained the rock-cut loculi. An opening in the apse wall leads to loculi now identified as the tombs of Joseph of Arimathea and Nicodemus. Around the interior of the Rotunda are twelve columns in groups of three each, alternating with four pairs of square piers.[92] The numbers have symbolic value: three for the Trinity; four for the Evangelists; twelve for the apostles. Two of the original columns preserved on the north side of the Rotunda are made from two halves of a monolithic column—that is, a column of a single piece of stone that was cut in half—which might have been taken from the Hadrianic temple. It is not clear if the column was used as a monolith in the Constantinian church and cut after a reconstruction in a later period, or if it was cut in half from the start.[93] The Byzantine Rotunda was roofed with a wooden cupola with a circular opening to the sky in the center.[94]

A Greek inscription on a marble slab of the fifth–sixth centuries found on the grounds of the Russian church of St. Mary Magdalene on the slope of the Mount of Olives commemorates a doorkeeper of the church.

Tomb belonging to Theodulus, who was doorkeeper of the Holy Anastasis of Christ and to Petrus, most God-fearing doorkeeper of the same (church), his son, and of all his (their) household.[95]

Doorkeepers were a minor order of clergy who were responsible for keeping the keys of the church, guarding the doors, and receiving visitors.[96] The Rotunda is the only part of Constantine's church still standing (Pl. 12B). However, over the centuries, it, too, has suffered tremendous damage. The floor level has risen, making the piers and columns appear stubby and truncated, the dome has been rebuilt repeatedly, and none of the original interior decoration—including marble veneer, mosaics, and gold and silver vessels—survives. The current edicule enclosing the tomb was constructed in 1809–1810.[97]

The Nea Church

The Madaba Map depicts a large basilica on the southeast side of the western cardo. This is the Nea (Greek for new) Church, an abbreviated form of its full name: the New Church of Mary, the Mother of God (Greek *Theotokos*), which was built by the emperor Justinian and dedicated on 20 November 543.[98] The Nea Church is described by Cyril of Scythopolis (*Life of St. Sabas* 72–73) and by Justinian's court biographer, Procopius (*Buildings* V, 6), and is mentioned by other early Christian writers.[99] In addition to the church, the complex included a monastery, a hostel for pilgrims, and a hospital. The church was damaged by the Sasanids and subsequently repaired but suffered even greater damage in an earthquake (perhaps the earthquake of 749). After being repaired again, it was destroyed, apparently some time in the ninth century after Charlemagne's reign, and was never rebuilt.[100]

Small parts of the church had been discovered previously, and its southeast corner can still be seen projecting outside the south wall of the Old City.[101] However, Avigad's excavations in the Jewish Quarter brought to light substantial portions of the building for the first time, in the same location shown on the Madaba Map.[102] The church was an enormous basilica measuring ca. 78 meters (255 feet) long × 52 meters (170 feet) wide.[103] There was a large apse at the east end of the nave and side chambers with smaller apses at the end of each aisle. The hall was entered at its west end from the western cardo by way of an atrium (courtyard).[104] The walls are constructed of alternating courses of stones and bricks, a technique typical of Byzantine buildings in Constantinople.[105] A huge monolith of red limestone (*mizzi ahmar*) that was left unfinished in a quarry by the Russian Compound because it cracked might have been intended for the Nea Church (Figure 9.5), which, according to Procopius, had "massive" columns "the

FIGURE 9.5 Unfinished column in the Russian Compound.
Credit: Photo by the author.

color of burning fire."[106] *Mizzi ahmar* does not appear to have been used in earlier (pre-Byzantine) buildings in Jerusalem, but the columns in the Church of the Nativity—which was rebuilt by Justinian—are made of this same type of stone, perhaps from the same quarry.[107]

The Nea Church was built on uneven ground that slopes down toward the south. To level the area, Justinian's architects constructed a platform supported on underground arches and vaults similar to Herod's extension of the Temple Mount, which is supported on "Solomon's Stables." The vaulted platform and other features of the church, including its large size, were intended to recall Solomon's temple, as Procopius's description makes clear. Procopius also states that

Justinian repatriated to Jerusalem the sacred vessels from the temple (including the menorah) that were taken to Rome in 70 CE. According to Procopius, the vessels were looted from the Temple of Peace in Rome and carried to North Africa by the Vandals but were recaptured by Justinian's general Belisarius, who brought them to Constantinople. In a 1960 article, Yohanan Lewy suggested identifying the Jerusalem church in which Justinian placed the sacred vessels with the Nea.[108] In this case, the vessels presumably would have been looted by the Sasanids and subsequently lost. More recently, however, Ra'anan Boustan argued convincingly that Procopius's account of the sacred vessels has no basis in reality and instead was invented to present Justinian and Belisarius's victory over the Vandals as analogous to the triumph celebrated by Vespasian and Titus after the fall of Jerusalem in 70 CE.[109] The story also reinforced the parallels between Justinian's construction of the Nea and Solomon's construction of the temple and broadcast the Christian supercessionist message that the temple had been replaced by the church, which now possessed the sacred vessels.

The Nea was also intended to compete with the Church of the Holy Sepulcher, to which it was connected by Justinian's extension of the western cardo. The extension facilitated processions and pilgrim traffic between the two churches. In fact, these are the only two buildings depicted in the Madaba Map as opening directly onto the western cardo.[110] Perhaps Justinian conceived of the Nea as an extension of or substitute for the Church of the Holy Sepulcher, which Christians believed had replaced the destroyed temple.[111] However, unlike the Church of the Holy Sepulcher and many of the other churches in Jerusalem, the Nea was not built on a spot with biblical associations. Instead, it was probably integrated into Jerusalem's liturgical calendar by linking it to the feast of the Presentation of Mary into the temple.[112]

The underground vaulted spaces below the Nea were used as cisterns. Here Avigad made a stunning discovery: the original dedicatory inscription of the church was still embedded in the wall (Figure 9.6). The inscription confirms that Justinian built the church, and is dated according to an indiction, which is a fifteen-year cycle used in the Byzantine calendar. The inscription, which is in Greek, reads,

> This work too was donated by our most pious Emperor Flavius Justinian, through the provision and care of Constantine, most saintly priest and abbot (Greek *hegumen*), in the thirteenth indiction.[113]

The "thirteenth indiction" refers to the thirteenth year of a fifteen-year indiction cycle. There were three thirteenth-year indictions during Justinian's reign: in 534/535, 549/550, and 564/565 CE. Avigad identified the indiction

FIGURE 9.6 The Nea Church inscription in the Israel Museum Jerusalem.
Credit: Photo by the author.

commemorated in the inscription as the first one in 534/535. However, a recent
discovery indicates that the indiction commemorated is almost certainly the
second one (549/550), or, less likely, the third one (564/565).[114] This discovery was made in a salvage excavation conducted in 2017, to the north of the
Damascus Gate, which brought to light a room paved with a mosaic floor.
Although the remains were badly damaged, most of a Greek dedicatory inscription is preserved in the mosaic.

> In the time of our most pious emperor Flavius Justinian, also this entire
> building Constantine, the most God-loving priest and abbot, established
> and raised, in the fourteenth indiction.[115]

The pottery and coins found in the excavations indicate that the floor dates to
the mid-sixth century, that is, the time of Justinian. The inscription refers to
the fourteenth indiction, which occurred twice under Justinian: in 535/536 and
550/551 CE.[116] The priest and abbot Constantine mentioned in the inscription
must be the same abbot commemorated in the Nea Church inscription. Since
Constantine apparently did not become the abbot of the Nea Church before

546–548, the fourteenth indiction in the newly discovered inscription must refer to 550/551. And since it is likely that Constantine dedicated the building associated with the newly discovered inscription when he was already abbot of the Nea Church, the thirteenth indiction mentioned in the Nea Church inscription must be the second one, in 549/550.[117] The room with the newly discovered inscription probably was in a Byzantine monastic complex to the north of the city (see below). Constantine might have founded this complex as a hostel for pilgrims arriving from that direction.[118]

The same Constantine is mentioned by John Moschus, a monk in the Judean Desert who lived in the second half of the sixth century and early seventh century.

> Abba Polychronios the priest told us that he had heard from Abba Constantine, who was higoumen [hegumen] of the new Lavra [laura = monastery] of Holy Mary the Mother of God, that one of the brethren died in the hospital at Jericho.[119]

An inscription in a Byzantine mosaic floor discovered at Jericho commemorates the burial of the abbot of a different church who donated to the Nea.

> Tomb of the most blessed Cyriac, priest and hegumen, who also founded the pious oratory of the holy and glorious martyr George and gave donation to the holiest new church of the glorious Mother of God in Jerusalem. He died in the month of December, the eleventh, fifteenth indiction, in the second year of the reign of our lord, Flavius Justinus (= 11 December 566 CE during the reign of Justin II).[120]

Mount Zion and the Citadel

Mount Zion originally denoted the Temple Mount and/or the southeastern hill: "Nevertheless David took the stronghold of Zion (Hebrew *metzudat zion*), which is now the city of David" (2 Sam 5:7). By the late Second Temple period, the name had been transferred to the southwestern hill, as Josephus indicates: "Of these hills that on which the upper city lay was far higher and had a straighter ridge than the other; consequently, owing to its strength it was called by King David—the father of Solomon the first builder of the temple—the Stronghold (Greek *Akra*), but we called it the upper agora" (*War* 5.137).[121]

Today Mount Zion is the southern part of the southwestern hill, which lies outside the walls of the Old City. The Madaba Map depicts a large basilica at this location, beyond the south end of the western cardo. This was the Church of Holy Zion, also known as the Church of the Holy Mother of Zion (Greek Hagia

Maria Sion) or the Mother of All Churches. The church was constructed in the mid to late fourth century on the spot where it was believed the resurrected Jesus appeared to his disciples (John 20:19) and where the apostles were filled with the Holy Spirit on Pentecost (Acts 2:1–4).[122] By the fifth century this spot was also venerated as the site of the Last Supper, which came to be called the Cenacle after Jerome (early fifth century) used the word *coenaculum* (from the Latin *ceno* ["I dine"]) in his Vulgate translation for the "upper room" where the meal took place (see Mk 14:15; Lk 22.12; Acts 1:13). The cenacle was in a small structure inside or next to the church complex.[123] By the sixth and seventh centuries, Christian tradition identified Mount Zion as the site of Mary's death (dormition).[124] And, by the tenth–eleventh centuries, the tomb of David had come to be located on Mount Zion, which by then was identified as "the City of David."[125] Ora Limor situates the roots of this tradition in the Byzantine period, when a memorial service was held on Mount Zion for David and James the Less—aka James the Lesser or James the Younger or James the son of Alphaeus (identified by some with James the Just, the brother of Jesus, who was the first bishop of Jerusalem). The linkage of David, the original founder of Zion, and James, the founder of the Church of Zion, the second Zion, eventually led Christians (and later, Jews and Muslims) to locate David's tomb on Mount Zion.[126] As David Clausen notes, unlike most other holy sites Mount Zion is not identified as the location of any events mentioned in the New Testament. Therefore, the sacredness of Mount Zion is based on traditions, some of which may have been preserved by the earliest Christian communities in Jerusalem.[127]

After being damaged by the Sasanids and subsequently repaired, the Church of Holy Zion was looted and burned in 966 CE.[128] By the mid-twelfth century, the church had been rebuilt by the Crusaders and dedicated to Sancta Maria in Monte Sion, but apparently was destroyed by Saladin at the end of that century.[129] The current Church of the Dormition on Mount Zion was built in 1898–1899, after the land was acquired by the German Kaiser Wilhelm II from the Ottoman sultan.[130] It was designed by Heinrich Renard, who conducted excavations prior to construction. Renard reconstructed the Byzantine church as a basilica with four rows of columns and three apses at the east end, and the Cenacle with "David's Tomb" as a southern annex to it.[131] One of the doorkeepers of the Byzantine church was buried in the Ben-Hinnom Valley (the area of the Akeldama tombs), as indicated by a Greek inscription over the tomb's entrance: "Tomb belonging to the doorkeepers of (the church) of Holy Sion."[132] Another tomb in the Ben-Hinnom Valley belonged to a German woman affiliated with the Byzantine church: "Tomb of Thecla (daughter) of Marulfus the German; (belonging to the church) of Holy Sion."[133]

Today a small two-story building to the south of the Church of the Dormition houses an empty stone sarcophagus (cenotaph) on the ground floor that is said to be the tomb of David, while the upper story is identified as the Cenacle. Although much of the current structure is medieval and later, the remains of earlier masonry and a niche in the north wall of the lower story (behind the sarcophagus) have led some scholars to speculate that the structure originally was an early synagogue. The upper story was rebuilt in the 1180s with ribbed vaults typical of Crusader architecture in Jerusalem, and a mihrab (prayer niche) was added to the south wall when it converted to a mosque in the fifteenth century.[134]

By the Byzantine period, other landmarks on the southwestern hill (Zion/ Sion) were associated with David, including the ruins of Herod's palace and the most prominent of the three adjacent Herodian towers, which became known as the Tower of David.[135] Two of the three towers are depicted on the Madaba Map to the right (south) of the west gate of the city (the site of the modern Jaffa Gate). Eventually the Tower of David gave its name to the fortified enclosure around it: David's Citadel, as it is called today. Because Christians identified the tower as part of David's palace, a tradition arose that this was where he composed the Psalms, committed the sin with Bathsheba, and repented after Nathan confronted him (2 Sam 11–12).[136]

During the Byzantine period, large numbers of monks who sought to emulate David's example of penitence lived in individual cells and monasteries in and around the Tower of David.[137] Epiphanius the Monk, writing ca. 750–800 CE, says: "And at the west gate of the Holy City is the Tower of David, in which he [David] sat in the dust and wrote the Psalter."[138] During the early Islamic period, Muslims continued to venerate the tower as a holy site, naming it the Mihrab Dawud (mihrab of David) after the prayer chamber (mihrab) mentioned in a variation of the 2 Samuel story that is related in the Qur'an (Sura 38:21).[139]

One of the monasteries in the vicinity of the Tower of David was founded by Peter the Iberian (ca. 411–491 CE).[140] Peter's homeland—the kingdom of Iberia or Kartli—corresponds roughly to the modern Republic of Georgia in the Caucasus.[141] By the latter part of the fifth century, Georgians were well-represented among Jerusalem's monastic communities.[142] Peter, whose name was Nabarnugios or Murvan before he became a monk, was a member of the Iberian royal family. At the age of twelve he was sent to Constantinople as a hostage, where he became acquainted with Eudocia and with Melania the Younger, who visited the city in 437.[143] Melania the Younger was the granddaughter of Melania the Elder, a Roman noblewoman from Spain who was related to the writer and poet Paulinus, the bishop of Nola in Italy.[144] As a young widow, Melania the Elder left Rome for the Egyptian desert, where she stayed with a group of monks. When the monks were banished to Palestine in the early 370s, Melania the Elder accompanied them to Jerusalem, where she built a pair of monasteries (one for men and one for women) and a hospice on the Mount of

Olives.[145] In 417, Melania the Younger arrived in Jerusalem and established a number of churches and monasteries, including a pair of monasteries (one for men and one for women) on the Mount of Olives. She spent much of the rest of her life in a monastic cell on the Mount of Olives, where she died in 439 CE, a year after Eudocia's arrival in the city.[146]

Perhaps with Melania the Younger's encouragement, Peter the Iberian escaped from Constantinople to Jerusalem in 437 or 438, where he became a monk on the Mount of Olives.[147] Around 444 CE, Peter moved to Gaza, where he was ordained as a priest. Seven years later he was appointed the Monophysite bishop of Maiumas, the port of Gaza.[148] The first centuries of Christianity were marked by doctrinal divisions and controversies, many of which focused on the nature of Jesus Christ. Whereas Monophysites believed that Jesus has only one nature, which is divine, in 451 CE the Council of Chalcedon (the fourth ecumenical council of the Christian church) declared the Orthodox dogma that Christ has two natures (divine and human) united in one person.

After Peter's death, a companion of his named John Rufus, who was a member of the Monophysite community in Maiumas, wrote his biography (*The Life of Peter the Iberian*).[149] Rufus relates that Peter founded a monastery in Jerusalem with a hospice for poor pilgrims "on a site above holy Sion in the place called the Tower of David."[150] Apparently, this is "the monastery of the Iberians in Jerusalem" that Procopius says was restored by Justinian.[151] In the Byzantine period, the term "Tower of David" referred to the area from the Citadel southward to Mount Zion.[152]

Possible remains associated with Peter the Iberian's monastery came to light in 1932, when John Iliffe conducted salvage excavations on the grounds of the YMCA (in West Jerusalem across the street from the King David Hotel).[153] These include a wine press and Byzantine cist graves cut into bedrock that were covered by stone slabs.[154] A Greek inscription on a limestone slab found near the cemetery reads: "Tomb belonging to Samuel, bishop of the Iberians, and to his monastery, which they bought in (the area of) David's Tower."[155] Iliffe suggested that the bishop named in the tombstone was a member of the monastery founded by Peter and that the cemetery served members of various Iberian monasteries near the Tower of David. Drawing on unpublished information from salvage excavations conducted in 1947 farther to the west, Yana Tchekhanovets proposes that the cist graves were located inside a large basilical church, which was part of a sprawling monastic complex that included wine and olive presses.[156] This monastery likely was one of the Iberian establishments in the vicinity of the Tower of David.[157]

A limestone slab in secondary use in the pavement of the courtyard of the Crusader tomb of the Virgin in Gethsemane (at the foot of the Mount of

Olives) is inscribed in Greek: "Tomb belonging to Ab . . . and Cericus the many-feeding(?) deacons(?) of the Anastasis, joint heirs of the Iberians. + Tomb of the Tower of David."[158] The inscription refers to a tomb belonging to the Iberian monastic community near the Tower of David. This tomb could have been in the Iberian cemetery on the grounds of the YMCA to the west of the city, or perhaps indicates that the Iberians also owned burial plots in Gethsemane.[159] The two men named in the inscription were Iberian clergy members at the Church of the Holy Sepulcher.[160]

In 1989–1993, Ronny Reich conducted salvage excavations outside Jaffa Gate in connection with the development of the Mamilla neighborhood. He discovered a mass burial consisting of heaps of human skeletons in a burial cave (crypt)—apparently the remains of Christians massacred by the Sasanids in 614 CE. An analysis of the skeletons indicates that the deceased were relatively young compared to contemporary cemetery populations, suggesting that they met their end in a sudden, tragic event. Female skeletons greatly outnumber males, perhaps because men would have been away fighting whereas the women stayed behind and were caught during the invasion. A small chapel in front of the cave is paved with a white mosaic decorated with three simple crosses. The chapel contained cross-shaped pendants, oil lamps, and approximately 130 coins, the latest of which is a gold issue of Phocas (602–610 CE).[161] A Greek inscription in the mosaic floor by the blocked-up entrance to the cave commemorates the anonymous dead: "For the salvation and succor of those whose names the Lord knows. Amen."[162]

Strategius relates that 24,518 Christians perished in the Pool of Mamilla, where they were penned up by the Persians.

> But he (the Persian leader) seized the remainder of the people and shut them up in the reservoir of Mamel [Mamila], which lies outside the city at a distance of about two stades from the tower of David. And he ordered sentinels to guard those thus confined in the moat. Oh my brethren, who can estimate the hardships and privations which befell the Christians on that day? For the multitude of people suffocated one the other, and fathers and mothers perished together owing to the confinement of the place. Like sheep devoted to slaughter, so were the crowd of believers got ready for massacre. Death on every side declared itself, since the intense heat, like fire, consumed the multitude of people, as they trampled on one another in the press, and many perished without the sword.[163]

This same pool is listed as one of the locations where a certain Thomas and his followers buried the dead: "Those whom they found they collected in great haste and with much zeal, and buried them in the grotto of Mamel."[164] It is possible that some of the heaps of bones found in burial caves to the north of the city (see below) are also the remains of Christians massacred by the Sasanids in 614.[165]

The Church of Siloam

In addition to uncovering large stretches of the Byzantine wall around the southwestern hill, Bliss and Dickie excavated the Church of Siloam. The church was built on the north side of the current Pool of Siloam at the outlet of the Siloam Tunnel, whereas the earlier (original) Pool of Siloam (Birket el-Hamra)—which had gone out of use and silted up—is located below it (to the southeast).[166] By the Byzantine period, the current pool was venerated as the spot where Jesus healed a blind man (John 9:1, 6–7). The church had an unusual layout due to the steep slope of the southeastern hill, which rises to the north: instead of being entered from the short end on the west, access was by way of an atrium on the north to a stepped narthex (porch) that descended to an arcade (row of arches) supported by piers along the building's north side. The church itself had four square piers supporting a dome over the center of the nave, which terminated on the east in an apse containing tiers of benches (a *synthronon*). The hall was paved with geometric mosaics and the apse was paved with marble tiles (*opus sectile*). An open portico along the church's south aisle overlooked the pool.[167]

In the early sixth century, a pilgrim named Theodosius wrote: "The Pool of Siloam is 100 paces from the pit where they cast the Prophet Jeremiah: it is inside the wall."[168] The Piacenza Pilgrim (ca. 570) reports: "Nowadays Siloam is included within the city, since the Empress Eudoxia (Eudocia) herself added walls to the city."[169] Because Bliss and Dickie attributed the construction of the wall around the southwestern hill to Eudocia, they understood the testimony of these pilgrims as indicating that she extended the wall as far as the Pool of Siloam to include the church.[170] Therefore, the Church of Siloam is thought to have been constructed by Eudocia in the mid-fifth century. The church apparently was damaged or destroyed by the Sasanids in 614; it is unclear if it was repaired and continued in use afterward.[171]

The Church of St. Stephen

Stephen is venerated as the first martyr (protomartyr) of Christianity. According to Acts 6–7, he was one of seven deacons appointed by the apostles to distribute food to Jerusalem's poor. Stephen's teachings angered the congregations of Diaspora Jews ("the synagogue of the Freedmen . . . , Cyrenians, Alexandrians, and others of those from Cilicia and Asia [Minor]"; Acts 6:9), who dragged him out of the city and stoned him to death for blasphemy (Acts 7:58–60).

Early Christian writers report that Stephen's remains were discovered in his native village of Caphargamala (Kafar Gamala) in 415 CE and brought to the Church of Holy Zion in Jerusalem.[172] The bones apparently were divided up among several churches around the city, and some were even sent to bishops around the Mediterranean as far away as Spain.[173] In 460, Stephen's remains were transferred from Mount Zion to the new Church of St. Stephen, which was built by Eudocia about 450 meters north of the site of the Damascus Gate.[174] By the late fifth century, the Church of St. Stephen was also identified as the spot where Stephen had been stoned.[175] As a native who was the "firstborn of the martyrs," Stephen had a special significance to Jerusalem's population.[176] The popularity of his cult is reflected by the cluster of monasteries, funerary chapels, and cemeteries that sprang up around the Church of St. Stephen. Nevertheless, even after Stephen's remains were transferred to Eudocia's church, he continued to be commemorated in an annual memorial service at the Church of Zion. In the early Islamic period, when pilgrims started avoiding the Church of St. Stephen because it had become a hospital for lepers, a tradition developed locating not only Stephen's tomb but the site of his stoning on Mount Zion.[177]

When Eudocia died in 460, shortly after the church's dedication, her body was laid to rest in the same burial cave as Stephen's.

> Nowadays Siloam is included within the city, since the Empress Eudoxia herself added walls to the city. She also built the basilica and tomb of Saint Stephen, and her own tomb is next to St. Stephen's, with twenty paces between the two. Saint Stephen's resting-place is outside the gate, and a bowshot from the road which leads westwards down to Joppa [Jaffa], Caesarea Palaestinae, and Diospolis [Lod].[178]

The church built by Eudocia was destroyed by the Sasanids in 614, perhaps because it was near the tunnels they dug under the city's north wall. It might have been replaced by a smaller chapel.[179] The remains of Eudocia's church—which was a basilica with a huge monastic complex that included two large crypts and numerous tombs—were discovered by the Dominican Fathers between 1885 and 1893, during construction of the current Church and Monastery (Couvent) of St. Étienne, which also house the École Biblique et Archéologique Française de Jerusalem.[180] A marble slab found in the vicinity of the Byzantine church is inscribed in Greek with a list of relics that Eudocia brought to Jerusalem: "These precious bones which the venerable Eudocia Augusta brought here (are those) of the most glorious martyrs . . . Callinicus, . . . , Domninus, . . . , Thecla

and . . . Glory be to these saints."[181] Another stone slab found inside the basilica bears a Greek inscription commemorating a deacon of the Church of the
Holy Sepulcher who apparently was buried at St. Stephen's: "Tomb belonging to Nonnus (son of) Onesimus, deacon of the Holy Anastasis and of its
monastery."[182]

Beginning in 1995, more than 15,000 human bones from a repository (numbered 6) in the largest crypt of the Byzantine church were analyzed as part
of a bioarchaeological project led by Susan Sheridan. The bones represent
the remains of at least 109–250 adults and 58 infants and children who were
interred in the crypt over a period of approximately 180 years.[183] Not surprisingly, an overwhelming majority of the adult bones (ninety-six percent) belong
to males, whose average reconstructed height is 162 centimeters (5 feet 4 inches)
to 168 centimeters (5 feet 6 inches).[184] The median age at death for adults was
between thirty and thirty-nine years, while the overall average age at death was
the mid-to-late forties. A large number of individuals were forty to forty-nine
years of age or older.[185] Stable isotope analyses of the bone collagen indicate
that bread, vegetables, and fruits were dietary staples for both men and women,
although animal protein such as eggs, cheese, milk, and possibly fish, fish sauce,
or meat was also regularly consumed.[186] In general, the men appear to have
been healthy, stocky, and muscular, suggesting this was an affluent monastic
community.[187]

Sheridan believes it is likely that the infants and children buried with the
monks were locals or perhaps lived at an orphanage run by the monastery.[188]
They ranged in age from seven months *in utero* to sixteen to eighteen years
old.[189] The infants consumed breastmilk for the first year of their lives and
were completely weaned at two to three years of age. Most of the children died
before the age of ten, with a peak mortality while weaning at one to three years
of age.[190] Ten to fifteen percent of the adults showed signs of considerable illness during childhood. All the individuals were part of the Near Eastern gene
pool.[191]

Although the adult men generally were healthy and robust, their lower limbs
show signs of severe arthritis and significant joint deterioration in the knees,
ankles, and toes that would have caused chronic pain.[192] Sheridan concludes
that the joint degeneration was caused by the act of genuflection, which involves
repeated kneeling. The bones indicate that individuals tended to push up with
the right knee when rising from the kneeling position.[193] The monks would have
considered the pain they endured a means of attaining salvation.[194] Sheridan's
analyses provide a fascinating glimpse into the everyday lives (and deaths) of the
population at St. Stephen's, and are consistent with literary descriptions of the
ascetic practices of Byzantine monks.[195]

The Church at the Sheep's Pool (or the Church of the Paralytic or Basilica of Saint Mary)

By the mid-fifth century, a church was built at the Sheep's Pool (Bezetha or Bethesda Pool), which is mentioned in John 5:2–9 as the site where Jesus healed an invalid (Figure 7.28). It also became identified as the place where the Virgin Mary was born because of an early Christian tradition that her father, Joachim, was responsible for supplying the temple with sacrificial sheep.[196] Excavations by the White Fathers, who own the property, indicate that the Byzantine church was a basilica, the western part of which was built on the partition wall separating the two basins of the pool.[197] A series of arches supporting the western extension was founded on the floor of the basins at a depth of 13 meters (43 feet) below the basilica.[198] A stone slab inscribed in Greek (perhaps the door of a tomb) discovered in secondary use in the pavement of the road outside the Lions' Gate nearby mentions a deacon of the church: "Tomb belonging to Amos, deacon of the Probatica (Church)."[199] The church at the Sheep's Pool probably was damaged by the Sasanids in 614 and subsequently repaired, but its condition may have deteriorated in the following centuries. The current church of St. Anne (the mother of Mary) was built by the Crusaders.[200]

Armenians in Byzantine Jerusalem

The kingdom of Armenia was the first state to adopt Christianity as its official religion in the early fourth century, since which time the Armenian Church has maintained a presence in Jerusalem.[201] *The List of Armenian Monasteries* compiled by Anastas Vardapet, which is preserved only in later copies but might have been composed in the sixth century, records seventy Armenian establishments in Jerusalem. Although the list includes churches such as the Holy Sepulcher which clearly were not established by Armenians, it reflects the extensive Armenian presence in the city in the sixth and seventh centuries.[202] One Armenian pilgrim, a man named Tiratur, scratched a graffito onto a marble slab that was found immediately to the west of Jaffa Gate—that is, in the vicinity of the Tower of David: "Lord have mercy upon Tiratur and Holy Resurrection(?) remember."[203]

During the Byzantine period, churches and monasteries, funerary chapels and cemeteries sprang up outside the walls of the Old City extending from the Mount of Olives and Mount Scopus on the east to the modern Musrara neighborhood to the northwest.[204] Some of these establishments are identified by inscriptions as Armenian, including a cluster north of the Damascus Gate, surrounding St. Stephen's.[205] Among them is a funerary chapel that was discovered in 1894 about 350 meters (1150 feet) northwest of the Damascus Gate, to the west of St. Stephen's. It was paved with a beautiful mosaic floor (the "Bird mosaic") measuring about 6.4 × 4 meters (21 × 13 feet), depicting a variety of birds and baskets of fruits inside grapevine medallions (Pl. 13A).[206] An Armenian inscription near the east end of the mosaic reads: "For the memorial and salvation of all Armenians whose names the Lord knows."[207] About 8 meters (25 feet) away from the "Bird mosaic," a marble slab broken into seven pieces was also inscribed in Armenian: "Having remembered Petros who made and Yohan who commissioned this cross."[208] Unfortunately, after its discovery this slab disappeared and is known only from written descriptions of the nineteenth century. It probably belonged to one of the tombs in the vicinity of the chapel.[209]

Recent excavations in the burial crypt under the floor of the "Bird mosaic" revealed a pile of fragmentary, disarticulated bones. Analyses indicate that at least seventeen individuals are represented, including three children (ranging from two to ten years old) and fourteen adults (ranging from fifteen to older than 40 years). Of the adults that could be sexed, four are male and three are female. The presence of children and equal numbers of males and females suggests these are the remains of civilians rather than soldiers, monks, or nuns. Whereas the mosaic and inscription are dated on stylistic grounds to the sixth to seventh centuries, radiocarbon dating provides a range from the fifth century to first half of the sixth century for the bones. This raises the possibility that the bones were brought to this crypt from elsewhere for reburial, or perhaps the mosaic floor and inscription are later additions to the funerary chapel.[210]

From 1948–1967, Jerusalem was divided by a wall, with the eastern part under Jordanian rule and the western part under Israeli rule. In 1967, Israel took control of East Jerusalem including the Old City during the Six-Day War, and, in the 1990s, constructed a major highway (1) along the former circuit of the wall to the north of the Old City. In advance of the work, salvage excavations were conducted from 1990–1992. The excavations brought to light remains of various periods including sections of the Third Wall and several monasteries, hostels, and a large cemetery of the Byzantine period.[211] One of these was an Armenian monastic complex with a small church or chapel on the eastern edge of the Musrara neighborhood. The apse was paved with marble tiles and the hall had a mosaic floor with a simple floral net pattern.[212] A Greek inscription in the mosaic in front of the apse reads: "In the days of Silvanus, the most God-loving deacon and abbot [Greek *hegemon*], the present mosaic(?) was made, and the apse and the annex of the church, for a length of . . . cubits and a height of 6 cubits. Remember him, o Lord, in Thy kingdom."[213] Crypts under the porch (narthex) contained human skeletal remains, including one filled with heaps of bones, and two tombstones inscribed in Armenian. One tombstone reads "Of

Petros of Sodk'" (a district in Eastern Armenia). According to Michael Stone, this is not the same Petros mentioned in the inscription found near the "Bird mosaic," as it is a common Armenian name.[214] The second tombstone, which is fragmentary, reads "(This is the tomb) of Abel."[215]

The monastery's reception hall was paved with a mosaic floor containing a medallion with an Armenian inscription: "I, Ewstat' the priest, laid this mosaic. (You) who enter this building, remember me and my brother Luke to Christ."[216] A coin found under the mosaic indicates that it was laid in the mid-seventh century, perhaps around the same time as the mosaic in the chapel. The complex appears to have expanded over the course of the sixth and seventh centuries, through the decades following the Muslim conquest.[217]

Not far from the Armenian monastic complex in Musrara, Eleazar Lipa Sukenik and Leo Aryeh Mayer's 1925 excavations brought to light a funerary chapel immediately north of the Third Wall, which was paved with a mosaic floor containing a Greek inscription: "Here lies Anatolia of Arabissos, the sister of the emperor(?), having valiantly fought the fight and consecrated herself to God. She fell asleep in the month of October, the 21st, of the third indiction."[218] Anatolia probably was related to—and perhaps was even the sister of—the emperor Maurice (Mauricius) (582–602), who was from Arabissos in Melitene (Lesser Armenia). The family had a history of benefactions to Jerusalem, including an upper church built by Maurice at the tomb of the Virgin on the Mount of Olives, which was destroyed before the Crusades.[219] In addition, Leah Di Segni identifies monograms on a group of sixth-century marble capitals in the Church of the Holy Sepulcher as the names of Maurice and his family. The capitals are now in secondary use in the Crusader arch connecting the Rotunda to the Catholicon. Di Segni proposes that they originated in an otherwise unknown renovation by Maurice to the Church of the Holy Sepulcher.[220]

After the general Phocas usurped the Byzantine throne in 602 and executed Maurice and six of his sons, other members of the royal family fled from Constantinople to Jerusalem. Among them were Maurice's sister Damiana, who became an abbess in Jerusalem, and her son Athenogenes, who was appointed bishop of Petra (in Jordan). Damiana and Maurice's niece founded a church in Jerusalem at the site venerated as the birthplace of the healing saints Cosmas and Damian. No remains of the church have been found, but it might be depicted on the Madaba Map on the spot now occupied by the "House of Veronica" at the sixth station of the Cross on the Via Dolorosa.[221] If Anatolia was related to Phocas, the inscription would date either to October 614 or October 629.[222] Perhaps her burial in this chapel instead of at the Church of St. Stephen indicates that the latter was in ruins after the Sasanid invasion in 614.[223]

The dedicatory inscription of Silvanus in the Armenian monastery in Musrara and the inscriptions associated with the Iberian monastic complex at the YMCA show that Greek was widely used by Armenians and Georgians. This makes it difficult to distinguish the presence of these communities when other ethnic identifiers are absent.[224] One example is a funerary chapel similar in size to the one with the "Bird mosaic," which may be part of the same complex. The chapel was discovered in 1901, 215 meters (705 feet) west-northwest of the Damascus Gate.[225] It was paved with a mosaic floor depicting Orpheus playing a lyre. According to Greek mythology, Orpheus had the ability to charm animals with his music. The mosaic shows him surrounded by animals as well as Pan and a centaur (hybrid creatures associated with Dionysos/Bacchus). Below is a panel with two elaborately dressed female figures labeled in Greek Theodosia and Georgia—presumably donors to the chapel who were buried there. A hunting scene is depicted below them. The mosaic, which probably dates to the sixth or seventh century, illustrates the continued popularity of Greek and Roman mythological stories long after the spread of Christianity. After its discovery, the Orpheus mosaic was removed from the chapel and taken to the Istanbul Archaeological Museum, where it is still displayed.[226]

Sukenik and Mayer followed the line of the Third Wall eastward to the point where it reaches the fence around the American School of Oriental Research (now the W. F. Albright Institute of Archaeological Research). Here they mention finding "remains of Byzantine buildings" and part of a mosaic floor.[227] In 1932, Byzantine tombs were discovered farther east on the grounds of the American School, behind the north wing of the building and adjacent to the tennis court. The tombs were excavated by Millar Burrows, the Director of the School at the time. They consisted of two units with a common wall. The northern unit was divided into two rooms with separate entrances, each containing four built compartments. The southern unit, which was also divided into two rooms containing built compartments, was larger, deeper, and had been roofed with vaults. It was entered through a doorway with heavy stone posts. The base of the wall around the southern unit sloped outward, apparently to support the weight of the vaults. The walls were poorly constructed of stone covered with plaster on the inside and cement on the outside.[228]

The compartments were filled with heaps of bones, mostly of adults but including a number of early adolescents and a few infants—a picture similar to St. Stephen's only a block away. Burrows estimated that the tombs contained at least a hundred burials and perhaps many more than that.[229] The finds included glass bottles and two intact large candlestick oil lamps dating to the second half of the sixth to seventh centuries, one with the Greek inscription "of the mother of God." There were scattered tesserae (mosaic cubes), but no remains of a mosaic floor were discovered. The tombs also contained two coins of Anastasius (490–518 CE).[230]

Because the school year was over and the students had departed, Burrows conducted the excavation with staff members and consulted with archaeologists such as John Crowfoot and Louis-Hugues Vincent, who happened to stop by.[231] Should the future opportunity arise to conduct further excavations on the grounds of the Albright Institute, the continuation of the Third Wall as well as additional Byzantine remains will undoubtedly be found—part of the extensive complex of monastic and funerary structures surrounding St. Stephen's.

The Ophel and Tyropoeon Valley

B. Mazar's 1968–1978 excavations south of the Temple Mount brought to light houses belonging to a sixth century residential quarter (Figures 9.7 and 9.8).[232] The spacious and sturdily built stone dwellings—which range in size from 400–685 square meters (4,305–7373 square feet)—were all the same type, consisting of two or three stories of rooms surrounding a central open-air courtyard. One house, part of which was excavated in the 1960s by Kathleen Kenyon, had a peristyle courtyard with two rows of columns that supported the overhanging roof.[233] The other courtyards had balconies surrounding the courtyard at the second story level, which were supported by small columns. Staircases inside the houses provided access to the upper stories and roofs.[234] Many of the houses had shops installed in the exterior walls. The shops faced onto narrow streets and alleys that ran north-south and east-west and separated the buildings.[235] The basement story, which was the coolest part of the house, was used for the storage of food and water. Every house had at least two cisterns with a capacity of 25–80 cubic meters (6,604–21,100 gallons) each, which were filled by rainwater channeled from the roof through terracotta pipes. The cisterns were hewn into the bedrock underneath the houses and were coated with thick layers of plaster to prevent seepage.[236]

The living rooms were on the second and third stories, while many of the ground floor rooms, which opened onto the central courtyard, contained workshop installations for crafts or light industry such as tanning, dyeing, and metalworking.[237] Kitchens and stables were also located on the ground floor. Much of the workshop activity and food preparation took place in the courtyard, which was paved with stone slabs or terracotta tiles.[238] One residence (in Area XVI) had a small triangular room adjoining a courtyard with a cistern. The courtyard was paved with a mosaic floor. An apparent toilet was found in the corner of the triangular room, accessed by four plastered steps, the uppermost of which had an opening cut in it. A channel underneath the opening passed

FIGURE 9.7 Plan of the Byzantine houses south of the Temple Mount (from E. Mazar 2007: 204, Fig. 18.3).
Credit: Prepared by the excavation's surveyors; reproduced with the permission of the Institute of Archaeology, the Hebrew University.

through the outer wall of the room and continued under the street outside the house. The excavators speculate that the cistern and possible toilet—which were accessible from the street through a doorway in the outer wall—might have been a public washroom.[239]

Many of the rooms had one or more stone arches to support the wooden beams of the ceiling and/or roof. The arches made it possible to use locally available wooden beams, which were too short to span the entire width of the room.[240] The roofs were coated with thick layers of plaster or covered with stone and had a small dome or rise in the center to facilitate the drainage of rainwater.[241] Some balconies apparently were covered with roof tiles, which were stamped with names or symbols indicating they were manufactured in ten different factories.[242] Some of the ground floor rooms were paved with plain mosaics or mosaics with simple geometric or floral designs. A few had Greek inscriptions, such as one that reads: "Good luck to those who live here."[243] It is likely that there were more elaborate mosaics in the upper floors which did not survive.[244] The houses were filled with a rich assortment of finds, including imported and locally produced pottery, glass vessels, coins, and metal, ivory,

FIGURE 9.8 A Byzantine house south of the Temple Mount.
Credit: Photo by the author.

and stone objects such as belt buckles, spindle whorls, beads and jewelry, cruci-
fixes, pins, and cosmetic items.

E. Mazar identifies a courtyard building located outside the southeast corner of the Temple Mount as a monastic establishment based on the finds, which
included a reliquary (a reused ossuary of the late Second Temple period), marble chancel screen fragments, an altar table, and numerous crosses. Specifically,
she proposes that it is the "Enclosed Convent of the Virgins" mentioned by
Theodosius (early sixth century), who described a closed monastery of reclusive
virgins "below the Pinnacle of the Temple" whose "food is let down to them
from the walls" (Theodosius, *The Topography of the Holy Land*, 143).[245] A large

Byzantine structure to the east of the monastic establishment and contemporary with it might be a hospice.[246]

Another courtyard building located outside the southwest corner of the Temple Mount (Area VI) was dubbed the "House of the Menorot" by the excavators.[247] An Umayyad palace (Building III) was later erected over this spot (see Chapter 10). Prior to the palace's construction, the area was leveled with a massive fill, which preserved the walls of the "House of the Menorot" to a height of two stories. However, during this process, the floors of the building were removed and, as a result, no finds were discovered in situ in any of the excavated rooms. The building is so-called because four seven-branched menorot (menorahs) (seven-branched candelabrums) were painted on walls or stones inside it. All four menorahs are painted in the same style in dark red paint. Two of the menorahs probably flanked a niche in the south wall of a room at the second story level. The other two menorahs were painted on a stone lintel on either side of a carved cross. E. Mazar is unable to verify B. Mazar's suggestion that the cross was covered with plaster when the menorahs were painted. According to her, the building was converted for use as a synagogue by Jewish settlers following the Sasanid Persian invasion in 614. In support, E. Mazar cites a document from the Cairo Geniza (a repository in Cairo's Ben Ezra synagogue) which indicates that a Jewish neighborhood existed in this area at the beginning of the early Islamic period. However, Jerome Murphy-O'Connor has pointed out that this document is four centuries later than in date and should not be taken at face value.[248] Even if we assume this information is reliable, there is a chronological problem with E. Mazar's suggestion, since the Cairo Geniza document refers to a Jewish settlement that was established in the southern part of the city after the Muslim conquest, not before. Although the painted menorahs could indicate Jewish occupation of this building after 614, it is puzzling that the niche flanked by menorahs, which E. Mazar identifies as a Torah Shrine is in the south wall instead of the north wall, facing the Temple Mount. And other finds from this building, such as the cross on the lintel, oil lamps with Christian inscriptions, and oil lamp handles in the shape of a cross suggest Christian (perhaps ecclesiastical?) occupation before 614. As the building's function after 614 is unknown, it may be more prudent to follow B. Mazar's original suggestion that it was a Jewish public building but not necessarily a synagogue.

The Byzantine residential quarter to the south of the Temple Mount extended southward on either side of a broad paved street along the Tyropoeon Valley.[249] Portions of the street and houses were brought to light in 1927 by John Crowfoot and George Fitzgerald, and, since 2003, in excavations in the Givati Parking Lot.[250] In the Givati Parking Lot, Doron Ben-Ami and Tchekhanovets discovered a large building (628), which they dubbed the "Late Roman peristyle building." This building contained multiple rooms surrounding a large open area with two adjacent courtyards, the western one surrounded by a peristyle.[251] The building covered an area of 2,000 square meters (21,528 square feet) or more, extending from the crest of the southeastern hill on the east down the slope of the Tyropoeon Valley on the west, where it rose to a height of two stories. Ben-Ami and Tchekhanovets cite the many roof tiles, over one hundred of which bear Tenth Legionary stamps, the building's interior decoration—including mosaics, frescoes, and stucco—and the rich finds, including a stone protome of a boxer and a gold earring with gemstones as evidence of the building's "clearly Roman nature."[252] Immediately to the south, across a two meter wide corridor or alley, the northernmost part of another spacious building (671) with the same orientation was excavated. Ben-Ami and Tchekhanovets conclude that the spacious residences were laid out in insulae that are typical of a Roman grid plan, and therefore are a feature of Aelia Capitolina.[253]

Although according to Ben-Ami and Tchekhanovets the Late Roman peristyle building was destroyed by the earthquake of 363, the associated pottery and coins indicate that it and Building 671 were constructed no earlier than the late fourth century—perhaps around the time that Eudocia fortified the city.[254] This date accords better with the discovery of Christian graffiti—including the Chi-Rho symbol (*christogram*) and the Greek word *kyrios* ("Lord")—written or incised on the plastered walls of the building.[255] By the first half of the sixth century, the Late Roman peristyle building ceased to be occupied and was filled with collapse. To the south, Building 671 (now designated Building 606) continued in use with modifications. After expanding the excavation area in 2008–2014, Ben-Ami and Tchekhanovets uncovered the southern wing of a large Byzantine administrative building (1821) at the north end of the Givati Parking Lot; two buildings (6592 and 6446) in the southeast; and a 6-meter-wide (20-foot) paved street running along the western side (Figure 9.9).

The walls of the Byzantine administrative building, which were preserved in spots to a height of over four meters, were covered with plaster and stucco. Ben-Ami and Tchekhanovets identify the building as the seat of a Byzantine official. A hoard of 264 gold coins minted in 610–613 found above the floor in one of the rooms and sealed with a layer of ash suggested to them that the building was destroyed in the Sasanid Persian invasion in 614. Perhaps the coins were issued by a temporary imperial mint in Jerusalem as funding for public needs.[256] The area between Building 1821 to the north and Buildings 6592 and 6446 to the south was covered with cultivated terraces with irrigation systems overlaid by a one meter thick layer of garden soil. The cultivated area appears to have continued to the north, where Benjamin Mazar describes a thick layer of dark garden soil dating to the Byzantine period under the Umayyad building south

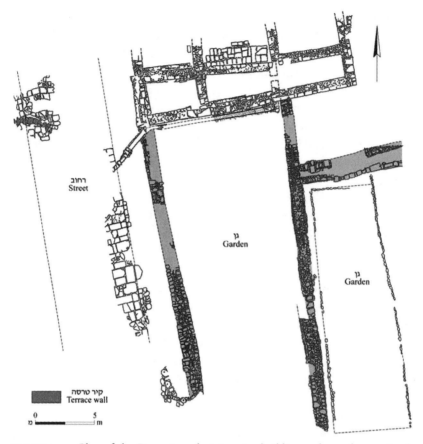

רחוב
Street

גן
Garden

גן
Garden

קיר טרסה
Terrace wall

0   5
מ   m

FIGURE 9.9 Plan of the Byzantine administrative building and paved street in the
Givati Parking Lot (from Ben-Ami and Tchekhanovets 2010b: Figure 5).
Credit: Ben-Ami and Tchekhanovets and reproduced courtesy of the Israel Antiquities
Authority.

of the Temple Mount.[257] Another series of agricultural terraces with earth fill
dating to the seventh century was found in Yigal Shiloh's excavations in Area K
farther to the south, suggesting that in this period large tracts of the southeastern
hill were under cultivation.[258] However, the pottery and coins indicate that the
Byzantine administrative building, the other buildings, and the paved street were
established in the first half of the sixth century and occupied until the second half
of the eighth century.[259] Therefore, although the hoard of gold coins might have
been deposited or hidden around the time of the Sasanid Persian invasion, the
building was not destroyed in 614.

The paved street on the western side of the Givati Parking Lot is the continuation of a Byzantine street lined by houses in the Tyropoeon Valley that was

excavated by Crowfoot and Fitzgerald approximately 50 meters (164 feet) to the southwest.[260] Crowfoot and Fitzgerald describe the walls, mosaic floor, and small finds in one house—dubbed "the house of Anastasius" after a name incised on a ceramic bowl lid—as so well-preserved that it gave "the illusive sense of intimacy with the former owners on whom we might be paying a discreetly curious visit."[261] Altogether, Crowfoot and Fitzgerald exposed the street for a length of nearly 40 meters (about 130 feet) (Pl. 6).[262] The construction of the street and houses along the western side of the Tyropoeon Valley posed a challenge to the Byzantine engineers as the steep slope was covered by the ruined walls and massive stone collapse of earlier structures, including the remains of the Akra. Houses were built on top of the collapse between ca. 300–550 CE (Crowfoot and Fitzgerald's "Lower Byzantine Level"). The rooms in the houses had arches spanning them to support the ceilings (like those found in the houses to the south of the Temple Mount).[263] When the Byzantine street and houses were constructed, the roofs of the houses of the "Lower Byzantine Level" were removed and the rooms were filled with stones mixed with potsherds and coins which clearly had been imported from middens elsewhere.[264] The houses along the street resemble those excavated by B. Mazar south of the Temple Mount.

Although Crowfoot and Fitzgerald dated the construction of the Byzantine street and houses to the late sixth to early seventh century, the latest coins found in sealed contexts indicate a date in the first half of the sixth century—that is, they are contemporary with the street and houses in the Givati Parking Lot. The construction of these structures in the first half of the sixth century, probably close to the mid-sixth century, attests to the intensive development of this part of the city during the reign of Justinian.[265] In both the Givati Parking Lot and Crowfoot and Fitzgerald's excavations, there is no evidence of destruction at the time of the Sasanid invasion in 614.[266]

To summarize: the Late Roman peristyle building and Building 671 in the Givati Parking Lot were constructed in the late fourth century or later, possibly around the time Eudocia fortified the city. By the first half of the sixth century, the Late Roman peristyle building ceased to be occupied and had collapsed, although the building to its south (671/606) continued in use with modifications. Shortly before the mid-sixth century, a large administrative building was constructed at the north end of the Givati Parking Lot along with other buildings to the south, separated by terraced gardens which are typical of Byzantine cities in the mid-sixth to seventh centuries. Shiloh's excavations indicate that other parts of the southeastern hill were under cultivation in the seventh century. To the west, a paved street lined by houses was established along the Tyropoeon Valley, indicating a significant development of Jerusalem's southeast sector during the reign of Justinian. The street provided access for pilgrims to the Church of Siloam at its southern end. The street, buildings, and gardens continued in use without interruption into the early Islamic period. Although the hoard of gold coins might have been hidden or deposited in 614 and apparently was never retrieved, the Byzantine administrative building was not destroyed at the time of the Sasanid Persian invasion, nor is there evidence that the other buildings were damaged in 614.

Blessings from Jerusalem

There was a brisk trade in pilgrim souvenirs at Jerusalem's holy sites in the Byzantine period. The souvenirs were called *eulogiae* (singular *eulogia*)—Greek for "blessings." *Eulogiae* are objects associated with a holy site, including relics or dirt or stones taken from it. During the Byzantine period, a variety of *eulogiae* ranging from containers for holy oil and dirt to oil lamps was marketed to pilgrims in Jerusalem. These objects were decorated with images, symbols, and messages that were intended to bear witness to the pilgrimage experience and enabled the owner to recall and relive it long afterward. Pilgrims believed that *eulogiae* retained their power of salvation after the pilgrimage ended and were like amulets that protected the owner from evil and cured and prevented sickness and disease.[267]

The best-known *eulogiae* from Jerusalem are ampullae (flasks) at Monza and Bobbio in northern Italy (Figure 9.10). According to tradition, this unique and homogeneous collection of metal flasks was presented to the Longobard queen Theodolinda at the beginning of the seventh century. As both the tradition and the scenes and inscriptions on the ampullae indicate, they originally contained holy oil from the tomb of Christ in the Church of the Holy Sepulcher. The inscriptions, which are in Greek, read: "Oil [of the] Tree of Life from the Holy Places of Christ" and "Blessing [of the] Lord from the Holy Places of Christ," sometimes accompanied by quotations from the New Testament. The scenes on the flasks depict various holy places or events: the Holy Sepulcher, the Golgotha cross, the Annunciation, the Nativity, the Crucifixion.[268] The high quality of workmanship indicates that they were intended as royal gifts.[269]

A different but related class of *eulogiae* is hexagonal glass bottles dating to the seventh century that are decorated with crosses and other symbols and contained holy oil from the Church of the Holy Sepulcher.[270] Dan Barag proposed that the hexagonal shape was inspired by the shape of the *ciboria* (canopies) above the tomb of Christ and Golgotha.[271] Another group of hexagonal and octagonal glass bottles is decorated with Jewish symbols such as the menorah, lulav, and ethrog (Figure 9.11). Perhaps they contained oil used by Jews in rituals on or around the Temple Mount, which would indicate that Jewish pilgrims to Jerusalem also

FIGURE 9.10 Monza-Bobbio ampulla.
Credit: Wikimedia Commons.

acquired *eulogiae*. It has been suggested that bottles decorated with symbols that are neither clearly Christian nor Jewish might have been used by Muslim visitors to the Temple Mount in the 690s, possibly in connection with the anointing of the Foundation Stone with oil.[272]

Some *eulogiae* might have been used by Christian pilgrims in ceremonies, processions, and liturgies at churches and other holy sites. For example, ceramic oil lamps typical of Byzantine Jerusalem have an oval body with raised lines on the shoulder surrounding the filling hole (Figure 9.12). They are called "candlestick lamps" because a design resembling a candlestick (menorah) or palm-branch decorates the nozzle. One variant of this type has a Greek inscription instead

FIGURE 9.11 Hexagonal glass bottle with Jewish symbols.
Credit: Metropolitan Museum of Art: www.metmuseum.orgartcollectionsearch465957.

of radiating lines on the shoulder.[273] Four different formulas appear among the inscriptions, one of which is "of the Mother of God [Theotokos]." Perhaps oil lamps with this formula were purchased by pilgrims who visited the Nea Church or other churches dedicated to Mary, the Mother of God, just as ceramic flasks from the shrine of Saint Menas in Egypt are inscribed "of Saint Menas." The evidence of the Menas flasks suggests that inscribed candlestick lamps were associated with specific churches or holy sites in Jerusalem.

By far the most common formula on inscribed candlestick lamps is "the light of Christ shines for all." I have suggested that these lamps were used in the ceremonies and rituals at the Church of the Holy Sepulcher. Already in 1900,

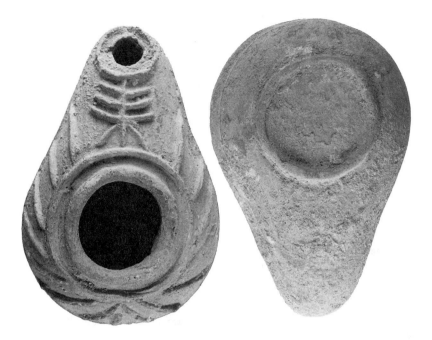

FIGURE 9.12 Large candlestick oil lamp.
Credit: Photo by David Hendin, Courtesy of David Hendin.

Clermont-Ganneau pointed out that this formula seems to have its source in the liturgy of St. Basil, employed by the Greek Orthodox at the ceremony of the Holy Fire at the Church of the Holy Sepulcher on Holy Saturday.[274] The Church of the Holy Sepulcher draws especially large crowds of pilgrims at Easter, when they come to celebrate Christ's resurrection. During the ceremony of the Holy Fire, which is one of the highlights of the Orthodox Easter ritual, light is passed by the Patriarch from the lamps that hang above the sepulcher through the crowd until everyone's lamps and candles are lit. Bernard the Monk, who visited Jerusalem ca. 870 CE, provides the earliest account of the ceremony of the Holy Fire.

> But it is worth saying what happens on Holy Saturday, the Vigil of Easter. In the morning the office begins in this church. Then, when it is over they go on singing *Kyrie eleison* ["Lord have mercy"] till an angel comes and kindles light in the lamps which hang above the sepulcher. The patriarch passes some of this light to the bishops and the rest of the people, and thus each one has light where he is standing.[275]

The lighting of lamps was also a feature of the *Lychnikon* or *Lucernare* ("Service of the Lamps"), a Vespers service described by Egeria toward the end of the fourth century.[276] The *Lychnikon* normally was held at 4:00 PM and was attended not only by the bishop and clergy but also by lay people and catechumens (converts to Christianity who had not yet been baptized). The service took place in the Rotunda and was illuminated by large numbers of lamps lit from the eternal flame in the tomb. From there the participants walked in a procession to the cross on Golgotha, connecting the complex's two focal points: the empty tomb, which confirmed Jesus's divine nature through his resurrection, and the cross, which bore witness to his crucifixion.[277] Perhaps oil lamps inscribed with a variant of the formula "the light of Christ shines for all" that adds "good evening" at the end were associated with the *Lychnikon* service.[278]

In the eyes of Byzantine pilgrims, objects associated with the tomb of Christ constituted a great "blessing." The Piacenza Pilgrim vividly describes taking oil as a "blessing" at the Church of the Holy Sepulcher.

> The tomb is hewn out of the living rock, or rather in the rock itself . . . and in the place where the Lord's body was laid, at the head, has been placed a bronze lamp. It burns there day and night, and we took a blessing from it, and then put it back . . . At the moment when the Cross is brought out of this small room for veneration, and arrives in the court to be venerated, a star appears in the sky, and comes over the place where they lay the Cross. It stays overhead whilst they are venerating the Cross, and they offer oil to be blessed in little flasks. When the mouth of one of the little flasks touches the Wood of the Cross, the oil instantly bubbles over, and unless it is closed very quickly it all spills out.[279]

Pilgrims could have used the inscribed candlestick lamps in the ceremonies and rituals at Jerusalem's churches and holy sites and taken them home as *eulogiae*, enabling them to relive the experience and preserve their protective powers. The importance of the Church of the Holy Sepulcher in relation to other sites might explain why candlestick lamps inscribed "the light of Christ shines for all" are so much more common than lamps with other formulas. The production of these inscribed lamps thus catered to the Christian pilgrim trade in Byzantine Jerusalem. Perhaps even some of the uninscribed candlestick lamps were purchased as *eulogiae*.[280]

Conclusion

Following the proclamation of the Edict of Milan and the construction of the Church of the Holy Sepulcher and the Eleona Church, Jerusalem underwent a rapid process of Christianization, benefiting from imperial patronage and an influx of clergy, monks, pilgrims, and immigrants. Churches and monasteries were established around the city and its environs, including the Church on Mount Zion and monastic cells in David's Tower (by the late fourth century); the Church of Siloam, the Church of St. Stephen, and the Church at the Sheep's Pool (by the mid-fifth century); and the Nea Church (mid-sixth century). In addition, by the mid-fifth century the city wall had been extended to the south to include the southeastern hill and the southern end of the southwestern hill, and spacious residences including a large peristyle building were erected south of the Temple Mount. By the mid-sixth century, the peristyle building had been replaced by a large administrative structure and the rest of the area was filled with prosperous residences separated by terraced gardens. Similar houses lined a paved street that led south to the Church of Siloam. By the sixth and seventh centuries the city was bursting at the seams, as other churches, chapels, monasteries, convents, and cemeteries covered the Mount of Olives and the areas outside the north and west walls of the city.

By the time the Madaba Map was made around 600 CE, Jerusalem was a jewel in the crown of the Byzantine Empire. The incense-filled churches were richly decorated with mosaics and marble veneer and equipped with bejeweled ecclesiastical vessels made of precious metals. The broad paved streets connecting the holy sites bustled with throngs of pilgrims and immigrants from as far away as Spain and the Caucasus. Shopkeepers and vendors catered to their needs, offering to sell food, souvenirs, guided tours, and lodging. Solemn processions—a common sight in the churches and streets—must have attracted dozens and even hundreds of participants.

In contrast to the Sasanid Persian invasion in 614, which damaged or destroyed many of Jerusalem's churches and monasteries and was accompanied by the massacre of many of its inhabitants, the transition to Muslim rule was peaceful. Christians continued to worship in churches and monasteries even as the new religion of Islam was introduced and spread. Approximately sixty years after the Muslim conquest, the Umayyads shifted the focus back to the Temple Mount by appropriating the site where the temples dedicated to the God of Israel had stood. Since then, the city has been dominated by two sacred structures only a half a kilometer (one-third of a mile) apart: the Dome of the Rock on the Temple Mount (Arabic *al-haram al-sharif*) and the Church of the Holy Sepulcher.

10

Early Islamic Jerusalem (800 CE)

ON CHRISTMAS DAY, 800 CE, Pope Leo III crowned Charlemagne emperor of the Holy Roman Empire. At the ceremony, which took place in Rome, the king was presented with the keys to the Church of the Holy Sepulcher and a banner of Jerusalem.[1] Charlemagne's decision to be crowned on this date may have been motivated by widespread apocalyptic expectations that the year 800 would usher in a new epoch in human history.[2] It was against this background that Charlemagne established intensive contacts with Harun al-Rashid (786–809), the Abbasid caliph whose empire included the province of Greater Syria (Arabic *Bilad al-Sham*).[3] Within this province, Jerusalem belonged to the district of Palestine (*Jund Filastin*), the capital of which originally was at Lod (ancient Lydda) and was moved to Ramla after its foundation by the Umayyads in 715–717.[4] The ties between Charlemagne and Harun al-Rashid were due, at least in part, to shared interests—the principle that the enemy of my enemy is my friend. For Charlemagne, the Abbasids helped keep the Byzantine Empire in check, while for Harun al-Rashid, the Frankish king was a buffer against the threat posed by the remaining Umayyads (the previous Islamic dynasty) in Spain.[5]

Historical Background

Despite the highly publicized contacts between Charlemagne and Harun al-Rashid, in 800 CE, Jerusalem was a Muslim city dominated by Islamic monuments. Over a century and a half had passed since it surrendered to the caliph Umar between 634–638—a peaceful negotiation that spared the city the kind of damage inflicted by the Sasanids in 614.[6] Throughout the Holy Land, the transition from Byzantine to Islamic rule was generally peaceful and was not accompanied by widespread destructions, nor was it followed by an immediate decline in population and prosperity. Umar was the second in a series of four elected caliphs who ruled the territories conquered by the Muslims after Muhammad's death in 632 CE. Jerusalem and the rest of Palestine fell to the Muslims during Umar's administration (634–644); Caesarea Maritima, the last major city, surrendered in 641 or 642. After the fourth caliph, Ali, was murdered in 661, Mu`awiyya founded the Umayyad dynasty, with its capital at Damascus.[7] By 711, the Umayyad caliphate extended as far west as Spain. In 749, a severe earthquake damaged or destroyed many of the settlements around the Sea of Galilee and the Jordan Valley, and, one year later (750), the Umayyad dynasty was overthrown by the Abbasids, who moved the imperial capital to Baghdad.[8]

Different types of literary works written by Christians and Muslims provide information about early Islamic Jerusalem. These include the accounts of Byzantine chroniclers, Christian pilgrims, and Christian clergy and monks who resided in the city and its environs. Among the Muslim sources is a world geography written ca. 985 by the Jerusalem native Ahmad ibn Muhammad al-Muqaddasi (or al-Maqdisi), and a travelogue written by a Persian named Nasir-i-Khusraw, who visited Jerusalem in 1047.[9] Other sources include documents from the Cairo Geniza (a repository in Cairo's Ben Ezra synagogue) which date to the eleventh century but contain information relating to the previous four centuries.[10]

The Muslims called (and still call) Jerusalem by various names. The earliest Islamic sources refer to the city as *Ilya* or *Iliya*, derived from Hadrian's foundation of Aelia Capitolina. The Arabic term *Bayt al-Maqdis*, corresponding to the Hebrew *Beit ha-Miqdash* ("the temple") originally denoted the Temple Mount and later was applied to the entire city (this is the source of al-Muqaddasi's name, which means "the Jerusalemite"). The Temple Mount became known as *al-haram al-sharif* (the Noble or Sacred Enclosure) or *al-Aqsa*, and Jerusalem came to be called *al-Quds*, the Arabic equivalent of the Hebrew *ha-Qodesh/ha-Qedusah* ("the holy")—terms that are still in use today.[11] These names reflect the Muslim reverence for Jerusalem as a holy city and the recognition of the Haram as the site of Solomon's temple and the place where David prayed.[12] This chapter uses the term Haram (pronounced "khah-RAHM") for the Temple Mount.

Muhammad is said to have first prayed facing Jerusalem, only later reorienting the direction of prayer (*qibla*) toward Mecca.[13] Eventually, Muslim tradition came to associate Jerusalem with Muhammad's night journey (*isra'*), an episode described in Sura (Chapter) 17:1 in the Qu`ran: "Exalted is He who took His Servant by night from *al-masjid al-haram* (the sacred enclosure in Mecca) to *al-masjid al-aqsā* (the Furthest Mosque), whose surroundings We have blessed, to show him of Our signs. Indeed, He is the Hearing, the Seeing."[14] Muhammad is said to have been carried on a winged horse-like beast called al-Buraq ("the lightning") and led by the angel Gabriel (Arabic *Jibrail*).[15] The term *al-masjid al-aqsa* (the Furthest Mosque) can be understood as denoting a physical space or a structure or even a heavenly temple. By the first half of the eighth century,

Muslim tradition identified it with the Haram in Jerusalem, where Muhammad is believed to have dismounted and prayed in the company of Abraham, Moses, Jesus, and the other prophets.[16]

By the tenth century, a separate tradition about Muhammad's miraculous ascent to heaven (mi'raj), which is not in the Qur'an, became connected with the night journey and was localized in Jerusalem.[17] According to this story, Muhammad first traveled to Jerusalem or the Haram (identified with the Furthest Mosque) and from there ascended to heaven, where the doctrinal principles of the new religion were revealed to him.[18] Eventually, the rocky outcrop (Foundation Stone) in the Dome of the Rock was identified as the site of Muhammad's ascent to heaven. The association of the Haram with Muhammad's night journey and ascension reflect expectations—common also among Jews and Christians—connecting Jerusalem to the Last Judgment at the End of Days.[19]

Although over time the number of Muslim inhabitants increased, in 800 CE Jerusalem was still home to a sizeable Christian population that encompassed diverse communities: the dominant Melkites (Greek Orthodox), who were represented by the Patriarch, as well as Syrian Jacobites and Egyptian Copts (both Monophysite churches), Armenians, Georgians, and Latins.[20] Under Muslim rule Jews were again permitted to reside in the city, and, by the ninth century, the Jewish population included both rabbinic Jews and Karaites (who reject rabbinic authority).[21] In fact, in the tenth century, al-Muqaddasi complained that "Everywhere [in Jerusalem] the Christians and Jews have the upper hand."[22] Early Islamic rulers were tolerant of other religions, although non-Muslims (dhimmis) were required to pay a personal poll tax (jizya) and were subject to other restrictions.[23]

Literary sources indicate that Christians clustered in the northwest part of the city, around the Church of the Holy Sepulcher, roughly corresponding to the modern-day Christian Quarter, and extending along the west side of the southwestern hill to Mount Zion, while Jews settled on the Ophel or on the southeastern hill.[24] The Muslim settlement focused on the Haram and was concentrated around its western and southern sides. Donald Whitcomb describes early Islamic Jerusalem—with Christians on the west and Muslims on the east—as a type of "twin city" that may have Arabian roots.[25]

Archaeological Evidence

When Jerusalem surrendered to the Muslims, it was a thoroughly Christian city filled with richly decorated churches and monasteries and bustling with clergy, monks, and pilgrims. A half a century later, the city was transformed by the Umayyads, who erected a series of buildings on and around the Haram—above all, the Dome of the Rock, which is still the city's most conspicuous monument. This building program was carried out by the caliphs ʿAbd al-Malik (685–705) and his son al-Walid (705–715). The Umayyads also rebuilt or repaired the city walls, which had been damaged by the Sasanids in 614.

The Haram: The Mosque of Umar

Several traditions suggest that Umar built a mosque in Jerusalem after the city surrendered.[26] The main source is an account attributed to a Gallic bishop named Arculf, who reportedly visited Jerusalem around 670: "However, in the celebrated place where once the temple (situated toward the east near the wall) arose in its magnificence, the Saracens [Arabs] now have a quadrangular prayer house. They built it roughly by erecting upright boards and great beams on some ruined remains. The building, it is said, can accommodate three thousand people at once."[27]

Arculf's account is preserved in *De locis sanctis* ("On the Holy Places"), a book written by Adomnán, the abbot of the remote island monastery of Iona off the west coast of modern Scotland.[28] Because is difficult to assess the reliability of the information attributed to Arculf, some scholars question whether he even existed. In this case, Arculf might have been a literary fiction (an invented character), even if Adomnán drew on the reports of travelers to Jerusalem.[29]

Some scholars argue that the lack of archaeological remains of the Mosque of Umar indicate there was no such building because the entire esplanade served as a mosque.[30] However, the evidence of absence is not decisive because a structure made of wood would leave few traces. The size of the mosque as reported by Arculf has also been questioned, as 3,000 could be a symbolic number derived from the Hebrew Bible.[31] Even scholars who believe there was a building called the Mosque of Umar disagree about its location: at the southern end of the Haram, or next to the Church of the Holy Sepulcher—a tradition based on late Christian sources.[32] In any case, by the early eighth century, the Mosque of Umar (if such a building existed) had been replaced or superseded by al-Aqsa Mosque, which was constructed at the southern end of the Haram.

The Haram: The Dome of the Rock (Qubbat al-Sakhra)

The Dome of the Rock (Arabic *Qubbat al-Sakhra*) sits on an elevated trapezoidal platform in the center of the Haram, approached on all sides by staircases. The current form of the staircases and the arcades at the top of them is a product of later centuries.[33] A dedicatory inscription by ʿAbd al-Malik inside the Dome of the Rock dates to AH 72 = 691/692 CE, indicating either when the project was begun or completed (AH = After the Hegira, referring to Muhammad's flight from Mecca to Medina in 622 CE).[34] Although most of the original exterior decoration has been replaced, the original structure and much of the interior decoration are intact, making it the earliest Muslim monument still standing anywhere in the world (Pl. 14A).[35]

The building is octagonal, with four entrances facing the four cardinal points. Inside it is divided into two concentric ambulatories (outer and inner) surrounding a circular central area with the rocky outcrop (Foundation Stone) in the center (Figures 10.1 and 10.2). The rocky outcrop is encircled by piers and columns that support a tall cylindrical drum with the dome above (Pl. 13B). The two ambulatories are separated by an octagonal arcade (series of arches) consisting of groups of columns between piers.[36] The diameter of the dome is equal to its height (ca. 20 meters/67 feet), which is also the length of each of the octagon's sides.[37] The building is 48 meters in diameter. The dome consists of an inner and outer wooden shell separated by a space; the current copper-plated dome is a product of the second half of the twentieth century.[38]

The polychrome tiles on the upper part of the exterior are a twentieth-century replacement for the original seventh-century glass mosaics, which are still preserved on the undersides of the arched passages above the four entrances.[39] The marble panels, which are split to display the veins decoratively, cover the lower part of the outer walls as well as the walls and piers inside (Pl. 14B). They are original, as are the marble columns and capitals, many of which were spoliated from ruined Byzantine churches and possibly from the second temple.[40] Inside, a continuous marble frieze above the marble panels is carved with vegetal motifs (such as winged palmettes, rosettes, flowers, and fruit) created by chiseling out the background around them, leaving the motifs in shallow relief. The background is painted in dark colors, so that the vegetal motifs not only project from the background but contrast with it—a decorative technique called *champlevé*.[41] Most of the rest of the interior decoration also dates to the seventh century, including the blue, green, and gold glass mosaics and white mother-of-pearl inlays on both faces of the octagonal arcade that separates the two ambulatories, on the circular arcade around the Foundation Stone, and on the drum of the dome (Pl. 15A).[42] Boaz Shoshan notes that "the approximately 1,200 square meters of mosaics [is] the largest preserved program of wall mosaics anywhere in the Mediterranean region before the 12th century."[43]

The use of marble sheathing on walls with colored and gold mosaics on the curvilinear surfaces above is common in Roman and Byzantine architecture. The mosaics in the Dome of the Rock depict richly bejeweled crowns, tiaras, bracelets, pendants, and necklaces; stylized plants and winged objects growing out of bejeweled amphoras (vases); and trees and date palms with fruit.[44] The crowns

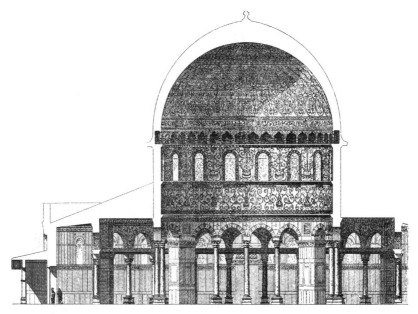

FIGURE 10.1 Section through the Dome of the Rock by Frederick Catherwood. Credit: Georg Dehio Gustav von Bezold, via Wikimedia Commons.

and jewels appear to represent the royal or imperial ornaments worn by Byzantine and Sasanid rulers and by Christ, the Virgin, and saints in Byzantine art, symbolizing the subjugation of these rival powers to the Muslims.[45]

Many early churches, synagogues, and mosques are basilicas—large rectangular buildings with rows of columns to support the roof—as these are ideally suited for congregational prayer and worship. In contrast, the Dome of the Rock is a centralized building, that is, a structure built around a central focal point—a plan characteristic of martyria (singular: martyrium) (see Chapter 9).[46] Whereas basilicas have pitched, tiled roofs supported on wooden trusses, centralized buildings typically have a dome representing the celestial sphere (the "dome of heaven"). Centralized buildings were designed to enable pilgrims to circumambulate an object of veneration in the center, as for example the tomb of Christ in the Rotunda of the Church of the Holy Sepulcher or the Foundation Stone in the Dome of the Rock. In fact, the Dome of the Rock copies not only the main elements of the Rotunda—a domed, circular core surrounded by an ambulatory (circular in the Rotunda and octagonal in the Dome of the Rock), with an additional octagonal ambulatory added around the Dome of the Rock—but also its dimensions: in both monuments the diameter of the dome is ca. 20 meters (65 feet) and the diameter of the ambulatory surrounding the inner circle is 38 meters (125 feet).[47] Although individuals can (and do) pray inside these structures, they

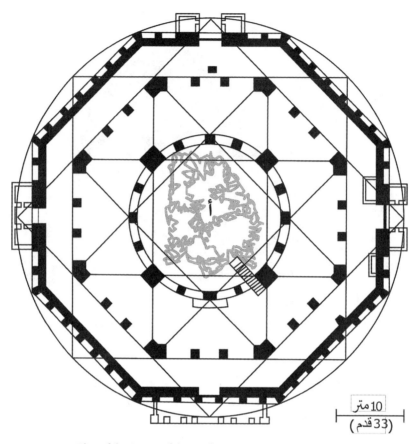

FIGURE 10.2 Plan of the Dome of the Rock.
Credit: ءارب, CC BY-SA 4.0, via Wikimedia Commons.

were not designed to accommodate congregational worship. This is why in the
Church of the Holy Sepulcher, Constantine's basilica (church) was paired with
the Rotunda, just as on the Haram, al-Aqsa Mosque (and perhaps before it, the
Mosque of Umar) was paired with the Dome of the Rock.[48] Indeed, the dedicatory inscription inside the Dome of the Rock refers to it not as a mosque but as a
qubba ("cube" = dome).[49] In addition to the similarities to martyria, the Dome of
the Rock's design recalls the Ka`aba in Mecca, which is also circumambulated by
pilgrims, albeit not inside a building.[50]

Although there is no doubt that the Dome of the Rock was built to enshrine
the Foundation Stone in its center, scholars disagree about why `Abd al-Malik
erected the structure. What was the significance of the rock to Muslims in the
seventh century? Different interpretations have been proposed based on the layout, decoration, and the inscriptions inside the building, as well as the testimony

of writers such as al-Muqaddasi and early Islamic traditions. Although the location of the rocky outcrop relative to the first and second temples is unclear, by the early Islamic period Jews and Muslims believed it was the Foundation Stone in the former temple(s) and therefore the navel (omphalos) of the earth.[51] They also identified it as Mount Moriah—the spot where Abraham offered his son for sacrifice (Isaac in Jewish tradition and Ishmael in Islamic tradition).[52] For seventh-century Muslims, therefore, the Dome of the Rock was a new temple built by the divinely appointed successor to David and Solomon, with Muhammad as the culminating link in the chain of biblical prophets. As the True Israel, Islam brings to fulfilment the requirements associated with the arrival of the End of Days.[53] The reconstruction of the "temple" countered Christian supersessionist claims based on the ruined state of the Temple Mount under Byzantine rule.[54] Writing in the tenth century, al-Muqaddasi says that his uncle told him the Dome of the Rock was built to compete with the Rotunda of the Church of the Holy Sepulcher: "And in like manner is it not evident how the Khalif ʿAbd al Malik, noting the greatness of the Dome of the (Holy Sepulcher called) Al Kumâmah and its magnificence, was moved lest it should dazzle the minds of the Muslims, and hence erected above the Rock, the Dome which now is seen there?" (al-Muqaddasi 159).[55] *Qubbat al-kumama* ("the dome of the garbage heap/dunghill") is a pejorative pun on the Arabic name of the Church of the Holy Sepulcher: *kanisat al-qiyama* ("the Church of the Resurrection").[56]

The Dome of the Rock's prominent location on the site of the former temples and its similarities in plan and decoration to early Christian martyria, above all the Rotunda of the Church of the Holy Sepulcher, were intended to express the triumph of Islam. This message is conveyed by a 240-meter-long (816-foot) inscription in a mosaic frieze that encircles the top of the intermediate octagon.[57] The inscription is contemporary with the building's construction except in one spot where the ninth century Abbasid caliph al-Maʾamun (full name: Abu al-Abbas ʿAbd Allah al-Maʾamun Ibn al-Rashid) replaced ʿAbd al-Malik's name with his own but without changing the original dedication date.[58] It combines the *basmala* (invocation: "In the name of God, the All-merciful, the All-compassionate") and *shahadah* (profession or affirmation of faith: "There is no god except God [Allah], alone, Muhammad is the Prophet of God [or messenger]") with quotations of passages from the Qurʿan that emphasize the fundamental principles of Islam and clarify the position of Jesus, Mary, and the other prophets in Islamic theology in relation to Christian beliefs.[59]

For example, the inscription quotes Qurʿan Sura 112:1–4: "*In the name of God, the All-merciful, the All-compassionate. There is no god but God alone. He has no partner. Say: 'He is God, the One. God, the Undivided. He did not give birth, nor was He born. There is no other equal to Him. Muhammad is the messenger* of God, may God bless him."[60] Other passages from the Qur`an (Suras 4 and 19) are aimed at "the People of the Book" (Christians and Jews) and state that God is one, Jesus is a prophet but not the son of God, and deny the doctrine of the Trinity:

> O people of the book, do not go beyond the bounds of your religion, nor say anything but the truth about God. The Messiah, Jesus son of Mary, was only the messenger of God and His word which He imparted to Mary, and a spirit from Him. So believe in God and his messengers and do not say "Three." Refrain, it is better for you. Rather, God is one God. Praise be to him that He should have a son! To Him belongs what is in the heavens and on the earth. God suffices as a Guardian. The Messiah does not disdain to be a servant of God nor do the nearby angels. Whoever disdains to serve him and is proud, He will gather to them to Him all together. O God, bless your messenger and servant, Jesus son of Mary. May peace be upon him the day he was born, the day he dies, and the day he is raised alive. That is Jesus, son of Mary, a statement of the truth about which you are in doubt. It is not for God to take a son. Glory be to Him![61]

These passages were aimed not only at Christians and Jews but were intended to educate new and potential converts to Islam.[62] The message aimed at Jews is that the Muslim caliph is the messiah who has fulfilled the expectations associated with the End of Days by rebuilding the temple.[63] Therefore, according to Oleg Grabar, the inscription expresses two themes: mission and eschatology.[64] Gülru Necipoğlu identifies three interrelated themes in the inscription and in `Abd al-Malik's overall building program on the Haram: the absolute sovereignty and mercy of God as judge, the privileged position of Muhammad, and the divine origin of earthly authority.[65]

The eschatological theme is expressed in other ways as well. For example, an inscription over the building's east entrance, which faces the Mount of Olives—the direction from which the messiah will come according to Jewish belief—refers to resurrection and judgment.[66] The octagonal shape of the Dome of the Rock likely reflects the association of the number eight with resurrection and Paradise.[67] Myriam Rosen-Ayalon notes that the jewels and floral motifs depicted in the mosaics allude to Paradise and the End of Days, with the trees representing the "Tree of Life," a motif that was symbolized in Christian art by the cross.[68] The colors of the mosaics also allude to these themes, with the blue border representing the ocean encircling the earth, green evoking the lush vegetation of paradise, and gold symbolizing the celestial sphere, arranged around the Foundation Stone and capped by the dome of heaven above.[69]

The belief that Jerusalem will be the site of the Last Judgment was shared by Jews, Christians, and Muslims, as was the identification of the "temple" building (first and second temples/Rotunda/Dome of the Rock) as the meeting point of heaven and earth.[70] Rosen-Ayalon concludes that the Dome of the Rock functions similarly to the Anastasis (Rotunda) by reestablishing the Haram and specifically the rocky outcrop—not the Church of the Holy Sepulcher—as the omphalos of the earth.[71] The crowns, jewels, and floral motifs in the mosaics might also have been intended to recall the rich decoration of Solomon's temple, thereby creating a visual linkage between the Dome of the Rock and its predecessor on the site.[72]

According to another view, ʿAbd al-Malik built the Dome of the Rock to divert pilgrimage from Mecca, which was under the control of a rival named Abdullah ibn al-Zubayr, thereby establishing Jerusalem as the main religious center of Islam. Scholars who reject this proposal question the reliability of the literary sources as well as the likelihood that ʿAbd al-Malik would have risked being branded a *kafir* (apostate) by challenging the primacy of the Kaʿaba in Mecca.[73] In response, Amikam Elad argues that ʿAbd al-Malik sought to emphasize Jerusalem's centrality by constructing the Dome of the Rock on the site of Solomon's temple and as a rival to Mecca, which was under rival control.[74]

As Elad notes, the different reasons that have been proposed for ʿAbd al-Malik's construction of the Dome of the Rock are not mutually exclusive and reflect the complexity of this monument. The similarities between the Dome of the Rock and the Kaʿaba, which consist of a sacred rock circumambulated by pilgrims, support the possibility that ʿAbd al-Malik intended Jerusalem to rival Mecca.[75] The identification of the rocky outcrop as Mount Moriah also connected Jerusalem to Abraham, whom Muslims consider to be the first true monotheist and whom, they believe, together with his son Ishmael, established the Kaʿaba as a sacred shrine.[76] Even if there was no intention to divert pilgrimage from Mecca, ʿAbd al-Malik's construction of the Dome of the Rock must be understood within the context of internal challenges to his authority by the Zubayrids, whom he defeated in 692 CE, and by the Kharijites—rebels who believed that judgment belongs to God alone.[77]

The Dome of the Rock blurs the boundaries of time and space by representing earthly and cosmic (heavenly) themes in the building's architecture and decoration, and by alluding to the past (Solomon's temple), present, and future (Final Judgment). It connects the caliph—the legitimate successor of David and Solomon and earthly king and judge—to God as the divine king and judge through the mediation of Muhammad, the last in the series of biblical prophets.[78] Although scholars disagree about Jerusalem's status relative to Mecca in the earliest phase of Islam and debate whether the influence of Jewish and Christian traditions indicates that significant numbers of Jews and Christians were among

Muhammad's followers, there is no doubt that the construction of the Dome of the Rock and other buildings by the Umayyads transformed the city's appearance and reflect its importance.[79] This was the Jerusalem visited by Charlemagne's delegations and, later, the Crusaders.

The Haram: al-Aqsa Mosque

Al-Aqsa Mosque is a hall for congregational worship and prayer at the southern end of the Haram (Figures 10.3 and 10.4). Because the only archaeological information comes from limited soundings under the floor conducted in the middle of the twentieth century by Robert Hamilton, the building's early construction history and original layout are murky. Hamilton distinguished three successive early buildings (Aqsa I, II, and III).[80] The earliest building (I) apparently was a rectangular hall with columns. Although Hamilton assigned Aqsa I to `Abd al-Malik and his son al-Walid I, some scholars now believe it was constructed by Mu`awiyya (in the 660s), arguing that the building is too crude to be contemporary with the Dome of the Rock. Instead, they assign Aqsa II, which is a larger building, to `Abd al-Malik and al-Walid.[81] Scholars also disagree on the size of Aqsa II: whereas Hamilton reconstructed the building as having fifteen aisles inside (separated by rows of columns), Rafi Grafman and Rosen-Ayalon estimate that it was over twice the size of the current mosque and would have extended for

FIGURE 10.3 Al-Aqsa Mosque.
Credit: Photo by the author.

FIGURE 10.4 Interior of al-Aqsa Mosque.
Credit: LoC Matson matpc 05895.

more than 100 meters (328 feet) along the southern end of the Haram—roughly the same area as Herod's Royal Stoa.[82]

The problems in determining the original size and layout of al-Aqsa Mosque are due to its location. Unlike the Dome of the Rock, which is founded on bedrock, al-Aqsa Mosque is built over the underground arches and vaults ("Solomon's Stables") that support the southern end of the esplanade. Because the hollow space under the mosque is not a stable foundation, the structure is prone to earthquake damage and has been rebuilt and repaired over time. The current building is largely the product of a renovation carried out after the earthquake of 1033.[83]

Papyri from Aphrodito in Egypt that date to the reign of al-Walid mention laborers, skilled workmen, and building materials from that country employed in the construction of "the mosque of Jerusalem."[84] Early Islamic sources written shortly before 800 describe al-Aqsa Mosque as a rectangular structure with a wide central nave flanked on either side by seven rows of arched columns (arcades) separating the aisles. The main *mihrab* with a niche indicating the *qibla* was in the south wall at the end of the nave. Fifteen doorways in the north wall provided access to the nave and aisles.[85]

Amazingly, roof and ceiling beams and panels made of cedar and cypress wood still survive from the late seventh–early eighth century mosque, although many of them have since been removed from the building. Some are elaborately carved in relief with floral motifs (vines, grape clusters and leaves, rosettes, and palmettes) and were painted in bright colors, traces of which are visible.[86] Because timbers for the construction and roofing of buildings are a scarce commodity in this region, they were often recycled, as is evident in the panels and beams from al-Aqsa Mosque. Some have cuttings indicating they originally were fitted into a different structure, and some are decorated with carvings that are pre-Islamic (Roman or Byzantine) in style. One beam has an inscription of the Byzantine period, which indicates that it originated in a church dedicated to St. Thomas the Apostle:[87] "In the time of the most holy archbishop and patriarch Peter and of the most God-beloved (X. priest and oeconomus?) this whole house [church] of Saint Thomas was erected (or, renewed) from the foun(dations. Year. . . ?)." The inscription can be dated precisely as the only patriarch in Jerusalem named Peter before the time of the Crusades officiated from 524–552 CE.[88] Other reused beams and panels presumably were also removed from nearby churches that were lying in ruins when al-Aqsa Mosque was constructed. Radiocarbon dating has confirmed that some of the wood dates to the Byzantine period, while some is even earlier, ranging from the ninth century BCE to the third–fourth centuries CE. The beams and panels must have originated in monuments in and around the Haram, such as Herod's Royal Stoa or perhaps even one of Solomon's structures (the temple or his palace), and they could have been reused in different buildings over time.[89]

The Haram: The Dome of the Chain (Qubbat al-Silsila)

To the east of the Dome of the Rock is an enigmatic monument called the Dome of the Chain (Pl. 14A). It is a small octagonal structure measuring 14 meters (46 feet) in diameter, with two concentric circles of columns: a central hexagon (six columns) supporting a central cupola, within an eleven-sided polygon (a hendecagon). Unlike the Dome of the Rock, the Dome of the Chain is open on all sides.[90] Although the structure is thought to be Umayyad, its precise date is unknown. Whereas many scholars believe it was constructed by 'Abd al-Malik, Lawrence Nees attributes the monument to Mu'awiyya's reign (661–680), when (he argues) the entire Haram served as a mosque (the Mosque of Umar). If this is correct, the Dome of the Chain would antedate the Dome of the Rock. Although much of the structure is original, the superstructure above the columns was later reworked, the original glass mosaics decorating the structure were replaced in the sixteenth century by glazed tiles, and the *mihrab* in the south side is a later addition.[91]

The function of the Dome of the Chain is unknown. The monument lies in the exact center of the Haram, at the intersection of the two main axes and next to the rocky outcrop (Foundation Stone). It is also aligned with a secondary *mihrab* in al-Aqsa Mosque (the main *mihrab* in the center of the south wall of al-Aqsa Mosque is farther to the west). Rosen-Ayalon suggests that this secondary *mihrab* was the *mihrab* in the Mosque of Umar, which she believes was located on this spot.[92] The location of the Dome of the Chain indicates that it might have marked the omphalos of the Haram and, therefore, of the world, with the other early Islamic monuments constructed in relation to this spot.[93]

According to later Islamic sources, the Dome of the Chain was a model for the Dome of the Rock, or was the place of Final Judgment, or was a treasury of the caliphate or local community.[94] It might be the dome "next to the Rock" where al-Walid's successor Sulayman was invested as caliph and distributed gifts to the populace.[95] According to one recent proposal, the monument indicated the *qibla* (direction of prayer) prior to the construction of the Dome of the Rock and was the spot where the caliph sat in judgment and led communal prayers. In this case, the term "chain"—an object that was a symbol of royal judgment, might reflect the structure's original function.[96]

The Umayyad Buildings Around the Southern and Western Sides of the Haram

In addition to the monuments they erected on the Haram, the Umayyads repaired the temenos wall and modified or rebuilt some of its gates, including the Golden Gate, the Huldah (Double and Triple) Gates, and perhaps Wilson's Arch, and probably the cryptoporticus under the southern end of the esplanade ("Solomon's Stables").[97] But by far the most important archaeological discovery of the Umayyad period in Jerusalem is four (or perhaps five) monumental buildings outside the southern and western walls of the Haram (Figures 10.5 and 10.6; Pl. 15B). The remains of one building (II) were first exposed in limited soundings by Kathleen Kenyon in 1961–1963 (Sites G and J). Roland de Vaux, who supervised the field work, suggested that the building was part of a Byzantine hospice connected to Justinian's Nea Church.[98] The rest of Building II as well as one or more buildings to its east (V–VII) and two buildings to its west (III–IV) came to light in Benjamin Mazar's 1968–1978 excavations. The discovery of these buildings came as a surprise as there was no previous hint of their existence from archaeology or literary sources.[99]

The buildings extend from the area outside (below and to the west of) Robinson's Arch on the west (which was destroyed in 70 CE) to the south side of the Haram and were located inside the Byzantine city wall around Mount Zion and the southeastern hill. By the eleventh–thirteenth centuries, the city wall had contracted to its current line, leaving most of the Umayyad buildings, which were

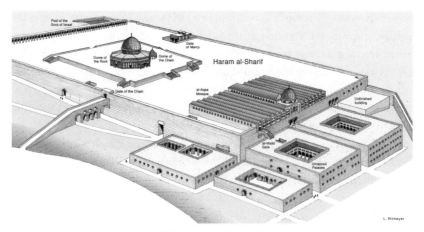

FIGURE 10.5 Reconstruction of the Umayyad Temple Mount and palaces.
Credit: © by Leen Ritmeyer.

FIGURE 10.6 Southwest corner of the Temple Mount with the wall of a monumental
Umayyad building (II) in the foreground.
Credit: Photo by the author.

now in ruins, outside it. The buildings were dismantled down to the foundations, the stones in their walls were robbed out for reuse, and the new city wall was constructed over the south wall of the building below Robinson's Arch (Building IV).[100]

Although the buildings differ in plan, they all have open courtyards surrounded by rooms. The courtyards were paved with stone and perhaps planted with trees.[101] Ornately carved pieces of marble fragments, colorful painted fresco fragments depicting floral motifs, and mosaic tesserae (cubes) indicate that the rooms were richly decorated.[102] The largest building (II), located at the southwest corner of the Haram, measures approximately 96 × 84 meters (315 × 275 feet) and has outer walls that are 2.75–3.10 meters (9–10 feet) thick. It consists of a central open courtyard surrounded by a colonnaded porch (a peristyle) and rows of elongated rooms on all four sides. The rooms measure between 17–20 meters (55–65 feet) long by 4–8 meters (13–26 feet) wide and likely were used for storage. Square piers at regular intervals along the long walls supported a vaulted ceiling and upper story, where the living quarters or public rooms were located.[103] B. Mazar and his assistant Meir Ben-Dov suggested that staircases on four sides of the complex (in narrow passages between the rooms on the north and south sides on the one hand, and the east and west sides on the other) provided access to a second story level. Each story was at least 6.5 meters (21 feet) high. The main gate was in the middle of the east side of the building, with other gates in the middle of the west and north sides. A bridge on the north side at the second story level provided direct access to al-Aqsa mosque.[104] The building was served by a sophisticated system of gutters and drainage channels for rainwater and waste.

A second building (III) located immediately to the west of Building II has a similar plan consisting of elongated rooms around a central peristyle courtyard. There is a row of six elongated rooms in the southeast corner of the building, and large square piers in the southwest corner supported a system of arches and vaults. The main gate was in the middle of the east side (directly opposite the west gate of Building II), with other gates in the middle of the north and west sides, as in Building II. And like Building II, Building III was equipped with a sophisticated drainage system.

In 1995–1997, renewed excavations conducted by Ronny Reich, Yaakov Billig, and Yuval Baruch revealed that Building III is larger than B. Mazar and Ben-Dov thought, measuring ca. 75 x 75 meters (246 × 246 feet).[105] It extends as far as the line of the eastern cardo along the Tyropoeon Valley, which Baruch and Reich suggest separated the administrative or government quarter from the civilian part of town. Baruch and Reich excavated four elongated rooms in the southeast corner of Building III that have square piers at regular intervals as in Building II. They note that these rooms contained deliberately dumped fills. In some cases, the fills were deposited in conjunction with the raising of the walls, and, in other cases, they were deposited after the walls were finished. In other words, the elongated rooms represent foundations that were filled with dumped material to level the area.

In Buildings II and III, the lower parts of the walls of the elongated rooms were constructed of a concrete mixture consisting of stones and gray lime mortar. This mixture was poured into a wood form or scaffolding. The upper parts of the walls were constructed of large, roughly cut stones, with small stones between them, held together by gray mortar containing charcoal. The walls were not plastered.[106]

To the north of Building III, B. Mazar and Ben-Dov uncovered part of a building (IV) to the west of the Haram and opposite Robinson's Arch. It differs in plan from the other two buildings in having two large courtyards surrounded by rows of square piers but no elongated rooms. Elongated rooms might have been used to create foundations in areas where the bedrock is very deep and steeply sloping, whereas square piers were employed in areas where the bedrock was close to the contemporary ground level.[107] Building IV incorporates the remains of a Roman legionary bath house, which seems to have remained in use as a bath house.

B. Mazar and Ben-Dov note that all three buildings had been robbed out, leaving only small sections of the walls and a few patches of floors surviving at or above ground level. Reich and Baruch also found little evidence of floors in Building III. Much of the robbing seems to have occurred in the Fatimid period (eleventh century).[108] Most of the floors on the ground story of the buildings were of stone. Because the flagstones were laid on a layer of terra rosa (soil), Ben-Dov suggests they were temporary floors meant to be replaced with mosaics. In some places, patches of mosaics were preserved, mostly of large white tesserae with no design or simple designs. In Building IV a pavement of large square polished flagstones was preserved.

B. Mazar and Ben-Dov assign the buildings to the Umayyad period based on the following considerations: (1) the buildings directly overlie houses from the end of the Byzantine period; (2) the plans of the buildings resemble Umayyad *qusur* (semi-fortified rural palaces), such as those at Khirbet al-Mafjar and Khirbet al-Minya; and (3) they date the finds from the drainage channels in the buildings to the Umayyad period. Specifically, B. Mazar and Ben-Dov attribute the construction of these buildings to al-Walid (705–715), the son of ʿAbd al-Malik (685–705).[109] They propose identifying Bab al-Walid, a gate in the Haram mentioned by al-Muqaddasi, with the gate leading from Building II to the south end of the Haram. If they are correct, this gate was still functioning in the tenth century. According to B. Mazar and Ben-Dov, the buildings were destroyed in the earthquake of 749.[110] Because there were no signs of collapse

(i.e., no piles of stones associated with the collapse of the walls) and few surviving floors, they conclude that construction halted before the completion of
the project: "The ambitious building program inaugurated in the days of Abd-
al-Malik was never fully consummated, so that several details of the Omayyad
buildings—including the final flooring—were never completed."[111]

In all the buildings, the excavators found evidence of later reoccupation,
which they associate with squatters, including later walls that incorporated spolia
and abutted the original walls, creating rooms that had no relationship to the
original building plan. The floors associated with this reoccupation were at a
higher level than the original floor level. In Building III, Baruch and Reich found
mosaic floors, some with simple designs at a higher level, which they associate
with this later reoccupation. Elsewhere Baruch and Reich describe lime or chalk
floors with ovens, thin walls, channels, and pits. B. Mazar and Ben-Dov, and
Baruch and Reich, date the reoccupation of these buildings to the Abbasid period
(late eighth to ninth century) based on the associated finds. Specifically, Baruch
and Reich describe the associated finds as including "glazed pottery and large
quantities of animal bones, especially sheep."[112] After this brief reoccupation, the
buildings were abandoned and robbed out.

According to B. Mazar and Ben-Dov, this grandiose Umayyad building
project was abandoned before the earthquake of 749 due to economic decline.
The unfinished buildings were brought down by the earthquake, which Ben-
Dov says caused cracked or warped foundations and walls, fallen columns, and
sunken floors. With the fall of the Umayyads and the rise of the Abbasid dynasty
the following year, the center of power shifted to the east, leaving Syria and
Palestine a backwater. In Ben-Dov's opinion, the archaeological remains indicate
that the Abbasids went out of their way to obliterate everything associated with
the Umayyads, including refraining from building on and around the Haram.[113]

However, although no final excavation reports have appeared in print, preliminary publications suggest a different sequence of events. First, Baruch and
Reich mention finding Umayyad coins in the foundation level fills in Building
III, including one dating to ca. 730 from inside the foundations of the courtyard's peristyle wall.[114] This indicates that construction of these buildings was
still underway during the reign of Hisham (724–743), assuming the project was
initiated by al-Walid, which is not surprising given the scale of the undertaking.
Second, the signs of damage described by Ben-Dov (cracked walls and warped
foundations, fallen columns, and sunken floors) could have been caused by a later
earthquake, perhaps that of 1033, which apparently damaged al-Aqsa mosque as
well (as a result, the number of gates into the mosque was reduced). It was after
this earthquake (in 1033) that the city walls were rebuilt, along the lines preserved

today, with the south wall of the Old City overlying the early Islamic buildings. The robbing activity must have occurred after this.

I also question the excavators' conclusion that all the buildings were unfinished (Ben-Dov describes them as "shells") when construction stopped. If this were the case, we would not expect the plumbing system to have been functioning. However, according to Ben-Dov, the sewage system in Building II, which included drainage pipes from the second story level was blocked with occupational debris and refuse. This debris included pottery types dating to the Abbasid period, indicating that the main phase of occupation continued at least into the ninth century.[115]

It appears, therefore, that these buildings were constructed in the latter part of the Umayyad period. Even if the project was initiated by al-Walid, work continued at least through the reign of Hisham. The construction of Buildings II, III, and IV seems to have been completed, unlike the buildings to the east (V–VII). It is not clear if the earthquake of 749 caused significant damage.[116] However, the ceramic evidence indicates that occupation continued into the Abbasid period. This scenario is supported by B. Mazar and Ben-Dov's identification of Bab al-Walid as the gate leading from Building II to the south end of the Haram, which, if they are correct, was still functioning in al-Muqaddasi's time. However, around this time or soon afterward, the buildings were abandoned and began to collapse, and some of the original floors and parts of the walls were robbed out. This was followed by a brief phase of reoccupation by a different population. Although this occupation is poorer than the original phase, the presence of mosaic floors indicates that the inhabitants were not squatters. I propose dating this occupation phase to the tenth to early eleventh century.[117] The earthquake of 1033 might have caused the damage noted by Ben-Dov, after which time the buildings were permanently abandoned and the remaining walls and floors were robbed out.[118]

The large size and lavish decoration of Building II, the alignment of its west wall with the west wall of the Haram and the bridge connecting it to al-Aqsa Mosque have led many scholars to identify it as an Umayyad palace—perhaps the palace of *Amir al-Mu'minim* (the "Commander of the Faithful") mentioned in the Aphrodito papyri with "the mosque of Jerusalem" as having been constructed using Egyptian laborers.[119] In this case, the building could be a type of early Islamic governor's residence called a *dar al-imara*, an identification supported by its resemblance to Umayyad palaces at other sites such as Khirbet al-Mafjar (near Jericho) and Khirbet al-Minya (by the Sea of Galilee).[120] This might explain why one of the names for Jerusalem in the early Islamic period was *al-Balat* ("the court" or "royal residence"), a term that derives from the Latin *palatium*—the source of our word "palace."[121] The absence of the fortification walls and towers that characterize other Umayyad palaces can be explained by Building II's location within Jerusalem's city walls.[122] The function of the other buildings is unknown, with proposed identifications ranging from administrative buildings to servants' quarters to storehouses to hostels or hospices for pilgrims.[123] According to some scholars, these buildings indicate that Mu'awiyya, the founder of the Umayyad dynasty, intended to make Jerusalem, not Damascus, his political capital.[124]

Some scholars have challenged the identification of these buildings as palaces or an administrative center on the grounds that, under the Umayyads, Ramla was the provincial capital whereas Jerusalem was a religious center but not a seat of government. Therefore, there would have been no need for a *dar al-imara* in Jerusalem.[125] They note that the dark, narrow rooms surrounding the central courtyards of Buildings II and III might be suitable as military barracks or for civilian occupation but are not appropriate for royal habitation.[126] Furthermore, the palace of *Amir al-Mu'minim* mentioned in the Aphrodito papyri might have been in Fustat in Egypt, not in Jerusalem.[127] These scholars also question the Umayyad date of the buildings, suggesting they might have been constructed in the Byzantine period and continued in use in the early Islamic period.[128] They argue that the Umayyad caliphs had neither the time nor the resources to carry out such a massive building project.[129] It also seems odd that literary sources of the early Islamic period, including al-Muqaddasi, make no mention of any such buildings.[130] Finally, according to these scholars, the lack of fortifications and the bridge connecting Building II with al-Aqsa Mosque would not be suitable for a caliph because the building would have been open and unsecure.[131] Accordingly, they propose that the buildings were used as hostels for Christian (and later, Muslim) pilgrims, living quarters for guest workers, storerooms, and/or workshops.[132]

Jacob Lassner has posed the most recent and detailed challenge to the identification of these buildings as palaces or an administrative center of the Umayyad period, going so far as to refer to them as "Islamic" in quotes and titling the relevant chapter in his book, "The So-Called Umayyad Administrative Center."[133] Lassner claims that the large buildings discovered above the Byzantine houses could have been built later in the Byzantine period and then continued in use in the early Islamic period.[134] However, although the function of these buildings may be open to debate, their Umayyad date is not. The coin of ca. 730 from the foundations of the peristyle of the courtyard in Building III suggests a construction date in the eighth century, not the seventh century. And, as noted above, the latest pottery types found in the drainage channels and in association with the main occupation of the buildings date to the ninth century, not the first half of the eighth century. Interestingly, the same scholars who question whether the Umayyad caliphs had the time and resources for a building project of this magnitude express no doubts that the Dome of the Rock was built in just a few years.[135]

Other evidence that the large buildings around the Haram were constructed in the Umayyad period comes from a Byzantine structure in Areas XV and XVII (southeast of the Temple Mount) identified by Eilat Mazar as a monastery (the "Enclosed Convent of the Virgins") and from another structure outside the southwest corner of the Temple Mount that she nicknamed the "House of the Menorot" (Area VI) (see Chapter 9).[136] Before Building III was constructed over the "House of the Menorot," the area was leveled with a massive fill that preserved the walls of the house to a height of two stories. During this process, the floors of the "House of the Menorot" were removed, and, as a result, no finds were discovered in situ in any of the excavated rooms.[137] The menorahs painted on the walls or stones inside the building support the excavators' proposal that the building was occupied by Jews after 614, as Jewish presence would be highly unlikely prior to the Sasanid invasion.

E. Mazar dates the construction of the Byzantine buildings south of the Temple Mount to the fourth century, citing the discovery of ninety-four coins under the floor of a house in Area XII (L12018), none of which postdates the years 393–395. However, since small bronze coins like these continued to circulate during the fifth century and first half of the sixth century, they provide a late fourth-century terminus post quem, not a fourth- or early fifth-century construction date for this house. Furthermore, the pottery found under the floors of the Byzantine buildings elsewhere to the south of the Temple Mount includes types that appeared in the mid-sixth century. Therefore, the ceramic evidence indicates that B. Mazar was correct in assigning the construction of these buildings to the reign of Justinian I (527–565) or later—part of the development of the southeast sector at this time.[138] This means that the large buildings above cannot date to the second half of the sixth or early seventh century, but instead are Umayyad.[139]

The monastic building suffered a violent destruction that left thick layers of burnt debris and collapse covering the floors and large numbers of whole but smashed vessels lying in situ. E. Mazar follows B. Mazar in associating this destruction with the Sasanid conquest of 614. However, many of the pottery types in the debris date from the mid-sixth century to the end of the seventh century, indicating that the destruction could have occurred at any time during the seventh century. A post-614 date is supported by the discovery of a coin of Constans II of 657/658 in the debris. Because the buildings in the other excavated areas were disturbed (e.g., the floors in the "House of the Menorot" were later removed and a thick fill was dumped), it is difficult to determine whether they suffered the same violent destruction. To the contrary, the fact that the "House of the Menorot" seems to have been occupied by Jews after 614 suggests that it was habitable, not in ruins. In other words, although it is possible that the monastic building was destroyed at the time of the Sasanid Persian invasion, the archaeological evidence indicates that the destruction could have occurred later in the seventh century, a possibility supported by the coin of Constans II from the debris. Furthermore, the painted menorahs in the "House of the Menorot" suggest that the house was not destroyed at the time of the Sasanid invasion but was occupied afterward by Jews. Two early channel-nozzle oil lamps, a type that dates to the seventh–early eighth centuries, were found in the "House of the Menorot." The fact that one of the lamps is almost complete suggests it is associated with the final phase of occupation in the house, prior to the construction of Building III above.[140] Alternatively, the lamp could have been deposited with the massive fills dumped to level the area when Building III was constructed. Either way, like the coin of Constans III, these oil lamps provide a seventh-century terminus post quem for the construction of Building III.

Altogether, the archaeological evidence indicates that the large buildings south and west of the Haram date to the Umayyad period, and likely to the first half of the eighth century. Although this evidence does not indicate their function, their size and decoration and the bridge connecting Building II to the Haram support the identification of these buildings as an administrative center.[141] I see no reason why Building II could not have served as the residence of the caliph in Jerusalem, even if the city was not a provincial capital. After all, the Umayyad caliphs built elaborate palaces for themselves at other sites that were not provincial capitals. Rulers typically constructed multiple palaces throughout their realms, often at sites that were not necessarily capitals or administrative centers. For example, in addition to his palace in the capital city of Jerusalem, Herod the Great had palaces and palatial buildings at Caesarea Maritima, Herodium, Jericho, Masada, Machaerus and other Judean desert refuges. It makes sense—as archaeologists have argued—to view the large buildings as an integral part of the Umayyad building program on the Haram.

The City Walls and Gates

The line of the city walls seems to have remained the same from the Byzantine period into the early Islamic period.[142] However, by the eleventh century, the wall on the south side of the city contracted to the current line of the Old City, leaving the southeastern hill and Mount Zion (the south end of the southwestern hill) outside it (Figure 10.7). This contraction is believed to have occurred after the earthquake of 1033, which probably necessitated the rebuilding of the walls.[143] The contraction of the walls indicates that Jerusalem's population declined, and, by the eleventh century, it numbered only around 10,000–20,000 inhabitants.[144]

After being breached by the Sasanids in 614, the city walls appear to have been left untouched for over a century. Some time in the first half of the eighth century,

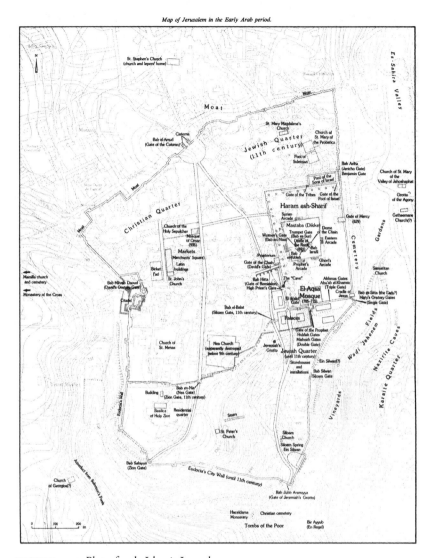

Map of Jerusalem in the Early Arab period.

FIGURE 10.7 Plan of early Islamic Jerusalem.
Credit: From E. Stern [ed.] 1993: 787, with permission of Carta.

apparently during the reign of Hisham, the damage was repaired, and the fortification system was overhauled.[145] The garbage that had accumulated in the breach
next to the Damascus Gate was cleared away to expose the stump of the wall, and
a patch was inserted to seal it (see Chapter 9). Pottery from the foundation trench
of the wall on the west side of the city, in the modern Armenian Garden, indicates
that it was constructed in the first half of the eighth century. In the courtyard of

FIGURE 10.8 Early Islamic round tower in the courtyard of the Citadel.
Credit: Photo by the author.

David's Citadel, a massive round tower measuring 9.8 meters (32 feet) in diameter was built, which either formed the southern part of an early Islamic citadel or was added to strengthen the existing line of wall (Figure 10.8).[146] As we have seen, Hisham may have been responsible for the construction of Building III and perhaps the other large buildings outside the Haram.

Hisham's successor Marwan II (744–750), a usurper to the throne who was the last Umayyad caliph, reportedly ordered the city walls dismantled, and additional damage might have been caused by the earthquake of 749.[147] Consequently, in the year 800, the walls would have been in a state of disrepair, with some sections still standing but others having been torn down or robbed out for their stones.[148] By the time al-Muqaddasi wrote in the tenth century, the city walls had been rebuilt.[149] He mentions eight gates (the Arabic word *bab* [pronounced like the name "Bob"] means "gate"), including those at the site of the modern Damascus Gate: Bab al-ʿAmud (the Gate of the Column); Jaffa Gate: Bab Mihrab Daʾud (the Gate of the Mihrab of David), named after David's Tower, which was called Mihrab Daʾud; and Lions' Gate: Bab Ariha (Jericho Gate).[150] On the south side of the city, Bab al-Balat (the Gate of the Court/Palace/Royal Residence) mentioned by al-Muqaddasi might have been in the vicinity of the modern Dung Gate, near the large buildings outside the Haram. Al-Muqaddasi also refers to the Bab al-Tih, which Charles Clermont-Ganneau proposed was the Bab al-Niya (the Nea Gate). Presumably it was near Justinian's Nea Church, likely at the south end of the western cardo.[151]

The Water Supply and Street Grid

The Gihon Spring and other sources that supplied Jerusalem with water in earlier periods continued to be used in the early Islamic period, including the cisterns under the Haram and the open-air reservoirs surrounding the city: Birket Isra`il (the Pool of Israel); Sulayman's Pool (the Bethesda/Bezetha/Sheep's Pool), the Pool of `Iyad (Hezekiah's Pool/the Amygdalon Pool/the Pool of the Towers), and the Pool of Siloam.[152] Private residences and public buildings were equipped with their own cisterns; for example, two large cisterns were added flanking the Damascus Gate, which collected run-off from the upper drainage basin of the Tyropoeon Valley. In addition, a channel added to the low-level aqueduct brought water to the large buildings outside the Haram. The conduit was laid in a deep horizontal groove cut into the Herodian temenos wall below Robinson's Arch.[153]

The major thoroughfares of the Roman and Byzantine periods continued in use in the early Islamic period, and their lines are preserved by the streets of the Old City today: Khan ez-Zeit/Beit ha-Bad Street follows the line of the western cardo, el-Wad Street/Rehov ha-Gai follows the line of the eastern cardo, and David Street/the Street of the Chain follows the line of the decumanus maximus.[154] However, over the centuries, repeated resurfacings and the accumulation of debris have caused the level of the streets to rise. In addition, the broad colonnaded thoroughfares of the Roman and Byzantine periods gradually were narrowed due to the encroachment of shops, houses, and other buildings. Pottery found in the drainage channels of the western cardo indicates that they silted up and went out of use in the late seventh to mid-eighth centuries.[155]

Hugh Kennedy has described the changes in street layout in Jerusalem and other Near Eastern cities as "the most complex and far reaching of the changes in urban design in late antiquity and the early Islamic period."[156] He notes that the layout of Roman and Byzantine cities, with broad colonnaded thoroughfares intersecting at right angles and open public squares and markets, provided an appearance of order. These features were also functional, as colonnaded streets separated pedestrians from wheeled traffic and covered sidewalks allowed for commercial activity even in inclement weather. In addition to the narrowing of broad colonnaded streets or their replacement altogether by shops and houses, over time, the large open marketplaces (agoras and forums) that characterized Roman and Byzantine cities disappeared. Instead, the markets and bazaars (*suqs*) of Islamic cities typically consist of narrow streets lined by the shops and stalls of merchants and vendors. Kennedy observes that, "Where large open markets did exist [in Islamic cities], they were to be found outside the gates and catered for livestock and food brought from the surrounding country by peasants or Bedouin. The high-status trades, fine textiles, jewelry, books, spices and the like were to be found in the *suqs* around the mosque, not in the open markets."[157] In recent times, a weekly sheep market was still held outside the northeast corner of the Old City walls, whereas the *suqs* are along the main streets inside the walls.

Although the disappearance of the broad colonnaded streets and open marketplaces of Roman and Byzantine cities has been viewed as evidence of decline and decay under Muslim rule, Kennedy cautions against making inappropriate value judgments. He notes that these changes were dictated by the needs of the inhabitants, not by administrative incompetence or aesthetic insensitivity.[158] For example, classical cities generally were not centers of industrial or commercial activity but instead depended on the participation of local landowners in civic life. The Roman urban elites derived much of their wealth from administration and tax collection, whereas merchants had a low social status.[159] In contrast, Islamic cities were hubs of commercial and trading activity and merchants enjoyed a high social status. The migration of commercial activity and trade into the walls was one factor in the transformation of cities from a Roman-Byzantine *polis* to an Islamic *madina*.[160]

Another factor that impacted the design of cities was the replacement of wheeled vehicles (carts and chariots) with camels and other pack animals as the main means of transporting goods in the Islamic world. Although from our perspective this may appear to be a step backward, transporting goods on pack animals is easier and less expensive than using wheeled vehicles, which require broad, flat, graded surfaces that must be maintained.[161] In contrast, camels, donkeys, and other pack animals can easily navigate narrow, winding, unpaved, uneven or stepped streets, alleys, and paths.[162] Consequently, when the broad colonnaded streets of Roman and Byzantine cities were no longer needed to accommodate wheeled traffic, they ceased to be maintained and disappeared.

Charlemagne and Jerusalem

By the mid-eighth century, Christians in Jerusalem began to seek the financial assistance and protection of Christian rulers in Europe. These contacts intensified under Charlemagne, who exchanged several delegations with the patriarch of Jerusalem and Harun al-Rashid.[163] Charlemagne's first delegation to the Abbasid caliph, sent in 797, consisted of two Frankish representatives named Lantfrid and Sigismund (or Sigimund), neither of whom survived the mission, and a Jewish interpreter named Isaac.[164] A few weeks after Charlemagne's coronation, a delegation sent by Harun al-Rashid arrived and announced that a gift of an African elephant was on its way. In 801, Isaac arrived at Aix-la-Chapelle (Aachen) with the elephant (named Abul Abaz), which died nine years later.[165]

In 799, a delegation sent by the patriarch of Jerusalem to Aix-la-Chapelle brought gifts to Charlemagne, who dispatched his own delegation to Jerusalem led by the palace priest Zacharias.[166] Zacharias returned to Rome on 23 December 800 with the keys to the Church of the Holy Sepulcher and the banner of Jerusalem.[167] These delegations are described in the Royal Annals of Charlemagne's court (*Annales Regni Francorum*), where the keys to the Church of the Holy Sepulcher are linked to the king's coronation.

> AD 800   The king released the monk of Jerusalem [sent to Charlemagne by the Patriarch of Jerusalem the previous year] and set him on his journey home, sending with him Zacharias, a priest of his palace, to take his gifts to the holy places. . . . On the same day Zacharias came to Rome on his way back from the East, along with two monks, one from the Mount of Olives and one from the monastery of St. Sabas, whom the patriarch of Jerusalem had sent to the king with Zacharias, to bring to him for blessing the keys of the Holy Sepulchre and of Calvary, and also those of the city itself and Mount Sion, along with a standard . . . . And the number of the years changed to 801.
>
> AD 801   On the holy day of Christmas itself [i.e. AD 800 in the Julian calendar], at a mass before the tomb of St Peter the apostle, Pope Leo placed a crown upon the king's head as he rose from prayer . . . and setting aside the title of patrician [Charlemagne] was named emperor and Augustus.[168]

While Charlemagne designed his capital at Aix-la-Chapelle as a "new Rome" and modeled his palace (which has disappeared) after that of Constantine, the first Christian emperor, he also cultivated an image as heir to David and Solomon through his patronage of the Christians and churches of Jerusalem.[169] Jerusalem's influence is evident in the design of the Palatine Chapel at the heart of Charlemagne's palace: an inner octagon surrounded by a sixteen-sided ambulatory (which still stands today). Although it was modeled after the Church of San Vitale in Ravenna, the chapel was also intended to recall the Rotunda of the Church of the Holy Sepulcher as well as the Dome of the Rock, which, perhaps by this time and certainly by the Crusades, was identified by Christians as Solomon's temple (see Chapter 11).[170] The master builder of the chapel, Odo of Metz, might be the same courtier nicknamed in some sources "Hiram"—the name of the king of Tyre who supplied cedars of Lebanon and skilled craftsmen for Solomon's temple (1 Kgs 5:18).[171] And Charlemagne's court biographer Einhard (or Eginhard), who wrote the *Life of Charles* in the early 830s, was nicknamed Bezalel, the figure said to have designed the biblical tabernacle (Exodus 35:30–33).[172]

The expectation that Charlemagne's investiture in the year 800 would usher in a new epoch in human history focused attention on Jerusalem—the site of the return of the messiah and the Last Judgment.[173] These apocalyptic and eschatological expectations are expressed in the layout and decoration of the Palatine Chapel. For example, the octagonal plan alludes to Christ's resurrection eight days after Palm Sunday, and the image of Christ enthroned in judgment in the cupola was inspired by the description of the apocalypse in Revelation 4:2.[174] The total length of the octagon and the sixteen-sided ambulatory is 44 meters (144 feet)—three times the octagon's diameter and height of 15 meters (48 feet)—corresponding to the number of cubits (144) mentioned in Revelation 21:17 as the length of Jerusalem's walls. One hundred forty-four stars surrounded the figure of Christ in the cupola, symbolizing the 144,000 souls saved at the apocalypse (Rev 7:4–8; 14:1).[175] These correspondences might even indicate that Charlemagne intended the Palatine Chapel to be a symbol of Jerusalem.[176]

Charlemagne's ties to Jerusalem and his patronage of its churches would have bolstered his claim to have ushered in a new era as ruler of a revived Christian Roman empire. These ties were solidified not only by Charlemagne's benefactions to Jerusalem but by the sacred relics enshrined in the Palatine Chapel, including, perhaps, a splinter from the Holy Cross and an ancient marble throne as well as the keys to the Church of the Holy Sepulcher.[177] The altar in the center of the octagon, with the figure of Christ seated in judgment above, was consecrated to the Trinity, an expression of Charlemagne's commitment to defending Catholic orthodoxy against heresies. One of these was adoptionism, a doctrine that considers Jesus to be God's "adopted son" instead of his "only begotten son."[178] Another controversy concerned the *filioque* (Latin: "and of the son"), a phrase that was added to the Nicene Creed by the Western church but was rejected by the Greeks, which states that the Holy Spirit proceeds not only from God but from his son Jesus: "And in the Holy Spirit, the Lord, the giver of life, who proceeds from the Father, who with the Father and the Son is adored and glorified, who proceeds from the Father *and the Son* (*filioque*)." The controversy over the *filioque* was a major cause of the schism between the Eastern (Orthodox) and Western churches.[179]

To determine how much money to send, Charlemagne sent a delegation to visit the churches and Christians in Jerusalem and elsewhere in the Holy Land.[180] The delegation compiled a list of churches and monasteries detailing the numbers of clerical and monastic personnel and the dimensions of the buildings in a group of documents written ca. 808. The report is titled the *Commemoratorium de Casis Dei vel Monasteriis*, commonly abbreviated as the *Breue* (pronounced BREH-veh) *commemoratorium*, or simply the *Commemoratorium*.[181] The measurements are recorded in dexters, which are approximately 1.5 meters (5 feet) each.[182] The *Commemoratorium* provides valuable information about the Christian population of Jerusalem and its churches and monasteries around 800, as illustrated by this excerpt:

> The book of the inventory of those houses of God and monasteries, which exist in the Holy City of Jerusalem, and in the surrounding country; and of the bishops, priests, deacons, monks, and all clergy, serving in those holy places of God; and of the convents of nuns.
>
> In the first place, there are at the Holy Sepulchre of the Lord, 9 priests, 14 deacons, 6 sub-deacons, 23 canons, 13 guardians, who are called *frage-lites*, 41 monks, 12 persons, who walk before the patriarch with tapers, 17 servants of the patriarch, 2 overseers (praepositi), 2 accountants (computarii), 2 notaries, 2 priests, who diligently watch over the Sepulchre of the Lord.
>
> There is one priest at Holy Calvary; at the place of the Cup of the Lord, 2 priests; at the place of the Holy Cross and of the Napkin, 2 priests and one deacon.
>
> There is a seneschal (syncellus) who keeps all things in order under the patriarch, 2 stewards (cellaria), one treasurer, one guardian of the cisterns (fontes), 9 porters. The total number is one hundred fifty, three hospitallers (hospitalibus) being excepted.[183]

The data in the *Commemoratorium* indicate that the number of clergy in the Jerusalem patriarchate had declined since its height in the sixth and seventh centuries, although Jerusalem still had over thirty churches and more than seven hundred monks and priests in its environs.[184]

BERNARD THE WISE, a Frankish monk who visited the Holy Land in 867, refers to the charitable foundations established by Charlemagne in Jerusalem:

> Then we went to the holy city of Jerusalem, where we were received in the hostel founded there by the glorious Emperor Charles, in which are received all pilgrims who speak the Latin tongue; adjoining to which is a church in honor of St. Mary, with a most noble library founded by the same emperor, with twelve dwellings, fields, vineyards and a garden in the Valley of Jehosaphat. In front of the hostel is a market, for which every one trading there pays yearly to him who provides it two gold pieces.[185]

The buildings mentioned by Bernard—including a church dedicated to St. Mary la Latine (St. Mary of the Latins, so named because of the use of Latin in the liturgy), a hostel for pilgrims, a monastery, a convent, and a library, and a marketplace—were in the Muristan Quarter, just south of the Church of the Holy Sepulcher. Apparently, there was also a church dedicated to John the Baptist.[186] The Muristan, which means "hospital" in Kurdish, is so-called because, in the twelfth century, the area was allocated to the Knights of the Order of Hospitallers. Charlemagne's buildings in the Muristan were destroyed in 1009 by the Fatimid caliph al-Hakim bi-ʿAmr Allah (original name: Abu Ali al-Mansur), whose order to raze the Church of the Holy Sepulcher ignited the Crusader quest to take the Holy Land.[187] Some of Charlemagne's ruined buildings might have been reconstructed after 1014 by Italian merchants from Amalfi.[188]

The Muristan Quarter is in the area of Aelia Capitolina's western forum. After Jerusalem fell to the Crusaders in 1099, the Hospitallers renovated the quarter, including constructing a Church of St. Mary la Latine in the northeast part and a Church of St. Mary la Grande to its west. During the Mamluk and Ottoman periods (thirteenth-twentieth centuries), the Muristan deteriorated and fell into ruin. In 1869, the Ottoman sultan gave the eastern part of the quarter to the Germans, who reconstructed the Crusader Church of St. Mary la Latine and dedicated it as the Lutheran Church of the Redeemer (see Chapter 11).

The location of Charlemagne's buildings within the Muristan is unknown. According to Dan Bahat, there are no remains of Charlemagne's buildings.[189] He situates the Church of St. Mary la Latine and Charlemagne's other buildings in the western part of the Muristan, whereas the Crusader Church of St. Mary la Latine and the modern Church of the Redeemer are on the northeast side.[190] Other scholars, however, place Charlemagne's buildings on the northeast side of the Muristan, where a pre-Crusader church dedicated to Mary might have stood.[191] In my opinion, the latter possibility is supported by the finds from excavations conducted in 1970–1974 by Ute Lux and Karel Vriezen under the Church of the Redeemer. They discovered a massive fill that had been deposited to level the area for a major building project, and an associated retaining wall. The latest pottery from the fill, which is early Islamic and medieval, raises the possibility that the building project dates to the time of Charlemagne. The excavators also found that the retaining wall had been rebuilt, perhaps, as I have suggested, by the merchants from Amalfi.[192]

Coins

The earliest coins minted by the Umayyads are often referred to by scholars as "Arab-Byzantine" because they imitate Byzantine types. The obverse shows an image of the emperor but without the cross depicted on Byzantine coins, and the reverse has a letter indicating the denomination (frequently the Greek letter M = 40 *nummi*). The first Umayyad coins were inscribed in Greek, which was soon replaced by Arabic.[193] In the decades that followed, diverse coin types were issued in different parts of the empire, influenced to varying degrees by Byzantine and Sasanid types.[194]

In 692–693 CE, after vanquishing Ibn al-Zubayr but still facing the Kharijite threat, ʿAbd al-Malik introduced a new series called the "Standing Caliph" because the obverse shows an image of the caliph standing with his sword, encircled by the *shahadah* (profession of faith).[195] The coins depict ʿAbd al-Malik as caliph and military leader, labeled "the leader/commander of the Faithful" (*amir al-muʾminim*) and "the caliph of God" (*khalifah allah*).[196] As Alan Walmsley observes, these coins linked the caliph with the prophet Muhammad and God.[197] By 693, ʿAbd al-Malik began to mint the first Islamic coins in gold as a substitute for the Byzantine gold currency that had been relied on until then.[198] The Standing Caliph series and the introduction of gold coinage were also a response to Byzantine gold solidi showing Christ holding the Gospels, which linked the emperor with Christ, God, and His Chosen Word.[199]

Small bronze coins of the Standing Caliph type were produced in various mints including Jerusalem.[200] The obverse of one issue depicts a bearded figure of the caliph standing in a long robe with his right hand on his sword, accompanied by the Arabic inscription "Muhammad is the messenger of God [Allah)]," and on the reverse the Greek letter M with the Arabic inscriptions "Filastin" (Palestine) and "Iliya/Ilya" (Aelia) (Figure 10.9).[201] It is unclear if the M indicates the coin's value, as it does on Byzantine coins, or is just a decorative imitation.[202]

Beginning in 696–697 CE, ʿAbd al-Malik instituted a sweeping monetary reform that eliminated most of the figured images and other Byzantine elements from Islamic coins.[203] In contrast to pre-reform coins, post-reform issues generally carry only Arabic inscriptions, usually with some version of the *shahadah* on one side and a Quranic statement (Sura 112) that emphasizes God's oneness and denies the Trinity (Figure 10.10).[204] These coins are described as "aniconic" (having no figured images) or "all-epigraphic" (having only writing). The elimination of figured images on coins contrasted Islam's "pure monotheism" with Christianity's (perceived) icon-filled idolatry, while the inscriptions conveyed Islam's core tenets of faith.[205] Nevertheless, some pious Muslims initially objected to the placement of Quranic verses with God's words on small pieces of metal that could be held by impure individuals or carried into impure spaces such as toilets.[206]

FIGURE 10.9 Arab-Byzantine Ilya bronze fals struck under the Umayyads, seventh century CE, showing a standing caliph with the Arabic inscription "there is no god but God alone" on the obverse, and an M with the Arabic inscription "Iliya Filastin" on the reverse, ANS Cultural Change 4.31. Photo ANS; Abraham D and Marian Scheuer Sofaer Collection at the Israel Museum.
Credit: Courtesy of David Hendin.

FIGURE 10.10 Umayyad post-reform bronze fals struck at Akka (Acre/Akko), seventh century CE; inscribed in Arabic on the obverse "There is no god but God alone" and on the reverse "Muhammad is the Messenger of God; in the name of God, this fals was struck at Akka," Cultural change 105. Photo ANS; Abraham D and Marian Scheuer Sofaer, Sofaer Collection at the Israel Museum.
Credit: Courtesy of David Hendin.

The post-reform coins were minted in gold (called a *dinar*, from the Roman *denarius*), silver (called a *dirham*, from the Greek *drachma*), and bronze (called a *fals*, from the Roman *follis*).[207] In contrast to Hellenistic and Roman coins, which show an image of the ruler on the obverse, until the second half of the eighth century, post-reform Islamic gold and silver coins did not even bear the name of the caliph. Instead, Qur`an Sura 112—the statement of God's unity—replaced the ruler's image as an expression of universal sovereignty, while the *shahadah* substituted for the religious symbols on Hellenistic and Roman coins.[208] The post-reform gold dinars not only differ from Byzantine gold solidi in having no figured images but used a different weight standard: 4.25 grams per coin instead of the Greek standard of 4.27–4.38 grams per coin. Payment in the lighter Islamic gold dinars was assessed by number instead of by weight, as was the case with their Byzantine counterparts. Because anyone using Byzantine solidi in this system would have lost money due to their heavier weight, they were soon superseded in the Islamic world by the lighter dinars.[209]

In the first half of the eighth century, a series of small bronze coins was minted in Jerusalem, which show a five-branched (or, more rarely, a seven-branched) candlestick on the obverse and the first half of the *shahadah* ("there is no god except Allah alone") on the reverse. The branched candlestick clearly alludes to the temple menorah, although the depiction on the coins differs in having a flat base and, sometimes, leaves attached to the stem (an element that reflects Christian traditions about the menorah). Dan Barag suggested that the candlestick was intended to give visual expression to Jerusalem as *Bayt al-Maqdis*—the temple.[210]

In 832 CE, during the reign of al-Ma'mun (the same Abbasid caliph who replaced `Abd al-Malik's name with his own in the dedicatory inscription in the Dome of the Rock), the first bronze coins inscribed with Jerusalem's Islamic name, *al-Quds*, were minted, marking another step in the city's transformation from *polis* to *madina*.[211]

Conclusion

Despite continued (but diminished) Christian presence and the survival of some churches and monasteries, Jerusalem in 800 CE bore little resemblance to the city that surrendered to the Muslims some 165 years earlier. The Temple Mount, which had been lying in ruins and used as a garbage dump by the Byzantine Christians, was transformed into *al-haram al-sharif*—a sacred precinct dominated by two Muslim monuments: the Dome of the Rock enshrining the Foundation Stone and al-Aqsa Mosque on the site of Herod's Royal Stoa. The area outside the southwest and south walls of the Haram was occupied by a series of massive, richly decorated, two-story-high buildings that were probably used for administrative purposes. Although still standing in some places, the city wall was in a state of disrepair and partial ruin. Inside the line of the wall, the broad colonnaded thoroughfares and open commercial spaces (forums) of the Roman and Byzantine periods had disappeared, replaced by narrow streets and alleys bustling with camels, pack animals, and push carts carrying goods to shops and stalls. The low-level aqueduct and large open-air reservoirs of earlier periods still supplied much of the water needed by the inhabitants. Thanks to the tolerant policy of the early Islamic rulers, Jews and Karaites were again part of the city's population, alongside Muslims and Christians.

Unfortunately, the cordial relations between East and West fostered by Harun al-Rashid and Charlemagne did not last. Two hundred years later, al-Hakim's order to dismantle the Church of the Holy Sepulcher ignited the Crusades, one of the bloodiest epochs in Jerusalem's history, and outbreaks of war and violence continue to the present day. However, the basic layout of the walled city is largely unchanged since 800 CE, and the Dome of the Rock remains Jerusalem's most iconic monument. The Temple Mount/Haram continues to be a bone of contention for those who seek to use it to legitimize religious or political claims. Indeed, control of the thirty-seven-acre esplanade lies at the heart of the current conflict, which cannot be resolved without understanding its roots in Jerusalem's long and complex history. As the dwelling place of the God of Israel and the site of the Last Judgment, the very thing that makes Jerusalem special also divides the followers of the three Abrahamic faiths.

II

Crusader Jerusalem (19 September 1187)

ON 19 SEPTEMBER 1187, Jerusalem's population was swollen with refugees seeking safety within the walls as Saladin's army advanced toward the city. The eighty-eight-year-long period of Frankish domination was about to end. The First Crusade had culminated on Friday, 15 July 1099, with the conquest of Jerusalem, which became the capital of the newly established kingdom, as reflected in its name: the Latin (or Frankish) Kingdom of Jerusalem.[1] Although the kingdom survived until the latter part of the thirteenth century, after 1187, the Franks never regained permanent control of Jerusalem.[2]

Historical Background

The Abbasids, who ruled Jerusalem in 800 CE, eventually were replaced by other Muslim powers, two of which vied for control of Palestine during the century preceding the arrival of the Crusaders: the Seljuk Turks, who were Sunni, and the Fatimids of Egypt, who were Shi`ites. Sunnis recognize the first four caliphs as Muhammad's rightful successors, whereas Shi`ites recognize only the legitimacy of Muhammad's son-in-law `Ali and his descendants.[3] Modern Iran is distinguished from most other Muslim countries in being overwhelmingly Shi`ite. In the eleventh century, Jerusalem went back and forth between the Fatimids (969–1073) and the Seljuks (1073–1098), and, just one year before the Crusaders arrived, the Fatimids had retaken the city.[4]

Although the underlying causes are obscure, it was the Fatimid caliph al-Hakim's dismantling of the Church of the Holy Sepulcher in 1009 that ignited the Crusader quest to take the Holy Land.[5] After proceeding southward along the coast and then inland from Jaffa, on the morning of 7 June 1099, the Crusaders caught their first glimpse of Jerusalem from Nabi Samwil (biblical Ramah), a tall hill 7.5 kilometers (24 miles) to the northwest that is venerated as the burial spot of the prophet Samuel. The Frankish moniker for the site—"Mount Joy" (*Montjoie* or *Mons Gaudii* in post-classical Latin)—reflects the jubilation they felt on seeing the city.[6] By that evening, the Crusaders were camped outside Jerusalem's north wall. The city's population—about 20,000 inhabitants—had been doubled by refugees sheltering inside the fortifications. The Crusader and Muslim forces were roughly equal in number, at approximately 40,000 each.[7] The Crusaders' initial attack on 13 June was easily repelled as they had prepared no scaling ladders due to a lack of wood in the area, apparently in the belief that God would miraculously bring the walls down. On 8 July, following a barefoot procession around the walls led by priests with crosses and holy relics, the Crusaders—having constructed three large siege towers with wood brought from Jaffa—mounted another assault. On Friday, 15 July, they succeeded in breaching the wall east of St. Stephen's Gate (Damascus Gate), roughly opposite the modern Rockefeller Museum, where a cross was later set up to mark the spot.[8] The Muslim and Jewish defenders, who took refuge in David's Tower, surrendered and negotiated a safe passage to the coastal city of Ascalon (Ashkelon). Over the next three days, the rest of the population—men, women, and children—was brutally slaughtered in one of the bloodiest massacres in Jerusalem's history. Muslim and Jewish captives were forced to clear out the corpses, which were piled in huge mounds outside the city. A half a year later, a Frankish visitor reported being overwhelmed by the stench of decaying flesh.[9] Joshua Prawer notes that the obliteration of Jewish communities by the Crusaders is reflected in the Cairo Geniza (a repository in Cairo's Ben Ezra synagogue), where the documentary record relating to the Holy Land ends in the first decade of the twelfth century.[10]

After the fall of the city, many of the Crusaders departed. Those remaining elected Godfrey de Bouillon as ruler with the title "Advocate of the Holy Sepulcher." Because the Franks had slaughtered, enslaved, or banished the inhabitants and banned Jews and Muslims from living in Jerusalem, it was nearly empty. The population gradually recovered as Eastern Christians were resettled from neighboring regions, while increasing numbers of pilgrims poured into the city. The security of the pilgrims was ensured by the Knights Templar and the Hospitallers—military orders of knights who were not clerics but lived according to monastic rule. They considered the killing of non-believers an act of piety, and participation in a crusade an act of penance. After initially being established in Jerusalem, the military orders spread rapidly throughout the Latin East and West.[11]

By the middle of the twelfth century, Jerusalem's population had grown to about 30,000, exceeding the pre-Crusader number.[12] The residents were divided into two main classes along socioeconomic lines: the Latin nobility and the burgesses (*burgenses/bourgeoisie*). The nobles comprised the high nobility and the barons and lesser knights (*chevaliers*). The rest of the Latin population were burgesses—non-noble tradespeople and property owners who were freemen. A lower class within the burgesses consisted of poor traders and people who owned no property.[13] Despite the ban on Jews and Muslims, Jerusalem's population was religiously and ethnically diverse, with communities of Franks (Latin Christians) from Gaul, Germany, Spain, Italy, and other European countries, and Eastern Christians including Greeks, Syrians, Armenians, Georgians, Jacobites, Copts, and Nestorians.[14]

Under Frankish rule, buildings were constructed throughout Jerusalem, the most important of which was the Church of the Holy Sepulcher. Ecclesiastical establishments and the arts benefited especially from the patronage of Melisende, who was Queen of Jerusalem from 1131–1153 and regent for her son Baldwin III from 1153–1161. Melisende was the daughter of King Baldwin II of Jerusalem and his wife, Morphia of Melitene, an Armenian princess. Soon after her marriage in 1130, Melisende became estranged from her husband Fulk V. Although Fulk attempted to assume full control of the kingdom, Melisende had the support of Jerusalem's feudal council (*Haute Cour*) and the church. After her husband was killed in a hunting accident in 1143, Melisende continued to rule the kingdom, which she shared with Baldwin III after he reached adulthood. When Baldwin III assumed the kingship by force in 1152, Melisende moved to Nablus. She died in 1161, around the time the Crusader kingdom was at its height. An extraordinary woman who lived an extraordinary life, Melisende was laid to rest in the Tomb of the Virgin in the Valley of Jehoshaphat in Jerusalem.[15]

In the last quarter of the twelfth century, the Crusader kingdom weakened. In 1185, incapacitated by leprosy, King Baldwin IV stepped down from the throne and died soon thereafter at the age of twenty-four. Since his successor Baldwin V was only seven years old, Raymond of Tripoli ruled the kingdom as regent. When Baldwin V died a year later, Guy of Lusignan, the husband of Baldwin IV's sister Sibylla, became king. The in-fighting between Guy and Raymond, both of whom claimed the throne, left the kingdom vulnerable as it faced its greatest threat: Saladin.[16] Saladin or Salah ed-Din (full name: al-Nasir Salah al-Din ibn Ayyub) was a Sunni Kurd who united Egypt and Syria under his rule and founded the Ayyubid dynasty.

Jerusalem's fate was sealed on 4 July 1187, three months before Saladin reached the city's walls, when the Crusader army was annihilated by Saladin's forces at the Battle of Hattin (or Hittin). The events leading up to that fateful day were set in motion when Saladin's forces crossed the Jordan River and took Tiberias. King Guy ordered the Frankish army—which, at ca. 20,000 strong, was half the size of Saladin's forces—to leave their encampment at le Saforie (Sepphoris) and march east toward Tiberias. Raymond, whose wife was holding out in Tiberias, argued against abandoning the easily defensible and well-watered position at le Saforie but was overruled. On Friday morning, 3 July, the Frankish troops set out for Tiberias. They marched eastward across the barren and windswept plateau of Hattin, which is dominated by two volcanic formations called the Horns of Hattin. The unrelenting heat of the midsummer sun beat down on the knights who were broiling in their suits of armor. Each wore a coat of chain mail (hauberk) over a gambeson (or gambison) (a quilted cotton waistcoat with a hood), chain mail hose on the legs, metal shoes on the feet and metal gauntlets on the arms, a solid iron helmet with nose-guard, and, over the body armor, a surcoat (a long, sleeveless coat) marked with a heraldic device. A sword and a dagger carried in scabbards were attached to a belt around the waist, and each knight held a shield in the left hand and a spear in the right hand. The horses were protected with chain mail covered with cloth.[17]

With access to the nearest major spring and the Sea of Galilee (a freshwater lake) blocked by Saladin's army, the parched and miserable Franks pitched camp for the night on the plateau. Their suffering intensified when Saladin had the dry brush covering the plateau set on fire. At dawn on Saturday, 4 July, having surrounded the Frankish troops, Saladin's forces attacked. The Franks were quickly overcome, many of them killed while trying to reach the Sea of Galilee, while others were taken captive. The relic of the True Cross, which had been carried into battle by the bishop of Acre (Akko), fell into Muslim hands and eventually disappeared.[18]

On 4 August, Saladin took Ascalon after a siege. With a full solar eclipse that day—an inauspicious omen—a delegation from Jerusalem arrived to negotiate terms of surrender. But they rejected Saladin's generous offer allowing them to retain control until the following Pentecost, when they would be required to surrender if the Frankish army could not save the city from the Muslim forces. The Franks could not conceive of relinquishing the city where their Savior had died for them. Proceeding northeast by way of Nabi Samwil, Saladin and his army reached the walls of Jerusalem on 20 September.[19]

The defenders were led by Balian of Ibelin, the lord of Nablus, one of the few Franks to escape from the Battle of Hattin. Saladin granted Balian safe passage to Jerusalem to rescue his wife Queen Maria and their children on condition that he stay only one night and not take up arms. But when Balian arrived, he was persuaded by the patriarch and other leaders to stay and take charge. Balian received Saladin's permission to be freed from his oath so he could remain in Jerusalem while his family was escorted to safety in Tyre. Although the city's population was swollen with refugees, there were almost no fighting men. In advance of Saladin's arrival, Balian knighted every noble-born boy over the age of fifteen as well as some thirty or forty burgesses. He had the countryside scoured for food and stripped the silver from the roof of the Church of the Holy Sepulcher to pay the new knights.[20]

On 30 September, the Muslims mounted their assault on the walls. After being repulsed on the northwest side of the city, they concentrated their attack on the northeast side, where they breached the wall at the same spot penetrated by the Franks eighty-eight years earlier. Quickly realizing that the situation was hopeless, Balian asked Saladin for terms of surrender. The Franks were given forty days to raise money to ransom themselves: ten dinars per man, five per woman, and one per child. Only a small number were able to afford the ransom; the others were freed without payment or were taken into captivity. With the surrender of the city on Friday, 2 October, and the departure of all the Latin Christian inhabitants by 10 November 1187, the Frankish occupation of Jerusalem effectively came to an end.[21]

Archaeological Evidence

We possess a wealth of literary sources about Crusader Jerusalem including ecclesiastical documents and pilgrims' accounts, chief among them *La Citez de Jherusalem*, a detailed description of the city written by an anonymous French pilgrim at the time of Saladin's conquest.[22] In addition, Jerusalem is depicted in a series of medieval European maps as a round city with four main gates in the cardinal directions and the major streets and buildings within.[23] The circular shape is intended to represent Jerusalem as an ideal city. The remains of Crusader structures—some of which no longer survive—were well-documented and studied by nineteenth- and twentieth-century explorers and scholars.[24] Aside from the Jewish Quarter (which was rebuilt after 1967), the modern Old City preserves the appearance of the Crusader city, with many of the buildings still standing and some continuing to serve their original purpose. As a result, we have a better understanding of Crusader Jerusalem than most other periods in the city's history.[25] Nevertheless, it is sometimes difficult to distinguish between Fatimid, Crusader, and Ayyubid remains as the pottery types of these periods often cannot be dated more precisely within a range of the eleventh to thirteenth centuries. In addition, we have little information about Frankish domestic architecture (private dwellings) in Jerusalem as nearly all the surviving Crusader structures are public (e.g., fortifications and gates, churches and monasteries, covered streets and market halls).

The City Wall and Gates

The present walls of the Old City, which were constructed by the Ottoman sultan Suleiman the Magnificent in the sixteenth century, follow the line of fortifications at the time of the Crusader conquest (Figure 11.1). This line, which was established under the Fatimids, excluded the southeastern hill and Mount Zion (the south end of the southwestern hill).[26] A dry, rock-cut moat created by the quarrying of stone for the wall and a forewall in front of segments of the fortification wall created additional barriers (Figure 11.2).[27] A Fatimid tower called Qasr al-Jalud (Goliath's Tower) or Tancred's Tower protected the vulnerable northwest side of the city. The Crusaders did not rebuild the walls but repaired them on a couple of occasions.[28] In addition, the Templars (who occupied the Temple Mount) erected a wall to protect the gates on the south side of the Temple Mount.[29]

There were four main gates in the Crusader city wall, one on each side: David's Gate on the west (modern Jaffa Gate), St. Stephen's Gate on the north (modern Damascus Gate), the Gate of Jehoshaphat (at or near the modern Lions' or St. Stephen's Gate) on the east, and Mount Zion Gate on the south. Smaller gates included St. Mary Magdalene's Postern (modern Herod's Gate) on the north; St. Lazarus's Postern on the northwest (near the present New Gate), which led to the St. Lazarus Hospital for lepers; Belcayre's or Beaucayre's Postern on the southwest (the name means "beautiful hill," referring to Mount Zion); and the Tanners' Gate or Iron Gate at the south end of the eastern cardo (Tyropoeon Valley). A gate with a massive tower excavated about 15 meters (49 feet) west of the present Dung Gate apparently represents the remains of the Tanners' Gate, which was so-called after the tanners' workshops located in its vicinity.[30]

David's Gate and St. Stephen's Gate were the main points of entry into the city. At the time of the Crusader conquest, David's Gate was set into the city wall adjoining the Tower of David. In the 1160s, the Tower of David was incorporated into a larger citadel, and David's Gate was moved farther west, to the present location of the Jaffa Gate.[31] The Franks also strengthened the Roman gate and towers at the Damascus Gate (St. Stephen's Gate) by adding a barbican (fortified outer gate and passage) at a ninety-degree angle, thereby forcing attackers to approach with their unshielded right side exposed. Remains of the barbican are visible outside the Roman gate.[32] Mount Zion Gate was at the south end of the cardo maximus (western cardo), about 100 meters (328 feet) east of the present Zion Gate. Excavations in 1974 exposed the gate's tower (Figure 11.3) and brought to light an Ayyubid (thirteenth-century) dedicatory inscription nearby, although an earlier gate likely stood on this spot. Later, after the gate was destroyed and the southern section of the cardo was no longer used, a new gate was built at the present location.[33]

The gates of the Temple Mount included the Golden Gate on the east, which was reserved for processions on Palm Sunday and the Feast of the Exaltation of the Cross, and the Beautiful Gate (*Porta Speciosa*) on the west, at the east end of David Street and the "Great Causeway" across the Tyropoeon Valley (see Chapter 8). A

Map of Jerusalem in the Crusader period.

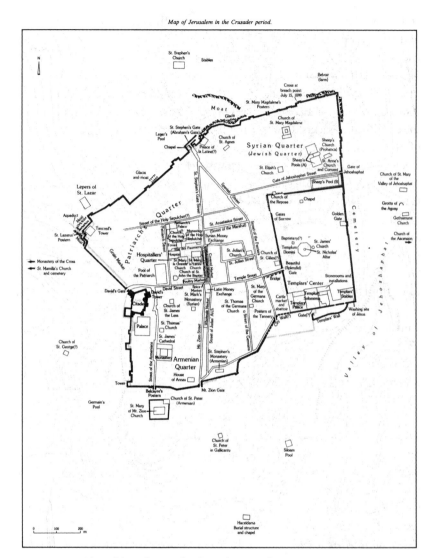

FIGURE 11.1 Plan of Jerusalem in the Crusader period.
Credit: from E. Stern (ed.), 1993: 788, with permission of Carta.

blocked portal with a single pointed arch called the Single Gate, about 32 meters
(105 feet) from the southeast corner of the Temple Mount, provided access to
Solomon's Stables (where the Templars stabled their horses). The eastern (Triple)
Hulda gate of the Herodian period was blocked with stones, while the western
(Double) gate, which was embellished in the early Islamic period, remained in
use (Figures 7.13 and 7.14). Its eastern portal was blocked and partly covered by
a large gate tower that enclosed and protected the passage through the western

FIGURE 11.2 The Crusader forewall and moat north of the Jaffa Gate.
Credit: Photo by the author.

portal, which was left open. This was the only direct access for the Templars from outside the city to their headquarters on the Temple Mount.[34]

The Tower of David and the Citadel

When the Franks took Jerusalem, the Citadel consisted of a massive tower built on the podium of the sole surviving Herodian tower, which had been identified as the Tower of David since the Byzantine period (Figure 7.18). Under the Crusaders, the tower belonged to the king and functioned as a fortified stronghold and administrative center, and it is depicted on Crusader coins and seals as

FIGURE 11.3 Remains of the tower of the Mount Zion Gate.
Credit: Photo by the author.

a symbol of Frankish rule. From 1101–1104, the Tower of David also served as the royal palace. In 1104, the king moved to al-Aqsa Mosque ("Solomon's Temple"), until 1118, when a new royal palace was built to the south of the Tower of David, in the same area where Herod's palace had been. In 1152, Queen Melisende took refuge inside the Tower of David when her son, Baldwin III, refused to accept the feudal court's decision to divide the kingdom between his mother and himself. Baldwin was unable to take the tower, and the stand-off ended when mother and son accepted a peace settlement. About a decade later, an expanded citadel with additional towers, walls, and forewalls was built around the Tower of David, in which Jerusalem's inhabitants took refuge during Saladin's siege. Demolished in the thirteenth century, the current Citadel is a product of rebuilding in the Mamluk and Ottoman periods, although it is thought to preserve many elements of the Crusader Citadel.[35]

The Main Streets, Markets, and Quarters
(Including the Temple Mount)

The streets and market halls of the Crusader city typically were covered with groin vaults (cross vaults shaped like an X), which are still preserved throughout the Old City. The four main gates led to the main streets, which were named after the gates and followed the lines of the Roman cardo maximus (western cardo) and decumanus maximus. The northern half of the western cardo was called St. Stephen's Gate Street (or St. Stephen's Street), while to the south of the intersection with the decumanus maximus it continued as two parallel streets: Mount Zion Street on the west (terminating at Mount Zion Gate; present day Habad Street) and, on the east, the Street of Judas's Arch (now the Street of the Jews), so-called because of a tradition that Judas Iscariot hanged himself from one of the arches over this street. The western half of the decumanus maximus was called David Street (a name it still retains today), and the eastern half was named Temple Street (now the Street of the Chain). The northern third of the eastern cardo (along the Tyropoeon Valley) was called Spanish Street, while its continuation, which terminated at the Tanners' Gate, was named the Street of the Furriers.[36]

Just north of the intersection of the western cardo (St. Stephen's Gate Street) and the decumanus maximus (David Street), the Crusaders established three parallel north-south streets along the cardo, each with its own market (the "Triple Market"), which have survived nearly intact. The Triple Market was built by Queen Melisende in 1152. Inscriptions next to some of the shops reading SCA ANNA (=Sancta Anna) connect them to the Convent of St. Anne (see below), where Melisende's sister Yvette (Joette) was a nun. Charles Clermont-Ganneau, who recorded the inscriptions, suggested that the convent received income from the rents of these shops.[37] The streets of the Triple Market were named, from west to east, the Street of Herbs (*Rue des Herbes*), the Street of Bad Cooking (*Malquisinat*), and the Covered Street (*Rue Couverte*). Herbs, fruit, and spices were sold on the Street of Herbs, and cloth was sold on the Covered Street. The Street of Bad Cooking offered cooked food to pilgrims and perhaps to residents. The preparation of food in bulk was a practical solution to the shortage of firewood, which made it expensive for use in private kitchens. Square shaft openings in the roof of the Street of Bad Cooking allowed the smoke to escape, while other streets have openings on the sides of the vaults (Figures 11.4 and 11.5). Immediately west of the Triple Market is a row of vaulted halls or shops. Other Crusader markets and buildings survive along Temple Street (the Street of the Chain), and along the southern part of the western cardo (in today's Jewish Quarter). Adrian Boas suggests that the latter, which is the route now walked by visitors to the western cardo, was established by the Franks in the thirteenth century.[38]

About midway between St. Stephen's Gate and David Street, another street called the Street of the Holy Sepulcher branched off to the west from St. Stephen's Gate Street (the western cardo), while Patriarch Street branched off to the north midway along David Street and intersected with the Street of the Holy Sepulcher. Together, these streets—the Street of the Holy Sepulcher on the north; Patriarch Street on the west; St. Stephen's Gate Street on the east; and David Street on the south—delineated the Patriarch's Quarter, which

FIGURE 11.4 Crusader street in the Triple Market with square shaft openings in the vaults.
Credit: Photo by the author.

overlaps with the modern Christian Quarter. The quarter is so-called because it was an autonomous area within the city administered by the patriarch. It was established as a predominantly Christian area in the eleventh century under an agreement between the Byzantine emperor and the Fatimid caliph. The buildings in the Patriarch's Quarter included the Church of the Holy Sepulcher and the Patriarch's palace to its northwest, as well as the Patriarch's pool (Hezekiah's pool). The pool was fed by another large reservoir also called the Patriarch's pool, which was located outside David's Gate in Mamilla.[39]

FIGURE 11.5 Crusader shops in the Triple Market with openings on the side of the vault.
Credit: Photo by the author.

The other quarters in the city were named after the populations that lived in them: the Syrian Quarter in the northeast (today the Muslim Quarter); the Armenian Quarter in the southwest, centered on the Cathedral Church of St. James; and the German Quarter in the southeast (the modern Jewish Quarter). Prior to the Crusader conquest, the Syrian Quarter had been inhabited by Jews (the *Juiverie*), who settled there after their neighborhood on Mount Zion was left outside the city walls in the eleventh century. The distinctions between the quarters were not rigid as Christians of different denominations and nationalities were co-mingled.[40]

The southern half of the Patriarch's Quarter had been the western forum of Aelia Capitolina. By the ninth century, a church dedicated to St. Mary la Latine, another church dedicated to John the Baptist, a hostel, a monastery, a convent, a library, and a marketplace were built in this area. These buildings were destroyed in 1009 by al-Hakim, and some might have been reconstructed after 1014 by Italian merchants from Amalfi (see Chapter 10). The area became known as the Muristan, which means "hospital" in Kurdish because under the Crusaders it was allocated to the Knights of the Hospitaller Order of St. John. The Hospitallers renovated the quarter, including constructing two Romanesque basilicas: a Church of St. Mary la Latine (or St. Mary Minor) in the northeast sector and a Church of St. Mary la Grande (St. Mary Major) to its west. A trefoil church dedicated to John the Baptist, the patron saint of the Hospitallers, was in the southwest sector. The other buildings included a large hospital and perhaps a second hospital for women, a bathhouse, the palace of the Grand Master of the Hospitallers, the knights' dormitory and refectory, stables, and a granary.[41] After the Crusader period, the Muristan deteriorated and fell into ruin. In 1869, the Ottoman sultan gave the eastern part of the quarter to the Germans, who reconstructed the Crusader Church of St. Mary la Latine and dedicated it as the Lutheran Church of the Redeemer in 1898 in the presence of Kaiser Wilhelm II. The Crusader cloister for Benedictine monks associated with the church still survives next to the modern church.[42] Nowadays visitors can climb to the top of the church's tower for a panoramic view of the Old City.

The Temple Mount was allocated to the Order of the Knights of the Temple—the Knights Templar. The Crusaders converted the Dome of the Rock into a church called "The Temple of the Lord" (*Templum Domini*). Al-Aqsa Mosque, which they called "Solomon's Temple" (*Templum Solomonis*), was used as the royal palace until 1119, when it became the Templars' headquarters. By ignoring the Muslim origin of these buildings and by-passing the Jewish past, the Crusaders not only Christianized the Temple Mount but presented themselves as the heirs to the biblical heritage, and, therefore, Christians—not Jews—as the True Israel. They covered the rocky outcrop (Foundation Stone) in the Dome of the Rock with marble slabs and enclosed it within an iron grille but made no other substantial changes. The grille, which might have been donated by Queen Melisende, and a pair of Frankish candelabra that were also in the Dome of the Rock, are now in the Islamic Museum on the Temple Mount (next to al-Aqsa Mosque).[43]

To the north of the Dome of the Rock the Crusaders erected an abbey (which was torn down by Saladin) to house the Augustinian monks in charge of the church. Al-Aqsa Mosque ("Solomon's Temple") was modified to serve as a royal palace (1104–1118), and later as the Templars' headquarters, with the addition of a dividing wall and apse to the mosque and the construction of new buildings including a cloister, church, refectories, storehouses, and granaries. The southern part of a Templar administrative building is preserved in a women's mosque and in the Museum of Islamic Art adjacent to al-Aqsa Mosque. The Templars used the underground arches and vaults that support the southern end of the Herodian esplanade as stables for their horses. Because they associated the structure with Solomon, the space became known as "Solomon's Stables." The Single Gate gave access to the stables. The Templars' headquarters in al-Aqsa Mosque were entered through the western (left-hand) portal of the Double Gate (Hulda Gate), by way of the tower that was added over the outside of the gate.[44]

After the Muslims took Jerusalem from the Crusaders, they reused carved Frankish architectural elements such as column capitals in repairs to al-Aqsa Mosque, the Dome of the Rock, and other buildings. In fact, a small octagonal monument about 20 meters (65 feet) northwest of the Dome of the Rock called the Dome of the Ascension of the Prophet Muhammad (*Qubbat al-Mi'raj*) is constructed almost entirely of carved Frankish stones. If it originally was constructed by the Crusaders and not by the Ayyubids, this structure might have been the baptistry of the "The Temple of the Lord" (the Dome of the Rock).[45]

The Order of the Teutonic Knights, which was a German branch of the predominantly French Order of the Hospitallers, was based in the southeastern part of the city. Their center included a hospital and a church dedicated to St. Mary, the excavated remains of which are visible today by Misgav Ladach Street in the Jewish Quarter (Figure 11.6).[46]

The Church of the Holy Sepulcher

Whereas in the Byzantine period public buildings had trussed wooden beams supporting a pitched, tiled roof—a form typical of basilicas—in the Crusader period these buildings usually had pointed arches and barrel or groin vaults constructed of stone. Meir Ben-Dov observes that stone arches and vaults provided a solution to roofing as timber became increasingly scarce due to the deforestation of the countryside. The Franks used stone arches and vaults to roof monumental private and public buildings and markets as well as streets, which had become narrow *suqs* instead of the broad colonnaded boulevards of the Byzantine period. The weight of the roof was concentrated onto the ribs of groin vaults and the spaces between them were filled with stones. Many Crusader churches are roofed with groin vaults, which are divided into bays, or with a combination of groin and barrel vaults.[47]

The thick stone walls, massive buttresses, stepped portals with clusters of columns and pilasters, carved voussoirs and archivolts around recessed windows,

FIGURE 11.6 The Church of St. Mary of the Order of Teutonic Knights in the Jewish Quarter.
Credit: Photo by the author.

pointed arches and groin vaults, and sculpted decoration of Crusader churches in Jerusalem reflect the influence of the Romanesque style, which was current in western Europe at the time of the First Crusade. However, Islamic and Byzantine influence is evident as well, as, for example, in the pointed arches, which were used in Islamic architecture. In other words, although Crusader art and architecture in Jerusalem are often described as "Romanesque," they represent a unique blend of local and foreign traditions.[48]

After al-Hakim's destruction of the Church of the Holy Sepulcher in 1009, only parts of the Rotunda remained standing. In 1048, the Byzantine emperor Constantine Monomachos received permission from the Fatimids to rebuild the church. The new structure was much smaller than its predecessor and introduced some important changes. The area that had been occupied previously by Constantine's basilica was not rebuilt, and since then it has remained outside the church (today the east end of Constantine's basilica is in the Alexander Nevsky Church). A large apse oriented to the east, which served as a modest prayer hall, was appended to the east side of the Rotunda. The remains of the apse are visible as brickwork on either side of the entrance to the main hall of the Crusader church from the Rotunda. To the east of the Rotunda was the Holy Garden, with

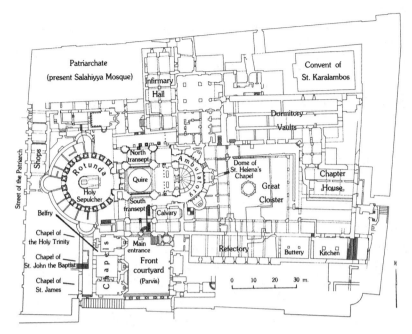

FIGURE 11.7 Plan of the Church of the Holy Sepulcher in the Crusader period.
Credit: From E. Stern [ed.] 1993: 796, with permission of the Israel Exploration Society

three small apsidal chapels along its east side, which were also oriented to the east. The entrance to the church was through a courtyard on the south side of the Holy Garden, as direct access from the western cardo was no longer possible. Three chapels were built along the west side of the courtyard. Many of these features were incorporated into the Crusader church.[49]

The quest to take the Church of the Holy Sepulcher was the motivating goal of the First Crusade. The current church's appearance is largely a product of the Crusader reconstruction, which was carried out during the reign of Queen Melisende. The rebuilt church was dedicated on 15 July 1149, fifty years after the Crusader conquest of Jerusalem (Figure 11.7).[50] Boas notes that the Crusaders modeled the building after the great Romanesque pilgrimage churches of the eleventh and twelfth centuries along the road from France to Santiago de Compostela—the cathedrals of Tours, Limoges, Conques, Toulouse, and Santiago—and concludes, "What the Franks did here is really quite remarkable."[51] These churches are characterized by a broad-aisled nave and transept, an ambulatory with radial chapels around the apse, and additional chapels on the east side of the transept. This design facilitated the movement of large numbers of pilgrims and allowed masses to be conducted in different parts of the building at the same time. But due to the lack of space between the Rotunda and the area to the east, in the Church of the Holy Sepulcher the nave and aisles were eliminated and the Choir (Quire) with a transept (now called the Catholicon) were built directly against the east side of the Rotunda. In other words, the Crusader church does not have a nave but only an aisled transept with an apse and ambulatory attached to the Rotunda, thereby uniting all the holy places within a single pilgrimage complex.[52] The piers of the north transept are built up against a row of columns from the courtyard of the Byzantine Holy Garden, which were incorporated into the Crusader church. A staircase between the eastern and southern chapels of the ambulatory descends to the chapel of St. Helena, and, from there, another staircase leads to the chapel of the Invention of the Cross (originally a quarry that was used as cistern under the nave of Constantine's basilica).

In the Crusader period, the Rotunda had a truncated, conical roof that was open to the sky, which was replaced by a dome after a great fire destroyed much of the church in 1808. The Franks added a stone screen with three holes to the front of the sepulcher inside the Rotunda, through which the tomb could be viewed, and the entrance to the eleventh-century edicule (the structure enshrining the tomb) was decorated with mosaics.[53] The chapel of Golgotha (Calvary) was also decorated with mosaics. The first eight Crusader kings of Jerusalem were interred in the chapel of Adam, below the chapel of Golgotha, and in the south arm of the transept. As Jaroslav Folda remarks, by placing the tombs of these kings "near that of Jesus Christ, the King of kings. . . . the venerable Church of the Holy Sepulchre—the most sacred pilgrimage site in Christendom—also became the pantheon of the Crusader kings."[54] The royal Crusader tombs, which were large stone sarcophagi (coffins), were removed by the Greek Orthodox after the 1808 fire.[55] Drawings and fragments of the sarcophagus of Baldwin V, who died in 1186 at the age of nine, indicate that it was more ornately decorated than those of the previous kings and was carved with the image of Christ between angels at the top.[56]

As in its eleventh-century predecessor, the main entrance to the Crusader Church of the Holy Sepulcher was through a courtyard to the south. The Franks added a Romanesque-style double portal in the south transept that was called the Gate of the Crucifixion, which might have been inspired by the appearance of the Golden Gate in the east wall of the Temple Mount (Figure 11.8). The right-hand portal has been blocked since the Ayyubid period (thirteenth century). A five-story-high belfry and, later, a bell tower, were added atop the chapel in the courtyard, on the west side of the portal. To the east of the church, above part of Constantine's former basilica, was a cloister for Augustinian canons (the monks who served in the church), which was centered on a large open courtyard.[57]

FIGURE 11.8 Main entrance to the Church of the Holy Sepulcher with the Crusader double portal and the Chapel of Golgotha (Calvary) on the right.
Credit: Photo by the author.

The Church of the Holy Sepulcher and other Crusader churches in Jerusalem were paved with stone floors, not mosaics. Elaborate carvings framed the recessed doors and windows, and clusters of columns and pilasters were topped with capitals sculpted with figures and vegetal designs. Two projecting horizontal cornices on the main (south) façade of the Church of the Holy Sepulcher—one between the lower and upper stories and the other along the top of the upper story—differ visibly in style from the Crusader reliefs and are thought to have originated in the temple built by Hadrian at this spot. The marble lintels above the double portal are carved in the Romanesque style but differ visibly from each other. The western (left) lintel depicts five episodes from the life of Jesus, from the raising of Lazarus to the Last Supper, which preceded the events commemorated within the church. The eastern (right) lintel is carved with vine scrolls containing mythological creatures such as sirens and centaurs. According to Nurith Kenaan-Kedar, the scenes on the western lintel convey a Christological message of the two natures of Christ (divine and human), while the eastern lintel represents the forces of evil (the devil and infidels) as a counterpart to the western lintel's message of triumph and salvation.[58] Both lintels are now in the Rockefeller Museum in Jerusalem.

The Church of St. Anne

With the exception of the Church of the Holy Sepulcher, Crusader churches typically are rectangular structures divided inside into a nave flanked by two aisles, which terminate at the east end in three apses contained within the outer wall. The nave and aisles are divided into bays roofed with barrel or groin vaults, and the nave rises to a greater height than the aisles as a clerestory.[59] One such church is the Benedictine Church of St. Anne, which Bahat aptly describes as "one of the most exquisite examples of Crusader architecture in the country."[60] The building, which was constructed over a ruined Byzantine church, is adjacent to the Sheep's Pool (Bezetha or Bethesda Pool) (Pl. 16). It is so-called because, according to Christian tradition, it was built on the site of the house of Anne and Joachim, where their daughter, the Virgin Mary, was born (see Chapter 9). A Crusader convent adjacent to the church derived considerable income from royal endowments, including rent from some of the shops in the Triple Market. It also benefited from royal patronage beginning in 1104, when King Baldwin I forced his estranged Armenian wife Arda to join the convent. Later, Yvette, the daughter of Baldwin II and sister of Queen Melisende, also entered the convent as a nun. Saladin converted the church into a Muslim school (*madrasa*). In 1761, it was sold to the Franciscans but was used mainly as a hostel for camel drivers entering the city through the Lions' Gate. In 1835, the governor of Jerusalem demolished part of the building and used the stones to build Ottoman barracks (now the Umariyya School) across the road. Subsequent attempts by the Muslims to restore it as a mosque failed, and, in 1856, the Ottoman sultan gave the building to France in gratitude for Napoleon III's support during the Crimean War. The church was restored soon thereafter by a French architect named Christophe-Edouard Mauss. Today it is administered by the White Fathers—a Catholic order so-called after the color of their robes.

Although its plan is typical of Crusader churches, the Church of St. Anne is unusual in having two windows above the main door in the west façade, one above the other. The upper window, which was round, was not restored. Boas points out that the arrangement of these windows was inspired by the south façade of the Church of the Holy Sepulcher, as was the large belfry in the southwest corner and, perhaps, the cupola (dome) at the junction of the nave and transept. The current small belfry was constructed by the French at a different spot over the base of a ruined minaret (tower of a mosque). The church's crypt is a cave venerated as the spot where the Virgin Mary was born. Although visitors today are impressed by the austerity of the interior, originally the walls were decorated with colorful mosaics and frescoes.[61]

Near the Church of St. Anne, the Crusaders rebuilt the Byzantine Church of St. Mary, which was supported on a wall separating the Sheep's Pool. By this time, the two reservoirs of the pool had silted up although they were still visible. The church had only one aisle supported on two rows of vaults, the upper of which served as a crypt.[62]

Water Supply

In addition to cisterns, the inhabitants of Crusader Jerusalem relied on various sources for their water supply, many of which originated in earlier periods. The Gihon spring and Pool of Siloam were still important sources, although the accumulation of sediment in the Siloam Tunnel impeded the flow of water. In addition, because the Gihon spring had become polluted its water was used mainly for irrigation, watering livestock, and industrial purposes.[63] The low-level aqueduct continued to function and supplied the pools on the Temple Mount.[64] Water was also stored in large reservoirs inside and outside the walls: the Patriarch's Pools (the Pool of Mamilla and Hezekiah's Pool), the Pool of Israel, and Germain's Pool. Germain's Pool (now the Sultan's Pool) was established in the 1170s, in the Ben-Hinnom Valley outside St. Stephen's Gate (Jaffa Gate). The pool is so-called after a philanthropist named Germain (or Germanus) who sponsored various projects to improve the city's water supply. It was a large reservoir consisting of two pools created by dams across the Ben-Hinnom Valley—a smaller upper pool and a larger lower pool. In the sixteenth century, the Ottoman sultan rebuilt the dam, giving rise to its current name.[65] Nowadays the Sultan's Pool is used as a venue for open-air concerts and performances.

Coins and Seals

Various currencies including Byzantine and Muslim coins circulated in the Crusader kingdom. As the royal seat, Jerusalem was the site of a mint, which might have been in or near the Tower of David or the palace. Because the economy of the Muslim East was based on gold, immediately after the conquest the Crusaders began to mint gold coins. Although the earliest specimens resemble Islamic dinars, by the 1130s–1140s the Franks began to produce a new series of gold coins called bezants (or besants), which circulated widely in the Latin East (Figure 11.9). Bezants were up to ten percent lighter in weight than dinars and have garbled Arabic inscriptions. In the 1140s, the Franks also began minting silver coins—low silver content (billon) deniers—supplementing the billon deniers from southern France and Italy, as well as small copper coins. The obverse of these coins has a Latin inscription and a cross, while the reverse depicts the Tower of David or the

FIGURE 11.9 Frankish gold bezants.
Credit: British Museum, CC BY-SA 3.0, via Wikimedia Commons.

edicule of the Church of the Holy Sepulcher. Crude, uninscribed cast lead tokens showing various motifs such as a cross, lion, mounted knight, heraldic shields, and monograms might have been used as unofficial currency or for gambling.[66]

Seals were used by the king, the Frankish nobility, royal and church officials, and the military orders to seal documents. The seal of Baldwin I, who succeeded Godfrey de Bouillon in 1100 and was the first Crusader ruler to be titled king, shows him enthroned on the obverse and, on the reverse, the Tower of David surrounded by David's Gate, the Dome of the Rock ("Temple of the Lord"), and the Church of the Holy Sepulcher. The seals of Baldwin's successors are similar, while the seals of church officials depict them seated or standing with a crosier.[67]

Conclusion

Under Frankish rule, medieval European features were introduced into Jerusalem's social and physical fabric. The military orders occupied some of the most prominent spots in the city. On the Temple Mount (Haram), the Knights Templar converted the Dome of the Rock into a church and al-Aqsa Mosque into their headquarters and used the crypotoporticus below as a stable for their horses. In the Muristan, adjacent to the Church of the Holy Sepulcher, the Hospitallers built churches and hospitals, while the Teutonic Knights established a hospital and church in the southeastern part of the city, opposite the Temple Mount. The Tower of David inside the Citadel functioned as a fortified stronghold and administrative center, and a royal palace was built to its south, in the same area where Herod's palace had been. The Church of the Holy Sepulcher was rebuilt, and new churches and monastic establishments were constructed around the city. Although Islamic and Byzantine stylistic influences are visible in the architecture and decoration of these churches, most of their features are typical of the Crusaders' homeland(s). The introduction of covered markets into the narrow *suqs* and the addition of elements such as barbicans to the fortifications further enhanced the city's medieval European appearance. Although the Crusaders had ethnically cleansed Jerusalem by slaughtering or banishing the Muslim and Jewish inhabitants, the Christian population was diverse, with communities of Latin Christians from around Europe as well as Eastern Christians.

After Saladin conquered Jerusalem, he restored the Dome of the Rock and al-Aqsa Mosque as Muslim monuments and converted some of the Crusader churches (such as the Church of St. Anne) to other purposes. Because the transition to Muslim rule was not accompanied by widespread destructions, many of the Frankish buildings and covered streets and markets continued to be used—some for their original functions—and have survived until today. Although Jerusalem was ravaged by wars, earthquakes, fires, and other disasters in the following centuries, including the dismantling of the walls by an Ayyubid caliph (which were later rebuilt by the Ottomans), the Old City still retains its medieval appearance. Despite the brief duration of their rule, the Crusaders left a lasting imprint upon the city.

Epilogue

BRITISH MANDATORY JERUSALEM
(11 DECEMBER 1917)

ON 11 DECEMBER 1917, following the withdrawal of Ottoman forces, General Edmund Allenby dismounted from his horse and entered the Jaffa Gate on foot to formally accept Jerusalem's surrender to the British Crown—a public display of piety captured in iconic early photographs (Figure E.1). Among the onlookers was T. E. Lawrence ("Lawrence of Arabia"), who was outfitted for the occasion in British military attire instead of his trademark Arabian robes: "While I was still with him, word came from Chetwode that Jerusalem had fallen; and Allenby made ready to enter in the official manner which the catholic imagination of Mark Sykes had devised. He was good enough, although I had done nothing for the success, to let Clayton take me along as his staff officer for the day. The personal Staff tricked me out in their spare clothes till I looked like a major in the British Army. Dalmeny lent me red tabs, Evans his brass hat; so that I had the gauds of my appointment in the ceremony of the Jaffa gate, which for me was the supreme moment of the war."[1]

Allenby's arrival hearkened back to Heraclius, who reportedly had displayed his humility by dismounting from his horse and removing his shoes and shirt, evoking David's and Jesus's triumphal entries. Less than two decades later, the caliph Umar is said to have entered the city on camel-back wearing simple camel hair garments, in a show of modesty that shocked the inhabitants who were accustomed to the extravagant displays of the ruling elite.[2] According to one account, when Jerusalem fell to the Crusaders, Godfrey de Bouillon emulated Heraclius's public demonstration of piety by entering the city barefoot and shirtless. By the eighteenth century it had become customary for Christian pilgrims to dismount from their horses at the city's gates—a practice that perhaps originated in the tradition about Godfrey.[3] Allenby's walk through the L-shaped passage of Jaffa Gate (which cannot accommodate wheeled traffic) was carefully choreographed to contrast with the 1898 visit by Kaiser Wilhelm II of Germany

FIGURE E.I General Allenby entering Jerusalem through Jaffa Gate.
Credit: Library of Congress; Digital ID: (b&w film copy neg.) cph 3b47734; LC-USZ62-93094.

and Prussia who, outfitted like a Crusader, rode a white stallion through a newly opened access road next to the gate, followed by the empress in her carriage.[4] It was during this visit that Wilhelm II oversaw the dedication of the Church of the Redeemer in the Muristan and acquired the land on which the Church of the Dormition on Mount Zion was built.[5]

Unlike his predecessors, Allenby approached Jerusalem not by way of the Mount of Olives and the Golden Gate to the east—the loci of messianic and eschatological expectations—but from the opposite direction.[6] Despite the

British government's efforts to tamp down any hint of a holy war, Jerusalem's surrender to Allenby was greeted enthusiastically by the public as a fulfilment of the Crusader quest. A flood of books and media coverage described Allenby and his soldiers as "modern" or "khaki" Crusaders. On 9 December 1917, the satirical magazine *Punch* published a cartoon captioned "The Last Crusade," showing Richard the Lionheart gazing at Jerusalem and exclaiming "My dream comes true!"[7] Perhaps no one drew a comparison to the Crusades more explicitly than Major Vivian Gilbert, the commander of a machine gun company, who wrote a memoir titled *The Romance of the Last Crusade: With Allenby to Jerusalem* (New York 1923).[8] The broad appeal of the Crusades in early twentieth-century Britain is illustrated by no less a figure than T. E. Lawrence, who wrote his 1910 undergraduate thesis on the topic of Crusader influence on European military architecture and claimed to be descended from a companion of Richard the Lionheart.[9]

And thus, the Franks left a lasting imprint not only on Jerusalem's physical appearance but on the popular imagination as well, with the British public viewing the city's surrender in 1917 as the culmination of the Crusader wars. Allenby's entry was rooted in millennia of precedent, from David to Jesus to Heraclius to Umar to Godfrey de Bouillon. As a result, Jerusalem, which for Christians is the center of universal salvation and the capital of a symbolic world empire, became part of the British Empire and the capital of Mandatory Palestine.[10] But the sun was already setting on the British Empire, and the British Mandate of Palestine did not survive for long. Just three decades after Allenby walked through the Jaffa Gate, the British, unable to stem the rising tide of violence between Jews and Arabs, relinquished the Mandate and withdrew from Palestine.

Walking Tours of Jerusalem

Jerusalem—especially the area in and around the Old City—is a compact city, and most of the sites mentioned in this book are within easy walking distance of each other. Here I suggest walking tours that include these sites. For all tours, wear comfortable shoes and bring a bottle of water. In the summer months, you will also need a hat and sunscreen. Some of the holy sites (such as the Church of the Holy Sepulcher) require modest dress for all visitors regardless of gender, meaning no shorts or bare knees and no bare shoulders. While walking through the Old City, secure your valuables such as wallets, purses, etc. from pickpockets (my husband once had a valuable camera lens stolen from a backpack that he was carrying). If you purchase souvenirs, always bargain with the shopkeeper for a lower price.

Before embarking on any tour, I recommend first going to the top of the Mount of Olives (in front of the Intercontinental Hotel) or Mount Scopus (by the Hebrew University) for a panoramic view of the city. From these vantage points, you will see the Temple Mount (Haram) and southeastern hill across the Kidron Valley, and the southwestern hill including Mount Zion rising behind to the west. I also recommend visiting the Israel Museum, where many of the artifacts mentioned in this book are displayed (e.g., the Caiaphas ossuary; the Theodotos inscription; the Ketef Hinnom amulets; the Nea church inscription; etc.).

The Southeastern Hill (City of David)

Begin from outside the Dung Gate. Following the sidewalk to the east (to the right of the Dung Gate as you are facing the gate), you will see al-Aqsa Mosque towering above the south wall of the Temple Mount, with Benjamin Mazar's excavations in front. From this spot, cross the encircling (east–west) road. You will see another road branching off to the south, which follows the Tyropoeon Valley. Walking south along the road, you will see the Givati Parking Lot excavations on your right. To the left, enter the City of David archaeological site (pay admission). This is a good place for a toilet break before embarking on your walk. Follow the steps to a lower level, along a walkway through and above the remains of the large stone structure. Continue eastward, walking down a long staircase overlooking the stepped stone structure and the Kidron Valley. At the bottom you can sit on benches in the shade, facing the Burnt Room House and, to the left, the House of Ahiel. Continuing upward along the walkway will take you to the entrance of Warren's Shaft. The way through the shaft is steep and, in some spots, dark and slippery, so watch your step. At the bottom you will emerge by the Rock-Cut Pool and the Pool Tower. The walkway continues to the entrance to the Gihon Spring. From there you can either enter the spring and walk through the Siloam Tunnel (through the water—bring a flashlight!) or through Channel II (which is dry). Emerge from Channel II through a turnstile (outside of which is another toilet facility) and continue walking south along the eastern slope of the southeastern hill. You will see the Middle Bronze Age-Iron Age mid-slope wall to your right (west) as you walk. The walkway will take you to the entrance of the recently excavated Hasmonean-Herodian–period Pool of Siloam, which is designed as a large *miqveh* surrounded on all sides by stepped bathing platforms. The paved street leading to the Temple Mount is across the pool from the main entrance; just above is the Siloam Church and the Pool of Siloam that lies at the outlet to the Siloam Tunnel. You can follow the paved street or the ancient sewer underneath it to the Western Wall plaza. Note that the walking through Channel II and the paved street/ancient sewer might make you uncomfortable if you are claustrophobic.

Jaffa Gate to the Jewish Quarter

Enter the Old City through the L-shaped passage of Jaffa Gate. Outside the gate to the north, notice the medieval forewall and moat below the pedestrian walkway. Once inside the gate, the Citadel with "David's Tower" will be on your right. Now or on another occasion, pay admission and visit the Citadel, which has a small museum and a view of the Temple Mount from the top of David's Tower. The First Wall with David's Tower and the early Islamic round tower are visible in the courtyard of the citadel. Outside the Citadel, follow the road to the right (south), encircling the Citadel to the Armenian Quarter. As the road narrows and enters a tunnel, the Armenian Garden (the area of Herod's palace) is on your right. After emerging from the tunnel, make your first left and follow the paved sidewalk as it winds to the east (through the Armenian Quarter), descending in steps toward the Jewish Quarter (down the east slope of the southwestern hill). Continue across the western cardo (visible below a pedestrian bridge) and straight ahead into a large open square that is at the center of the modern Jewish Quarter. On the other side of the square, enter the Wohl Archaeological Museum (this is off a side road that leads into the square). After paying admission, walk through the Herodian-period mansions, marveling at the interior decoration and displayed artifacts (note: as of March 2022, the Wohl Archaeological Museum is closed for two years, so check on its status before you go). At the other end, emerge through a turnstile and turn left, where you will see a large staircase. The "Burnt House" is up the steps and to the right. Following the steps down (right or east) leads to a panoramic view overlooking the southwest side of the Temple Mount. Continue now or on another occasion to B. Mazar's excavations around the southern and western sides of the Temple Mount (including the early Islamic palaces/administrative buildings) or to the Western Wall plaza (from the men's section of the Western Wall, enter Wilson's Arch and the Great Causeway and the entrance to the tunnels along the west side of the Temple Mount) (note: check if advance reservations are needed to enter the tunnels along the western side of the Temple Mount). There are public toilet facilities at the Western Wall plaza.

Damascus Gate Along the Western Cardo to the Church of the Holy Sepulcher

Enter the Old City through the Damascus Gate. As you cross the bridge just outside the present gate (which is Ottoman), you will see part of the Hadrianic, triple-arched gateway below and to the left. On the other side (inside) of the gate, you will emerge into an open area bustling with vendors (above the original Hadrianic oval plaza). At the end of the open area, two roads branch off: the left-hand road follows the Tyropoeon Valley south (the line of the eastern cardo) to the Temple Mount (emerging at the Western Wall plaza). Take the right-hand road, which follows the line of the western cardo, through the *suq* (marketplace). Watch on your right for a break in the shops, which will take you to the Russian Alexander Hospice (Alexander Nevsky Church). Ring the bell and pay a small admission fee to enter the basement, where you can see the remains of Hadrian's western forum, including part of the triple-arched gateway, the pavement of the forum, and the Roman basilica constructed of reused Herodian masonry (which was converted by Constantine into the basilica of the Church of the Holy Sepulcher). Notice the threshold next to the corner of the basilica with a large poster of Jesus carrying the cross; this is venerated by the church as the gate in the Second Wall through which Jesus was led to be crucified. Around the corner to the right, behind the threshold, you can see columns that lined the western cardo.

Across from the Russian Alexander Hospice, you will see the Lutheran Church of the Redeemer, which is in the Muristan. The Church of the Redeemer is worth visiting as it is modeled after the Crusader-period Church of St. Anne (by the Sheep's Pools next to the Via Dolorosa, north of the Temple Mount). The bell tower of the church affords a panoramic view over the Old City. Emerging from the Russian Alexander Hospice, continue to the right (west), which will take you through a gate into the open paved space in front of the main entrance to the Church of the Holy Sepulcher, which dates to the Crusader period (the original entrance into Constantine's basilica was from the western cardo). The small domed structure above and to the right of the entrance is the chapel of Golgotha (Calvary). Entering the church, you will see a large flat stone venerated as the spot where Jesus's body was anointed (the stone of unction). Immediately inside and to the right of the entrance, climb a steep, narrow set of steps to the chapel of Golgotha (which is divided among the Catholic and Greek Orthodox churches), where you can see part of the rock of Golgotha behind glass. Exit by descending another set of steps and enter the chapel of Adam immediately below the chapel of Golgotha. The rock of Golgotha is visible behind glass; the vertical crack or split is venerated as a crack through which Jesus's blood flowed on to and resurrected Adam. From the chapel of Adam, go back out to the curved corridor (ambulatory) that encircles the nave of the Crusader basilica, noticing the typical late Romanesque style architecture including the clustered columns, ribbed ceiling vaults, and the chapels radiating off the ambulatory. As you round the bend in the ambulatory, you will see steps descending to the Chapel of St. Helena and the Armenian Chapel of St. Vartan (where the fourth-century CE pilgrim graffito was found—not open to the public), and, at the bottom of the steps, the Chapel of the Invention of the Cross. Go back up the steps and continue along the ambulatory, around the north side of the nave of the Crusader basilica and into the Rotunda. From here you can look inside the nave of the Crusader church (now a Greek Orthodox church) and see the edicule with the tomb inside (unless you are a religious pilgrim, you may wish to skip entering the edicule due to the long lines). Most of the tomb is controlled by the Greek Orthodox, but a small corner in the rear is in the custody of the Coptic (Egyptian) church, whose priest will be happy to show you their corner of the remains. By the rear side of the edicule, enter a decrepit chapel off the western side of the Rotunda that belongs to the Syrian Orthodox church. A small opening at the far end of the chapel wall leads to part of a rock-cut tomb with loculi (the so-called tomb of Joseph of Arimathea)—evidence that this was the site of a Jewish cemetery in the first century CE. Re-enter the Rotunda and continue around it and exit through the entrance to the church.

From the Albright Institute and Third Wall to the Church of the Sisters of Zion

Begin at the W. F. Albright Institute on 26 Salah ed-Din Street in East Jerusalem. The institute is gated, so if you wish to visit, contact the Director in advance (aiar.org). Walk westward—that is, away from—the institute, along the right side of a road that passes by the St. George Hotel (on the left side of the road). After passing the hotel (on the left) and a series of small shops (on the right), you will see a couple of large, battered stone blocks on the right side of the sidewalk. These are part of the Third Wall. At the rotary a little further along, in front of the former American consulate in East Jerusalem, you will see another block of the Third Wall in an excavated trench. The continuation of the wall is visible straight ahead (to the west), past the rotary. But, instead of following it, turn left (south) at the rotary, past a gas station (on the left) and a mosque (on the right). The mosque lies roughly on the site of the northern arch. Follow the road (Nablus Road) southward, passing on the left (east) the École Biblique/ Church of St. Stephen and then the Garden Tomb. At the end of the road, you will reach the Damascus Gate. Enter the Damascus Gate and take the left-hand road along the Tyropoeon Valley. After going through an arched passage with shops, take your first major left turn onto the Via Dolorosa. The Austrian Hospice will be at the corner on your left; they have a café with excellent apple strudel. Follow the Via Dolorosa as it ascends toward the Church of the Sisters of Zion (a convent), which is on the left (north) side of the road. Herod's Antonia fortress would have been on the right (south) side of the road. You will see the Arch of Ecce Homo spanning the Via Dolorosa; the north part of the arch, which is in the church's sanctuary, can be seen by going up steps to a room on the left side of the Via Dolorosa. Continue along and make your first left to enter the convent (after turning the corner, on the left). Pay admission and enter the building. This is a good place for a toilet break. After the toilets, proceed inside, looking at the exhibits, and follow the steps down (careful—they are dark and slippery) into the Struthion Pools. Emerge from the pools via another set of steps onto the Lithostratos pavement. You will see games incised on the paving stones (it was common in antiquity to incise gameboards in paving stones in public spaces—this has nothing to do with the Roman soldiers casting lots for Jesus's clothing) and striations in the paving stones to prevent wheeled traffic from slipping and sliding. Exit the complex through another set of steps and a turnstile, emerging back onto the Via Dolorosa. Turning left (east) will take you to the Church of St. Anne and the Sheep's Pools (on the right/north), ending at the Lions' Gate. Turning right (west) will take you back along the Via Dolorosa, where you can turn left (south) to follow the Tyropoeon Valley to the Western Wall plaza. Or you can turn right (west) off the Tyropoeon Valley to continue with the Via Dolorosa to the western cardo and the Church of the Holy Sepulcher.

Timeline

BCE

ca. 3500–2200: Early Bronze Age; Jerusalem first settled

ca. 2000–1550: Middle Bronze Age II; Jerusalem (*Rushalimum*) mentioned in the Egyptian Execration Texts

ca. 1550–1200: Late Bronze Age; Jerusalem (*Urusalim*) mentioned in the el-Amarna letters.

ca. 1200: Beginning of the Iron Age; the Israelite tribes enter Canaan and settle the hill country, and the Philistines establish a kingdom on the southern coastal plain

ca. 1005–928 BCE: The United Kingdom/United Monarchy (kingdom of David and Solomon)

ca. 960: Solomon builds the first temple

ca. 928: After Solomon's death, the United Kingdom splits into Israel (north) and Judah (south)

722: The kingdom of Israel falls to Assyria

701: The Assyrians invade Judah, destroy Lachish, and besiege Jerusalem (under King Hezekiah)

639–609: Deuteronomistic reforms under Josiah, king of Judah

612: The Assyrian empire collapses, replaced as the dominant Near Eastern power by the Neo-Babylonian empire

586: The end of the Iron Age; the Babylonians destroy Jerusalem and Solomon's temple and disperse the Judahite (Judean) elite

539: King Cyrus II of Persia issues an edict allowing the exiled Judeans to return to their homeland and rebuild the temple

516: The second Jerusalem temple is consecrated

ca. 450: Ezra and Nehemiah in Jerusalem

332: Alexander the Great conquers Judea (Yehud)

198: Judea comes under Seleucid rule

167: Antiochus IV Epiphanes outlaws Judaism and dedicates the Jerusalem temple to Olympian Zeus, leading to the outbreak of the Maccabean Revolt

164: Antiochus IV rescinds his edict outlawing Judaism, and the Jerusalem temple is rededicated to the God of Israel, but the Maccabean Revolt continues

by 140: The Maccabees establish an independent Jewish kingdom ruled by their descendants (the Hasmoneans). In the decades that follow, the Hasmoneans increase the size of their kingdom through territorial expansion

ca. 80: A sectarian community settles at Qumran (the site associated with the Dead Sea Scrolls)

63: The Roman general Pompey annexes the Hasmonean kingdom

40: The Parthians invade Syria-Palestine; Herod flees to Rome and is appointed king of Judea

37: Herod defeats Mattathias Antigonus

31: Octavian defeats Mark Antony and Cleopatra at the battle of Actium; afterward he reconfirms Herod as king of Judea and increases the size of Herod's kingdom

4: Herod dies and his kingdom is divided among three of his sons

CE

6: Herod's son Archelaus is deposed and replaced by the Romans with prefects or procurators who establish their base of administration at Caesarea Maritima

26–36: Pontius Pilate is the Roman prefect and executes Jesus

37–44: Rule of Herod Agrippa I, the grandson of Herod the Great and his Hasmonean wife Mariamme

44–66: All of Herod the Great's former kingdom is placed under the administration of Roman procurators

62/63: James the Just (brother of Jesus) is executed by the Jewish Sanhedrin in Jerusalem and Paul is executed in Rome

66: The First Jewish Revolt against Rome begins

67: Galilee is subdued by the Romans and Josephus surrenders to Vespasian

68: The sectarian settlement at Qumran is destroyed and the community flees, depositing the Dead Sea Scrolls in the nearby caves

69: Vespasian becomes Roman emperor, leaving his son Titus in charge of taking Jerusalem

70: Jerusalem falls to the Romans and the second temple is destroyed, marking the official end of the First Jewish Revolt. The Tenth Legion is stationed permanently in Jerusalem.

115–117: The Diaspora Revolt (during the reign of Trajan)

ca. 135: Jerusalem is rebuilt by Hadrian as Aelia Capitolina after the Second Jewish Revolt against the Romans (Bar Kokhba revolt)

ca. 300: The Tenth Legion is transferred from Jerusalem to Aila (modern Aqaba)

313: Constantine and Licinius issue the Edict of Milan, legalizing Christianity

324: Constantine establishes Constantinople (formerly Byzantium) as the new capital of the Roman Empire

395: The Roman Empire splits into West and East (East = the Byzantine Empire)

527–565: Reign of the Byzantine emperor Justinian

614: The Sasanid Persian conquest of Palestine

622: Muhammad's flight (*hegira*) from Mecca to Medina

634–641/2: The Muslim conquest of Palestine (Jerusalem surrenders by 638)

661–750: The Umayyad dynasty rules Palestine from their capital in Damascus

691/2: The Umayyad caliph ʿAbd al-Malik dedicates the Dome of the Rock

750: The Abbasid dynasty overthrows the Umayyads and moves the capital to Baghdad

Christmas Day, 800 CE: Charlemagne is crowned emperor of the Holy Roman Empire

1009: The Fatimid caliph al-Hakim orders the Church of the Holy Sepulcher dismantled

15 July 1099: Jerusalem falls to the Crusaders

2 October 1187: Balian of Ibelin surrenders Jerusalem to Saladin

11 December 1917: General Edmund Allenby accepts the surrender of Jerusalem to the British Crown

1947–1948: The British Mandate ends, Palestine is partitioned, and the State of Israel is established

Notes

PREFACE

1. Matt Adams, personal communication (2 March 2022).
2. Küchler 2014 provides broad and detailed coverage but differs in being organized by site and is published only in German.
3. Tehillah Lieberman in Lawler 2021a: 347.

INTRODUCTION: TOPOGRAPHY AND SOURCES

1. Sophronius of Jerusalem, *Anacreonticon* 20:1; from Wilkinson 1977: 91.
2. Wilkinson 1977: 7; R. Schick 1995: 58–61.
3. Unless otherwise indicated, all biblical citations are from the NRSV.
4. For the term "God of Israel," see Stahl 2020.
5. Patrich and Edelcopp 2013: 322 n. 1. It was also called the mountain of the house of the Lord (e.g., Micah 4:1); see Bahat 2020: 15.
6. This identification first occurs in 2 Chronicles 3:1; see Patrich and Edelcopp 2013: 322 n. 1; Levine 2002: 41. According to Bahat 2020: 17, Moriah derives from the Hebrew root for "to found/establish."
7. Vincent 2004: 157–62; Hurowitz 2009: 18–20. "Zion" can denote both the Temple Mount and all of Jerusalem, see Bahat 2020: 15.
8. Cahill 2003a: 13–14; references in Magness 2019: 40–41.
9. Ben-Dov 2002: 13; Cahill 2003a: 16.
10. A quarter of the total rainfall is in the month of January; Boas 2001: 171.
11. Ben-Arieh 1984: 74–79; Ben-Dov 2002: 14–15.
12. Estimates of the spring's output vary widely; see Reich 2021c: 9; Reich 2021a: 245; Sneh et al. 2010: 59; Ben-Dov 2002: 15.
13. Gill 1996: 3.

14. Gill 1996: 9–11; Reich 2021c: 5; Cahill 2003a: 15. Mizzi Ahmar is exposed along the lower eastern slope of the southeastern hill, while the upper eastern slope and crest are Meleke.

15. Reich 2004: 127.

16. Gill 1996: 17; Reich 2021c: 5–9; Cahill 2003a: 15–16. According to Reich 2021c: 9–14, "Gihon" was never the name of the spring (which is called in Arabic `En Umm ed-Daraj ["the spring of the mother of the stairs"]). Instead, he argues that from the Iron Age II through the early Roman period, Gihon was a technical term for the Canaanite (Bronze Age) water system, while the name Shelah/Shiloah/Siloam denoted the spring and/or the pool at the south end of the southeastern hill. Reich proposes that, before the Iron Age II, the spring was known as Ein Shemesh.

17. Finkelstein 2011: 189.

18. Ben-Dov 2002: 4–5.

19. Cahill 2003a: 14, speculates that "Jerusalem's prominence during the Iron Age may have been due, at least in part, to its position guarding the northern end of a bottleneck on the north-south route that followed the watershed through the center of the region."

20. Huffmon 1999: 756. Demsky 2021: 69, identifies *yeru* as a verb in the third person; Elitzur 2014: 192, 195, argues that the city's name from the beginning meant "a place of peace and tranquility" and that *yeru* referred to a certain topographical, landscape, or agricultural entity in the vicinity of Jerusalem.

21. Murphy-O'Connor 2012a: 1; Huffmon 1999: 756.

22. Pullan et al. 2013: 76–77.

23. See, e.g., Cahill 2003a: 14 (12 acres). Reich 2021b: 57, estimates that the southeastern hill covers an area of ca. 28 acres based on recent discoveries indicating the presence of remains extending farther to the east and west than was previously thought.

24. Cahill 2003a: 15.

25. Ben-Dov 2002: 11.

26. Gibson and Har-Peled 2019: 124–25.

27. Josephus, *War* 5.67; from Thackeray 2006: 23 (Vol. IV). Unless otherwise indicated, all translations of Josephus are from the Loeb Classical Library editions.

28. Geva 2003: 503.

29. Ben-Arieh 1984: 14.

30. Ben-Arieh 1984: 14; although the quarters existed earlier, the current names go back to the nineteenth century. According to Peters 2011: 5, the Christian Quarter was first established in the northwest part of the Old City in the 1160s, three decades before the Crusades, whereas Ben-Arieh says it is not mentioned in European travelers' writings before 1806.

31. Pullan et al. 2013: 50–51, 59.

32. Ben-Arieh 1984: 25.

33. Crowfoot and Fitzgerald 1929: 7; Cahill 2003a: 18.

34. De Groot and Bernick-Greenberg 2012: 141–43.

35. For periodization in biblical historiography, see Machinist 2019 (with a discussion of the book of Daniel on pp. 226–31) and see the essays in the same volume for systems of periodization in other ancient cultures.

36. See Hammond and Scullard 1970: 521.

37. Ikram and Dodson 1998: 8–10, provide the following conjectural dates: Old Kingdom: 2663–2195 BCE; Middle Kingdom: 2066–1650 BCE; New Kingdom: 1549–1069. The Old Kingdom is preceded by the Archaic Period (3050–2663 BCE); the First Intermediate Period (2195–2066 BCE) separates the Old and Middle Kingdom; and the Second Intermediate Period (1650–1549 BCE) separates the Middle and New Kingdom.

38. Lawler 2021a: 345.

39. Pullan et al. 2013: 34–35.

40. Pullan et al. 2013: 76–101; Lawler 2021a: 298–300. Also see the Emek Shaveh website at https://emekshaveh.org/en/ (accessed 15 October 2021).

41. See Lawler 2021a; Kletter 2020; Galor 2017; Abu El-Haj 2002.

42. Halpern 1988 claims that some of the biblical writers were historians who "meant to furnish fair and accurate representations of Israelite antiquity" (p. 3). Lipiński 2020: 1, is more skeptical of the "historical value" of some of the information even in the books of the Former Prophets—Joshua, Judges, 1–2 Samuel, and 1–2 Kings. For an excellent discussion (relating to 1–2 Kings), see Grabbe 2017: 6–14, 82–84, 95, who concludes, "The Greeks questioned their myths and traditions in a way for which we have no evidence among Jewish historians. . . . Unlike history writing as it developed in the Greco-Roman period . . . the DH shows no evidence of applying critical thought or analysis and its ultimate aim was theological, not the telling of history. We cannot consider the DH as 'history' in the same sense as modern critical history or even in the sense as written by Herodotus or Polybius" (pp. 84, 95).

43. See, e.g., Finkelstein and Silberman 2001.

1. THE EXPLORERS

1. Twain 1996: 558.

2. Twain 1996: 559–60. Ben-Arieh 1984: 25, notes that "The crowded clusters of domes so typical of the Old City skyline were a constant source of wonderment to Western travelers"; see pp. 98–101 for lepers' huts in the Old City in the nineteenth century.

3. Silberman 1982: 4.

4. Twain 1996: 582.

5. Ben-Arieh 1979: 15.

6. Avni and Galor 2011: x.

7. Silberman 1982: 14; Ben-Arieh 1979: 21.

8. Silberman 1982: 15–16; Ben-Arieh 1979: 21.

9. Ben-Arieh 1979: 27, 30–31, 67.

10. Ben-Arieh 1979: 67–69; Ben-Arieh 1984: 107–11; Silberman 1982: 45.

11. Ben-Arieh 1979: 79.

12. Ben-Arieh 1979: 79–82.

13. Ben-Arieh 1979: 94–102.

14. Ben-Arieh 1979: 91.

15. Hallote 2006: 8–13.

16. Robinson and Smith 1841: 384; Section VII.1.

17. Robinson and Smith 1841: 395–96; Section VII.2.

18. Silberman 1982: 43; Robinson and Smith 1841: 423–24.

19. Silberman 1982: 43; Robinson and Smith 1841: 424–27. The stones had been noted previously by Catherwood; see Gibson 2021: 2–3.

20. Robinson and Smith 1841: 465–66.

21. Robinson and Smith 1841: 528–38.

22. Reich 2011a: 13, 16.

23. Robinson and Smith 1841: 500–3.

24. Ben-Arieh 1979: 85; Silberman 1982: 47.

25. Ben-Arieh 1979: 153.

26. Ben-Arieh 1979: 91, 153; Silberman 1982: 62.

27. Ben-Arieh 1979: 111–17; Ben-Arieh 1984: 184–86.

28. Silberman 1982; 65; Cohen-Hattab and Shoval 2015: 30; Peters 2011: 13. For pilgrimage versus other types of travel, see Cohen-Hattab and Shoval 2015: 2–4; Trotter 2019: 76 n. 2.

29. Silberman 1982: 46.

30. Hallote 2006: 29–31; Cohen-Hattab and Shoval 2015: 27.

31. Silberman 1982: 65.

32. Magness 2019b: 32–33. For a recent account of de Saulcy's work in Jerusalem, see Lawler 2021a: 3–19.

33. Silberman 1982: 67.

34. Silberman 1982: 67.

35. Silberman 1982: 69.

36. Silberman 1982: 71.

37. Cotton et al. 2010: 166, no. 123 (Yardeni/Price/Misgav); Kloner and Zissu 2007: 234; Ben-Ami and Tchekhanovets 2011a: 238.

38. Silberman 1982: 71.

39. Silberman 1982: 72.

40. Caubet 1997: 495.

41. Silberman 1982: 80; Ben-Arieh 1979: 184; Gibson 2011: 26. For a recent account of Wilson's activities in Jerusalem, see Lawler 2021a: 20–38.

42. Hallote 2006: 22, 27, 49.

43. Hallote 2006: 48. For diseases in the city in the nineteenth century, see Ben-Arieh 1984: 94–96.

44. Hallote 2006: 22–23, 49.
45. Silberman 1982: 82; Gibson and Jacobson 1996: 14.
46. Silberman 1982: 83; Ben-Arieh 1979: 184–85; Gibson 2011: 26–28.
47. Ben-Arieh 1979: 184; Silberman 1982: 87; Hodson 1997b: 345–46; Gibson 2011: 26–28.
48. Silberman 1982: 84. The arch had been identified previously as part of a bridge by Titus Tobler; see Warren 1876: 368; Gibson 2021: 2; E. Mazar 2011c: 76.
49. Gibson 2011: 36; for the PEF's relationship to the Palestine Association, which existed from 1804–1834, see pp. 30–31.
50. Silberman 1982: 86–89; Ben-Arieh 1979: 191, 195.
51. Silberman 1982: 89–90; Gibson 2011: 37.
52. Hodson 1997b: 346; Gibson and Jacobson 1996: 14.
53. Silberman 1982: 90; Ben-Arieh 1979: 199; Gibson and Jacobson 1994: 15. For a recent account of Warren's activities in Jerusalem, see Lawler 2021a: 38–67.
54. Silberman 1982: 92–95; Ben-Arieh 1979: 199, 203; Warren and Conder 1889: 148, 183; Gibson 2011: 43.
55. Hodson 1997a: 330–31.
56. Reich 2011a: 20–24; Gibson and Jacobson 1996: 15.
57. Ben-Arieh 1979: 203; Silberman 1982: 94; Magness 2019b: 34.
58. For the personal relationship between Wilson and Warren, see Gibson 2021: 9–13.
59. Ben-Arieh 1979: 210; Magness 2019b: 34.
60. Silberman 1982: 124; Magness 2019b: 35.
61. Silberman 1982: 124, 126; Gibson and Jacobson 1996: 14–15.
62. Silberman 1982: 126.
63. Gibson and Jacobson 1996: 17.
64. Silberman 1982: 106–11; Silberman 1997: 37; Reich 2011a: 25–27.
65. Cotton et al. 2010: 45 (Price).
66. Dershowitz 2021a: 2, 5–6.
67. Dershowitz 2021a: 10.
68. Silberman 1982: 131–46.
69. Dershowitz 2021a; 2021b; Dershowitz and Tabor 2021.
70. It appears that most scholars reject Dershowitz's argument that the Shapira fragments were authentic; see, e.g., Klawans 2022; Richey 2022; Hendel and Richelle 2021. For an overview of the Shapira affair in light of Dershowitz's claim, see Press 2021.
71. Cook 1923; also see his obituary in the *Journal des Débats*, 14 March 1923, p. 4.
72. James Davila, "The Shapira Fragments Raise their Mouldering Heads Again," 4 November 2014; https://paleojudaica.blogspot.com/2013_11_03_archive.html#810475699851573000) (accessed 13 October 2021).
73. Ben-Arieh 1979: 133.
74. Gibson 2011: 40.

75. Ben-Arieh 1979: 117.

76. Ben-Arieh 1984: 115, 186–88.

77. Ben-Arieh 1979: 117–18.

78. Astafieva 2020. I thank David Gurevich for this reference.

79. Reich 2011a: 27–32.

80. For Schick, see Gurevich 2019; Lawler 2021a: 71–82, 93–95; Silberman 1982: 151–52; Ben-Arieh 1979: 213; Masterman 1902. David Gurevich informs me that Schick did not accept the identification of the remains as the Second Wall (personal communication April 2022).

81. https://www.palestine-studies.org/sites/default/files/jq-articles/Conrad_Schick__JQ_67_0.pdf

82. Gibson and Jacobson 1996: 17, 20.

83. Silberman 1982: 127; Barkay 1986: 44; Gibson and Jacobson 1996: 14.

84. See Peters 2011: 14, about the Protestant desire to have "an unmediated relation to the Bible" rather than experiencing holy places overlaid by Orthodox or Catholic churches.

85. Pullan et al. 2013: 55; Barkay 1996: 42–43.

86. C. Gordon 1888: 289–90.

87. Silberman 1982: 152–53; Frantzman and Kark 2008: 6–9.

88. Barkay 1986.

89. Frantzman and Kark 2008: 5.

90. Lawler 2021a: 88–93; Hallote 2006: 46–48, 55–57 (for a biography of Bliss, see pp. 85–191); Silberman 1982: 150; Blakely 1993: 110–11.

91. Hallote 2006: 88–89, 99–105; Silberman 1982: 150; Moorey 1991: 30–31.

92. Hallote 2006: 126–134.

93. Silberman 1982: 153.

94. Silberman 1982: 156.

95. Silberman 1982: 155.

96. Hallote 2006: 127–28; Silberman 1982: 156; Bliss 1977: 278; Reich 2011a: 46–48.

97. Bliss 1977: 278.

98. Reich 2011a: 50.

99. Hallote 2006: 132; Silberman 1982: 157.

100. Bliss 1977: 279; Hallote 2006: 130.

101. Reich 2011a: 47.

102. Blakely 1997: 332–33. Bliss also interviewed Prince Faisal of Saudi Arabia for the *New York Times* during his brief tenure as King of Hejaz; see Hallote 2006: 176–80, and 172 for Allenby's close ties to James Henry Breasted.

103. Silberman 1982: 163; Tubb 2015: 6–7.

104. Tubb 2015: 10; Silberman 1982: 164; Thomas 1984: 34; Dever 1997.

105. Gibson 2015: 37–38; Tubb 2015: 16–17; Thomas 1984: 34; Macalister and Duncan 1926: 9.

106. For different views, see the papers in Wolff (ed.) 2015; Thomas 1984: 34–35; Wolff 2015; Dever 1997: 391. Moorey 1991: 32, says "The Gezer excavations suffered from the worst practices of the time."

107. Macalister and Duncan 1926: 73–74; Reich 2011a: 89; Gibson 2011: 49.

108. Murphy-O'Connor 1997; Albright 1961; Sellers 1961.

109. Lawler 2021a: 98–112; Silberman 1982: 180–88.

110. Reich 2011a: 59–68, 281; Vincent 1911.

111. Reich 1997: 342–43; Vandier 2004: xxix–xxx; Reich 2004: 124; Lawler 2021a: 114–18. Weill was not only the first Jewish archaeologist to excavate in Jerusalem, but in Palestine.

112. Reich 2011a: 70; Reich 2004: 123–24.

113. Reich 1997: 343; Reich 2004: 126; Gadot 2022a: 288.

114. Reich 1997: 343; Reich 2011a: 72–75; Shanks (ed.) 2004: 86–89.

115. Reich 1997: 343; Vandier 2004: xxx.

116. Reich 2011a: 85–86.

117. Vandier 2004: xxxi.

118. Silberman 1982: 200, 271; Reich 2011b: 117, 119; Reich 2011a: 86–87.

119. Silberman 1982: 200, 217; Reich 2011b: 120.

120. Reich 2011b: 122–24; IES website: https://www.israelexplorationsociety.com/ (accessed 16 October 2021).

121. E. Crowfoot 1997: 72–73.

122. E. Crowfoot 1997: 72; Reich 2011a: 93–100.

123. Moorey 1997: 491.

124. For Hamilton's biography, see the obituary by Moorey 1997.

125. See Hamilton 1944.

126. Albright 1949: 13.

127. For Kenyon's biography, see Tushingham 1997; Prag 1992; Moorey 1991: 60–64, 94–99, 122–26.

128. Gibson 2011: 50–52; Reich 2011a: 112–14.

129. Reich 2011a: 106, notes that Kenyon's last season was conducted in the summer of 1967, after the war.

130. Lawler 2021a: 130.

131. For the IAA, see Seligman 2011.

132. A. Mazar 1997.

133. https://www.timesofisrael.com/fearless-pioneering-biblical-archaeologist-eilat-mazar-dies-at-64/ (accessed 16 October 2021).

134. Avigad 1954.

135. Avigad 1983.

136. Meyers 1997; Geva 2000: 32.

137. For Shiloh's biography, see Lawler 2021a: 158–63; T. Shiloh 1997; Reich 2011a: 124–42. For an obituary, see Abraham Rabinovitch, "Israeli Archaeologist

Yigal Shiloh: A Warrior on the Walls of Jerusalem," *The Jerusalem Post*, Monday, 16 November 1987, p. 3.

138. Herb Keinon, "Posters Curse Late Archaeologist," *The Jerusalem Post*, week of 16 November 1987.

139. For archaeologists working in Jerusalem in more recent years, see Lawler 2021a: 164–355; Reich 2011a: 118–269. For a summary of all excavations on the southeastern hill with maps and references, see Reich 2021b: 21–64.

2. JEBUSITE JERUSALEM (1050 BCE)

1. For scant Chalcolithic remains (but no architecture), see Maeir 2011: 171–72; Cahill 2003a: 19; E. Mazar 2009: 20–21. De Groot and Bernick-Greenberg 2012: 143–44, posit a sedentary settlement in the Neolithic and Chalcolithic periods. Flint tools found in the vicinity of the Gihon spring indicate that it has been in use since the Epipaleolithic Period (ca. 18,000–14,000 BP [Before Present]); Reich 2021c: 8; also see Lipiński 2020: 7. For a tiny Neolithic flint arrowhead from recent excavations on Mount Zion, see https://www.haaretz.com/archaeology/2022-07-28/ty-article/neolithic-arrowhead-no-larger-than-fingernail-is-oldest-artifact-ever-found-in-jerusalem/00000182-454e-d473-a7ca-fdcefd680000 (accessed 24 December 2022).

2. Greenberg 2019: 188.

3. De Groot and Bernick-Greenberg 2012: 123–30, 144; Cahill 2003a: 19–20; Reich 2011a: 282; Maeir 2011: 172. Reich questions whether Jerusalem was inhabited between the EB I and MB II (p. 284), whereas Maeir states, "Throughout the entire Early Bronze Age, Jerusalem was inhabited" (p. 174).

4. Vincent 1911: 24–28; Pl. X.

5. Huffmon 1999: 756; Ben-Dov 2002: 23; B. Mazar 1993: 698; Bahat 2011b: 18, 20. Na'aman 1992: 279, disagrees due to the missing 'aleph at the beginning of the name, but Lipiński 2020: 10, notes that the initial vowel is generally not indicated even in genuine Egyptian words. Greenberg 2019: 186, cautions against using the Execration Texts as an accurate reflection of political geography.

6. Ben-Dov 2002: 30–31; Bahat 2011b: 18. Lipiński 2020: 11–12, identifies both names as Amorite.

7. Bahat 2011b: 18; Meiron 2019: 5.

8. Bryan 1997.

9. Izre'el 1997: 86–87; Reich 2011a: 288. An additional 2–3 letters sent from Gath mention Jerusalem; see Lipiński 2020: 18. Maeir 2011: 179 n. 7, rejects the suggestion of others that *Urusalim* is not Jerusalem.

10. From Moran 1992: 328.

11. Coote 2000; Pitard 1998: 65.

12. Fortner 2000: 87.

13. Michalowski 2000; Meiron 2019: 5. Lipiński 2020: 13, 21, identifies the entire population including the Jebusites as Amorites. Greenberg 2019: 187–88, concludes that the term Amorite "should be taken as an indication of shared values and mutually recognized expressions of status."

14. Greenberg 2019: 237, estimates 900–1,200. Geva 2014a: 135–137, estimates 500–700; but Geva 2019: 7, estimates 1,000. Lipiński 2020: 13, 20, estimates 880–1,100 in the MB II and 1,750 in the Late Bronze Age. Reich 2011a: 288, and Geva 2019: 12, note the apparent disconnect between the historical sources and archaeological remains.

15. Prag 2018: 15, including a possible fortification wall at the north end in Kenyon's Site H. For the absence of remains in the Givati Parking Lot, see Ben-Ami 2014: 15.

16. Greenberg 2019: 225–26, 236–38. Also see Prag 2018: 16, 19.

17. Reich and Shukron 2021b: 360; Reich and Shukron in E. Stern 2008: 1801; Reich and Shukron 2004.

18. Reich and Shukron 2021b: 360; Reich and Shukron 2021d: 674, 677; Reich 2011a: 306; Meiron 2019: 11–12; Geva 2019: 5; Gill 1996: 13–18; Ariel and de Groot 2000: 165; Ussishkin 2016: 146.

19. Reich and Shukron 2021b: 358–59; Reich and Shukron 2021d: 677; Reich 2011a: 161, 183; Ariel and Lender 2000: 15; Ariel and de Groot 2000: 164–66; Cahill 2003a: 25.

20. Reich and Shukron 2021b: 358–60, propose that Channel II was an early attempt to redirect the water from the spring to the southwest side of the southeastern hill and was soon replaced by Siloam Tunnel. Also see Reich and Shukron 2021b: 335; Reich and Shukron 2021d: 664; Meiron 2019: 11; Cahill 2003a: 24 including n. 47.

21. Reich and Shukron 2004; Ussishkin 2016: 142–43; contra Reich 2011a: 306; but see Reich 2018: 116.

22. Reich 2011a: 235; Ussishkin 2016: 142–43; Reich, Shukron, and Lernau 2019: 42.

23. Ussishkin 2016: 143. Also see McKinny et al. 2021: 656–57.

24. Reich 2011a: 155.

25. Reich 2011a: 155–56.

26. Reich 2011a: 156; Meiron 2019: 8–10.

27. Reich, Shukron, and Lernau 2019: 42; also see Reich and Shukron 2021b: 351–52.

28. Reich 2011a: 253. Alon de Groot (personal communication, February 2022) points out that Pool Tower/Fortified Corridor still stood in the ninth century BCE, contradicting the proposal that Warren's Shaft was hewn to provide an exit from the system.

29. Grossberg 2014: 209–210, argues that Warren's Shaft provided access to water brought to its base from the spring instead of to the rock-cut pool.

30. Reich 2011a: 253; Meiron 2019: 10.

31. Reich 2011a: 257, 260; Reich, Sharon, and Lernau 2019: 42–43.

32. Prag 2018: 15, 19.

33. Meiron 2019: 5; de Groot and Bernick-Greenberg 2012: 147.
34. Prag 2018: 18; Ussishkin 2016: 136.
35. Reich 2011a: 260–61; Ussishkin 2016: 138.
36. Reich, Shukron, and Lernau 2019: 43–44, with an alternative proposal that Kenyon's Wall 3 represents a later extension of the fortifications to the north or south.
37. Gadot and Uziel 2017: 130–31. Prag 2018: 16–19, concludes that Wall 3 dates to the Middle Bronze Age but was part of the fortifications protecting the spring and citadel above, not a city wall.
38. Cahill 2003a: 21–23; de Groot and Bernick-Greenberg 2012: 45–47, 106–7; de Groot 2012: 147.
39. Reich 2011a: 260–61; Ussishkin 2016: 142, who argues that the wall postdates the Middle Bronze Age.
40. Reich 2011a: 177–181; Ussishkin 2016: 142; Ben-Ami 2014: 17.
41. Shiloh 1984: 23–24.
42. Ussishkin 2016: 147.
43. De Groot and Bernick-Greenberg 2012:147–48.
44. Reich 2011a: 252, 260–61; Geva 2019: 5.
45. Prag 2018: 19.
46. Regev et al. 2017.
47. Reich 2018; Reich and Shukron 2021d: 664.
48. Ussishkin 2016: 146.
49. For a response to Ussishkin's claims regarding the Iron Age I, see Cahill 2003a: 75–76. Also see Wightman 2022, who concludes (inter alia), that the mid-slope wall and Spring Tower are originally Middle Bronze Age in date.
50. Reich 2018: 116.
51. Gill 2011; Gill 1996: 13–16; Ussishkin 2016: 147. Meiron 2019: 6, argues that the chisel marks on the walls of the different parts of Warren's Shaft indicate it was cut artificially, although in my opinion the marks could also indicate the widening of existing karstic features.
52. For an extramural MB II structure, see Reich and Shukron 2021d: 663.
53. Greenberg 2019: 238.
54. For an overview, see Cline 2014.
55. Greenberg 2019: 341–43, 346–47; "What is important is that, whatever the nature of its political transformations, 'civilization' did not 'collapse'; people in the Levant continued living their Bronze Age lives until new technologies, new relations of production and new forms of political legitimacy converged in the new, Iron Age, millennium" (346).
56. However, Maeir 2011: 181, notes that there is no archaeological evidence for the arrival of a new population in Jerusalem at this time.
57. Hackett 1998: 208; Faust 2006: 186.

58. Faust 2006: 65–66.

59. Faust 2006: 163–64; Redmount 1998: 97; Stager 1998: 124–25; Cline 2014: 6–7; Lasine 2000: 658.

60. Uziel and Szanton 2015: 243–45; for the opposite view, see Ben-Ami 2014: 16.

61. Greenberg 2019: 263–64, 272, 282.

62. Greenberg 2019: 286–87.

63. Prag 2018: 24–25; Greenberg 2019: 328. For the lack of LB sherds around the Gihon spring, see Reich 2011a: 304–6.

64. Cahill 2003a: 31–33, 77; de Groot and Bernick-Greenberg 2012: 149–50, suggest that "the Late Bronze Age inhabitants of Jerusalem probably reused the Middle Bronze Age fortifications." In contrast, Finkelstein et al. 2007: 160, and Ben-Ami 2014: 16, say there is no evidence that the MB fortifications continued in use in the LB.

65. E. Mazar 2009: 16, 26–42.

66. Keel 2015: 525.

67. E. Mazar et al. 2010; E. Mazar 2011a:137–40.

68. Macalister and Duncan 1926: 37–68; Cahill 2003a: 34–35 n. 69.

69. These are the components described by Cahill 2003a: 34–36; E. Mazar 2015b: 186–87, calls the terraces the "Initial Component" and the overlying rubble and stepped mantle the "Upper Component."

70. Cahill 2003a: 34; E. Mazar 2015b: 174–85.

71. Cahill 2003a: 40; E. Mazar 2015b: 175; E. Mazar 2009: 63.

72. Cahill 2003a: 40–41.

73. Macalister and Duncan 1926: 52–53; Cahill 2003a: 34–35 n. 69.

74. Kenyon 1974:95, 100–1; E. Mazar 2015b: 178–79.

75. Kenyon 1974: 192–93; E. Mazar 2015b: 174–75.

76. Cahill 2003a: 40; E. Mazar 2015b: 177–78; E. Mazar 2009: 64.

77. Cahill 2003a: 44–45, 52–530; Reich 2011a: 132–33, 306–7; Maeir 2011: 179–80.

78. Prag 2018: 34; also see E. Mazar 2015b: 177–78.

79. Finkelstein 2011: 192–93; Finkelstein et al. 2007.

80. E. Mazar 2015b: 179–85; E. Mazar 2009: 14–16.

81. As noted by Cahill 2003a: 53: "the rampart's size and structural complexity suggest that it skirted a fortress or citadel that housed the city's administrative-religious complex—that is, a feature that can reasonably be reconstructed as having occupied the highest point in the town." E. Mazar 2009: 12, says this area was extramural before the time of David.

82. According to *Gesenius' Hebrew and Chaldee Lexicon*, the word is "specially used of the stridulous sound of water flowing down violently, as in cataracts, aqueducts" (Tregelles 1857: 714)

83. Vincent 2004. E. Mazar 2019a: 51, identifies a water channel behind the stepped stone structure as the *tsinnor*, but this makes no sense because she dates the channel

to the time of David, which means it would not have existed at the time of his conquest.

84. Reich 2011a: 295–96; Meiron 2019: 6–7.
85. Reich 2011a: 296.
86. Prag 2018: 59.
87. Bahat 2011b: 22.
88. Chausidis 2018; Greenberg 2019: 238, 328–29, who refers to the sacred hill/mountain above the spring but without specifying if he is referring to the crest of the hill above or to the Temple Mount.
89. Barkay 1996; Bahat 2011b: 20.
90. Maeir 2011: 180–81.
91. De Groot and Bernick-Greenberg 2012: 149–50.
92. Vincent 2004: 184. Also see Maeir 2011: 180–81; Prag 2018: 24–25.

3. ISRAELITE JERUSALEM (930 BCE)

1. Greenberg 2019: 347.
2. Meyers 1998: 223 (map).
3. For a recent discussion of the dates of David and Solomon's reigns, see Patrich et al. 2021: 340–34; also see Meyers 1998: 225. Halpern 2000: 318, gives David's dates as ca. 1010–970 BCE. Lipiński 2020: 27, dates the combined reigns of David and Solomon to ca. 960–928/927 BCE. Handy 1997 concludes that the earliest possible date for Solomon's reign is 973 BCE and the latest possible date for his death is 930 BCE (p. 105).
4. Finkelstein and Silberman 2001: 123–45; Meyers 1998: 245, Halpern 2000: 321; Alhström 1993: 480–490 and Map 14. Lipiński 2018, 54, claims that "David's effective rule did not extend beyond Jerusalem, the Judaean highland, and the surrounding areas."
5. Biran and Naveh 1995: 13.
6. Biran and Naveh 1993; Biran and Naveh 1995; Cahill 2003a: 55; Finkelstein and Silberman 2001: 129.
7. A. Mazar 1990: 369; Alhström 1993: 541; van der Toorn 2009: 26. For a good introduction, see Friedman 1987.
8. Redmount 1998: 85. Halpern 1988: 269, argues that the ancient Israelites distinguished myth from history and fact from fiction.
9. For a recent discussion, see Machinist 2020.
10. See, e.g., Ahlström 1993: 541.
11. De Groot and Bernick-Greenberg 2012: 150.
12. See, e.g., E. Mazar 2009: 13; 36 n. 79; de Groot and Bernick-Greenberg 2012: 150, 153; Ariel and de Groot 2000: 160; Ussishkin 2012: 106; and see below.
13. Meyers 1998: 253–55; Cahill 2003a: 73, 76; de Groot and Bernick-Greenberg 2012: 141–43.

14. Meyers 1998: 253; E. Mazar 2009: 43; Murphy-O'Connor 2012a: 6.

15. E. Mazar 2009: 31–32, 43; Huffmon 1999: 756.

16. Hurowitz 2009: 20; Bahat 2020: 27.

17. Honigman 2014: 150.

18. Hackett 1998: 209–11.

19. Hurowitz 2009: 15.

20. For example, *War* 5.412; see Magness 2008: 205–6, 215.

21. See Modrzejewski 1997; Bohak 1996; van der Toorn 2019.

22. Biran 1994: 159–209; Campbell 1998: 282–83.

23. See de Vaux 1965: 312; Meyers 1998: 263.

24. For Jedidiah, see Tregelles 1857: 333 (*Gesenius*).

25. de Vaux 1965: 312; Gerstenberger 2011: 145.

26. Ahlström 1993: 500, and Grabbe 2017: 43, suggest an association of Solomon's name with the god Shalem. Huffmon 1999: 756–57, says the name "Solomon" probably means "His (David's?) Peace" or "His (the deceased's) Healthiness."

27. Hurowitz 2009: 17; King and Stager 2001: 335–36; A. Mazar 1990: 376–77; Ritmeyer 2006: 279–93; Bahat 2020: 28–29.

28. Aharoni 1993: 83; Herzog 1997: 175.

29. Kisilevitz 2015; Kisilevitz and Lipschits 2020. Another excavation season was conducted in August 2021.

30. Kisilevitz and Lipschits 2020: 300, report that the building has been excavated for a length of 21 meters (69 feet).

31. See https://www.haaretz.com/israel-news/judahite-temple-by-jerusalem-may-have-housed-statue-of-canaanite-god–1.10330237 (accessed 28 October 2021).

32. Ritmeyer 2006: 293, mentions only one courtyard. Bahat 2020: 32, says there were "one or more" courtyards.

33. Ritmeyer 2006: 292–93.

34. Ritmeyer 2006: 284; Hurowitz 2009.

35. Ritmeyer 2006: 289; it also contained Aaron's rod and the manna pot.

36. Hurowitz 2009: 30; Ritmeyer 2006: 289–90.

37. Ritmeyer 2006: 285–86.

38. See de Vaux 1965; 313–19; King and Stager 2001: 330–34; A. Mazar 1990: 376–78; Meyers 1998: 263–64; Hurowitz 2009: 20–31; Ritmeyer 2006: 279–93. Patrich 2011: 206, argues that the rocky outcrop enshrined in the Dome of the Rock was not inside the first and second temples.

39. Hurowitz 2009: 24, 27.

40. Hurowitz 2009: 31.

41. A. Mazar 1990: 378–79; Meyers 1998: 256.

42. Macalister and Duncan 1926: 52–53; Cahill 2003a: 34–35 n. 69.

43. E. Mazar 2015b: 184; E. Mazar 2009: 36–37.

44. The identification was first proposed by Kenyon (1974:100–1). For a recent overview, see McKinny et al. 2021, who identify the Millo with the massive fortifications surrounding the Gihon spring and the large stone structure at the crest of the hill above with the Stronghold of Zion (2 Sam 5:9) (see p. 660 n. 70). Also see Atkinson 2000a: E. Mazar and B. Mazar 1989: IX; E. Mazar 2009: 13; E. Mazar 2011a: 40; Stager 1982.

45. Ben-Dov 2002: 12, 50, interprets the Millo as fill dumped to connect the southeastern hill, the Ophel, and the Temple Mount, and identifies the Millo with the Ophel; also see Atkinson 2000a. A. Mazar 1990: 379–80, also identifies the Millo as an artificial fill dumped in the saddle between the southeastern hill and the Temple Mount.

46. Cahill 2003a: 56–57.

47. See, e.g., Prag 2018: 34; Finkelstein et al. 2007: 152.

48. Strata 14 and 13 in Shiloh's excavations; Cahill 2003a: 56–66.

49. Cahill 2003a: 66.

50. Notice, for example, the Black-on-Red (BoR) spherical jug or flask in Cahill 2003a: 59, figure 1.13a:15, a type which Herzog and Singer-Avitz 2015: 217, say "first appear[s] in Judah in the late Iron IIA. Their floruit is in the early 9th century BCE, and they decline in the Iron IIB." This BoR jug is close to E. Stern 2015: 464, Pl. 4.1.13:4; 441–42. Also compare the complete, red-slipped bowl from Stratum 14 in Cahill 2003a: 59, figure 1.13a: 9, to Herzog and Singer-Avitz 2015: 237, Pl. 2.4.9: 14, which is Iron Age IIB. And, contrary to the claim of Finkelstein et al. 2007: 152, the pottery from the earliest floor of the Burnt Room House includes not "only sherds" but complete or nearly complete vessels, or at least some complete or nearly complete profiles; see Cahill 2003a: 59, figure 1.13a:3, 6, 9. Finkelstein 2011: 192, dismisses this pottery without apparent basis as coming from "a fill or a make-up for the construction of the later building."

51. Cahill 2003a: 44–54.

52. See E. Mazar 2009: 37, 40–42, also citing the large quantity of Iron Age I sherds.

53. E. Mazar 2009: 18, 41; Steiner 1993: 24, 28–29; Cahill 2003a: 42–53.

54. Cahill 2003a: 45.

55. E. Mazar 2011a: 40.

56. E. Mazar 2015b: 187: "the Large Stone Structure and the Stepped Stone Structure are actually a single, immense complex."

57. E. Mazar 2009: 17–18.

58. Lawler 2021a: 202–4, 283–88.

59. E. Mazar 2009: 43–65; E. Mazar 2019a: 47–48.

60. E. Mazar 2009: 38–39, 52.

61. E. Mazar 2009: 47; also see Reich 2011a: 265–66, 307, who speculates that the structure dates to the Middle Bronze Age.

62. Finkelstein 2011: 193.

63. See, e.g., E. Mazar 2009: 50–51, 53, 55: "Later additions to the structure (Pavement 717, W22) have been dated by pottery associated with them to the Iron Age IIA (the tenth century BCE)" (p. 55); Iron Age IIA pottery found under a bench-like installation (p. 51).

64. Finkelstein et al. 2007 date the lower part of the stepped stone structure to the ninth–eighth centuries BCE and the upper part (together with Macalister and Duncan's "Jebusite" wall and the large stone structure) to the Hasmonean period.

65. E. Mazar 2009: 38; Reich 2011a: 267. This is rejected by de Groot and Bernick-Greenberg 2012: 149: "there is no need to see in these remains a nomadic encampment" and by Finkelstein et al. 2007: 147. E. Mazar 2019a: 46–48, identifies the large stone structure as a "new significant addition to the already existing Canaanite-Jebusite Palace-Fortress . . . built by King David"—which seems to contradict her repeated claims that this was an open area without any structures before the time of David.

66. E. Mazar 2009: 38–39, and Finkelstein et al. 2007: 148, discuss the C14-dated olive pits and bone, which they say provide a ninth-century terminus post quem.

67. E. Mazar 2009: 59–61; E. Mazar 2019a: 48. The "Crucibles Layer" was found only in the eastern part of the structure.

68. E. Mazar 2009: 40–41, 61; E. Mazar 2018: 323.

69. See Mullins and Yannai 2019: 152; 160; 211, Pl. 3.23:4.

70. E. Mazar 2018: 323.

71. A. Mazar 2015: 38–39.

72. E. Mazar 2019a: 35; E. Mazar 2019b: 61.

73. The bilbil is Base Ring I (BR I); see E. Mazar 2009: 34; E. Mazar 2019a: 46. It resembles Artzy 2015: 369, Pl. 4.2:14:3, who says (p. 343) says that BR I first appears in the Late Bronze Age (LB) IA, is more characteristic of the LB IB, and continues into the LB IIA, albeit in smaller quantities. She dates the LB IIA-B to 1400–1200 BCE (p. 339).

74. E. Mazar 2009: 61–62, dates the bowl to the Iron Age IIA and says it dates the surface to the tenth century at the earliest, but it is virtually identical to an IA I bowl illustrated by A. Mazar 2015: 23, Pl. 1.1.1:14.

75. E. Mazar 2009: 62; see A. Mazar 2015: 13–14; 41, Pl. 1.1.12: 1–4.

76. E. Mazar 2009: 51–52, 54; there is also a radiocarbon-dated bone from this context (p. 52 n. 122). The pottery (illustrated on p. 54) includes a number of bowls with a hand-burnished red slip and a BoR jug, which are characteristic of the Iron Age IIA (ca. 980/950–830/800); see Herzog and Singer-Avitz 2015: 214–15, 217.

77. Contrary to her claim that they are bonded; see E. Mazar 2009: 17, 57–58; E. Mazar 2019a: 48.

78. Thackeray 2006: 45 (Vol. IV) glosses the term as "hump."

79. Tregelles 1857: 645 (*Gesenius*); Atkinson 2000b: 990; E. Mazar 2011a: 71.

80. Rollston 2000: 887.

81. In the passages cited in this paragraph, I added the definite article, which appears in the Hebrew.

82. *War* 5.145; from Thackeray 2006: 45 (Vol. IV).

83. Warren and Conder 1884: 226–33; Prag 2018: 38–39; E. Mazar and B. Mazar 1989; E. Mazar, Solomon; E. Mazar 2015a; E. Mazar 2018.

84. E. Mazar 2011a: 39–150; E. Mazar 2015a: 459–69; E. Mazar 2019a: 56–62.

85. See, e.g., de Groot and Bernick-Greenberg 2012: 159; Gadot and Uziel 2017: 137, who simply refer to these structures as "non-domestic."

86. Except for the Extra Tower, which E. Mazar dates to the eighth century. For a discussion, see Prag 2018: 38–39. Geva 2019: 11, cites E. Mazar's identification and dating of the gate.

87. E. Mazar 2011a: 68–72, 147; E. Mazar 2015a: 461.

88. See Herzog and Singer-Avitz 2015: 235, Pl. 2.4.8:5; 217, whose dates for the Iron Age IIA are 980/950–830/800; also see Cahill 2003a: 70.

89. E. Mazar 2011a: 69–71.

90. E. Mazar 2015a: 461.

91. E. Mazar and B. Mazar 1989: 58.

92. Mazar 2011a: 71–72, 148.

93. E. Mazar 2011a: 108, 130–34.

94. My emphasis; E. Mazar 2011a: 99.

95. See, e.g., Cahill 2003a: 22–23 including nn. 41–42, 71, 79, who points out that "Reich and Shukron's discovery of at least one floor surface dating to the final phase of the Iron Age built up to the exterior wall of one of these towers proves undisputedly that at least one of these towers remained standing until then" (p. 71); de Groot and Bernick-Greenberg 2012, 150, 153; Ariel and de Groot 2000: 160; Uziel and Szanton 2015: 245. Finkelstein et al. 2007: 160; Ussishkin 2012: 106; and Ben-Ami 2014: 16, reject this possibility.

96. Prag 2018: 42.

97. E. Mazar 2011a: 120–21, 127; E. Mazar 2015a: 464, 469; E. Mazar 2019a: 58–59. E. Mazar 2018: 321, says "the Straight Wall was an integral part of the Early Iron Age IIA Solomonic Wall." E. Mazar 2011a: 125–27, says the Straight Wall is contemporary with the Royal Structure and identifies it as the "Mikstoa" of Neh 3:25; also see E. Mazar 2015a: 464, 469.

98. Kenyon 1974: 114–15; Pl. 37; the attribution to Solomon was Yadin's. Also see A. Mazar 1990: 465; Steiner 1993: 48, fig. 5.8; E. Mazar 2011a: 38; de Groot and Bernick-Greenberg 2012: 153.

99. See, e.g., McKinny et al. 2020: 4, 10.

100. Prag 2018: 38.

101. Cahill 2003a: 69–70 including n. 143.

102. E. Mazar 2011a: 142–43; E. Mazar 2015a: 468; E. Mazar 2019a: 57–58, 62.

103. Ca. 38 × 20 meters (125 × 65 feet); see E. Mazar 2018: 325.

104. E. Mazar 2018: 324; E. Mazar 2015a: 465.

105. E. Mazar 2018: 323; figure III.1.2.

106. For parallels, see Herzog and Singer-Avitz 2015: 228, Pl. 2.4.3:3 (from Arad XI), which they describe as "a common form" (p. 261).

107. See Herzog and Singer-Avitz 2015: 214 n. 8. Keimer 2019: 15, dates the IA IIA to ca. 980−840 BCE.

108. E. Mazar 2018: 329−76; IA IIA pottery is listed from a foundation trench of Unit II (p. 354).

109. E. Mazar 2015a: 465−69; 462 Plan III.1.2.

110. E. Mazar 2015a: 467−68; E. Mazar 2019a: 59−62.

111. For parallels from Samaria, see Tappy 2015: 193; 205 Plate 2.3.7:2, 3, 5, dated to the end of the Iron Age IIB (Samaria Period IV). Also see Herzog and Singer-Avitz 2015: 242 Plate 2.4.13:1 (Beersheba II).

112. According to Alon de Groot (personal communication, February 2022), unpublished Iron Age IIA pottery was found in structures north of the Straight Wall; he also notes that the structures discussed here have not yet been fully published.

113. Ben-Ami 2014; Prag 2018: 35.

114. Lawler 2021a: 300−4.

115. Ben-Ami 2014: 16−17 (where an Iron Age IIA date is cited); Ben-Ami and Misgav 2016: 103* (where an Iron Age IB date is cited).

116. Ben-Ami 2014: 16−17; Prag 2018: 38.

117. Shalev et al. 2019: 53−55, 64, who note that the hewing of the terraces in the early Iron Age could have obliterated earlier remains (p. 67). Crowfoot and Fitzgerald 1929: 18−19, mention the bedrock shelves.

118. Shalev et al. 2020: 153−56.

119. De Groot and Bernick-Greenberg 2012: 1 (Strata 15−14).

120. De Groot and Bernick-Greenberg 2012: 34−35, 101−3, 152, 170−71.

121. Ben-Ami 2014: 7−11; Prag 2018: 36; also see similar chalices from Moza.

122. Geva 2014a: 137−38.

123. Finkelstein 2011: 192−93; Finkelstein et al. 2007.

124. Finkelstein et al. 2011.

125. Finkelstein et al. 2011: 8.

126. Barkay and Dvira 2012: 67−68; Barkay and Zweig 2007: 36−37; Geva and de Groot 2017: 34−39.

127. Finkelstein et al. 2011: 10, who suggest that the cisterns under the Temple Mount provided water for the settlement, but most (if not all) of them date to the Second Temple period or later. There are no biblical references to cisterns in Solomon's temple; see Patrich 2020: 275. For the problem of placing the original settlement at such a distance from the Gihon spring, see Geva and de Groot 2017: 42−43.

128. Geva and de Groot 2017; Gadot and Uziel 2017; Ussishkin 2012: 104; de Groot and Bernick-Greenberg 2012: 148.

129. Jamieson-Drake 1991: 136–45.
130. For example, Finkelstein and Silberman 2001: 143, attribute the creation of this story to the Deuteronomistic historian (DH).
131. Cahill 2003a: 77.
132. Meyers 1998: 255.

4. JUDAHITE JERUSALEM (587 BCE)

1. Campbell 1998: 273–74.
2. Lipiński 2018: 134–37; Campbell 1998: 281; Ahlström 1993: 551, calls them "national shrines." Bethel is only 17 kilometers (10 miles) north of Jerusalem.
3. Ahlström 1993: 547.
4. See Lipschits 2005: 272–304, 362, 367–68. Lipiński 2020: 2, dates the work to after Josiah's reforms, "probably around 500 BC, when the Temple of Jerusalem had been rebuilt."
5. See Campbell 1998. Cogan 1998: 322, says Kings is mainly a product of the late seventh century and Chronicles was written in the fourth century BCE. Leith 1998: 373, 401, also dates Chronicles to the fourth century. Lipiński 2020: 2–3, dates it to the late Persian or early Hellenistic period.
6. Campbell 1998: 276; Leith 1998: 401; Gerstenberger 2011: 144–45.
7. Campbell 1998: 281–82.
8. Cogan 1998: 324; the population of Samaria was deported in 720. For the Assyrian policy versus Babylonian, see Lipschits 2005: 187.
9. Lipiński 2020: 67, argues that Hezekiah did not rebel but withheld the annual tribute to the Assyrians.
10. For the walls, see 2 Chr 32:5; Isa 22:9; and the discussion in Ariel and de Groot 2000: 160–61. For the water system, see below.
11. For speculations on why, see Ahlström 1993: 713–14.
12. Cogan 1998: 331–35.
13. Cogan 1998: 325–26; but Ahlström 1993: 703–6, and Edelman 2008, question Hezekiah's supposed reforms.
14. Cogan 1998: 335–40; Ahlström 1993: 730–39.
15. Lipiński 2020: 86–87; Cogan 1998: 340.
16. Ahlström 1993: 770–79.
17. For an opposing view see Ahlström 1993: 775–77, who concludes that "the 'law book' of the Josianic period was neither part of the Book of Deuteronomy, nor of any other known biblical book" (p. 777).
18. Cogan 1998: 345–46; Ahlström 1993: 615–16.
19. Ahlström 1993: 766, speculates that, under Josiah, Judah was a vassal of Egypt; Kletter 1996: 6, rejects the possibility that Josiah rebelled against Egypt; Lipschits 2005: 363, thinks that Necho was on his way to aid the Assyrians.
20. See Cline 2000.

21. Cogan 1998: 348–52; Leith 1998: 371; Ahlström 1993: 788–93; Lipschits 2005: 42–84, 70–71; Lipiński 2020: 90–96.

22. Cogan 1998: 348–53; Lipschits 2005: 42–84, 367.

23. Jer 40; see Cogan 1998: 355–56; Lipschits 2005: 84–97.

24. Cogan 1998: 356–57; Ahlström 1993: 798–99; Lipschits 2005: 187, 190, 216–18.

25. Ariel and de Groot 2000: 160; de Groot 2012: 158; Prag 2018: 42. For the recent discovery of additional sections of this wall, see Vukosavović et al. 2021.

26. See Re'em 2018: 249 (with A. de Groot). Uziel and Szanton 2015: 247–48, argue that the expansion began in the ninth century; but Geva 2003b: 515; Avigad and Geva 2000: 24, 81–82, and Avigad 1983: 55, date it to the eighth century. Also see Reich 2011a: 313. Finkelstein 2011: 195, attributes the growth entirely to an influx of refugees.

27. Reich and Shukron 2021d: 664–71; Geva 2019: 8–9. However, the claim that this wall (W501 in Area J and W10 in Area A) supported a terrace on which the houses were built is contradicted by the fact that it postdates the development of the residential quarter, which would require the wall and houses to be contemporary in date. Bocher 2021: 49–50, argues that this wall, as well as narrower north–south walls that were uncovered in the vicinity, are not fortifications but instead were agricultural terraces or supported the adjacent (water) Channels I and II.

28. Reich and Shukron 2021d: 667; Chalaf and Uziel 2018: 27*; Reich 2011a: 179; de Groot 2012: 158–59; Cahill 2003a: 68; Ariel and de Groot 2000: 158–61, 164, who attribute the wall to Hezekiah.

29. Geva 2003b: 511–12. For a section of this wall discovered recently in the Kishle (Ottoman police headquarters), by the Citadel, see Re'em 2019: 137–39.

30. Avigad and Geva 2000: 81; Geva 2003b: 514; de Groot, Geva, and Yezerski 2003: 16; Re'em 2018: 249 (with A. de Groot). For the earlier remains, see Geva 2003b: 512–13, 518.

31. Geva 2003b: 503, 512; Avigad and Geva 2000: 81; Avigad 1983: 57.

32. Avigad 1983: 59; Avigad and Geva 2000: 45; Geva 2003b: 512.

33. Avigad and Geva 2000: 82; Geva 2003b: 515–16.

34. Avigad and Geva 2000: 82; Geva and Avigad 2000a (Area W): 148–57; Geva and Avigad 2000b (Area X–2): 212–15; Geva 2003b: 510–16; de Groot, Geva, and Yezerski 2003: 16.

35. Geva 2003b: 513–14.

36. Avigad and Geva 2000: 82; Geva and Avigad 2000a (Area W): 134, 155; Geva 2003b: 513, 523.

37. Geva 2003b: 516–17.

38. Geva 2003b: 505, 517–18; Weksler-Bdolah and Szanton 2014; Weksler-Bdolah 2013: 186, who, however, notes the paucity of datable artifacts associated with the dam wall by the Pool of Siloam.

39. Geva 2003b: 515.

40. Avigad 1983: 54; Geva 2003b: 518.

41. De Groot 2012: 168; Geva 2014a: 137–41; Geva 2003b: 518–19.

42. Geva 2003b: 519–20.

43. Geva 2014a: 137–41; Geva 2003b: 518–19.

44. Geva 2003b: 520–21; de Groot 2012: 160–61; Re'em 2018: 249 (with A. de Groot); Mendel-Geberovich, Chalaf, and Uziel 2020: 175.

45. Ariel and de Groot 2000: 162; Chalaf and Uziel 2018: 27*–28*.

46. Reich and Shukron 2021d: 670; Geva 2003b: 522; de Groot 2012: 158, 168; Chalaf and Uziel 2018: 28*.

47. De Groot 2012: 161.

48. Geva 2014a: 139–41; Geva 2003b: 518–19; de Groot 2012: 165, 167–68.

49. E. Mazar and B. Mazar 1989: 44–45; E. Mazar 2018: 176; E. Mazar 2011a: 58–60.

50. E. Mazar and B. Mazar 1989: 29, 39–40; E. Mazar 2018: 176; E. Mazar 2011a: 60–61.

51. See the discussion in Chapter 3; E. Mazar and B. Mazar 1989: 34, 60; E. Mazar 2011a: 70.

52. E. Mazar and B. Mazar 1989: IX, 14–21, 59; E. Mazar 2011a: 44–48.

53. E. Mazar 2018: 176–83; E. Mazar and Ben-Arie 2018: 254–56; E. Mazar 2015a: 628–40.

54. Shalev et al. 2021: 22; Shalev et al. 2020: 156–59; Mendel-Geberovich et al. 2019: 156–57.

55. See Mendel-Geberovich et al. 2019: 163–65.

56. Ben-Ami and Misgav 2016: 106*–107*; http://www.cityofdavid.org.il/en/news/elihana-bat-gael-seal (accessed on 22 January 2022).

57. Prag 2018: 43–47; Karlin and Mazar 2015: 549–51; Ben-Ami and Tchekhanovets 2015b.

58. See Lipschits 2011.

59. De Groot 2012: 170. For a rebuttal of Lipschits's (2011) proposal that proto-Aeolic capitals were introduced into the vassal kingdoms of Judah, Moab, and Ammon from Assyria in the late eighth century, see Kletter 2015: 55–64.

60. Prag 2018: 47–48; de Groot 2012: 169, who both note the discovery of ashlars found in the rubble in Kenyon's Area A.

61. Mendel-Geberovich et al. 2019: 167.

62. For Kenyon's excavations, see Prag 2018: 27–34.

63. Shiloh 1984: 18–19; Cahill and Tarler 1994: 37–38.

64. Gibson 2022b: 11–15; de Groot and Bernick-Greenberg 2012: 22, photo 14; p. 99, Photos 111–112; 172, 347, 352, 351, figure 10.3; Cahill and Tarler 1994: 38. Vincent 1911: 29, identified another seat discovered by the Parker Expedition. A perforated stone block that appears to be an unfinished toilet seat was recently discovered built into the Iron Age II fortification wall midway down the east slope of the southeastern hill; see Vukosavović et al. 2021: 10*–11*.

65. Billig et al. 2021: 84.

66. See Gibson 2022b: 11–15; de Groot 2012: 172; Ganor and Kreimerman 2019; Liraz 2018. But not at Tell es-Saidiyeh; see Chapman 1992: 4. For ancient toilets and toilet habits, see Magness 2011b: 130–44.

67. Cahill et al. 1991.

68. Langgut 2021.

69. Magness 2018: 125*.

70. Langgut 2021: 4. Dvorjetski 2016: 74, concludes that only "people of means" had private toilet facilities. However, de Groot 2012: 172, notes that the toilets in the City of David were not limited to palaces or public buildings but were a common feature of the urban architecture of the Iron Age city. Also see Gibson 2022b: 17, who proposes that private toilets may have been more common but have not been found because they had wooden seats.

71. Shiloh 1984: 19.

72. Shiloh 1984: 19–20.

73. Sapir-Hen et al. 2021: 111.

74. Sapir-Hen et al. 2021: 113–14.

75. Sapir-Hen et al. 2021: 115–16.

76. https://www.timesofisrael.com/archaeologists-unearth–1st-jerusalem-evidence-of-quake-from-bibles-book-of-amos/; https://www.haaretz.com/archaeology/.premium. MAGAZINE-fact-checking-the-book-of-amos-there-was-a-huge-quake-in-eighth-century-b-c-e–1.6807298 (accessed 23 January 2022).

77. For the dates of Amos's activities and the earthquake, see Andersen and Freedman 1989: 19, 183, 193–99.

78. For Josephus's reference to the earthquake during Uzziah's reign, see Meyers and Meyers 1993: 428.

79. Uziel and Szanton 2015: 247.

80. De Groot and Bernick-Greenberg 2012: 45–48; de Groot 2012: 157.

81. De Groot and Bernick-Greenberg 2012: 84.

82. De Groot and Bernick-Greenberg 2012: 99.

83. Ariel and de Groot 2000: 156; Cahill 2003a: 67–68; de Groot 2012: 161; Reich 2011a: 179.

84. De Groot 2012: 162–65.

85. De Groot and Bernick-Greenberg 2012: 22–29; de Groot 2012: 166; Cahill and Tarler 1994: 37.

86. De Groot and Bernick-Greenberg 2012: 22.

87. Shiloh's Areas E3 and E1; see de Groot and Bernick-Greenberg 2012: 79–82; de Groot 2012: 169.

88. De Groot 2012: 168.

89. Geva 2003b: 509.

90. Geva 2003b: 523; de Groot et al. 2003: 16.

91. Billig et al. 2021.

92. Reich 2011a: 216–17; Reich et al. 2019: 34–35.

93. Sukenik and Shamir 2018.

94. Reich et al. 2007: 153–56; Reich 2011a: 210–17.

95. Reich et al. 2007: 161.

96. Reich et al. 2007: 162–63; Reich 2011a: 214–15.

97. Reich et al. 2007: 162; Reich et al. 2019: 36–37.

98. Mendel-Geberovic et al. 2020.

99. Mendel-Geberovich et al. 2020: 178–79.

100. Reich et al. 2019: 35.

101. Tütken et al. 2021.

102. Reich et al. 2007: 157–60; Reich 2011a: 215–16, 310–11.

103. Reich et al. 2007: 160.

104. H. Lernau and O. Lernau 1992.

105. H. Lernau and O. Lernau 1992: 134–37.

106. Reich 2011a: 310–311; Reich et al. 2007: 163.

107. Adler and Lernau 2021: 14–15, 20–21.

108. Tütken et al. 2021. At least twenty-nine of the sharks' teeth are fossils; see Adler and Lernau 2021: 15 (asterisked note).

109. https://phys.org/news/2021–07-city-david-sharks-teeth-mystery.html (accessed 23 October 2021).

110. Sneh et al. 2010: 60; Shiloh 1984: 23.

111. See Sneh et al. 2010; Reich 2011a: 137, 186.

112. Sneh et al. 2010: 60; Shiloh 1984: 23; Reich 2011a: 183; Reich and Shukron 2002.

113. Sneh et al. 2010: 60; Shiloh 1984: 23; Reich 2011a: 183; Reich and Shukron 2002.

114. Reich and Shukron 2021d: 678; Reich 2011a: 198–200.

115. Reich 2011a: 204.

116. Ariel and Lender 2000: 17–18; the southern end of the Siloam Channel was put out of use by the Siloam Tunnel.

117. Sneh et al. 2010: 61.

118. Geva 2019: 8.

119. Ariel and de Groot 2000: 159–60; Reich and Shukron 2004: 217.

120. Ariel and de Groot 2000: 161.

121. Reich and Shukron 2011c; Weksler-Bdolah 2013: 175–76; McKinny et al. 2021: 657 n. 60.

122. From Amiran 1976: 78.

123. See Reich 2011a: 316; Rendsburg and Schniedewind 2010.

124. See Gadot and Uziel 2017: 135.

125. Reich and Shukron 2011a. McKinny et al. 2021: 658 n. 61, say Reich and Shukron's claim is "difficult to accept."

126. Sneh et al. 2010.

127. Frumkin et al. 2003; Mendel-Geberovich et al., 2020: 178 n. 14.

128. Reich 2011a: 35–36.
129. https://www.timesofisrael.com/israeli-official-turkey-agrees-to-return-ancient-hebrew-inscription-to-jerusalem/
130. Cahill 2003b: 92, says that Barkay identifies *mmšt* with Ramat Rahel.
131. Cahill 2003b: 89.
132. Avigad 1983: 43; see Cahill 2003b: 88.
133. Avigad 1983: 44; Mazar and Ben-Arie 2018: 255.
134. E. Mazar 2018: 180, 184–85; Mazar and Ben-Arie 2018: 255–56.
135. Cahill 2003b: 93.
136. Cahill 2003b: 88, 90–91.
137. Cahill 2003b 91–92.
138. Prag 2018: 47, 50.
139. For Arnona, see https://www.timesofisrael.com/huge-kingdom-of-judah-governm ent-complex-found-stones-throw-from-us-embassy/ (accessed 23 October 2021).
140. Kletter 1996: 41, 47.
141. Gilbert-Peretz 1996: 32.
142. Gilbert-Peretz 1996: 32.
143. Moorey 2003: 60.
144. Moorey 2003: 48, 60, describes the breasts as "pendulous" and extremely exaggerated. Also see Darby 2014: 56–57, who says, "The prominence of the breasts has been greatly over-exaggerated" (p. 321).
145. Darby 2014: 219.
146. Moorey 2003: 58.
147. Moorey 2003: 63.
148. Moorey 2003: 59–61, 64; Kletter 1996: 27 (who argues against toys on p. 73).
149. Moorey 2003: 49.
150. See Moorey 2003: 62–63.
151. Moorey 2003: 49, 51; Kletter 1996: 62.
152. See Kletter 1996: 75–77, 81; Moorey 2003: 48. Lipiński 2018: 139–44, and Lipiński 2020: 104–7, argues that "Asherah" denotes a shrine or sanctuary, especially with a sacred tree or grove, not a goddess.
153. Darby 2014: 214, 215, 322, 404. Kletter 1996: 81, also concludes they were protective figures, although he identifies them with Asherah.
154. Darby 2014: 394–95, 400.
155. Moorey 2003: 67. But Kletter 1996: 79–80, argues that the JPFs represent only one figure and likely had one basic function.
156. De Groot 2012: 170.
157. Darby 2014: 256.
158. Moorey 2003: 66–67. Darby 2014: 219, notes correlations between Neo-Assyrian texts describing magical rituals and the deposition of the Jerusalem figurines; she also cautions about the use of the term "apotropaic" (p. 14).

159. Moorey 2003: 48; Darby 2014: 395.
160. E. Mazar and B. Mazar 1989: XI; Rahmani 1981b: 232.
161. E. Mazar and B. Mazar 1989: XI; Rahmani 1981b: 233.
162. Rahmani 1981b: 231–33.
163. Reich 2011a: 26–27, 73–74; Avigad in Stern 1993: 713; Rahmani 1981b: 232.
164. Clausen 2016: 13–15; Limor 1988.
165. For a survey, see Barkay 2000.
166. Lipschits 2005: 215.
167. Geva in Stern 1993: 715.
168. E. Mazar and B. Mazar 1989: X–XI, 49–55.
169. Geva 2003b: 536 n. 9; Rahmani 1981b: 232.
170. Ussishkin 1986. The basic study of the monumental tombs in the Kidron Valley is Avigad 1954. Also see Geva in Stern 1993: 713; Barkay 2000: 248–55.
171. For the three types, see Ussishkin 1986: 229–37.
172. Avigad 1954: 18–36; Avigad 1993: 712; Ussishkin 1986: 47–63.
173. Avigad 1954: 9–17; Avigad 1993: 712; Ussishkin 1986: 173–84; Layton 1990: 633–37.
174. Clermont-Ganneau 1899: 305–13 (the quote is from p. 307); Reich 2011a: 25.
175. Clermont-Ganneau 1899: 313; Layton 1990: 638.
176. Avigad 1953: 143.
177. Avigad 1953: 146. Rahmani 1981b: 233, says that in addition to a secondary wife, an *amah* was a kind of female official.
178. Barkay 2000: 254.
179. Avigad 1953: 130–32; Avigad 1954: 16. Clermont-Ganneau 1899: 313, was the first to suggest this was the tomb of Shebna. For other proposals, see Layton 1990: 638–39, who believes the identification with Shebna is correct; also see Mendel-Geberovich et al. 2020: 175. Na'aman 2016, suggests that the Tomb of the Steward did not belong to the Shebna mentioned in Isaiah and interprets Isaiah's condemnation as referring to the construction by Shebna of a tomb within the city walls.
180. Avigad 1955: 166.
181. Ussishkin 1969: 21.
182. Barkay 2000: 255–60; Barkay et al. 1994; Geva in Stern 1993: 714. A thorough study of these tombs by Lufrani 2019 came to my attention after this book went to press.
183. Barkay 2000: 257. The metal box was never photographed or fully published, and it was stolen from the collection of the Dominicans during World War I.
184. Geva in Stern 1993: 715; Barkay 2000: 262–70.
185. Barkay 2000: 265–69; Barkay 1994; Barkay and Kloner 1986.
186. For undisturbed Iron Age tombs, see Reich 1994: 111–12.
187. Barkay 1994: 96.

188. Barkay 1994: 96–102.
189. Barkay 2000: 267–69; Barkay 1994: 102–5.
190. Barkay et al. 2004: 61.
191. Barkay et al. 2004: 68.
192. Barkay et al. 2004: 68.
193. Ussishkin 1986: 276–77.

5. POST-EXILIC (PERSIAN) JERUSALEM (333 BCE)

1. Blenkinsopp 2009: 44–45.
2. Lipschits 2005: 211. Geva 2003b: 524, describes the Babylonian destruction of Jerusalem as "comprehensive and total."
3. Cogan 1998: 357–58; Lipschits 2005: 59–62; Edelman 2006: 236; Blenkinsopp 2009: 118.
4. Grabbe 2004: 355.
5. Leith 1998: 378–79; Grabbe 2004: 215–16.
6. Leith 1998: 377–79. Some scholars doubt the Persian king issued a separate decree for the Jews like the one in Ezra; see Grabbe 2004: 271–75, 342–43, 355; Lipschits 2005: 122–23.
7. From Pritchard 1955: 316.
8. Leith 1998: 375; Cogan 1998: 363–64; Grabbe 2004: 91.
9. Ezra 1:8; 5:14; see Leith 1998: 387. Cogan 1998: 357, says that Zerubbabel led the first wave. Blenkinsopp 2009: 32, observes that the identification of Sheshbazzar with Shenazzar "would be accepted by few today"; also see Blenkinsopp 1988: 78–79; Grabbe 2004: 276; Levine 2002: 12–13.
10. Leith 1998: 380, 388; Grabbe 2004: 276–77; Patrich 2009: 39.
11. Levine 2002: 17–18; Leith 1998: 391–92, who describes the arrangement as a theocracy; Grabbe 2004: 279–80. Honigman 2014: 162, 172, says the division of power "was probably not established prior to the second half of the fifth century."
12. Smith-Christopher 2000.
13. Leith 1998: 390–91.
14. Grabbe 2004: 230–31; Gerstenberger 2011: 198.
15. Leith 1998: 390–93. Levine 2002: 18, dates the consecration to 12 March 515 BCE. Grabbe 2004: 284–85, 356, notes that construction likely continued to the end of the fifth century; also see Honigman 2014: 161.
16. Grabbe 2004: 281; Eshel, 2000: 330; Levine 2002: 17–18.
17. See the gloss to Zech 3:8 in the NRSV (p. 1272). For discussions, see Grabbe 2004: 281–82; Eshel, 2000: 330; Blenkinsopp 2009: 156, 181.
18. Grabbe 2004: 295–98.

19. Leith 1998: 407; Levine 2002: 29; Blenkinsopp 1988: 152–57. Ezra is said to be a Zadokite priest (Ezra 7:2). Adler 2022b: 190–97, 206–7, argues that Ezra-Nehemiah present an idealized picture rather than a historical reality of the Persian period.

20. Leith 1998: 373; Levine 2002: 20; Eshel 2000: 332 n. 26; 335 including n. 35; Blenkinsopp 2009: 110, who dates Ezra's arrival to 458 BCE (p. 48); Blenkinsopp 1988: 65, 140–44. Edelman 2005, argues that the temple was rebuilt by Zerubbabel and Nehemiah (whom she claims were contemporaries) in the mid-fifth century during the reign of Artaxerxes I, not during the reign of Darius I. Also see Honigman 2014: 168, who notes that the conflation of Nehemiah's reconstruction of the city wall and Ezra's reforms was the work of later editors.

21. Leith 1998: 373; Blenkinsopp 2009: 86. For reviews of the sources, see Williamson 2004: 3–24; Grabbe 2004: 70–130, who dates Ezra-Nehemiah no earlier than the beginning of the Hellenistic period (p. 72); on p. 359 he says Ezra-Nehemiah was "probably finished in the third century"; Gerstenberger 2011: 33–37, 141–425 (who dates it to the fifth–fourth centuries). For the relationship between the books of Ezra-Nehemiah and Chronicles, see Blenkinsopp 2009: 163–66; Williamson 2004: 244–70; Levine 2002: 7 including n. 15; 41; Blenkinsopp 1988: 47–54.

22. See Blenkinsopp 2009: 90–116; Grabbe 2004: 78–80, 294; Leith 1998: 409.

23. Levine 2002: 23, notes that whereas the book of Nehemiah says the walls were rebuilt in fifty-two days, Josephus says it took two years and four months.

24. Leith 1998: 410–11; Grabbe 2004: 298–300.

25. Leith 1998: 410; Grabbe 2004: 315, 356; Blenkinsopp 2009: 10.

26. Blenkinsopp 2009: 67–71; Grabbe 2004: 171, 313–16; Levine 2002: 21–22.

27. Blenkinsopp 2009: 157.

28. Leith 1998: 385; Grabbe 2004: 171, 287; Lipschits 2005: 119.

29. Grabbe 2004: 316.

30. Blenkinsopp 2009: 144–45.

31. Also see Exodus 34: 11–16. Blenkinsopp 2009: 67.

32. Blenkinsopp 2009: 67–71; 143–45; Levine 2002: 22.

33. See, for example, Ezra 2:64, which reports that 42,360 exiles accompanied Ezra; also see Leith 1998: 385; Grabbe 2004: 274. For the "myth of the empty land," see Blenkinsopp 2009: 44–45.

34. Lipschits 2005: 125, 368, 372–73; Grabbe 2004: 274, 287–88, 355. Blenkinsopp 2009: 45–46, says that the idea of a depopulated land "flies in the face of political and social realities," and notes that it was not in the conquerors' interests to devastate the land.

35. Grabbe 2004: 139.

36. Lipschits 2005: 154–84, 373–74 (map on p. 183); Grabbe 2004: 138.

37. Leith 1998: 384; Grabbe 2004: xxi, 134. Lipschits 2005: 270, says "the number of inhabitants of the kingdom of Judah as it came to an end was approximately

110,000, and the population of Yehud province was approximately 30,000"; also see Lipschits and Tal 2007: 47. Finkelstein 2008: 507, estimates only ca. 15,000.

38. Geva 2014a: 142–43; Lipschits 2009: 2–3; Finkelstein 2008: 506–7; Grabbe 2004: 30. Leith 1998: 384, estimates 1,750 at the time of Alexander's conquest. Levine 2002: 33, estimates 4,000–5,000.

39. Blenkinsopp 2009: 59; Blenkinsopp 1988: 67.

40. See Blenkinsopp 2009: 19–28; Meyers and Meyers 1987: xxix.

41. For references, see Magness 2019b: 213 n. 9.

42. Leith 1998: 368, 387; Grabbe 2004: 167–71.

43. Grabbe 2004: 359.

44. Grabbe 2004: 360; Leith 1998: 401.

45. Blenkinsopp 2007; Blenkinsopp 2009: 189–227.

46. Honigman 2014: 144–76; Ariel 2019: 27–28.

47. Shalev et al. 2021: 18. For an overview of the archaeological evidence for Persian-period Jerusalem, see Ristau 2016: 13–88 (chapter 2). Finkelstein 2018: 12, limits the Persian- and early Hellenistic-period settlement to the center of the ridge of the southeastern hill (ca. 20–25 dunams), with a population of only ca. 400–500. He argues that the settlement was unfortified and that the description of Nehemiah's wall was inserted into the text by Hasmonean redactors (pp. 19, 22).

48. According to Levine 2002: 9, the document in Ezra 1 was intended to be written and read aloud, while Ezra 6 was only written; on pp. 10–11 he suggests that Ezra 1 was directed toward the Jewish community while Ezra 6 was an internal government document.

49. Also see Josephus, *Ant.* 11.99; see Patrich 2009: 40. The gloss to Ezra 6:3 in the NRSV (p. 655) says the temple would have measured 27 × 9 × 14 meters (90 × 30 × 45 feet).

50. See below; Patrich 2020: 282–83; Patrich and Edelcopp 2013: 328–29.

51. E. Mazar 2011c: 258–59; Bahat 2020: 33; Ritmeyer 2006: 174–75, 197–98; Shalev et al. 2020: 168 n. 10; Galor and Bloedhorn 2013: 60. Levine 2002: 88, attributes the courses to Jonathan the Maccabee. Patrich and Edelcopp 2013 state that "there is no evidence to confirm the hypothesis that the eastern wall of the Herodian precinct was originally built already in the First Temple period." They claim that the line of the current east wall of the Temple Mount was first established by John Hyrcanus I (p.353), but have no explanation for the lowest courses by the Golden Gate, which they only say "seem to be pre-Herodian" (p. 352).

52. Patrich 2009: 39–40; Grabbe 2004: 217.

53. Bahat 2020: 35.

54. Patrich and Edelcopp 2013: 329; Bahat 2020: 35. *Rehov* is translated in Tregelles 1857: 764 (*Gesenius*) as "an open space or forum."

55. Patrich 2009: 41.

56. Dates: Nickelsburg 2005: 198; 138–130 BCE; Bar-Kochva 2010: 53–54 n. 83; last quarter of the second century BCE; Honigman 2014:73; second half of the second century BCE. Also see Patrich 2020: 278 n. 43.

57. From Charles 1969: 103.

58. Honigman 2014, who says the author modeled his description of Jerusalem after the ideals presented in Aristotle's *Constitution of the Athenians*.

59. Patrich 2009: 41. Honigman 2004: 79–80, suggests the reference is to the Gihon spring.

60. Approximately forty cisterns are known. See Reich 2021a: 251; Gibson and Jacobson 1996: 229–32, who say that some of the cisterns date back at least to the Iron Age.

61. Ritmeyer 2006: 221–32; Patrich 2020: 275–81; Gibson and Jacobson 1994; Gibson and Jacobson 1996: 14, 17, 20.

62. Patrich 2020: 275–81.

63. Leith 1998: 396, 410–11; Bahat 2015: 16; Bahat 2011a: 99–101.

64. Bar-Kochva 2010: 465 including n. 51; Bahat 2011a.

65. Edelman 2006: 207; Patrich 2020: 281–82, 323; Ritmeyer 2006: 191, 195; J. Schwartz 1996.

66. Eshel 2000; Simons 1952: 437–58.

67. Eshel 2000: 333 including n. 30. In contrast, Williamson 2004: 69–70, argues that "the name of a gate need not be taken from the feature to which it immediately leads."

68. Eshel 2000: 338, places this gate on the north side of the Temple Mount because he believes the fish market was located nearby. Avi-Yonah 1954b: 242, places it at the northwest corner of the Temple Mount because fish were brought to the city from that direction.

69. For a possible Iron Age gate on the west side of the southeastern hill, see Chapter 6.

70. Eshel 2000: 338; Avi-Yonah 1954b: 242.

71. Avi-Yonah 1954b: 242–43.

72. Geva 2003b: 524–25; Lipschits 2005: 212–13. For scattered Persian-period remains outside the southeastern hill, see Barkay 2008: 49–50.

73. Lipschits 2005: 213.

74. Grabbe 2004: 302, says this is an exaggeration.

75. Eshel 2000: 341; Finkelstein 2008: 502.

76. Ben-Dov 2002: 87.

77. Ussishkin 2012: 124.

78. Eshel 2000: 334, figure 1; 341; Avi-Yonah 1954b.

79. See Yoram Tsafrir's "maximalist" reconstruction in Ussishkin 2012: 121, figure 7.

80. Ussishkin 2012: 124.

81. Eshel 2000: 334, figure 1; 336–38.

82. Geva 2012: 75–76. For a different reconstruction, see Avi-Yonah 1954b.

83. Ussiskhkin 2012: 109, 120–24, argues that the Bronze Age wall on the west side of the southeastern hill was not rebuilt and reused in the early Iron Age. Ariel 2021a: 268, says that this wall was still "fully functional" when Antiochus VII Sidetes besieged Jerusalem ca. 133 BCE (see Chapter 6).

84. Eshel 2000: 338–39.

85. See, e.g., Simons 1952: 443, figure 56, who, however, thought the southwestern hill was settled; Ussishkin 2012: 124–25.

86. Ussishkin 2012: 125, proposes that the reconstruction was "symbolic," but this does not account for the investment of resources and manpower. See Geva 2012: 73–76.

87. For different proposals, see Ben-Dov 2002: 86–87; Geva 2003b: 505–6; Geva 2012.

88. A. Mazar 2000: 199. Reich 2021c: 15, proposes identifying it with the Siloam Tunnel.

89. A. Mazar 2000: 229.

90. De Groot and Wexler-Bdolah 2014: 133–35.

91. A. Mazar 2000: 228.

92. A. Mazar 2000: 225, 230, who identifies the old pool as a pool by the Gihon spring that went out of use when the Siloam Tunnel was hewn. Also see McKinny et al. 2021: 658.

93. A. Mazar 2000: 228, 230; Eshel 2000: 339.

94. A. Mazar 2000: 230; Shanks 2004: 34–38.

95. Eshel 2000: 340. A. Mazar 2000: 230, says that the name must derive from the period before the water was diverted from the spring into the Siloam Tunnel.

96. Although the stretch of the "Broad Wall" uncovered by Avigad is farther west; see Avigad 1983: 62; Geva 2003b: 512.

97. Grafman 1974; Williamson 2004: 70–71; Geva 2012:74.

98. Macalister and Duncan 1926: 37–68. For the Persian-period walls, see Ristau 2016: 21–66.

99. Kenyon 1974: 192.

100. Prag 2018: 52–53, 55 figure 3.33; Kenyon 1974: 183, 191–92; Wightman 1993: 105.

101. Kenyon 1974: 183–84; 191–92; Prag 2018: 52–57.

102. De Groot 2012: 176; Eshel 2000: 339.

103. Lipschits 2009: 17; Reich and Shukron 2004: 217; Reich and Shukron 2021a: 298, 360.

104. De Groot 2012: 176.

105. Shiloh 1984: 20; Prag 2018: 52–55.

106. Shiloh 1984: 21.

107. Shiloh 1984: 20.

108. Kenyon 1974: 183. See Prag 2018: 52–57; Steiner 2011: 308. Ussiskhkin 2012: 117–18, claims that this wall postdates the Persian period.

109. Steiner 2011: 308–11; Prag 2018: 55–56.

110. Steiner 2011: 313.

111. E. Mazar 2015b: 179–81, 189–202.

112. E. Mazar 2009: 73–77; E. Mazar 2015b: 189–92.

113. E. Mazar 2009: 47, 74–75; E. Mazar 2015b: 198–202.

114. E. Mazar 2015b: 192.

115. E. Mazar 2015b: 190–92.

116. E. Mazar 2009: 75–76.

117. E. Mazar 2009: 75–76.

118. E. Mazar 2015b: 34–35, 201.

119. E. Mazar 2009: 74–75; E. Mazar 2015b: 31–33, 201.

120. Raban-Gerstel et al. 2015: 74–75.

121. Wapnish and Hesse 2008: 542, 545.

122. Wapnish and Hesse 2008: 547–48.

123. Wapnish and Hesse 2008: 561–62; J. Schwartz 2004: 249, 252–53.

124. Wapnish and Hesse 2008: 562; J. Schwartz 2004: 248.

125. Stager 2008.

126. See Wapnish and Hesse 2008: 559–60.

127. Taylor 2000; Wapnish and Hesse 2008: 562; J. Schwartz 2004: 246–49.

128. See Taylor 2000.

129. See Magness 2011b: 44–53.

130. Edelman 2006. I thank Andrea Berlin for bringing this reference to my attention.

131. Edelman 2006: 212–13, notes that "the Shabbat transgressions were not a pre-existing condition like the others. They had developed during Nehemiah's absence and were being initiated by citizens of Jerusalem and by resident foreigners" (p. 213).

132. Reich 2011a: 327–28.

133. See, e.g., Finkelstein 2009: 6; Steiner 2011: 313; de Groot 2012: 175.

134. De Groot 2012: 173, although it is not clear how he knows that the fill abuts the wall. Cahill and Tarler 1994: 41, state that Kenyon discovered LB deposits on the bedrock close to the inner face of the wall, suggesting it might be much earlier than the Persian period; see Kenyon 1974: 95, 183 (who does not make this claim).

135. Steiner 2011.

136. E. Mazar 2015b: 190, describes it as giving the impression of "hasty work."

137. Geva 2012: 69–73; Geva 2019: 14, who states, "Nothing in the finds justifies the dating of the Northern Tower to the Persian period." Ariel 2019: 46, says the mid-slope wall was in use by the time of Antiochus VII's siege but does not explain if he is following Geva in identifying this as the Persian-period wall or thinks it is the First Wall (with the remains of the Akra above being separate).

138. Geva 2015: 61.

139. Geva 2012: 70; Geva 2015: 61; E. Mazar 2015b: 193–94. Although both refer to the possibility of the wall abutting the tower (and therefore the tower predating

the wall), this seems impossible as the tower would had to have been built up against the wall.

140. Szanton and Zilberstein 2015: 36*, 38*; Geva 2019: 14. Ariel 2021a: 234, expresses reservations about the identification with the Akra.

141. E. Mazar 2015b: 201, says the accumulated layers excavated by Shiloh just down the slope from (east of) the north tower would not have reached a height sufficient for the deep foundations posited by Geva.

142. E. Mazar 2015b: 35; unfortunately, she does not publish the pottery from the foundation trench separately from the clay layer (L1208); see p. 227.

143. *Pace* Geva 2015: 70 n. 14, who rules out a Persian-period date and says the tower cannot be any earlier than the Hasmonean period.

144. E. Mazar 2015b: 201.

145. See, e.g., de Groot 2012: 176; Ariel and de Groot 2000: 159.

146. Finkelstein 2008; Finkelstein 2009. For responses, see Ussishkin 2012: 118–20; Barkay 2008: 51–53.

147. De Groot 2012: 175.

148. Lipschits 2009; Barkay 2008: 50, who notes that the peaceful transition from the Persian to early Hellenistic period also contributed to the paucity of identifiable remains.

149. De Groot 2012: 175–76; Lipschits 2009: 12, 17, 19; Ristau 2016: 14–21.

150. Lipschits 2009: 19.

151. Lipschits 2009: 20. Levine 2002: 25, and Barkay 2008: 51, estimate the total area including the Temple Mount at 120–130 dunams (30–32 acres).

152. Ristau 2016: 73; he does not include the Givati Parking Lot. Reich and Shukron 2021d: 679, conclude that the Persian-period settlement was limited to the southern part of the southeastern hill.

153. Ristau 2016: 73.

154. De Groot and Bernick-Greenberg 2012: 21–22; de Groot 2012: 166.

155. De Groot and Bernick-Greenberg, 2012: 20–21; de Groot 2012: 166; Ariel et al., 2000: 59–62.

156. De Groot 2012: 176; Ariel et al. 2000: 59—all of whom associate the quarrying with the construction of the First Wall, which makes no sense since the chips are mostly in Stratum 9 of the Persian period; see Lipschits 2009: 15–16.

157. Shalev et al. 2021: 22; Shalev et al. 2020: 160–61.

158. Shalev et al. 2020: 160. For early Persian pottery from the Givati Parking Lot, see Shalev et al. 2019: 60–62.

159. Shalev et al. 2021: 23–25; Shalev et al. 2020.

160. Shalev et al. 2020: 167, also note that, by the late Iron Age, large cisterns appear to have been cut into the rock west of the Temple Mount as settlement expanded to the west. For small quantities of Persian pottery from Shiloh's Area H in the Tyropoeon Valley, see de Groot and Michaeli 1992: 50.

161. Shalev et al. 2021: 34; Zilberstein 2021: 48; Szanton and Zilberstein 2015: 31*; Shalev et al. 2020: 166–69; Ristau 2016: 22–23.

162. Ariel and Shoham 2000.

163. Ariel and Shoham 2000: 138; Lipschits 2005: 176; Lipschits and Vanderhooft 2011: xvi, 760–64; Geva 2018: 33.

164. Lipschits and Vanderhooft 2011: 60; *pace* Ariel and Shoham 2000: 138, who remark on the "variety of wares."

165. Lipschits and Vanderhooft 2011: 759, 761.

166. Lipschits 2009: 12; Prag 2018: 57.

167. Rappaport 1984: 25.

168. Meshorer 1985: 6.

169. Ristau 2016: 70.

170. *Against Apion*, 1.22, 187–89; see Levine 2002: 38, 49. For Yehud coins, see Meshorer 1982: 13–34; Hendin 2010: 113–36; Mildenberg 1979; Grabbe 2004: 64–67.

171. Adler 2022b: 199; Hendin 2010: 122, 133 no. 1071; Levine 2002: 35, 38–39.

172. Barkay 1994: 98–99. Barkay 2008: 50, says that some of the tombs at Ketef Hinnom were used into the early Hellenistic period.

173. Barkay 1994: 101–2.

174. Levine 2002: 41.

175. Levine 2002: 43.

6. HASMONEAN JERUSALEM (64 BCE)

1. For bibliographical references to the historical background presented here, in addition to those cited in the endnotes, see Magness 2018: 93–116.

2. For the argument that biblical laws were not widely observed until the Pentateuch was adopted and promoted by the Hasmoneans as a means of unifying the Jewish population after the Maccabean revolt, see Adler 2022b: 229–31, 232–33.

3. There is a huge corpus of scholarly literature on Hellenization. For a discussion, see Levine 2002: 46.

4. Blenkinsopp 2009: 148–49, argues that the Zadokite high priesthood originated in the Babylonian exile.

5. For discussions, see Honigman 2014: 530–67, who attributes the revolt to economic distress and political destabilization; Atkinson 2016: 25; Levine 2002: 78–80. For other references, see Coşkun 2021: 270 n. 3.

6. For the origins of this holiday, see Atkinson 2016: 27; Levine 2002: 82–84.

7. For a recent survey of the Hasmoneans, see Atkinson 2016.

8. *Ant.* 13.257–58; from Marcus 1943: 357 (Vol. IX). For a discussion of the "Jewishness" of converted Idumaeans focusing on Herod the Great, see Cohen 1999: 13–27. Atkinson 2016: 68–69, says the literary and archaeological evidence indicates that the Idumaeans submitted peacefully to John Hyrcanus I.

9. Schürer 1973–1986: 217–18. For a recent discussion, see Leibner 2021: 124. However, since Josephus does not say who conquered Galilee, Levine 2002: 91 n. 1, suggests it might have been John Hyrcanus I. Atkinson 2016: 87–97, concludes, "There is no evidence of a forced Judaization of the Galilee during the reign of Aristobulus" (p. 96), and "Jewish expansion in Iturean territory appears to have been a gradual process" (p. 97); also see Chancey 2014: 115–16.

10. See Atkinson 2016: 131–32.

11. See Atkinson 2016: 134–35.

12. *Hist.* 5.9:1; from M. Stern 1980: 28 (Vol. 2) (transl. C. H. Moore, LCL).

13. See Adler 2022b: 233–34. In contrast, Blenkinsopp 2009: 189–227, traces the origins of sectarianism back to Ezra and Nehemiah's reforms.

14. For recent studies on the Pharisees, see Sievers and Levine 2021.

15. Levine 2002: 121.

16. *War* 5.145; from Thackeray 2006: 45 (Vol. IV).

17. For the relationship of the Temple Scroll to sectarian literature, see Schiffman and Gross 2021: 6–7. Crawford 2000: 28–29, believes its influence on the Qumran sect was limited.

18. 11QT 46:13–16. See Magness 2021: 122–23.

19. Yadin 1983: 302–3 (Vol. 1); *pace* Gibson 2007: 25*, Yadin did not interpret Bethso as "a place of sewers."

20. See Yadin 1983: 303–4 (Vol. 1). Others have rejected the association with an Essene quarter; see, for example, Gibson 2007; Binder 1999: 457.

21. Pixner 1989: 96–99; Pixner 1997; Pixner and Chen 1989; Riesner 1989; Binder 1999: 457–58. For the sectarian view regarding the impurity of excrement, see Magness 2021: 127–33.

22. See Gibson 2007: 32* n. 18; cited by Pixner 1997: 65–66.

23. For references, see Yadin 1983: 302–3 (Vol. 1); Gibson 2007.

24. For Josephus's use of 1–2 Maccabees and other sources, see Honigman 2014: 18–19; Bar-Kochva 2010: 165, 186–93, 448. For overviews of 1–2 Maccabees and Josephus as sources on the Hasmonean period, see Bar-Kochva 2010: 151–93.

25. Eckhardt 2021: 349; Nickelsburg 2005: 102; Honigman 2014: 21; Bar-Kochva 2010: 151–52, 162–64. Berlin and Kosmin 2021: 406, say it is a work of an "historian working in the circle of John Hyrcanus [I]."

26. Bar-Kochva 2010: 170.

27. Nickelsburg 2005: 106–10. Honigman 2014: 13–78, who also attributes 2 Macc to a member of the Hasmonean court.

28. From Danby 2013: 591.

29. Ritmeyer 2006: 173; Patrich 2011: 210–11 n. 17. According to Bahat 2020: 41, 49, 1 cubit was no more than 44–45 cms (17 inches).

30. See Ritmeyer 2006: 147.

31. Ritmeyer 2006: 186–94; Patrich and Edelcopp 2013: 338, 351–53; Bahat 2020: 52. Also see Jerome Murphy O'Connor, cited in Ritmeyer 2006: 196–97. For other theories, see Patrich and Edelcopp 2013: 329 n. 17.

32. Patrich and Edelcopp 2013: 333, 340–41; Ritmeyer 2006: 145. Levine 2002: 239 n. 96, identifies the ʿazarah as the Women's Court in Herod's temple. According to Bahat 2006: 304, and Bahat 2020: 52–54, before Herod expanded the Temple Mount, gentiles were forbidden from entering it altogether.

33. Ritmeyer 2006: 193–94; Klein 2000: 446; Bahat 2020: 36–38.

34. Schiffman and Gross 2021: 9–10. Crawford 2000: 26, dates it between 350 and 175 BCE. For a discussion relating to Ezekiel, see Yadin 1983: 190–92 (Vol. 1).

35. Schiffman 2008: 227.

36. Schiffman 2008: 217; Crawford 2000: 34.

37. Patrich and Edelcopp 2013: 339, who propose that John Hyrcanus I established the square for "ideological reasons" and was influenced by these works. Ritmeyer 2006: 194, suggests that Ezekiel was influenced by the existing square Temple Mount, which he dates to Hezekiah's time.

38. Patrich 2011: 213.

39. Ritmeyer 2006: 242, 244. Patrich 2011: 205–6, claims that the rocky outcrop enshrined in the Dome of the Rock is not the Foundation Stone.

40. Ritmeyer 2006: 258–60, 265–68, 277.

41. Patrich 2011: 205–8.

42. The cistern is numbered 5 on Charles Wilson's map. Gibson and Jacobson 1996: 135–38, number it Cistern 28.

43. From Danby 2013: 598; also see m. ʿErubin 10:14. Patrich 2011: 207–11; Ritmeyer 2006: 227–28. Charles Warren proposed that the western end of the cistern was located under the altar and was used to drain the blood of sacrifices; see Gibson and Jacobson 1996: 136. Bahat 2020: 86–88, identifies the circular cisterns on the Temple Mount as Hellenistic, and Cistern 5 as Herodian.

44. Patrich 2011: 210, a proposal first made by Conrad Schick; see Gibson and Jacobson 1996: 138.

45. Patrich 2011: 224–25. He argues that the temple was oriented toward the rising sun on the date of its dedication, allowing its light to flood the interior on that day every year; see Patrich et al. 2021: 352, 360. Gibson and Jacobson 1996: 138, reject this possibility on the grounds that *Beth Horadath ha-Mayim* ("the place for draining the water") is mentioned in the Mishnah in connection with the dimensions of the temple sanctuary (*heikhal*), which is thought to be on or near the Foundation Stone in the Dome of the Rock (Patrich divorces the temple from the stone), and because the cistern's width does not match that mentioned in the Mishnah.

46. E. Mazar 2011c: 182–95, 259; Ritmeyer 2006: 102–5, 207–20; Patrich and Edelcopp 2011: 329 n. 17, 353–54; Bahat 2020: 49–50.

47. Geva 2018: 32 n. 13; Gibson 2021: 7. For an overview, see E. Mazar 2011c: 177–95.

48. Bar-Kochva 2010: 465; Bahat 2015: 17.

49. J. Schwartz 1996; Bahat 2013: 274; Bahat 2015: 14–15, 17–18 n. 22, 16.

50. Bahat 2015: 14–15; Levine 2002: 112–13.

51. Bahat, 2011a: 103–4; Bahat 2013: 274, 285 nn. 7, 9; Bahat 2015: 14–15, who proposes that the northern part of the *baris* was incorporated in the Antonia.

52. Bahat 2013: 273–85; Bahat 2020: 53, 70, 72; Bahat 2015: 15; Bahat 2011a: 103–4; Geva in E. Stern 1993: 742. Also see Gurevich 2017: 117, 130 n. 4, who refers to them as the "Twin Pools."

53. Ritmeyer 2006: 216–19; also see Levine 2002: 113.

54. Cabaret 2022: 37–43. I am grateful to Dominique-Marie Cabaret for generously giving me a copy of the English-language translation of his book (2022) immediately after its publication.

55. Geva 2003b: 526–27, 534; Geva 2015: 66, 68; Geva 2018: 45–47, 49.

56. Geva 2014a: 143; Levine 2002: 106.

57. Levine 2002: 111; Geva 2014a: 143, who estimates 8,000 and adds another 2,000 if the Second Wall dates to the Hasmonean period.

58. *War* 5.142–143; from Thackeray 2006: 45 (Vol. IV).

59. Geva 2003b: 529–34; Geva 2015: 62; Geva 2018: 36–45; Re'em 2018: 62, 241, 247; Re'em 2019: 140; Zelinger 2019: 284–85.

60. Geva 2003b: 530–33; Geva 2018: 40–42; Re'em 2018: 241–42, 248; Re'em 2019: 140.

61. As is the south tower at the top of the stepped stone structure on the southeastern hill; see Geva 2015: 61; Geva 2018: 38.

62. Geva 2003b: 533; Geva 1994: 158–60.

63. Geva 2018: 42–43. Also see Uziel, Lieberman, and Solomon 2017: 242. The dating of the arched bridge called the Great Causeway to after 70 CE raises the question of how the low-level aqueduct connected to the Temple Mount because the top of the dam wall was lower than the aqueduct. See Geva 2019: 26; Onn and Weksler-Bdolah 2019: 121–22.

64. Regev et al. 2020: 8.

65. Onn and Weksler-Bdolah 2016.

66. Weksler-Bdolah 2006–2007:172–73.

67. See Weill's Gate P in Reich 2004: 34–38; Weksler-Bdolah 2006–2007: 173, 188, who says that the southern gate is Hasmonean and was replaced in the first century CE by another gate some 60 meters (197 feet) to the south, at the point where the first wall turns to climb the southwestern hill, which connects with the paved road along the Tyropoeon Valley; Weksler-Bdolah and Szanton 2014; Szanton and Zilberstein 2015: 38*.

68. Geva 2003b: 533–34; Geva 2018: 43–45; Ariel 2019: 28; Ariel 2021a: 260–63.

69. Ariel 2021a: 260–64, 267.

70. Josephus, *Ant.* 13.247; see Atkinson 2016: 55–59; Schürer 1973–1986: 203–4 (Vol. I); Levine 2002: 102; Ariel 2021a: 232, 262–63.

71. Geva 2003b: 534; Geva 2015: 65, 68; Geva 2018: 44–45; also see Ariel 2021a: 267.

72. 1 Macc 16:23; see Geva 2015: 65; Ariel 2019: 39; Atkinson 2016: 57–58 n. 53, 62–67.

73. See Regev et al. 2020: 14, who attribute construction to Alexander Jannaeus.

74. See Geva 1994; Sivan and Solar 1994.

75. Sivan and Solar 1994: 173–74; Geva in E. Stern 1993: 727; Yuzefovsky 2018; Ariel 2021a: 243–44.

76. Mazis and Wright 2018: 206, 215–16, 224; Ariel 2019: 31–34; Ariel 2021a: 251–52.

77. *War* 5.136; from Thackeray 2006: 41 (Vol. IV).

78. *War* 5.146; from Thackeray 2006: 45 (Vol. IV). For other references to the Second Wall in Josephus, see Wightman 1993: 182.

79. See Geva and Avigad 2000b: 234; Geva 2018: 50; Geva 2003b: 532, with references to other proposals; he notes that if Avigad is correct, it would leave the Christian Quarter outside the wall. Kloner 2020: 419, locates it farther west.

80. See Cabaret 2022: 11–24; Geva 2011: 299; Geva 2018: 50–51; Wightman 1993: 181–84; Kloner 2020: 419–22, 430–37, who dates the construction of the Second Wall to ca. 100 BCE and reconstructs its circuit from east of the Citadel to the Antonia (not reaching the Damascus Gate).

81. For a discussion, see Levine 2002: 109–10.

82. Geva 2018: 50; Cabaret 2022: 18–19, 31.

83. *Ant.* 14.470, 476–77. See Ariel 2019: 43 n. 86; Wightman 1993: 184, who suggests the Second Wall was built by Antipater after Pompey's siege.

84. Geva and Avigad 2000a: 134, 176 (where Geva relates this to the Second Wall); Geva and Avigad 2000b: 215–18, 231–35; Geva 2003a: 113–14, 150 (pottery deposited in a short time—in a generation or two—in the second half of the second century and the very beginning of the first century BCE); 534–35 (where he relates this to the Second Wall), including references to earth fills of the first century BCE at other points along the First Wall on the southwestern hill—in the Citadel and along the western side of the hill (p. 534); Geva 1994: 159 (the Citadel). However, Geva 2019: 15, dates all these dumps to the end of the early Roman period (first century CE).

85. Geva 2018: 51; Bahat 2013: 274, 303, 308. However, Geva 2011: 307, says "The [Second] wall certainly was constructed at some point in the first century BCE, though the lack of specific historical evidence and the fact that no clear remains of the wall were uncovered make it difficult to establish whether it was built by the Hasmoneans or Herod."

86. Geva 2003b: 534; Geva 1994: 159.

87. See Bar-Kochva 2010: 455–58, who shows that Josephus's account of Simon leveling the hill is unsupported. Atkinson 2016: 45 n. 92, says that "the traditional date of the siege is from 143–141 BCE."

88. Letter of Aristeas 100–114, and a decree of Antiochus III preserved in Josephus. See Levine 2002: 66 n. 82; Bar-Kochva 2010: 53–54 n. 83; 462–65; Ritmeyer 2006: 201–2; Wightman 1993: 185.

89. Levine 2002: 75–78; Geva 2018: 30 n. 5; Zilberstein 2021: 49 n. 9.

90. Bar-Kochva 2010: 445–65.

91. Ben-Ami and Tchekhanovets 2016; Zilberstein 2021; Shalev et al. 2019. But Ariel 2021a: 234, 268–70, associates the wall and glacis with the earlier (pre-First Wall) fortifications around the southeastern hill, not the Akra.

92. Kenyon 1974: 194–99.

93. Zilberstein 2021: 50.

94. Zilberstein 2021: 40; Zilberstein 2019: 31–37. According to Shalev et al. 2019, the tower is separate from the wall, while the wall consists of two parts: an earlier south wall (W7109) to which the north wall (W7009) was added. They propose that the south wall originally terminated in an opening or gate at its north end, which was later blocked by the addition of the north wall. They also note different construction styles or stages in the north wall.

95. Zilberstein 2021: 39–42; Zilberstein 2019: 37–40.

96. Zilberstein 2021: 46–47; Zilberstein 2019: 40; Ariel 2021a: 237–38.

97. Zilberstein 2021: 45, 48–51; Zilberstein 2019: 40–41; Shalev et al. 2021: 21; Ben-Ami and Tchekhanovets 2015a.

98. Zilberstein 2021: 49.

99. Ariel 2019: 35–36, 49; Ariel 2021a: 238–40.

100. See Zilberstein 2021: 50–51.

101. Zilberstein 2021: 50–51; Ariel 2021a: 239.

102. Crowfoot and Fitzgerald 1929; see Zilberstein 2021: 49 n. 9; Ben-Ami and Tchekhanovets 2016: 26*.

103. Crowfoot and Fitzgerald 1929: 4.

104. Crowfoot and Fitzgerald 1929: 13, 17, 18–19.

105. Crowfoot and Fitzgerald 1929: 17. Zilberstein 2019: 47, agrees that the construction with large boulders is earlier, while the elongated ashlars are Hellenistic.

106. Crowfoot and Fitzgerald 1929: 15–16, 21–22. Ussishkin 2012: 109–15, rejects the identification of this structure as a gate and dates it to the late Second Temple period; for other views, see Steiner 2011: 314; Ristau 2016: 44–62. Prag 2018: 51, believes that Crowfoot and Fitzgerald's gate was part of an eighth-century line of wall. Geva 2012: 74, says it is a Hasmonean-period gate that presumably preserves the line of an earlier (Iron Age) line of fortifications.

107. Crowfoot and Fitzgerald 1929: 20, 64–71 ("Low Level").

108. Crowfoot and Fitzgerald 1929: 106; Ristau 2016: 61.

109. Crowfoot and Fitzgerald 1929: 15, 19, 64–65; Ristau 2016: 61.

110. The other coins are unidentified; Crowfoot and Fitzgerald 1929: 104–5. Ristau 2016: 61 n. 44, connects the coins to the destruction of the Akra by Alexander

Jannaeus. Zilberstein 2019: 46, notes that a house (no. 47) found to the west of the gate was dated by Crowfoot and Fitzgerald to the late second–early first century BCE.

111. Crowfoot 1929a; Crowfoot 1929b; Crowfoot 1929c. Also see Zilberstein 2019: 41–47; Ristau 2016: 47–62.

112. Crowfoot 1929a: 14; Crowfoot 1929c: 159–60.

113. Crowfoot 1929c: 159.

114. Crowfoot 1929c: 155.

115. Crowfoot 1929c: 160.

116. Shiloh 1984: 20–21 (Stratum 7).

117. Shiloh 1984: 21; followed by Steiner 2011.

118. Ben-Ami and Tchekhanovets 2016: 25*–27*.

119. Crowfoot 1929c: 160–61; Macalister and Duncan 1926: 69–73.

120. See Steiner 2011: 301 figure 3.

121. Szanton and Zilberstein 2015: 36*, 38*.

122. Crowfoot and Fitzgerald 1929: 23, citing Louis-Hugues Vincent, *Topographie de l'Ancienne Jérusalem des Origines à Titus* (1912). Ariel 2019: 46–48, says that the lower [gravel] glacis was added to the old Iron Age wall on the western side of the southeastern hill as a second line of defense before Antiochus VII's siege, with the First Wall on the southwestern hill functioning as an "outwork." Ariel does not explicitly associate the glacis with the Akra but only with a reuse of the Iron Age fortifications on the western side of the southeastern hill, nor does he cite Crowfoot and Fitzgerald.

123. *Ant.* 20.189–191.

124. Geva 2015: 66–68; Geva 2018: 47–48.

125. For overviews, see Netzer 2006: 42–72; Netzer 2018: 11–63. For the final report, see Netzer 2001.

126. Gurevich 2017: 124.

127. For the high-level aqueduct, see Chapter 7. For the Hasmonean date of the low-level aqueduct, see A. Mazar 2002: 237, who suggests that it dates to the time of John Hyrcanus I or Alexander Jannaeus (following a suggestion by Joseph Patrich). Billig 2002: 249, dates it between Alexander Jannaeus's and Herod's time; also see Weksler-Bdolah 2011: 23.

128. C. Schick 1878, especially 160–69. See A. Mazar 2002: 211; for two other aqueducts that fed Solomon's Pools, see pp. 213–17, 223–26.

129. A. Mazar 2002: 230.

130. A. Mazar 2002: 211–12.

131. Weksler-Bdolah 2011: 22.

132. A. Mazar 2002: 213, 231.

133. A. Mazar 2002: 217; Billig 2002: 245.

134. A. Mazar 2002: 217, 241–43.

135. A. Mazar 2002: 220–23; Geva 2018: 42–43 n. 42, who responds to Weksler-Bdolah's (2011) proposal that the aqueduct did not cross at the Tyropoeon Valley but continued northward and entered the Temple Mount at the northwest corner.

136. A. Mazar 2002: 220–23; Reich 2021a: 248.

137. For an overview of Jewish ritual purity, see Adler 2022b: 50–86.

138. Adler 2022b: 61–66, 82–83.

139. Adler 2011: 51–62; Reich 2013: 15–17; Adler 2022b: 83.

140. For the expansion of purity observance, see Levine 2002: 139–42.

141. Reich 2013: 209.

142. Finkielsztejn 1999: 21*.

143. Geva 2018: 35; Ariel 1990: 14, 19, 21; Finkielsztejn 1999: 21*–24*, 28*.

144. See Geva 2018: 35; Finkielsztejn 1999: 27*.

145. Finkielsztejn 2021: 196. However, amphoras and handles without stamps that postdate the mid-second century BCE are found on the southeastern hill; see Ariel 2000: 268.

146. Ariel 2019: 43; Ariel 2021a: 260–64; Finkielsztejn 2021: 202. Also see Atkinson 2016: 56; Antiochus VII surrounded Jerusalem with a rampart and agger and seven siege camps and attacked the north wall with one hundred mobile siege engines.

147. Ariel 2021a: 253–58.

148. Ariel 2000: 267, documented only thirty-two Greek stamped handles from the Jewish Quarter excavations versus 330 from excavations in the City of David—only 2.5 percent of the total found in Jerusalem.

149. Ariel 2000: 267.

150. Geva 2018: 35.

151. For discussions, see Ariel and Strikovsky 1990; Ariel 2000: 276–80; Finkielsztejn 1999: 31*–32*.

152. Avigad 1983: 88.

153. See Geva 2018: 32–35; Lipschits and Vanderhooft 2011: 593–757; Levine 2002: 95; Hendin 2010: 169–70; Ariel 2021b: 238; Meshorer 1982: 50–51.

154. Geva 2018: 34.

155. Geva 2018: 35.

156. Ariel 2021b: 227, 235; see this same article for earlier coins minted while Hyrcanus I was still a vassal to Antiochus VII Sidetes; Atkinson 2016: 62. Syon 2021: 179 n. 4, does not agree that the earlier coins were minted by Hyrcanus I.

157. Meshorer 1982: 58; also see Ariel 2021b: 232.

158. Meshorer 1982: 59.

159. Meshorer 1982: 58.

160. Atkinson 2016: 101–2.

161. Hendin 2010: 195–96; Meshorer 1982: 82–83.

162. Josephus, *Ant.* 13.398; *War* 1.105–106.

163. Hendin 2010: 196; Meshorer 1982: 82.

164. Ariel 2021b: 237.

165. Ariel 2021b: 220–21, who does not think the flower on Hasmonean coins is a lily.

166. Levine 2002: 142–43. Also see Adler 2022b: 111–12; Ariel 2021b: 237; Hendin 2010: 172–76.

167. Hendin 2010: 163, 185–201.

168. Levine 2002: 97; see 114–15 for the meaning of the council of the Jews.

169. Hendin 2010: 208–16; Meshorer 1982: 92–97.

170. For a discussion and references, see Magness 2011: 145–58.

171. Josephus, *Ant.* 13:210–11; from Marcus 1943: 331–33 (Vol. IX).

172. See Rahmani 1967; Rahmani 1982: 45–46; Barag 2010.

173. Avigad 1954: 66–73.

174. Barag 2010: 159, dates the tomb to ca. 135–31 BCE; Rahmani 1967: 94, dates it from the time of Alexander Jannaeus to Herod.

175. From Barag 2010: 149, 151.

176. Barag 2010: 151.

177. Barag 2010: 152, 159–60.

178. Barag 2010: 154.

179. Adler 2022b: 165.

180. Barag 2010: 152–53; Rahmani 1967: 69–70.

181. Rahmani 1967: 96–97.

182. Barag 2010: 153–54.

183. Barag 2010: 155; however, the individuals mentioned in the inscriptions cannot be Onias III and his brother Jason, who lived in the first half of the second century BCE, decades before the tomb was constructed.

184. Barag 2010: 155, 159–60.

185. Rahmani 1967: 93–94.

186. See Magness 2019b: 184.

187. Rahmani 1967: 93–94.

188. Barag 2010: 150.

189. Barag 2010: 149–150, 159.

190. *Iasonis Pagus* is mentioned in the Georgian Lectionary for 15 July; see Be'eri and Levi 2018: 27; Arubas and Goldfus 2005: 11; Tsafrir et al. 1994: 151. The surviving manuscripts date to the tenth century but include information that goes back to the fifth and sixth centuries; see Buchinger 2021: 117–18; Shalev-Hurvitz 2015: 19; Verhelst 2006: 430.

191. Be'eri and Levi 2018: 27.

192. Solimany et al. 2011: 71*.

193. Demsky 2021.

7. HERODIAN JERUSALEM (MARCH 70 CE)

1. For the historical background in this chapter including references, see Rogers 2021; Magness 2019b: 118–40. Additional references are cited here in the endnotes.

2. Levine 2002: 342–43, estimates 60,000–70,000; Geva 2014a: 144–48, estimates 20,000 or less.

3. For Josephus including references, see Magness 2019b: 18–24. For Nicolaus of Damascus, who was Josephus's main source on Herod, see Czajkowski and Eckhardt 2021.

4. However, Josephus's works were (re)appropriated by Jews in the tenth century, when a Hebrew paraphrase called the *Sefer Yosippon* (or *Sepher Josippon*) was composed in Southern Italy, see Dönitz 2016; Bowman 2022 (I was unable to obtain Bowman's book before submitting this manuscript).

5. Levine 2002: 155.

6. Macrobius, *Saturnalia* 2.4.11; see Rogers 2021: 20, 559 n. 42.

7. See Magness 2019a: 283–85.

8. For Herod's tomb at Herodium with references, see Magness 2019a.

9. *Ant.* 18.118; from Feldman 1965: 83 (Vol. XII).

10. For the argument that Pontius Pilate was appointed prefect in 18/19 CE, see D. Schwartz 1992: 182–201.

11. See Kokkinos 1998: 271–304.

12. Goodman 2007: 76–85.

13. See Hendin 2010: 290.

14. *War* 2.224; from Thackeray 1997: 411 (Vol. I).

15. *War* 2.254–255; from Thackeray 1997: 423 (Vol. I).

16. *Hist.* V.12.3; from M. Stern 1980: 30 (Vol. 2).

17. *War* 5.25; from Thackeray 2006: 11 (Vol. III).

18. Soncino translation.

19. *War* 5.362, 375; from Thackeray 2006: 113, 119 (Vol. III).

20. *War* 5.449, 451; from Thackeray 2006: 143 (Vol. III).

21. Josephus, *War* 5.512–513; from Thackeray 2006: 161 (Vol. III).

22. Rogers 2021: 350–51, says that Josephus's report of cannibalism (which is a common literary trope among Greek and Roman authors) was intended to distract readers from Titus's responsibility for allowing the destruction of the temple by showing that it was God's punishment to Jews who had become subhuman.

23. From Danby 2013: 200.

24. *War* 6.120; from Thackeray 2006: 213 (Vol. III).

25. *Chronica* II.30:7; from M. Stern 1980: 64–67 (Vol. 2).

26. Rogers 2021: 353–54, 359.

27. Ben-Shahar 2015; Rogers 2021: 359; Patrich 2009: 69; Levine 2002: 410.

28. *War* 6.404; from Thackeray 2006: 295 (Vol. III).

29. From Isaac 2010: 11–12.

30. Isaac 2010: 12.
31. *War* 6.420; from Thackeray 2006: 299 (Vol. III).
32. Hendin 2010: 225.
33. For a list of Herod's buildings in Jerusalem and dates of construction, see Richardson 1999: 197–98.
34. Levine 2002: 281.
35. Richardson 1999: 202.
36. See Magness 2019a.
37. See Magness 2008: 206.
38. Jacobson 2007: 147–48.
39. Levine 2002: 223; Patrich 2009: 50; Jacobson 2007: 149, who also mentions Philo.
40. Levine 2002: 223–24.
41. Levine 2002: 224–25.
42. Binder 1999: 122; Bourgel 2021: 25 n. 8.
43. For debates about the temple's existence motivated by political considerations, see Lawler 2021a: 261–65.
44. Jacobson 2007: 151–52 including n. 33. For Josephus's description of Herod's buildings as marble, see Peleg-Barkat 2017: 120 n. 68.
45. Patrich 2009: 38; Jacobson 2007: 149–50. Levine 2002: 196 n. 33, says that generally a cubit was close to a half-yard.
46. Jacobson 2007: 152.
47. Levine 2002: 242; Patrich 2009: 58.
48. Levine 2002: 242; Patrich 2009: 58, 59; Jacobson 2007: 152–53.
49. Patrich 2009: 59; Levine 2002: 242.
50. From Danby 2013: 167.
51. Bahat 2020: 19; Ritmeyer 2006: 242; Geva in E. Stern 1993: 743.
52. Levine 2002: 238; Ritmeyer 2006: 244.
53. Patrich 2011: 205–6.
54. Levine 2002: 239–41; Patrich 2009: 55; Jacobson 2007: 153–54, who says (p. 155) that women could not go beyond the Women's Court.
55. Levine 2002: 241 n. 109, says there were seven or eight gates; Patrich 2009: 55, says there were ten.
56. Levine 2002: 235, 241–42; Patrich 2009: 55–56.
57. Levine 2002: 239–40; Patrich 2009: 55.
58. Patrich 2009: 55.
59. t. Kippurim (Yoma) 2:4; m. Yoma 3:10; m. Middoth 2:3. Josephus does not refer to Nicanor's gate by name but mentions it was of Corinthian bronze (*War* 5.201); see Jacobson 2007: 155.
60. Patrich and Edelcopp 2013: 346–47; Levine 2002: 238–39. Jacobson 2007: 155, says the Women's Court probably projected east of the elevated platform and was level with the rest of the esplanade.

61. Levine 2002: 329; Patrich 2009: 393 n. 81.

62. Jos., *Ant.* 15.424; see Patrich 2009: 55.

63. Jacobson 2007: 154–55; Bahat 2020: 55.

64. Jacobson 2007: 156.

65. Jacobson 2007: 156–57. Patrich and Edelcopp 2013: 345–46, identify this as "The Second Sacred Precinct" going back to Simon the Just. Similarly, Bahat 2006: 304, and Bahat 2020: 52–54, identifies the area outside the *soreg* with the Herodian expansion; he says that before then the entire Temple Mount was off-limits to gentiles.

66. See Price in Cotton et al. 2010: 43, no. 2.

67. From Price in Cotton et al. 2010: 43, no. 2.

68. From Marcus and Wikgren 2004: 459 (Vol. X).

69. See Jacobson 2007: 156.

70. Price in Cotton et al. 2010: 41; Patrich 2009; Patrich and Edelcopp 2013: 344; Levine 2002: 228. Bahat 2020: 16, and O. Grabar 2005: 203, give slightly different dimensions. Gurevich 2017: 116, suggests that the esplanade is asymmetrical because, when Herod expanded it, he had to take into account preexisting structures to the north, specifically, Birket Isra`il and the Antonia Fortress.

71. Patrich 2009: 50; also see E. Mazar 2011c: 90.

72. Geva in E. Stern 1993: 738.

73. But none on the northeast side; see Geva in E. Stern 1993: 738.

74. Ritmeyer and Ritmeyer 1989a: 29–33; Reich and Billig 2000: 348; Reuven and Shalev 2011.

75. E. Mazar 2011c: 112–18; Bahat 2020: 67–68.

76. For this stretch of wall, see E. Mazar 2011c: 74.

77. Bahat 2007.

78. Ritmeyer and Ritmeyer 1989a: 26–27.

79. Bahat 2020: 24–25; Geva in E. Stern 1993: 739; Ritmeyer and Ritmeyer 1989a: 26; Jacobson 2007: 157–58.

80. Geva in E. Stern 1993: 739; Rosen-Ayalon in E. Stern 1993: 792; Ben-Dov 2002: 353–55; Ritmeyer 2006: 98–99. Bahat 2020: 95, and Bahat 2019: 256, 261–62, argues that the current structure dates to the eleventh century (Fatimid period) but replaced an earlier, "probably Herodian" subterranean structure.

81. See https://tmsifting.org/en/; https://www.salon.com/2001/09/29/intifada/ (both accessed 2 December 2021); Ben-Dov 2002: 354–56; Lawler 2021a: 227–33, 243–58, 277–79. Bahat 2019: 257–61, 263, proposes that the fill was dumped after the earthquake of 1033 to restore the level of the southern part of the Temple Mount platform to its original height.

82. See Jacobson 2007: 168–69. Patrich and Edelcopp 2013: 341, date this portico to the Hasmonean period and claim it was at a lower level than the rest of the Outer Court (Temple Mount).

83. The immediately preceding passages in Acts 3 (1–10), in which Peter heals a cripple near the Beautiful Gate, suggest that Solomon's Portico was nearby; see Aist 2009: 156–57.

84. See Peleg-Barkat 2017, who calls it the Royal Portico; on p. 112 she says this is one of the earliest examples of a building combining the features of Greek stoas and Roman basilicas.

85. Peleg-Barkat 2017: 95–96; Patrich 2009: 62; Levine 2002: 233–35.

86. Levine 2002: 232; Patrich 2009: 63, who compares the Temple Mount to a Caesareum—a complex dedicated to the imperial cult; Jacobson 2007: 162, 164; Reuven 2011; Bahat 2020: 58.

87. For the argument that this change was made earlier, see Hendin 2010: 476–79.

88. Hendin 2010: 481; Ariel and Fontanille 2012: 41.

89. See Magness 2011b: 101–3.

90. See Peleg-Barkat 2017: 95–96; Ritmeyer and Ritmeyer 1989a: 29.

91. E. Mazar 2011c: 178–79 (who thinks the current gate is the product of an Umayyad reconstruction); Bahat 2020: 60–62, 94–95 (who dates Solomon's Stables to the eleventh century, noting that the floor level is higher than the threshold of the Eastern Arch).

92. E. Mazar 2011c: 162–70; Peleg-Barkat 2017: 139, 165 nn. 20, 24; Levine 2002: 229–30 including n. 40; Gibson 2021: 15; Geva in E. Stern 1993: 743; Bahat 2020: 63, 114–17 (who says the Shushan Gate was not on this spot because the Mishnah's reference indicates it was pre-Herodian).

93. Weksler-Bdolah and Onn 2022: 206–7; E. Mazar 2011c: 92–96.

94. For the controversies surrounding the exploration and opening of this tunnel by the Israeli authorities, see Lawler 2021a: 233–41.

95. In distinction from the Southern Master Course (or "Grand Course") at the street level in the south temenos wall, which runs from the western (Double) gate to the southeast corner; see Geva in E. Stern 1993: 738; Bahat 2020: 80; E. Mazar 2011c: 201–13.

96. E. Mazar 2011c: 90; Patrich 2009: 50; Bahat 2020: 73.

97. E. Mazar 2011c: 91–92; Bahat 2020: 73.

98. E. Mazar 2011c: 76–89.

99. Onn, Weksler-Bdolah, and Patrich 2019; Onn, Weksler-Bdolah, and Patrich 2016; Onn and Weksler-Bdolah 2016; Levine 2002: 325.

100. Onn and Weksler-Bdolah 2019: 108; Onn and Weksler-Bdolah 2016; Weksler-Bdolah, Onn, and Rosenthal-Heginbottom 2009. Levine 2002: 230 n. 49, says that the Mishnah might have confused the Kiponos Gate with a gate in the temple that Herod named after Marcus Agrippa; see *War* 1.416. E. Mazar 2011c: 67, suggests identifying Barclay's Gate with the Kiponos Gate, which Geva in E. Stern 1993: 742, says is erroneous. Bahat 2020: 42, locates the Kiponos Gate at the Gate of the Chain.

101. Kogan-Zehavi 1997; Onn and Weksler-Bdolah 2019: 109.

102. Onn, Weksler-Bdolah, and Bar-Nathan 2011; Onn and Weksler-Bdolah 2010; Weksler-Bdolah, Onn, and Heginbottom 2009; Uziel et al. 2017: 240–41, 244, 258.

103. Regev et al. 2020: 10, 12. In contrast, Lieberman et al. 2019: 178, say that the original narrower arch predates Herod's expansion of the Temple Mount, was doubled in width as part of the Herodian expansion, and note that the current arch is integrated into this wall. Also see Uziel et al. 2019, who do not give a precise date for either phase. Onn and Weksler-Bdolah 2019: 113, document evidence of an early phase of Wilson's Arch that collapsed, perhaps in the earthquake of 30 CE, and was rebuilt as part of Herod's expansion of the Temple Mount (which continued after his death).

104. Levine 2002: 201–3.

105. Spielman 2020: 19–20 n. 9; Lichtenberger 2006; Levine 2002: 205–206, 320. Cabaret 2022: 59–91, locates the theater in the Bezetha quarter.

106. Spielman 2020: 26–28; Lichtenberger 2006: Patrich 2002; Levine 2002: 192.

107. Reich and Billig 2000: 350–52.

108. Uziel et al. 2017: 248. Lichtenberger 2006: 293, suggests a second-century or later date for the seats based on their profile.

109. E. Mazar 2011c: 60–68; Jacobson and Gibson 1997: 138; Ritmeyer and Ritmeyer 1989a: 27–29.

110. Ritmeyer and Ritmeyer 1989a: 27–29.

111. See Lawler 2021a: 132–37.

112. See E. Mazar 2011c: 37–60.

113. An arrangement that Charles Warren had proposed; see Gibson 2021: 3–7; also see Ritmeyer and Ritmeyer 1989a: 29–31; Reich and Billig 2000: 340–43.

114. Peleg-Barkat 2017: 163 n. 1; Bahat 2020: 93; as the Mishnah's description apparently refers to gates in the pre-Herodian Temple Mount, it is not clear if the name Huldah was still used in Herod's time.

115. E. Mazar 2011c: 213–220, 226–38; Peleg-Barkat 2017: 121. Ritmeyer and Ritmeyer 1989b: 51, argue that it originally was a triple gate; also see Ritmeyer and Ritmeyer 1989a: 35–36; Bahat 2020: 81–83, 137–40, says it originally was a double gate and dates the triple passage to after the 1033 earthquake.

116. From Danby 2013: 590. Ritmeyer and Ritmeyer 1989b: 51, and Ritmeyer and Ritmeyer 1989a: 37, argue that the Double Gate was used for entry and exit while the Triple Gate was used by priests.

117. See Peleg-Barkat 2017: 121–63.

118. Geva in E. Stern 1993: 738; Ritmeyer and Ritmeyer 1989a: 36.

119. Baruch and Reich 2019: 88–93, who propose that sacrificial animals were brought to the Temple Mount by way of the ramp.

120. Also see Josephus, *Ant.* 20.219. See Price in Cotton et al. 2010: 41, 46–47; Levine 2002: 224–25; Patrich 2009: 50; Richardson 1999: 197; Bahat 2020: 57. This passage uses the Greek term *naos* (temple building) rather than *hieron* (sacred precinct/Temple Mount).
121. Reich 2015: 404; Reich and Shukron 2011b: 68–69; Szanton et al. 2019: 151; Peleg-Barkat 2017: 91, with other references.
122. Reich and Billig 2000: 343–45; Szanton et al. 2019: 148 n. 1.
123. Geva 2019: 19.
124. Geva in E. Stern 1993: 742; Bahat 2020: 57, 67.
125. Josephus, *War* 1.649–51; also see *Ant.* 17:148–67; from Thackeray 1997: 309 (Vol. I).
126. See Richardson 1999: 15–18; Bourgel 2021: 25–28; Gibson and Nagorsky 2016: 155*.
127. Although Jonathan Bourgel 2021 claims it must be one of the temple building's portals because Josephus refers to the "great gate of the naos" in *Ant.* 17.151, in *War* 1.651 Josephus says the young men let themselves down on ropes from the roof of the *hieron*. The rest of Bourgel's argument, which is based on the inaccessibility of the eagle to the public, therefore falls.
128. See Ariel and Fontanille 2012: 115–19, 172–73.
129. *War* 1.654; from Thackeray 1997: 311 (Vol. I).
130. See, e.g., Long 2013: 136–38; Yuval-Hacham 2007: 73–74.
131. Rogers 2021: 20.
132. Josephus, *War* 5.244.
133. Netzer 2006: 120–21; Levine 2002: 194–95.
134. Geva in E. Stern 1993: 742–43. Netzer 2006: 120–26, reconstructs a larger fortress that extended southward into the Temple Mount.
135. Benoit 1976; Benoit 1971. For recent discussions, see Weksler-Bdolah 2020: 100–2; Mazor 2017: 76–78. Cabaret 2022: 110–75, argues that the arch is Herodian but was reused in Hadrian's time.
136. Benoit 1976: 87; Benoit 1971: 167; but see Isaac 2010: 6.
137. Geva in E. Stern 1993: 736; Levine 2002: 198–201; Re'em 2018: 49, 53; Re'em 2019: 140–42.
138. Re'em 2018: 53–62, 247.
139. Josephus, *War* 6.413; from Thackeray 2006: 297 (Vol. III).
140. Re'em 2018: 240.
141. Geva 1981.
142. Geva in E. Stern 1993: 727.
143. Onn and Weksler-Bdolah 2019: 120; Levine 2002: 324.
144. See Avigad 1983.
145. See Geva 2021.

146. The palatial mansion was undergoing renovation at the time of its destruction in 70; see Geva 2021: 13, 73.

147. Geva 2021: 72.

148. Many scholars now prefer to avoid the term "Romanization" because it is a colonial legacy that implies one-way influence from the conquerors to the natives; see, e.g., Mattingly 2004.

149. Levine 2002: 390. Reich 2021a: 260, says that *miqva'ot* have been found in every private house excavated in Jerusalem, and in some cases more than one *miqveh*. Altogether, over 170 *miqva'ot* have been documented in Jerusalem; see Gurevich 2017: 122. For discussions of stone vessels with references, see Gibson 2022a; Adler 2022b: 66–71, 83–84; Adler 2022a; Magness 2011b: 70–74.

150. It was found in a fill between two Herodian floors in Area A; see Avigad 1983: 147.

151. Geva 2010: 64.

152. J. Schwartz 2010; Reich 2006: 350.

153. Avigad 1983: 120–39; Geva 2010: 60, 66–68, including skeletal remains dating to 70 from other excavations around Jerusalem.

154. Geva 2010: 66–68. Also see the critique by Abu el-Haj 2002: 143–45.

155. Broshi 1976b: 84; Broshi 1976a.

156. See Magness 2011b: 10. For figured images in other contexts or media in Jerusalem, see Adler 2022b: 96–101.

157. Greenhut 2011: 288–89.

158. See Levine 2002: 316 n. 9, with references to Josephus and Tacitus.

159. Magen 1994: 286.

160. Robinson and Smith 1841: 464–67; Wightman 1993: 163–67.

161. Sukenik and Mayer 1930; Sukenik and Mayer 1944.

162. Spiezer forthcoming; Geva in E. Stern 1993: 744–45; Tzaferis et al. 1994.

163. Geva in E. Stern 1993: 744; Tzaferis et al. 1994: 288.

164. Geva in E. Stern 1993: 744–45.

165. Sukenik and Mayer 1944; Geva in E. Stern 1993: 745; also see Cabaret 2022: 181–83.

166. Josephus, *War* 5.133, 147.

167. *War* 5.159–160; from Thackeray 2006: 49 (Vol. III).

168. Geva in E. Stern 1993: 745.

169. Geva 2011: 301; Avner and Arbib 2016: 89.

170. Geva in E. Stern 1993: 745.

171. Josephus, *War* 5.156–158.

172. Avner and Arbib 2016.

173. For a ballista stone found by the southern face of this wall near the Albright Institute, see Sukenik and Mayer 1930: 25, 43–44; for another from Kenyon's Area T, see Hamrick 1985: 222; 528 Pl. 184.

174. Levine 2002: 314–15; Geva 2011: 300.

175. *War* 5.148–49, 151; from Thackeray 2006: 47 (Vol. III).

176. Weksler-Bdolah 2011: 187; Geva 2011: 300–1.
177. Geva 2011: 301, calls this the central hill.
178. Geva 2011: 308; Levine 2002: 337; Cabaret 2022: 59 n. 203. In *War* 2.530, Josephus says the quarter was called Bezetha *and* Caenopolis.
179. Geva in E. Stern 1993: 745; Geva 2011: 307–8.
180. Shiloh 1984: 20–21 (Stratum 7).
181. Cahill and Tarler 1994: 42.
182. See Gadot 2022b: 9–11; Gadot 2022a: 288–89. Reich and Shukron 2021d: 684, estimate that the landfill contains at least 200,000 cubic meters (7 million cubic feet) of debris.
183. Gadot 2022a: 295–96; Bar-Oz et al. 2007; Reich and Shukron 2003, who, however, do not associate Shiloh's Stratum 7 with the Akra's glacis and therefore identify it as part of the dump (p. 13); see Szanton and Zilberstein 2015: 37*.
184. Spiciarich and Sapir-Hen 2022: 212; Bouchnick et al. 2021: 484; Bar-Oz et al. 2007: 5.
185. Spiciarich and Sapir-Hen 2022: 213–16, whose statement (p. 214) that none of the animals at the north end of the landfill survived to old age seems to be contradicted by the representation of young caprines in smaller numbers (only forty-four percent) than adults in this area; see Bouchnick et al. 2021: 484. Another difference between the two parts of the landfill is the discovery of hundreds of chalk (stone) vessel fragments at the south end compared with only two from the north end; see Gadot 2022a: 291.
186. Lernau 2022: 240.
187. Bar-Oz et al. 2007: 1.
188. Gadot 2022a: 290; Reich and Shukron 2021d: 681; Bar-Oz et al. 2007: 7–8; Reich 2011a: 329. Machline 2022: 60–61, notes that the greater number of ceramic types as well as more stone vessels at the south end of the southeastern hill apparently reflects their origin in household waste rather than temple sacrifices.
189. Reich 2011a: 147, 329; Reich and Shukron 2021c: 204; Reich and Shukron 2021d: 679. Prag's suggestion (2018: 78), following Kenyon, that the cooking pots belonged to the "camps of enslaved prisoners and refugees who were used in the Roman destruction and clearance of the city following the sack in AD 70" not only seems far-fetched, but is contradicted by Reich's observation that the cooking pots were deposited in distinct layers in which chronological and typological distinctions could be made, indicating they had accumulated over a long period.
190. Reich and Shukron 2003: 16–17.
191. Geva 2021: 76.
192. See Gurevich 2017.
193. A. Mazar 2002: 228.
194. A. Mazar 2002: 228.
195. Amit 2002: 253–54.

196. A. Mazar 2002: 223; Amit 2002: 246–60.

197. Yechezkel et al. 2021: 922–23.

198. A. Mazar 2002: 229–30; Gurevich 2017: 124.

199. A. Mazar 2002: 212–13.

200. *War* 2.175; from Thackeray 1997: 391 (Vol. I); also see *Ant.* 18.60, which mentions a distance of 200 furlongs. For a discussion see Levine 2002: 216 n. 109.

201. See Gurevich 2017, who notes that the reservoirs were created by damming the valley beds (p. 112).

202. See Weksler-Bdolah 2020: 148–49; Levine 2002: 214–15; Reich 2021a: 251–52. Gibson 2007: 27, following Broshi 1992, places the Serpent's Pool to the north of the Old City based on its proximity to Herod's monument in *War* 5.108, but the reference there is to Herod's monuments (plural), whereas *War* 5.507 refers to Herod's monument in the singular but not to the Serpent's Pool. Therefore, the pool's location is unknown; see Gurevich 2017: 110, 130 n. 11. Cabaret 2020: 216–19; Bahat 2011b: 40; Levine 2002: 214 figure 55, place it to the west of the city.

203. See von Wahlde 2006; Anderson, 2006; Magness 2016; Frey 2018: 59–95, who concludes "even if the Fourth Gospel displays numerous historiographical devices and elements of authentication, this cannot prove the claim of a more accurate historical reference . . . these . . . can also be fictional elements introduced with the intention of crafting a credible story" (p. 95).

204. Gurevich 2017: 130 n. 3.

205. Gibson 2005: 286. For a different suggestion, see Cabaret 2022: 92–93.

206. Murphy-O'Connor 2012b: 430.

207. See Gibson 2005.

208. Gibson 2005: 287, identifies the northern basin as an *'otsar*, but Adler 2014, argues that no such arrangement existed. Also see the objection by Greenhut 2011: 272 n. 3.

209. Gibson 2005: 271.

210. See Magness 2016; Murphy-O'Connor 2012b: 430.

211. See Magness 2016.

212. I thank George van Kooten for bringing this to my attention (email communications). See Wilkinson 1977: 170; *pace* Murphy-O'Connor 2012b: 430, who dismisses their testimony as simply repeating John's narrative.

213. Onomasticon 240; from Belayche 1970: 163 (Klostermann edition).

214. Sermon on the Paralytic 2; from McCauley and Stephenson 1970: 209 (vol. 2); also see Aist 2009: 150.

215. Meshorer 1989: 56–57.

216. Belayche 1970: 168–69.

217. See Magness 2016.

218. Reich and Shukron 2011c: 244; Reich and Shukron 2019; Geva 2019: 16. Also see Lawler 2021a: 280–83, 291–92.

219. Reich and Shukron 2011c: 244, 249.

220. Reich and Shukron 2011c: 248; Reich and Shukron 2019: 80. The Qumran sect differed from other Jews in wearing clothing while immersing due to modesty concerns; see Magness 2021: 234, 237.

221. Reich and Shukron 2011c: 244–45; Reich and Shukron 2019: 79.

222. Reich and Shukron 2011c: 247; Reich and Shukron 2019: 79.

223. Wilkinson 1978: 121–25; Reich and Shukron 2011c: 250; Weksler-Bdolah 2013: 175–76; A. Mazar 2000: 225.

224. See Weill's Gate P in Reich 2004: 34–38; Weksler-Bdolah 2013: 173, 188.

225. Weksler-Bdolah 2013: 173, 188; Weksler-Bdolah and Szanton 2014; Szanton and Zilberstein 2015: 38*.

226. Reich and Shukron 2011c: 245.

227. Reich and Shukron 2011c: 252.

228. Reich and Shukron 2011c: 246.

229. Reich and Shukron 2011c: 250–52.

230. Reich and Shukron 2011c: 253; Reich and Shukron 2019: 82–83.

231. *War* 6.370; from Thackeray 2006: 285 (Vol. III).

232. Ariel 2022: 235.

233. Szanton et al. 2019: 150–51, who date the latter coin to 30/31 CE; Kogan-Zehavi 1997: 104.

234. Szanton et al. 2019: 161.

235. Reich and Shukron 2011c: 253.

236. *Ant.* 20.219, 222; from Feldman 1965: 117–19 (Vol. XIII).

237. Szanton et al. 2019: 161.

238. See Kokkinos 1998: 318–19. Ariel 2022: 235, argues that the street must have been completed before 41/42 CE.

239. https://www.cnn.com/2019/07/01/middleeast/friedman-pilgrimage-road-opening-intl; Lawler 2021a: 307–21.

240. Ir David/El-Ad at https://www.cityofdavid.org.il/en/The-Ir-David-Foundation; opposed by Emek Shaveh at https://emekshaveh.org/en/. Also see Lawler 2021a: 206–7, 291–304.

241. See Lawler 2021a: 292–97. For a response, see Reich and Shukron 2011c: 251.

242. Also see Acts 11:20; Levine 2002: 370–71; Levine 2000: 52–53.

243. Tosefta Megillah 2:17; from Neusner 2003: 36.

244. See Kloppenborg 2006: 236–37.

245. The stone table from the first-century Magdala synagogue is an exception; see Avshalom-Gorni and Najar 2013.

246. See Shanks 2004: 84–93. For discussions, see Hachlili 2013: 523–26; Price in Cotton et al. 2010: 54–55; Levine 2000: 54–56; Binder 1999: 104–9.

247. Price in Cotton et al. 2010: 54 no. 9.

248. Price in Cotton et al. 2010: 54, rejects a later date as "unconvincing." For a discussion, see Kloppenborg 2006.

249. Clermont-Ganneau 1920: 193; Price in Cotton et al. 2010: 54–55.

250. Levine 2002: 397.

251. Levine 2000: 54–56.

252. As originally proposed by Clermont-Ganneau 1920: 193, 195–97; also see Levine 2000: 53–54; Trotter 2019: 98.

253. Kloppenborg 2006: 263–65.

254. Erich Gruen points out that the assumption that Vettenos is a Latin name is unproved (oral communication November 2021).

255. Avigad 1983: 191; Gorin-Rosen and Katsnelson 2006, 430.

256. For a discussion and references, see Magness 2011b: 66–70.

257. Ariel and Fontanille 2012: 1, 100–4; Hendin 2010: 227.

258. Ariel and Fontanille 2012: 188.

259. Hendin 2010: 233–34, who rejects the identification as the cap of the Dioscuri; Ariel and Fontanille 2012: 100–4, 186, who argue these were minted in Jerusalem with Herod's other coins.

260. Hendin 2010: 262–72, 278–310.

261. See Hendin 2010: 338–64.

262. See Hendin 2010: 346–47.

263. Hendin 2010: 411.

264. For coins perhaps commemorating the Roman victory over the Jews minted by Agrippa II, see Hendin 2010: 286–87.

265. Reich 2006: 350, 368, 376.

266. Reich 2006: 372.

267. Reich 2006: 346, 376.

268. Reich 2006: 376–77.

269. Reich 2006: 342.

270. For this section, including any references not cited here, see Magness 2011b: 145–80.

271. See Rahmani 1994.

272. Rahmani 1981a; 1982: 43–45.

273. See Kloner and Zissu 2007; Hachlili 2005; Rahmani 1982.

274. See Hachlili 2005: 30–34; Rahmani 1982: 46–48; Avigad 1954: 37–138.

275. Barag 2003: 84–89; Avigad 1954: 37–59, 73–76.

276. From Barag 2003: 92. Also see Avigad 1954: 59–66.

277. Barag 2003: 92.

278. See Hachlili 2005: 168.

279. Avigad 1983: 162–65; Avigad 1954: 79–90.

280. Avigad 1954: 66. Barag 2003: 94–95, 105, dates it to the half century after ca. 132/131 BCE.
281. Barag 2003: 98–99.
282. Barag 2003: 99.
283. Avigad 1954: 91–138.
284. Avigad 1954: 127–30, 138; also see Barag 2003: 98.
285. Zias and Puech 2005: 149, 152, 161–62; Barag 2003: 99–101.
286. Zias and Puech 2005: 161–62; it is not clear why they say James's burial was not located in the tomb of Bene Hezir.
287. Barag 2003: 102–4.
288. Zias and Puech 2005: 160–61.
289. Barag 2003: 107.
290. Barag 2003: 107.
291. Zias and Puech 2005: 163.
292. See Magness 2019a.
293. See Lawler 2021a: 335–44.
294. See Josephus, *Ant.* 20.17–96. For a recent study, see Marciak 2018; also see Rogers 2021: 104–5. For information on Helena, see Ben-Ami and Tchekhanovets 2011a: 237–38.
295. See Trotter 2019: 105–6.
296. From Danby 2013: 165–66.
297. See Ben-Ami and Tchekhanovets 2011a: 234–36; Ben-Ami and Tchekhanovets 2019: 268–69; Ben-Ami and Tchekhanovets 2011b. For a more cautious approach, see Marciak 2018: 34–36. Geva 2019: 14, says there are "no signs of architectural grandeur or small finds" identifying this as Helena's palace.
298. *Ant.* 20.95; from Feldman 1965: 51 (Vol. XIII).
299. *War* 5.147; from Thackeray 2006: 45–47 (Vol. III); also see *War* 5.55, 119.
300. Description of Greece [Arcadia] 8.16:4–5; from Jones 1933: 427–29.
301. See Kloner and Zissu 2007: 231; Marciak 2018: 39. For Jerome, see Wilkinson 1977: 49, 9.1.
302. For a recent reevaluation of the tomb, see Marciak 2018: 36–45; also see Cabaret 2022: 183–90.
303. Adler 2009: 57.
304. Kloner and Zissu 2007: 232; but Marciak 2018: 42, doubts there was any such device.
305. Kloner and Zissu, 2007: 233.
306. Yardeni/Price/Misgav in Cotton et al. 2010: 165 no. 123. Marciak 2018: 44, notes that this name does not correspond with Helena.
307. Yardeni/Price/Misgav in Cotton et al. 2010: 166; Kloner and Zissu 2007: 234; Ben-Ami and Tchekhanovets 2011a: 238. Marciak 2018: 44, relying on the anthropological analyses of Pruner-Bey in the mid-nineteenth century

and Dussaud in 1912, identifies the remains as a young woman and therefore not Helena.

308. Kloner and Zissu 2007: 234. Yardeni/Price/Misgav in Cotton et al. 2010: 166, state: "If indeed the present sarcophagus is that of Queen Helena, then only her semitic name, and not her Greek one, was inscribed. But the whole matter remains shrouded in uncertainty." Marciak 2018: 44–45, identifies the tomb as belonging to the royal family of Adiabene, but argues that it was not Helena but another member of the family who was interred in the inscribed sarcophagus. For the suggestion—based on recent (unpublished) work at the site by Jean-Baptiste Humbert—the tomb was commissioned by Herod Agrippa I and acquired by the royal family of Adiabene, see Cabaret 2022: 188–89; Lawler 2021b. In my opinion, Herod Agrippa I would have been laid to rest in his family's dynastic mausoleum at Herodium; see Magness 2019a: 286.

309. m. Middoth 1:4; 2:6. See Trotter 2019: 106.

310. Kloner and Zissu 2007: 179.

311. Kloner and Zissu 2007: 181.

312. Price/Misgav in Cotton et al. 2010: 140 no. 98.

313. See Price/Misgav in Cotton et al. 2010: 309–34; Avni and Greenhut 1996.

314. Avni and Greenhut 1996: 2.

315. Avni and Greenhut 1996: 19.

316. Avni and Greenhut 1996: 26–27.

317. Avni and Greenhut 1996: 32.

318. Shadmi 1996: 41.

319. Price/Misgav in Cotton et al. 2010: 309–10; Avni and Greenhut 1996: 34.

320. Cotton et al. 2010: 310 (Price/Misgav); 314 no. 291 (Price); 327 no. 304 (Price/Misgav); Avni and Greenhut 1996: 31; Ilan 1996: 59, reads "of Eiras of Sel[e]uc[ia], (or daughter of) Sel[e]uc[us]."

321. From Danby 2013: 88. See Avni and Greenhut 1996: 35; Ilan 1996: 66. But Price/Misgav in Cotton et al. 2010: 327, say "It cannot of course be known for certain whether this is the same Ariston, or whether this Ariston died in Apamea or Jerusalem. It should be noted that the Apamea of this Ariston is not necessarily the main city by that name in Syria."

322. Price in Cotton et al. 2010: 320–21 no. 297; Ilan 1996: 61–62.

323. Ilan 1996: 66, 68; Price/Misgav in Cotton et al. 2010: 327–28 no. 304.

324. Shadmi 1996: 45, 51.

325. Price in Cotton et al. 2010: 316 no. 293. For a different reading, see Ilan 1996: 60–61.

326. Price in Cotton et al. 2010: 328–29 no. 305.

327. Price in Cotton et al. 2010: 317.

328. For Rome, see Patterson 2000: 266.

329. Ben-Arieh and Coen-Uzzielli 1996: 77.

330. Ilan 1996: 68.
331. Price/Misgav in Cotton et al. 2010: 310.
332. Avni and Greenhut 1996: 12.
333. See Magness 2011b: 155–64.
334. See Magness 2011b: 164–72.
335. Tzaferis 1985: 50.
336. See Magness 2011b: 174–80.
337. *Ant.* 20:200; from Feldman 1965: 109 (Vol. XIII).
338. *Apud* Eusebius, *Hist. eccl.* 2.23:15–18; from Lake 1926: 175.
339. See Magness 2011b: 172–74.
340. See Magness 2005a.

8. ROMAN JERUSALEM (AELIA CAPITOLINA) (200 CE)

1. Avi-Yonah 1977: 110.
2. Barclay 1996: 78–81.
3. See Yadin 1963; Yadin 1971; Schäfer 2003: Applebaum 1976.
4. Eck 1999: 81, estimates that 12–13 legions (in full force or represented by *vexillationes*) were deployed to Judea.
5. Mor 2003: 127–29. For possible archaeological evidence that the revolt impacted a Galilean Jewish village, see Leibner 2018: 628; also see Eck 1999: 81, 88.
6. Eck 2003: 160.
7. Avi-Yonah 1977: 114; Avi-Yonah 1984: 12–13; Mor 2003; Eck 1999: 88–89.
8. See Di Segni and Tsafrir 2012: 408, 440–46. For Hadrian's edict banning Jews from Aelia and its environs, see Avi-Yonah 1984: 50–51, 163–64; Isaac 2010: 23–25; Belayche 1970: 112–13; Belayche 2021: 288; Sivan 2021: 290.
9. Sivan 2021: 291; Drijvers 2021: 371.
10. Isaac 2010: 101–6.
11. Cotton Paltiel and Ecker 2019; also see Cassibry 2018: 258.
12. Cotton Paltiel and Ecker 2019.
13. Weksler-Bdolah 2020: 21; Isaac 2010: 25–26.
14. See Isaac 2010 Capitolina: 15–17. Geva in E. Stern 1993: 759, and Geva 2014a: 148, states categorically that "Following the destruction of Jerusalem in 70 CE, the city had no Jewish inhabitants"; while Tsafrir 2009: 75–77, says that Jews and Christians returned to the ruined city shortly after its destruction in 70.
15. Bar-Nathan and Sklar-Parnes 2007: 58. For other references, see Weksler-Bdolah 2020: 187 n. 40.
16. Bar-Nathan and Sklar-Parnes 2007: 60–61.
17. *War* 5.50–51; from Thackeray 2006: 17–19 (Vol. III).
18. Bar-Nathan and Sklar-Parnes 2007: 63.
19. Natural History 5.70. See Cotton 2007: 12*–13*.
20. Cotton 2007: 16*–18*.

21. Bar-Nathan and Sklar-Parnes 2007: 64.
22. Bar-Nathan and Sklar-Parnes 2007: 63.
23. *War* 7.5; from Thackeray 2006: 307 (Vol. III); also see *War* 7.17.
24. Weksler-Bdolah 2020: 32, argues for an irregular polygonal shape.
25. For a response to Hillel Geva's view that the camp was temporary and unfortified, see Weksler-Bdolah 2020: 42.
26. Weksler-Bdolah 2020: 22.
27. Weksler-Bdolah 2020: 49–50; Magness 2020: 904.
28. See Weksler-Bdolah 2020: 6–14, 23; Eliav 2005: 105–6.
29. Seligman 2017.
30. *War* 7.1–2; from Thackeray 2006: 307 (Vol. III); see Isaac 2010: 14.
31. Weksler-Bdolah 2020: 24, 150. Billig 2002: 249, says that the low-level aqueduct did not function during the Roman period, whereas A. Mazar 2002: 238, states that it was in continuous use until the beginning of the twentieth century.
32. See Weksler-Bdolah 2020: 6–14, 22–23; Cabaret 2022: 215–17.
33. Weksler-Bdolah 2020: 32–38.
34. Magness 2020: 905.
35. See E. Mazar 2011b; Stiebel 1999.
36. Weksler-Bdolah 2020: 129.
37. Stiebel 2011b; Stiebel 2011a: 342–44.
38. Cagnat and Besnier 1921: no. 21.
39. Isaac 2010: 26; Stiebel 2011a: 344.
40. Unlike Stiebel, Mazar includes the Temple Mount in the camp; see Stiebel 1999; E. Mazar 2011b: 1–8; E. Mazar 2015a: 2. Stiebel 1999: 89, notes that Jewish and Christian pilgrimage indicates the Temple Mount was not a military zone.
41. Stiebel 1999: 90–91; E. Mazar 2011b: 7.
42. Weksler-Bdolah 2020: 129.
43. Eck in Cotton et al. 2012: 63–64, no. 760.
44. See Avi-Yonah 1954a; Donner 1992; Piccirillo and Alliata 1999.
45. From Eck in Cotton et al. 2012: 31, no. 728; also see Hamilton 1944: 22–23.
46. According to Eck in Cotton et al. 2012: 30–31.
47. Wightman 1989: 35; Wightman 1993: 171.
48. The column was still a landmark in the tenth century, when it was mentioned by al-Muqaddasi; see Heidemann 2010: 180.
49. For the final report, see Weksler-Bdolah and Onn 2019b; Rosenthal-Heginbottom 2019; Weksler-Bdolah and Onn 2021.
50. Weksler-Bdolah and Onn 2019a: 166, reconstruct the eastern cardo with colonnades on both sides. Geva 2019: 27, argues that as there is no clear evidence of an eastern colonnade, there probably was only a colonnade on the western side, as depicted in the Madaba Map.

51. Weksler-Bdolah 2019b; Weksler-Bdolah and Onn 2017a; Weksler-Bdolah 2020: 85.

52. Weksler-Bdolah 2019b: 29–88; Weksler-Bdolah and Onn 2021; Weksler-Bdolah and Onn 2017a: 21; Weksler-Bdolah 2014: 54–56.

53. Di Segni and Weksler-Bdolah 2012.

54. Weksler-Bdolah 2019a: 199; Weksler-Bdolah 2014: 50, 52.

55. Weksler-Bdolah 2019a: 199–200; Weksler-Bdolah 2014: 56; Rosenthal-Heginbottom 2014: 657.

56. Weksler-Bdolah 2020: 58, 90; Weksler-Bdolah 2019a: 198.

57. Historia Romana LXIX.12–13; from M. Stern 1980: 392 (Vol. 2) (transl. E. Cary, LCL).

58. Historia Ecclesiastica IV.6.3–4; from Cotton Paltiel and Ecker 2019: 692; also see M. Stern 1980: 396 (Vol. 2).

59. Weksler-Bdolah 2020: 53–54; Bar-Nathan and Bijovsky 2008. Isaac 2010: 19, rejects the coin evidence as inconclusive (but without including Shu`afat).

60. For the most recent argument in favor of this view, see Cotton Paltiel and Ecker 2019.

61. Cotton Paltiel and Ecker 2019: 685; Irshai 2006: 97.

62. See Weksler-Bdolah 2020: 51; Capponi 2010; Di Segni 2014. M. Stern 1980: 395 (Vol. 2), dismisses these sources.

63. See Weksler-Bdolah and Onn 2017a: 21–22. Di Segni 2014: 448–49, cites Weksler-Bdolah's claim that work on the eastern cardo was under way well before Hadrian's visit in 129/130 CE.

64. Baker 2012; also see Weksler-Bdolah 2020: 51 n. 3. For a response, see Di Segni 2014. Cotton Paltiel and Ecker 2019: 692, cite Baker as conclusively showing that Epiphanius's testimony is *not* evidence of an earlier visit by Hadrian.

65. See Rosenthal-Heginbottom 2019: 238, whose dating is also based on the absence of certain types, including stamped roof tiles. She clarifies that the Roman pottery could be characterized more accurately as "military" since the Jerusalem kiln works were separate from the legionary camp (p. 2 n. 2; Rosenthal-Heginbottom 2017: 285).

66. The pottery types include a common type of local oil lamp (round discus lamps) that ranges in date from the late first to third centuries, examples of which were found in fills underlying the eastern cardo's flagstones. See Rosenthal-Heginbottom 2019: 115; 236, who notes that their presence initially led the excavators to date the deposit to the late second–early third centuries. Also see Rosenthal-Heginbottom 2017: 321, where she acknowledges the long range of many of the same types, which were found in a cistern on the southwestern hill. Whereas in earlier publications burnt seeds from the dump are said to be radio-carbon dated to 5–125 CE and 20–135 CE—a key piece of evidence for Weksler-Bdolah's argument in favor of a pre–130 CE date—in the final report they are

dated to 30/45 BCE–220/230 CE. See Boaretto 2021: 160, 163, who cites a cali-
brated age with a ± 2σ standard deviation (95.4 percent probability) of 30/45
BCE–220/230 CE for the seeds, which is consistent with the dates obtained from
other (charcoal) samples in the dump. She concludes that a range of 1–250 CE
"can be considered as the *terminus post quem* of the laying of the flagstones of the
[eastern] Cardo" (p. 162).

67. Rosenthal-Heginbottom 2019: 1, 280, says the material originated in "nearby liv-
    ing quarters." However, the presence of late Second Temple-period types, even
    if in relatively small numbers (Rosenthal-Heginbottom 2019: 218; see, for exam-
    ple, pp. 232–33), suggests the pottery was brought from mixed deposits on the
    southwestern hill. For an example of such a deposit on the southwestern hill, see
    Rosenthal-Heginbottom 2017.

68. See Magness 2020: 906–10. Weksler-Bdolah and Peleg-Barkat 2022 attribute the
    unfinished state of monuments around Aelia Capitolina to the outbreak of the
    Bar-Kokhba Revolt and/or to Hadrian's death.

69. Weksler-Bdolah 2014: 56.

70. See, for example, Rosenthal-Heginbottom 2017: 286, 320–21, who says that a
    deposit from a cistern on the southwestern hill, which she associates with living
    quarters of Roman officers in an unknown but nearby location, "points to habita-
    tion debris from the time-span of 70–150 CE approximately; on the other hand
    the building activities in the early years of Hadrian permit to set the date between
    70-ca. 120 CE" (p. 286).

71. Weksler-Bdolah 2019a: 199–200. See Gorin-Rosen 2021: 27; Katsnelson 2021: 69.

72. Weksler-Bdolah 2020: 54.

73. Gutfeld 2017: 44; Avigad 1983: 226–27. Weksler-Bdolah and Onn 2019a: 166 and
    Weksler-Bdolah 2019a: 197, note that the paving stones in the northern half of the
    western cardo resemble those in the eastern cardo, whereas the paving stones in
    the southern half of the western cardo are laid in a different manner, supporting
    Avigad's later dating of this section.

74. Weksler-Bdolah 2020: 137, 145, 208–9.

75. Weksler-Bdolah 2020: 26–28, 70–71, 180–82.

76. See Weksler-Bdolah 2020: 60–65.

77. Avigad 1983: 207; also see Gutfeld 2017: 47; Magness 2000: 330.

78. Hamilton 1944; see Weksler-Bdolah 2020: 62; Geva in E. Stern 1993: 761–62.

79. For various excavations along the Old City walls, see Weksler-Bdolah 2020: 138
    n. 32. For the evidence from Hamilton's excavations, see Magness 2011a: 89, 93.

80. For the following discussion, see Magness and Davies 2023.

81. Avner and Arbib 2016.

82. Mazor 2017: 80–81, objects that the triple-arched gateway at the Damascus Gate
    fits the profile of a city gate (at the entrance to a city), not a gate within the city.

83. Clermont-Ganneau 1903: 486–95; Clermont-Ganneau 1905: 188–99. Geva in E. Stern 1993: 762, erroneously gives the date of discovery as 1864 and mistakenly states that Clermont-Ganneau associated the inscriptions with a monumental gateway at this spot.

84. See Gibson and Nagorsky 2016: 158*–62*.

85. Savignac 1904; see Gibson and Nagorsky 2016: 158*–61*.

86. See Magness 2000: 331; Eck in Cotton et al. 2012: 13–15 no. 715.

87. Avner et al. 2014; Weksler-Bdolah 2020: 57.

88. From Cotton Paltiel and Ecker 2019: 689; Antoniniana was added later by a second hand.

89. Eck in Cotton et al. 2012: 16–17 no. 717.

90. See Gibson and Nagorsky 2016: 158*. Others have suggested a monumental column or equestrian statue base instead; see Cotton Paltiel and Ecker 2019: 690; Ecker 2019: 112, 114 (who associates the inscriptions with two different monuments); Eck in Cotton et al. 2012:14.

91. Magness 2000: 333.

92. See Magness 2000: 333; Weksler-Bdolah 2020: 56 n. 27; Mazor 2017: 78–79.

93. Ecker 2019: 114–15.

94. Ecker 2019: 114.

95. Letter heights: Inscription 1: ca. 13–11.5 centimeters (5–4.5 inches) (see Eck in Cotton et al. 2012: 13 no. 715; Cotton Paltiel and Ecker 2019: 688). Inscription 2: ca. 14–10.5 centimeters (5.5–4 inches) (see Eck in Cotton et al. 2012: 16 no. 717). Inscription dedicated to Septimius Severus: 12.5–10 (5–4) centimeters high (see Eck in Cotton et al. 2012, 19–20 no. 719). Inscription of unknown date: 11.5 centimeters (4.5 inches) high (see Eck in Cotton et al. 2012: 20–22 no. 720).

96. Ecker 2019: 114.

97. Weksler-Bdolah 2020: 57.

98. For the date, see Cotton Paltiel and Ecker 2019: 687.

99. See Cassibry 2018: 258 n. 75: "soldiers were expected to possess some knowledge of Latin, the army's basic language of command here, as well as basic literacy" (describing Lambaesis and Timgad).

100. From Cassibry 2018: 259 n. 78; found near the northern gate (CIL 8, 17843).

101. See Magness 2000: 334. For references, see Segal 1997: 131.

102. From Stinespring 1934: 16 and Welles 1938: 401–02 no. 58.

103. Gibson and Nagorsky 2016: 163*–65*.

104. Sukenik and Mayer 1930: 27–35; Sheet 9.

105. https://aiar.org/home/about/about-the-building/ (accessed 31 January 2022).

106. Ecker 2019: 113.

107. Sukenik and Mayer 1944: 145; at the eastern edge of the Albright Institute's courtyard they found a section of wall and a tower.

108. Personal communication from Matt Adams (2 March 2022).

109. See Avner et al. 2014: 96.

110. See Gibson and Nagorsky 2016: 158*.

111. See https://www.npr.org/2019/03/04/699969357/u-s-closes-jerusalem-consul ate-that-gave-palestinians-a-link-to-washington (accessed 31 January 2022).

112. Ben-Arieh and Netzer 1974: 98–100. For additional sections of the wall and another tower discovered in 1990–1992, see Tzaferis et al. 1994: 287–89.

113. Hamrick 1985: 217; Trenches T.I.1 and T.1.2.

114. See Wightman 1993: 166; Tower 161 = his Tower 4; the Salah ed-Din tower = his Tower 6.

115. See Cabaret 2022: 194.

116. For supplementary dedications to the arches at Timgad, see Cassibry 2018: 263–64.

117. See Weksler-Bdolah 2020: 57; M. Stern 1980: 395 (Vol. 2).

118. Cassibry 2018: 258; also see Isaac 1998: 103, "evidence from other colonies leads one to suppose that Aelia was furnished with walls at the time of the foundation."

119. See Avni 2005; Avni 2017, especially pp. 124–28, 130. Ecker 2019: 115, says the necropolis lay to the north of the *campus*. Weksler-Bdolah and Di Segni 2020: 96–97, note the presence of Roman burials of the late first–early second centuries between the north wall of the Old City and the northern line and suggest that burial in this area ceased after Aelia Capitolina was established.

120. Wightman 1993: 205–6. Weksler-Bdolah 2006–2007, argues that the city was unwalled until ca. 400–450.

121. 592: "Inside Sion, within the wall"; 593: "As you leave there and pass through the wall of Sion"; from Wilkinson 1981: 157–58; for the pilgrim of Bordeaux see below. Isaac 2010: 21, cites John Rufus (ca. 500 CE), whose works are preserved only in a later Syriac translation "of mediocre quality," who says the city was sparsely inhabited and had no walls until they were rebuilt by Constantine (*The Life of Peter the Iberian*; see Isaac 2010, 21; Weksler-Bdolah 2006–2007: 98–99 nn. 18–19). For John Rufus, see Wilkinson 1977: 4. This does not negate the possibility that Hadrian intended the northern line to be the north wall of Aelia Capitolina, if indeed it was abandoned relatively quickly and never completed. In any case, Rufus would be referring to the construction of the current line of the north wall of the Old City.

122. The free-standing arch at Gerasa might have been designed to be set later into an extended line of city wall that was never built around a planned Hadrianic quarter; see Kraeling 1938: 50; Segal 1997:132; Magness 2000, 334.

123. Uziel et al. 2019: 249.

124. Weksler-Bdolah 2020: 35–38; Onn and Weksler-Bdolah 2019: 116–20; Magness 2020: 906; Weksler-Bdolah and Onn 2017b.

125. Weksler-Bdolah and Onn 2017b: 85 n. 17.

126. Eck in Cotton et al. 2012: 27–28 no. 725; Onn, Weksler-Bdolah, and Bar-Nathan 2011.

127. Uziel et al. 2019: 245.
128. Uziel et al. 2019: 247.
129. Uziel et al. 2019: 247–48; Regev et al. 2020: 11–12/17.
130. Rives 1995: 39–41.
131. For a review of the opinions and scholarship, see Eliav 1997.
132. Historia Romana 69.12.1; from M. Stern 1980: 392 (Vol. 2) (transl. E. Cary, LCL).
133. See Isaac 2010: 19–20; Eliav 2005: 86–87; Eliav 1997: 128–29 including n. 10, who suggests the reference to the Temple Mount was added by Xiphilinius.
134. See, e.g., Belayche 2021: 275–76; Murphy-O'Connor 1994: 415. For a response, see Mango 1992: 2.
135. *Pace* Eliav 1997: 142, who argues that the expression "temple of the god" "bears the stamp of a Christian writer such as Xiphilinius." Eliav does not distinguish between *hieron* and *naos*. Furthermore, it seems clear that in the passage under discussion, *tou theo* is used to distinguish the deity previously worshiped from Jupiter, to whom the new temple was dedicated.
136. From Wilkinson 1981: 156–57.
137. Weksler-Bdolah 2020: 117; Mango 1992: 3. The Latin word *aedes* denotes a temple building that is less elaborate than a *templum* (Cassell's Latin Dictionary); also see Eliav 1997: 88–89.
138. Murphy-O'Connor 1994: 409; Bahat 2011b: 73–74.
139. From Eck in Cotton et al. 2012: 17–18 no. 718, who rejects the possibility that this base was associated with the statue mentioned by the pilgrim.
140. See Weksler-Bdolah 2020: 118.
141. Commentary on Matthew 24.15; from Scheck 2008: 272. Jerome uses the Latin word *templum* to denote the temple.
142. Commentary on Isaiah 2.9; from Scheck 2015: 99; see also Murphy-O'Connor 1994: 408.
143. Whitby and Whitby 1989: ix–x.
144. Dindorf 1832: 474. See Vincent and Abel 1914: 6–19 (Fasc. 1); Isaac 2010: 20, including the entire passage in Greek in n. 82; Weksler-Bdolah 2020: 110–11.
145. Isaac 2010: 20; Weksler-Bdolah 2020: 110.
146. See Weksler-Bdolah 2020: 110–11; Isaac 2010: 20. For a full discussion, see Eliav 2005: 89–91.
147. See Flusin 1992; Mango 1992: 2; Eliav 2005: 91.
148. See, e.g., Belayche 2021: 276; Murphy-O'Connor 1994: 415; Eliav 2005: 91–92; Tsafrir 2009: 82; Weksler-Bdolah 2020: 118 including references in n. 149.
149. Weksler-Bdolah 2020: 37, 119; Onn and Weksler-Bdolah 2019: 121; Weksler-Bdolah and Onn 2017b: 92–94.
150. It also negates Eliav's claim (2005: 116–24) that the Temple Mount was left in ruins and was not part of Aelia Capitolina.
151. See Magness 2008.

152. Weksler-Bdolah 2020: 37–38, 123.

153. See Eck in Cotton et al. 2012: 15 no. 761; 19–20 no. 719; 20–22 no. 720; B. Mazar 1969: 9; Avi-Yonah 1969. Stiebel 1999: 86–87, dates the Severan inscription to 198–199 CE and associates it with the south gate of the legionary camp, which he locates to the southwest of the Temple Mount).

154. Cabaret 2022: 110–75, 249–64, identifies the arch of Ecce Homo as a gate added by Herod the Great to the Second Wall after his expansion of the Temple Mount. He argues that Hadrian reused the arch of Ecce Homo, which, he says, was left standing because it provided access to the northeastern side of the city and covered it with a pavement (the Lithostratos). However, contrary to Cabaret's claim, H.-M. Coüasnon's discovery that the north pier of the arch of Ecce Homo is founded on bedrock rather than on the Lithostratos does not prove that the pavement is later than the arch, as one would expect the arch's foundations to sit on bedrock. In fact, Coüasnon's conclusion that the pavement and the arch are contemporary contradicts Cabaret's dating of the arch of Ecce Homo to Herod's time—one of the linchpins in his reconstruction of the city. Eliav 2005: 99, 112–13, identifies the arch of Ecce Homo as the east gate of Aelia Capitolina.

155. See Belayche 1970: 163–67; Weksler-Bdolah 2020: 126; Eliav 2005: 111–16, who places this area outside the city.

156. See Magness 2003.

157. See Coüasnon 1974: 12, who admits that the basilica is hypothetical; other scholars believe the entire north side of the forum was occupied by the temenos of the temple.

158. For these and other remains in and around the Church of the Holy Sepulcher, see Patrich 2016: 142–43; Geva in E. Stern 1993: 779–80.

159. See Gibson and Taylor 1994: 67; Patrich 2016: 142; Geva in E. Stern 1993: 779; Coüasnon 1974: 42, 45, 47.

160. See Weksler-Bdolah 2020: 71–74, 124; Geva in E. Stern 1993: 763.

161. Life of Constantine, III.26:2–3; from Cameron and Hall 1999: 132.

162. Ecclesiastical History II.1:3; from Walford 1855: 50.

163. See Weksler-Bdolah 2020: 125; Gibson and Taylor 1994: 68; Drijvers 2021: 374.

164. Hieronymus, Epistolae 58.3; from Murphy-O'Connor 1994: 409. See Murphy-O'Connor 1994; Belayche 2021: 276–79; Belayche 1970: 136–54; Krüger 2021: 196–97. For a review of the evidence, see Gibson and Taylor 1994: 68, who reject the identification with the Capitolium and argue that the temple of Venus included a number of statues, shrines, and altars.

165. See Gibson and Taylor 1994: 69.

166. Following Virgilio Corbo; see Cabaret 2022: 267–310, who contends that there was a visual connection between the Capitolium at the western forum and the statue of Hadrian on the Temple Mount; Belayche 2021: 276–78; Belayche 1970: 145–54; Patrich 2016: 141–42. Gibson and Taylor 1994: 65, 68, and Bahat

2011b: 75, argue that the rock of Golgotha projected above the pavement of the temenos while the rock-cut tomb was buried within it.

167. Following Charles Coüasnon; see Weksler-Bdolah 2020: 124; Geva in E. Stern 1993: 763.

168. Belayche 1970: 140.

169. Cabaret 2022: 267–310; Murphy-O'Connor 1994: 411; Belayche 1970: 141. This view seems to be especially popular among Francophone scholars—but not only; see, e.g., Bahat 2020: 102–6, 112–13; Bahat 2011b: 74, who dates Wilson's Arch to the early Islamic period and claims that it therefore would not have provided access to a Hadrianic shrine or temple on the Temple Mount.

170. Eliav 2005: 124, also claims that the area of the modern Christian Quarter was the religious and economic center of Aelia Capitolina.

171. Magness 2008: 207.

172. Be'eri and Levi 2019: 201–3; Be'eri and Levi 2018: 30, 32, 35; Rosenthal-Heginbottom 2015: 615–16. As at Shu'afat, Jews lived on Jerusalem's periphery between the two revolts.

173. For publications and references, see Magness 2005b; Magness 2020: 908; Be'eri and Levi 2018; Rosenthal-Heginbottom 2019.

174. Rosenthal-Heginbottom 2019: 280–81, argues that some of the legionary types have local prototypes.

175. Magness 2005b: 108.

176. Rosenthal-Heginbottom 2017: 320; Rosenthal-Heginbottom 2015: 616; Ben Zeev 2005: 219–57.

177. Magness 2010a: 121.

178. For the production of stamped roof tiles by private workshops in Jerusalem after ca. 200, see Weksler-Bdolah et al. 2022.

179. Hendin 2010: 372–73.

180. For a discussion, see Hendin 2010: 377–82, who clarifies that the coin "depicts a messianic version of a rebuilt Jerusalem temple. It no doubt bore some similarity to Herod's temple but it would be an error to describe it as a depiction of Herod's temple or the second temple" (email communication, 18 March 2022).

181. Hendin 2010: 368–71.

182. Geva in E. Stern 1993: 759; Drijvers 2021: 371.

183. Avi-Yonah 1977: 108–17, 127–80.

184. Meshorer 1985: 60; Meshorer 1989: 21.

185. Meshorer 1985: 60; Meshorer 1989: 22.

186. Meshorer 1985: 60–61.

187. Meshorer 1985: 81.

188. Geva 2014a: 149. Drijvers 2021: 369, says the colony was only two-fifths the size of the former city and had no more than 10,000–12,000 inhabitants.

9. BYZANTINE JERUSALEM (633 CE)

1. Avni 2014: 109.
2. For Julian, see Avi-Yonah 1984: 185–204; Tsafrir 2009: 86–87.
3. Schick 1882.
4. Reuven 2007.
5. Di Segni in Cotton et al. 2012: 95–96 no. 790, who says that, although a fourth-century date fits, the inscription could also be later. For other proposals, see Bahat 2020: 111.
6. Reich and Billig in E. Stern 2008: 1811.
7. Ehrman and Jacobs 2004: 70.
8. Ehrman and Jacobs 2004: 68.
9. Avi-Yonah 1984: 213–14.
10. Avi-Yonah 1984: 227–28.
11. Avi-Yonah 1984: 218–20.
12. Stemberger 2006: 300.
13. For an overview of ancient synagogues, see Levine 2000.
14. Tsafrir 2009: 98.
15. Avi-Yonah 1984: 269–70; Milwright 2016: 34.
16. Scholars disagree on the exact year; see Nees 2016: 5–6.
17. Wilkinson 1977: 3; Drijvers 2021: 382–83. Di Segni and Tsafrir 2012: 419, provide slightly different dates for Eudocia's visit (439) and settlement in Jerusalem (443 or 441).
18. Geva 2014: 150–51; Seligman 2021: 240.
19. Avni 2014: 138; Di Segni and Tsafrir 2012: 412.
20. Wilkinson 1977: 91 n. 1; Tsafrir 2009: 94. For the etymology, see Demsky 2021: 69–70.
21. Nees 2016: 26–27, suggests this is not entirely accurate but is a literary trope.
22. *Demonstratio Evangelica* (Proof of the Gospel) 8.3.12; from Ferrar 1920: 141 (Vol. 2); also see Tsafrir 2009: 78.
23. Tsafrir 2009: 84; also see Irshai 2006: 100–2.
24. See Weksler-Bdolah 2006–2007: 99–100; Wightman 1993: 215–16.
25. From Wilkinson 1977: 53; also see 3–4.
26. Tsafrir 1999: 159.
27. Wilkinson 1977: 161.
28. Tsafrir 1999: 158.
29. See Aist 2009: 82–90.
30. Geva in E. Stern 1993: 772, dates the entire wall to ca. 300, while Weksler-Bdolah 2006–2007 and Weksler-Bdolah 2020: 138 n. 34, dates it to ca. 400–450.
31. See Wightman 1993: 210–24; Geva in E. Stern 1993: 770–72; Weksler-Bdolah 2006–2007. A portion of the wall on Mount Zion was re-excavated by Yehiel Zelinger (2019: 285–86).

32. E. Mazar and Lang 2015: 337–39; E. Mazar 2007: 181–200.

33. From Wightman 1993: 209; also see Weksler-Bdolah 2006–2007: 101.

34. See Wightman 1993: 209–10; Weksler-Bdolah 2006–2007: 100–1.

35. Weksler-Bdolah 2006–2007: 101–103; Weksler-Bdolah 2020: 138. For a recent overview, see Asutay-Effenberger and Weksler-Bdolah 2022: 88–102. Zelinger 2019: 286–87, says the associated finds support a date in the time of Eudocia (ca. 445–460 CE).

36. Avigad 1983: 226–27; Gutfeld 2017: 44; Gutfeld 2012a: 479–96.

37. Weksler-Bdolah 2020: 137, 145, 208–9; Gutfeld 2017: 47; Gutfeld, 2012a: 481.

38. See R. Schick 1995: 33–48.

39. *Chronicon Paschale* 614; from Whitby and Whitby 1989: 156.

40. For Sebeos's account, see Thomson 1999: 68–70; for commentary, see Howard-Johnston 1999: 207. For Antiochus Strategius's account, see Conybeare 1910.

41. Conybeare 1910: 514–16.

42. R. Schick 1995: 34.

43. Avi-Yonah 1993; R. Schick 1995: 35.

44. From Conybeare 1910: 515.

45. Barkay 1994: 89–90.

46. R. Schick 1995: 34–39.

47. See Hamilton 1944: Magness 2011a: 89–93.

48. Wightman 1989; Wightman 1993: 12–15; Magness 2011a: 88–89.

49. From Conybeare 1910: 506.

50. Clermont-Ganneau 1898: 37.

51. Sebeos, 115; from Thomson 1999: 69.

52. See Clermont-Ganneau 1898: 45.

53. See Clermont-Ganneau 1898: 35, 53.

54. Magness 2011a: 89–93.

55. For the date of Heraclius's entry to Jerusalem, see Kaegi 1992: 74–77; R. Schick 1995:50; Drijvers 2021: 386; Milwright 2016: 34.

56. Drijvers 2021: 386.

57. v. 170; from Wilkinson 1977: 83; for the Piacenza Pilgrim, see pp. 6–7.

58. Wilkinson 1977: 161; also see Mango 1992: 15.

59. Wilkinson 1977: 161; Aist 2009: 97–98; Greisiger 2022: 300–3.

60. Bahat 2020: 116; Bahat 2011b: 87; Bahat 1999, who suggests the Madaba Map may date as late as the seventh–eighth centuries. Mango 1992: 15, says it would be "rather odd" if the Golden Gate had been built by the Muslims ca. 700 CE only to be blocked up by ca. 800.

61. Tsafrir 2009: 99.

62. Di Segni and Tsafrir 2012: 419; Gibson and Taylor 1994: 84; Wilkinson 1977: 175; Aist 2009: 64–65. The earliest accounts, by Gelasius of Caesarea and Ambrose,

Bishop of Milan, date to the late fourth century; see Trampedach 2022a: 23; Ehrman and Jacobs 2004: 65–66.

63. Geva in E. Stern 1993: 779. Both Biddle 1999: 65, and Coüasnon 1974: 15–16, say the consecration took place on 17 September, not 14 September. Wilkinson 1977: 175, says the dedication ceremonies took place from 13 to 20 September and that construction was completed just before 348. Shalev-Hurvitz 2015: 60, dates the consecration to 14 September; see 60–69 for a discussion of how long construction lasted, which she estimates took no longer than a decade (p. 76).

64. Wilkinson 1977: 175.

65. See Biddle 1999: 56, 58, 66; Coüasnon 1974: 13–14.

66. Biddle 1999: 55, 69.

67. Wilkinson 1977: 175; Coüasnon 1974: 17; Patrich 2016: 153; R. Schick 1995: 327–29.

68. Wilkinson 1977: 212, dates *The Life* to after 337; Coüasnon 1974: 15, 21, says it was written between 337 and 340.

69. See, e.g., Tsafrir 1999: 160; Donner 1992: 90. Gibson and Taylor 1994: 77, 84, argue that the tomb was not originally enshrined as a domed structure and that instead there was a dome over a spot in the basilica that was venerated as the place where the cross reportedly was discovered.

70. Wilkinson 1977: 177; Prawer 1996: 326–27; Ousterhout 1990: 45–50.

71. Life of Constantine III.33.1; from Cameron and Hall 1999: 135; also see 284–85.

72. Kaplony 2002: 47.

73. Bahat 2011b: 79.

74. Geva in E. Stern 1993: 779.

75. Coüasnon 1974: 42–43; Geva in E. Stern 1993: 780; Patrich 2016: 141–42.

76. Coüasnon 1974: 37–38. For the evolution of the term "martyrium/martyrion" in relation to the Church of the Holy Sepulcher, see Ousterhout 1990.

77. Geva in E. Stern 1993: 780.

78. Geva in E. Stern 1993: 780.

79. Gibson and Taylor 1994: 11–17, 24, 51–56; Patrich 2016: 141; Seligman and Avni 2019: 241, who also document a large, previously unknown structure (perhaps a baptistery) on the north side of the complex, which was part of the original fourth-century church.

80. Gibson and Taylor 1994: 85 (who do not refer to it as a cistern).

81. Broshi and Barkay 1985: 125–28 (inscription on p. 125); Broshi 1993 (inscription on p. 121). Eck in Cotton et al. 2012: 92 no. 787, reads it as "Lord, we have come." Gibson and Taylor 1994: 25–48, 80, argue that the drawing dates to the second century CE and was not made by a Christian pilgrim.

82. Broshi 1993: 121–22.

83. Bahat 2011b: 79; Geva in E. Stern 1993: 781; Patrich 2016: 145.

84. Bahat 2011b: 79.

85. Mark 15:22; Matthew 27:33; Luke 23:33; John 19:17–18. See Aist 2009: 115. Gibson and Taylor 1994: 56–60, argue that the name "Golgotha" originally denoted the entire area of the church before being restricted to the rocky outcrop alone (the Rock of Calvary).
86. Wilkinson 1977: 177; Coüasnon 1974: 42; Patrich 1993: 108, who notes that the entrance today is via a staircase built after the fire of 1808, which blocks the eastern of the two Crusader portals to the church.
87. Gibson and Taylor 1994: 59; Aist 2009: 116–17; Prawer 1996: 328; Ousterhout 1990: 47.
88. Wilkinson 1977: 177; Coüasnon 1974: 39–40, 50; Patrich 1993: 109; Aist 2009: 116–17; Gibson and Taylor 1994: 57–59.
89. Biddle 1999: 69; Krüger 2021: 208–9.
90. Patrich 1993: 106–7.
91. Geva in E. Stern 1993: 781; Shalev-Hurvitz 2015: 42.
92. Geva in E. Stern 1993: 781; Wilkinson 1977: 176.
93. Geva in E. Stern 1993: 781; Patrich 1993: 107–8; Krüger 2021: 210–13.
94. Geva in E. Stern 1993: 781; Bahat 2011b: 79. For a recent discussion, see Krüger 2021: 214–18.
95. Di Segni in Cotton et al. 2012: 293–94 no. 913.
96. Di Segni in Cotton et al. 2012: 344–45.
97. Biddle 1999: 9; Shalev-Hurvitz 2015: 43–44.
98. Di Segni 2012: 261.
99. See Trampedach 2022b: 164–68; Gutfeld 2012b: 246–49; Tsafrir 2000: 150–54.
100. Destruction date from Geva in E. Stern 1993: 776. R. Schick 1995: 332–33; McCormick 2011: 160–61; Bahat 1996: 89. Trampedach 2022b: 178–79, suggests that the church vanished from Jerusalem's sacred topography because it was not associated with a biblical site.
101. Tsafrir 2000: 154–55.
102. See Gutfeld 2012b; Avigad 1993.
103. McCormick 2011: 105–11; Gutfeld 2012b: 226; Geva in E. Stern 1993: 777.
104. Gutfeld 2012b: 226–27.
105. Avigad 2012b: 132–33.
106. Procopius, *Buildings* 5, 6, 19–22; see Tsafrir 2000: 162–63; Trampedach 2022b: 167–68.
107. Trampedach 2022b: 168.
108. Lewy 1960.
109. Boustan 2008: 357–62; also see Trampedach 2022b: 176–78.
110. Amitzur 1996; Drijvers 2021: 385.
111. Amitzur 1996: 168–70.
112. Trampedach 2022b: 170–74.
113. From Di Segni 2012: 259.

114. Di Segni 2012; Di Segni and Gellman 2017.

115. Di Segni and Gellman 2017: *31.

116. Di Segni and Gellman 2017: *31; Justinian died shortly after the beginning of the next indiction in 565/566.

117. Di Segni and Gellman 2017: *33; also see Trampedach 2022b: 166.

118. Di Segni and Gellman 2017: *34–*35.

119. The Spiritual Meadow 6; translated by Wortley; from Gutfeld 2012b: 248.

120. Translated by Di Segni; from Gutfeld 2012b: 250.

121. From Thackeray 2006: 43 (Vol. III); see Clausen 2016: 57.

122. See Clausen 2016: 9–10, 15, 36; Wilkinson 1977: 171; Geva in E. Stern 1993: 778; Aist 2009: 138, 144–45. For traditions about a small Jewish or Jewish-Christian community on Mount Zion before the fourth century, see Irshai 2006: 97 n. 18; Clausen 2016: 17–27.

123. For the earliest evidence of this tradition, see Clausen 2016: 27, 40; Wilkinson 1977: 172; Aist 2009: 145–46.

124. Clausen 2016: 54.

125. McKinny et al. 2021: 653. Scholars disagree about whether Josephus's reference to the Tomb of David in *Ant.* 16. 179, 181 places it on Mount Zion; see Clausen 2016: 57, 58; Wilkinson 1977: 171; Limor 1988.

126. Limor 1988.

127. Clausen 2016: 17–34.

128. Geva in E. Stern 1993: 778; Clausen 2016: 59; Aist 2009: 175; R. Schick 1995: 37, 335–36.

129. Clausen 2016: 69, 80.

130. Clausen 2016: 135.

131. Renard 1900: 18–19; Clausen 2016: 139–142; Geva in E. Stern 1993: 778. Vincent has only one apse and places "David's Tomb" in the building's southeast corner; see Clausen 2016: 142–47; McCormick 2011: 102–3.

132. From Di Segni in Cotton et al. 2012: 344–45 no. 968.

133. From Di Segni in Cotton et al. 2012: 346–47 no. 970.

134. See Clausen 2016: 152–93, who rejects the possibility that this is an early synagogue. Also see Limor 1988: 453; Folda 2008: 66.

135. Busse 1994: 151; Clausen 2016: 30; Wilkinson 1977: 155.

136. Wilkinson 1977: 155; Busse 1994: 142, 152.

137. Busse 1994: 160, notes that it was common for anchorites in Syria to isolate themselves in towers.

138. Epiphanius, II.1 D; from Wilkinson 1977: 117; see Busse 1994: 153–54.

139. Busse 1994: 145–46, 154.

140. See Tchekhanovets 2018: X.

141. Wilkinson 1977: 4; Tchekhanovets 2018: IX.

142. Di Segni and Tsafrir 2012: 436–40; Verhelst 2006: 430; Tchekhanovets 2018: 1; Linder 1996: 147–52.
143. Wilkinson 1977: 4.
144. For Paulinus, see Trout 1999; Ehrman and Jacobs 2004: 468.
145. Bahat 2011b: 78; Bitton-Ashkelony 2021: 352.
146. Wilkinson 1977: 2–3; R. Schick 1995: 355; Bitton-Ashkelony 2021: 354.
147. Tchekhanovets 2018: 23; Bitton-Ashkelony 2021: 354–55.
148. Wilkinson 1977: 4; Di Segni in Cotton et al. 2012: 382; Tchekhanovets 2018: 23–24.
149. See Tchekhanovets 2018: 22–23; Bitton-Ashkelony 2021: 357.
150. Life of Peter 45; from Wilkinson 1977: 155. See Tchekhanovets 2018: 23.
151. Buildings, 356, IX.6; from Wilkinson 1977: 76. See Tchekhanovets 2018: 13.
152. Iliffe 1935: 79.
153. Iliffe 1935. See Tchekhanovets 2018: 156–69.
154. The wine press was misidentified by Iliffe as part of a monastic building; see Tchekhanovets 2018: 156–58.
155. From Di Segni in Cotton et al. 2012: 381–83 no. 1000. Also see Iliffe 1935: 78; Tchekhanovets 2018: 166.
156. Tchekhanovets 2018: 166–69.
157. See Iliffe 1935: 77–79; Di Segni in Cotton et al. 2012: 382.
158. From Di Segni from Cotton et al. 2012: 355–56 no. 977; also see Tchekhanovets 2018: 189.
159. Tchekhanovets 2018: 189.
160. Di Segni in Cotton et al. 2012: 356; Tchekhanovets 2018: 189.
161. Reich 1996; Reich 1994: 117–18; Nagar 2002.
162. Di Segni in Cotton et al. 2012: 245 no. 869.
163. From Conybeare 1910: 508; also see p. 515.
164. From Conybeare 1910: 514.
165. See Avni 2005: 381.
166. Reich 2021a: 253–54.
167. See Bliss and Dickie 1898: 177–91; Geva in E. Stern 1993: 772–73.
168. The Topography of the Holy Land 8b; from Wilkinson 1977: 66; also see p. 5.
169. v. 176, 25; from Wilkinson 1977: 84.
170. Bliss and Dickie 1898: 193.
171. Aist 2009: 153 n. 497; R. Schick 1995: 337–38. The remains of the church now lie on the route of the first-century CE street connecting the Pool of Siloam and the Temple Mount; see Lawler 2021a: 314–15.
172. Wilkinson 1977: 2; Aist 2009: 146. For Lucianus's account, see Ehrman and Jacobs 2004: 360–65.
173. Ehrman and Jacobs 2004: 360. Eudocia took some to Constantinople in 439; see Drijvers 2021: 383.

174. Wilkinson 1977: 162; also see Sheridan 2020: 83.
175. See Theodosius, *The Topography of the Holy Land*, 141, 8(a), in Wilkinson 1977: 66; also see p. 162.
176. See Méndez 2017.
177. Limor 1988: 461.
178. The Piacenza Pilgrim, v. 176.25; from Wilkinson 1977: 84.
179. Wilkinson 1977: 162; R. Schick 1995: 35, 342–43.
180. Geva in E. Stern 1993: 782; also see Sheridan 2020: 83.
181. From Di Segni in Cotton et al. 2012: 127–28 no. 816.
182. From Di Segni in Cotton et al. 2012: 267–69 no. 888; it is not clear if the monastery mentioned is the one at St. Stephen's or at the Holy Sepulcher.
183. Sheridan 2019: 156. Lufrani 2019 questions some of Sheridan's conclusions.
184. Gregoricka and Sheridan 2013: 66; Sheridan 2019: 156.
185. Sheridan 1999: 20, 30; Gregoricka and Sheridan 2013: 66; Sheridan 2020: 107.
186. Gregoricka and Sheridan 2013: 68–69.
187. Sheridan 1999: 30–36; Sheridan 2019: 156; Sheridan 2020: 87.
188. Sheridan 2019: 172–79.
189. Sheridan 2019: 171.
190. Sheridan 2019: 160, 171.
191. Sheridan 2019: 171–72.
192. Sheridan 2020: 87, 89.
193. Sheridan 2020: 92.
194. Sheridan 2020: 107.
195. See Sheridan 2020: 86–87.
196. Aist 2009: 153.
197. Geva in E. Stern 1993: 781; Wilkinson 1977: 170; Aist 2009: 151.
198. Bahat 2011b: 81.
199. From Di Segni in Cotton et al. 2012: 360–61 no. 980, who notes that a lector and deacon of the church are mentioned by John Rufus, Plerophories 18, PO 8, 35–37, in a passage in which Peter the Iberian relates a miracle that he witnessed when he was living in Jerusalem.
200. Wilkinson 1977: 170; Aist 2009: 154; R. Schick 1995: 333–34.
201. Verhelst 2006: 430; Tchekhanovets 2018: IX, 1.
202. Tchekhanovets 2018: 20–21; also see Linder 1996: 157–59.
203. From Michael Stone in Cotton et al. 2012: 120–21 no. 810A; Tchekhanovets 2018: 118–20.
204. See Avni 2005: 381–84; Tchekhanovets 2018; R. Schick 2005.
205. Tchekhanovets 2018: 78.
206. Schick and Bliss 1894; Avi-Yonah in E. Stern 1993: 782; Bahat 2011b: 84; Tchekhanovets 2018: 78–84; Re'em et al 2021: 119*.
207. From Stone in Cotton et al. 2012: 122–23 no. 812. See Tchekhanovets 2018: 80.

208. Stone in Cotton et al. 2012: 123–24 no. 813; Re'em et al. 2021: 122*. See Schick and Bliss 1894: 260.

209. Tchekhanovets 2018: 80–81.

210. Re'em et al. 2021: 125*–29*, who suggest that these individuals were not of Armenian origin because there is no evidence of an Armenian lay community in Byzantine and early Islamic Jerusalem. However, Di Segni and Tsafrir 2012: 432–36, who Re'em et al. cite, assume that many Armenian pilgrims settled in Jerusalem.

211. See Tzaferis et al. 1994.

212. Amit and Wolff 1994: 294.

213. From Di Segni in Cotton et al. 2012: 115–16 no. 809. See Amit and Wolff 1994: 294; Tchekhanovets 2018: 87.

214. Stone in Cotton et al. 2012: 124. Also see Tchekhanovets 2018: 87–89; Amit and Wolff 1994: 295.

215. From Stone in Cotton et al. 2012: 250 no. 874. Also see Amit and Wolff 1994: 295–96; Tchekhanovets 2018: 89–90.

216. From Stone in Cotton et al. 2012: 129–30 no. 817. See Amit and Wolff 1994: 296.

217. Amit and Wolff 1994: 296–97.

218. From Di Segni in Cotton et al. 2012: 251–52 no. 875; Sukenik and Mayer 1930: 38, 46–47.

219. R. Schick 1995: 14, 353.

220. Di Segni 2011: 357–59.

221. Wilkinson 1977: 161, Map 12b; R. Schick 1995: 14, 332.

222. Di Segni in Cotton et al. 2012: 252. R. Schick 1995: 44, says the later date is more likely.

223. R. Schick 1995: 331.

224. Tchekhanovets 2018: 2, 78, 93, 242.

225. Vincent 1901: 436; Tchekhanovets 2018: 78, 93.

226. Vincent 1901; Di Segni in Cotton et al. 2012: 255–56 no. 878; Avi-Yonah in E. Stern 1993: 782; Bahat 2011b: 84.

227. Sukenik and Mayer 1930: 42.

228. Burrows 1932: 31–34.

229. Burrows 1932: 34–35.

230. Burrows 1932: 29–30, 32.

231. Burrows 1932: 28.

232. See Ben-Dov 1982: 243–59, who says (p. 246) that eighteen houses were excavated; E. Mazar 2003; E. Mazar 2007 (who says on p. XI that eleven houses were uncovered); B. Gordon 2007: 201, says that nine residential buildings were identified in the excavations. His number appears to be correct as he says that in some cases the remains are fragmentary and may have been part of the same dwelling. For the dating of these buildings, see Magness 2011a: 97. Excavations

by E. Mazar in 2009 and 2012–2013 brought to light additional remains; see E. Mazar 2015a: 1–455.

233. E. Mazar 20087: 99–112.

234. B. Gordon 2007: 202.

235. E. Mazar 2007: XI; B. Gordon 2007: 207.

236. Ben-Dov 1982: 249.

237. Ben-Dov 1982: 248; E. Mazar 2007: 63–69; B. Gordon 2007: 206–7.

238. Ben-Dov 1982: 252.

239. E. Mazar 2007: 3–14; for the toilet (L14997), see pp. 14–15. Ben-Dov 1982: 249, says the seat was built to hold a chamber pot, but this makes no sense as there would be no need for a drain below.

240. Ben-Dov 1982: 253–54; E. Mazar 2007: XIII.

241. Ben-Dov 1982: 255.

242. Ben-Dov 1982: 255. B. Gordon 2007: 202, does not associate the tiles with balconies.

243. From Di Segni in Cotton et al. 2012: 99 no. 792. See Ben-Dov 1982: 251–52.

244. E. Mazar 2007: XIII.

245. From Wilkinson 1977: 66; see E. Mazar 2003: 3–67. Magness 2011a: 96, argues that the finds from the building do not support its identification as the Enclosed Convent. Murphy-O'Connor 2005 questions the identification of this building as a monastery. For its possible depiction on the Madaba Map, see Bahat 2020: 105.

246. E. Mazar 2003: 78–85.

247. E. Mazar 2003: 163–86; Magness 2011a: 96–97.

248. Murphy-O'Connor 2005: 129.

249. B. Gordon 2007: 208.

250. Tchekhanovets 2022: 305, with references.

251. For references and discussion, see Magness 2023.

252. Ben-Ami and Tchekhanovets 2019: 270–72.

253. Ben-Ami and Tchekhanovets 2017: 67.

254. See Magness 2023: 82*–84*.

255. Sharabi, Tchekhanovets, and Ben Ami 2020, who associate the graffiti with "non-Christians" (p. 300).

256. See Bijovsky 2020; Ben-Ami 2020b: 48–50; Ben-Ami and Tchekhanovets 2010a; Ben-Ami, Tchekhanovets, and Bijovsky 2010.

257. B. Mazar 1971: 12; 7, figure 8. The garden soil was outside the southwest end of the Temple Mount, to the west of the western (Double) Huldah Gate and the buildings shown in E. Mazar 2015a: 2 Plan 1.

258. Ariel and Magness 1992: 73–74 (Area K1, Phases 3C–3A); Magness 1992a: 163.

259. See Magness 2023: 85*–88*. However, the street was narrowed in the early Islamic period and there is evidence of industrial activity in the adjacent buildings; see Tchekhanovets 2022: 309.

260. Crowfoot and Fitzgerald 1929; see Magness 1992b.

261. Crowfoot and Fitzgerald 1929: 37.

262. Crowfoot and Fitzgerald 1929: 41.

263. For an analysis, see Magness 1993: 56–59.

264. Crowfoot and Fitzgerald 1929: 39–40.

265. Tchekhanovets 2022: 309.

266. See Magness 1992b; Magness 2023: 88*.

267. Filipová 2014: 12–13; Magness 1996: 43*.

268. Barag 1970: 46–47.

269. See A. Grabar 1958; Magness 1996: 43*.

270. Barag 1970; Barag 1971.

271. Barag 1971: 62.

272. See Raby 1999.

273. See Loffreda 1989; Magness 1996.

274. Magness 1996: 41*.

275. *A Journey to the Holy Places and Babylon* 315, 11; from Wilkinson 1977: 142–44; also see p. 13.

276. See Shalev-Hurvitz 2015: 34; Magness 1996: 41*; and, more generally, Verhelst 2006 on the Jerusalem liturgy.

277. Shalev-Hurvitz 2015: 34–35, 53.

278. Magness 1996: 41*.

279. v. 171–172; from Wilkinson 1977: 83.

280. Magness 1996: 42*–43*.

10. EARLY ISLAMIC JERUSALEM (800 CE)

1. Gil 1996c: 14.

2. Fried 2016: 377, 398, 409, 420, 431. In the Carolingian calendar, the year was 801.

3. Fried 2016: 400–1.

4. Gil 1996c: 10.

5. Wilkinson 1977: 12; McCormick 2011: 196. Fried 2016: 404, notes that Frankish writers refer to Harun al-Rashid as king of the Persians, not as a Saracen or Moor, thereby associating the Abbasids with the Sasanids, who were the treaty partners of the Byzantine emperors from Justinian on. Umayyad rule in Spain—initially an emirate and later a caliphate—was based in Córdoba.

6. See Gil 1996c: 6–9. For the date of surrender, see Nees 2016: 5–7, who notes it is doubtful that Umar ever visited Jerusalem.

7. Elad 1995: 23.

8. Gil 1996c: 13.

9. O. Grabar 1996: 8–12; Kaplony 2002: 6–13; Lassner 2017: 7–15; Whitcomb 2011: 402–3; Linder 1996: 121; Le Strange 1965: 1–12. Muqaddasi's full name was Shams ed-Din Ibn Abdullah (Bahat 2011b: 88).

10. Gil 1996c: 104. For the Cairo Geniza documents, see Goitein 1967–1993.

11. Lassner 2017: 6–7; Busse 1991: 33–34; Gil 1996c: 10; O. Grabar 1996: 112; Neuwirth 2021: 435. The name al-Quds originated in the ninth century; see Barag 1988–89: 46–47; Bahat 2020: 123

12. Kaplony 2002: 38, 214–24; Le Strange 1965: 90; O. Grabar 1996: 113; O. Grabar 1959: 40–41; Berger 2012: 39, 41–42. For Jerusalem's importance in Quranic tradition, see Neuwirth 2021.

13. Elad 1995: 30–33; Gil 1996b: 3, 163; Hasson 1996: 352; O. Grabar 1996: 47–48.

14. From Milwright 2016: 26. Also see Gil 1996c: 4. For the term *isra* ', which means "exodus," see Neuwirth 2021: 439–40.

15. Gil 1996c: 4; Le Strange 1965: 89. For discussions, see Lassner 2017: 33–59; Hasson 1996: 353–59.

16. Nees 2016: 10–11; Milwright 2016: 26, 256; Neuwirth 2021: 442; Rosen-Ayalon 1989: 5; Kaplony 2002: 33–37. Kaplony 2009: 120, describes *al-masjid al-aqsa* as a greater mosque (the whole Haram) and a smaller mosque (al-Aqsa Mosque), or a mosque within a mosque. Shoshan 2021: 469, argues that the traditions associating the spot with the *isra'* developed after the buildings were constructed; also see Milwright 2016: 256. But Necipoğlu 2008: 43–44, identifies both the *isra* ' and *mi'raj* as "integral to 'Abd al-Malik's grand narrative."

17. Shalev-Hurvitz 2015: 316–18, 321; Gil 1996c: 4; O. Grabar 1996: 113–14, 157. O. Grabar 1959: 38, 53, 61, dates these traditions to the time of al-Walid. Busse 1968: 442, 459–60, says they antedate the tenth century.

18. Busse 1991: 1; Rabbat 1989: 12.

19. O. Grabar 1996: 48; Sharon 2009: 286–88.

20. See Linder 1996. O. Grabar 1996: 132–166, estimates that Christians were still the majority in 725, but changed in make-up over time with more coming from western Asia and the Caucasus.

21. See Gil 1996b; Ben-Shammai 1996. Shoshan 2021: 463, says the numbers were small at first but increased around 800 CE, when the Palestinian *yeshiva* moved from Tiberias to Jerusalem.

22. From Le Strange 1965: 86.

23. Gil 1996a: 101–11.

24. Avni 2011: 392; Whitcomb 2011: 405; Ben-Shammai 1996: 208.

25. Whitcomb 2011: 412–15; for a critique, see Lassner 2017: 105–6 n. 15.

26. See Nees 2016: 8–13; O. Grabar 1996: 112; Kaplony 2002: 29–30; Gil 1996b: 167.

27. The Holy Places, vv. 226–227; from Nees 2016: 33–34.

28. Nees 2016: 3, 33, 38; the information about how Arculf came to be in Iona comes from Bede.

29. Nees 2016: 43–45, 56–57; Hoyland and Waidler 2014: 787–90, who believe that Arculf was a real person.

30. Nees 2016: 11, 17–18, 34–35. But if this is so, why is the Mosque of Umar not preserved in later Islamic tradition as one of the names for the Haram?

31. Nees 2016: 52.

32. Shoshan 2021: 465.

33. Rosen-Ayalon 1989: 30; Bahat 1996: 84; Bahat 2020: 16–17, who says the elevated platform did not exist before the Islamic period.

34. Shoshan 2021: 467. Milwright 2016: 165, 214, believes the date indicates the year of foundation, with planning beginning a year or two before 691–692 and completion in the mid–690s. Some scholars propose that the project was initiated by Mu'awiya and completed by 'Abd al-Malik; see the discussions in Lassner 2017: 81–95; Elad 1995: 44–45; Shalev-Hurvitz 2015: 296 n. 2. Blair 1992: 68, dates the construction to 692–702 CE.

35. Rosen-Ayalon 1996: 388; Rosen-Ayalon 1989: 14; Grabar 1996: 52. But Nees 2016: 102, quoting O. Grabar, points out that the building's current appearance is largely the product of modern reconstruction or reworking. For Ottoman renovations, see Necipoğlu 2008: 57–81.

36. Milwright 2016: 49–51; O. Grabar 1959: 34.

37. Rosen-Ayalon 1996: 390. Shalev-Hurvitz 2015: 45, notes that the height of the Rotunda of the Church of the Holy Sepulcher to the top of the dome also equaled the diameter of its inner circle.

38. Nees 2016: 102; Milwright 2016: 51; Rosen-Ayalon in E. Stern: 1993: 790. Bahat 2020: 164, says the Umayyad dome was gold-plated and that there are iron bars between the two shells.

39. Milwright 2016: 55.

40. Rosen-Ayalon 1996: 397–99.

41. Rosen-Ayalon 1989: 22–24; Rosen-Ayalon 1996: 401.

42. Rosen-Ayalon in E. Stern 1993: 790; Rosen-Ayalon 1989: 17; Rosen-Ayalon 1996: 404; Milwright 2016: 51.

43. Shoshan 2021: 467.

44. Rosen-Ayalon 1989: 15–16; Milwright 2016: 57.

45. O. Grabar 1959: 48, 52. In contrast, Milwright 2016: 257, finds it difficult to find "even an implied reference to the concept of victory." Bahat 2020: 166, says that the crowns might also allude to the Dome of the Rock as the successor to the temple of the house of David.

46. Milwright 2016: 254; O. Grabar 1996: 107–9, 114; Sharon 2009: 293, who describes it as a "shrine."

47. Shalev-Hurvitz 2015: 45, 319; Blair 1992: 70, who notes that in both buildings there is an internal alternation of piers and columns.

48. Nees 2016: 32; Kaplony 2009: 119, who notes that there are no references to con-
    gregational prayer anywhere on the Haram outside of al-Aqsa Mosque. Also see
    Shalev-Hurvitz 2015: 311, although on p. 332 she observes that the Anastasis oper-
    ated as an independent church. Rosen-Ayalon 1989: 6, 71, points to a similar pair-
    ing between Solomon's temple and palace, and later, Herod's temple and the Royal
    Stoa, although these do not seem to be analogous.
49. Rosen-Ayalon 1989: 6; Rosen-Ayalon 1996: 389.
50. O. Grabar 1996: 106; Shalev-Hurvitz 2015: 320; Shoemaker 2012: 234–35. Lassner
    2017: 158–59, claims the ambulatories in the Dome of the Rock are too narrow to
    accommodate masses of pilgrims.
51. Nees 2016: 148; Necipoğlu 2008: 36, 38, who argues there was a "pre-existing cult
    of the Rock."
52. Sharon 2009: 289, 294; Lassner 2017: 34–36; Kaplony 2002: 45, 346–63; Kaplony
    2009: 109, 116, who notes that the rock is "especially loaded with Temple Traditions";
    O. Grabar 1959: 38–40, 43, 46; Shalev-Hurvitz 2015: 301–3, 317. Another Islamic
    tradition identifies Mount Moriah at or near the Ka'aba in Mecca; see Shoemaker
    2012: 252, 256, who suggests this tradition arose after Mecca surpassed Jerusalem in
    importance for Muslims; also see Neuwirth 2021: 456.
53. See Necipoğlu 2008: 39; Rabbat 1989: 14, 17; Kaplony 2009: 108; Lassner 2017: 172,
    citing Moshe Sharon; Milwright 2016: 31, 42. However, Milwright 2016: 255–56,
    notes that there is no mention of David, Solomon, or Abraham in the inscriptions
    in the Dome of the Rock, and therefore the connection to the earlier temples and
    Mount Moriah might not have been obvious to the Umayyad elite; also see Nees
    2016: 26–27.
54. Sharon 2009: 295; Kaplony 2002: 119; Kaplony 2009: 112–13.
55. From Le Strange 1965: 117–18.
56. Le Strange 1965: 208; Lassner 2017: 178; Necipoğlu 2008: 30.
57. O. Grabar 1996: 56; also see Necipoğlu 2008: 48. For a recent study, see
    Milwright 2016.
58. O. Grabar 1996: 64, 162.
59. O. Grabar 1959: 54; O. Grabar 1996: 66–67; Sharon 2009: 292–93; Milwright
    2016: 72–74, 239–40; see pp. 228–29 for the relationship between the Quranic
    quotes in the inscription and the text of the Qur'an. Bacharach 2010: 2, 7, notes
    that different versions of the *shahadah* were used over time.
60. From Milwright 2016: 71; also see p. 69.
61. From Milwright 2016: 72; also see O. Grabar 1959: 53.
62. O. Grabar 1959: 55, 56, who says the inscription has a "missionary Character" and is
    an expression of superiority; also see Bacharach 2010: 7. But Rosen-Ayalon 1989: 16,
    notes that Christians were forbidden to enter the building.
63. Kaplony 2009: 114; Shalev-Hurvitz 2015: 320; Necipoğlu 2008: 36, who says,
    "This process of resanctification underscored Islam's position as heir to previous

Abrahamic monotheistic faiths, while at the same time asserting it supremacy as the last divine revelation." Milwright 2016: 240, 256–57, 262–63, claims that the universal message is of a "true" Islam under the caliph in preparation for the End of Days.

64. O. Grabar 1996: 66; qualified in O. Grabar 2005: 227–28. Sharon 2009: 286–88, 298–99, while noting that Muslims absorbed Jewish and Christian traditions identifying Jerusalem as the site of the Last Judgment, says the inscriptions exalt Islam and contain anti-Christian polemics but suggest no connection to the Day of Judgment.

65. Necipoğlu 2008: 45, 49.

66. O. Grabar 1996: 65–66. But Shalev-Hurvitz 2015: 317, finds "problematic" the idea that it was the site of the "Last Judgment."

67. Rosen-Ayalon 1989: 66.

68. Rosen-Ayalon 1989: 52–53, 60; also see Milwright 2016: 262.

69. Nees 2016: 150; Necipoğlu 2008: 54, 56.

70. Nees 2016: 159; Necipoğlu 2008: 35, 38.

71. Rosen-Ayalon 1989: 67, 71–72. Also see Shalev-Hurvitz 2015: 334; Kaplony 2009: 359; Busse 1968: 455; Necipoğlu 2008: 48.

72. Lassner 2017: 160–73. But Milwright 2016: 257, argues that there is no explicit reference to Solomon's temple.

73. See Goitein 1950; O. Grabar 1959: 35–36; Elad 1995: 158–59; Necipoğlu 2008: 37.

74. Elad 1995: 163. Also see Shalev-Hurvitz 2015: 312–15; Milwright 2016: 216–17, 258, who notes that this proposal makes the most sense if the building was begun before 692. Elad's proposal is rejected by Shoemaker 2012: 243; and by Lassner 2017: 121–50, 159. O. Grabar 2005: 219–20, says that the sources cited by Elad are unreliable.

75. Shalev-Hurvitz 2015: 321.

76. Lassner 2017: 28, 158; Rabbat 1989: 14.

77. See Heidemann 2010: 187–88; Bacharach 2010: 9, 12–14.

78. Necipoğlu 2008: 56.

79. See Hasson 1996: 349–67; compare Shoemaker 2012: 197–25 and Lassner 2017: 19, 123.

80. Hamilton 1949. For a summary of the building's later phases with references, see Shalev-Hurvitz 2015: 298 n. 9.

81. Milwright 2016: 27–28; Johns 1999: 62–69; Rosen-Ayalon 1989: 6.

82. Milwright 2016: 27; Grafman and Rosen-Ayalon 1999: 6; Rosen-Ayalon in E. Stern 1993: 791. For a critique of Grafman and Rosen-Ayalon, see Nees 2016: 15.

83. Rosen-Ayalon 1989: 14; Kaplony 2009: 121; Bahat 1996: 82–83.

84. Rosen-Ayalon 1989: 6; Prag 2008: 104.

85. Rosen-Ayalon 1996: 395.

86. Rosen-Ayalon 1996: 407–8.

87. See Schick 1995: 348–49.
88. Avi-Yonah 1944: 162–65.
89. Reuven 2013; Liphschitz et al. 1997; Lev-Yadun 1992.
90. Nees 2016: 58–99; Rosen-Ayalon 1996: 392; O. Grabar 1996: 130.
91. Nees 2016: 59–61, 97; Rosen-Ayalon in E. Stern 1993: 790.
92. Rosen-Ayalon 1989: 27; Milwright 2016: 25–26.
93. Rosen-Ayalon 1989: 29; Nees 2016: 64.
94. Nees 2016: 61; Grabar 1996: 130–31.
95. Necipoğlu 2008: 41.
96. Nees 2016: 62, 84–85.
97. Ben-Dov in E. Stern 1993: 792–93; Bahat 1996: 73–74.
98. Prag 2008: 101–2.
99. Rosen-Ayalon 1989: 8; Ben-Dov in E. Stern 1993: 793.
100. Bahat 2011b: 97–98; Ben-Dov 1971: 42; Rosen-Ayalon 1989: 8; Prag 2008: 158–59.
101. Ben-Dov in E. Stern 1993: 794; Ben-Dov 1982: 305–6.
102. Ben-Dov 1971: 41–43; Ben-Dov 1982: 294, 304, 311–12.
103. Prag 2008: 120, 160.
104. See E. Mazar 2011c: 280–81; Bahat 2020: 146, figure 6.26. Prag 2008: 117, notes that the springing of the arch was 8 meters (26 feet) above the level of the Umayyad street along the south wall of the Haram, which in turn was 4 meters (13 feet) above the floor of Building II, which means the building's walls were at least 12 meters (39 feet) high.
105. Baruch and Reich 1999. For the following analysis with references, see Magness 2010b: 147–53.
106. Also see Prag 2008: 123–30.
107. Ben-Dov 1982: 309 (describing Building II).
108. See Prag 2008: 158.
109. Rosen-Ayalon 1989: 10, dates Building II to the reign of ʿAbd al-Malik.
110. They wrote 747/748, but we now know the earthquake occurred in 749.
111. Ben-Dov 1985: 312.
112. Reich and Baruch 1999: 139 (my translation from the Hebrew).
113. Ben-Dov 1985: 293, 323.
114. Also see Nees 2016: 23–24.
115. See Magness 2010b: 152; Prag 2008: 158–61; Avni 2014: 136–37.
116. See Prag 2008: 158.
117. See also Prag 2008: 158.
118. Also see Avni 2014: 137.
119. Rosen-Ayalon 1989: 8; Ben-Dov 1971: 43; Prag 2008: 104.
120. Rosen-Ayalon 1989: 9–10.
121. Le Strange 1965: 84; Ben-Dov 1971: 43 n. 16. Alternatively, the word might refer to a pavement, perhaps of the Haram; Bahat 2020: 123.

122. Lassner 2017: 117.

123. Rosen-Ayalon 1989: 8; Bahat 2011b: 91; Ben-Dov 1971: 43; O. Grabar 1996: 129.

124. See Lassner 2017: 96–97, 102.

125. Sharon 2009: 306–7; O. Grabar 1996: 304–5; O. Grabar 2005: 223–24.

126. O. Grabar 1996: 128–29. This argument is invalid as the ground floor rooms were for storage. Prag 2008: 160, suggests that Building II was an "urban administrative center."

127. Sharon 2009: 304–5; see also Lassner 2017: 108–9.

128. Lassner 2017: 105 n. 15, 106.

129. Sharon 2009: 304, 307–8.

130. Lassner 2017: 109; this assumes the reference in the Aphrodito papyri is not to Jerusalem.

131. Lassner 2017: 112–13, 116; O. Grabar 1996: 130, says it could be a gate for women (!). Prag 2008: 122–23, 160, also notes that the three entrances suggest the building had a "more accessible function . . . than is normal for a palace" (p. 123).

132. Lassner 2017: 117–18.

133. Lassner 2017: 96–120.

134. Lassner 2017: 111.

135. See Lassner 2017: 94. His association of the fifteen lime kilns with the initial construction of Building II (p. 119) is contradicted by Ben-Dov's statement (1982: 306) that they were "found among its ruins."

136. See E. Mazar 2003. For the following analysis with references, see Magness 2011a: 94–98.

137. E. Mazar 2003: 183.

138. Magness 2011a: 97.

139. *Pace* Sharon 2009: 308; Lassner 2017: 106–7, 110–11, 120.

140. E. Mazar 2003: 183; Shapira and Peleg 2003: 188–90 (Pl. II.4:9–10). See Magness 2011a: 97–98.

141. See O. Grabar 1996: 129.

142. Bahat 1996: 41.

143. Bahat 1996: 43–44. Also see Wightman 1993: 235–236; Avni 2014: 116–18.

144. Geva 2014a: 154; Avni 2014: 158.

145. Magness 1991.

146. Magness 1991: 214; Avni 2014: 119.

147. Wightman 1993: 235.

148. Wightman 1993: 235–36.

149. Wightman 1993: 237.

150. Bahat 1996; 46; O. Grabar 1996: 139.

151. Bahat 1996: 48; also see Wightman 1993: 230–31.

152. Bahat 1996: 65–66; Avni 2014: 145.

153. Bahat 1996: 67.

154. Bahat 1996: 49–52; Avni 2014: 119–20.
155. Magness 2012: 286.
156. Kennedy 1985: 11.
157. Kennedy 1985: 13.
158. Kennedy 1985: 17.
159. Kennedy 1985: 23–24.
160. Kennedy 1985: 25.
161. Bulliet 1975: 217, 226.
162. Kennedy 1985: 26; Bulliet 1975: 9, 22–26, 227.
163. Fried 2016: 400–2; Runciman 1935: 607; Graboïs 1981: 792; Linder 1996: 133.
164. Runciman 1935: 607; Fried 2016: 401.
165. Runciman 1935: 608–9; Fried 2016: 403, 447; McKitterick 2008: 286–87, who says the elephant died eight years later. Some publications give the year as 802 instead of 801.
166. Runciman 1935: 609; Fried 2016: 403–4.
167. Runciman 1935: 609–10; Bahat 1996: 60–61.
168. From Loyn and Percival 1975: 40–41; also see Runciman 1935: 607.
169. Fried 2016: 344–50; McCormick 2011: 185–96; Kaplony 2002: 47.
170. Fried 2016: 351–52, 370; Prawer 1996: 333; McCormick 2011: 192.
171. Fried 2016: 351.
172. Fried 2016: 3, 353. For Einhard, see Loyn and Percival 1975: 11.
173. McCormick 2011: 193.
174. Fried 2016: 357–58, 373–77; McCormick 2011: 195.
175. Fried 2016: 358.
176. Fried 2016: 382–83; 370.
177. Fried 2016: 364–65.
178. Fried 2016: 369, 378–79; McKitterick 2008: 311–12.
179. For a history of the controversy, see Siecienski 2010. Also see Fried 2016: 369; McKitterick 2008: 311–15, who notes on p. 341 that the liturgy recited in the Palatine Chapel included the *filioque*.
180. Fried 2016: 446; McCormick 2011: 166–67.
181. McCormick 2011: xv, xx, 3, 177; Watson 2013: 23; Aist 2009: 20; Wilkinson 1977: 12.
182. Watson 2013: 32.
183. From Watson 2013: 24. For another translation, see Wilkinson 1977: 137–38.
184. McCormick 2011: 25, 46–47, 73 (who says the religious population was 405 persons); Linder 1996: 137. Avni 2014: 113, says Christian presence declined only in the tenth and eleventh centuries.
185. From Runciman 1935: 614. For other translations, see Bahat 1996: 61; Wilkinson 1977: 142; McCormick 2011: 81–82.
186. Bahat 2011b: 94–95; Bahat 1996: 62; Avni 2014: 129.

187. Bahat 1996: 61.
188. Bahat 1996: 63–64.
189. Bahat 1996: 61–62.
190. Bahat 1996: 62, 64.
191. See McCormick 2011: 84–85.
192. See Magness 1995: 88–89.
193. Meshorer 1996: 415; Bates 1986: 239–42 (phases one and two).
194. See Heidemann 2010.
195. Heidemann 2010: 170, 175; Milwright 2016: 230; Walmsley 2007: 61; Bates 1986: 238–39.
196. Bacharach 2010: 14.
197. Walmsley 2007: 61.
198. Bacharach 2010: 9–10.
199. Walmsley 2007: 61–62; Bates 1986: 243–49; Milwright 2016: 230.
200. Bates 1986: 254.
201. Meshorer 1996: 416–17.
202. Meshorer 1996: 414–16.
203. Bates 1986: 239, 255; Milwright 2016: 235; Heidemann 2010: 184.
204. Meshorer 1996: 416; Walmsley 2007: 62; Blair 1992: 67; Milwright 2016: 238–39; Bacharach 2010: 16.
205. Lassner 2017: 121.
206. Bacharach 2010: 22–23, who connects this opposition to resistance to Marwanid "absolutism."
207. Walmsley 2007: 62–63.
208. Heidemann 2010: 186.
209. Bacharach 2010: 19–22, 25.
210. Barag 1988–89.
211. Meshorer 1996: 419.

II. CRUSADER JERUSALEM (19 SEPTEMBER 1187)

1. It was also called the "Kingdom of Jerusalemites" and the "Kingdom of David," establishing a conscious tie to the biblical past; see Prawer 1972: 39. Kedar and Pringle 2009: 135, note that this was first time since 70 CE that Jerusalem was a capital city.
2. Boas 2001: 37, defines "Frank" as a term used by Easterners in the Crusader period to denote anyone from the West. However, Folda 2008: 26, clarifies that Franks legally were Christians of the law of Rome, and therefore anyone, even Muslims, could become a Frank and enjoy the same legal rights if they converted to Catholicism.
3. For this section, see Boas 2001: 8–40; Prawer 1988: 1–64; Prawer 1972: Runciman 1971; Benvenisti 1970: 3–49.
4. Boas 2001: 8–9; Prawer 1988: 1–2.

5. For a discussion of the possible causes, see Gil 1996c: 23–24.

6. Gibson and Har-Peled 2019: 115–17, say that the Crusaders arrived at Nabi Samwil on 15 June, whereas Boas 2001: 9, Prawer 1988: 17, and Benvenisti 1970: 35, say it was on 7 June.

7. Boas 2001: 9; Benvenisti 1970: 36.

8. Boas 2001: 10–12; Benvenisti 1970: 36–37.

9. Boas 2001: 12–13; Prawer 1988: 20–25; Benvenisti 1970: 38. Among those massacred were hundreds or possibly thousands of Muslims who took refuge on the roof of al-Aqsa Mosque after being granted protection by the Norman Crusader Tancred; see Kedar and Pringle 2009: 133–34. Contemporary descriptions of the massacre might have been intended to evoke an apocalyptic scenario; see Boas 2001: 13 (citing a proposal by Benjamin Z. Kedar).

10. Prawer 1988: 43.

11. Boas 2001: 26–29; Prawer 1988: 19–24; Prawer 1972: 37; 252–79; Benvenisti 1970: 3. The Order of the Hospitallers was established before the Crusaders arrived but were formally recognized by the Pope in 1113; Folda 2008: 29.

12. Boas 2001: 15. Benvenisti 1970: 26, notes that the number was about the same as Jerusalem's population at the end of the nineteenth century and was roughly equivalent to the number of residents within the walls of the Old City in 1970.

13. Boas 2001: 36–37; Prawer 1972: 60–85; Benvenisti 1970: 28.

14. Reiner 1999: 50 (who mentions visits by Jewish pilgrims); Prawer 1988: 46–49. According to Boas 2001: 39–40, small numbers of Muslims and Jews were present in the city in the twelfth century, mainly as merchants, craftspeople, and pilgrims. Benvenisti 1970: 40, says that Muslims but not Jews resettled in the city.

15. Folda 2008: 29–47; Benvenisti 1970: 11.

16. Folda 2008: 56, 66; Boas 2001: 15.

17. Boas 1999: 170–74, who says the armor weighed twenty-five pounds; Benvenisti 1970: 373, who says the armor weighed approximately thirty kilograms; Prawer 1972: 334–39.

18. Runciman 1971: 460 (Vol. 2); for the Battle of Hattin, see 456–60.

19. Boas 2001: 15.

20. Boas 2001: 15–16; Benvenisti 1970: 42–43.

21. Kedar and Pringle 2009: 149; Boas 2001: 16; Bahat 1990: 101–2; Benvenisti 1970: 43–46. Jerusalem was under Crusader control again for a decade in the thirteenth century (1229–1239); see Boas 2001: 19–20.

22. For this section, see Boas 2001; also see Boas 1999; Bahat 1990: 90–103; Bahat in Geva 1993: 795–800; Benvenisti 1970: 49–391.

23. Bahat 1990: 96, 102, proposes that all the round maps are copies of a twelfth-century original, whereas the Cambrai Map, which depicts the city as square, is based on a different source.

24. Boas 2001: 2, 41–42.

25. Bahat 1990: 90; also see Boas 2001: 4; Benvenisti 1970: 49.

26. Boas 2001: 8, 43; Bahat 1990: 87–88; Benvenisti 1970: 51.

27. Boas 2001: 46–48.

28. Boas 2001: 44, 69–70; Bahat 1990: 92.

29. Boas 2001: 47–48.

30. Boas 2001: 49–68; Bahat 1990: 92–93; Benvenisti 1970: 52, who says the Crusader Citadel "almost coincided" with the Mamluk and Turkish Citadel.

31. Boas 2001: 50–53.

32. Boas 2001: 53–56.

33. Boas 2001: 56–58.

34. Kedar and Pringle 2009: 146–47; Boas 2001: 63–68; Bahat 1990: 89.

35. Boas 2001: 73–80; Bahat 1990: 93, 96; Benvenisti 1970: 52–53.

36. Boas 2001: 136–40.

37. See Boas 2001: 147.

38. Boas 2001: 140–55. For the markets, also see Benvenisti 1970: 55–56.

39. Boas 2001: 24, 83–85; Bahat 1990: 93, 97; Benvenisti 1970: 54.

40. Boas 2001: 83, 88–89; Bahat 1990: 97; Benvenisti 1970: 54.

41. Boas 2001: 85–88, 121–25, 156–60; Bahat 1990: 96; Benvenisti 1970: 58–62.

42. https://www.church-of-the-redeemer-jerusalem.info/

43. Boas 1999: 156–57; Kedar and Pringle 2009: 136–41.

44. Boas 2001: 89–93, 109–10, 163–64; Bahat 1990: 97; Benvenisti 1970: 64–68.

45. Folda 2008: 45, 65; Kedar and Pringle 2009: 141–46.

46. Boas 2001: 89, 125–26, 160; Bahat 1990: 97; Benvenisti 1970: 63–64.

47. Ben-Dov 1999: 85–86, who says the Franks adopted this method of construction from the Muslims.

48. Kühnel 1999: 166–68; Folda 2008: 68.

49. Bahat 1990: 88.

50. Folda 2008: 38–45.

51. Boas 2001: 103–4.

52. Boas 2001: 105.

53. The current edicule, which is the product of a reconstruction after the fire of 1808, preserves the main elements of the medieval structure; see Folda 2008: 25.

54. Folda 2008: 23.

55. Boas 2001: 106–8, 180; Bahat 1990: 94–95. For Frankish graves and cemeteries in Jerusalem, see Boas 2001: 180–88; Benvenisti 1970: 31–34.

56. Folda 2008: 66; Boas 1999: 233; the fragments are now in the Greek Patriarchate Museum in Jerusalem.

57. Boas 2001: 25, 106; Bahat 1990: 94. Prawer 1972: 428, says that the belfry was not part of the original plan but was added later.

58. Kenaan-Kedar 1999: 184–85. Prawer 1972: 433–37; Folda 2008: 42, 44, who relates the vine-scroll motif on the right lintel to the Cross of Christ as the Tree of Life.

59. Kühnel 1999: 165.
60. Bahat 1990: 99.
61. Boas 2001: 114–19; Bahat 1990: 99.
62. Bahat 1990: 99.
63. Boas 2001: 171–72.
64. Boas 2001: 173.
65. Boas 2001: 173–74; Benvenisti 1970: 56–57.
66. Boas 1999: 185–88; Prawer 1972: 382–91; Folda 2008: 29, 47, 50, who notes that Baldwin III introduced the motif of the Tower of David, which is where he succeeded in wresting power from his mother Melisende. It was Amalric, Baldwin III's younger brother, who introduced the motif of the Rotunda of the Church of the Holy Sepulcher.
67. Boas 1999: 189.

EPILOGUE: BRITISH MANDATORY JERUSALEM
(11 DECEMBER 1917)

1. Lawrence 1926: 453.
2. Gil 1996c: 7.
3. Greisiger 2022: 299, 307, 311–13; Goldhill 2009: 142–46.
4. Bar-Yosef 2005: 263–64; Greisiger 2022: 311–13; Goldhill 2009: 139–40.
5. Greisiger 2022: 309; Goldhill 2009: 141. Wilhelm II also commissioned the Augusta Victoria Hospital on the Mount of Olives, named in honor of his wife, as a guest house for German pilgrims and a malaria hospital. In 1914, it became the headquarters of the Ottoman army, and, in 1917, Allenby made it the British army's headquarters; see https://jerusalem.lutheranworld.org/content/history-91. The hospital's tower is one of the landmarks towering over the city from the top of the Mount of Olives.
6. Greisiger 2022: 313.
7. Bar-Yosef 2005: 247–94; Greisiger 2022: 313; Goldhill 2009: 143. For the cartoon, see https://magazine.punch.co.uk/image/I0000K4BBqRuNY20 (p. 415).
8. Bar-Yosef 2014: 51.
9. Bar-Yosef 2005: 256–57.
10. Greisiger 2022: 300.

References

Abu El-Haj, Nadia. 2002. *Facts on the Ground. Archaeological Practice and Territorial Self-Fashioning in Israeli Society* (Chicago: University of Chicago Press).

Adler, Yonatan. 2009. "Ritual Baths Adjacent to Tombs: An Analysis of the Archaeological Evidence in Light of the Halakhic Sources," *Journal for the Study of Judaism* 40: 55–73.

Adler, Yonatan. 2011. *The Archaeology of Purity: Archaeological Evidence for the Observance of Ritual Purity in Erez-Israel from the Hasmonean Period Until the End of the Talmudic Era (164 BCE–400 CE)* (unpublished PhD dissertation; Ramat-Gan: Bar-Ilan University, Department of Land of Israel Studies and Archaeology) (in Hebrew).

Adler, Yonatan. 2014. "The Myth of the *ʾôṣār* in Second Temple-Period Ritual Baths: An Anachronistic Interpretation of a Modern-Era Innovation," *Journal of Jewish Studies* 65: 263–83.

Adler, Yonatan. 2022a. "The Chalk Vessels," in Y. Gadot (ed.), *The Landfill of Early Roman Jerusalem: The 2013–2014 Excavations in Area D3* (University Park, PA: Eisenbrauns), 97–122.

Adler, Yonatan. 2022b. *The Origins of Judaism: An Archaeological-Historical Reappraisal* (The Anchor Yale Bible Reference Library) (New Haven, CT: Yale University Press).

Adler, Yonatan, and Omri Lernau. 2021. "The Pentateuchal Dietary Proscription Against Finless and Scaleless Aquatic Species in Light of Ancient Fish Remains," *Tel Aviv* 48.1: 5–26.

Aharoni, Miriam. 1993. "Arad: The Israelite Citadels," in E. Stern (ed.), *The New Encyclopedia of Archaeological Excavations in the Holy Land* (New York: Simon & Schuster), 82–87.

Ahlström, Gösta W. 1993. *The History of Ancient Palestine* (Minneapolis: Fortress).

Aist, Rodney. 2009. *The Christian Topography of Early Islamic Jerusalem* (Belgium: Brepols).

Albright, William Foxwell. 1949. *The Archaeology of Palestine* (London: Pelican Books).

Albright, William Foxwell. 1961. "In Memory of Louis-Hugues Vincent," *Bulletin of the American Schools of Oriental Research* 164: 2–4.

Amiran, Ruth. 1976. "The Water Supply of Israelite Jerusalem," in Y. Yadin (ed.), *Jerusalem Revealed: Archaeology in the Holy City 1968–1974* (Jerusalem: Israel Exploration Society), 75–78.

Amit, David. 2002. "New Data for Dating the High-Level Aqueduct, the Wadi el Biyar Aqueduct, and the Herodion Aqueduct," in D. Amit, J. Patrich, and Y. Hirschfeld (eds.), *The Aqueducts of Israel* (Portsmouth, RI: Journal of Roman Archaeology Supplementary Series Number 46), 253–66.

Amit, David, and Samuel R. Wolff. 1994. "An Armenian Monastery in the Morasha Neighborhood, Jerusalem," in H. Geva (ed.), *Ancient Jerusalem Revealed* (Jerusalem: Israel Exploration Society), 293–98.

Amitzur, Hagi. 1996. "Justinian's Solomon's Temple in Jerusalem," in M. Poorthuis and Ch. Safrai (eds.), *The Centrality of Jerusalem: Historical Perspectives* (Kampen, The Netherlands: Kok Pharos), 160–75.

Andersen, Francis I., and David Noel Freedman. 1989. *Amos: A New Translation with Introduction and Commentary* (The Anchor Bible) (New York: Doubleday).

Anderson, Paul N. 2006. "Aspects of Historicity in the Gospel of John: Implications for Investigations of Jesus and Archaeology," in J. H. Charlesworth (ed.), *Jesus and Archaeology* (Grand Rapids, MI: Eerdmans), 587–618.

Applebaum, Shimon. 1976. *Prolegomena to the Study of the Second Jewish Revolt (A.D. 132–135)* (Oxford: BAR Supplementary Series 7).

Ariel, Donald T. 1990. "Imported Stamped Amphora Handles," in D. T. Ariel (ed.), *Excavations at the City of David 1978–1985 Directed by Yigal Shiloh, Volume II: Imported Stamped Amphora Handles, Coins, Worked Bone and Ivory, and Glass* (Qedem 30) (Jerusalem: The Hebrew University), 13–88.

Ariel, Donald T. 2000. "Imported Greek Stamped Amphora Handles," in H. Geva (ed.), *Jewish Quarter Excavations in the Old City of Jerusalem Conducted by Nahman Avigad, 1969–1982, Volume I: Architecture and Stratigraphy: Areas A, W and X-2, Final Report* (Jerusalem: Israel Exploration Society), 267–83.

Ariel, Donald T. 2013. "The Stamped Amphora Handles," in D. Ben-Ami (ed.), *Jerusalem: Excavations in the Tyropoeon Valley (Giv'ati Parking Lot), Vol. I* (IAA Reports No. 52) (Jerusalem: Israel Antiquities Authority), 327–37.

Ariel, Donald T. 2019. "New Evidence for the Dates of the Walls of Jerusalem in the Second Half of the Second Century BC," *Electrum, Studies in Ancient History* 26: 25–52.

Ariel, Donald T. 2021a. "Archaeological Evidence for the Siege of Jerusalem by Antiochus VII Sidetes," in C. Feyel and L. Graslin (eds.), *Les derniers Séleucides et leur territoire: Actes du colloque international organisé à Nancy les 20–22 novembre 2019* (Études nancéennes d'histoire grecque 4) (Nancy-Paris: de Boccard), 232–79.

Ariel, Donald T. 2021b. "John Hyrcanus I's First Autonomous Coins," in A. M. Berlin and P. J. Kosmin (eds.), *The Middle Maccabees: Archaeology, History, and the Rise of the Hasmonean Kingdom* (Atlanta: SBL Press), 215–39.

Ariel, Donald T. 2022. "Coins from the Excavation near Warren's Gate, Jerusalem," `*Atiqot* 106: 235–37.

Ariel, Donald T., and Alon de Groot (eds.). 1996. *Excavations at the City of David 1978–1985 Directed by Yigal Shiloh, Volume IV: Various Reports* (Qedem 35) (Jerusalem: The Hebrew University).

Ariel, Donald T., and Alon de Groot. 2000. "The Iron Age Extramural Occupation at the City of David and Additional Observations on the Siloam Channel," in D. T. Ariel (ed.), *Excavations at the City of David 1978–1985 Directed by Yigal Shiloh, Volume V: Extramural Areas* (Qedem 40) (Jerusalem: The Hebrew University), 155–69.

Ariel, Donald T., and Jean-Philippe Fontanille. 2012. *The Coins of Herod: A Modern Analysis and Die Classification* (Leiden: Brill).

Ariel, Donald T., and Yeshayahu Lender. 2000. "Area B: Stratigraphic Report," in D. T. Ariel (ed.), *Excavations at the City of David 1978–1985 Directed by Yigal Shiloh, Volume V: Extramural Areas* (Qedem 40) (Jerusalem: The Hebrew University), 1–32.

Ariel, Donald T., and Jodi Magness. 1992. "Area K," in A. de Groot, A., and D. T. Ariel (eds.), *Excavations at the City of David 1978–1985 Directed by Yigal Shiloh, Volume III: Stratigraphical, Environmental, and Other Reports* (Qedem 33) (Jerusalem: The Hebrew University), 63–97.

Ariel, Donald T., and Yair Shoham. 2000. "Locally Stamped Handles and Associated Body Fragments of the Persian and Hellenistic Periods," in D. T. Ariel et al. (eds.), *Excavations at the City of David 1978–1985 Directed by Yigal Shiloh, Volume VI: Inscriptions* (Qedem 41) (Jerusalem: The Hebrew University), 137–69.

Ariel, Donald T., and Aryeh Strikovsky. 1990. "Imported Stamped Amphora Handles: Appendix," in D. T. Ariel (ed.), *Excavations at the City of David 1978–1985 Directed by Yigal Shiloh, Volume II: Imported Stamped Amphora Handles, Coins, Worked Bone and Ivory, and Glass* (Qedem 30) (Jerusalem: The Hebrew University), 25–28.

Ariel, Donald T., Hannah Hirschfeld, and Neta Savir. 2000. "Area D1: Stratigraphic Report," in D. T. Ariel (ed.), *Excavations at the City of David 1978–1985 Directed by Yigal Shiloh, Volume V: Extramural Areas* (Qedem 40) (Jerusalem: The Hebrew University), 33–89.

Armstrong, Karen. 1996. *Jerusalem, One City Three Faiths* (New York: Alfred A. Knopf).

Artzy, Michal. 2015. "Late Bronze Age I-*II* Cypriot Imports," in S. Gitin (ed.), *The Ancient Pottery of Israel and Its Neighbors from the Iron Age Through the Hellenistic Period, Volume 3* (Jerusalem: Israel Exploration Society), 339–79.

Arubas, Benny, and Haim Goldfus. 2005. "Introduction to the Excavations," in B. Arubas and H. Goldfus (eds.), *Excavations on the Site of the Jerusalem International Convention Center (Binyanei Ha'uma): A Settlement of the Late First to Second Temple Period, the Tenth Legion's Kilnworks, and a Byzantine Monastic Complex.*

The Pottery and Other Small Finds (Portsmouth, RI: Journal of Roman Archaeology Supplementary Series Number 60), 11–16.

Astafieva, Elena. 2020. "Found and Buy, Study and Appropriate, Build and Reconfigure: The Three Stages in Turning the 'Coptic domain' in Jerusalem into the Church of Saint Alexander Nevsky (1856–1896)," *European Journal of Turkish Studies* http://journals.openedition.org/ejts/6195; doi:https://doi.org/10.4000/ejts.6195.

Asutay-Effenberger, Neslihan, and Shlomit Weksler-Bdolah. 2022. "Delineating the Sacred and the Profane: The Late-Antique Walls of Jerusalem and Constantinople," in K. M. Klein and J. Wienand (eds.), *City of Caesar, City of God: Constantinople and Jerusalem in Late Antiquity* (Berlin: Walter de Gruyter), 71–110.

Atkinson, Kenneth. 2000a. "Millo," in D. N. Freedman (ed.), *Eerdmans Dictionary of the Bible* (Grand Rapids, MI: Eerdmans), 901.

Atkinson, Kenneth. 2000b. "Ophel," in D. N. Freedman (ed.), *Eerdmans Dictionary of the Bible* (Grand Rapids, MI: Eerdmans), 990.

Atkinson, Kenneth. 2016. *A History of the Hasmonean State, Josephus and Beyond* (London: Bloomsbury).

Avi-Yonah, Michael. 1944. "Greek Inscriptions from Ascalon, Jerusalem, Beisān, and Hebron," *The Quarterly of the Department of Antiquities in Palestine* 10: 160–65.

Avi-Yonah, Michael. 1954a. *The Madaba Mosaic Map* (Jerusalem: Israel Exploration Society).

Avi-Yonah, Michael. 1954b. "The Walls of Nehemiah: A Minimalist View," *Israel Exploration Journal* 4: 239–48.

Avi-Yonah, Michael. 1969. "The Latin Inscription from the Excavations in Jerusalem," in B. Mazar (ed.), *The Excavations in the Old City of Jerusalem: Preliminary Report of the First Season, 1968* (Jerusalem: Israel Exploration Society), 22–24.

Avi-Yonah, Michael. 1977. *The Holy Land from the Persian to the Arab Conquest (536 B.C.–A.D. 640): A Historical Geography* (Grand Rapids, MI: Baker Book House).

Avi-Yonah, Michael. 1984. *The Jews Under Roman and Byzantine Rule* (Jerusalem: Magnes).

Avi-Yonah, Michael. 1993. "Church on Giv'at Ram," in E. Stern (ed.), *The New Encyclopedia of Archaeological Excavations in the Holy Land* (New York: Simon & Schuster), 784.

Avigad, Nahman. 1953. "The Epitaph of a Royal Steward from Siloam Village," *Israel Exploration Journal* 3.3: 137–52.

Avigad, Nahman. 1954. *Ancient Monuments in the Kidron Valley* (Jerusalem: Bialik Institute) (in Hebrew).

Avigad, Nahman. 1955. "The Second Tomb-Inscription of the Royal Steward," *Israel Exploration Journal* 5.3: 163–66.

Avigad, Nahman. 1983. *Discovering Jerusalem* (Nashville: Thomas Nelson).

Avigad, Nahman. 1993. "The Nea: Justinian's Church of St. Mary, Mother of God Discovered in the Old City of Jerusalem," in Y. Tsafrir (ed.), *Ancient Churches Revealed* (Jerusalem: Israel Exploration Society), 128–35.

Avigad, Nahman, and Gabriel Barkay, 2000. "The *lmlk* and Related Seal Impressions," in H. Geva (ed.), *Jewish Quarter Excavations in the Old City of Jerusalem Conducted by Nahman Avigad, 1969–1982, Vol. I* (Jerusalem: Israel Exploration Society), 243–66.

Avigad, Nahman, and Hillel Geva, 2000. "Area A–Stratigraphy and Architecture, Iron Age *II* Strata 9–7," in H. Geva (ed.), *Jewish Quarter Excavations in the Old City of Jerusalem Conducted by Nahman Avigad, 1969–1982, Vol. I* (Jerusalem: Israel Exploration Society), 44–82.

Avner, Rina, and Kfir Arbib, 2016. "New Excavations in the Russian Compound and Their Importance for the Study of the 'Third Wall' and the Battle over Jerusalem," in G. D. Stiebel et al. (eds.), *New Studies on the Archaeology of Jerusalem and Its Region, Vol. 10* (Jerusalem: Israel Antiquities Authority), 83–95 (in Hebrew).

Avner, Rina, Roi Greenwald, Avner Ecker, and Hannah M. Cotton. 2014. "A New-Old Monumental Inscription from Jerusalem Honoring Hadrian," in G. D. Stiebel, O. Peleg-Barkat, D. Ben-Ami, and Y. Gadot (eds.), *New Discoveries in Jerusalem and Its Region, Vol. 8* (Jerusalem: Israel Antiquities Authority), 96–101 (in Hebrew).

Avni, Gideon. 2005. "The Urban Limits of Roman and Byzantine Jerusalem: A View from the Necropoleis," *Journal of Roman Archaeology* 18: 373–97.

Avni, Gideon. 2011. "From Hagia Polis to Al-Quds: The Byzantine-Islamic Transition in Jerusalem," in K. Galor and G. Avni (eds.), *Unearthing Jerusalem: 150 Years of Archaeological Research in the Holy City* (Winona Lake, IN: Eisenbrauns), 387–98.

Avni, Gideon. 2014. *The Byzantine-Islamic Transition in Palestine: An Archaeological Approach* (New York: Oxford University Press).

Avni, Gideon. 2017. "The Necropoleis of *Aelia Capitolina*: Burial Practices, Ethnicity, and the City Limits," in G. Avni and G. D. Stiebel (eds.), *Roman Jerusalem: A New Old City* (Portsmouth, RI: Journal of Roman Archaeology Supplementary Series Number 105), 123–30.

Avni, Gideon, and Katharina Galor. 2011. "Unearthing Jerusalem: 150 Years of Archaeological Research," in K. Galor and G. Avni (eds.), *Unearthing Jerusalem: 150 Years of Archaeological Research in the Holy City* (Winona Lake, IN: Eisenbrauns), ix–xix.

Avni, Gideon and Zvi Greenhut. 1996. *The Akeldama Tombs: Three Burial Caves in the Kidron Valley, Jerusalem* (IAA Reports No. 1; Jerusalem, Israel Antiquities Authority).

Avshalom-Gorni, Dina, and Arfan Najar. 2013. "Migdal," *Hadashot Arkheologiyot* 125, at https://www.hadashot-esi.org.il/report_detail_eng.aspx?id=2304&mag_id=120.

Bacharach, Jere. 2010. "Signs of Sovereignty: The 'Shahāda,' Qur'anic Verses, and the Coinage of ʿAbd al-Malik," *Muqarnas* 27: 1–30.

Bahat, Dan. 1990. *The Illustrated Atlas of Jerusalem* (Jerusalem: Carta).

Bahat, Dan. 1996. "The Physical Infrastructure," in J. Prawer and H. Ben-Shammai (eds.), *The History of Jerusalem: The Early Muslim Period, 638–1099* (Jerusalem: Yad Izhak Ben-Zvi), 38–100.

Bahat, Dan. 1999. "The Golden Gate and the Date of the Madaba Map," in M. Piccirillo and E. Alliata (eds.), *The Madaba Map Centenary, 1897–1997: Travelling Through the Byzantine Umayyad Period. Proceedings of the International Conference Held in Amman, 7–9 April 1997* (Jerusalem: Studium Biblicum Franciscanum), 254–56.

Bahat, Dan. 2006. "Jesus and the Herodian Temple Mount," in J. H. Charlesworth (ed.), *Jesus and Archaeology* (Grand Rapids, MI: Eerdmans), 300–8.

Bahat, Dan. 2007. "When Did Jews Begin to Pray at the Temple Mount?," in J. Aviram, D. Bahat, G. Barkay, Y. Ben-Arieh, and M. Broshi (eds.), *Eretz-Israel: Archaeological, Historical and Geographical Studies* 28 (Jerusalem: Israel Exploration Society), 235–38 (in Hebrew with English summary on p. 17*).

Bahat, Dan. 2011a. "The *Baris* in Jerusalem," in S. C. Mimouni and G. Nahon (eds.), *Jérusalem antique et médiévale: Mélanges en l'honneur d'Ernst-Marie Lapperousaz* (Paris: Peeters), 99–104.

Bahat, Dan. 2011b. *The Carta Jerusalem Atlas: Third Updated and Expanded Edition* (Jerusalem: Carta).

Bahat, Dan. 2013. *The Jerusalem Western Wall Tunnel* (Jerusalem: Israel Exploration Society).

Bahat, Dan. 2015. "The Fortress Called Baris that Became the Antonia?," in Z. Weiss (ed.), *Eretz-Israel 31* (Ehud Netzer Volume) (Jerusalem: Israel Exploration Society), 12–19 (in Hebrew).

Bahat, Dan. 2019. "A New Look at the History of Solomon's Stables," in H. Geva (ed.), *Ancient Jerusalem Revealed: Archaeological Discoveries, 1998–2018* (Jerusalem: Israel Exploration Society), 255–63.

Bahat, Dan. 2020. *The Temple Mount: The Holy Precinct in Jerusalem* (Jerusalem: Israel Exploration Society) (in Hebrew).

Baker, Renan. 2012. "'On Weights and Measures' §14: Hadrian's Journey to the East and the Rebuilding of Jerusalem," *Zeitschrift für Papyrologie und Epigraphik* 182: 157–57.

Bar-Kochva, Bezalel. 2010. *Judas Maccabeus: The Jewish Struggle Against the Seleucids* (New York: Cambridge University Press).

Bar-Nathan, Rachel, and Gabriela Bijovsky. 2008. "The Emperor Plowing: Cause or Effect? A Hadrianic Coin from Excavations at Shu'afat and the Foundation of Aelia Capitolina," *Israel Numismatic Journal* 13: 139–50.

Bar-Nathan, Rachel, and Deborah A. Sklar-Parnes. 2007. "A Jewish Settlement in Orine Between the Two Revolts," in J. Patrich and D. Amit (eds.), *New Studies in the Archaeology of Jerusalem and Its Region* (Jerusalem: Israel Antiquities Authority), 57–64 (in Hebrew).

Bar-Oz, Guy, Ram Bouchnik, Ehud Weiss, Lior Weissbrod, Daniella E. Bar-Yosef Mayer, and Ronny Reich. 2007. "'Holy Garbage': A Quantitative Study of the City-Dump of Early Roman Jerusalem," *Levant* 39.1: 1–12.

Bar-Yosef, Eitan. 2005. *The Holy Land in English Culture 1799–1917: Palestine and the Question of Orientalism* (Oxford: Clarendon).

Bar-Yosef, Eitan. 2014. "Theatre, Masculinity, and Class in the First World War, Vivian Gilbert Performs the Last Crusade," *TDR: The Drama Review* 58.2: 51–71.

Barag, Dan. 1970. "Glass Pilgrim Vessels from Jerusalem: Part I," *Journal of Glass Studies* 12: 35–63.

Barag, Dan. 1971. "Glass Pilgrim Vessels from Jerusalem: Parts *II* and *III*," *Journal of Glass Studies* 13: 45–63.

Barag, Dan. 1988–89. "The Islamic Candlestick Coins of Jerusalem," *Israel Numismatic Journal* 10: 40–48.

Barag, Dan. 2003. "The 2000–2001 Exploration of the Tombs of Benei Ḥezir and Zechariah," *Israel Exploration Journal* 53.1: 78–110.

Barag, Dan. 2010. "The Tomb of Jason Reconsidered," in Z. Weiss, O. Irshai, J. Magness, and S. Schwartz (eds.), *"Follow the Wise": Studies in Jewish History and Culture in Honor of Lee I. Levine* (Winona Lake, IN: Eisenbrauns), 145–61.

Barclay, John M. G. 1996. *Jews in the Mediterranean Diaspora from Alexander to Trajan (323 BCE–117 CE)* (Berkeley: University of California Press).

Barkay, Gabriel. 1986. "The Garden Tomb: Was Jesus Buried Here?," *Biblical Archaeology Review* 12.2: 40–57.

Barkay, Gabriel. 1994. "Excavations at Ketef Hinnom in Jerusalem," in H. Geva (ed.), *Ancient Jerusalem Revealed* (Jerusalem: Israel Exploration Society), 85–106.

Barkay, Gabriel. 1996. "A Late Bronze Age Egyptian Temple in Jerusalem?," *Israel Exploration Journal* 46: 23–43.

Barkay, Gabriel. 2000. "The Necropolis of Jerusalem in the First Temple Period," in S. Ahituv and A. Mazar (eds.), *The History of Jerusalem: The Biblical Period* (Jerusalem: Yad Itzhak Ben-Zvi), 195–232 (in Hebrew).

Barkay, Gabriel. 2008. "Additional Views of Jerusalem in Nehemiah's Days," in D. Amit and G. D. Stiebel (eds.), *New Studies on the Archaeology of Jerusalem and Its Region, Vol. 2* (Jerusalem: Israel Antiquities Authority), 48–54 (in Hebrew).

Barkay, Gabriel, and Amos Kloner. 1986. "Jerusalem Tombs from the Days of the First Temple," *Biblical Archaeology Review* 12.2: 22–57.

Barkay, Gabriel, Amos Kloner, and Amihai Mazar. 1994. "The Northern Necropolis of Jerusalem During the First Temple Period," in H. Geva (ed.), *Ancient Jerusalem Revealed* (Jerusalem: Israel Exploration Society), 119–27.

Barkay, Gabriel, Marilyn J. Lundberg, Andrew G. Vaughn, and Bruce Zuckerman. 2004. "The Amulets from Ketef Hinnom: A New Edition and Evaluation," *Bulletin of the American Schools of Oriental Research* 334: 41–71.

Barkay, Gabriel, and Yitzhak Shimon Dvira. 2012. "New Discoveries in the Temple Mount Sifting Project, Second Preliminary Report," in E. Meiron (ed.), *Studies in the City of David and Early Jerusalem: Proceedings of the Thirteenth Congress* (Jerusalem: Megalim), 48–96 (in Hebrew).

Barkay, Gabriel, and Yitzhak Zweig. 2007. "New Discoveries in the Temple Mount Sifting Project, Second Preliminary Report," in E. Meiron (ed.), *Studies in the City of David and Early Jerusalem: Proceedings of the Eighth Congress* (Jerusalem: Megalim), 27–66 (in Hebrew).

Baruch, Yuval, and Ronny Reich. 1999. "Renewed Excavations at the Ummayyad Building *III*," in A. Faust and E. Baruch (eds.), *Ingeborg Rennert Center for Jerusalem Studies: New Studies on Jerusalem, Proceedings of the Fifth Conference, December 23rd 1999* (Ramat-Gan: Bar-Ilan University), 128–40 (in Hebrew).

Baruch, Yuval, and Ronny Reich. 2019. "Second Temple Period Finds from the New Excavations in the Ophel, South of the Temple Mount," in H. Geva (ed.), *Ancient Jerusalem Revealed: Archaeological Discoveries, 1998–2018* (Jerusalem: Israel Exploration Society), 84–93.

Bates, Michael L. 1986. "History, Geography and Numismatics in the First Century of Islamic Coinage," *Revue Suisse de Numismatique* 65: 231–62.

Be'eri, Ron, and Danit Levi. 2018. "Pottery Production in Jerusalem in the Second Temple Period Until The Second Jewish Revolt in Light of the Crown Plaza Hotel and Jerusalem International Convention Center Excavations," *Cathedra* 168: 7–38 (in Hebrew).

Be'eri, Ron, and Danit Levi. 2019. "Roman Period Workshops at the Crowne Plaza Hotel at Giv`at Ram," in H. Geva (ed.), *Ancient Jerusalem Revealed: Archaeological Discoveries, 1998–2018* (Jerusalem: Israel Exploration Society), 195–205.

Belayche, Nicole. 1970. *Iudaea-Palaestina: The Pagan Cults in Roman Palestine (Second to Fourth Century)* (Tübingen: Mohr Siebeck).

Belayche, Nicole. 2021. "The Religious Life at Aelia Capitolina (ex-Jerusalem) in Roman Times (Hadrian to Constantine)," in K. Heyden and M. Lissek with A. Kaufmann (eds.), *Jerusalem II: Jerusalem in Roman-Byzantine Times* (Tübingen: Mohr Siebeck), 265–90.

Ben-Ami, Doron. 2013. *Jerusalem: Excavations in the Tyropoeon Valley (Giv`ati Parking Lot), Vol. I* (IAA Reports No. 52) (Jerusalem: Israel Antiquities Authority).

Ben-Ami, Doron. 2014. "Notes on the Iron *IIA* Settlement in Jerusalem in Light of Excavations in the Northwest of the City of David," *Tel Aviv* 41: 3–19.

Ben-Ami, Doron. 2020a. "Stratigraphy and Architecture," in D. Ben-Ami and Y. Tchekhanovets (eds.), *Jerusalem: Excavations in the Tyropoeon Valley (Giv`ati Parking Lot), Volume II: The Byzantine and Early Islamic Periods. Part 1: Stratum V: The Byzantine Period* (IAA Reports No. 66/1) (Jerusalem: Israel Antiquities Authority), 5–68.

Ben-Ami, Doron. 2020b. "Stratigraphy and Architecture," in D. Ben-Ami and Y. Tchekhanovets (eds.), *Jerusalem: Excavations in the Tyropoeon Valley (Giv`ati Parking Lot), Volume II: The Byzantine and Early Islamic Periods. Part 2: Strata IV-I: The Early Islamic Period* (IAA Reports No. 66/2) (Jerusalem: Israel Antiquities Authority), 271–373.

Ben-Ami, Doron, and Haggai Misgav. 2016. "A Late Iron Age *II* Administrative Building Excavated in the City of David," in S. Ganor, I. Kreimerman, K. Streit, and M. Mumcuoglu (eds.), *From Sha`ar Hagolan to Shaaraim: Essays in Honor of Prof. Yosef Garfinkel* (Jerusalem: Israel Exploration Society), 103*–118* (in Hebrew).

Ben-Ami, Doron, and Yana Tchekhanovets. 2010a. "The 'Givati Parking Lot'; Roman Period Discoveries and Finds," in E. Meiron (ed.), *City of David: Studies of Ancient Jerusalem, The 11th Annual Conference* (Jerusalem: Megalim), 25*–37*.

Ben-Ami, Doron, and Yana Tchekhanovets. 2010b. "Jerusalem, Giv`ati Parking Lot," *Hadashot Arkheologiyot* 122, at http://www.hadashot-esi.org.il/report_detail_eng.aspx?id=1377&mag_id=117.

Ben-Ami, Doron, and Yana Tchekhanovets. 2011a. "Has the Adiabene Royal Family "Palace" Been Found in the City of David?," in K. Galor and G. Avni (eds.), *Unearthing Jerusalem: 150 Years of Archaeological Research in the Holy City* (Winona Lake, IN: Eisenbrauns), 231–39.

Ben-Ami, Doron, and Yana Tchekhanovets. 2011b. "The Lower City of Jerusalem on the Eve of Its Destruction, 70 C.E.: A View from Hanyon Givati," *Bulletin of the American Schools of Oriental Research* 364: 61–85.

Ben-Ami, Doron, and Yana Tchekhanovets. 2013. "A Roman Mansion Found in the City of David," *Israel Exploration Journal* 63: 164–73.

Ben-Ami, Doron, and Yana Tchekhanovets. 2015a. "The Gaps Close: The Late Hellenistic Period in the City of David," *Eretz-Israel 31* (Ehud Netzer Volume) (Jerusalem: Israel Exploration Society), 30–37 (in Hebrew).

Ben-Ami, Doron, and Yana Tchekhanovets. 2015b. "A New Fragment of Proto-Aeolic Capital from Jerusalem," *Tel Aviv* 42: 67–71.

Ben-Ami, Doron, and Yana Tchekhanovets. 2016. "'Then They Built up the City of David with a High, Strong Wall and Strong Towers, and It Became Their Citadel' (I Maccabees 1:33)," in E. Meiron (ed.), *City of David Studies of Ancient Jerusalem* 11, 19*–29*.

Ben-Ami, Doron, and Yana Tchekhanovets. 2017. "The Southward Expansion of Aelia Capitolina in the Late Roman Period," in G. Avni and G. D. Stiebel (eds.), *Roman Jerusalem: A New Old City* (Portsmouth, RI: Journal of Roman Archaeology Supplementary Series Number 105), 65–71.

Ben-Ami, Doron, and Yana Tchekhanovets. 2019. "The Givati Excavation Project 2007–2015: From the Iron Age to the Early Islamic Period," in H. Geva (ed.), *Ancient Jerusalem Revealed: Archaeological Discoveries, 1998–2018* (Jerusalem: Israel Exploration Society), 264–78.

Ben-Ami, Doron, and Yana Tchekhanovets. 2020a. *Jerusalem: Excavations in the Tyropoeon Valley (Giv`ati Parking Lot), Volume II: The Byzantine and Early Islamic Periods. Part 1: Stratum V: The Byzantine Period* (IAA Reports No. 66/1) (Jerusalem: Israel Antiquities Authority).

Ben-Ami, Doron, and Yana Tchekhanovets. 2020b. *Jerusalem: Excavations in the Tyropoeon Valley (Giv`ati Parking Lot), Volume II: The Byzantine and Early Islamic Periods. Part 2: Strata IV-I: The Early Islamic Period* (IAA Reports No. 66/2) (Jerusalem: Israel Antiquities Authority).

Ben-Ami, Doron, Yana Tchekhanovets, and Gabriela Bijovsky. 2010. "New Archaeological and Numismatic Evidence for the Persian Destruction of Jerusalem in 614 CE," *Israel Exploration Journal* 60.2: 204–21.

Ben-Arieh, Roni, and Tania Coen-Uzzieli. 1996. "The Pottery," in G. Avni and Z. Greenhut (eds.), *The Akeldama Tombs: Three Burial Caves in the Kidron Valley, Jerusalem* (IAA Reports No. 1; Jerusalem, Israel Antiquities Authority), 73–93.

Ben-Arieh, Sara, and Ehud Netzer. 1974. "Excavations Along the 'Third Wall' of Jerusalem, 1972–1974," *Israel Exploration Journal* 24: 97–107.

Ben-Arieh, Yehoshua. 1979. *The Rediscovery of the Holy Land in the Nineteenth Century* (Detroit: Wayne State University Press).

Ben-Arieh, Yehoshua. 1984. *Jerusalem in the 19th Century: The Old City* (New York: St. Martin's).

Ben-Dov, Meir. 1971. "The Omayyad Structures Near the Temple Mount," in B. Mazar (ed.), *The Excavations in the Old City of Jerusalem Near the Temple Mount: Preliminary Report of the Second and Third Seasons, 1969–1970* (Jerusalem: Israel Exploration Society), 37–44.

Ben-Dov, Meir. 1982. *In the Shadow of the Temple: The Discovery of Ancient Jerusalem* (New York: Harper and Row).

Ben-Dov, Meir. 1999. "Churches in the Crusader Kingdom of Jerusalem," in S. Rozenberg (ed.), *Knights of the Holy Land: The Crusader Kingdom of Jerusalem* (Jerusalem: Israel Museum), 83–93.

Ben-Dov, Meir. 2002. *Historical Atlas of Jerusalem* (New York: Continuum).

Ben-Shahar, Meir. 2015. "When was the Second Temple Destroyed? Chronology and Ideology in Josephus and in Rabbinic Literature," *Journal for the Study of Judaism* 46: 547–73.

Ben-Shammai, Haggai. 1996. "The Karaites," in J. Prawer and H. Ben-Shammai (eds.), *The History of Jerusalem: The Early Muslim Period, 638–1099* (Jerusalem: Yad Izhak Ben-Zvi), 201–24.

Ben Zeev, Miriam Pucci. 2005. *Diaspora Judaism in Turmoil, 116/117 CE: Ancient Sources and Modern Insights* (Leuven: Peeters).

Benoit, Pierre. 1971. "L'Antonia d'Hérod le Grand et le Forum Oriental de'Aelia Capitolina," *Harvard Theological Review* 64: 135–67.

Benoit, Pierre. 1976. "The Archaeological Reconstruction of the Antonia Fortress," in Y. Yadin (ed.), *Jerusalem Revealed: Archaeology in the Holy City 1968–1974* (Jerusalem: Israel Exploration Society), 87–89.

Benvenisti, Meron. 1970. *The Crusaders in the Holy Land* (Jerusalem: Israel Universities Press).

Berger, Pamela. 2012. *The Crescent on the Temple; The Dome of the Rock as Image of the Ancient Jewish Sanctuary* (Leiden: Brill).

Berlin, Andrea M., and Paul J. Kosmin. 2021. "Conclusion: The Maccabean Rise to Power, in Archaeological and Historical Context," in A. M. Berlin and P. J. Kosmin (eds.), *The Middle Maccabees: Archaeology, History, and the Rise of the Hasmonean Kingdom* (Atlanta: SBL Press), 391–407.

Biddle, Martin. 1999. *The Tomb of Christ* (Gloustershire: Sutton Publishing).

Bieberstein, Klaus. 2017. *A Brief History of Jerusalem From the Earliest Settlement to the Destruction of the City in AD 70* (Wiesbaden: Harrassowitz).

Bijovsky, Gabriela. 2020. "A Hoard of *Solidi* of Heraclius," in D. Ben-Ami and Y. Tchekhanovets (eds.), *Jerusalem: Excavations in the Tyropoeon Valley (Giv`ati Parking Lot), Volume II: The Byzantine and Early Islamic Periods. Part 1: Stratum V: The Byzantine Period* (IAA Reports No. 66/1) (Jerusalem: Israel Antiquities Authority), 183–200.

Billig, Ya`akov. 2002. "The Low-Level Aqueduct to Jerusalem: Recent Discoveries," in D. Amit, J. Patrich, and Y. Hirschfeld (eds.), *The Aqueducts of Israel* (Portsmouth, RI: JRA Supplementary Series Number 46), 245–52.

Billig, Ya`akov, Liora Freud, and Efrat Bocher. 2021. "A Royal Mansion from the First Temple Period at Armon Ha-Naẓiv," in Y. Zelinger, O. Peleg-Barkat, J. Uziel, and Y. Gadot (eds.), *New Studies in the Archaeology of Jerusalem and Its Region, Collected Papers, Vol. XIV* (Jerusalem: Israel Antiquities Authority), 77–100 (in Hebrew).

Binder, Donald D. 1999. *Into the Temple Courts: The Place of the Synagogues in the Second Temple Period* (Atlanta: Society of Biblical Literature).

Biran, Avraham. 1994. *Biblical Dan* (Jerusalem: Israel Exploration Society).

Biran, Avraham, and Joseph Naveh. 1993. "An Aramaic Stele Fragment from Tel Dan," *Israel Exploration Journal* 43.2–3: 81–98.

Biran, Avraham, and Joseph Naveh. 1995. "The Tel Dan Inscription: A New Fragment," *Israel Exploration Journal* 45.1: 1–18.

Bitton-Ashkelony, Brouria. 2021. "Monastic Networks in Byzantine Jerusalem," in K. Heyden and M. Lissek with A. Kaufmann (eds.), *Jerusalem II: Jerusalem in Roman-Byzantine Times* (Tübingen: Mohr Siebeck), 345–61.

Blair, Sheila S. 1992. "What is the Date of the Dome of the Rock?," in J. Raby and J. Johns (eds.), *Bayt al-Maqdis: `Abd al-Malik's Jerusalem, Part One* (Oxford: Oxford University Press), 59–87.

Blakely, Jeffrey A. 1993. "Frederick Jones Bliss, Father of Palestinian Archaeology," *Biblical Archaeologist* 56.3: 110–15.

Blakely, Jeffrey A. 1997. "Bliss, Frederick Jones," in E. M. Meyers (ed.), *The Oxford Encyclopedia of Archaeology in the Near East, Vol. 1* (New York: Oxford University Press), 332–33.

Blenkinsopp, Joseph. 1988. *Ezra-Nehemiah, A Commentary* (Philadelphia; Westminster).

Blenkinsopp, Joseph. 2007. "The Development of Jewish Sectarianism from Nehemiah to the Hasidim," in O. Lipschits, G. N. Knoppers, and R. Albertz (eds.), *Judah and the Judeans in the Fourth Century B.C.E.* (Winona Lake, IN: Eisenbrauns), 385–404.

Blenkinsopp, Joseph. 2009. *Judaism: The First Phase. The Place of Ezra and Nehemiah in the Origins of Judaism* (Grand Rapids, MI: Eerdmans).

Bliss, Frederick J. 1977. *The Development of Palestine Exploration Being the Ely Lectures for 1903* (New York: Arno Press).

Bliss, Frederick J., and Archibald C. Dickie. 1898. *Excavations at Jerusalem, 1894–97* (London: Palestine Exploration Fund).

Blomme, Yves. 1978. *Aelia Capitolina: Jérusalem à l'époque romaine* (Jerusalem: EBAF).

Boaretto, Elisabetta. 2021. "Radiocarbon Dating of the Roman Refuse Dump and the Eastern Cardo," in S. Weksler-Bdolah and A. Onn (eds.), *Jerusalem, Western Wall Plaza Excavations Volume III: The Roman and Byzantine Periods: Small Finds from the Roman Refuse Dump and Other Contexts* (IAA Reports No. 67) (Jerusalem: Israel Antiquities Authority), 159–64.

Boas, Adrian. 1999. *Crusader Archaeology: The Material Culture of the Latin East* (New York: Routledge).

Boas, Adrian. 2001. *Jerusalem in the Time of the Crusades: Society, Landscape and Art in the Holy City under Frankish Rule* (New York: Routledge).

Bohak, Gideon. 1996. *Joseph and Aseneth and the Jewish Temple in Heliopolis* (Atlanta: Scholars).

Bocher, Efrat. 2021. "The Fortifications of the Eastern Slopes of the City of David in Areas A and J: A Reappraisal," in Y. Zelinger et al. (eds.), *New Studies in the Archaeology of Jerusalem and Its Region: Collected Papers, Volume XIV* (Jerusalem: Israel Antiquities Authority), 39–52 (in Hebrew).

Bouchnick, Ram, Guy Bar-Oz, and Ronny Reich. 2021. "Area L, The Faunal Remains," in Ronny Reich and Eli Shukron (eds.), *Excavations in the City of David: Jerusalem (1995–2010), Areas A, J, F, H, D and L, Final Report* (University Park, PA: Eisenbrauns), 482–89.

Bourgel, Jonathan. 2021. "Herod's Golden Eagle on the Temple Gate: A Reconsideration," *Journal of Jewish Studies* 72.1: 23–44.

Boustan, Ra'anan S. 2008. "The Spoils of the Jerusalem Temple at Rome and Constantinople," in G. Gardner and K. L. Osterloh (eds.), *Antiquity in Antiquity: Jewish and Christian Pasts in the Greco-Roman World* (Tübingen: Mohr Siebeck), 327–72.

Bowman, Steven B. 2022. *Sepher Yosippon: A Tenth-Century History of Ancient Israel* (Detroit: Wayne State University Press).

Broshi, Magen. 1976a. "Excavations in the House of Caiaphas, Mount Zion," in Y. Yadin (ed.), *Jerusalem Revealed: Archaeology in the Holy City 1968–1974* (Jerusalem: Israel Exploration Society), 57–60.

Broshi, Magen. 1976b. "Excavations on Mount Zion, 1971–1972," *Israel Exploration Journal* 26: 81–88.

Broshi, Magen. 1992. "The Serpent's Pool and Herod's Monument: A Reconsideration," *Maarav* 8: 213–22.

Broshi, Magen. 1993. "Excavations in the Holy Sepulchre in the Chapel of St. Vartan and the Armenian Martyrs," in Y. Tsafrir (ed.), *Ancient Churches Revealed* (Jerusalem: Israel Exploration Society), 118–22.

Broshi, Magen, and Gabriel Barkay. 1985. "Excavations in the Chapel of St. Vartan in the Holy Sepulchre," *Israel Exploration Journal* 35.2–3: 108–28.

Broshi, Magen, and Shimon Gibson. 1994. "Excavations Along the Western and Southern Walls of the Old City of Jerusalem," in H. Geva (ed.), *Ancient Jerusalem Revealed* (Jerusalem: Israel Exploration Society), 147–55.

Bryan, Betsy. 1997. "Amarna, Tell-el," in E. M. Meyers (ed.), *The Oxford Encyclopedia of Archaeology in the Near East, Vol. 1* (New York: Oxford University Press), 82–86.

Buchinger, Harald. 2021. "Liturgy and Topography in Late Antique Jerusalem," in K. Heyden and M. Lissek with A. Kaufmann (eds.), *Jerusalem II: Jerusalem in Roman-Byzantine Times* (Tübingen: Mohr Siebeck), 117–88.

Bulliet, Richard W. 1975. *The Camel and the Wheel* (Cambridge, MA: Harvard University Press).

Burrows, Millar. 1932. "The Byzantine Tombs in the Garden of the Jerusalem School," *Bulletin of the American Schools of Oriental Research* 47: 28–35.

Busse, Heribert. 1968. "The Sanctity of Jerusalem in Islam," *Judaism* 17: 441–68.

Busse, Heribert. 1991. "Jerusalem in the Story of Muhammad's Night Journey and Ascension," *Jerusalem Studies in Arabic and Islam* 14: 1–40.

Busse, Heribert. 1994. "The Tower of David/Miḥrāb Dāwūd, Remarks on the History of a Sanctuary in Jerusalem in Christian and Islamic Times," *Jerusalem Studies in Arabic and Islam* 17 (1994): 142–65.

Cabaret, Dominique-Marie. 2020. *La topographie de la Jérusalem antique. Essais sur l'urbanisme fossile, défenses et portes. IIᵉ s. av. - IIᵉ s. ap. J.-C.* (Leuven: Peeters).

Cabaret, Dominique-Marie. 2022. *The Topography of Ancient Jerusalem 2nd Century BC–2nd Century AD: Essays on the Urban Planning Record, Defences and Gates* (Leuven: Peeters).

Cagnat, Rene, and Maurice Besnier. 1921. *L'Année épigraphique, revue des publications épigraphiques relatives à l'antiquité romaine* (Paris: Presses Universitaires de France).

Cahill, Jane M. 2003a. "Jerusalem at the Time of the United Monarchy: The Archaeological Evidence," in A. G. Vaughn and A. E. Killebrew (eds.), *Jerusalem in Bible and Archaeology: The First Temple Period* (Atlanta: Society of Biblical Literature), 13–80.

Cahill, Jane M. 2003b. "Rosette Stamp Seal Impressions," in H. Geva (ed.), *Jewish Quarter Excavations in the Old City of Jerusalem Conducted by Nahman Avigad, 1969–1982, Vol. 2* (Jerusalem: Israel Exploration Society), 85–98.

Cahill, Jane M., and David Tarler. 1994. "Excavations Directed by Yigal Shiloh at the City of David, 1978–1985," in H. Geva (ed.), *Ancient Jerusalem Revealed* (Jerusalem: Israel Exploration Society), 31–45.

Cahill, Jane, Karl Reinhard, David Tarler, and Peter Warnock. 1991. "It Had to Happen: Scientists Examine Remains of Ancient Bathroom," *Biblical Archaeology Review* 17: 64–69.

Cameron, Averil, and Stuart G. Hall. 1999. *Eusebius: Life of Constantine. Introduction, Translation, and Commentary* (Oxford: Clarendon).

Campbell, Jr., Edward F. 1998. "A Land Divided: Judah and Israel from the Death of Solomon to the Fall of Samaria," in M. D. Coogan (ed.), *The Oxford History of the Biblical World* (New York: Oxford University Press), 273–319.

Capponi, Livia. 2010. "Hadrian in Jerusalem and Alexandria in 117," *Athenaeum, Studi di Letteratura e Storia dell'Antichità pubblicati sotto gli auspice dell'Università di Pavia* 98: 489–501.

Cassibry, Kimberly. 2018. "Reception of the Roman Arch Monument," *American Journal of Archaeology* 12.3: 245–75.

Caubet, Annie. 1997. "Saulcy, Félicien de," in E. M. Meyers (ed.), *The Oxford Encyclopedia of Archaeology in the Near East, Vol. 4* (New York: Oxford University Press), 495.

Chalaf, Ortal, and Joe Uziel. 2018. "Beyond the Walls: New Findings on the Eastern Slope of the City of David and Their Significance for Understanding the Urban Development of Late Iron Age Jerusalem," in E. Meiron (ed.), *City of David Studies of Ancient Jerusalem* 13: 18*–31*.

Chancey, Mark A. 2014. "The Ethnicities of Galileans," in D. A. Fiensy and J. R. Riley (eds.), *Galilee in the Late Second Temple and Mishnaic Periods, Volume 1: Life, Culture, and Society* (Minneapolis: Fortress), 112–28.

Chapman, Rupert. 1992. "A Stone Toilet Seat Found in Jerusalem in 1925," *Palestine Exploration Quarterly* 124.1: 4–8.

Charles, Robert H. 1969. *The Apocrypha and Pseudepigrapha of the Old Testament in English: Volume II: Pseudepigrapha* (Oxford: Clarendon [reprint of the first edition, 1913]).

Chausidis, Nikos. 2018. "Threshing Floor as a Symbolic Paradigm of the Ancient Observatories," in Dejan Gjorgjievski (ed.), *Giving Gifts to God: Evidences [sic] of Votive Offerings in the Sanctuaries, Temples, and Churches, Proceedings of the 1st & 2nd International Archaeological Conference "KOKINO," Held in Skopje & Kumanovo, 2016–2017* (Kumanovo: NI Museum), 39–48.

Clausen, David Christian. 2016. *The Upper Room and Tomb of David: The History, Art and Archaeology of the Cenacle on Mount Zion* (Jefferson, NC: McFarland & Company).

Clermont-Ganneau, Charles. 1896. *Archaeological Researches in Palestine During the Years 1873–1874, Vol. 2* (London: Palestine Exploration Fund).

Clermont-Ganneau, Charles. 1898. "The Taking of Jerusalem by the Persians, A.D. 614," *Palestine Exploration Fund Quarterly Statement*: 38–54.

Clermont-Ganneau, Charles. 1899. *Archaeological Researches in Palestine During the Years 1873–1874, Vol. 1* (London: Palestine Exploration Fund).

Clermont-Ganneau, Charles. 1903. "Inscriptions de Palestine," *Comptes rendus des séances de l'Académie des Inscriptions et Belles-Lettres* 47.6: 479–95.

Clermont-Ganneau, Charles. 1920. "Découverte a Jérusalem d'une synagogue de l'epoque hérodienne," *Syria* 1: 190–97.

Clermont-Ganneau, Charles. 1905. *Recueil d'archéologie orientale, Vol. VI* (Paris: Ernest Leroux).

Cline, Eric H. 2000. *The Battles of Armageddon, Megiddo and the Jezreel Valley from the Bronze Age to the Nuclear Age* (Ann Arbor: University of Michigan Press).

Cline, Eric H. 2004. *Jerusalem Besieged: From Ancient Canaan to Modern Israel* (Ann Arbor: University of Michigan Press).

Cline, Eric H. 2014. *1177 B.C.: The Year Civilization Collapsed* (Princeton, NJ: Princeton University Press).

Cogan, Mordechai. 1998. "Into Exile: From the Assyrian Conquest of Israel to the Fall of Babyon," in M. D. Coogan (ed.), *The Oxford History of the Biblical World* (New York: Oxford University Press), 321–65.

Cohen, Shaye J. D. 1999. *The Beginnings of Jewishness: Boundaries, Varieties, Uncertainties* (Berkeley: University of California Press).

Cohen-Hattab, Kobi, and Noam Shoval. 2015. *Tourism, Religion, and Pilgrimage in Jerusalem* (New York: Routledge).

Conybeare, Frederick Cornwallis. 1910. "Antiochus Strategos' Account of the Sack of Jerusalem in A.D. 614," *The English Historical Review* 25: 502–17.

Cook, Stanley A. 1923. "The Late M. Charles Clermont-Ganneau," *Palestine Exploration Fund Quarterly Statement*: 137–39.

Coote, Robert B. 2000. "Habiru, Apiru," in D. N. Freedman (ed.), *Eerdmans Dictionary of the Bible* (Grand Rapids, MI: Eerdmans), 549–51.

Corbo, Virgilio C. 1981. *Il Santo Sepolcro di Gerusalemme: Aspetti archeologici dale origini al period crociato. Vol. II: Tavole con annotazione in italiano e in inglese* (Collectio Maior 29) (Jerusalem: Studium Biblicum Franciscanum).

Coşkun, Altay. 2021. "Seleucid Throne Wars: Resilience and Disintegration of the Greatest Successor Kingdom from Demetrius I to Antiochus *VII*," in A. M. Berlin and P. J. Kosmin (eds.), *The Middle Maccabees: Archaeology, History, and the Rise of the Hasmonean Kingdom* (Atlanta: SBL Press), 269–91.

Cotton, Hannah M. 2007. "The Administrative Background to the New Settlement Recently Discovered near Giv'at Shaul, Ramallah-Shu'afat Road," in J. Patrich and D. Amit (eds.), *New Studies in the Archaeology of Jerusalem and Its Region* (Jerusalem: Israel Antiquities Authority), 12*–18*.

Cotton Paltiel, Hannah M., and Avner Ecker. 2019. "Reflections on the Foundation of Aelia Capitolina," in G. A. Cecconi, R. L. Testa, and A. Marcone (eds.), *The Past as Present: Essays on Roman History in Honour of Guido Clemente* (Studi e Testi Tardoantichi, Profane and Christian Culture in Late Antiquity 17) (Turnhout, Belgium: Brepols), 681–95.

Cotton, Hannah M., Leah Di Segni, Werner Eck, Benjamin Isaac, Alla Kusnir-Stein, Haggai Misgav, Jonathan Price, Israel Roll, and Ada Yardeni. 2010. *Corpus Inscriptionum Iudaea/Palaestinae, Vol. 1, Jerusalem, Part 1: 1–704* (Berlin: Walter de Gruyter).

Cotton, Hannah M., Leah Di Segni, Werner Eck, Benjamin Isaac, Alla Kushnir-Stein, Haggai Misgav, Jonathan J. Price, and Ada Yardeni. 2012. *Corpus Inscriptionum Iudaea/Palaestinae, Vol. 1, Jerusalem, Part 2: 705–1120* (Berlin: Walter de Gruyter).

Coüasnon, Charles. 1974. *The Church of the Holy Sepulchre in Jerusalem* (London: Oxford University Press).

Crawford, Sidnie White. 2000. *The Temple Scroll and Related Texts* (Sheffield: Sheffield Academic).

Crowfoot, Elisabeth. 1997. "Crowfoot, John Winter," in E. M. Meyers (ed.), *The Oxford Encyclopedia of Archaeology in the Near East, Vol. 2* (New York: Oxford University Press), 72–73.

Crowfoot, John W. 1929a. "Excavations on Ophel, 1928. Preliminary Report to December 8," *Palestine Exploration Fund Quarterly Statement*: 9–16.

Crowfoot, John W. 1929b. "Sixth Progress Report. Covering the Period from December 3 to 22, 1928," *Palestine Exploration Fund Quarterly Statement*: 75–77.

Crowfoot, John W. 1929c. "Excavations on Ophel, 1928. Preliminary Report," *Palestine Exploration Fund Quarterly Statement*: 150–66.

Crowfoot, John W., and George M. Fitzgerald. 1929. *Excavations in the Tyropoeon Valley: Jerusalem, 1927* (Annual of the Palestine Exploration Fund 5) (London: Palestine Exploration Fund).

Czajkowski, Kimberley, and Benedikt Eckhardt. 2021. *Herod in History: Nicolaus of Damascus and the Augustan Context* (New York: Oxford University Press).

Danby, Herbert. 2013. *The Mishnah: Translated from the Hebrew with Introduction and Brief Explanatory Notes* (Peabody MA: Hendrickson).

Darby, Erin. 2014. *Interpreting Judean Pillar Figurines: Gender and Empire in Judean Apotropaic Ritual* (Tübingen: Mohr Siebeck).

de Groot, Alon. 2012. "Discussion and Conclusions," in A. de Groot and H. Bernick-Greenberg (eds.), *Excavations at the City of David Vol. VIIa-b, Area E* (Qedem 53–54) (Jerusalem: The Hebrew University), 141–84.

de Groot, Alon, and Donald T. Ariel (eds.). 1992. *Excavations at the City of David Vol. III, Stratigraphical, Environmental, and Other Reports* (Qedem 33) (Jerusalem: The Hebrew University).

de Groot, Alon, and Hannah Bernick-Greenberg. 2012. "Stratigraphy," in A. de Groot and H. Bernick-Greenberg (eds.), *Excavations at the City of David Vol. VIIa-b, Area E* (Qedem 53–54) (Jerusalem: The Hebrew University), 9–138.

de Groot, Alon, and Dan Michaeli. 1992. "Area H: Stratigraphic Report," in A. de Groot and D. T. Ariel (eds.), *Excavations at the City of David 1978–1985 Directed by Yigal Shiloh, Volume III: Stratigraphical, Environmental, and Other Reports* (Qedem 33) (Jerusalem: The Hebrew University), 35–53.

de Groot, Alon, and Shlomit Wexler-Bdolah. 2014. "The Slopes of Mt. Zion and the Siloam Pool (Birket el-Hamrah): An Issue Concerning Jerusalem's Topography in the Persian Period," in E. Baruch and A. Faust (eds.), *New Studies on Jerusalem* 20 (Ramat-Gan: Bar-Ilan University), 131–39 (in Hebrew).

de Groot, Alon, Hillel Geva, and Irit Yezerski. 2003. "Iron Age *II* Pottery," in H. Geva (ed.), *Jewish Quarter Excavations in the Old City of Jerusalem Conducted by Nahman Avigad, 1969–1982, Vol. 2* (Jerusalem: Israel Exploration Society), 1–49.

de Saulcy, Félicien. 1882. *Jérusalem* (Paris: Vve A. Morel et cie).

de Vaux, Roland. 1965. *Ancient Israel, Volume 2: Religious Institutions* (New York: McGraw-Hill).

Demsky, Aharon. 2021. "The 'Hananiah bar Daedalus from Yerushalayim' Inscription," *Eretz-Israel 34* (Ada Yardeni Volume) (Jerusalem: Israel Exploration Society), 67–72 (in Hebrew).

Dershowitz, Idan. 2021a. "The Valediction of Moses: New Evidence on the Shapira Deuteronomy Fragments," *Zeitschrift für die alttestamentliche Wissenschaft* 133.1: 1–22.

Dershowitz, Idan. 2021b. *The Valediction of Moses: A Proto-Biblical Book* (Tübingen: Mohr Siebeck).

Dershowitz, Idan, and James D. Tabor. 2021. "The Shapira Scrolls: The Case for Authenticity," *Biblical Archaeology Review* 47.4: 47–53.

Dever, William G. 1997. "Macalister, Robert Alexander Stewart," in E. M. Meyers (ed.), *The Oxford Encyclopedia of Archaeology in the Near East, Vol. 3* (New York: Oxford University Press), 390–91.

Di Segni, Leah. 2011. "Epigraphic Finds Reveal New Chapters in the History of the Church of the Holy Sepulcher in the 6th Century," in K. Galor and G. Avni (eds.), *Unearthing Jerusalem: 150 Years of Archaeological Research in the Holy City* (Winona Lake, IN: Eisenbrauns), 351–60.

Di Segni, Leah. 2012. "Greek Dedicatory Inscription from the Vaulted Structure of the Nea Church," in O. Gutfeld (ed.), *Jewish Quarter Excavations in the Old City of Jerusalem Conducted by Nahman Avigad, 1969–1982, Volume V: The Cardo (Area X) and the Nea Church (Areas D and T), Final Report* (Jerusalem: Israel Exploration Society), 259–67.

Di Segni, Leah. 2014. "Epiphanius and the Date of Foundation of Aelia Capitolina," *Liber Annuus* 64: 441–51.

Di Segni, Leah, and David Gellman. 2017. "A Justinian Inscription North of Byzantine Jerusalem, and Its Importance for the Dating of the Nea Church Inscription," in Y. Gadot, Y. Zelinger, K. Cytryn-Silverman, and J. Uziel (eds.), *New Studies on the Archaeology of Jerusalem and Its Region: Collected Papers, Volume XI* (Jerusalem: Israel Antiquities Authority), *27–*37.

Di Segni, Leah, and Yoram Tsafrir. 2012. "The Ethnic Composition of Jerusalem's Population in the Byzantine Period (312–638 CE)," *Liber Annuus* 62: 405–54.

Di Segni, Leah, and Shlomit Weksler-Bdolah. 2012. "Three Military Bread Stamps from the Western Wall Plaza Excavations, Jerusalem," ʿ*Atiqot* 70: 21*–31*.

Dindorf, Ludwig August (ed.). 1832. *Chronicon Paschale: Editio Dindorf* (Bonn: Weber).

Dönitz, Saskia. 2016. "Sefer Yosippon (Josippon)," in H. H. Chapman and Z. Rodgers (eds.), *A Companion to Josephus* (Malden, MA: John Wiley & Sons), 382–89.

Donner, Herbert. 1992. *The Mosaic Map of Madaba: An Introductory Guide* (Kampen: Kok Pharos).

Drijvers, Jan Willem. 2021. "Jerusalem–Aelia Capitolina: Imperial Intervention, Patronage and Munificence," in K. Heyden and M. Lissek with A. Kaufmann (eds.), *Jerusalem II: Jerusalem in Roman-Byzantine Times* (Tübingen: Mohr Siebeck), 365–87.

Dvorjetski, Estēe. 2016. "Public Health in Ancient Palestine, Historical and Archaeological Aspects of Lavatories," in A. E. Killebrew and G. Fassbeck (eds.), *Viewing Ancient Jewish Art and Archaeology: VeHinnei Rachel–Essays in Honor of Rachel Hachlili* (Leiden: Brill), 48–100.

Eck, Werner. 1999. "The Bar Kokhba Revolt: The Roman Point of View," *Journal of Roman Studies* 89: 76–89.

Eck, Werner. 2003. "Hadrian, the Bar Kokhba Revolt, and the Epigraphic Transmission," in P. Schäfer (ed.), *The Bar Kokhba War Reconsidered* (Tübingen: Mohr Siebeck), 152–70.

Ecker, Avner. 2019. "The Training Ground (*Campus*) of the Legio X Fretensis in Jerusalem/Aelia Capitolina–A Possible Identification North of the Damascus Gate," *Electrum* 26: 109–17.

Eckhardt, Benedikt. 2021. "Reading the Middle Maccabees," in A. M. Berlin and P. J. Kosmin (eds.), *The Middle Maccabees: Archaeology, History, and the Rise of the Hasmonean Kingdom* (Atlanta: SBL Press), 349–62.

Edelman, Diana. 2005. *The Origins of the Second Temple: Persian Imperial Policy and the Rebuilding of Jerusalem* (New York: Routledge).

Edelman, Diana. 2006. "Tyrian Trade in Yehud under Artaxerxes I: Real or Fictional? Independent or Crown Endorsed?," in O. Lipschits and M. Oeming (eds.), *Judah and the Judeans in the Persian Period* (Winona Lake, IN: Eisenbrauns), 207–46.

Edelman, Diana. 2008. "Hezekiah's Alleged Cultic Centralization," *Journal for the Study of the Old Testament* 32.4: 395–434.

Ehrman, Bart D., and Andrew S. Jacobs. 2004. *Christianity in Late Antiquity 300–450 C.E., A Reader* (New York: Oxford University Press).

Elad, Amikam. 1995. *Medieval Jerusalem and Islamic Worship: Holy Places, Ceremonies, Pilgrimage* (Leiden: Brill).

Eliav, Yaron Z. 1997. "Hadrian's Actions in the Jerusalem Temple Mount According to Cassius Dio and Xiphilini Manus," *Jewish Studies Quarterly* 4: 125–44.

Eliav, Yaron Z. 2005. *God's Mountain: The Temple Mount in Time, Place, and Memory* (Baltimore: Johns Hopkins University Press).

Elitzur, Yoel. 2014. "The Biblical Names of Jerusalem," *Maarav* 21.1–2: 189–201.

Eshel, Hanan. 2000. "Jerusalem Under Persian Rule: The City's Layout and the Historical Background," in S. Ahituv and A. Mazar (eds.), *The History of Jerusalem: The Biblical Period* (Jerusalem: Yad Izhak Ben-Zvi), 327–43 (in Hebrew).

Faust, Avraham. 2006. *Israel's Ethnogenesis: Settlement, Interaction, Expansion and Resistance* (London: Equinox).

Feldman, Louis H. (transl.). 1965. *Josephus: Jewish Antiquities, Books XVIII-XX* (Vols. XII-XIII) (Cambridge, MA: Harvard University Press) (Loeb Classical Library).

Ferrar, W. J. 1920. *The Proof of the Gospel Being the Demonstratio Evangelica of Eusebius of Caesarea, Vols. 1–2* (New York: Macmillan).

Filipová, Alžběta. 2014. "The Memory of Monza's Holy Land Ampullae; from Reliquary to Relic, or There and Back Again," in A. Filipová, Alžběta, Z. Frantová, and F. Lovino (eds.), *Objects of Memory, Memory of Objects: The Artworks as a Vehicle of the Past in the Middle Ages* (Brno: Masaryk University Press), 10–25.

Finkelstein, Israel. 2008. "Jerusalem in the Persian (and Early Hellenistic) Period and the Wall of Nehemiah," *Journal for the Study of the Old Testament* 32.4: 501–20.

Finkelstein, Israel. 2009. "Persian Period Jerusalem and Yehud: A Rejoinder," *The Journal of Hebrew Scriptures* 9, Article 24.

Finkelstein, Israel. 2011. "Jerusalem in the Iron Age: Archaeology and Text; Reality and Myth," in K. Galor and G. Avni (eds.), *Unearthing Jerusalem: 150 Years of Archaeological Research in the Holy City* (Winona Lake, IN: Eisenbrauns), 189–201.

Finkelstein, Israel. 2018. *Hasmonean Realities Behind Ezra, Nehemiah, and Chronicles: Archaeological and Historical Perspectives* (Atlanta: Society of Biblical Literature).

Finkelstein, Israel, and Neil Asher Silberman. 2001. *The Bible Unearthed: Archaeology's New Vision of Ancient Israel and the Origin of Its Sacred Texts* (New York: The Free Press).

Finkelstein, Israel, Ze'ev Herzog, Lily Singer-Avitz, and David Ussishkin. 2007. "Has King David's Place in Jerusalem Been Found?," *Tel Aviv* 34: 142–64.

Finkelstein, Israel, Ido Koch, and Oded Lipschits. 2011. "The Mound on the Mount: A Possible Solution to the 'Problem with Jerusalem,'" *Journal of Hebrew Scriptures* 11, article 12 (2011): 1–24 (doi:10.5508/jhs.v11a12).

Finkielsztejn, Gerald. 1999. "Hellenistic Jerusalem: The Evidence of the Rhodian Amphora Stamps," in A. Faust and E. Baruch (eds.), *New Studies on Jerusalem: Proceedings of the Fifth Conference, December 23rd 1999* (Ramat Gan: Bar-Ilan University), 21*–36*.

Finkielsztejn, Gerald. 2021. "Contribution of the Rhodian Eponyms Amphora Stamps to the History of the Maccabees: The Data," in A. M. Berlin and P. J. Kosmin (eds.), *The Middle Maccabees: Archaeology, History, and the Rise of the Hasmonean Kingdom* (Atlanta: SBL Press), 193–214.

Flusin, Bernard. 1992. "L'esplanade du Temple à l'arrivée des Arabes d'après deux récits byzantins," in J. Raby and J. Johns (eds.), *Bayt al-Maqdis: 'Abd al-Malik's Jerusalem* (Oxford: Oxford University Press), 17–31.

Folda, Jaroslav. 2008. *Crusader Art: The Art of the Crusaders in the Holy Land, 1099–1291* (Burlington, VT: Lund Humphries).

Fortner, John D. 2000. "Araunah," in D. N. Freedman (ed.), *Eerdmans Dictionary of the Bible* (Grand Rapids, MI: Eerdmans), 87.

Franken, Hendricus J., and Margreet Steiner. 1990. *Excavations in Jerusalem 1961–1967: II. The Iron Age Extramural Quarter on the South-East Hill* (Oxford: Oxford University Press).

Frantzman, Seth J., and Ruth Kark. 2008. "General Gordon, the Palestine Exploration Fund, and the Origins of "Gordon's Calvary" in the Holy Land," *Palestine Exploration Quarterly* 140.2: 1–18.

Frey, Jörg. 2018. *Theology and History in the Fourth Gospel: Tradition and Narration* (Waco, TX: Baylor University Press).

Fried, Johannes. 2016. *Charlemagne* (transl Peter Lewis) (Cambridge, MA: Harvard University Press).

Friedman, Richard Elliott. 1987. *Who Wrote the Bible?* (Englewood Cliffs, NJ: Prentice Hall).

Frumkin, Amos, Aryeh Shimron, and Jeff Rosenbaum. 2003. "Radiometric Dating of the Siloam Tunnel, Jerusalem," *Nature* 425: 169–71.

Furstenberg, Yair. 2020. "Jesus Against the Laws of the Pharisees: The Legal Woe Sayings and Second Temple Intersectarian Discourse," *Journal of Biblical Literature* 139.4: 769–88.

Gadot, Yuval. 2022a. "Committing the Kidron's Western Slopes to Garbage Disposal: Jewish Urbanism Under Roman Hegemony," in Y. Gadot (ed.), *The Landfill of Early Roman Jerusalem: The 2013–2014 Excavations in Area D3* (University Park, PA: Eisenbrauns), 287–300.

Gadot, Yuval. 2022b. "Introduction," in Y. Gadot (ed.), *The Landfill of Early Roman Jerusalem: The 2013–2014 Excavations in Area D3* (University Park, PA: Eisenbrauns), 3–13.

Gadot, Yuval, and Joe Uziel. 2017. "The Monumentality of Iron Age Jerusalem Prior to the 8th Century BCE," *Tel Aviv* 44: 123–40.

Galor, Katharina. 2017. *Finding Jerusalem: Archaeology Between Science and Ideology* (Berkeley: University of California Press).

Galor, Katharina, and Gideon Avni (eds.). 2011. *Unearthing Jerusalem: 150 Years of Archaeological Research in the Holy City* (Winona Lake, IN: Eisenbrauns).

Galor, Katharina, and Hanswulf Bloedhorn. 2013. *The Archaeology of Jerusalem From the Origins to the Ottomans* (New Haven, CT: Yale University Press).

Ganor, Saar, and Igor Kreimerman. 2019. "An Eighth-Century B.C.E. Gate Shrine at Tel Lachish, Israel," *Bulletin of the American Schools of Oriental Research* 381: 211–36.

Gerstenberger, Erhard S. 2011. *Israel in the Persian Period: The Fifth and Fourth Centuries B.C.E.* (transl. Siegfried S. Schatzmann) (Biblical Encyclopedia; Atlanta: Society of Biblical Literature).

Geva, Hillel. 1981. "The 'Tower of David'–Phasael or Hippicus?," *Israel Exploration Journal* 31: 57–65.

Geva, Hillel. 1994. "Excavations at the Citadel of Jerusalem, 1976–1980," in H. Geva (ed.), *Ancient Jerusalem Revealed* (Jerusalem: Israel Exploration Society), 156–67.

Geva, Hillel. 2000. *Jewish Quarter Excavations in the Old City of Jerusalem Conducted by Nahman Avigad, 1969–1982, Vol. I: Architecture and Stratigraphy: Areas A, W and X-2, Final Report* (Jerusalem: Israel Exploration Society).

Geva, Hillel. 2003a. *Jewish Quarter Excavations in the Old City of Jerusalem Conducted by Nahman Avigad, 1969–1982, Vol. II: The Finds from Areas A, W and X-2, Final Report* (Jerusalem: Israel Exploration Society).

Geva, Hillel. 2003b. "Summary and Discussion of Findings from Areas A, W and X-2," in H. Geva (ed.), *Jewish Quarter Excavations in the Old City of Jerusalem Conducted by Nahman Avigad, 1969–1982, Vol. II* (Jerusalem: Israel Exploration Society), 501–52.

Geva, Hillel. 2006. *Jewish Quarter Excavations in the Old City of Jerusalem Conducted by Nahman Avigad, 1969–1982, Vol. III: Area E and Other Studies, Final Report* (Jerusalem: Israel Exploration Society).

Geva, Hillel. 2010. "Stratigraphy and Architecture," in H. Geva (ed.), *Jewish Quarter Excavations in the Old City of Jerusalem Conducted by Nahman Avigad, 1969–1982, Vol. IV. The Burnt House of Area B and Other Studies, Final Report* (Jerusalem: Israel Exploration Society), 1–90.

Geva, Hillel. 2011. "On the "New City" of Second Temple Period Jerusalem: The Archaeological Evidence," in K. Galor and G. Avni (eds.), *Unearthing Jerusalem: 150 Years of Archaeological Research in the Holy City* (Winona Lake, IN: Eisenbrauns), 299–312.

Geva, Hillel. 2012. "Remarks on the Archaeology of Jerusalem in the Persian Period," in D. Amit, G. D. Stiebel, O. Peleg-Barkat, and D. Ben-Ami (eds.), *New Studies in the Archaeology of Jerusalem and Its Region: Collected Papers, Volume VI* (Jerusalem: Israel Antiquities Authority), 66–79 (in Hebrew).

Geva, Hillel. 2014a. "Jerusalem's Population in Antiquity: A Minimalist View," *Tel Aviv* 41: 131–60.

Geva, Hillel. 2014b. *Jewish Quarter Excavations in the Old City of Jerusalem Conducted by Nahman Avigad, 1969–1982, Vol. VI: Areas J, N, Z and Other Studies, Final Report* (Jerusalem: Israel Exploration Society).

Geva, Hillel. 2015. "Hasmonean Jerusalem in the Light of Archaeology–Notes on Urban Topography," in Z. Weiss (ed.), *Eretz-Israel 31* (Ehud Netzer Volume) (Jerusalem: Israel Exploration Society), 57–75 (in Hebrew with English summary on 184*-85*).

Geva, Hillel. 2017. *Jewish Quarter Excavations in the Old City of Jerusalem Conducted by Nahman Avigad, 1969–1982, Vol. VII: Areas Q, H, O-2 and Other Studies, Final Report* (Jerusalem: Israel Exploration Society).

Geva, Hillel. 2018. "Hasmonean Jerusalem in the Light of Archaeology, Notes on Urban Topography," *Journal of Hellenistic Pottery and Material Culture* 3: 30–60.

Geva, Hillel. 2019. "Archaeological Research in Jerusalem from 1998 to 2018: Findings and Evaluations," in H. Geva (ed.), *Ancient Jerusalem Revealed: Archaeological Discoveries, 1998–2018* (Jerusalem: Israel Exploration Society), 1–31.

Geva, Hillel. 2021. *Jewish Quarter Excavations in the Old City of Jerusalem Conducted by Nahman Avigad, 1969–1982, Vol. VIII: Architecture and Stratigraphy: The Palatial Mansion (Areas F-2, P and P-2), Final Report* (Jerusalem: Israel Exploration Society).

Geva, Hillel, and Nahman Avigad. 2000a. "Area W–Stratigraphy and Architecture," in H. Geva (ed.), *Jewish Quarter Excavations in the Old City of Jerusalem Conducted by Nahman Avigad, 1969–1982, Vol. I* (Jerusalem: Israel Exploration Society), 131–97.

Geva, Hillel, and Nahman Avigad. 2000b. "Area X-2–Stratigraphy and Architecture," in H. Geva (ed.), *Jewish Quarter Excavations in the Old City of Jerusalem Conducted by Nahman Avigad, 1969–1982, Vol. I* (Jerusalem: Israel Exploration Society), 199–242.

Geva, Hillel, and Alon De Groot. 2017. "The City of David Is Not on the Temple Mount After All," *Israel Exploration Journal* 67.1: 32–49.

Gibson, Shimon. 2005. "The Pool of Bethesda in Jerusalem and Jewish Purification Practices of the Second Temple Period," *Proche-Orient Chrétien* 55: 270–93.

Gibson, Shimon. 2007. "Suggested Identifications for 'Bethso' and the 'Gate of the Essenes' in the Light of Magen Broshi's Excavations on Mount Zion," in J. Patrich and D. Amit (eds.), *New Studies on the Archaeology of Jerusalem and Its Region, Vol. 1* (Jerusalem: Israel Antiquities Authority), 25–33.

Gibson, Shimon. 2011. "British Archaeological Work in Jerusalem Between 1865 and 1967: An Assessment," in K. Galor and G. Avni (eds.), *Unearthing Jerusalem: 150 Years of Archaeological Research in the Holy City* (Winona Lake, IN: Eisenbrauns), 23–57.

Gibson, Shimon. 2015. "The Disputed Legacy of R. A. S. Macalister's Archaeological Explorations in Palestine," in Samuel R. Wolff (ed.), *Villain or Visionary: R. A. S. Macalister and the Archaeology of Palestine* (New York: Routledge), 24–41.

Gibson, Shimon. 2021. "Archival Notes on Robinson's Arch and the Temple Mount/ Haram al-Sharif in Jerusalem," *Palestine Exploration Quarterly* 153:3: 1–22 (https:// doi.org/10.1080/00310328.2020.1805907).

Gibson, Shimon. 2022a. "Common and Uncommon Jewish Purity Concerns in City and Village in Early Roman Palestine and the Flourishing of the Stone Vessel Industry: A Summary and Discussion," *Journal for the Study of Judaism* 53: 157–97.

Gibson, Shimon. 2022b. "An Iron Age Stone Toilet Seat (the 'Throne of Solomon') from Captain Montagu Brownlow Parker's 1909–1911 Excavations in Jerusalem," Palestine Exploration Quarterly: 1–23 (https://doi.org/10.1080/00310328.2022.2111492).

Gibson, Shimon, and Misgav Har-Peled. 2019. "On the Location of *Mons Gaudii* in Northern Jerusalem," *Strata: Bulletin of the Anglo-Israel Archaeological Society* 37: 113–40.

Gibson, Shimon, and David Jacobson. 1994. "The Oldest Datable Chambers on the Temple Mount in Jerusalem," *Biblical Archaeologist* 57.3: 150–60.

Gibson, Shimon, and David Jacobson. 1996. *Below the Temple Mount in Jerusalem: A Sourcebook on the Cisterns, Subterranean Chambers and Conduits of the Ḥaram al-Sharīf* (Oxford: BAR International Series 637).

Gibson, Shimon, and Alla Nagorsky. 2016. "On the So-Called Head of Hadrian and a Hypothetical Roman Triumphal Arch on the North Side of Jerusalem," in J. Patrich, O. Peleg-Barkat, and E. Ben-Yosef (eds.), *Arise, Walk Through the Land: Studies in the Archaeology and History of the Land of Israel in Memory of Yizhar Hirschfeld on the Tenth Anniversary of his Demise* (Jerusalem: Israel Exploration Society), 149*–72*.

Gibson, Shimon, and Joan E. Taylor. 1994. *Beneath the Church of the Holy Sepulchre Jerusalem: The Archaeology and Early History of Traditional Golgotha* (Palestine Exploration Fund Monograph Series Maior 1) (London: Committee of the Palestine Exploration Fund).

Gil, Moshe. 1992. *A History of Palestine, 634–1099* (translated from the Hebrew by Ethel Broido) (New York: Cambridge University Press).

Gil, Moshe. 1996a. "The Authorities and the Local Population," in J. Prawer and H. Ben-Shammai (eds.), *The History of Jerusalem: The Early Muslim Period, 638–1099* (Jerusalem: Yad Izhak Ben-Zvi), 101–20.

Gil, Moshe. 1996b. "The Jewish Community," in J. Prawer and H. Ben-Shammai (eds.), *The History of Jerusalem: The Early Muslim Period, 638–1099* (Jerusalem: Yad Izhak Ben-Zvi), 163–200.

Gil, Moshe. 1996c. "The Political History of Jerusalem During the Early Muslim Period," in J. Prawer and H. Ben-Shammai (eds.), *The History of Jerusalem: The Early Muslim Period, 638–1099* (Jerusalem: Yad Izhak Ben-Zvi), 1–37.

Gilbert-Peretz, Diana. 1996. "Ceramic Figurines," in D. T. Ariel and A. de Groot (eds.), *Excavations at the City of David 1978–1985 Directed by Yigal Shiloh, Volume IV: Various Reports* (Qedem 35) (Jerusalem: The Hebrew University), 29–84.

Gill, Dan. 1996. "The Geology of the City of David and Its Ancient Subterranean Waterworks," in D. T. Ariel and A. de Groot (eds.), *Excavations at the City of David 1978–1985 Directed by Yigal Shiloh, Volume IV: Various Reports* (Qedem 35) (Jerusalem: The Hebrew University), 1–28.

Gill, Dan. 2011. "The MBII Warren Shaft Water Well in the City of David, Jerusalem," *New Studies on Jerusalem* 17: 7–42 (in Hebrew).

Goitein, Shelomo Dov. 1950. "The Historical Background of the Erection of the Dome of the Rock," *Journal of the American Oriental Society* 70.2: 104–8.

Goitein, Shelomo Dov. 1967–1993. *A Mediterranean Society: The Jewish Communities of the Arab World as Portrayed in the Documents of the Cairo Geniza*, Vols. 1–6 (Berkeley: University of California Press).

Goldhill, Simon. 2009. *Jerusalem: City of Longing* (Cambridge, MA: Harvard University Press).

Goodman, Martin. 2007. *Rome and Jerusalem: The Clash of Ancient Civilizations* (New York: Alfred A. Knopf).

Gordon, Ben. 2007. "The Byzantine Quarter South of the Temple Mount Enclosure," in E. Mazar (ed.), *The Temple Mount Excavations Vol. III: The Byzantine Period* (Qedem 46) (Jerusalem: The Hebrew University), 201–15.

Gordon, Charles G. 1888. *Letters of C. G. Gordon to His Sister M. A. Gordon* (London: Macmillan).

Gorin-Rosen, Yael. 2021. "Glass Finds," in S. Weksler-Bdolah and A. Onn (eds.), *Jerusalem, Western Wall Plaza Excavations Volume I: The Roman and Byzantine Remains: Architecture and Stratigraphy* (IAA Reports No. 63) (Jerusalem: Israel Antiquities Authority), 27–67.

Gorin-Rosen, Yael, and Natalya Katsnelson. 2006. "Refuse of a Glass Workshop of the Second Temple Period from Area J," in H. Geva (ed.), *Jewish Quarter Excavations in the Old City of Jerusalem Conducted by Nahman Avigad, 1969–1982. Volume III: Area E and Other Studies, Final Report* (Jerusalem: Israel Exploration Society), 411–60.

Grabar, André. 1958. *Ampoules de Terre Sainte (Monza-Bobbio)* (Paris: Librairie C. Klincksieck).

Grabar, Oleg. 1959. "The Umayyad Dome of the Rock in Jerusalem," *Ars Orientalis* 3: 33–62.

Grabar, Oleg. 1996. *The Shape of the Holy: Early Islamic Jerusalem* (Princeton, NJ: Princeton University Press).

Grabar, Oleg. 2005. *Jerusalem: Constructing the Study of Islamic Art, Volume IV* (Burlington, VT: Ashgate/Variorum).

Grabar, Oleg, and Benjamin Z. Kedar (eds.). 2009. *Where Heaven and Earth Meet: Jerusalem's Sacred Esplanade* (Austin: University of Texas Press).

Grabbe, Lester L. 2004. *A History of the Jews and Judaism in the Second Temple Period. Volume 1, Yehud: A History of the Persian Province of Judah* (New York: T & T Clark).

Grabbe, Lester L. 2017. *1 & 2 Kings: History and Story in Ancient Israel. An Introduction and Study Guide* (London: Bloomsbury T&T Clark).

Graboïs, Aryeh. 1981. "Charlemagne, Rome and Jerusalem," *Revue belge de philologie et d'histoire* 59.4: 792–809.

Grafman, Raphael. 1974. "Nehemiah's 'Broad Wall,'" *Israel Exploration Journal* 24.1: 50–51.

Grafman, Rafi, and Myriam Rosen-Ayalon. 1999. "The Two Great Syrian Umayyad Mosques: Jerusalem and Damascus," *Muqarnas* 16: 1–15.

Greenberg, Raphael. 2019. *The Archaeology of the Bronze Age Levant From Urban Origins to the Demise of City-States, 3700–1000 BCE* (New York: Cambridge University Press).

Greenhut, Zvi. 2011. "A Domestic Quarter from the Second Temple Period on the Lower Slopes of the Central Valley (Tyropoeon)," in K. Galor and G. Avni (eds.), *Unearthing Jerusalem*: 150 Years of Archaeological Research in the Holy City (Winona Lake, IN: Eisenbrauns), 257–93.

Gregoricka, Lesley A., and Susan G. Sheridan. 2013. "Ascetic or Affluent? Byzantine Diet at the Monastic Community of St. Stephen's, Jerusalem from Stable Carbon and Nitrogen Isotopes," *Journal of Anthropological Archaeology* 32: 63–73.

Greisiger, Lutz. 2022. "From 'King Heraclius, Faithful in Christ' to 'Allenby of Armageddon': Christian Reconquistadores Enter the Holy City," in K. M. Klein and J. Wienand (eds.), *City of Caesar, City of God: Constantinople and Jerusalem in Late Antiquity* (Berlin: Walter de Gruyter), 295–321.

Grossberg, Asher. 2014. "New Observations on the Siloam Water System: Tunnels VI and VIII," *Tel Aviv* 41: 205–21.

Gurevich, David. 2017. "The Water Pools and the Pilgrimage to Jerusalem in the Late Second Temple Period," *Palestine Exploration Quarterly* 149.2: 103–34.

Gurevich, David. 2019. "Digging in the Archives: Methodological Guidelines on Conrad Schick's Documents at the PEF and the Study of Archaeology," *Strata: Bulletin of the Anglo-Israel Archaeological Society* 37: 141–62.

Gutfeld, Oren (ed.). 2012a. *Jewish Quarter Excavations in the Old City of Jerusalem Conducted by Nahman Avigad, 1969–1982, Volume V: The Cardo (Area X) and the Nea Church (Areas D and T), Final Report* (Jerusalem: Israel Exploration Society).

Gutfeld, Oren. 2012b. "The Nea Church (Areas D, T)–Stratigraphy and Architecture," in O. Gutfeld (ed.), *Jewish Quarter Excavations in the Old City of Jerusalem Conducted by Nahman Avigad, 1969–1982, Volume V: The Cardo (Area X) and the Nea Church (Areas D and T), Final Report* (Jerusalem: Israel Exploration Society), 141–250.

Gutfeld, Oren. 2017. "From *Aelia Capitolina* to *Hagia Polis Hierosalima*: Changes in the Urban Layout of Jerusalem," in G. Avni and G. D. Stiebel (eds.), *Roman Jerusalem: A New Old City* (Portsmouth, RI: Journal of Roman Archaeology Supplementary Series Number 105), 41–50.

Hachlili, Rachel. 2005. *Jewish Funerary Customs, Practices and Rites in the Second Temple Period* (Leiden: Brill).

Hachlili, Rachel. 2013. *Ancient Synagogues: Archaeology and Art: New Discoveries and Current Research* (Leiden: Brill).

Hackett, Jo Ann. 1998. "'There Was No King in Israel': The Era of the Judges," in M. D. Coogan (ed.), *The Oxford History of the Biblical World* (New York: Oxford University Press), 177–218.

Hallote, Rachel. 2006. *Bible, Map, and Spade: The American Palestine Exploration Society, Frederick Jones Bliss, and the Forgotten Story of Early American Biblical Archaeology* (New Jersey: Gorgias Press).

Halpern, Baruch. 1988. *The First Historians: The Hebrew Bible and History* (University Park: Pennsylvania State University Press).

Halpern, Baruch. 2000. "David," in D. N. Freedman (ed.), *Eerdmans Dictionary of the Bible* (Grand Rapids, MI: Eerdmans), 318–22.

Hamilton, Robert W. 1944. "Excavations Against the North Wall of Jerusalem, 1937–38," *Quarterly of the Department of Antiquities in Palestine* 10: 1–54.

Hamilton, Robert W. 1949. *The Structural History of the Aqsa Mosque* (Oxford: Oxford University Press).

Hammond, Nicholas G. L., and Howard H. Scullard (eds.). 1970. *The Oxford Classical Dictionary* (Oxford: Clarendon [second edition]).

Hamrick, Emmett Willard. 1985. "The Northern Barrier Wall in Site T," in A. D. Tushingham (ed.), *Excavations in Jerusalem 1961–1967, Volume I* (Toronto: Royal Ontario Museum), 215–32.

Handy, Lowell K. 1997. "On the Dating and Dates of Solomon's Reign," in L. K. Handy (ed.), *The Age of Solomon: Scholarship at the Turn of the Millennium* (Leiden: Brill), 96–105.

Hasson, Izhak. 1996. "The Muslim View of Jerusalem, The Qurʾān and Ḥadīth," in J. Prawer and H. Ben-Shammai (eds.), *The History of Jerusalem: The Early Muslim Period, 638–1099* (Jerusalem: Yad Izhak Ben-Zvi), 349–85.

Heidemann, Stefan. 2010. "The Evolving Representation of the Early Islamic Empire and Its Religion of Coin Imagery," in A. Neuwirth, N. Sinai, and M. Marx (eds.), *The Qurʾān in Context: Historical and Literary Investigations into the Qurʾānic Milieu* (Leiden: Brill), 149–95.

Hendel, Ronald S., and Matthieu Richelle. 2021. "The Shapira Scrolls: The Case for Forgery," *Biblical Archaeology Review* 47.4: 39–46.

Hendin, David. 2010. *Guide to Biblical Coins, Fifth Edition* (New York: Amphora Books).

Herzog, Zeʾev. 1997. "Arad: Iron Age Period," in E. M. Meyers (ed.), *The Oxford Encyclopedia of Archaeology in the Near East, Vol. 1* (New York: Oxford University Press), 174–76.

Herzog, Zeʾev, and Lily Singer-Avitz. 2015. "Iron Age IIA-B: Judah and the Negev," in S. Gitin (ed.), *The Ancient Pottery of Israel and Its Neighbors from the Iron Age Through the Hellenistic Period, Volume 1* (Jerusalem: Israel Exploration Society), 213–55.

Hodson, Yolande. 1997a. "Warren, Charles," in E. M. Meyers (ed.), *The Oxford Encyclopedia of Archaeology in the Near East, Vol. 5* (New York: Oxford University Press), 330–31.

Hodson, Yolande. 1997b. "Wilson, Charles William," in E. M. Meyers (ed.), *The Oxford Encyclopedia of Archaeology in the Near East, Vol. 5* (New York: Oxford University Press), 345–46.

Honigman, Sylvie. 2004. "La description de Jérusalem et de la Judée dans la Lettre d'Aristée," *Estratto da Athenaeum–Studi di Letteratura e Storia dell'Antichità* 92: 73–101.

Honigman, Sylvie. 2014. *Tales of High Priests and Taxes: The Books of the Maccabees and the Judean Rebellion Against Antiochos IV* (Berkeley: University of California Press).

Howard-Johnston, James. 1999. *The Armenian History Attributed to Sebeos, Part II: Historical Commentary* (Liverpool: Liverpool University Press).

Hoyland, Robert G., and Sarah Waidler. 2014. "Adomnán's De Locis Sanctis and the Seventh-Century Near East," *English Historical Review* CXXIS No. 539: 787–807.

Huffmon, Herbert B. 1999. "Shalem," in K. van der Torn, B. Becking, and P. W. van der Horst (eds.), *Dictionary of Deities and Demons in the Bible* (Grand Rapids, MI: Eerdmans), 755–57.

Hurowitz, Victor Avigdor. 2009. "Tenth Century BCE to 586 BCE: The House of the Lord (*Beyt YHWH*)," in O. Grabar and B. Z. Kedar (eds.), *Where Heaven and Earth Meet: Jerusalem's Sacred Esplanade* (Jerusalem: Yad Ben-Zvi 2009), 15–35.

Ikram, Salima, and Aidan Dodson. 1998. *The Mummy in Ancient Egypt: Equipping the Dead for Eternity* (London: Thames and Hudson).

Ilan, Tal. 1996. "The Ossuary and Sarcophagus Inscriptions," in G. Avni and Z. Greenhut (eds.), *The Akeldama Tombs: Three Burial Caves in the Kidron Valley, Jerusalem* (IAA Reports No. 1; Jerusalem, Israel Antiquities Authority), 57–72.

Iliffe, John H. 1935. "Cemeteries and a 'Monastery' at the Y.M.C.A., Jerusalem," *Quarterly of the Department of Antiquities in Palestine* 4: 72–80.

Irshai, Oded. 2006. "From Oblivion to Fame: The History of the Palestinian Church (135–303 CE), in O. Limor and G. Stroumsa (eds.), *Christians and Christianity in the Holy Land: From the Origins to the Latin Kingdoms* (Turnhout, Belgium: Brepols), 91–139.

Isaac, Benjamin. 1998. *The Near East under Roman Rule, Selected Papers* (Leiden: Brill 1998).

Isaac, Benjamin. 2010. "Jerusalem–An Introduction," in H. M. Cotton et al. (eds.), *Corpus Inscriptionum Iudaea/Palaestinae, Vol. 1, Jerusalem, Part 1* (Berlin: Walter de Gruyter), 1–37.

Izre`el, Shlomo. 1997. "Amarna Tablets," in E. M. Meyers (ed.), *The Oxford Encyclopedia of Archaeology in the Near East, Vol. 1* (New York: Oxford University Press), 86–87.

Jacobson, David. 2007. "The Jerusalem Temple of Herod the Great," in N. Kokkinos (ed.), *The International Conference: The World of the Herods and the Nabataeans held at the British Museum, 17–19 April 2001, Volume 1* (Stuttgart: Franz Steiner Verlag), 145–76.

Jacobson, David, and Shimon Gibson. 1997. "The Original Form of Barclay's Gate," *Palestine Exploration Quarterly* 129.2: 138–49.

Jamieson-Drake, David W. 1991. *Scribes and Schools in Monarchic Judah: A Socio-Archaeological Approach* (JSOT 109) (Sheffield: Sheffield Academic).

Jeremias, Joachim. 1969. *Jerusalem in the Time of Jesus* (Philadelphia: Fortress).

Johns, Jeremy. 1999. "The 'House of the Prophet' and the Concept of the Mosque," in J. Johns (ed.), *Bayt al-Maqdis: Jerusalem and Early Islam* (Oxford: Oxford University Press), 59–112.

Jones, W. H. S. 1933. *Pausanias: Description of Greece, Books VI-VIII.21 (Vol. III)* (Cambridge, MA: Harvard University Press) (Loeb Classical Library).

Kaegi, Walter E. 1992. *Byzantium and the Early Islamic Conquest* (New York: Cambridge University Press).

Kaplony, Andreas. 2002. *The Ḥaram of Jerusalem, 324–1099: Temple, Friday Mosque, Area of Spiritual Power* (Stuttgart: Franz Steiner).

Kaplony, Andreas. 2009. "635/638–1099: The Mosque of Jerusalem (*Masjid Bayt al-Maqdis*)," in O. Grabar and B. Z. Kedar (eds.), *Where Heaven and Earth Meet: Jerusalem's Sacred Esplanade* (Jerusalem: Yad Ben-Zvi), 101–31.

Karlin, Margo, and Eilat Mazar. 2015. "A Proto-Aeolic Capital from the Ophel," in E. Mazar (ed.), *The Ophel Excavations to the South of the Temple Mount 2009–2013: Final Reports Volume I* (Jerusalem: Shoham Academic Research and Publication), 549–52.

Katsnelson, Natalya. 2021. "Glass Finds from the 2017 Excavation Season," in S. Weksler-Bdolah and A. Onn (eds.), *Jerusalem, Western Wall Plaza Excavations Volume I: The Roman and Byzantine Remains: Architecture and Stratigraphy* (IAA Reports No. 63) (Jerusalem: Israel Antiquities Authority), 69–98.

Kedar, Benjamin Z., and Denys Pringle. 2009. "1099–1187: The Lord's Temple (*Templum Domini*) and Solomon's Palace (*Palatium Salomonis*)," in O. Grabar and B. Z. Kedar (eds.), *Where Heaven and Earth Meet: Jerusalem's Sacred Esplanade* (Jerusalem: Yad Ben-Zvi 2009), 133–49.

Keel, Othmar. 2015. "Glyptic Finds from the Ophel Excavations 2009–2013," in E. Mazar (ed.), *The Ophel Excavations to the South of the Temple Mount 2009–2013: Final Reports Volume I* (Jerusalem: Shoham Academic Research and Publication), 475–529.

Keimer, Kyle H. 2019. "Jerusalem in the First Temple Period," in S. A. Mourad, N. Koltun-Fromm, and B. Der Matossian (eds.), *Routledge Handbook on Jerusalem* (New York: Routledge), 15–24.

Kenaan-Kedar, Nurith. 1999. "The Two Lintels of the Church of the Holy Sepulcher in Jerusalem," in S. Rozenberg (ed.), *Knights of the Holy Land: The Crusader Kingdom of Jerusalem* (Jerusalem: Israel Museum), 177–85.

Kennedy, Hugh. 1985. From Polis to Madina: Urban Changes in Late Antique and Early Islamic Syria," *Past and Present* 106: 3–27.

Kenyon, Kathleen M. 1974. *Digging Up Jerusalem* (London: Ernst Benn Ltd.).

King, Philip J., and Lawrence E. Stager. 2001. *Life in Biblical Israel* (Louisville: Westminster John Knox).

Kisilevitz, Shua. 2015. "The Iron *IIA* Judahite Temple at Tel Moẓa," *Tel Aviv* 42: 147–64.

Kisilevitz, Shua, and Oded Lipschits. 2020. "Tel Moẓa: An Economic and Cultic Center from the Iron Age *II* (First Temple Period)," in H. Khalaily, A. Re'em, J. Vardi, and I. Milevski (eds.), *The Mega Project at Motza (Moẓa): The Neolithic and Later Occupations up to the 20th Century, New Studies in the Archaeology of Jerusalem and Its Region, Supplementary Volume* (Jerusalem: Israel Antiquities Authority), 295–312.

Klawans, Jonathan. 2022. "Shapira's Deuteronomy, Its Decalogue, and Dead Sea Scrolls Authentic and Forged," *Dead Sea Discoveries* 29: 199–227.

Klein, Konstantin M., and Johannes Wienand (eds.). 2022. *City of Caesar, City of God: Constantinople and Jerusalem in Late Antiquity* (Berlin: Walter de Gruyter).

Klein, Ralph W. 2000. "Ezekiel, Book of," in D. N. Freedman (ed.), *Eerdmans Dictionary of the Bible* (Grand Rapids, MI: Eerdmans), 446–48.

Kletter, Raz. 1996. *The Judean Pillar-Figurines and the Archaeology of Asherah* (Oxford: BAR International Series 636).

Kletter, Raz. 2015. "A Clay Shrine Model," in R. Kletter, I. Ziffer, and W. Zwickel (eds.), *Yavneh II: The 'Temple Hill' Repository Pit. Fire Pans, Kernos, Naos, Painted Stands, 'Plain' Pottery, Cypriot Pottery, Inscribed Bowl, Dog Bones, Stone Fragments, and Other Studies* (Fribourg: Academic Press/Göttingen: Vandenhoeck & Ruprecht), 28–84.

Kletter, Raz. 2020. *Archaeology, Heritage and Ethics in the Western Wall Plaza, Jerusalem: Darkness at the End of the Tunnel* (New York: Routledge).

Kloner, Amos. 2020. "The Contribution of Walls and Fortifications to Shaping the Urban Plan and Layout of the City," in I. Gafni, R. Reich, and J. Schwartz (eds.), *The History of Jerusalem: The Second Temple Period 332 BCE–70 CE, Volume Two* (Jerusalem: Yad Izhak Ben-Zvi), 413–44 (in Hebrew).

Kloner, Amos, and Boaz Zissu. 2007. *The Necropolis of Jerusalem in the Second Temple Period* (Leuven: Peeters).

Kloppenborg, John S. 2006. "The Theodotos Synagogue Inscription and the Problem of First-Century Synagogue Buildings," in J. H. Charlesworth (ed.), *Jesus and Archaeology* (Grand Rapids, MI: Eerdmans), 236–82.

Kogan-Zehavi, Elena. 1997. "Jerusalem, Hashalshelet Street," *Excavations and Surveys in Israel* 16: 104–6.

Kokkinos, Nikos. 1998. *The Herodian Dynasty: Origins, Role in Society and Eclipse* (Sheffield: Sheffield Academic Press).

Kraeling, Carl H. 1938. "Introduction *III*. The History of Gerasa," in C. H. Kraeling (ed.), *Gerasa: City of the Decapolis* (New Haven, CT: American Schools of Oriental Research), 27–69.

Krüger, Jürgen. 2021. "Die Grabeskirche: Entstehung und Entwicklung bis in frühislamische Zeit," in K. Heyden and M. Lissek with A. Kaufmann (eds.), *Jerusalem II: Jerusalem in Roman-Byzantine Times* (Tübingen: Mohr Siebeck), 189–222.

Küchler, Max. 2014. *Ein Handbuch und Studienreiseführer zur Heligen Stadt* (Göttingen: Vandenhoeck & Ruprecht [second edition]).

Kühnel, Bianca. 1999. "Crusader Art and the Holy Land," in S. Rozenberg (ed.), *Knights of the Holy Land: The Crusader Kingdom of Jerusalem* (Jerusalem: Israel Museum), 163–75.

Lake, Kirsopp (transl.). 1926. *Eusebius: The Ecclesiastical History, Volume I* (Cambridge, MA: Harvard University Press) (Loeb Classical Library).

Langgut, Dafna. 2021. "Mid-7th Century BC Human Parasite Remains from Jerusalem," *International Journal of Paleopathology* 36: 1–6.

Lasine, Stuart. 2000. "Israel," in D. N. Freedman (ed.), *Eerdmans Dictionary of the Bible* (Grand Rapids, MI: Eerdmans), 655–59.

Lassner, Jacob. 2017. *Medieval Jerusalem: Forging an Islamic City in Spaces Sacred to Christians and Jews* (Ann Arbor: University of Michigan Press).

Lawler, Andrew. 2021a. *Under Jerusalem: The Buried History of the World's Most Contested City* (New York: Doubleday).

Lawler, Andrew. 2021b. "Who Built the Tomb of the Kings?," *Biblical Archaeology Review* 47.4: 30–38.

Lawrence, T. E. 1926. *The Seven Pillars of Wisdom, A Triumph* (London: Jonathan Cape).

Layton, Scott C. 1990. "The Steward in Ancient Israel: A Study of Hebrew (ʾăšer) ʿal-habbayit in Its Near Eastern Setting," *Journal of Biblical Literature* 109.4: 633–49.

Le Strange, Guy. 1965. *Palestine Under the Moslems: A Description of Syria and the Holy Land from A.D. 650 to 1500, Translated from the Works of Medieval Arab Geographers* (Beirut: Khayats).

Leibner, Uzi. 2018. *Khirbet Wadi Ḥamam: A Roman-Period Village and Synagogue in the Lower Galilee* (Qedem Reports 13) (Jerusalem: The Hebrew University).

Leibner, Uzi. 2021. "Galilee in the Second Century B.C.E.: Material Culture and Ethnic Identity," in A. M. Berlin and P. J. Kosmin (eds.), *The Middle Maccabees: Archaeology, History, and the Rise of the Hasmonean Kingdom* (Atlanta: SBL Press), 123–44.

Leith, Mary Joan Winn. 1998. "Israel Among the Nations: The Persian Period," in M. D. Coogan (ed.), *The Oxford History of the Biblical World* (New York: Oxford University Press), 367–419.

Lernau, Omri. 2022. "Fish Remains," in Y. Gadot (ed.), *The Landfill of Early Roman Jerusalem: The 2013–2014 Excavations in Area D3* (University Park, PA: Eisenbrauns), 235–42.

Lernau, Hanan, and Omri Lernau. 1992. "Fish Remains," in A. de Groot and D. T. Ariel (eds.), *Excavations at the City of David 1978–1985 Directed by Yigal Shiloh, Volume III: Stratigraphical, Environmental, and Other Reports* (Qedem 33) (Jerusalem: The Hebrew University), 131–47.

Lev-Yadun, Simcha. 1992. "The Origin of the Cedar Beams from Al-Aqsa Mosque: Botanical, Historical and Archaeological Evidence," *Levant* 24: 201–8.

Levine, Lee I. 2000. *The Ancient Synagogue: The First Thousand Years* (New Haven, CT: Yale University Press).

Levine, Lee I. 2002. *Jerusalem: Portrait of the City in the Second Temple Period (538 B.C.E.–70 C.E.)* (Philadelphia: Jewish Publication Society).

Lewy, Yohanan Hans. 1960. "The Fate of the Temple Implements After the Destruction of the Second Temple," *Studies in Jewish Hellenism* (Jerusalem: Bialik Institute), 255–58 (in Hebrew).

Lichtenberger, Achim. 2006. "Jesus and the Theater in Jerusalem," in J. H. Charlesworth (ed.), *Jesus and Archaeology* (Grand Rapids, MI: Eerdmans), 283–99.

Lieberman, Tehillah, Avi Solomon, and Joe Uziel. 2019. "Wilson's Arch: 150 Years of Archaeological and Historical Exploration," in H. Geva (ed.), *Ancient Jerusalem Revealed* (Jerusalem: Israel Exploration Society), 173–83.

Limor, Ora. 1988. "The Origins of a Tradition: King David's Tomb on Mount Zion," *Traditio* 44: 453–62.

Linder, Amnon. 1996. "Christian Communities in Jerusalem," in J. Prawer and H. Ben-Shammai (eds.), *The History of Jerusalem: The Early Muslim Period, 638–1099* (Jerusalem: Yad Izhak Ben-Zvi), 121–62.

Liphschitz, Nili, Gideon Biger, Georges Bonani, and W. Wolfli. 1997. "Comparative Dating Methods: Botanical Identification and 14C Dating of Carved Panels and Beams from the Al-Aqsa Mosque in Jerusalem," *Journal of Archaeological Science* 24: 1045–50.

Lipiński, Edward. 2018. *A History of the Kingdom of Israel* (Leuven: Peeters).

Lipiński, Edward. 2020. *A History of the Kingdom of Jerusalem and Judah* (Leuven: Peeters).

Lipschits, Oded. 2005. *The Fall and Rise of Jerusalem: Jerusalem Under Babylonian Rule* (Winona Lake, IN: Eisenbrauns).

Lipschits, Oded. 2009. "Persian Period Finds from Jerusalem: Facts and Interpretations," *The Journal of Hebrew Scriptures* 9, Article 20.

Lipschits, Oded. 2011. "The Origin and Date of the Volute Capitals from the Levant," in I. Finkelstein and N. Na`aman (eds.), *The Fire Signals of Lachish: Studies in the Archaeology and History of Israel in the Late Bronze Age, Iron Age, and Persian Period in Honor of David Ussishkin* (Winona Lake, IN: Eisenbrauns), 203–25.

Lipschits, Oded, and Oren Tal. 2007. "The Settlement Archaeology of the Province of Judah: A Case Study," in O. Lipschits, G. N. Knoppers, and R. Albertz (eds.), *Judah and the Judeans in the Fourth Century B.C.E.* (Winona Lake, IN: Eisenbrauns), 33–52.

Lipschits, Oded, and David S. Vanderhooft. 2011. *Yehud Stamp Impressions: A Corpus of Inscribed Impressions from the Persian and Hellenistic Periods in Judah* (Winona Lake, IN: Eisenbrauns).

Liraz, Elad. 2018. "A Second Cult Room at the Lachish Gate?," *Near Eastern Archaeology* 81.4: 269–75.

Loffreda, Stanislao. 1989. *Lucerne bizantine in Terra Santa con iscrizioni in Greco* (Jerusalem: Franciscan Printing Press).

Long, Fredrick J. 2013. "Roman Imperial Rule Under the Authority of Jupiter-Zeus: Political-Religious Contexts and the Interpretation of 'The Ruler of the Authority of the Air' in Ephesians 2:2," in Stanley E. Porter and Andrew Pitts (eds.), *The Language of the New Testament: Context, History, and Development* (Leiden: Brill), 113–54.

Loyn, H. R., and John Percival. 1975. *The Reign of Charlemagne: Documents on Carolingian Government and Administration* (London: Edward Arnold).

Lufrani, Riccardo. 2019. *The Saint-Etienne Compound Hypogea (Jerusalem)* (Göttingen: Vandenhoeck & Ruprecht).

Macalister, Robert A. S., and John G. Duncan. 1926. *Excavations on the Hill of Ophel, Jerusalem* (Annual of the Palestine Exploration Fund 4) (London: Palestine Exploration Fund).

Machinist, Peter. 2019. "Periodization in Biblical Historiography," in J. Baines, H. van der Blom, Y. S. Chen, and T. Rood (eds.), *Historical Consciousness and the Use of the Past in the Ancient World* (Sheffield: Equinox), 215–37.

Machinist, Peter. 2020. "Writing and Rewriting the History of Ancient Israel: Some Preliminary Expectorations," in I. Kalimi (ed.), *Writing and Rewriting History in Ancient Israel and Near Eastern Cultures* (Wiesbaden: Harrassowitz), 5–16.

Machline, Hélène. 2022. "The Pottery," in Y. Gadot (ed.), *The Landfill of Early Roman Jerusalem: The 2013–2014 Excavations in Area D3* (University Park, PA: Eisenbrauns), 37–67.

Maeir, Aren M. 2011. "The Archaeology of Early Jerusalem: From the Late Proto-Historic Periods (ca. 5th Millennium) to the End of the Late Bronze Age (ca. 1200 B.C.E.)," in K. Galor and G. Avni (eds.), *Unearthing Jerusalem: 150 Years of Archaeological Research in the Holy City* (Winona Lake, IN: Eisenbrauns), 171–87.

Magen, Menahem. 1994. "Excavations at the Damascus Gate, 1979–1984," in H. Geva (ed.), *Ancient Jerusalem Revealed* (Jerusalem: Israel Exploration Society), 281–86.

Magness, Jodi. 1991. "The Walls of Jerusalem in the Early Islamic Period," *The Biblical Archaeologist* 54.4: 208–17.

Magness, Jodi. 1992a. "Late Roman and Byzantine Pottery from Areas H and K," in A. de Groot and D. T. Ariel (eds.), *Excavations at the City of David 1978–1985 Directed by Yigal Shiloh, Volume III: Stratigraphical, Environmental, and Other Reports* (Qedem 33) (Jerusalem: The Hebrew University), 149–83.

Magness, Jodi. 1992b. "A Reexamination of the Archaeological Evidence for the Sasanian Persian Destruction of the Tyropoeon Valley," *Bulletin of the American Schools of Oriental Research* 287: 67–74.

Magness, Jodi. 1993. *Jerusalem Ceramic Chronology circa 200–800 C.E.* (Sheffield: Sheffield Academic Press).

Magness, Jodi. 1995. "Review of K. J. H. Vriezen, *Die Ausgrabungen unter der Erlöserkirche im Muristan, Jerusalem (1970–1974)* (Wiesbaden: Harrassowitz Verlag, 1994)," *Bulletin of the American Schools of Oriental Research* 298: 87–89.

Magness, Jodi. 1996. "Blessings from Jerusalem: Evidence for Early Christian Pilgrimage," *Eretz-Israel 25* (Joseph Aviram Volume) (Jerusalem: Israel Exploration Society), 37*–45*.

Magness, Jodi. 2000. "The North Wall of Aelia Capitolina," in L. E. Stager, J. A. Greene, and M. D. Coogan (eds.), *The Archaeology of Jordan and Beyond: Essays in Honor of James A. Sauer* (Winona Lake, IN: Eisenbrauns) 328–39.

Magness, Jodi. 2003. "A Mithraeum in Jerusalem?," in G. C. Bottini, L. Di Segni, and L. D. Chrupcała (eds.), *One Land–Many Cultures: Archaeological Studies in Honour of Stanislao Loffreda ofm* (Jerusalem: Franciscan Printing Press), 163–71.

Magness, Jodi. 2005a. "Ossuaries and the Burials of Jesus and James," *Journal of Biblical Literature* 124.1: 121–54.

Magness, Jodi. 2005b. "The Roman Legionary Pottery," in B. Arubas and H. Goldfus (eds.), *Excavations on the Site of the Jerusalem International Convention Center (Binyanei Ha'uma): A Settlement of the Late First to Second Temple Period, the Tenth Legion's Kilnworks, and a Byzantine Monastic Complex. The Pottery and Other Small Finds* (Portsmouth, RI: Journal of Roman Archaeology Supplementary Series Number 60), 69–191.

Magness, Jodi. 2008. "The Arch of Titus at Rome and the Fate of the God of Israel," *Journal of Jewish Studies* 59.2: 201–17.

Magness, Jodi. 2010a. "Early Islamic Pottery: Evidence of a Revolution in Diet and Dining Habits?" in S. R. Steadman and J. C. Ross (eds.), *Agency and Identity in the Ancient Near East: New Paths Forward* (London: Equinox), 117–26.

Magness, Jodi. 2010b. "Early Islamic Urbanism and Building Activity in Jerusalem and at Hammath Gader," in J. Haldon (ed.), *Money, Power, and Politics in Early Islamic Syria: A Review of Current Debates* (Burlington, VT: Ashgate), 147–63.

Magness, Jodi. 2011a. "Archaeological Evidence for the Sasanian Persian Invasion of Jerusalem," in K. G. Holum and H. Lapin (eds.), *Shaping the Middle East: Jews, Christians, and Muslims in an Age of Transition, 400–800 C.E.* (University Park: Pennsylvania State University Press), 85–98.

Magness, Jodi. 2011b. *Stone and Dung, Oil and Spit: Jewish Daily Life in the Time of Jesus* (Grand Rapids, MI: Eerdmans).

Magness, Jodi. 2012. "Late Roman and Byzantine Pottery from the Cardo and the Nea Church," in O. Gutfeld (ed.), *Jewish Quarter Excavations in the Old City of Jerusalem Conducted by Nahman Avigad, 1969–1982, Volume V: The Cardo (Area X) and the Nea Church (Areas D and T), Final Report* (Jerusalem: Israel Exploration Society), 282–300.

Magness, Jodi. 2016. "Sweet Memory: Archaeological Evidence of Jesus in Jerusalem," in K. Galinsky (ed.), *Memory in Ancient Rome and Early Christianity* (New York: Oxford University Press), 324–43.

Magness, Jodi. 2018. "More Than Just Filth: The Impurity of Excrement in Biblical and Early Jewish Traditions," in A. Ben-Tor, E. Stern, and J. Magness (eds.), *Eretz-Israel 33: Lawrence E. Stager Volume* (Jerusalem: Israel Exploration Society), 124*–132*.

Magness, Jodi. 2019a. "Herod the Great's Self-Representation Through his Tomb at Herodium," *Journal of Ancient Judaism* 10.3: 258–287.

Magness, Jodi. 2019b. *Masada: From Jewish Revolt to Modern Myth* (Princeton, NJ: Princeton University Press).

Magness, Jodi. 2020. "Hadrian's Jerusalem: Review of Shlomit Weksler-Bdolah, *Aelia Capitolina–Jerusalem in the Roman Period in Light of Archaeological Research*," *Journal of Roman Archaeology* 33: 903–12.

Magness, Jodi. 2021. *The Archaeology of Qumran and the Dead Sea Scrolls* (Grand Rapids, MI: Eerdmans [second edition]).

Magness, Jodi. 2023. "The Development of Jerusalem's Southeast Sector in the Late Roman and Byzantine Periods," in O. Gutfeld, A. Mazar. O. Peleg-Barkat, and S. Weksler-Bdolah (eds.), *Eretz-Israel 35: Hillel Geva Volume* (Jerusalem: Israel Exploration Society), 88*–98* (in press).

Magness, Jodi, and Gwyn Davies. 2023. "Jerusalem's Northern Defences Under Hadrian," *Palestine Exploration Quarterly* 155.3: 204–16 (doi:10.1080/00310328.2022.203060).

Mango, Cyril. 1992. "The Temple Mount, AD 614–638," in J. Raby and J. Johns (eds.), *Bayt al-Maqdis: 'Abd al-Malik's Jerusalem* (Oxford: Oxford University Press), 1–16.

Marciak, Michał. 2018. "Royal Converts from Adiabene and the Archaeology of Jerusalem," *Göttingen Forum für Altertumswissenschaft* 21: 29–58.

Marcus, Ralph (transl.). 1943. *Josephus: Jewish Antiquities Books XII–XIII (Vol. IX)* (Cambridge, MA: Harvard University Press) (Loeb Classical Library).

Marcus, Ralph (transl.), and Allen Wikgren (completed and ed.). 2004. *Josephus: Jewish Antiquities Books XIV–XV (Vol. X)* (Cambridge, MA: Harvard University Press) (Loeb Classical Library).

Masterman, Ernest W. G. 1902. "The Important Work of Dr. Conrad Schick," *The Biblical World* 20: 146–48.

Mattingly, David. 2004. "Being Roman: Expressing Identity in a Provincial Setting," *Journal of Roman Archaeology* 17: 5–25.

Mazar, Amihai. 1990. *Archaeology of the Land of the Bible: 10,000–586 B.C.E.* (New York: Doubleday).

Mazar, Amihai. 1997. "Mazar, Benjamin," in E. M. Meyers (ed.), *The Oxford Encyclopedia of Archaeology in the Near East, Vol. 3* (New York: Oxford University Press), 442.

Mazar, Amihai. 2000. "Jerusalem's Water Supply in the First Temple Period," in S. Ahituv and A. Mazar (eds.), *The History of Jerusalem: The Biblical Period* (Jerusalem: Yad Izhak Ben-Zvi), 195–232 (in Hebrew).

Mazar, Amihai. 2002. "A Survey of the Aqueducts to Jerusalem," in D. Amit, J. Patrich, and Y. Hirschfeld (eds.), *The Aqueducts of Israel* (Portsmouth, RI: JRA Supplementary Series Number 46), 210–44.

Mazar, Amihai. 2015. "Iron Age I: Northern Coastal Plain, Galilee, Samaria, Jezreel Valley, Judah, and Negev," in S. Gitin (ed.), *The Ancient Pottery of Israel and Its Neighbors from the Iron Age Through the Hellenistic Period, Vol. 1* (Jerusalem: Israel Exploration Society), 5–70.

Mazar, Benjamin. 1969. *The Excavations in the Old City of Jerusalem: Preliminary Report of the First Season, 1968* (Jerusalem: Israel Exploration Society).

Mazar, Benjamin. 1971. *The Excavations in the Old City of Jerusalem Near the Temple Mount: Preliminary Report of the Second and Third Seasons, 1969–1970* (Jerusalem: Israel Exploration Society).

Mazar, Benjamin. 1975. *The Mountain of the Lord, Excavating in Jerusalem* (New York: Doubleday).

Mazar, Benjamin. 1993. "Jerusalem, The Early Periods and the First Temple Period," in E. Stern (ed.), *The New Encyclopedia of Archaeological Excavations in the Holy Land* (New York: Simon & Schuster), 698–701.

Mazar, Eilat. 1989. "Royal Gateway to Ancient Jerusalem Uncovered," *Biblical Archaeology Review* 15.3: 38–46, 48–51.

Mazar, Eilat. 2003. *The Temple Mount Excavations in Jerusalem 1968–1978 Directed by Benjamin Mazar, Final Reports Volume II: The Byzantine and Early Islamic Periods* (Qedem 43) (Jerusalem: The Hebrew University).

Mazar, Eilat. 2007. *The Temple Mount Excavations Vol. III: The Byzantine Period* (Qedem 46) (Jerusalem: The Hebrew University).

Mazar, Eilat. 2009. *The Palace of King David: Excavations at the Summit of the City of David, Preliminary Report of Seasons 2005–2007* (Jerusalem: Shoham Academic Research and Publication).

Mazar, Eilat. 2011a. *Discovering the Solomonic Wall in Jerusalem: A Remarkable Archaeological Adventure* (Jerusalem: Shoham Academic Research and Publication).

Mazar, Eilat. 2011b. *The Temple Mount Excavations Vol. IV: The Tenth Legion in Aelia Capitolina* (Qedem 52) (Jerusalem: The Hebrew University).

Mazar, Eilat. 2011c. *The Walls of the Temple Mount* (Jerusalem: Shoham Academic Research and Publication).

Mazar, Eilat. 2015a. *The Ophel Excavations to the South of the Temple Mount 2009–2013: Final Reports Volume I* (Jerusalem: Shoham Academic Research and Publication).

Mazar, Eilat. 2015b. *The Summit of the City of David Excavations 2005–2008: Final Reports Vol. I* (Jerusalem: Shoham Academic Research and Publication).

Mazar, Eilat. 2018. *The Ophel Excavations to the South of the Temple Mount 2009–2013: Final Reports Volume II* (Jerusalem: Shoham Academic Research and Publication).

Mazar, Eilat. 2019a. "Excavations at the Summit of the City of David Hill, 2005–2008," in H. Geva (ed.), *Ancient Jerusalem Revealed: Archaeological Discoveries, 1998–2018* (Jerusalem: Israel Exploration Society), 45–53.

Mazar, Eilat. 2019b. "The Royal Quarter Built by King Solomon in the Ophel of Jerusalem in Light of Recent Excavations (2009–2013)," in H. Geva (ed.), *Ancient Jerusalem Revealed: Archaeological Discoveries, 1998–2018* (Jerusalem: Israel Exploration Society), 54–66.

Mazar, Eilat, and Tzachi Lang. 2015. "The Byzantine Wall," in E. Mazar (ed.), *The Ophel Excavations to the South of the Temple Mount 2009–2013: Final Reports Volume I* (Jerusalem: Shoham Academic Research and Publication), 337–54.

Mazar, Eilat, and Reut Livyatan Ben-Arie. 2018. "Hebrew Seal Impressions (Bullae) from the Ophel, Area A2009," in E. Mazar (ed.), *The Ophel Excavations to the South of the Temple Mount 2009–2013: Final Reports Volume II* (Jerusalem: Shoham Academic Research and Publication), 247–88.

Mazar, Eilat, and Benjamin Mazar. 1989. *Excavations in the South of the Temple Mount: The Ophel of Biblical Jerusalem* (Qedem 29) (Jerusalem: The Hebrew University).

Mazar, Eilat, Wayne Horowitz, Takayoshi Oshima, and Yuval Goren. 2010. "A Cuneiform Tablet from the Ophel in Jerusalem," *Israel Exploration Journal* 60.1: 4–21.

Mazis, Matasha, and Nicholas L. Wright. 2018. "Archers, Antiochos *VII* Sidetes, and the 'BE' Arrowheads," *Bulletin of the American Schools of Oriental Research* 380: 205–29.

Mazor, Gabriel. 2017. "Monumental Arches and City Gates in *Aelia Capitolina*: An Urban Appraisal," in G. Avni and G. D. Stiebel (eds.), *Roman Jerusalem: A New Old City* (Portsmouth, RI: Journal of Roman Archaeology Supplementary Series Number 105), 73–81.

McCauley, Leo P. and Anthony A. Stephenson (transl.). 1969–1970. *The Works of Saint Cyril of Jerusalem (The Fathers of the Church: A New Translation)*, Vols. 1–2 (Washington, DC: Catholic University of America Press).

McCormick, Michael. 2011. *Charlemagne's Survey of the Holy Land: Wealth, Personnel, and Buildings of a Mediterranean Church Between Antiquity and the Middle Ages* (Washington, DC: Dumbarton Oaks).

McKinny, Chris, Aharon Tavger, Nahshon Szanton, and Joe Uziel. 2021. "The Setting of the Assassination of King Joash of Judah: Biblical and Archaeological Evidence for Identifying the House of Millo," *Journal of Biblical Literature* 140.4: 643–62.

McKinny, Chris, Aharon Tavger, Deborah Cassuto, Casey Sharp, Matthew J. Suriano, Steven M. Ortiz, and Itzhaq Shai. 2020. "Tel Burna After a Decade of Work: The Late Bronze and Iron Ages," *Near Eastern Archaeology* 83.1: 4–15.

McKitterick, Rosamond. 2008. *Charlemagne: The Formation of a European Identity* (New York: Cambridge University Press).

Meiron, Eyal. 2019. "Jerusalem from Its Beginnings to the End of the Bronze Age," in S. A. Mourad, N. Koltun-Fromm, and B. Der Matossian (eds.), *Routledge Handbook on Jerusalem* (New York: Routledge), 3–14.

Mendel-Geberovich, Anat, Yiftah Shalev, Efrat Bocher, Nitsan Shalom, and Yuval Gadot. 2019. "A Newly Discovered Personal Seal and Bulla from the Excavations of the Giv`ati Parking Lot, Jerusalem," *Israel Exploration Journal* 69.2: 154–74.

Mendel-Geberovich, Anat, Ortal Chalaf, and Joe Uziel. 2020. "The People Behind the Stamps: A Newly-Found Group of Bullae and a Seal from the City of David, Jerusalem," *Bulletin of the American Schools of Oriental Research* 384: 159–82.

Méndez, Hugo. 2017. "Stephen the Martyr (Acts vi-viii) in the Early Jerusalem Lectionary System," *Journal of Ecclesiastical History*: 22–39.

Meshorer, Ya`akov. 1982. *Ancient Jewish Coinage, Volume I: Persian Period Through Hasmonaeans* (New York: Amphora Books).

Meshorer, Ya`akov. 1985. *City-Coins of Eretz-Israel and the Decapolis in the Roman Period* (Jerusalem: Israel Museum).

Meshorer, Ya`akov. 1989. *The Coinage of Aelia Capitolina* (Jerusalem: Israel Museum).

Meshorer, Ya`akov. 1996. "Coins of Jerusalem Under the Umayyads and the `Abbāsids," in J. Prawer and H. Ben-Shammai (eds.), *The History of Jerusalem: The Early Muslim Period, 638–1099* (Jerusalem: Yad Izhak Ben-Zvi), 413–19.

Meyers, Carol. 1998. "Kinship and Kingship: The Early Monarchy," in M. D. Coogan (ed.), *The Oxford History of the Biblical World* (New York: Oxford University Press), 221–71.

Meyers, Carol. 2000. "Haggai, Book of," in D. N. Freedman (ed.), *Eerdmans Dictionary of the Bible* (Grand Rapids, MI: Eerdmans), 539–40.

Meyers, Carol L., and Eric M. Meyers. 1987. *Haggai, Zechariah 1–8: A New Translation with Introduction and Commentary* (The Anchor Bible) (New York: Doubleday).

Meyers, Carol L., and Eric M. Meyers. 1993. *Zechariah 9–14: A New Translation with Introduction and Commentary* (The Anchor Bible) (New York: Doubleday).

Meyers, Eric M. (ed.). 1997. *The Oxford Encyclopedia of Archaeology in the Near East*, Vols. 1–5 (New York: Oxford University Press).

Meyers, Eric M. 1997. "Avigad, Nahman," in E. M. Meyers (ed.), *The Oxford Encyclopedia of Archaeology in the Near East, Vol. 1* (New York: Oxford University Press), 238.

Michalowski, Piotr. 2000. "Amorites," in D. N. Freedman (ed.), *Eerdmans Dictionary of the Bible* (Grand Rapids, MI: Eerdmans), 55–56.

Mildenberg, Leo. 1979. "Yehud: A Preliminary Study of the Provincial Coinage of Judaea," in O. Mørkholm and N. M. Waggoner (eds.), *Greek Numismatics and Archaeology: Essays in Honor of Margaret Thompson* (Wetteren: Éditions NR), 183–96.

Milwright, Marcus. 2016. *The Dome of the Rock and Its Umayyad Mosaic Inscriptions* (Edinburgh: Edinburgh University Press).

Modrzejewski, Joseph M. 1997. *The Jews of Egypt: From Rameses II to Emperor Hadrian* (Princeton, NJ: Princeton University Press).

Montefiore, Simon S. 2011. *Jerusalem: The Biography* (London: Weidenfeld and Nicolson).

Moorey, Peter Roger Stuart 1991. *A Century of Biblical Archaeology* (Cambridge: Lutterworth).

Moorey, Peter Roger Stuart 1997. "Robert William Hamilton 1905–1995," *Proceedings of the British Academy* 94: 491–509.

Moorey, Peter Roger Stuart 2003. *Idols of the People: Miniature Images of Clay in the Ancient Near East: The Schweich Lectures of the British Academy 2001* (London: British Academy).

Mor, Menahem. 2003. "The Geographical Scope of the Bar-Kokhba Revolt," in Peter Schaëfer (ed.), *The Bar Kokhba War Reconsidered* (Tübingen: Mohr Siebeck), 107–31.

Moran, William L. (transl. and ed.). 1992. *The Amarna Letters* (Baltimore: Johns Hopkins University Press).

Mourad, Suleiman A., Naomi Koltun-Fromm, and Bedross Der Matossian (eds.). 2019. *Routledge Handbook on Jerusalem* (New York: Routledge).

Mullins, Robert A., and Eli Yannai. 2019. "Late Bronze Age I-*II*," in S. Gitin (ed.), *The Ancient Pottery of Israel and Its Neighbors from the Middle Bronze Age Through the Late Bronze Age, Volume 3* (Jerusalem: Israel Exploration Society), 151–257.

Murphy O'Connor, Jerome. 1994. "The Location of the Capitol in Aelia Capitolina," *Revue Biblique* 101–3: 407–15.

Murphy O'Connor, Jerome. 1997. "Vincent, Louis-Hugues," in E. M. Meyers (ed.), *The Oxford Encyclopedia of Archaeology in the Near East, Vol. 5* (New York: Oxford University Press), 303–4.

Murphy O'Connor, Jerome. 2005. "Review of E. Mazar, *The Temple Mount Excavations in Jerusalem 1968–1978, Volume II*," *Revue Biblique* 112: 126–30.

Murphy O'Connor, Jerome. 2012a. *Keys to Jerusalem* (Oxford: Oxford University Press).

Murphy O'Connor, Jerome. 2012b. "Recensions: '*Sainte-Anne de Jérusalem. La Piscine Probatique de Jésus à Saladin. Le Projet Béthesda (1994–2010)*,' ed. C. Dauphin (Spécial de *Proche-Orient Chrétien* 2011)," *Revue Biblique* 119.3: 429–433.

Na'aman, Nadav. 1992. "Canaanite Jerusalem and Its Central Hill Country Neighbors in the Second Millennium B.C.E.," *Ugarit Forschungen* 24: 275–91.

Na'aman, Nadav. 2016. "A Violation of Royal Prerogative: The Shebna Prophecy (Isaiah 22.15–19) in Context," *Journal for the Study of the Old Testament* 40.4: 451–65.

Nagar, Yossi. 2002. "Human Skeletal Remains from the Mamilla Cave, Jerusalem," '*Atiqot* 43: 141–48.

Necipoğlu, Gülru. 2008. "The Dome of the Rock as Palimpsest: 'Abd al-Malik's Grand Narrative and Sultan Süleyman's Glosses," *Muqarnas* 25: 17–105.

Nees, Lawrence. 2016. *Perspectives on Early Islamic Art in Jerusalem* (Leiden: Brill).

Netzer, Ehud. 2001. *Hasmonean and Herodian Palaces at Jericho: Final Reports of the 1973–1987 Excavations. Volume I: Stratigraphy and Architecture* (Jerusalem: Israel Exploration Society).

Netzer, Ehud. 2006. *The Architecture of Herod, the Great Builder* (Tübingen: Mohr Siebeck).

Netzer, Ehud. 2018. *The Palaces of the Hasmoneans and Herod the Great: Reprinted and Expanded Edition* (Jerusalem: Israel Exploration Society).

Neusner, Jacob. 2003. *Rabbinic Narrative: A Documentary Perspective, Volume IV: The Precedent and the Parable in Diachronic View* (Leiden: Brill).

Neuwirth, Angelika. 2021. "*Al-masjid al-aqṣā*–The Qur'anic New Jerusalem," in K. Heyden and M. Lissek with A. Kaufmann (eds.), *Jerusalem II: Jerusalem in Roman-Byzantine Times* (Tübingen: Mohr Siebeck), 435–57.

Nickelsburg, George W. E. 2005. *Jewish Literature Between the Bible and the Mishnah* (Minneapolis: Fortress [second edition]).

Onn, Alexander, and Shlomit Weksler-Bdolah. 2010. "Wilson's Arch and the Great Causeway in the Second Temple and Roman Periods in Light of Recent Excavations," *Qadmoniot* 149: 109–22 (in Hebrew).

Onn, Alexander, and Shlomit Weksler-Bdolah. 2016. "Jerusalem, The Western Wall Tunnels," *Hadashot Arkheologiyot* 128, at https://www.hadashot-esi.org.il/report_detail_eng.aspx?id=25120&mag_id=124 (accessed on 8 April 2021).

Onn, Alexander, and Shlomit Weksler-Bdolah. 2019. "Wilson's Arch and the Giant Viaduct West of the Temple Mount During the Second Temple and Late Roman Periods in Light of Recent Excavation," in H. Geva (ed.), *Ancient Jerusalem Revealed: Archaeological Discoveries, 1998–2018* (Jerusalem: Israel Exploration Society), 104–22.

Onn, Alexander, Shlomit Weksler-Bdolah, and Rachel Bar-Nathan. 2011. "Jerusalem, The Old City, Wilson's Arch and the Great Causeway, Preliminary Report," *Hadashot Arkheologiyot* 123, at https://www.hadashot-esi.org.il/report_detail_eng.aspx?id=1738&mag_id=118 (accessed on 8 April 2021).

Onn, Alexander, Shlomit Weksler-Bdolah, and Joseph Patrich. 2016. "A Herodian Triclinium with Fountain Along the Road Leading to the Temple Mount," *Qadmoniot* 151 (2016): 39–48 (in Hebrew).

Onn, Alexander, Shlomit Weksler-Bdolah, and Joseph Patrich. 2019. "A Herodian Triclinium with Fountain on the Road Ascending to the Temple Mount from the West," in H. Geva (ed.), *Ancient Jerusalem Revealed: Archaeological Discoveries, 1998–2018* (Jerusalem: Israel Exploration Society), 123–35.

Ousterhout, Robert. 1990. "The Temple, the Sepulchre, and the Martyrion of the Savior," *Gesta* 29.1: 44–53.

Patrich, Joseph. 1993. "The Early Church of the Holy Sepulchre in the Light of Excavations and Restoration," in Y. Tsafrir (ed.), *Ancient Churches Revealed* (Jerusalem: Israel Exploration Society), 101–17.

Patrich, Joseph. 2002. "Herod's Theater in Jerusalem–A New Proposal," *Israel Exploration Journal* 52.2: 231–39.

Patrich, Joseph. 2009. "538–70 CE: The Temple (*Beyt Ha-Miqdash*) and Its Mount," in O. Grabar and B. Z. Kedar (eds.), *Where Heaven and Earth Meet: Jerusalem's Sacred Esplanade* (Austin: University of Texas Press), 36–71.

Patrich, Joseph. 2011. "The Location of the Second Temple and the Layout of Its Courts, Gates, and Chambers: A New Proposal," in K. Galor and G. Avni (eds.), *Unearthing Jerusalem: 150 Years of Archaeological Research in the Holy City* (Winona Lake, IN: Eisenbrauns), 205–29.

Patrich, Joseph. 2016. "An Overview on the Archaeological Work in the Church of the Holy Sepulchre," in D. Vieweger and Shimon Gibson (eds.), *The Archaeology and History of the Church of the Redeemer and the Muristan in Jerusalem: A Collection of Essays from a Workshop on the Church of the Redeemer and Its Vicinity Held on 8th/9th September 2014 in Jerusalem* (Oxford: Archaeopress), 139–61.

Patrich, Joseph. 2020. "The Temple and Its Mount: Location and Layout," in I. Gafni, R. Reich, and J. Schwartz (eds.), *The History of Jerusalem: The Second Temple Period 332–70 CE, Volume One* (Jerusalem: Yad Izhak Ben-Zvi), 263–326 (in Hebrew).

Patrich, Joseph, Jonathan Devor, and Roy Albag. 2021. *"Awake, Why Sleepest Thou, O Lord? Arise, Cast Us Not Off for Ever"* (Ps. 44: 24): On Jerusalem Temple Orientation, Inauguration and the Sunrise," in S. E. Binder, E. Ratzon, Y. Shivtiel (eds.), *TE'UDA XXXII–XXXIII: "A Work of Wisdom" (Exod. XXXII–XXXIII 35:33). Studies in Honor of Professor Bezalel Bar-Kochva, Part A*, 339–372 (in Hebrew).

Patrich, Joseph, and Marcos Edelcopp. 2013. "Four Stages in the Evolution of the Temple Mount," *Revue Biblique* 120–3: 321–61.

Patterson, John. 2000. "Living and Dying in the City of Rome: Houses and Tombs," in J. Coulston and H. Dodge (eds.), *Ancient Rome: The Archaeology of the Eternal City* (Oxford: Oxford University School of Archaeology Monograph 54), 259–89.

Peleg-Barkat, Orit. 2017. *The Temple Mount Excavations in Jerusalem 1968–1978 Directed by Benjamin Mazar, Final Reports Volume V: Herodian Architectural Decoration and King Herod's Royal Portico* (Qedem 57) (Jerusalem: The Hebrew University).

Peters, Francis E. 1985. *Jerusalem: The Holy City in the Eyes of Chroniclers, Visitors, Pilgrims, and Prophets* (Princeton, NJ: Princeton University Press).

Peters, Francis E. 2011. "Where Three Roads Meet: Jewish, Christian, and Muslim Pilgrimage to Jerusalem," in K. Galor and G. Avni (eds.), *Unearthing Jerusalem: 150 Years of Archaeological Research in the Holy City* (Winona Lake, IN: Eisenbrauns), 1–19.

Piccirillo, Michele, and Eugenio Alliata (eds.). 1999. *The Madaba Map Centenary, 1897–1997: Travelling Through the Byzantine Umayyad Period. Proceedings of the International Conference Held in Amman, 7–9 April 1997* (Jerusalem: Studium Biblicum Franciscanum).

Pitard, Wayne T. 1998. "Before Israel: Syria-Palestine in the Bronze Age," in M. D. Coogan (ed.), *The Oxford History of the Biblical World* (New York: Oxford University Press), 33–77.

Pixner, Bargil. 1989. "The History of the 'Essene Gate' Area," *Zeitschrift des Deutschen Palästina-Vereins* 105: 96–104.

Pixner, Bargil. 1997. "Jerusalem's Essene Gateway: Where the Community Lived in Jesus's Time," *Biblical Archaeology Review* 23.3: 22–31, 64–66.

Pixner, Bargil, and Doron Chen. 1989. "Mt. Zion: The 'Gate of the Essenes' Re-excavated," *Zeitschrift des Deutschen Palästina-Vereins* 105: 85–95.

Prag, Kay. 1992. "Kathleen Kenyon and Archaeology in the Holy Land," *Palestine Exploration Quarterly* 124.2: 109–23.

Prag, Kay. 2008. *Excavations by K. M. Kenyon in Jerusalem 1961–1967. V: Discoveries in Hellenistic to Ottoman Jerusalem* (Oxford: Oxbow).

Prag, Kay. 2017. *Excavations by K. M. Kenyon in Jerusalem 1961–1967. VI: Sites on the Edge of the Ophel* (Oxford: Oxbow).

Prag, Kay. 2018. *Re-Excavating Jerusalem: Archival Archaeology* (Oxford: Oxford University Press).

Prawer, Joshua. 1972. *The Latin Kingdom of Jerusalem: European Colonialism in the Middle Ages* (London: Weidenfeld and Nicolson).

Prawer, Joshua. 1988. *The History of the Jews in the Latin Kingdom of Jerusalem* (Oxford: Clarendon).

Prawer, Joshua. 1996. "Christian Attitudes Towards Jerusalem in the Early Middle Ages," in J. Prawer and H. Ben-Shammai (eds.), *The History of Jerusalem: The Early Muslim Period, 638–1099* (Jerusalem: Yad Izhak Ben-Zvi), 311–48.

Prawer, Joshua, and Haggai Ben-Shammai (eds.). 1996. *The History of Jerusalem: The Early Muslim Period, 638–1099* (Jerusalem: Yad Izhak Ben-Zvi).

Press, Michael. 2021. "The Myth of Moses Shapira," *Ancient Jew Review* at https://www.ancientjewreview.com/read/2021/8/31/the-myth-of-moses-shapira (accessed 16 October 2021).

Pritchard, James B. 1955. *Ancient Near Eastern Texts Relating to the Old Testament with Supplement* (Princeton, NJ: Princeton University Press).

Pullan, Wendy, Maximilian Sternberg, Lefkos Kyriacou, Craig Larkin, and Michael Dumper. 2013. *The Struggle for Jerusalem's Holy Places* (New York: Routledge).

Raban-Gerstel, Noa, Nuha Agha, Lidar Sapir-Hen, and Guy Bar-Oz. 2015. "The Dog Burials: Zooarchaeological, Taphonomic, and Pathological Analysis," in E. Mazar (ed.), *The Summit of the City of David Excavations 2005–2008: Final Reports Vol. I* (Jerusalem: Shoham Academic Research and Publication), 486–96.

Rabbat, Nasser. 1989. "The Meaning of the Umayyad Dome of the Rock," *Muqarnas* 6: 12–21.

Raby, Julian. 1999. "In Vitro Veritas: Glass Pilgrim Vessels from 7th-Century Jerusalem," in J. Johns (ed.), *Bayt al-Maqdis: Jerusalem and Early Islam, Oxford Studies in Islamic Art IX. Part Two* (Oxford: Oxford University Press), 113–90.

Rahmani, Levy Yitzhak. 1967. "Jason's Tomb," *Israel Exploration Journal* 17.2: 61–100.

Rahmani, Levy Yitzhak. 1981a. "Ancient Jerusalem's Funerary Customs and Tombs, Part One," *Biblical Archaeologist* 44.3: 171–77.

Rahmani, Levy Yitzhak. 1981b. "Ancient Jerusalem's Funerary Customs and Tombs, Part Two," *Biblical Archaeologist* 44.4: 229–35.

Rahmani, Levy Yitzhak. 1982. "Ancient Jerusalem's Funerary Customs and Tombs, Part Three," *Biblical Archaeologist* 45.1: 43–53.

Rahmani, Levy Yitzhak. 1994. *A Catalogue of Jewish Ossuaries in the Collections of the State of Israel* (Jerusalem: Israel Antiquities Authority).

Rappaport, Uriel. 1984. "Numismatics," in W. D. Davies and L. Finkelstein (eds.), *The Cambridge History of Judaism, Volume I: Introduction: The Persian Period* (New York: Cambridge University Press), 25–59.

Redmount, Carol A. 1998. "Bitter Lives: Israel in and out of Egypt," in M. D. Coogan (ed.), *The Oxford History of the Biblical World* (New York: Oxford University Press), 79–121.

Re'em, Amit. 2018. *The Qishle Excavation in the Old City of Jerusalem* (Jerusalem: Israel Exploration Society).

Re'em, Amit. 2019. "First and Second Temple Period Fortifications and Herod's Palace in the Jerusalem Kishle Compound," in H. Geva (ed.), *Ancient Jerusalem Revealed: Archaeological Discoveries, 1998–2018* (Jerusalem: Israel Exploration Society), 136–44.

Re'em, Amit, Ghaleb Abu Diab, Jacques Neguer, Yossi Nagar, Elisabetta Boaretto, and Yana Tchekhanovets. 2021. "New Archaeological Study of the Armenian 'Birds Mosaic' Chapel in Jerusalem," in Y. Zeilinger, O. Peleg-Barkat, J. Uziel, and Y. Gadot (eds.), *New Studies in the Archaeology of Jerusalem and Its Region, Collected Papers, Volume XIV* (Jerusalem: Israel Antiquities Authority), 119*–40*.

Regev, Johanna, Joe Uziel, Tehillah Lieberman, Avi Solomon, Yuval Gadot, Doron Ben-Ami, Lior Regev, and Elisabetta Boaretto. 2020. "Radiocarbon Dating and Microarchaeology Untangle the History of Jerusalem's Temple Mount: A View from Wilson's Arch," *Plos One*: 1–17, at https://journals.plos.org/plosone/article?id=10.1371/journal.pone.0233307.

Regev, Johanna, Joe Uziel, Nahshon Szanton, and Elisabetta Boaretto. 2017. "Absolute Dating of the Gihon Spring Fortifications, Jerusalem," *Radiocarbon* 59.4: 1171–93.

Reich, Ronny. 1994. "The Ancient Burial Ground in the Mamilla Neighborhood," in H. Geva (ed.), *Ancient Jerusalem Revealed* (Jerusalem: Israel Exploration Society), 111–18.

Reich, Ronny. 1996. "God Knows Their Names, Mass Christian Grave Revealed in Jerusalem," *Biblical Archaeology Review* 22.2: 26–33, 60.

Reich, Ronny. 1997. "Weill, Raymond," in E. M. Meyers (ed.), *The Oxford Encyclopedia of Archaeology in the Near East, Vol. 5* (New York: Oxford University Press), 342–43.

Reich, Ronny. 2004. "Raymond Weill's Excavations in the City of David (1913–1914): A Reassessment," in H. Shanks (ed.), *The City of David: Revisiting Early Excavations* (Washington, DC: Biblical Archaeology Society), 123–52.

Reich, Ronny. 2006. "Stone Scale Weights of the Late Second Temple Period from the Jewish Quarter," in H. Geva (ed.), *Jewish Quarter Excavations in the Old City of Jerusalem Conducted by Nahman Avigad, 1969–1982, Vol. III* (Jerusalem: Israel Exploration Society), 329–88.

Reich, Ronny. 2011a. *Excavating the City of David: Where Jerusalem's History Began* (Jerusalem: Israel Exploration Society).

Reich, Ronny. 2011b. "The Israel Exploration Society (IES)," in K. Galor and G. Avni (eds.), *Unearthing Jerusalem: 150 Years of Archaeological Research in the Holy City* (Winona Lake, IN: Eisenbrauns), 117–24.

Reich, Ronny. 2013. *Miqwa'ot (Jewish Ritual Baths) in the Second Temple, Mishnaic and Talmudic Periods* (Jerusalem: Yad Yitzhak Ben-Zvi) (in Hebrew).

Reich, Ronny. 2015. "The Construction and Destruction of Robinson's Arch at the Temple Mount in Jerusalem," *Eretz-Israel 31* (Ehud Netzer Volume) (Jerusalem: Israel Exploration Society, 2015), 398–407 (in Hebrew with English summary on 195*).

Reich, Ronny. 2018. "The Date of the Gihon Spring Tower in Jerusalem," *Tel Aviv* 45: 114–19.

Reich, Ronny. 2021a. "The Cultic and Secular Use of Water in Roman and Byzantine Jerusalem," in K. Heyden and M. Lissek with A. Kaufmann (eds.), *Jerusalem II: Jerusalem in Roman-Byzantine Times* (Tübingen: Mohr Siebeck), 243–64.

Reich, Ronny. 2021b. "Excavations in the City of David," in Ronny Reich and Eli Shukron (eds.), *Excavations in the City of David: Jerusalem (1995–2010), Areas A, J, F, H, D and L, Final Report* (University Park, PA: Eisenbrauns), 21–64.

Reich, Ronny. 2021c. "A Moment in Which to Be Born," in Ronny Reich and Eli Shukron (eds.), *Excavations in the City of David: Jerusalem (1995–2010), Areas A, J, F, H, D and L, Final Report* (University Park, PA: Eisenbrauns), 3–20.

Reich, Ronny, and Yaacov Billig. 1998. "Jerusalem. Robinson's Arch. The Jerusalem Archaeological Park of the Second Temple Period," *Excavations and Surveys in Israel* 18: 88–90.

Reich, Ronny, and Yaacov Billig. 2000. "Excavations near the Temple Mount and Robinson's Arch, 1994–1996," in H. Geva (ed.), *Ancient Jerusalem Revealed* (Jerusalem: Israel Exploration Society), 340–52.

Reich, Ronny, and Eli Shukron. 1999. "Light at the End of the Tunnel, Warren's Shaft Theory of David's Conquest Shattered," *Biblical Archaeology Review* 25.1: 22–33, 72.

Reich, Ronny, and Eli Shukron. 2002. "Reconsidering the Karstic Theory as an Explanation to the Cutting of Hezekiah's Tunnel in Jerusalem," *Bulletin of the American Schools of Oriental Research* 325: 75–80.

Reich, Ronny, and Eli Shukron. 2003. "The Jerusalem City-Dump in the Late Second Temple Period," *Zeitschrift des Deutschen Palästina-Vereins* 119: 12–18.

Reich, Ronny, and Eli Shukron. 2004. "The History of the Gihon Spring in Jerusalem," *Levant* 36: 211–23.

Reich, Ronny, and Eli Shukron. 2011a. "The Date of the Siloam Tunnel Inscription," *Tel Aviv* 38.2 (2011): 147–57.

Reich, Ronny, and Eli Shukron. 2011b. "Excavations in Jerusalem beneath the Paved Street and in the Sewage Channel next to Robinson's Arch," *Qadmoniot* 142: 66–73 (in Hebrew).

Reich, Ronny, and Eli Shukron. 2011c. "The Pool of Siloam in Jerusalem of the Late Second Temple Period and Its Surroundings," in K. Galor and G. Avni (eds.), *Unearthing Jerusalem: 150 Years of Archaeological Research in the Holy City* (Winona Lake, IN: Eisenbrauns), 241–55.

Reich, Ronny, and Eli Shukron. 2019. "The Second Temple Period Siloam Pool," in H. Geva (ed.), *Ancient Jerusalem Revealed: Archaeological Discoveries, 1998–2018* (Jerusalem: Israel Exploration Society), 73–83.

Reich, Ronny, and Eli Shukron. 2021a. *Excavations in the City of David: Jerusalem (1995–2010), Areas A, J, F, H, D and L, Final Report* (University Park, PA: Eisenbrauns).

Reich, Ronny, and Eli Shukron. 2021b. "Area F, Stratigraphy and Architecture," in Ronny Reich and Eli Shukron (eds.), *Excavations in the City of David: Jerusalem (1995–2010), Areas A, J, F, H, D and L, Final Report* (University Park, PA: Eisenbrauns), 267–364.

Reich, Ronny, and Eli Shukron. 2021c. "Area J, Stratigraphy and Architecture," in Ronny Reich and Eli Shukron (eds.), *Excavations in the City of David: Jerusalem (1995–2010), Areas A, J, F, H, D and L, Final Report* (University Park, PA: Eisenbrauns), 171–214.

Reich, Ronny, and Eli Shukron. 2021d. "Synthesis and Summary," in Ronny Reich and Eli Shukron (eds.), *Excavations in the City of David: Jerusalem (1995–2010), Areas A, J, F, H, D and L, Final Report* (University Park, PA: Eisenbrauns), 663–93.

Reich, Ronny, Eli Shukron, and Omri Lernau. 2007. "Recent Discoveries in the City of David, Jerusalem," *Israel Exploration Journal* 57.2: 153–69.

Reich, Ronny, Eli Shukron, and Omri Lernau. 2019. "Recent Discoveries in the City of David," in H. Geva (ed.), *Ancient Jerusalem Revealed: Archaeological Discoveries, 1998–2018* (Jerusalem: Israel Exploration Society), 32–44.

Reiner, Elchanan. 1999. "Jews in the Crusader Kingdom of Jerusalem" in S. Rozenberg (ed.), *Knights of the Holy Land: The Crusader Kingdom of Jerusalem* (Jerusalem: Israel Museum), 49–59.

Renard, Heinrich. 1900. "Die Marienkirchen auf dem Brege Sion in ihrem Zusammenhung mit dem Abendmahlssaale," *Das Heilige Land* 44: 3–23.

Rendsburg, Gary A., and William M. Schniedewind. 2010. "The Siloam Tunnel Inscription: Historical and Linguistic Perspectives," *Israel Exploration Journal* 60.2: 188–203.

Reuven, Peretz. 2007. "A Statue of an Eagle with a Medallion Containing a Monogram Found on the Temple Mount," in J. Aviram, D. Bahat, G. Barkay, Y. Ben-Arieh, and M. Broshi (eds.), *Eretz-Israel: Archaeological, Historical and Geographical Studies 28* (Jerusalem: Israel Exploration Society), 206–10 (in Hebrew with English summary on pp. 16*-17*).

Reuven, Peretz. 2011. "A Comparison of the Temple Mount Compound with Other Sacred Precincts from the Classical Period," in E. Mazar (ed.), *The Walls of the Temple Mount* (Jerusalem: Shoham Academic Research and Publication), 289–91.

Reuven, Peretz. 2013. "Wooden Beams from Herod's Temple Mount: Do They Still Exist?," *Biblical Archaeology Review* 39.3: 40–47.

Reuven, Peretz, and Yiftaḥ Shalev. 2011. "The Pilasters in the Temple Mount Walls," in E. Mazar (ed.), *The Walls of the Temple Mount* (Jerusalem: Shoham Academic Research and Publication), 293–302.

Richardson, Peter. 1999. *Herod, King of the Jews and Friend of the Romans* (Minneapolis: Fortress).

Richey, Madadh. 2022. "Review of Idan Dershowitz, *The Valediction of Moses: A Proto-Biblical Book* (Tübingen: Mohr Siebeck, 2021)," *AJS Review* 46.2: 405–7.

Riesner, Rainer. 1989. "Josephus' 'Gate of the Essenes' in Modern Discussion," *Zeitschrift des Deutschen Palästina-Vereins* 105: 105–9.

Ristau, Kenneth A. 2016. *Reconstructing Jerusalem: Persian-Period Prophetic Perspectives* (Winona Lake, IN: Eisenbrauns).

Ritmeyer, Leen. 2006. *The Quest: Revealing the Temple Mount in Jerusalem* (Jerusalem: Carta).

Ritmeyer, Kathleen, and Leen Ritmeyer. 1989a. "Reconstructing Herod's Temple Mount in Jerusalem," *Biblical Archaeology Review* 15.6: 23–42.

Ritmeyer, Kathleen, and Leen Ritmeyer. 1989b. "Reconstructing the Triple Gate," *Biblical Archaeology Review* 15.6: 49–53.

Rives, James B. 1995. *Religion and Authority in Roman Carthage from Augustus to Constantine* (Oxford: Clarendon).

Robinson, Edward. 1856. *Later Biblical Researches in Palestine and in the Adjacent Regions* (New York: Arno).

Robinson, Edward, and Eli Smith. 1841. *Biblical Researches in Palestine, Mount Sinai and Arabia Petraea: A Journal of Travels in the Year 1838* (Boston: Crocker & Brewster).

Rogers, Guy Maclean. 2021. *For the Freedom of Zion: The Great Revolt of Jews Against Romans, 66–74 CE* (New Haven, CT: Yale University Press).

Rollston, Chris A. 2000. "Mesha," in D. N. Freedman (ed.), *Eerdmans Dictionary of the Bible* (Grand Rapids, MI: Eerdmans), 887–88.

Rosen-Ayalon, Myriam. 1989. *The Early Islamic Monuments of al-haram al-sharīf: An Iconographic Study* (Qedem 28) (Jerusalem: The Hebrew University).

Rosen-Ayalon, Myriam. 1996. "Art and Architecture in Jerusalem in the Early Islamic Period," in J. Prawer and H. Ben-Shammai (eds.), *The History of Jerusalem: The Early Muslim Period, 638–1099* (Jerusalem: Yad Izhak Ben-Zvi), 386–412.

Rosenthal-Heginbottom, Renate. 2014. "Dating the Jerusalem Rilled-Rim and Arched-Rim Basins," in N. Poulou-Papadimitriou, E. Nodarou, and V. Kilikoglou (eds.), *LRCW 4, Late Roman Coarse Wares, Cooking Wares and Amphorae in the Mediterranean. Archaeology and Archaeometry, The Mediterranean: A Market Without Frontiers* (Oxford: BAR International Series 2616[I]), 657–64.

Rosenthal-Heginbottom, Renate. 2015. "The Kiln Works of the *Legio Decima Fretensis*: Pottery Production and Distribution," in L. Vagalinski and N. Sharankov (eds.), *Limes XXII: Proceedings of the International Congress of Roman Frontier Studies* (Sofia: National Archaeological Institute), 611–17.

Rosenthal-Heginbottom, Renate. 2017. "Selected Pottery from the Late Second Temple Period and Aelia Capitolina from Area F-6," in H. Geva (ed.), *Jewish Quarter Excavations in the Old City of Jerusalem Conducted by Nahman Avigad, 1969–1982, Vol. VII* (Jerusalem: Israel Exploration Society), 284–351.

Rosenthal-Heginbottom, Renate. 2019. *Jerusalem: Western Wall Plaza Excavations Volume II: The Pottery from the Eastern Cardo* (IAA Reports No. 64) (Jerusalem: Israel Antiquities Authority).

Runciman, Steven. 1935. "Charlemagne and Palestine," *The English Historical Review* 50: 606–19.

Runciman, Steven. 1971. *A History of the Crusades 2: The Kingdom of Jerusalem* (Harmondsworth: Penguin).

Sapir-Hen, Lidar, Joe Uziel, and Ortal Chalaf. 2021. "Everything but the Oink: On the Discovery of an Articulated Pig in Iron Age Jerusalem and Its Meaning to Judahite Consumption Practices," *Near Eastern Archaeology* 84.2: 110–19.

Savignac, Raphaël P. 1904. "Inscription romaine et sépultures áu nord de Jérusalem," *Revue Biblique* 1.1: 90–98.

Schäfer, Peter (ed.). 2003. *The Bar Kokhba War Reconsidered* (Tübingen: Mohr Siebeck, 2003).

Scheck, Thomas P. (transl.). 2008. *St. Jerome: Commentary on Matthew* (Washington, DC: Catholic University of America Press).

Scheck, Thomas P. (transl.). 2015. *St. Jerome: Commentary on Isaiah, Including St. Jerome's Translation of Origen's Homilies 1–9 on Isaiah* (New York: The Newman Press).

Schick, Conrad. 1878. "Die Vasserversorgung der Stadt Jerusalem," *Zeitschift des Deutschen Palästina-Vereins* 1: 132–76.

Schick, Conrad. 1882. "Newly Found Figure Found in the Haram Wall," *Palestine Exploration Fund Quarterly Statement*: 171.

Schick, Conrad, and Frederick J. Bliss. 1894. "Discovery of a Beautiful Mosaic Pavement with Armenian Inscription, North of Jerusalem," *Palestine Exploration Quarterly* 26.4: 257–61.

Schick, Robert. 1995. *The Christian Communities of Palestine from Byzantine to Islamic Rule: A Historical and Archaeological Study* (Princeton, NJ: The Darwin Press).

Schiffman, Lawrence H. 2008. *The Courtyards of the House of the Lord: Studies on the Temple Scroll* (ed. F. García Martínez; Leiden: Brill).

Schiffman, Lawrence H., and Andrew D. Gross. 2021. *The Temple Scroll 11Q19, 11Q20, 11Q21, 4Q524, 5Q21 with 4Q365a and 4Q365 frag. 23* (Leiden: Brill).

Schürer, Emil. 1973–1986. *The History of the Jews in the Age of Jesus Christ, Vols. 1–3* (rev. and ed. G. Vermes, F. Millar, and M. Goodman; Edinburgh: T & T Clark).

Schwartz, Daniel R. 1992. *Studies in the Jewish Background of Christianity* (Wissenschaftliche Unterschungen zum Neuen Testament 60) (Mohr Siebeck: Tübingen).

Schwartz, Daniel R. 2006. "'Stone House,' Birah, and Antonia During the Time of Jesus," in J. H. Charlesworth (ed.), *Jesus and Archaeology* (Grand Rapids, MI: Eerdmans), 341–48.

Schwartz, Joshua. 1996. "The Temple in Jerusalem, Birah and Baris in Archaeology and Literature," in M. Poorthuis and Ch. Safrai (eds.), *The Centrality of Jerusalem: Historical Perspectives* (Kampen, The Netherlands: Kok Pharos), 28–49.

Schwartz, Joshua. 2004. "Dogs in Jewish Society in the Second Temple Period and in the Time of the Mishnah and Talmud," *Journal of Jewish Studies* 55.2: 246–77.

Schwartz, Joshua. 2010. "Bar Qatros and the Priestly Families of Jerusalem," in H. Geva (ed.), *Jewish Quarter Excavations in the Old City of Jerusalem Conducted by Nahman Avigad, 1969–1982. Volume IV: The Burnt House of Area B and Other Studies, Final Report* (Jerusalem: Israel Exploration Society), 308–19.

Segal, Arthur. 1997. *From Function to Monument: Urban Landscapes of Roman Palestine, Syria and Provincia Arabia* (Oxford: Oxbow).

Seligman, Jon. 2011. "The Departments of Antiquities and the Israel Antiquities Authority (1918–2006): The Jerusalem Experience," in K. Galor and G. Avni (eds.), *Unearthing Jerusalem: 150 Years of Archaeological Research in the Holy City* (Winona Lake, IN: Eisenbrauns), 125–46.

Seligman, Jon. 2017. "'Absence of Evidence' or 'Evidence of Absence'? Where was Civilian *Aelia Capitolina*, and was Jerusalem the Site of the Legionary Camp?," in G. Avni and G. S. Stiebel (eds.), *Roman Jerusalem: A New Old City* (Portsmouth, RI: Journal of Roman Archaeology Supplementary Series Number 105), 107–16.

Seligman, Jon. 2021. "The Economy of Jerusalem from the Second to Seventh Centuries," in K. Heyden and M. Lissek with A. Kaufmann (eds.), *Jerusalem II: Jerusalem in Roman-Byzantine Times* (Tübingen: Mohr Siebeck), 225–42.

Seligman, Jon, and Gideon Avni. 2019. "New Excavations and Studies in the Holy Sepulcher Compound," in H. Geva (ed.), *Ancient Jerusalem Revealed: Archaeological Discoveries, 1998–2018* (Jerusalem: Israel Exploration Society), 238–46.

Sellers, Ovid R. 1961. "Louis-Hugues Vincent," *The Biblical Archaeologist* 24.2: 62–64.

Shadmi, Tamar. 1996. "The Ossuaries and the Sarcophagus," in G. Avni and Z. Greenhut (eds.), *The Akeldama Tombs: Three Burial Caves in the Kidron Valley, Jerusalem* (IAA Reports No. 1; Jerusalem, Israel Antiquities Authority), 41–55.

Shalev, Yiftah, Nitsan Shalom, Efrat Bocher, and Yuval Gadot. 2020. "New Evidence on the Location and Nature of Iron Age, Persian and Early Hellenistic Period Jerusalem," *Tel Aviv* 47: 149–72.

Shalev, Yiftah, David Gellman, Efrat Bocher, Liora Freud, Naomi Porat, and Yuval Gadot. 2019. "The Fortifications Along the Western Slope of the City of David: A New Perspective," in O. Peleg, Y. Zelinger, Y. Uziel, and Y. Gadot (eds.), *New Studies in the Archaeology of Jerusalem and Its Region* 13 (Jerusalem: Israel Antiquities Authority), 51–70 (in Hebrew).

Shalev, Yiftah, Efrat Bocher, Helena Roth, Débora Sandhaus, Nitsan Shalom, and Yuval Gadot. 2021. "Jerusalem in the Early Hellenistic Period: New Evidence for Its Nature and Location," in A. M. Berlin and P. J. Kosmin (eds.), *The Middle Maccabees: Archaeology, History, and the Rise of the Hasmonean Kingdom* (Atlanta: SBL Press), 17–36.

Shalev-Hurvitz, Vered. 2015. *Holy Sites Encircled: The Early Byzantine Concentric Churches of Jerusalem* (New York: Oxford University Press).

Shanks, Hershel (ed.). 2004. *The City of David: Revisiting Early Excavations, English Translation of Reports by Raymond Weill and L.-H. Vincent, Notes and Comments by Ronny Reich* (Washington, DC: Biblical Archaeology Society).

Shanks, Hershel. 1995. *Jerusalem: An Archaeological Biography* (New York: Random House).

Shapira, Lior, and Orit Peleg. 2003. "Byzantine and Early Islamic Pottery Lamps from the "House of the Menorot" in Area VI," in E. Mazar (ed.), *The Temple Mount Excavations in Jerusalem 1968–1978 Directed by Benjamin Mazar, Final Reports Volume II: The Byzantine and Early Islamic Periods* (Qedem 43) (Jerusalem: The Hebrew University), 187–90.

Sharabi, Lena Naama, Yana Tchekhanovets, and Doron Ben Ami. 2020. "Early Christian Graffiti from Fourth-Century Jerusalem," in A. Coniglio and A. Ricco (eds.), *Holy Land, Archaeology on Either Side: Archaeological Essays in Honor of Eugenio Alliata ofm.* (Jerusalem: Franciscan Printing Press).

Sharon, Moshe. 2009. "Shape of the Holy," *Studia Orientalia* 107: 283–310.

Sheridan, Susan G. 1999. "'New Life the Dead Receive': The Relationship Between Human Remains and the Cultural Record for Byzantine St. Stephen's," *Revue Biblique* 106: 1–38.

Sheridan, Susan G. 2019. "Coming of Age at St. Stephen's: Bioarchaeology of Children at a Byzantine Jerusalem Monastery (5th-7th centuries CE)," in S. Flynn (ed.), *Children in the Bible and Ancient World: Comparative and Historical Methods in Reading Ancient Children* (London: Routledge), 150–94.

Sheridan, Susan G. 2020. "Pious Pain: Repetitive Motion Disorders from Excessive Genuflection at a Byzantine Jerusalem Monastery," in S. G. Sheridan and L. A. Gregoricka (eds.), *Purposeful Pain: The Bioarchaeology of Intentional Suffering* (New York: Springer), 81–117.

Shiloh, Tamar. 1997. "Shiloh, Yigal," in E. M. Meyers (ed.), *The Oxford Encyclopedia of Archaeology in the Near East, Vol. 5* (New York: Oxford University Press), 29–30.

Shiloh, Yigal. 1984. *Excavations at the City of David I, 1978–1982* (Qedem 19) (Jerusalem: The Hebrew University).

Shoemaker, Stephen J. 2012. *The Death of a Prophet: The End of Muhammad's Life and the Beginnings of Islam* (University Park: University of Pennsylvania Press).

Shoshan, Boaz. 2021. "The Islamic Conquest: Continuity and Change," in K. Heyden and M. Lissek with A. Kaufmann (eds.), *Jerusalem II: Jerusalem in Roman-Byzantine Times* (Tübingen: Mohr Siebeck), 459–74.

Silberman, Neil A. 1982. *Digging for God and Country: Exploration in the Holy Land, 1799–1917* (New York: Doubleday).

Silberman, Neil A. 1997. "Clermont-Ganneau, Charles," in E. M. Meyers (ed.), *The Oxford Encyclopedia of Archaeology in the Near East, Vol. 2* (New York: Oxford University Press), 37.

Siecienski, Edward. 2010. *The Filioque: History of a Doctrinal Controversy* (New York: Oxford University Press).

Sievers, Joseph, and Amy-Jill Levine (eds.). 2021. *The Pharisees* (Grand Rapids, MI: Eerdmans).

Simons, Jan. 1952. *Jerusalem in the Old Testament: Researches and Theories* (Leiden: Brill).

Sivan, Hagith. 2021. "The Making of Memory: Jerusalem and Palestinian Jewry in Late Antiquity," in K. Heyden and M. Lissek with A. Kaufmann (eds.), *Jerusalem II: Jerusalem in Roman-Byzantine Times* (Tübingen: Mohr Siebeck), 291–310.

Sivan, Renée, and Giora Solar. 1994. "Excavations in the Jerusalem Citadel, 1980–1988," in H. Geva (ed.), *Ancient Jerusalem Revealed* (Jerusalem: Israel Exploration Society), 168–76.

Smith-Christopher, Daniel L. 2000. "Zerubbabel," in D. N. Freedman (ed.), *Eerdmans Dictionary of the Bible* (Grand Rapids, MI: Eerdmans), 1418–19.

Sneh, Amihai, Ram Weinberger, and Eyal Shalev. 2010. "The Why, How, and When of the Siloam Tunnel Reevaluated," *Bulletin of the American Schools of Oriental Research* 359: 57–65.

Solimany, Gideon, Rafeh Abu Raya and Ronny Reich. 2011. "A Burial Cave from the Early Roman Period on Diskin Street, Jerusalem," `Atiqot 65: 93–103 (in Hebrew with English summary on pp. 71*–72*).

Spiezer, Yosef. Forthcoming. "Re-mapping by GIS of the Course of Jerusalem's Third Wall and the Northeastern Sites Along It," *Israel Exploration Journal*.

Spiciarich, Abra, and Lidar Sapir-Hen. 2022. "Faunal Remains," in Y. Gadot (ed.), *The Landfill of Early Roman Jerusalem: The 2013–2014 Excavations in Area D3* (University Park, PA: Eisenbrauns), 195–233.

Spielman, Loren R. 2020. *Jews and Entertainment in the Ancient World* (Tübingen: Mohr Siebeck).

Stager, Lawrence E. 1982. "The Archaeology of the East Slope of Jerusalem and the Terraces of the Kidron," *Journal of Near Eastern Studies* 41.2: 111–21.

Stager, Lawrence E. 1998. "Forging an Identity: The Emergence of Ancient Israel," in M. D. Coogan (ed.), *The Oxford History of the Biblical World* (New York: Oxford University Press), 123–75.

Stager, Lawrence E. 2008. "Dogs and Healing in Phoenician Ashkelon," in L. E. Stager, J. D. Schloen, and D. M. Master (eds.), *Ashkelon 1: Introduction and Overview (1985–2006)* (Winona Lake, IN: Eisenbrauns), 565–68.

Stahl, Michael J. 2020. "The 'God of Israel' in Judah's Bible: Problems and Prospects," *Journal of Biblical Literature* 139.4: 721–45.

Steiner, Margreet. 1993. *Excavations by Kathleen M. Kenyon in Jerusalem 1961–1967. III: The Settlement in the Bronze and Iron Ages* (London: Sheffield Academic Press).

Steiner, Margreet. 2011. "The Persian Period City Wall of Jerusalem," in I. Finkelstein and N. Na`aman (eds.), *The Fire Signals of Lachish: Studies in the Archaeology and History of Israel in the Late Bronze Age, Iron Age, and Persian Period in Honor of David Ussishkin* (Winona Lake, IN: Eisenbrauns), 307–15.

Stemberger, Gunter. 2006. "Christians and Jews in Byzantine Palestine," in O. Limor and G. Stroumsa (eds.), *Christians and Christianity in the Holy Land: From the Origins to the Latin Kingdoms* (Turnhout, Belgium: Brepols), 239–319.

Stern, Ephraim (ed.). 1993. *The New Encyclopedia of Archaeological Excavations in the Holy Land*, Vols. 1–4 (New York: Simon & Schuster), s.v. "Jerusalem," 698–804.

Stern, Ephraim (ed.). 2008. *The New Encyclopedia of Archaeological Excavations in the Holy Land, Vol. 5* (New York: Simon & Schuster), s.v. "Jerusalem," 1801–37.

Stern, Ephraim. 2015. "Iron Age I-II: Phoenician Pottery," in S. Gitin (ed.), *The Ancient Pottery of Israel and Its Neighbors from the Iron Age Through the Hellenistic Period, Volume 1* (Jerusalem: Israel Exploration Society), 435–82.

Stern, Menahem. 1980. *Greek and Latin Authors on Jews and Judaism: Edited with Introductions, Translations and Commentary, Vols. 1–3* (Jerusalem: Israel Academy of Sciences and Humanities).

Stiebel, Guy D. 1999. "The Whereabouts of the Xth Legion and the Boundaries of Aelia Capitolina," in A. Faust and E. Baruch (eds.), *New Studies on Jerusalem* 5, 68–103 (in Hebrew).

Stiebel, Guy D. 2011a. "Metal Finds from the Temple Mount Excavations," in E. Mazar (ed.), *The Temple Mount Excavations Vol. IV: The Tenth Legion in Aelia Capitolina* (Qedem 52) (Jerusalem: The Hebrew University), 333–45.

Stiebel, Guy D. 2011b. "A Military Die from the Bakery," in E. Mazar (ed.), *The Temple Mount Excavations Vol. IV: The Tenth Legion in Aelia Capitolina* (Qedem 52) (Jerusalem: The Hebrew University), 229–31.

Stiebel, Guy D. 2013. "The Military Equipment," in D. Ben-Ami (ed.), *Jerusalem: Excavations in the Tyropoeon Valley (Giv'ati Parking Lot), Vol. I* (IAA Reports No. 52) (Jerusalem: Israel Antiquities Authority), 297–304.

Stinespring, W. F. 1934. "The Inscription of the Triumphal Arch at Jerash," *Bulletin of the American Schools of Oriental Research* 56: 15–16.

Sukenik, Eleazar Lipa. 1927. "Note on the North Wall of Jerusalem," *Bulletin of the American Schools of Oriental Research* 26: 8–9.

Sukenik, Eleazar Lipa, and Leo Aryeh Mayer. 1930. *The Third Wall of Jerusalem: An Account of Excavations* (Jerusalem: The Hebrew University).

Sukenik, Eleazar Lipa, and Leo Aryeh Mayer. 1944. "A New Section of the Third Wall, Jerusalem," *Palestine Exploration Quarterly* 76.1: 145–51.

Sukenik, Naama, and Orit Shamir. 2018. "Fabric Imprints on the Reverse of Bullae from the Ophel, Area A2009," in E. Mazar (ed.), *The Ophel Excavations to the South of the Temple Mount 2009–2013: Final Reports Volume II* (Jerusalem: Shoham Academic Research and Publication), 281–88.

Syon, Danny. 2021. "The Hasmonean Settlement in Galilee: A Numismatic Perspective," in A. M. Berlin and P. J. Kosmin (eds.), *The Middle Maccabees: Archaeology, History, and the Rise of the Hasmonean Kingdom* (Atlanta: SBL Press), 177–92.

Szanton, Nahshon, and Ayala Zilberstein. 2015. "'The Second Hill, which Bore the Name of Acra, and Supported the Lower City. . .' A New Look at the Lower City of Jerusalem in the End of the Second Temple Period," in E. Meiron (ed.), *City of David Studies of Ancient Jerusalem* 11: 29*–47*.

Szanton, Nahshon, Moran Hagbi, Joe Uziel, and Donald T. Ariel. 2019. "Pontius Pilate in Jerusalem: The Monumental Street from the Siloam Pool to the Temple Mount," *Tel Aviv* 46: 147–66.

Tappy, Ron E. 2015. "Iron Age *IIA*-B: Samaria," in S. Gitin (ed.), *The Ancient Pottery of Israel and Its Neighbors from the Iron Age Through the Hellenistic Period, Volume 1* (Jerusalem: Israel Exploration Society), 189–211.

Taylor, Michelle Ellis. 2000. "Dog," in D. N. Freedman (ed.), *Eerdmans Dictionary of the Bible* (Grand Rapids, MI: Eerdmans), 352.

Tchekhanovets, Yana. 2018. *The Caucasian Archaeology of the Holy Land: Armenian, Georgian and Albanian Communities Between the Fourth and Eleventh Centuries CE* (Leiden: Brill).

Tchekhanovets, Yana. 2022. "Excavations on the Southwestern Margins of Giv`ati Parking Lot, Jerusalem: Markers of Byzantine-Early Islamic Transition," `*Atiqot* 106: 303–38.

Thackeray, Henry St. John (transl.). 1997. *Josephus: The Jewish War, Books 1–2 (Vol. I)* (Cambridge, MA: Harvard University Press) (Loeb Classical Library).

Thackeray, Henry St. John (transl.). 2006. *Josephus: The Jewish War, Books III-VII* (Vols. *II–III*) (Cambridge, MA: Harvard University Press) (Loeb Classical Library).

Thomas, Page A. 1984. "*BA* Portrait: The Success and Failure of Robert Alexander Stewart Macalister," *Biblical Archaeologist* 47.1: 33–35.

Thomson, R. W. 1999. *The Armenian History Attributed to Sebeos, Part I* (Liverpool: Liverpool University Press).

Trampedach, Kai. 2022a. "The Making of the Holy Land in Late Antiquity," in K. M. Klein and J. Wienand (eds.), *City of Caesar, City of God: Constantinople and Jerusalem in Late Antiquity* (Berlin: Walter de Gruyter), 11–38.

Trampedach, Kai. 2022b. "A New Temple of Solomon in Jerusalem? The Construction of the Nea Church (531–543) by Emperor Justinian," in K. M. Klein and J. Wienand (eds.), *City of Caesar, City of God: Constantinople and Jerusalem in Late Antiquity* (Berlin: Walter de Gruyter), 161–81.

Tregelles, Samuel Prideaux. 1857. *Gesenius' Hebrew and Chaldee Lexicon to the Old Testament Scriptures, with Additions and Corrections from the Author's Thesaurus and Other Works* (Grand Rapids, MI: Eerdmans).

Trotter, Jonathan R. 2019. *The Jerusalem Temple in Diaspora Jewish Practice and Thought During the Second Temple Period* (Leiden: Brill).

Trout, Dennis E. 1999. *Paulinus of Nola: Life, Letters, and Poems* (Berkeley: University of California Press).

Tsafrir, Yoram. 1999. "The Holy City of Jerusalem in the Madaba Map," in M. Piccirillo and E. Alliata (eds.), *The Madaba Map Centenary, 1897–1997: Travelling Through the Byzantine Umayyad Period. Proceedings of the International Conference Held in Amman, 7–9 April 1997* (Jerusalem: Studium Biblicum Franciscanum), 155–63.

Tsafrir, Yoram. 2000. "Procopius and the Nea Church in Jerusalem," *Antiquité tardive* 8: 149–64.

Tsafrir, Yoram. 2009. "70–638: The Temple-less Mountain," in O. Grabar and B. Z. Kedar (eds.), *Where Heaven and Earth Meet: Jerusalem's Sacred Esplanade* (Austin: University of Texas Press), 73–99.

Tsafrir, Yoram, Leah Di Segni, and Judith Greene, with contributions by Israel Roll and Tsvika Tsuk. 1994. *Tabula Imperii Romani Iudaea-Palaestina: Eretz-Israel in the Hellenistic, Roman and Byzantine Periods, Map and Gazetteer* (Jerusalem: The Israel Academy of Sciences and Humanities).

Tubb, Jonathan N. 2015. "R. A. S. Macalister: Villain or Visionary?," in Samuel R. Wolff (ed.), *Villain or Visionary: R. A. S. Macalister and the Archaeology of Palestine* (New York: Routledge), 5–19.

Tütken, Thomas, Michael Weber, Irit Zohar, Hassan Helmy, Nicolas Bourgon, Omri Lernau, Klaus Peter Jochum, and Guy Sisma-Ventura. 2021. "Strontium and Oxygen Isotope Analyses Reveal Late Cretaceous Shark Teeth in Iron Age Strata in the Southern Levant," *Frontiers in Ecology and Evolution* doi:10.3389/fevo.2020.570032, at https://www.frontiersin.org/articles/10.3389/fevo.2020.570032/full (accessed 10/11/2021).

Tushingham, A. Douglas. 1985. *Excavations in Jerusalem 1961–1967, Volume I* (Toronto: Royal Ontario Museum).

Tushingham, A. Douglas. 1997. "Kenyon, Kathleen Mary," in E. M. Meyers (ed.), *The Oxford Encyclopedia of Archaeology in the Near East, Vol. 5* (New York: Oxford University Press), 279–80.

Twain, Mark. 1996. *The Innocents Abroad* (New York: Oxford University Press).

Tzaferis, Vassilios. 1985. "Crucifixion–The Archaeological Evidence," *Biblical Archaeology Review* 11.1: 44–53.

Tzaferis, Vassilios, Nurit Feig, Alexander Onn, and Eli Shukron. 1994. "Excavations at the Third Wall, North of the Jerusalem Old City," in H. Geva (ed.), *Ancient Jerusalem Revealed* (Jerusalem: Israel Exploration Society), 287–92.

Ussishkin, David. 1969. "On the Shorter Inscription from the 'Tomb of the Royal Steward,'" *Bulletin of the American Schools of Oriental Research* 196: 16–22.

Ussishkin, David. 1986. *The Village of Silwan: The Necropolis from the Period of the Judean Kingdom* (Jerusalem: Yad Itzhak Ben-Zvi) (in Hebrew).

Ussishkin, David. 2012. "On Nehemiah's City Wall and the Size of Jerusalem During the Persian Period: An Archaeologist's View," in I. Kalimi (ed.), *New Perspectives on Ezra-Nehemiah: History and Historiography, Text, Literature, and Interpretation* (Winona Lake, IN: Eisenbrauns), 101–30.

Ussishkin, David. 2016. "Was Jerusalem a Fortified Stronghold in the Middle Bronze Age?–An Alternative View," *Levant* 48.2: 135–51.

Uziel, Joe, Tehillah Lieberman, and Avi Solomon. 2017. "Two Years of Excavation Beneath Wilson's Arch: New Discoveries and Ponderings," in Y. Gadot et al. (eds.), *New Studies on the Archaeology of Jerusalem and Its Region* 11: 239–61 (in Hebrew).

Uziel, Joe, Tehillah Lieberman, and Avi Solomon. 2019. "The Excavations beneath Wilson's Arch: New Light on Roman Period Jerusalem," *Tel Aviv* 46: 237–66.

Uziel, Joe, and Nahshon Szanton. 2015. "Recent Excavations Near the Gihon Spring and Their Reflection on the Character of Iron *II* Jerusalem," *Tel Aviv* 42: 233–50.

van der Toorn, Karel. 2009. *Scribal Culture and the Making of the Hebrew Bible* (Cambridge, MA: Harvard University Press).

van der Toorn, Karel. 2019. *Becoming Diaspora Jews: Behind the Story of Elephantine* (New Haven, CT: Yale University Press).

Vandier, Jacques. 2004. "An Obituary of Raymond Weill," in H. Shanks (ed.), *The City of David: Revisiting Early Excavations* (Washington, DC: Biblical Archaeology Society), xxix–xxxii.

Vaughn, Andrew G., and Ann E. Killebrew (eds.). 2003. *Jerusalem in Bible and Archaeology: The First Temple Period* (Atlanta: Society of Biblical Literature).

Verhelst, Stéphane. 2006. "The Liturgy of Jerusalem in the Byzantine Period," in O. Limor and G. Stroumsa (eds.), *Christians and Christianity in the Holy Land: From the Origins to the Latin Kingdoms* (Turnhout, Belgium: Brepols), 421–62.

Vilnay, Zev. 1973. *Legends of Jerusalem* (Philadelphia: Jewish Publication Society).

Vincent, Louis-Hugues. 1901. "Chronique: une mosaïque byzantine a Jérusalem," *Revue Biblique* 10.3: 436–44.

Vincent, Louis-Hugues. 1911. *Underground Jerusalem: Discoveries on the Hill of Ophel (1909–11)* (London: Horace Cox).

Vincent, Louis-Hugues. 2004. "Zion and the City of David," in H. Shanks (ed.), *The City of David* (Washington, DC: Biblical Archaeology Society), 157–62.

Vincent, Louis-Hugues, and Félix-Marie Abel. 1914. *Jérusalem: Recherches de topographie, d'archéologie et d'histoire. II: Jérusalem nouvelle, Fasc.1–2* (Paris: Gabalda).

Vincent, Louis-Hugues, and M.-A. Steve. 1954–6. *Jérusalem de l'Ancien Testament* (Paris: Gabalda).

von Wahlde, Urban C. 2006. "Archaeology and John's Gospel," in J. H. Charlesworth (ed.), *Jesus and Archaeology* (Grand Rapids, MI: Eerdmans), 523–86.

Vukosavović, Filip, Ortal Chalaf, and Joe Uziel. 2021. "'And You Counted the Houses of Jerusalem and Pulled Houses Down to Fortify the Wall' (Isaiah 22:10): The Fortifications of Iron Age *II* Jerusalem in Light of New Discoveries in the City of David," in Y. Zelinger et al. (eds.), *New Studies in the Archaeology of Jerusalem and Its Region: Collected Papers, Volume XIV* (Jerusalem: Israel Antiquities Authority), 1*–16*.

Walford, Edward (transl.). 1855. *The Ecclesiastical History of Sozomen: Comprising a History of the Church from A.D. 324 to A.D. 440* (London: Henry G. Bohn).

Walmsley, Alan. 2007. *Early Islamic Syria: An Archaeological Assessment* (London: Bloomsbury).

Wapnish, Paula, and Brian Hesse. 2008. "The Ashkelon Dog Burials: Data and Interpretations," in L. E. Stager, J. D. Schloen, and D. M. Master (eds.), *Ashkelon 1: Introduction and Overview (1985–2006)* (Winona Lake, IN: Eisenbrauns), 541–64.

Warren, Charles. 1876. *Underground Jerusalem* (London: Richard Bentley and Son).

Warren, Charles, and Claude Reignier Conder. 1884. *The Survey of Western Palestine, V: Jerusalem* (London: PEF).

Warren, Charles, and Claude Reignier Conder. 1889. *The Survey of Western Palestine: Memoirs of the Topography, Orography, Hydrography and Archaeology, IV: Jerusalem* (London: PEF).

Watson, C. M. 2013. "Commemoratorium De Casis Dei Vel Monasteriis," *Palestine Exploration Quarterly* 45.1: 23–33.

Weill, Raymond. 1947. *La Cité de David* (Paris: Paul Geuthner).

Weksler-Bdolah, Shlomit. 2006–2007. "The Fortifications of Jerusalem in the Byzantine Period," *ARAM* 18–19: 85–112.

Weksler-Bdolah, Shlomit. 2011. "The Route of the Second Temple Period's 'Lower Aqueduct' and Where it Entered the Temple Mount," *Cathedra* 140: 19–46 (in Hebrew).

Weksler-Bdolah, Shlomit. 2013. "The Fortifications of Jerusalem South of the Pool of Siloam–New Discoveries," in G. D. Stiebel, O. Peleg-Barkat, D. Ben-Ami, S. Weksler-Bdolah, and Y. Gadot (eds.), *New Discoveries in the Archaeology of Jerusalem* 7 (Tel Aviv: Tel Aviv University Press), 171–93 (in Hebrew).

Weksler-Bdolah, Shlomit. 2014. "The Foundation of Aelia Capitolina in Light of New Excavations Along the Eastern Cardo," *Israel Exploration Journal* 64.1: 38–62.

Weksler-Bdolah, Shlomit. 2019a. "The Cardo in Urban Context," in S. Weksler-Bdolah and A. Onn (eds.), *Jerusalem, Western Wall Plaza Excavations Volume I: The Roman and Byzantine Remains: Architecture and Stratigraphy* (IAA Reports No. 63) (Jerusalem: Israel Antiquities Authority), in S. Weksler-Bdolah and A. Onn, *Jerusalem, Western Wall Plaza Excavations Volume I: The Roman and Byzantine Remains: Architecture and Stratigraphy* (IAA Reports No. 63) (Jerusalem: Israel Antiquities Authority), 195–200.

Weksler-Bdolah, Shlomit. 2019b. "The Eastern Cardo in the Roman and Byzantine Periods (Strata *XII-X*)," in S. Weksler-Bdolah and A. Onn (eds.), *Jerusalem, Western Wall Plaza Excavations Volume I: The Roman and Byzantine Remains: Architecture and Stratigraphy* (IAA Reports No. 63) (Jerusalem: Israel Antiquities Authority), 29–115.

Weksler-Bdolah, Shlomit. 2020. *Aelia Capitolina: Jerusalem in the Roman Period* (Leiden: Brill).

Weksler-Bdolah, Shlomit, and Leah Di Segni 2020. "A Latin Epitaph of a Soldier from Magen's Excavations in Damascus Gate and the Burial Grounds of Jerusalem Between 70 and 130 CE," *Israel Exploration Journal* 70.1: 90–98.

Weksler-Bdolah, Shlomit, and Alexander Onn. 2017a. "Colonnaded Streets in *Aelia Capitolina*: New Evidence from the Eastern *Cardo*," in G. Avni and G. D. Stiebel (eds.), *Roman Jerusalem: A New Old City* (Portsmouth, RI: Journal of Roman Archaeology Supplementary Series Number 105), 11–22.

Weksler-Bdolah, Shlomit, and Alexander Onn. 2017b. "The Temple Mount at the Time of *Aelia Capitolina*: New Evidence from 'the Giant Viaduct,' " in G. Avni and G. D. Stiebel (eds.), *Roman Jerusalem: A New Old City* (Portsmouth, RI: Journal of Roman Archaeology Supplementary Series Number 105), 83–95.

Weksler-Bdolah, Shlomit, and Alexander Onn. 2019a. "A First Temple Period Building and the Roman Eastern Cardo in the Western Wall Plaza," in H. Geva (ed.), *Ancient Jerusalem Revealed: Archaeological Discoveries, 1998–2018* (Jerusalem: Israel Exploration Society), 153–68.

Weksler-Bdolah, Shlomit, and Alexander Onn. 2019b. *Jerusalem, Western Wall Plaza Excavations Volume I: The Roman and Byzantine Remains: Architecture and Stratigraphy* (IAA Reports No. 63) (Jerusalem: Israel Antiquities Authority).

Weksler-Bdolah, Shlomit, and Alexander Onn. 2021. *Jerusalem, Western Wall Plaza Excavations Volume III: The Roman and Byzantine Periods: Small Finds from the Roman Refuse Dump and Other Contexts* (IAA Reports No. 67) (Jerusalem: Israel Antiquities Authority).

Weksler-Bdolah, Shlomit, and Alexander Onn. 2022. "Herodian Pavement (Esplanade?) and Later Remains near Warren's Gate, West of the Temple Mount," `Atiqot 106: 195–209.

Weksler-Bdolah, Shlomit, and Orit Peleg-Barkat. 2022. "Unfinished Business: What Caused the Sudden Cessation of the Construction Works During the Foundation of Aelia Capitolina?," in W. Atrash, A. Overman, and P. Gendelman (eds.), *Cities, Monuments and Objects in the Roman and Byzantine Levant: Studies in Honour of Gabi Mazor* (Oxford: Archaeopress), 138–47.

Weksler-Bdolah, Shlomit, and Nahshon Szanton. 2014. "Jerusalem, Silwan," *Hadashot Arkheologiyot* 126, at https://www.hadashot-esi.org.il/report_detail_eng.aspx?id=10572&mag_id=121.

Weksler-Bdolah, Shlomit, Alexander Onn, and Renate Rosenthal-Heginbottom. 2009. "The Eastern Cardo and the Wilson Bridge in Light of New Excavations–The Remains from the Second Temple Period and from Aelia Capitolina," in L. Di Segni, Y. Hirschfeld, J. Patrich, and R. Talgam (eds.), *Man Near a Roman Arch: Studies Presented to Prof. Yoram Tsafrir* (Jerusalem: Israel Exploration Society), 135–59 (in Hebrew).

Weksler-Bdolah, Shlomit, Alexander Onn, Brigitte Ouahnouna, and Shua Kisilevitz. 2009. "Jerusalem, the Western Wall Plaza Excavations, 2005–2009," *Hadashot Arkheologiyot* 121, at https://www.hadashot-esi.org.il/report_detail_eng.aspx?id=1219&mag_id=115.

Weksler-Bdolah, Shlomit, Rachel Bar-Nathan, Anat Cohen-Weinberger, and Leah Di Segni. 2022. "'(Work) of CILO': An Impression of a Roman-Period Private Stamp from the Western Wall Tunnels," `Atiqot 106: 239–55.

Welles, C. Bradford. 1938. "The Inscriptions," in C. H. Kraeling (ed.), *Gerasa: City of the Decapolis* (New Haven, CT: American Schools of Oriental Research), 355–494.

Wheatley, Paul. 2001. *The Places Where Men Pray Together: Cities in Islamic Lands, Seventh Through the Tenth Centuries* (Chicago: University of Chicago Press).

Whitby, Michael, and Mary Whitby. 1989. *Chronicon Paschale, 284–628 AD* (Liverpool: Liverpool University Press).

Whitcomb, Donald. 2011. "Jerusalem and the Beginnings of the Islamic City," in K. Galor and G. Avni (eds.), *Unearthing Jerusalem: 150 Years of Archaeological Research in the Holy City* (Winona Lake, IN: Eisenbrauns), 399–416.

Wightman, Gregory J. 1989. *The Damascus Gate, Jerusalem: Excavations by C.-M. Bennett and J. B. Hennessy at the Damascus Gate, Jerusalem, 1964–66* (Oxford: BAR International Reports 519).

Wightman, Gregory J. 1993. *The Walls of Jerusalem from the Canaanites to the Mamluks* (Sydney: Meditarch).

Wightman, Gregory J. 2022. "The Disappearing Walls of Jerusalem? Observations on the Bronze and Iron Age Fortifications and Waterworks on the East Slope of the City of David," *Levant* (ahead-of-print 1–17): https://doi.org/10.1080/00758 914.2022.2061814.

Wilkinson, John. 1977. *Jerusalem Pilgrims Before the Crusades* (Jerusalem: Ariel).

Wilkinson, John. 1978. "The Pool of Siloam," *Levant* 10: 116–25.

Wilkinson, John. 1981. *Egeria's Travels to the Holy Land* (Jerusalem: Ariel [revised edition]).

Williamson, Hugh G. M. 2004. *Studies in Persian Period History and Historiography* (Tübingen: Mohr Siebeck).

Wilson, Charles W., and Charles Warren. 1871. *The Recovery of Jerusalem* (London: R. Bentley).

Wolff, Samuel R. (ed.). 2015. *Villain or Visionary: R. A. S. Macalister and the Archaeology of Palestine* (New York: Routledge).

Wolff, Samuel R. 2015. "R. A. S. Macalister: A Retrospective after 100 Years," *Near Eastern Archaeology* 78.2: 104–10.

Yadin, Yigael. 1963. *The Finds from the Bar-Kokhba Period in the Cave of Letters* (Jerusalem: Israel Exploration Society).

Yadin, Yigael. 1971. *Bar-Kokhba: The Rediscovery of the Legendary Hero of the Last Jewish Revolt Against Imperial Rome* (London: Weidenfeld and Nicolson).

Yadin, Yigael. 1983. *The Temple Scroll, Volumes 1–3* (Jerusalem: Israel Exploration Society).

Yechezkel, Azriel, Yoav Negev, Amos Frumkin, and Uzi Leibner. 2021. "The Shaft Tunnel of the Biar aqueduct of Jerusalem: Architecture, Hydrology, and Dating," *Geoarchaeology*: 897–924.

Yezerski, Irit, and Hillel Geva. 2003. "Iron Age II Clay Figurines," in H. Geva (ed.), *Jewish Quarter Excavations in the Old City of Jerusalem Conducted by Nahman Avigad, 1969–1982, Vol. 2* (Jerusalem: Israel Exploration Society), 63–84.

Yuval-Hacham, Noa. 2007. "'Like an Eagle Who Rouses His Nestlings': The Meaning of the Eagle Motif in Ancient Synagogues in the Golan and Galilee," *Cathedra* 124 (Jerusalem: Yad Yitzhak Ben-Zvi), 65–80 (Hebrew).

Yuzefovsky, Baruch. 2018. "Lead Sling Bullets," in Amit Re'em (ed.), *The Qishle Excavation in the Old City of Jerusalem* (Jerusalem: Israel Exploration Society), 199–200.

Zelinger, Yehiel. 2019. "The Line of the Southern City Wall of Jerusalem in the Early Periods," in H. Geva (ed.), *Ancient Jerusalem Revealed: Archaeological Discoveries, 1998–2018* (Jerusalem: Israel Exploration Society), 279–88.

Zias, Joe, and Émile Puech. 2005. "The Tomb of Absalom Reconsidered," *Near Eastern Archaeology* 68.4: 148–65.

Zilberstein, Ayala. 2019. "'On the Walls of the City of David': The Line of the Western Fortification Wall of the Hill of the City of David in the Hellenistic Period in the Light of New Discoveries," *New Discoveries in the Archaeology of Jerusalem and Its Region* 13: 31–50 (in Hebrew).

Zilberstein, Ayala. 2021. "Hellenistic Military Architecture from the Giv`ati Parking Lot Excavations, Jerusalem," in A. M. Berlin and P. J. Kosmin (eds.), *The Middle Maccabees: Archaeology, History, and the Rise of the Hasmonean Kingdom* (Atlanta: SBL Press), 37–52.

Index

For the benefit of digital users, indexed terms that span two pages (e.g., 52–53) may, on occasion, appear on only one of those pages.

Note: Figures are indicated by *f* following the page number